Recommended by **Teachers**
Trusted by **Toppers**

All in One

BUSINESS STUDIES
Class 12

EVERYTHING YOU NEED TO SCORE

- Simplified NCERT Theory
- All Types of Exam Pattern Questions
- CBQs; MCQs, A-R, Case Based
- Board Questions Upto 2025
- Sample Question Papers

CBSE Exams 2026

Author
Ishita Agarwal

arihant
SUCCESS AND NOTHING LESS

ARIHANT PRAKASHAN

(School Division Series)

卐 *ADMINISTRATIVE & PRODUCTION OFFICES*

Regd. Office

'Ramchhaya' 4577/15, Agarwal Road, Darya Ganj, New Delhi -110002

Tele: 011- 47630600, 43518550; Fax: 011- 23280316

卐 *Head Office*

Kalindi, TP Nagar, Meerut (UP) - 250002, Tel: 0121-7156203, 7156204

卐 *SALES & SUPPORT OFFICES*

Agra, Ahmedabad, Bengaluru, Bareilly, Chennai, Delhi, Guwahati, Hyderabad, Jaipur, Jhansi, Kolkata, Lucknow, Nagpur & Pune.

PO No : TXT-XX-XXXXXXX-X-XX

Published By Arihant Publications (India) Ltd.

For further information about the books published by Arihant, log on to www.arihantbooks.com or e-mail at info@arihantbooks.com

Follow us on

卐 *PRICE* ₹ 500.00

PRODUCTION TEAM

Publishing Managers
Mahendra Singh Rawat & Keshav Mohan

Cover Designer
Salman Shaikh

Inner Designer
Ankit Prajapati

Project Head
Saurabh Gupta

Page Layouting
Amit Bansal

Proof Reader
Apoorvi

Index *cum* Study Planner

PART A Principles and Functions of Management

One Book- Endless Features
to Help you Succeed

01
CHAPTER

Nature and Significance of Management

"Management is the process of working with and through others to effectively achieve organisational objectives by efficiently using limited resources in the changing environment." — *Kreitner*

YOUR STUDY GOALS

1.1 Concept of Management

Management can be defined as "a process of getting things done with the aim of achieving goals effectively and efficiently."

The above definition focuses on three terms given below

In this Chapter

At the start of each chapter, all the topics of the chapter have been listed, so that students may know what they are going to study.

1.1 Concept of Management

Management can be defined as "a process of getting things done with the aim of achieving goals effectively and efficiently."

The above definition focuses on three terms given below

1. **Management as Process** It is considered as process as it includes a series of functions such as planning, organising, staffing, directing and controlling.
2. **Management needs Effectiveness** Effectiveness in management is concerned with doing the right task, completing activities and achieving goals within the prescribed time limit.
3. **Management to be Done Efficiently** Efficiency is concerned with doing the task correctly and with minimum cost, least wastage and maximum utilisation of resources.

Complete Theory in Each Chapter

Each chapter has Complete, Easy to Understand and Simplified theory covering latest syllabus and latest NCERT Textbook. Theory is developed in such a way that it is suitable for all types of learners.

Management Principles vs Principles of Pure Science

- Management principles are flexible, required to be applied creatively and have to keep pace with the changing environment while principles of pure science are rigid, applied in absolute or static manner and do not have to be adaptive to changing environment.

Management Principles vs Techniques of Management

- Management principles are flexible and act as guidelines for decision-making or taking actions while techniques are less flexible and are methods or procedures involving a series of steps to achieve desired goals.

Management Principles vs Values

- Management principles are guidelines, technical in nature and formed through research in work situations while values are ethical and general rules for individual behaviour which are formed through common practice.

Boxed Matter

Information in the boxes is given to focus on important points related to the concepts.

Nature of Principles of Management

Following points characterise the nature of principles of management

Nature of Principles of Management
- Universal applicability
- General guidelines
- Formed by practice and experimentation
- Flexible
- Mainly behavioural
- Cause and effect relationship
- Contingent

1. **Universal Applicability** The principles can be applied in all types of organisations, business as well as non-business whether small or large, manufacturing or service sector.
2. **General Guidelines** The principles are general guidelines to action and decision-making, but they do not provide readymade solutions as the business situations are ever changing or dynamic and are a result of multiple factors.
3. **Formed by Practice and Experimentation** The principles are developed after thorough research work on the basis of experiences, observation and experimentation of managers.
4. **Flexible** The principles can be adapted and modified by the practicing managers as per the demands of the situations as they are man-made principles.
5. **Mainly Behavioural** Since the principles aim at influencing complex human behaviour, they are mainly behavioural in nature. They help in motivating and inspiring the human beings working in an organisation.
6. **Cause and Effect Relationship** The principles establish cause and effect relationship as they tell us if a particular principle is applied in a particular situation, which can be its likely effect.
7. **Contingent** Their applicability depends upon the prevailing situation at a particular point of time.

Flowchart

To quickly recall the concepts, flow charts are given at many places.

One Book- Endless Features

to Help you Succeed

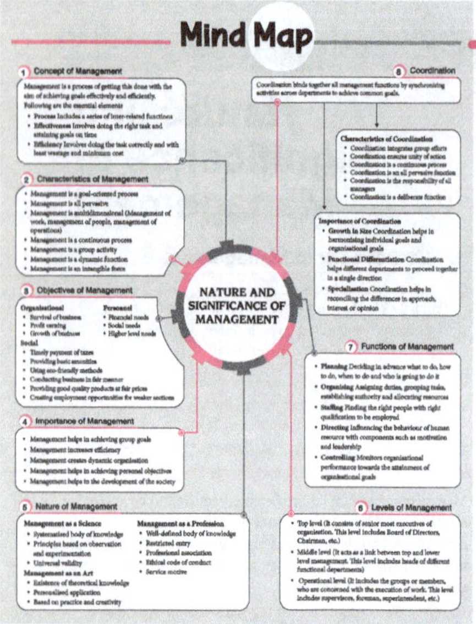

Mind Map

A quick revision visual tool for the complete chapter.

Exam Pattern Questions

To make students completely prepared for examination, Exam Pattern Questions are provided after theory. There questions cover all types of questions, like; MCQs, Case Based Questions, Assertion-Reason, SA & LA Type Questions. All the questions are fully explained helping students to understand, how to write the answers to get full marks in the exam.

Case Studies

To give the students a practice of applying their knowledge, each chapter has a separate section carrying case studies.

EXAM PATTERN QUESTIONS

Objective Type Questions

Multiple Choice Questions (MCQs)

1. "In order to be successful, an organisation must change its goals according to the needs of the environment." Identify the characteristic of management highlighted in the statement. **Competency Based Que**

(a) Management is dynamic
(b) Management is goal-oriented process
(c) Management is a group activity
(d) Management is all pervasive

Identify the feature of management.

(a) Management is multi-dimensional
(b) Management is all pervasive
(c) Management is a continuous process
(d) Management is a dynamic function

6. Identify the characteristic of management illustrated by the below picture in which the heads of all departments have contributed towards the company's growth.

Case Study Based Questions

Short Case Studies

Case Study 1

Shreya works as a designer in an export house. As per the terms of an order received by the export house, she has to get 100 units of denim jackets made in 15 days @ ₹ 2,000 per jacket.

She is able to complete her target production in 20 days because in order to complete the order in 15 days, she would have made the workers work over time. As a result, the cost of production per jacket may have increased by ₹ 100.

In the context of the above case, "Is Shreya efficient in her work? Explain by giving a suitable reason in support of your answer."

Shreya's decision to prioritise regular working hours for her workers may have contributed to a more sustainable and equitable work environment.

However, the increased production costs incurred by extending the production timeline suggest a potential inefficiency in her work.

Case Study 2

Mahesh is the Chief Executive Officer of 'Kidzania Garments Ltd.' Due to festive season, Mahesh got an additional order of 10,000 garments which he had to supply within two days. Due to his goodwill in the market, he did not want to lose the order. So, he decided to achieve the target by operating on double shifts. He achieved the target and supplied the order within two days.

One Book- Endless Features

to Help you Succeed

Self Assessment Test

Complete Test of chapter in Exam format.

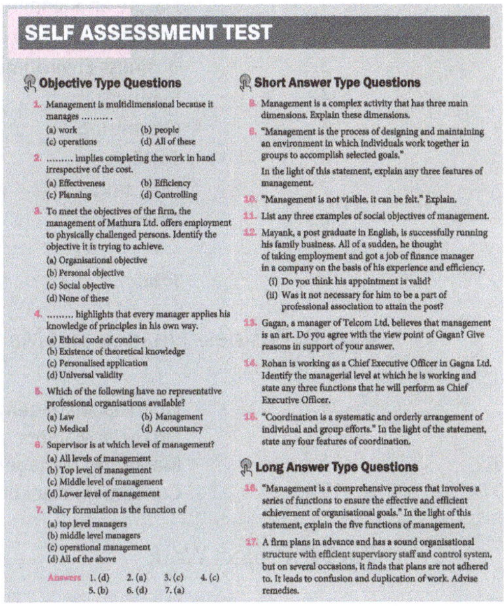

SELF ASSESSMENT TEST

Objective Type Questions

1. Management is multidimensional because it manages ....
   (a) work (b) people
   (c) operations (d) All of these
2. .... implies completing the work in hand irrespective of the cost.
   (a) Effectiveness (b) Efficiency
   (c) Planning (d) Controlling
3. To meet the objectives of the firm, the management of Mathura Ltd. offers employment to physically challenged persons. Identify the objective it is trying to achieve.
   (a) Organisational objective
   (b) Personal objective
   (c) Social objective
   (d) None of these
4. .... highlights that every manager applies his knowledge of principles in his own way.
   (a) Ethical code of conduct
   (b) Existence of theoretical knowledge
   (c) Personalised application
   (d) Universal validity
5. Which of the following have no representative professional organisations available?
   (a) Law (b) Management
   (c) Medical (d) Accountancy
6. Supervisor is at which level of management?
   (a) All levels of management
   (b) Top level of management
   (c) Middle level of management
   (d) Lower level of management
7. Policy formulation is the function of
   (a) top level managers
   (b) middle level managers
   (c) operational management
   (d) All of the above

Answers 1. (d) 2. (a) 3. (c) 4. (c) 5. (b) 6. (d) 7. (a)

Short Answer Type Questions

8. Management is a complex activity that has three main dimensions. Explain these dimensions.
9. "Management is the process of designing and maintaining an environment in which individuals work together in groups to accomplish selected goals."
   In the light of this statement, explain any three features of management.
10. "Management is not visible, it can be felt." Explain.
11. List any three examples of social objectives of management.
12. Mayank, a post graduate in English, is successfully running his family business. All of a sudden, he thought of taking employment and got a job of finance manager in a company on the basis of his experience and efficiency.
    (i) Do you think his appointment is valid?
    (ii) Was it not necessary for him to be a part of professional association to attain the post?
13. Gagan, a manager of Telcom Ltd. believes that management is an art. Do you agree with the view point of Gagan? Give reasons in support of your answer.
14. Rohan is working as a Chief Executive Officer in Gagna Ltd. Identify the managerial level at which he is working and state any three functions that he will perform as Chief Executive Officer.
15. "Coordination is a systematic and orderly arrangement of individual and group efforts." In the light of the statement, state any four features of coordination.

Long Answer Type Questions

16. "Management is a comprehensive process that involves a series of functions to ensure the effective and efficient achievement of organisational goals." In the light of this statement, explain the five functions of management.
17. A firm plans in advance and has a sound organisational structure with efficient supervisory staff and control system, but on several occasions, it finds that plans are not adhered to. It leads to confusion and duplication of work. Advise remedies.

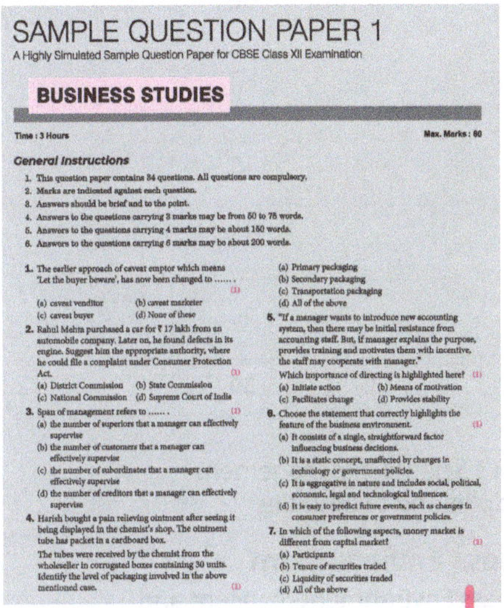

SAMPLE QUESTION PAPER 1

A Highly Simulated Sample Question Paper for CBSE Class XII Examination

BUSINESS STUDIES

Time : 3 Hours Max. Marks : 80

General Instructions

1. This question paper contains 34 questions. All questions are compulsory.
2. Marks are indicated against each question.
3. Answers should be brief and to the point.
4. Answers to the questions carrying 3 marks may be from 50 to 75 words.
5. Answers to the questions carrying 4 marks may be about 150 words.
6. Answers to the questions carrying 6 marks may be about 200 words.

1. The earlier approach of caveat emptor which means 'Let the buyer beware', has now been changed to .... (1)
   (a) caveat venditor (b) caveat marketer
   (c) caveat buyer (d) None of these
2. Rahul Mehta purchased a car for ₹ 17 lakh from an automobile company. Later on, he found defects in its engine. Suggest him the appropriate authority, where he could file a complaint under Consumer Protection Act. (1)
   (a) District Commission (b) State Commission
   (c) National Commission (d) Supreme Court of India
3. Span of management refers to .... (1)
   (a) the number of superiors that a manager can effectively supervise
   (b) the number of customers that a manager can effectively supervise
   (c) the number of subordinates that a manager can effectively supervise
   (d) the number of creditors that a manager can effectively supervise
4. Harish bought a pain relieving ointment after seeing it being displayed in the chemist's shop. The ointment tube has packet in a cardboard box.
   The tubes were received by the chemist from the wholeseller in corrugated boxes containing 30 units. Identify the level of packaging involved in the above mentioned case. (1)
   (a) Primary packaging
   (b) Secondary packaging
   (c) Transportation packaging
   (d) All of the above
5. "If a manager wants to introduce new accounting system, then there may be initial resistance from accounting staff. But, if manager explains the purpose, provides training and motivates them with incentive, the staff may cooperate with manager."
   Which importance of directing is highlighted here? (1)
   (a) Initiate action (b) Means of motivation
   (c) Facilitates change (d) Provides stability
6. Choose the statement that correctly highlights the feature of the business environment. (1)
   (a) It consists of a single, straightforward factor influencing business decisions.
   (b) It is a static concept, unaffected by changes in technology or government policies.
   (c) It is aggregative in nature and includes social, political, economic, legal and technological influences.
   (d) It is easy to predict future events, such as changes in consumer preferences or government policies.
7. In which of the following aspects, money market is different from capital market? (1)
   (a) Participants
   (b) Tenure of securities traded
   (c) Liquidity of securities traded
   (d) All of the above

Sample Question Papers

To make students practice of examination in real sense, there are 3 Sample Question Papers at the end. All these Sample Questions Papers are exactly prepared on the latest syllabus & pattern of examination.

Latest Course *Structure*

Paper: One | Time: 3 Hrs | Max. Marks : 80

S.No.	Units	Marks
Part A: Principles and Functions of Management		
1.	Nature and Significance of Management	
2.	Principles of Management	16
3.	Business Environment	
4.	Planning	14
5.	Organising	
6.	Staffing	
7.	Directing	20
8.	Controlling	
	Total	**50**
Part B: Business Finance and Marketing		
9.	Financial Management	15
10.	Financial Markets	
11.	Marketing Management	15
12.	Consumer Protection	
Part C: Project Work		20
	Total	**50**

PART A Principles and Functions of Management

UNIT 1 Nature and Significance of Management

- Management-concept, objectives, and importance
- Management as Science, Art and Profession
- Levels of Management
- Management Functions-planning, organizing, staffing, directing and controlling
- Coordination- concept and importance

UNIT 2 Principles of Management

- Principles of Management- concept and significance
- Fayol's principles of management
- Taylor's Scientific Management- principles and techniques

UNIT 3 Business Environment

- Business Environment- concept and importance
- Dimensions of Business Environment- Economic, Social, Technological, Political and Legal
- Demonetization - concept and features

UNIT 4 Planning

- Concept, importance and limitation
- Planning process
- Single use and standing plans. Objectives, Strategy, Policy, Procedure, Method, Rule, Budget and Programme

UNIT 5 Organising

- Concept and importance
- Organising process

- Structure of Organisation- Functional and divisional concept. Formal and informal organisation- concept
- Delegation- Concept, elements and importance
- Decentralization- Concept and importance

UNIT 6 Staffing

- Concept and importance of staffing
- Staffing as a part of Human Resource Management concept
- Staffing process
- Recruitment process
- Selection process
- Training and Development- Concept and importance, Methods of training- on the job and off the job - vestibule training, apprenticeship training and internship training

UNIT 7 Directing

- Concept and importance
- Elements of directing
- Motivation- Concept, Maslow's hierarchy of needs, Financial and non-financial incentives
- Leadership- Concept, styles- authoritative, democratic and laissez faire
- Communication- Concept, formal and informal communication; barriers to effective communication, how to overcome the barriers

UNIT 8 Controlling

- Concept and importance
- Relationship between planning and controlling
- Steps in process of control

PART B Business Finance and Marketing

UNIT 9 Financial Management

- Concept, role and objectives of Financial Management
- Financial decisions- Investment, financing and dividend- Meaning and factors affecting
- Financial Planning- Concept and importance
- Capital Structure- Concept and factors affecting capital structure
- Fixed and Working Capital- Concept and factors affecting their requirements

UNIT 10 Financial Markets

- Financial Markets: Concept.
- Money market : Concept
- Capital market and its types (primary and secondary).
- Stock Exchange- Functions and trading procedure
- Securities and Exchange Board of India (SEBI) - Objectives and functions

UNIT 11 Marketing

- Marketing - Concept, functions and philosophies
- Marketing Mix – Concept and elements
- Product - Branding, labelling and packaging - Concept
- Price-Concept, Factors determining price
- Physical Distribution - Concept, components and channels of distribution
- Promotion – Concept and elements; advertising, personal selling, sales promotion, public relations

UNIT 12 Consumer Protection

- Concept and importance of consumer protection
- The Consumer Protection Act 2019
- Meaning of consumer
- Rights and responsibilities of consumers
- Who can file a complaint ?
- Redressal machinery
- Remedies available
- Consumer awareness- Role of consumer organizations and Non-Governmental Organizations (NGOs).

UNIT 13 Project Work

PART A PRINCIPLES AND FUNCTIONS OF MANAGEMENT

01

CHAPTER

Nature and Significance of Management

"Management is the process of working with and through others to effectively achieve organisational objectives by efficiently using limited resources in the changing environment."

— *Kreitner*

YOUR STUDY GOALS

1.1 Concept of Management
1.2 Characteristics of Management
1.3 Objectives of Management
1.4 Importance of Management
1.5 Nature of Management
1.6 Levels of Management
1.7 Functions of Management
1.8 Coordination

YOUR PRACTICE GOAL

- Objective Type Questions (68 Qs ; MCQs, A-R, Statements, Matching)
- Subjective Type Questions (14 SAs, 5 LAs)
- Case Study Based Questions (Short Case Studies-13, Long Case Studies-6)
- Self Assessment Test (7 MCQs, 8 SAs, 2 LAs)

1.1 Concept of Management

Management can be defined as "a process of getting things done with the aim of achieving goals effectively and efficiently."

The above definition focuses on three terms given below

1. **Management as Process** It is considered as process as it includes a series of functions such as planning, organising, staffing, directing and controlling.
2. **Management needs Effectiveness** Effectiveness in management is concerned with doing the right task, completing activities and achieving goals within the prescribed time limit.
3. **Management to be Done Efficiently** Efficiency is concerned with doing the task correctly and with minimum cost, least wastage and maximum utilisation of resources.

Effectiveness vs Efficiency

Effectiveness, aims to achieve goals within time while *efficiency* is concerned with optimum utilisation of resources and achieving the goal with minimum cost. So, completing the task in time with minimum cost is desirable.

Real World Examples to Understand Effectiveness and Efficiency

- **Effectiveness without Efficiency** A company needs to produce 10,000 units of Smart TVs in one month. The manager works extra hours, hires more workers and meets the target, but the production cost skyrockets. Here, the manager is *effective* (met the goal) **but not** *efficient* (used too many resources).
- **Efficiency without Effectiveness** Another company has the same target of 10,000 units. The manager reduces costs by cutting corners but produces only 8,000 units by the end of the month. This manager is *efficient* (saved resources) **but not** *effective* (didn't meet the goal).

1.2 Characteristics of Management

The elements given below are considered as characteristics of management

1. **Management is a Goal-oriented Process** Management aims to achieve certain organisational goals by uniting everyone's efforts in the organisation. These goals should be simple and clearly stated. Different organisations have different goals to accomplish.
2. **Management is All Pervasive** It is universally applicable in all types of organisation whether political, economic or social.
3. **Management is Multi-dimensional** Management is a complex activity which comprises of three main dimensions, that are as follows
   (i) **Management of Work** It is concerned with performance of various activities/tasks in an organisation.
   (ii) **Management of People** It refers to management of human resources, which are the most important asset for an organisation.
   (iii) **Management of Operations** It refers to the activities of production cycle, which entails the flow of input material and transforms the input into desired output.

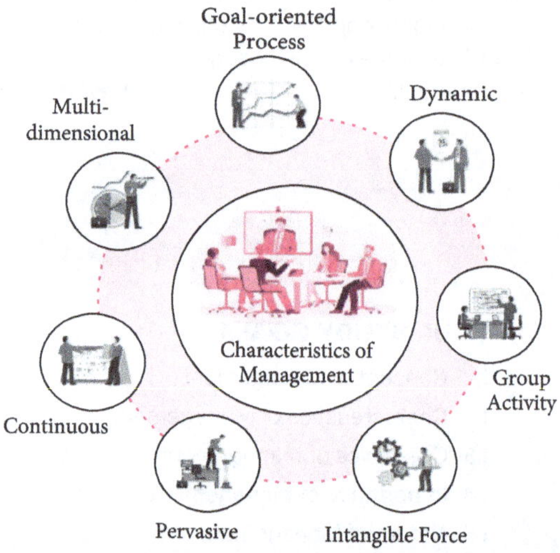

4. **Management is a Continuous Process** Management is an ongoing process of continuous, composite, but separate functions (planning, organising, staffing, directing and controlling).
5. **Management is a Group Activity** Through coordination and teamwork, management unites the efforts of individuals to achieve organisational goals, alongwith the growth and development of individuals as needs and opportunities change.
6. **Management is a Dynamic Function** Every organisation interacts with its external environment which includes social, economic and political factors. An organisation must adapt itself and its goals according to the needs of the environment.
7. **Management is an Intangible Force** Management is like an invisible force that can be felt through a well-run organisation. When there is order, discipline and happy employees, it shows that management is effective.

1.3 Objectives of Management

Management has to achieve following objectives in an effective and efficient manner. These can be grouped as follows

Objectives of Management

- **Organisational**
  - **Survival** Ensure that organisation earns enough revenue to cover costs.
  - **Profit** Achieve profitability to cover risks and sustain operations.
  - **Growth** Expand activities in terms of sales, products and employees.
- **Personnel**
  - Satisfy employees' financial, social and personal growth needs while aligning personal goals with organisational objectives.
- **Social**
  - Create jobs, provide amenities, offer quality products, pay taxes, use eco-friendly methods and conduct business fairly.

Organisational Objective

Tesla aims to drive growth and profitability through constant innovation and market expansion. In 2023,the company introduced the Tesla Model S Plaid, the fastest production car in the world, which significantly boosted sales and market share.

Social Objective

Starbucks aims to positively impact the communities it serves. One of its notable social initiatives is the "Starbucks College Achievement Plan," which offers 100% tuition coverage for its employees through Arizona State University's online programme.

1.4 Importance of Management

1. **Management helps in Achieving Group Goals** Management unites the resources together and give common direction to the efforts of all individuals towards achieving those goals.
2. **Management increases Efficiency** Managers seek to reduce costs and increase productivity through better planning, organising, directing, staffing and controlling the activities of the organisation.
3. **Management creates a Dynamic Organisation** Management helps individuals adapt to changes in the ever-changing environment to maintain the organisation's competitive edge.
4. **Management helps in Achieving Personal Objectives** A manager leads and motivates team members to achieve personal goals while contributing to organisational objectives, fostering team spirit, cooperation and commitment.
5. **Management helps in the Development of Society** Management aims to develop both the organisation and society by fulfilling social obligations alongside achieving organisational objectives.

Case Study
Importance of Management

- Imagine Innovate Inc. has a new goal – to launch a groundbreaking AI-powered gadget in the next six months. The CEO gathers all departments: R&D, marketing, production and sales. Through meticulous planning and coordination, each team member knows their role, ***ensuring all efforts are directed towards this ambitious goal.***
- Innovate Inc. wants to reduce production costs. The operations manager implements a new resource management system, optimises workflows and trains employees. ***As a result, production costs drop and productivity soars.***
- The tech industry is ever-changing and Innovate Inc. needs to adapt quickly. The HR manager introduces continuous learning programmes, while the leadership fosters a culture of innovation. ***Employees embrace change, driving the company to stay ahead of the curve.***
- Jane, a software developer at Innovate Inc., dreams of becoming a project leader. Her manager provides her the leadership training. ***By aligning her personal goals with the company's objectives,*** Jane becomes a crucial part of the team's success, achieving her dream while contributing to the company's growth.
- Innovate Inc. believes in ***social responsibility***. The management team initiates community development projects, such as tech education programmes. This not only helps the community but also builds a positive company image and loyal customer base.

1.5 Nature of Management

Different management thinkers have different views, as some authors describe it as a science, while same consider it as an art. Moreover, some practitioners believe that management is going towards the way of profession.

Nature of Management	Related Features		
Management as an Art	**Existence of Theoretical Knowledge** Management is grounded in principles and extensive literature across various areas like finance and marketing.	**Personalised Application** Management mirrors art, as each manager applies principles differently based on their creativity and individuality, combining practice with innovation.	**Based on Practice and Creativity** Management benefits from continuous application of principles, leading to unique management styles and improved skills.
Management as a Science	**Systematised Body of Knowledge** Science has a structured body of knowledge with principles based on cause and effect relationships. Similarly, management has its own organised set of theories, principles, vocabulary and concepts.	**Principles Based on Experimentation** In management, principles are developed through observation and practice, but they cannot always be precisely tested or replicated due to the unpredictable nature of human behaviour. Hence, management is considered an inexact science.	**Universal Validity** Scientific principles are universally applicable. In contrast, management principles are not universally valid; they need to be adapted according to different situations and contexts.
Management as a Profession	**Well-defined Body of Knowledge** Management has established principles and knowledge, which can be acquired through courses like MBA and BBA at institutions such as IIM.	**Restricted Entry** Management does not have strict entry requirements, though management degrees from reputable institutions are increasingly valued.	**Professional Association** In management, associations like AIMA exist but are not mandatory for practice.
		Ethical Code of Conduct Professions follow a strict ethical code. Management lacks a formal ethical code and there are no specific rules guiding managers' conduct.	**Service Motive** This feature is not present completely as the primary motive of management is to help organisation achieve its stated goal, which can be profit maximisation for a business enterprise and service for a hospital.

Conclusion

Management is an 'art' as it fulfills all the criteria of being an art. Thus, we can conclude that "management is an art of getting things done through people."

Management cannot be cosidered as exact or pure science but we can call it as an **inexact science or social science.**

Management does not possess all the characteristics of profession. Thus, it should be considered that it is not a full-fledged profession, but is moving at a pace in the direction of becoming a profession.

1.6 Levels of Management

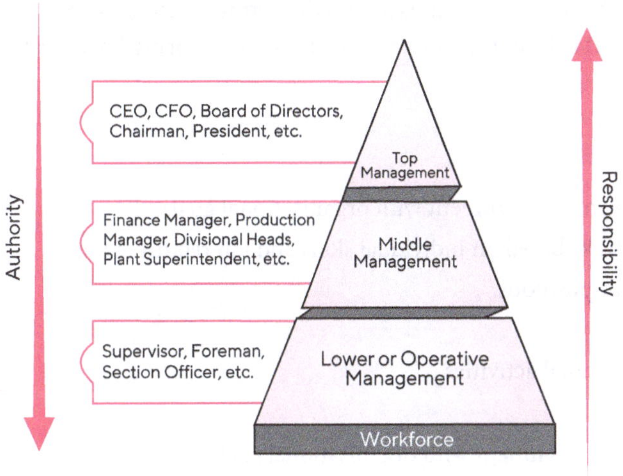

1. **Top Level Management**
   - Strive for the business's welfare and survival and formulate goals and policies.
   - Integrate and coordinate departmental activities to achieve overall objectives.
   - Analyse the business environment and its implications and oversee all activities.
2. **Middle Level Management**
   - Interpret policies set by top management.
   - Select, appoint and evaluate middle and supervisory level employees.
   - Assign duties and responsibilities to lower level managers.
3. **Operational or Supervisory Level**
   - Communicate middle managers' instructions to workers, minimise material wastage and maintain output quality and safety standards.
   - Represent workers' grievances and suggestions to management, ensure safe and proper working

1.7 Functions of Management

Management is a dynamic process, in which every manager has to perform various functions (i.e. POSDC). They are

1. **Planning** Decides in advance what to do, how, when and who will do it. Bridges the gap between current and future positions by setting goals and devising efficient ways to achieve them.

   e.g. A company creates a detailed strategy to launch a new product in the market within the next six months.
2. **Organising** Assigns duties, groups tasks, establishes authority and allocates resources. Defines who will do what, where and when and promotes efficiency and effectiveness through proper organisational structure.

   e.g. The project manager assigns specific tasks to team members and establishes deadlines for each phase of the project.
3. **Staffing** Fills positions with qualified personnel. Involves recruitment, selection, placement and training, ensuring the right people are employed at the right time.

   e.g. The HR department recruits a new marketing manager with five years of experience in the industry.

4. **Directing** Involves leading, influencing, communicating, supervising and motivating employees to achieve targets. Key components include motivation and leadership.

   e.g. The supervisor motivates the sales team with a performance-based incentive programme to achieve their quarterly targets.

5. **Controlling** Monitors performance against goals, identifies deviations and takes corrective actions to align actual performance with plans.
   e.g. The quality control manager reviews production reports and implements corrective actions to ensure the products meet the company's standards.

1.8 Coordination

Coordination binds together all management functions by synchronising activities across departments to achieve common goals. While sometimes viewed as a separate function, it is fundamental to management, ensuring harmony among individual efforts for group goals.

Coordination is essential in management for these reasons

1. **Needed for All Function**
   - **Planning** Coordination starts during the planning stage to ensure alignment with organisational goals.
   - **Organising** It helps structure the organisation and assign tasks based on individual skills and job requirements.
   - **Staffing** Ensures that the right people are placed in the right positions.
   - **Directing** Coordinates efforts to execute plans effectively.
   - **Controlling** Addresses discrepancies between planned and actual activities.
2. **Needed at All Levels**
   - **Top Level Managers** Coordinate overall activities and ensure alignment with organisational goals.
   - **Middle Level Managers** Facilitate coordination between different departments.
   - **Lower Level Managers** Oversee and coordinate the activities of workers to ensure adherence to plans.

Coordination as the Essence of Management

At Nexus Tech, the R&D, marketing and sales teams worked in perfect harmony to launch their new smartphone. The R&D team provided timely updates on product features, enabling marketing to craft accurate promotional materials, while sales strategised effectively based on real-time information.

This seamless coordination resulted in a successful product launch, highlighting coordination as the essence of effective management.

Characteristics of Coordination

1. **Integrates Group Efforts** Coordination binds diverse interests into purposeful activities, ensuring that group efforts align with plans to achieve common goals.
2. **Ensures Unity of Action** It aligns the efforts of individuals, departments and levels towards a shared purpose, ensuring that everyone works in the same direction to achieve organisational goals.

3. **Continuous Process** Coordination starts with planning and continues through all stages, including execution and control, as an ongoing process in the organisation.
4. **All Pervasive Function** Required at all levels and functions due to the interdependence of activities, coordination prevents overlapping and chaos.
5. **Responsibility of All Managers** Every manager, from top to lower level, is responsible for coordinating efforts to ensure smooth execution of plans.
6. **Deliberate Function** Managers must actively create and maintain coordination by directing efforts. Without coordination, cooperation may be wasted and without cooperation, there may be employees' dissatisfaction.

Importance of Coordination

Through coordination, managers reconcile differences in timing, interest or effort, etc. There is also a need to harmonise individual goals and organisational goals.

Following points highlight the importance of coordination

Points	Explanation	Example
Growth in Size	As an organisation grows, aligning the diverse habits, backgrounds and goals of employees with common objectives becomes crucial. Coordination helps harmonise individual goals with organisational goals to improve efficiency.	A large company with multiple branches needs to ensure all employees work towards the same goals.
Functional Differentiation	Departments with their own objectives and strategies can cause conflicts, making coordination essential. Proper coordination ensures departments work together towards common goals.	The marketing department and production department may have different goals, but need to work together.
Specialisation	Specialisation and technology can cause conflicts among specialists who may believe only they can judge situations. Coordination helps reconcile differences in approach, interest or opinion among specialists and others in the organisation.	IT specialists may not listen to input from marketing specialists, causing friction.

Mind Map

NATURE AND SIGNIFICANCE OF MANAGEMENT

1 Concept of Management

Management is a process of getting this done with the aim of achieving goals effectively and efficiently.

Following are the essential elements

- **Process** Includes a series of inter-related functions
- **Effectiveness** Involves doing the right task and attaining goals on time
- **Efficiency** Involves doing the task correctly and with least wastage and minimum cost

2 Characteristics of Management

- Management is a goal-oriented process
- Management is all pervasive
- Management is multidimensional (Management of work, management of people, management of operations)
- Management is a continuous process
- Management is a group activity
- Management is a dynamic function
- Management is an intangible force

3 Objectives of Management

Organisational

- Survival of business
- Profit earning
- Growth of business

Personnel

- Financial needs
- Social needs
- Higher level needs

Social

- Timely payment of taxes
- Providing basic amenities
- Using eco-friendly methods
- Conducting business in fair manner
- Providing good quality products at fair prices
- Creating employment opportunities for weaker sections

4 Importance of Management

- Management helps in achieving group goals
- Management increases efficiency
- Management creates dynamic organisation
- Management helps in achieving personal objectives
- Management helps in the development of the society

5 Nature of Management

Management as a Science

- Systematised body of knowledge
- Principles based on observation and experimentation
- Universal validity

Management as an Art

- Existence of theoretical knowledge
- Personalised application
- Based on practice and creativity

Management as a Profession

- Well-defined body of knowledge
- Restricted entry
- Professional association
- Ethical code of conduct
- Service motive

8 Coordination

Coordination binds together all management functions by synchronising activities across departments to achieve common goals.

Characteristics of Coordination

- Coordination integrates group efforts
- Coordination ensures unity of action
- Coordination is a continuous process
- Coordination is an all pervasive function
- Coordination is the responsibility of all managers
- Coordination is a deliberate function

Importance of Coordination

- **Growth in Size** Coordination helps in harmonising individual goals and organisational goals
- **Functional Differentiation** Coordination helps different departments to proceed together in a single direction
- **Specialisation** Coordination helps in reconciling the differences in approach, interest or opinion

7 Functions of Management

- **Planning** Deciding in advance what to do, how to do, when to do and who is going to do it
- **Organising** Assigning duties, grouping tasks, establishing authority and allocating resources
- **Staffing** Finding the right people with right qualification to be employed
- **Directing** Influencing the behaviour of human resource with components such as motivation and leadership
- **Controlling** Monitors organisational performance towards the attainment of organisational goals

6 Levels of Management

- Top level (It consists of senior most executives of organisation. This level includes Board of Directors, Chairman, etc.)
- Middle level (It acts as a link between top and lower level management. This level includes heads of different functional departments)
- Operational level (It includes the groups or members, who are concerned with the execution of work. This level includes supervisors, foreman, superintendent, etc.)

EXAM PATTERN QUESTIONS

Objective Type Questions

Multiple Choice Questions (MCQs)

1. **"In order to be successful, an organisation must change its goals according to the needs of the environment." Identify the characteristic of management highlighted in the statement.** **Competency Based Que**

(a) Management is dynamic
(b) Management is goal-oriented process
(c) Management is a group activity
(d) Management is all pervasive

2. **Choose the incorrect statement from the following about the multi-dimensional nature of management.**

(a) The multi-dimensional nature of management includes overseeing various aspects such as people, operations and strategic planning
(b) Effective management requires a focus solely on optimising operational processes without regard to people's management
(c) Management must balance different dimensions, including managing work processes, human resources and organisational goals
(d) The multi-dimensional nature of management involves integrating diverse functions like marketing, finance and human resources

3. **"It is the process of designing and maintaining an environment in which individuals, working together in groups, efficiently accomplish selected aims." Identify the process.** **CBSE 2025**

(a) Management (b) Organising
(c) Staffing (d) Directing

4. **Most of the organisations these days have adapted themselves to changing environment. To reach and engage with the target customers, they started to have a strong presence on social media like Facebook, Instagram, etc.**

From the following, identify the feature of management being highlighted

(a) Management is a group activity
(b) Management is a continuous process
(c) Management is multi-dimensional
(d) Management is a dynamic function

5. **The activities involved in managing the enterprise are common to all organisations whether economic, political or social.**

Identify the feature of management.

(a) Management is multi-dimensional
(b) Management is all pervasive
(c) Management is a continuous process
(d) Management is a dynamic function

6. **Identify the characteristic of management illustrated by the below picture in which the heads of all departments have contributed towards the company's growth.**

(a) Management is pervasive
(b) Management is multi-dimensional
(c) Management is a group activity
(d) Management is a dynamic function

7. **The management of a bag manufacturing company has recently changed. Due to this, an improvement can be felt in the way company functions. Now, targets are met according to plans, whereas, earlier deadlines were never given importance. Now there is orderliness, instead of chaos in the organisation and the employees are happy and satisfied.**

From the following, identify the characteristic of management which is highlighted in the above case. **CBSE 2023; Competency Based Que**

(a) Management is dynamic
(b) Management is a continuous process
(c) Management is a group activity
(d) Management is an intangible force

8. **Akshara runs a business in the name of 'AK Solutions' in a well reputed area of her city where people provide spaces to students as library, as study centres and as training and event centres to businesses. Akshara provides only conference halls to big and small enterprises for their meetings and events. Suddenly, in July 2024, floods affected some libraries and study centres in her neigbouring area.**

The exams were fast approaching and students were facing a lot of problems as these study centres and libraries had to be closed. Taking advantage of this opportunity and to help the students 'AK Solutions' adapted itself to the needs of the environment, they decided to convert some of their conference halls into libraries and study centres. They also decided to provide food and other facilities required by the students at subsidised rates. This initiative increased their business manifold and earned them significant goodwill. The feature of management highlighted in the above case is **CBSE 2025; Competency Based Que**

(a) management is a continuous process
(b) management is an intangible force
(c) management is a dynamic function
(d) management is a group activity

9. Neeraj is the Director of 'Tulip Public School' having 2000 students. There are two headmasters one for senior classes and another for junior classes. 50 teachers are under the supervision of the Senior headmaster and 60 teachers under the supervision of the junior headmaster.

No teacher working under the supervision of the senior headmaster is happy and satisfied, which is affecting the result of the senior classes.

On the other hand the teachers working under the supervision of the junior headmaster are performing their duties willingly and achieving their objectives. All the teachers are happy and satisfied. The Director, Neeraj can feel how nicely the junior headmaster was managing his classes. The characteristic of management discussed above is **CBSE 2023; Competency Based Que**

(a) management is a goal-oriented process
(b) management is a dynamic function
(c) management is an intangible force
(d) management is a continuous process

10. 'TechPro Solutions' is an IT company with a goal to provide innovative software solutions to businesses. On the other hand, 'Carewell Foundation' is a healthcare non-profit organisation focused on offering free medical services to rural areas.

Both organisations rely on their management to coordinate and unite the efforts of their teams to achieve their respective goals.

The characteristic of management being discussed here is **Competency Based Que**

(a) management is a group activity
(b) management is goal-oriented
(c) management is pervasive
(d) management is a multi-dimensional activity

11. Rahul is the operations manager at a manufacturing company. He was recently praised for implementing a new system that reduced waste and improved the accuracy of production processes, all while keeping the costs under control. His team has managed to produce higher-quality products with fewer resources, meeting all deadlines.

The company appreciated how tasks were performed accurately and with minimal costs. What quality was Rahul demonstrating by performing tasks accurately and with minimal costs? **Competency Based Que**

(a) Effectiveness (b) Coordination
(c) Process (d) Efficiency

12. Rohan's company's target production is 6,000 units in a year. To achieve this target the manager has to operate on double shifts due to power failure most of the time. The manager is able to produce 6,000 units but at a higher production cost. In the above case, tell the status of the manager. **Competency Based Que**

(a) Manager was effective
(b) Manager was efficient
(c) Manager was effective but not efficient
(d) Manager was efficient but not effective

13. Akash works as a production manager in 'Elite Enterprises' manufacturing LED lights. Due to festive season, there is lot of demand for their lights.

Akash was given the task of producing 100 units of LED lights @ ₹ 200 per unit within 5 days for an urgent order.

Akash was able to achieve the target of 100 units of LED lights within 5 days @ ₹ 220 per unit.

Identify from the following whether Akash is **CBSE 2023; Competency Based Que**

(a) efficient only
(b) effective only
(c) Both efficient and effective
(d) Neither efficient nor effective

14. Aparna and Priyanka are working in 'Shreya Industries', a company dealing in readymade garments for women. Each of them was assigned the responsibility of producing 10 dresses each within 5 days at a cost of ₹ 1,000 per dress.

Aparna was able to produce 10 dresses at a cost of ₹ 1,100 per dress within 5 days, whereas Priyanka was able to produce only 8 dresses at a cost of ₹ 900 per dress in 5 days.

Which of the following statements is correct with respect to the above? **CBSE 2024 C**

(a) Aparna is efficient but Priyanka is effective
(b) Aparna is effective but Priyanka is efficient
(c) Both Aparna and Priyanka are effective
(d) Both Aparna and Priyanka are efficient

15. Tech Inc. is a renowned IT consulting firm known for its commitment to achieving high performance and growth. The company emphasises setting clear goals and measuring performance against these goals.

It regularly evaluates its progress and adapts its strategies to ensure that its objectives are met efficiently. This focus on achieving targets and improving overall performance aligned with the company's strategic direction.

The objective of management being met by Tech Inc. is **Competency Based Que**

(a) social (b) personnel
(c) organisational (d) Both social and personnel

16. Bonfast Cement Ltd. supports 7 villages with housing facilities, schools, safe drinking water, health and hygiene. The company sends its employees to visit a nearby village every 15 days to provide support and to see whether the facilities provided are being implemented on ground.

The objective which 'Bonfast Cement Ltd.' is trying to achieve is **CBSE 2024; Competency Based Que**

(a) personal objective (b) social objective
(c) organisational objective (d) economic objective

17. 'Saras Dairy' started using environment-friendly 'Bilona' method of making ghee, unlike other dairies which were using modern methods involving machines and chemicals. By doing this, 'Saras Dairy' is providing employment to hundreds of illiterate people in the rural areas. Which objective of management is 'Saras Dairy' trying to achieve? **Competency Based Que**

(a) National objective (b) Personal objective
(c) Social objective (d) Economic objective

18. A multinational sweets and snacks company had been into catering business for the last many years. To add to its prospects and to grow in the long-run, it wants to increase its sales volume, the number of products and capital investment.

The organisational objective of management it seeks to achieve is **CBSE 2024; Competency Based Que**

(a) survival (b) profit
(c) growth (d) corporate social responsibility

19. 'Alfanzo Ltd.' is achieving all its objectives in an effective and efficient manner. It is earning enough revenue to cover costs and the risks of the business. Now the company wants to increase the sales volume, the capital investment, the number of employees and the number of products also. By doing this, the management wants to achieve its following objective. **CBSE 2023; Competency Based Que**

(a) Survival (b) Profit
(c) Personal (d) Growth

20. The below picture depicts some of the steps taken by the organisation. Identify the objective of organisation which is being fulfilled by these steps.

(a) Social objective (b) Profit objective
(c) Survival objective (d) Personal objective

21. Indian Railways has launched a new broad gauge solar power train which is going to be a path breaking leap towards making trains greener and more environment friendly.

The solar power DEMU (Diesel Electric Multiple Unit) has 6 trailer coaches and is expected to save about 21,000 liters of diesel and ensure a cost saving of ₹ 12,00,000 per year.

Name the objective of management achieved by Indian Railways in the above case. **NCERT Modified; Competency Based Que**

(a) Social objective (b) Personal objective
(c) Strategic objective
(d) Organisational objective

22. GreenEarth Solutions, a leading environmental consulting firm, is deeply committed to reducing the environmental impact of businesses and promoting sustainability. The company has taken multiple initiatives, such as running awareness campaigns about waste management and offering eco-friendly solutions to local communities.

It also partners with non-profits to support reforestation projects and works with government bodies to improve environmental regulations. These efforts reflect the company's dedication to contributing positively to society and protecting the environment.

The objective of management being met by GreenEarth Solutions is **Competency Based Que**

(a) organisational
(b) personnel
(c) social
(d) Both organisational and personnel

23. 'BetaTech Pvt Ltd' has been successfully operating in the tech industry, meeting all its targets efficiently and maintaining a healthy profit margin. The company has now set its sights on expanding its market presence by launching new products, entering international markets and increasing its workforce. The management aims to boost its market share and solidify its position in the industry through this expansion.

The objective of management being pursued by BetaTech Pvt Ltd. is **Competency Based Que**

(a) survival (b) profit
(c) personal (d) growth

24. 'EcoMart Supermarket' has introduced an initiative to reduce plastic waste by encouraging customers to bring their own reusable bags. Additionally, the supermarket has replaced plastic packaging with biodegradable materials across all its product lines. Through these efforts, EcoMart aims to contribute to environmental sustainability while also educating customers on the importance of reducing plastic consumption.

The objective of management achieved by EcoMart in the above case is **Competency Based Que**

(a) Social objective (b) Personal objective
(c) Strategic objective (d) Organisational objective

25. TX Group is rolling out an initiative to help create wealth for its employees through the implementation of Employee Stock Option. Through motivation and leadership the management will help individuals to develop team spirit, cooperation and commitment to the success of the group. The following importance of management is highlighted above **Competency Based Que**

(a) Management helps in achieving personal objectives
(b) Management helps in the development of society
(c) Management creates a dynamic organisation
(d) Management increases efficiency

26. Management helps in providing good quality products and services, creating employment opportunities, adopting new technology for the greater good of the people and leads the path towards growth and development.

This highlights the following point of importance of management. **CBSE 2023**

(a) Management helps in achieving group goals
(b) Management creates a dynamic organisation
(c) Management helps in the development of society
(d) Management helps in achieving personal objectives

27. Priya Sharma, a seasoned operations manager, was tasked with improving the efficiency of her team in a manufacturing plant. She observed the workflow and noticed several bottlenecks. Priya decided to implement a new process based on her extensive experience and intuition about the team's strengths and weaknesses. She customised her approach by experimenting with different strategies and monitoring their effectiveness.

Her solutions were innovative and tailored specifically to the unique needs of her team, showcasing her ability to adapt management principles to real-world challenges.

The nature of management highlighted in the above case is **Competency Based Que**

(a) management as a science
(b) management as an art
(c) management both as an art and as a science
(d) management as a profession

28. The newly appointed production manager of Saheb Ltd., a firm manufacturing toys, Mr. Ahrawat noticed that the workers in the factory were not giving their best as the physical conditions in the factory were not good.

He conducted an experiment to see the effect of improvement in the physical conditions in the factory on the performance of the workers, by providing adequate ventilation and water facilities. He observed that the fatigue level of the workers reduced.

The nature of management being highlighted in the above case is **CBSE SQP 2025**

(a) management as science
(b) management as profession
(c) management as an art (d) Both (a) and (c)

29. "Management has its own vocabulary of terms and concepts. Managers need to communicate with one another with the help of a common vocabulary for the better understanding of their work situation."
Which of the following features is highlighted in the above statement? **CBSE 2023**

(a) Principles based on experimentation
(b) Systematised body of knowledge
(c) Universal validity
(d) Personalised application

30. Which of the following features of 'Management as an art' highlights that every manager applies his knowledge of principles in his own way to deal with a given situation? **CBSE 2023**

(a) Ethical code of conduct
(b) Existence of theoretical knowledge
(c) Personalised application
(d) Universal validity

31. Rahul Verma, a marketing head for a fast-growing startup, was given the responsibility to boost the company's brand recognition. With his creative flair, Rahul devised a unique campaign by leveraging social media trends and analysing consumer behaviour. He crafted engaging content, adjusted strategies based on feedback and intuitively understood what would appeal to the target audience. His ability to think outside the box and tailor his methods according to the company's needs demonstrated his expertise in applying management principles creatively.

The nature of management highlighted in the above case is **Competency Based Que**

(a) Management as a science (b) Management as an art
(c) Management both as an art and as a science
(d) Management as a profession

32. The primary focus of ....management is to manage the daily operations and provide guidance to employees.

(a) top level (b) middle level
(c) lower level (d) strategic

33. With respect to levels of management, choose the incorrect statement from the following. **CBSE 2024**

(a) Operational level management is responsible for maintaining safety standards in the organisation
(b) At middle level management, managers ensure that their department has the necessary personnel
(c) Chief Executive Officer at top level management is responsible for all activities of first line managers
(d) Top level management is responsible for all the activities of the business and for its impact on the society

34. Which of the following responsibilities is associated with top level management?

(a) They ensure that their department has the necessary personnel
(b) They interact with the actual workforce and pass on instructions of the middle management to the workers
(c) They cooperate with other departments for smooth functioning of the organisation
(d) They analyse the business environment and its implications for the survival of the firm

35. Which of the following is not a function of middle level management? **CBSE 2024 C**

(a) To interpret the policies framed by the top management
(b) To ensure that their department has the necessary personnel
(c) To coordinate the activities of different departments
(d) To assign necessary duties and responsibilities to the personnel in their departments

36. The image below shows the organisational structure of a company. Identify the level of management represented by the role of President.

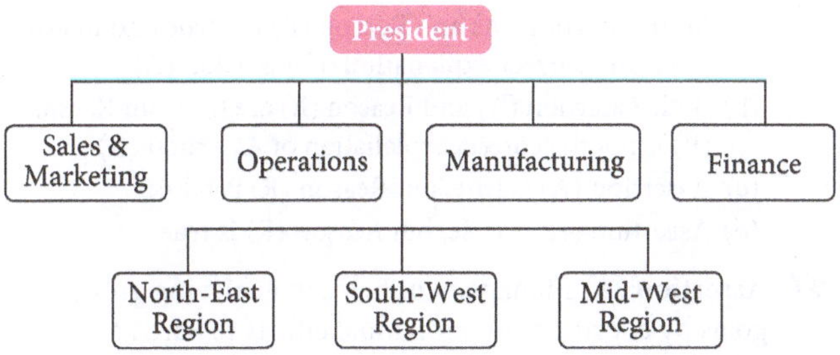

(a) Top level management (b) Middle level management
(c) Lower level management (d) Supervisory management

37. To determine whether decisions have been effectively implemented into desired actions, which management function should be performed?

(a) Planning (b) Organising
(c) Directing (d) Controlling

38. Identify the function of management depicted in the given picture.

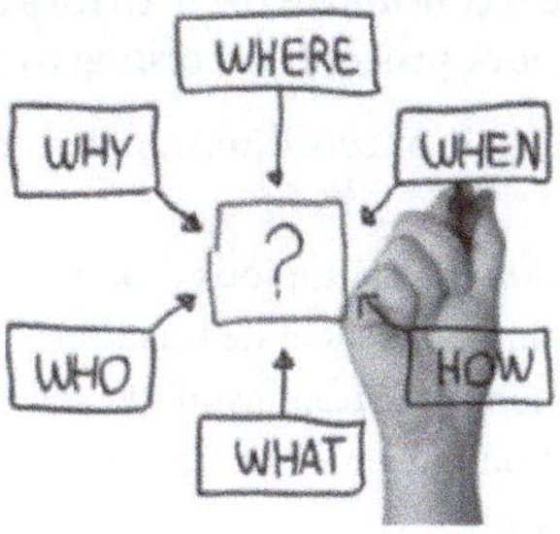

(a) Planning (b) Organising
(c) Staffing (d) Directing

39. The picture given below depicts chaos in the organisation. The absence of which concept results in such chaos?

(a) Motivation (b) Coordination
(c) Communication (d) Planning

40. At XYZ Ltd., the production, marketing and finance departments had been working independently, leading to delays and miscommunication. To solve this, the management decided to bring all department heads together for regular coordination meetings. These meetings helped align the efforts of all departments, ensuring they worked towards the same organisational goals. As a result, tasks were completed more efficiently and the company saw an improvement in overall performance.
Which characteristic of coordination is being emphasised in this scenario where different departments are working together towards the same goal?

Competency Based Que

(a) Coordination ensures unity of action
(b) Coordination is an all pervasive function
(c) Coordination is a deliberate function
(d) Coordination is the responsibility of all managers

41. **In an organisation, coordination is the function of every manager. Top level managers need to coordinate with their subordinates to ensure that the overall plans of the organisation are duly carried out.**

Middle level managers coordinate with both the top level and the supervisory level managers. Supervisory level managers coordinate the activities of workers to ensure that work proceeds according to plans.

The characteristic of coordination discussed in the above para is **CBSE 2023**

(a) coordination is a continuous process
(b) coordination is a deliberate function
(c) coordination is the responsibility of all managers
(d) coordination integrates group efforts

42. **EcoFresh Ltd., a company specialising in eco-friendly products, faced challenges in launching a new product line. The marketing, production, and R&D departments were working on different aspects of the product, but there was a lack of alignment and communication between them. The marketing team developed a campaign that did not match the product's features, while the production team faced delays due to uncoordinated feedback from R&D.**

Realising the issue, the management implemented a coordination system where representatives from each department met regularly to ensure that all teams were aligned with the product's goals and timelines.

This improved communication led to a successful product launch and enhanced overall efficiency.

The importance of coordination highlighted in the above case is **Competency Based Que**

(a) It ensures effective communication between departments
(b) It helps in reducing the cost of production
(c) It promotes individual performance
(d) It increases the number of products manufactured

Direction *Read the following case study and answer the questions 43 to 46 on the basis of the same*

Sana is the branch manager of ABC Handicrafts Pvt. Ltd. The company's objective is to promote the sales of Indian handloom and handicraft products. It sells fabrics, furnishings, readymades and household items are made out of traditional Indian fabrics. Sana decides quantities, variety, colour and texture of all the above items and then allocates resources for their purchase from different suppliers.

She appoints a team of designers and crafts' people in the company, who developed some prints for bed covers in bright colour on silk.

Although the products looked very attractive and impressive, they were relatively expensive on, the front of affordability for an average customer. Sana suggested that they should keep the silk bed covers for special festive occasions and offer the cotton bed covers on a regular basis to keep costs under control.

43. **"She appoints a team of designers and crafts' people in the company, who developed some prints for bed covers in bright colour on silk." Which function of management is highlighted in this context?**

(a) Controlling (b) Staffing
(c) Planning (d) Directing

44. **In the above case "company's objective is to promote the sales of Indian handloom and handicraft products." The above line focuses on which feature of management?**

(a) Management is an intangible force
(b) Management is a goal-oriented process
(c) Management is pervasive in nature
(d) Management is a continuous process

45. **With reference to the above case, at which level of management Sana is working?**

(a) Lower level (b) Top level
(c) Middle level (d) Shop floor

46. **"Sana suggested that they should keep the silk bed covers for special festive occasions and offer the cotton bed covers on a regular basis to keep costs under control." Which function of management is highlighted in this context?**

(a) Controlling (b) Staffing
(c) Organising (d) Planning

Assertion-Reason

Direction (Q.No. 47 to 56) *Read the following Assertion (A) and Reason (R) and choose the correct alternative from the following*

Alternatives

(a) Both Assertion (A) and Reason (R) are true and Reason (R) is the correct explanation of Assertion (A)
(b) Both Assertion (A) and Reason (R) are true, but Reason (R) is not the correct explanation of Assertion (A)
(c) Assertion (A) is true, but Reason (R) is false
(d) Assertion (A) is false, but Reason (R) is true

47. **Assertion** (A) Management helps in achieving group goals by coordinating individual efforts towards a common purpose.

Reason (R) Management is only concerned with planning and organising resources but not with directing or controlling activities.

48. **Assertion** (A) Management is fundamentally a group activity because it involves coordinating and directing the efforts of people to achieve organisational goals.

Reason (R) Management as a group activity primarily focuses on individual performance rather than collective team efforts.

49. **Assertion** (A) Management is termed as a process because it involves a series of continuous and interrelated functions such as planning, organising, leading and controlling.

Reason (R) Management is termed as a process because it focuses exclusively on short-term operational tasks and ignores long-term strategic planning.

50. **Assertion** (A) Management focuses on both efficiency and effectiveness to ensure that organisational resources are used optimally and that goals are achieved.

Reason (R) Efficiency is concerned only with the speed of operations, while effectiveness is solely about achieving goals without considering resource utilisation.

51. **Assertion** (A) Management aims to achieve social, financial and personal objectives to ensure comprehensive organisational success.

Reason (R) Social objectives focus on community engagement, while financial objectives concentrate solely on profitability.

52. **Assertion** (A) Effective management is crucial for achieving organisational goals and ensuring efficiency.

Reason (R) The primary importance of management is solely focused on reducing operational costs.

53. **Assertion** (A) Management is considered a science because it uses systematic and empirical methods to achieve objectives.

Reason (R) Science is characterised by its ability to predict and control events through established principles and laws.

54. **Assertion** (A) Management operates at three levels i.e. top level, middle level and lower level management.

Reason (R) Each level of management has distinct roles and responsibilities to ensure the smooth functioning of the organisation.

55. **Assertion** (A) Coordination is the deliberate effort by managers to ensure that individuals and departments work towards the achievement of organisational goals.

Reason (R) Coordination is a natural and automatic process that occurs without any managerial intervention.

56. **Assertion** (A) Coordination is essential for ensuring that all parts of an organisation work together effectively.

Reason (R) Coordination is important only for large organisations and has minimal impact on small businesses.

Two Statements Based MCQs

Direction (Q.No. 57 to 64) *Read the following statements carefully and choose the correct alternative*

Alternatives

(a) Statement I is correct and Statement II is incorrect
(b) Statement II is correct and Statement I is incorrect
(c) Both the statements are correct
(d) Both the statements are incorrect

57. **Statement I** Management is multi-dimensional.

Statement II The activities involved in managing an enterprise are common to all organisations whether economic, social or political. **CBSE 2023**

58. **Statement I** Achieving organisational objectives requires alignment between employee's personal objectives and the company's strategic goals.

Statement II Personal objectives should be prioritised over organisational objectives for an effective management strategy.

59. **Statement I** In order to survive, an organisation must earn enough revenues to cover cost.

Statement II Management increases effectiveness by reducing cost and increasing productivity.

60. **Statement I** Management as a science relies on established principles and systematic methods to achieve organisational goals.

Statement II Management as a science emphasises creativity and intuition over empirical evidence and systematic analysis.

61. **Statement I** The nature of management includes its universal applicability across various types of organisations and industries.

Statement II Management is only relevant in large organisations and is not applicable to small businesses.

62. **Statement I** Operational level managers are responsible for the welfare and survival of the organisation.

Statement II The authority and responsibility of supervisory level managers are limited according to plans drawn by middle level management.

63. **Statement I** Planning is a function of management that involves setting goals and deciding on the actions required to achieve them.

Statement II Coordination is part of the organising function and does not involve setting goals or deciding actions.

64. Statement I Coordination ensures that different departments work together harmoniously towards common organisational goals.

Statement II Coordination is a function that is primarily handled by top management and does not concern middle or lower management.

Matching

65. Match the following statements with their correct options

Column I (Statements)	Column II (Importance of Management)
A. Achieving organisational goals	(i) Management ensures that resources such as time, money and manpower are used efficiently and effectively.
B. Optimum utilisation of resources	(ii) Management guides and directs efforts to accomplish the organisation's objectives and goals.
C. Facilitating growth and innovation	(iii) Management helps the people in adapting to the changes in business environment.
D. Creates a dynamic organisation	(iv) Management encourages new ideas, methods and improvements to foster progress and development.

Codes

	A	B	C	D
(a)	(ii)	(i)	(iv)	(iii)
(b)	(iii)	(ii)	(i)	(iv)
(c)	(i)	(iii)	(ii)	(iv)
(d)	(iv)	(ii)	(i)	(iii)

66. Match the following features of management with its classification as a profession, art or science

Column I (Features)	Column II (Classification)
A. Systematic knowledge	(i) Management involves the application of specialised skills and techniques to handle specific organisational challenges and achieve desired results.
B. Application of skills	(ii) Management adheres to established standards and ethical practices, often guided by professional bodies and codes of conduct.
C. Code of conduct	(iii) Management relies on systematic, empirical knowledge and principles derived from research and experience.
D. Universal validity	(iv) Principles of management are not exact like scientific principles.

Codes

	A	B	C	D
(a)	(iii)	(i)	(ii)	(iv)
(b)	(ii)	(iii)	(i)	(iv)
(c)	(i)	(ii)	(iv)	(iii)
(d)	(iii)	(ii)	(iv)	(i)

67. Match the levels of management given in Column I with the functions performed at each level given in Column II CBSE 2024

Column I	Column II
A. Top level management	(i) They directly oversee the efforts of the workforce.
B. Middle level management	(ii) They ensure that their department has the necessary personnel.
C. Operational management	(iii) They are responsible for the welfare and survival of the organisation.

Codes

	A	B	C
(a)	(i)	(ii)	(iii)
(b)	(iii)	(ii)	(i)
(c)	(iii)	(i)	(ii)
(d)	(ii)	(iii)	(i)

68. Match the following management functions with their correct options given in Column II

Column I (Functions)	Column II (Descriptions)
A. Planning	(i) Making sure that right people, with the right qualification are available at the right places.
B. Organising	(ii) Determining what needs to be done, how, and by whom to accomplish the goals.
C. Controlling	(iii) Arranging resources and tasks in a structured manner to achieve the objectives.
D. Staffing	(iv) Ensuring that the organizational goals are achieved by monitoring performance and making necessary adjustments.

Codes

	A	B	C	D
(a)	(ii)	(iii)	(i)	(iv)
(b)	(i)	(iii)	(ii)	(iv)
(c)	(ii)	(iii)	(iv)	(i)
(d)	(ii)	(i)	(iii)	(iv)

Answers

1. (a) Management is dynamic
2. (b) Management involves balancing all aspects, including human resources, work processes, and organisational goals.
3. (a) Management
4. (d) management is a dynamic function
5. (b) Management is all pervasive
6. (c) Management is a group activity
7. (d) Management is an intangible force
8. (c) management is a dynamic function
9. (c) management is an intangible force
10. (b) management is goal-oriented
11. (d) Efficiency
12. (c) Manager was effective but not efficient
13. (b) effective only
14. (b) Aparna is effective but Priyanka is efficient
15. (c) organisational
16. (b) social objective
17. (c) Social objective
18. (c) growth
19. (d) Growth
20. (a) Social objective
21. (a) Social objective
22. (c) social
23. (d) growth
24. (a) Social objective
25. (a) Management helps in achieving personal objectives
26. (c) Management helps in the development of society.
27. (b) management as an art
28. (a) management as science
29. (b) Systematised body of knowledge
30. (c) Personalised application
31. (b) Management as an art
32. (c) lower level
33. (c) Top level management, such as the Chief Executive Officer (CEO), is responsible for setting the overall direction of the organisation and making strategic decisions, but they do not directly manage the activities of first line managers.
34. (d) They analyse the business environment and its implications for the survival of the firm
35. (c) To coordinate the activities of different departments
36. (a) Top level management
37. (d) Controlling
38. (a) Planning
39. (b) Coordination
40. (a) Coordination ensures unity of action
41. (c) coordination is the responsibility of all managers
42. (a) It ensures effective communication between departments
43. (b) Staffing
44. (b) Management is a goal-oriented process
45. (c) Middle level
46. (a) Controlling
47. (c) Management is not limited to just planning and organising. It also includes directing and controlling activities, which are essential functions to ensure that goals are met effectively and efficiently.
48. (c) Management inherently values the group activity over isolated individual performance to achieve organisational objectives effectively.
49. (c) Assertion (A) is true, but Reason (R) is false
50. (c) Assertion (A) is true, but Reason (R) is false
51. (b) Both Assertion (A) and Reason (R) are true, but Reason (R) is not the correct explanation of Assertion (A)
52. (c) Effective management impacts goals and efficiency broadly, not just cost reduction.
53. (b) Management uses systematic methods, but not all aspects of management can be predicted or controlled like in pure sciences.
54. (a) Both Assertion (A) and Reason (R) are true and Reason (R) is the correct explanation of Assertion (A)
55. (c) Coordination is not an automatic process but requires active managerial involvement.
56. (c) Coordination is crucial for all organisations, not just large ones.
57. (c) Both the statements are correct
58. (a) Prioritising personal objectives over organisational ones is not effective for achieving organisational goals.
59. (a) Management increases efficiency by reducing costs and increasing productivity.
60. (a) Creativity and intuition are more associated with management as an art.
61. (a) Management is applicable to all types of organisations.
62. (b) The responsibility for the overall welfare and survival of the organisation typically rests with top level management.
63. (a) Coordination involves aligning and integrating efforts across different functions and levels to achieve those goals.
64. (a) Coordination is crucial at all levels of management, not just at the top level.
65. (a) (ii) (i) (iv) (iii)
66. (a) (iii) (i) (ii) (iv)
67. (b) (iii) (ii) (i)
68. (c) (ii) (iii) (iv) (i)

Subjective Questions

Short Answer Type Questions

1. State any four characteristics of management. **CBSE 2024**

Or Explain the following features of management.

(i) Management is a goal-oriented process

(ii) Management is a continuous process **CBSE 2025**

Or Name any two important characteristics of management. **NCERT**

Ans. Following are the characteristics of management

(i) **Management is a Continuous Process**
Management is an ongoing process of continuous, composite, but separate functions (planning, organising, staffing, directing and controlling). These functions are simultaneously performed by all managers on a continuous basis.

(ii) **Management is a Group Activity**
An organisation is a collection of diverse individuals with different needs. Through coordination and teamwork, management unites the efforts of individuals to achieve organisational goals, alongwith the growth and development of individuals as needs and opportunities change.

(iii) **Management is a Dynamic Function**
Every organisation interacts with its external environment which includes social, economic and political factors. In order to survive or achieve success, an organisation must change itself and its goals according to the needs of the environment.

(iv) **Management is an Intangible Force**
Management is an unseen force whose presence can be felt when an organisation functions. Orderliness, discipline, happy and satisfied employees, all reflect the presence of effective management.

(v) **Management is a Goal-oriented Process**
The basic aim of management is to achieve the organisational goals. These should be simple and clearly stated. Different organisations have different set of goals. Management achieve these goals through uniting the efforts of the individuals in the organisation.

2. 'Management is multidimensional' is one of the features of management. Explain its following dimensions

(i) Management of work

(ii) Management of people **CBSE 2025**

Or Why is management considered to be a multi-dimensional concept? **NCERT**

Ans. Management is considered to be a multi-dimensional concept due to the following points

(i) **Management of Work**
It is concerned with performance of various activities/ tasks in an organisation. e.g. Manufacturing a product in a factory, treating patients in a hospital, etc.
Management translates this work in terms of goals to be achieved and assigns the means to achieve it.
This is done in terms of problems to be solved, decisions to be made, plans to be established, budgets to be prepared, responsibilities to be assigned and authority to be delegated.

(ii) **Management of People**
It refers to management of human resources, which are the most important asset for an organisation.
Management of people implies two things
- Dealing with employees as individuals with diverse needs and behaviour.
- Dealing with individuals as a group of people.

(iii) **Management of Operations**
It refers to the activities of production cycle, which entails the flow of input material and transforms the input into desired output.
It is interlinked with both management of work and management of people.

3. Explain efficiency and effectiveness in the context of management.

Ans. Effectiveness, in management, is concerned with doing the right task, completing activities and achieving goals within the prescribed time limit. It is basically concerned with end result.
Efficiency is concerned with doing the task correctly and with minimum cost, least wastage and maximum utilisation of resources.
Management is concerned with the efficient use of resources to get the maximum output, as it reduces costs and lead to higher profits.

4. There are different objectives of business and economics objectives are one among them. Explain these economic objectives.

Ans. Following are the economic objectives of business

(i) **Survival**
The most important objective of every business is to survive. Management must seek to ensure organisation's survival, which can be possible only if organisation earns enough revenue to cover its costs.

(ii) **Profit**
It is the incentive or reward for carrying out a business. Management must ensure that the organisation makes profit, which provides a vital incentive for organisation's continued continued successful operation. Profit is essential to cover costs and risks of the business.

(iii) **Growth**
Business organisations must grow and expand their activities which can be measured in terms of sales, profits, number of products, number of employees, etc. Growth indicates the ability of an organisation to fully exploit its potential opportunities.

5. Explain the following terms
(i) Social objectives of management
(ii) Personnel objectives of management

Or **Explain the various objectives of management.**
CBSE 2024 C

Ans. Following are the objectives of management

(i) **Organisational or Economic Objective**
The main objective of any organisation should be to utilise human and material resources to the maximum possible advantage. It includes

- Survival • Profit • Growth

(ii) **Social Objectives of Management**
These objectives deal with the commitment of an organisation towards the society. It involves creating employment opportunities for disadvantaged sections of society, providing basic amenities like schools and creches to employees, providing good quality products at reasonable prices, timely payment of taxes, using eco-friendly methods of production and conducting business in fair and careful manner.

(iii) **Personnel Objectives of Management**
These objectives are related with satisfying the personal needs of the employees having different personalities, backgrounds, experiences and objectives.

These objectives involve

- Financial needs, by giving competitive salary and perks.
- Social needs, by peer recognition.
- Higher level needs, by providing opportunities for personal growth and development.

6. Management is a profession like accounting, medicine and law as it also has a well-defined body of knowledge. Yet management does not qualify to be a full-fledged profession? Why? **Competency Based Que**

Ans. Management does not qualify to be a full-fledged profession because of the following reasons

(i) **Restricted Entry**
Entry into a profession is restricted through an examination or educational degree. In management, no such restriction is there to appoint a manager. Anyone can become a manager irrespective of the educational qualification.

(ii) **Professional Association**
All professionals are bound to be a part of a professional association which regulates entry, grants certificate of practice and enforces a code of conduct. This feature is also not applicable to management.

Though, there are certain management associations in India like All India Management Association (AIMA), but they do not have the statutory backing and membership to these associations is not mandatory for managers.

(iii) **Ethical Code of Conduct**
All professions are subject to an ethical code of conduct which guides the behaviour of its members. However, in management, no such rules and regulations are framed to guide the managers through a code of conduct.

(iv) **Service Motive**
The basic motive of each profession is to provide dedicated and committed service to its clients. This feature is also not present in management completely, as the primary motive of management is to help organisation achieve its stated goal, which can be profit maximisation for a business enterprise and service for a hospital.

7. "Art is concerned with personal application of knowledge." In the light of this statement, compare all the features of management with art and prove that it is an art. **Competency Based Que**

Ans. Following is the comparison of all the features of management with art

(i) **Existence of Theoretical Knowledge**
Art is based on the existence of theoretical knowledge and principles of concept necessary for practice.

This characteristic is present in management as it has certain principles and techniques alongwith lots of literature available in various areas of management like finance, marketing, etc. that the manager has to specialise in.

(ii) **Personalised Application**
Art is a personalised concept, as use of principles and theories differs from person to person, giving rise to different styles of application.

Management also possess this feature, as every manager learn same principles and theories of management, but each manager manages things and people in his own unique way depending on how creative they are.

A good manager works through a combination of practice, creativity, imagination, initiative and innovation.

(iii) **Based on Practice and Creativity**
Art lies in creative application of existing theoretical knowledge, which improves with consistent practice, creativity, imagination, innovation and initiative.

This feature also applies to management, as manager improves his skills and gains vast experience with the continuous application of management principles. This gives rise to different styles of management.

Thus, we can say that management is an 'art', as it fulfills all the criteria of being an art. Hence, we can conclude that "management is an art of getting things done through people."

8. **Why is management an inexact science? Explain.**

Or **Why management is not considered as pure science?**

Ans. Management is an inexact science because of the following reasons

(i) **Systematised Body of Knowledge**
Science is a systematised body of knowledge consisting of principles and theories based on cause and effect relationship.

Like science, there is a systematised body of knowledge in management, consisting of theories, principles, vocabulary and concepts.

(ii) **Principles Based on Experimentation**
Scientific principles are developed through observation and then tested through repeated experimentation under controlled conditions. This feature is not fully applicable to management. Though, principles of management have been developed over a period of time based on observation and experimentation, but it deals with human beings whose behaviour cannot be accurately predicted or replicated.

(iii) **Universal Validity**
Scientific principles are valid and applicable universally. This feature is also not fully applicable to management. Principles of management are not exact like scientific principles. Their application and use is not universal. They have to be modified according to a given situation.

Hence, it can be concluded that management cannot be considered as exact or pure science but we can call it as an inexact science or social science.

9. **"They are responsible for interpreting the policies formulated by top level management."**
Identify the level of management and state some of its functions. Competency Based Que

Ans. Middle level management is responsible for interpreting the policies formulated by top level management.

Some of the functions are as follows

(i) To ensure that their department has the necessary personnel.

(ii) To assign necessary duties and responsibilities to them.

(iii) To motivate them to achieve desired objectives.

(iv) To cooperate with other departments for smooth functioning of the organisation.

10. **State any four functions performed by top level management.** CBSE 2024

Ans. Following are the functions performed by top level management

(i) To strive for welfare and survival of business.

(ii) To formulate overall organisational goals and policies of the business.

(iii) To integrate diverse elements and coordinate the activities of different departments according to the overall objectives of the organisation.

(iv) To analyse the business environment and its implications for the survival of the firm.

11. **Give any four functions which are performed by a plant superintendent.**

Ans. Following are the functions which are performed by a plant superintendent

(i) To directly oversee the efforts of the workforce.

(ii) To interact with actual workforce and pass on middle level managers' instructions to the workers.

(iii) To ensure that wastage of materials is minimised, output quality and safety standards are maintained.

The quality and quantity of output depends on the hardwork, discipline and loyalty of workers.

(iv) To represent workers' grievances and suggestions before the management.

12. **"Coordination is needed at all levels of management and it is the responsibility of all managers." Explain how.**

Ans. Coordination is needed at all the three levels of management.

The work at every level is performed by a group of people, that is why, it is required at all the three levels, *viz.*

(i) **Top Level**
It requires coordination to integrate all the activities performed by middle and lower level of management.

(ii) **Middle Level**
This level requires coordination to balance the activities performed by different individuals.

(iii) **Lower Level**
This level requires coordination to bind the efforts of all workers towards the achievement of goals.

13. **"Coordination is the essence of management." Do you agree? Give reasons.** NCERT

Ans. Yes, I agree. Coordination is the essence of management because of the following reasons

(i) **Coordination is Needed to Perform All the Functions of Management**
Coordination begins at the planning stage when top management plans for the entire organisation. The organisational structure is developed through plans.

Through coordination, people are staffed in organisational structure, based on the required skills and abilities of an individual and jobs are assigned to them. To ensure that plans are properly executed, directing is required. If any discrepancy arises between actual and realised activities, then such discrepancy is taken care of at controlling stage.

(ii) **Coordination is Needed at All Levels of Management**
Top level coordinates the activities of the whole organisation, keeping in view the desired goals. Middle level managers coordinate the activities of different departments. Lower level managers coordinate activities of workers to ensure that work proceeds as per plans.

14. Justify how coordination is
(i) a continuous process.
(ii) an all pervasive function.

Ans.
(i) **Coordination is a Continuous Process**
Coordination is a never ending process whose need is felt at each and every step in the organisation. It starts with planning and continues till controlling.

(ii) **Coordination is an All Pervasive Function**
Coordination is required at all levels, departments and functions of management due to the interdependent nature of various activities.

Absence of coordination at any level, gives rise to overlapping of activities and chaos.

Long Answer Type Questions

15. "Management act as a crucial factor in steering an organisation towards its strategic goals, productivity and ensuring its competitive advantage."

In the light of this statement, explain the importance of management. **Competency Based Que**

Or **Explain any four points of significance of management for an organisation.** **CBSE 2024 C**

Ans. Management plays an important role in the following ways

(i) **Management helps in Achieving Group Goals**
Every organisation has a set of goals to be achieved. Management unites the resources together and give common direction to the efforts of all individuals towards achieving those goals.

(ii) **Management increases Efficiency**
Managers seek to reduce costs and increase productivity through better planning, organising, directing, staffing and controlling the activities of the organisation.

(iii) **Management creates a Dynamic Organisation**
Every organisation works in an ever-changing environment and individuals resist such change. Thus, management helps people adapt to these changes, so that an organisation is able to maintain its competitive edge.

(iv) **Management helps in Achieving Personal Objectives**
A manager leads and motivates his team members in such a way that each individual is able to achieve his/her personal goals while contributing towards organisational objectives.

Through motivation and leadership, the management helps the individuals to develop team spirit, cooperation and commitment to group success.

(v) **Management helps in the Development of Society**
An organisation has number of objectives towards diverse groups. Alongwith the development of organisation, management also aims to develop society by giving due importance to social obligations.

Effective management helps to create employment, provide good quality products at reasonable price, use eco-friendly methods of production etc. which contribute towards the growth and development of society.

16. Differentiate between top level, middle level and lower level of management on any four basis.

Ans. Following are the differences between top level, middle level and lower level management (any four)

Basis	Top Level Management	Middle Level Management	Supervisory Level Management
Time Range	It covers long span of period.	It covers intermediate range.	It is concerned with short period.
Skills	It requires creative skills.	It needs persuasive skills.	It is concerned with operative skills.
Evaluation	It is difficult to evaluate its achievement.	It is less difficult to evaluate its performance.	It is easy to evaluate its performance.
Policy Formulation	It is concerned with the formulation of policies to a greater extent.	It is moderately concerned with policy formulation.	It is least concerned with policy formulation.
Nature	It is determinative. It is more administrative than managerial.	It is more executory and managerial than administrative.	It is operative. It is more supervisory than managerial.

17. In the grand tapestry of organisational success, management weaves its influence through various critical functions.
Identify and elaborate on the five fundamental functions of management that contribute to achieving organisational objectives and sustaining growth?

Ans. Following are the five functions of management that contribute to achieving organisational objectives and sustaining growth

(i) **Planning**
It is the process of deciding in advance what to do, how to do, when to do and who is going to do it. It bridges the gap between where we are and where we want to reach, i.e. future position that the management wants to achieve.

All managers start with deciding in advance the organisational goals and developing a way of achieving them efficiently and effectively.

(ii) **Organising**
It is the process of assigning duties, grouping tasks, establishing authority and allocating resources required to carry out a specific plan.
It decides who will do a particular task, where and when it will be done.
It involves grouping of various tasks into manageable departments and establishes an authority and reporting relationship within the organisational hierarchy.
Proper organisational techniques help in the accomplishment of work and promote both the efficiency of operations and the effectiveness of results.

(iii) **Staffing**
It is the process of filling all positions in an organisation with adequate and qualified personnel. It is related to finding the right people with right qualification to be employed at a right place and at right time.

This is also known as human resource function and involves activities like recruitment, selection, placement, training, etc.

(iv) **Directing**
This function is related with leading, influencing, communicating, supervising and motivating employees towards the attainment of planned targets.

It is concerned with influencing the behaviour of human resource. Motivation and leadership are two key components of directing.

(v) **Controlling**
This function monitors organisational performance towards the attainment of organisational goals. In this function, manager compares the actual performance with the planned performance and look towards finding the deviations, if any. Manager, then takes corrective actions to keep the actual performance as per plan.

18. Explain the term 'coordination' and its importance in management.

Ans. Coordination is the force that binds all the functions of management. It involves synchronisation of all activities of different departments towards the accomplishment of common goal.

It is sometimes considered as a separate function of management. However, it is the essence of management, to achieve harmony among individual efforts towards the accomplishment of goals.

Following points indicate the importance of coordination in management

(i) **Growth in Size**
As organisation grows, it employs larger number of individuals who have different habits of work, background, goals, etc. Thus, there arises a need to synchronise the efforts of all individuals towards achieving the common organisational goals. To improve efficiency, coordination helps in harmonising the individual goals and organisational goals.

(ii) **Functional Differentiation**
Functions of an organisation are divided into departments, divisions arid sections. All the departments have their own objectives, strategies and policies. Thus, there is a chance of conflict. Such a situation can only be handled by establishing proper coordination between the departments, so that they proceed together in a single direction for attainment of common organisational goals.

(iii) **Specialisation**
Increasing complexities of modern technology and diversity of tasks have given rise to high degree of specialisation. Specialists think that they only are qualified, perfect and able to judge the situation. Thus, they are not interested in listening to advice from others.

This sometimes leads to conflict amongst different specialists as well as others in an organisation. In order to avoid such kind of conflicts, coordination is required to reconcile the differences in approach, interest or opinion of the specialists.

19. "Coordination plays an important role in integrating the efforts of various departments." In the light of this statement, explain five characteristics of coordination.

Or **Explain any four features of coordination.** **CBSE 2024 C**

Or **Explain the following features of coordination**
(i) Coordination integrates group efforts
(ii) Coordination is the responsibility of all managers **CBSE 2025**

Ans. Following are the characteristics of coordination

(i) **Coordination integrates Group Efforts**
Coordination is always required where a group of people work towards a common goal. It binds unrelated or diverse interests into purposeful work activity.

It gives a common focus to group effort to ensure that performance is as per plans.

(ii) **Coordination ensures Unity of Action**
Coordination aims to unite the efforts of every individual, departments and levels for the realisation of a common purpose. It leads to action of all individuals in one common direction towards achieving organisational goals.

(iii) **Coordination is an All Pervasive Function**
Coordination is required at all levels, departments and functions of management due to the interdependent nature of various activities. Absence of coordination at any level, gives rise to overlapping of activities and chaos.

(iv) **Coordination is the Responsibility of All Managers**
Coordination is the function of every manager in the organisation.
Top level managers coordinate to ensure that overall policies are duly carried out, middle level managers coordinate with the top and supervisory levels and lower level managers coordinate the activities of its workers to ensure that work proceeds as per plans.

(v) **Coordination is a Deliberate Function**
Coordination does not establish itself, rather it is deliberately created by managers, by directing the efforts of individuals working under their guidance.

Cooperation in the absence of coordination may lead to wasted effort and coordination without cooperation may lead to dissatisfaction among employees.

Case Study Based Questions

Short Case Studies

Case Study 1

Shreya works as a designer in an export house. As per the terms of an order received by the export house, she has to get 100 units of denim jackets made in 15 days @ ₹ 2,000 per jacket.

She is able to complete her target production in 20 days because in order to complete the order in 15 days, she would have made the workers work over time. As a result, the cost of production per jacket may have increased by ₹ 100.

In the context of the above case, "Is Shreya efficient in her work? Explain by giving a suitable reason in support of your answer."

Ans. In assessing Shreya's efficiency in her work, we need to consider her ability to meet the production target within the specified time frame and at the expected cost.

Shreya's completion of the production target of 100 units of denim jackets demonstrates her effectiveness in delivering the desired output. However, her inability to complete the order within the originally specified time frame of 15 days raises concerns about her efficiency.

While Shreya was able to complete the production in 20 days, she had to extend the production timeline due to not making the workers work overtime.

This decision likely led to increased production costs, as she mentions that completing the order in 15 days would have resulted in a higher cost of production per jacket by ₹ 100.

Efficiency, in this context, would involve completing the production target within the specified time frame while minimising costs.

Shreya's decision to prioritise regular working hours for her workers may have contributed to a more sustainable and equitable work environment.

However, the increased production costs incurred by extending the production timeline suggest a potential inefficiency in her work.

Case Study 2

Mahesh is the Chief Executive Officer of 'Kidzania Garments Ltd.' Due to festive season, Mahesh got an additional order of 10,000 garments which he had to supply within two days. Due to his goodwill in the market, he did not want to lose the order. So, he decided to achieve the target by operating on double shifts. He achieved the target and supplied the order within two days.

But due to double shifts, his cost of production was higher than the regular production cost.

(i) Identify the two concepts of management discussed in the above para.

(ii) Explain the concepts identified in (i).

Ans.

(i) The two concepts of management discussed in the case are effectiveness and efficiency.

(ii) Following is the explanation of the two concepts

- **Effectiveness**
This refers to the extent to which an organisation achieves its goals and objectives. In the case, Mahesh's decision to operate on double shifts was aimed at effectively meeting the additional order of 10,000 garments within the tight deadline. Despite the increased cost, he was successful in achieving the target and fulfilling the order, demonstrating effectiveness in meeting his goal.

- **Efficiency**
  This relates to the optimal use of resources to achieve a goal with minimal waste. In this case, while Mahesh was effective in meeting the target, the cost of production was higher due to the double shifts. This indicates a decrease in efficiency because the increased production cost implies that resources were not used in the most cost-effective manner.

Case Study 3

Nisha had given some old dresses of her own to her house-helper Beenu. After a few days, Nisha was happily surprised when she saw Beenu wearing one of the dresses beautifully refurbished. On enquiry, Beenu told Nisha that this was done by her daughter who had just completed her Class 12th studies. Beenu also told Nisha that she was a little concerned as her daughter did not want to study further. Nisha was very much impressed by the creativity of Beenu's daughter, so she decided to setup a small business for her.

Nisha bought 15 sewing machines and appointed 15 girls to refurbish the old dresses. Nisha also arranged old dresses from various sources and employed a person who will sell these dresses at a very low cost for the one's who could not purchase new dresses due to their low income. Nisha divided the girls in three equal groups, each having five sewing machines.

Each group was given a target of refurbishing 150 old dresses in a fortnight with a cost of ₹ 30 per dress. After a fortnight, Nisha who was supervising this business with Beenu was informed that Group I was able to meet the target by refurbishing 150 old dresses at a cost of ₹ 30 per dress. Group II was able to refurbish 150 old dresses at a cost of ₹ 35 per dress, whereas Group III could refurbish only 140 old dresses but at a cost of ₹ 27 per dress.

CBSE 2025

(i) Identify the concepts of management discussed above for each of the three groups giving reason in support of your answer.
(ii) Give meaning of the concepts identified in (i) above and state which one is important for the management and why?

Ans.

(i) The concepts of management discussed for each of the three groups are

- Group I **Efficiency and Effectiveness**
  This group successfully met the target of refurbishing 150 dresses within the given cost of ₹ 30 per dress.

  Efficiency is about minimising costs while maximising output and effectiveness is about achieving the target.
- Group II **Effectiveness but not Efficiency**
  This group was able to refurbish 150 dresses (meeting the target), which means they were effective. However, they exceeded the cost limit by refurbishing at ?35 per dress, which means they were not efficient in utilising resources.
- Group III **Efficiency but not Effectiveness**
  This group completed the work at a lower cost of ₹ 27 per dress (better efficiency). However, they could only refurbish 140 dresses instead of 150, meaning they did not achieve their goal and were not effective.

(ii) Effectiveness, in management, is concerned with doing the right task, completing activities and achieving goals within the prescribed time limit. It is basically concerned with end result.

Efficiency is concerned with doing the task correctly and with minimum cost, least wastage and maximum utilisation of resources.

Case Study 4

The general manager of a reputed organisation, Mr. Agastaya Lokhande, made the following announcement at the annual general meeting of the company. "When we think of a brand, we think of reputation, but the reputation is made or broken by the quality of products and customer representation.

If people are miserable, they can't give their best work and the brand suffers. On the contrary, positive results can be observed if there is job satisfaction, effective and efficient functioning."

CBSE SQP 2025

(i) Identify and explain the feature of management discussed by Mr. Agastaya in his announcement.
(ii) Explain any three reasons that make management important to any organisation.

Ans.

(i) The feature of management discussed by Mr. Agastaya in his announcement is 'management is an intangible force'.

Management is an unforeseen force whose presence can be felt when an organisation functions. Orderliness, discipline, happy and satisfied employees, all reflect the presence of effective management.

(ii) **Importance of Management**

- **Management helps in Achieving Group Goals**
  Every organisation has a set of goals to be achieved. Management unites the resources together and give common direction to the efforts of all individuals towards achieving those goals.
- **Management Increases Efficiency**
  Managers seek to reduce costs and increase productivity through better planning, organising, directing, staffing and controlling the activities of the organisation.

- **Management creates a Dynamic Organisation**
  Every organisation works in an ever-changing environment and individuals resist such change. Thus, management helps people adapt to these changes, so that an organisation is able to maintain its competitive edge.

Case Study 5

Kamal, Khan and Devid are partners in a firm engaged in the distribution of dairy products in Madhya Pradesh. Kamal is a holder of Senior Secondary School Certificate from Central Board of Secondary Education with Business Studies as one of his elective subjects.

Khan had done his post graduation in Hindi literature and Devid in Dairy Farming. One day there was a serious discussion between Khan and Devid regarding the nature of 'Management as a science'.

Khan argued that management was not a science whereas Devid was of the opinion that management is a Science. Kamal intervened and corrected both Khan and Devid about the nature of management as a Science with the help of his knowledge of business studies.

Explain, how Kamal would have been able to satisfy both Khan and Devid?

Ans. Kamal would have satisfied both Khan and Devid by giving the following points for considering management as a science

(i) **Existence of a Systematised Body of Knowledge**

Like science, management has its own theory, techniques and principles. It also draws some principles from various disciplines such as Economics, Sociology, Psychology and Mathematics. So this feature of science is present in management.

(ii) **Principles based on Observation and Experimentation**

Management principles have been developed on the basis of scientific observation and experiments in different types of organisation.

(iii) **Universal Validity and Application**

The principles of management are not as exact as the principles of science and their application and their use is not universal. They have to be modified according to a given situation. However, they provide managers with certain standardised techniques that can be used in different situations irrespective of the area, region and country.

Conclusion Management cannot be considered as exact or pure science but we can call it as an inexact science or social science.

Case Study 6

Three friends, Aman, Ashish and Ashi after completing their MBA from a reputed management institute, formed a start-up named 'Solutions'.

The goal of the start-up was to make a social and environmental impact through its services. 'Solutions' supports social business ideas to improve living conditions in slums of Mumbai.

As all the three friends are specialised in social work, they adopted three different slums of Mumbai and started educating the slum dwellers in their own creative manner. Aman used 'playway method', Ashish used 'music' as a method of learning while Ashi used 'activity based method of learning'.

They used basic knowledge in their unique manner and were able to educate the slum dwellers. It implies that skillful and personal application of acquired knowledge varies from individual to individual in achieving desired results.

(i) Identify and state the nature of management discussed in the above case. **CBSE 2024**

(ii) Quoting lines from the above para, state any two features of nature of management identified in (i) above.

Ans.

(i) The nature of management discussed is management as an art.

Management as an art involves the skillful and personal application of acquired knowledge and techniques to achieve desired results.

(ii) Following are the features of management as an art

- **Personal Application of Knowledge**
  "It implies that skillful and personal application of acquired knowledge varies from individual to individual in achieving desired results."
  This line highlights that management as an art involves the personal touch and unique application of knowledge by individuals to achieve the desired outcomes.
- **Practice and Creativity**
  "Aman used 'playway method,' Ashish used 'music' as a method of learning while Ashi used 'activity-based method of learning."
  This demonstrates that each individual applied their creative and innovative methods to address the same objective, showcasing how management as an art involves unique, creative approaches.

Case Study 7

Monika, Rashmi and Garima are childhood friends. After completing their education, Monika joined a school as a teacher. Rashmi joined a firm as a Chartered Accountant and Garima as a General Manager in a Multinational Company.

After a long time in a re-union function of the school, they met each other. Rashmi said that they were all professionals now.

Garima told Rashmi that she can say this about Monika and herself, but not about her since Manager is not considered a full fledged professional.

Why did Garima say that she was not a professional ? State any three points in support of your answer. **CBSE 2023**

Ans. Following are the reasons that indicate that Garima is not a professional (any three)

(i) **Restricted Entry**
Entry into a profession is restricted through an examination or educational degree. In management, no such restriction is there to appoint a manager. Anyone can become a manager irrespective of the educational qualification.

(ii) **Professional Association**
All professionals are bound to be a part of a professional association which regulates entry, grants certificate of practice and enforces a code of conduct. This feature is also not applicable to management. Though, there are certain management associations in India like All India Management Association (AIMA), but they do not have the statutory backing and membership to these associations is not mandatory for managers.

(iii) **Ethical Code of Conduct**
All professions are subject to an ethical code of conduct which guides the behaviour of its members. However, in management, no such rules and regulations are framed to guide the managers through a code of conduct.

(iv) **Service Motive**
The basic motive of each profession is to provide dedicated and committed service to its clients. This feature is also not present in management completely, as the primary motive of management is to help organisation achieve its stated goal, which can be profit maximisation for a business enterprise and service for a hospital.

Case Study 8

Alex, Jordan and Sam are three friends working in the same company, each holding a managerial position at a different level. They often meet to discuss their work. One day, during their conversation

Alex said, "Lately, I've been facing challenges motivating the staff on the shop floor. I've decided to buy two new machines and realise that I need to lead by example."

Jordan mentioned, "I'm struggling to understand the precise needs of my department. I need to communicate various policies to our employees so they are aware of our company's objectives. Additionally, I have to coordinate with heads of other departments to understand their needs."

Sam stated, "I'm responsible for long-term planning. I know that I am ultimately accountable for all activities and extensive planning is necessary for formulating policies and strategies."

Based on this conversation, identify the different levels of management to which these three friends belong.

Ans. Alex belongs to Lower Level of Management
Lower level manager works at the shop floor level. Shop floor is the place where workers work and machines are kept.

Jordan belongs to Middle Level Management
Middle level manager decides the number of employees to be required in his department. He also has to coordinate with other departmental heads though at the same level.

Sam belongs to the Top Level of Management
Top level manager is required to plan for long-term basis. He is responsible for all the activities in the organisation. Policies and strategies are formulated by the top management.

Case Study 9

Rahul Mukerjee has recently joined AMV Ltd., a company manufacturing refrigerators. He found that his department was under-staffed and other departments were not cooperating with his department for smooth functioning of the organisation.

Therefore, he ensured that his department has the required number of employees and its cooperation with other departments is improved.

(i) Identify the level at which Rahul Mukerjee was working.
(ii) Also, state three more functions required to be performed by Rahul Mukerjee at this level.

Ans.

(i) The level at which Rahul Mukherjee was working is middle level management.

(ii) Functions that are required to be performed by Rahul Mukherjee at this level are

- To assign duties and responsibilities to lower level managers.
- To motivate them to achieve desired objectives.
- To cooperate with other departments for smooth functioning of organisation.
- To interpret the policies framed by top management.

Case Study 10

After completing his MBA degree, Aman joined a multinational company Zevovya Ltd. His job demands long hours and commitment to the organisation. He is responsible for integrating diverse elements and coordinating all the activities of the business and for its impact on society. His job is complex and stressful. **CBSE 2023**

(i) Identify the level of management at which Aman joined the organisation.
(ii) State any two functions to be performed by Aman at this level other than those discussed in the para.

Ans.

(i) The level of management at which Aman joined the organisation is top level management.

(ii) Following are the functions that are to be performed by Aman at this level

- To strive for welfare and survival of business.
- To formulate overall organisational goals and policies of the business.

Case Study 11

Gamma Ltd. aims to achieve flawless coordination across its various organisational functions. They focus on synchronising all company activities and understand that coordination is crucial. During the planning phase for the year, they ensure that there is harmony between the organisation's goals and those of each department. When hiring employees, they evaluate their efficiency before determining their compensation. In the final month of production, they repeatedly check for deviations between set targets and actual production. In the above scenario, while the primary focus is on coordination, various management functions are also highlighted.

(i) Define the term 'management'.

(ii) Identify the three management functions illustrated in the scenario where coordination is evident.

Ans.

(i) Management is a process of getting things done with the aim of achieving goals effectively and efficiently.

(ii) The management functions highlighted in the case are as follows

- **Planning**
  This function is performed by ensuring that there is harmony between the organisation's goals and those of each department. It is the process of deciding in advance what to do, how to do, when to do and who is going to do it.
- **Staffing**
  This function is performed by evaluating the efficiency of employees before determining their compensation. It is the process of filling all positions in an organisation with adequate and qualified personnel.
- **Controlling**
  This function is performed by checking for deviations between set targets and actual production. This function monitors organisational performance towards the attainment of organisational goals.

Case Study 12

Vortico Fabrics' was started by Ashish in 2001 to sell bed sheets, towels, comforters, pillows, cushions, bath mats, etc. It is now a famous name and its branches are across India.

To manage the work all over India, it has eight teams-two each for North, South, East and West India. Ashish spends a considerable amount of time to develop an orderly pattern of group efforts among different teams and to secure unity of action in pursuit of a common purpose.

To ensure suitable allocation of tasks to the various members of the teams and to see that the tasks are performed with harmony among the members, he tries to balance the different teams at different locations. **CBSE 2024**

(i) Identify and explain the concept of management discussed in the above para.

(ii) Also, explain any one point of importance of the concept identified in (i) above.

Ans.

(i) The concept of management discussed in the case is coordination. Coordination is the force that binds all the functions of management. It involves synchronisation of all the activities of different departments towards the accomplishment of common goal.

(ii) Coordination plays an important role in case of functional differentiation. Functions of an organisation are divided into departments, divisions and sections.

All the departments have their own objectives, strategies and policies.

Thus, there is a chance of conflict. Such a situation can only be handled by establishing proper coordination between the departments, so that they proceed together in a single direction for attainment of common organisational goals.

Case Study 13

Company X is facing a lot of problems these days. It manufactures white goods like washing machines, microwave ovens, refrigerators and air conditioners. The company's margins are under pressure and the profits and market share are declining.

The production department blames marketing for not meeting sales targets and marketing blames production department for producing goods, which are not of good quality meeting customers expectations.

The finance department blames both production and marketing for declining return on investment and bad marketing. What quality of management do you think the company is lacking? Explain briefly. What steps should the company's management take to bring the company back on track? **NCERT**

Ans. Coordination is missing in Company X. All the departments are not coordinating with each other and that is why, they end up in blaming each other for the poor performance.

To bring coordination, management should take the following steps

(i) After the goals are established, they should be communicated to all departments well in advance to understand goals' importance and their specific roles.

(ii) Managers ensure that all departments coordinate with each other.

(iii) Whenever there is difference of interest, the managers should try and strike a balance so that they all work in the same direction.

(iv) Meetings between the departmental heads of production, marketing, finance, etc, should be organised on a regular basis and in routine to solve problems when they emerge.

Long Case Studies

Case Study 14

Vikram is the General Manager at GreenTech Solutions, a company that specialises in sustainable energy solutions. GreenTech Solutions is dedicated to balancing profitability with social responsibility. Vikram's leadership is central to achieving this balance through various strategic initiatives that clearly illustrate key features of management.

Vikram's approach to management emphasises that it is a group activity. To meet the company's social objectives, Vikram fosters collaboration across different departments. For instance, he coordinates with the research and development team to create affordable solar energy solutions and works closely with the community outreach team to ensure these solutions effectively reach local households. This cross-departmental collaboration showcases how management involves integrating efforts from various parts of the organisation to achieve common goals.

Moreover, Vikram demonstrates that management exists at all levels throughout the organisation. He ensures that social responsibility is embedded in all aspects of GreenTech Solutions' operations. For example, the company's ethical supply chain management practices are integrated into every procurement decision, reflecting the pervasive nature of management principles. Additionally, the comprehensive employee welfare program is implemented across all departments, indicating that management practices influence every level of the organisation.

To support these objectives, Vikram has implemented several initiatives

- **Affordable Solar Energy Solutions** The company's program to provide solar energy to local communities not only helps reduce household energy costs but also aligns with the company's environmental goals.
- **Job Creation and Skill Development** Training centers are established in underdeveloped regions, providing local residents with skills in renewable energy technology, which supports economic development and builds a skilled workforce.
- **Ethical Supply Chain Management** GreenTech Solutions partners only with suppliers who follow fair labor practices and environmental standards, demonstrating the company's commitment to ethical business practices.
- **Employee Welfare Programmes** Vikram has introduced health benefits, educational assistance and wellness activities, ensuring that employee welfare is prioritised across the organisation.

(i) State the social objectives identified in the case.

(ii) Identify two features of management highlighted in the case.

(iii) Give any two examples of social objectives.

Ans.

(i) Following are the social objectives identified in the case

- **Affordable Solar Energy Solutions**
  Providing solar energy to local communities reduces energy costs and supports environmental sustainability.
- **Job Creation and Skill Development**
  Establishing training centers to develop skills in renewable energy technology creates job opportunities and promotes economic development in underdeveloped regions.

(ii) Following are the features of management highlighted in the case

- **Management is a Group Activity**
  Vikram's coordination between various departments for initiatives like solar energy solutions and community outreach demonstrates how management involves integrating efforts from different parts of the organisation.
  An organisation is a collection of diverse individuals with different needs. Through coordination and teamwork, management unites the efforts of individuals to achieve organisational goals, alongwith the growth and development of individuals as needs and opportunities change.
- **Management is Pervasive**
  The ethical supply chain management and employee welfare programs implemented across all levels of the organisation illustrate that management practices are embedded throughout the company's operations. Management is necessary to conduct all types of activities whether it is a business or non-business activity.

  It is universally applicable in all types of organisation whether political, economic or social.

(iii) Following are the examples of social objectives
- To make available employment opportunities.
- To save environment from getting polluted.

Case Study 15

Dynamic Innovations Ltd. is a technology firm specialising in cutting-edge software solutions and IT consulting. Over the past few years, the company has expanded rapidly but faces significant challenges in maintaining its competitive position and ensuring employee satisfaction.

The management team, comprising four key individuals, is working diligently to address both economic and personal objectives.

Current Scenario

The team at Dynamic Innovations is focused on various aspects of the company's operations

Ravi, the Operations Manager, is primarily concerned with ensuring the company's stability and longevity. He is implementing cost-reduction strategies and optimising resource allocation to ensure that the company's revenue covers its operational costs and secures its survival in the competitive market.

Meera, the Financial Analyst, is focused on enhancing profitability. She is exploring new revenue streams, investing in innovative technologies, and analysing financial performance to ensure the company remains profitable and can reward its employees effectively.

Raj, the HR Manager, is dedicated to addressing the financial needs of employees. He is responsible for revising salary structures, introducing performance bonuses and ensuring that compensation packages are competitive to motivate and retain staff.

Anita, the Learning and Development Coordinator, is working on fulfilling the higher-level needs of employees. She is organising training programmes, professional development workshops and career advancement opportunities to help employees grow and achieve their personal and professional goals.

Identify and explain the objectives of management fulfilled by Ravi, Meera, Raj and Anita respectively.

Ans. Following are the objectives of management that have been indicated in the case

(i) Ravi is working to fulfil the survival objective of organisation. The most important objective of every business is to survive. Management must seek to ensure organisation's survival, which can be possible only if organisation earns enough revenue to cover its costs.

(ii) Meera is working to fulfil the fulfil the profit objective of organisation. It is the incentive or reward for carrying out a business. Management must ensure that the organisation makes profit, which provides a vital incentive for organisation's continued successful operation. Profit is essential to cover costs and risks of the business.

(iii) Raj is working to fulfil the financial needs motive as part of the personal objective. Financial needs are being fulfilled by giving competitive salary and perks.

(iv) Anita is working to fulfil the higher level needs motive as part of the personal objective. Higher level needs are being fulfilled by providing opportunities for personal growth and development.

Case Study 16

Two ambitious friends, Sana and Mihir, having passion for creating innovative software applications, established a tech start-up named 'Quick Solutions'. Their software was developed in such a way that it caters to the needs of all sections. Since its inception, 'Quick Solutions' was earning enough revenue to cover the costs.

They faced countless challenges from competing with large and well-established companies. But they learned from their mistakes and continuously improved their product. Slowly, their software gained recognition for its quality and uniqueness and the company started making profits.

It was a big incentive for Sana and Mihir for the continued successful operation of the enterprise.

Within two years, the customer base increased manifold. Now, Sana and Mihir decided to make additional capital investment and hired more employees. They invested in research and development and expanded their product line to meet emerging market demands.

'Quick Solutions' ultimately became the industry leader because of the tireless efforts of Sana and Mihir.

Quoting lines, identify and state the objectives of management discussed in the above case which 'Quick Solutions' seeks to achieve. **CBSE 2024**

Ans. In the case of 'Quick Solutions', the objectives of management that are evident include

(i) **Survival**

"Since its inception, 'Quick Solutions' was earning enough revenue to cover the costs."

This reflects the objective of survival, as the company needed to ensure it earned sufficient revenue to cover its costs and sustain operations.

(ii) **Profit**

"Slowly, their software gained recognition for its quality and uniqueness and the company started making profits. It was a big incentive for Sana and Mihir for the continued successful operation of the enterprise."

This demonstrates the importance of profit as an incentive and reward for the continued operation and success of the business.

(iii) **Growth**

"Sana and Mihir decided to make additional capital investment and hired more employees. They invested in research and development and expanded their product line to meet emerging market demands."

This illustrates the objective of growth, as the company expanded its activities, increased its customer base, and developed new products.

Case Study 17

Priya is the Operations Manager at EcoClean Ltd., a company specialising in eco-friendly cleaning products. EcoClean Ltd. prides itself on its commitment to sustainability and innovation.

Priya's role is crucial in ensuring the smooth operation of the company's production processes, maintaining high standards of quality control and managing the supply chain effectively. Under Priya's leadership, the production team has been working diligently to streamline operations. She has implemented a new system for inventory management that reduces waste and ensures that resources are used efficiently.

Priya conducts regular team meetings to ensure that all members are aligned with the company's goals and understand their roles in achieving these objectives. Her efforts to coordinate the team's activities help everyone work towards a unified vision of reducing the company's carbon footprint and increasing its market share.

Priya is also focused on improving efficiency within the company.

She frequently analyses production workflows and identifies areas where processes can be optimised.

Recently, she introduced new technologies that automate repetitive tasks, which has significantly increased the production rate and reduced operational costs. Her commitment to continuous improvement ensures that EcoClean Ltd. operates at peak efficiency, benefitting from cost savings and enhanced productivity.

In addition to her focus on internal operations, Priya is proactive in adapting to industry trends and regulatory changes. The eco-friendly cleaning product market is highly dynamic, with frequent updates in environmental regulations and consumer preferences.

Priya stays informed about these changes and adjusts the company's strategies accordingly. e.g. When new regulations were introduced regarding the use of certain chemicals, Priya quickly led her team in reformulating products to comply with the new standards.

This adaptability helps EcoClean Ltd. stay competitive and maintain its reputation as a leader in the sustainable products sector.

Quoting lines from the above paragraph, list and explain three reasons that have made management so important.

Ans. Following are the reasons that indicate the importance of management

(i) **Management helps in Achieving Group Goals**

"She conducts regular team meetings to ensure that all members are aligned with the company's goals and understand their roles in achieving these objectives."

By keeping the team well-coordinated and focused on common objectives, Priya ensures that everyone works together towards the company's goals, thereby facilitating the achievement of organisational targets.

Every organisation has a set of goals to be achieved. Management unites the resources together and give common direction to the efforts of all individuals towards achieving those goals.

(ii) **Management increases Efficiency**

"She frequently analyses production workflows and identifies areas where processes can be optimised."

Priya's efforts to streamline operations and implement new technologies to automate tasks enhance productivity and reduce costs.

This continuous focus on process improvement highlights the role of management in increasing organisational efficiency.

Managers seek to reduce costs and increase productivity through better planning, organising, directing, staffing and controlling the activities of the organisation.

(iii) **Management creates a Dynamic Organisation**

"Priya stays informed about these changes and adjusts the company's strategies accordingly."

Priya's enterprising approach to adapting to industry trends and regulatory changes ensures that EcoClean Ltd. remains competitive in a rapidly evolving market. This ability to adapt and respond to external changes is a key aspect of effective management.

Every organisation works in an everchanging environment and individuals resist such change. Thus, management helps people adapt to these changes, so that an organisation is able to maintain its competitive edge.

Case Study 18

A company wants to modify its existing product in the market due to decreasing sales. You can imagine any product about which you are familiar. What decisions/steps should each level of management take to give effect to this decision? **NCERT**

Ans. The three levels of management will work together towards the modification of the product with the motive of increasing sales.

(i) Decisions to be taken by top level management are

- Direction of modification, after scanning the environment.
- Drafting sales targets and various sales plans and sales incentives.
- How to enhance the value of the product in qualitative terms.
- Thinking of the financial requirements.
- Marketing and promotional techniques required for fastening the sales.

(ii) Decisions to be taken by middle level management are

- Interpretation of the policies framed by top management to the lower level management.
- Hiring necessary personnel with the required qualities and qualifications.
- Assigning responsibility as per capability and establishing the superior-subordinate relationship.
- Motivating people to achieve the desired results.
- Cooperating with the team members as well as with other departments.
- Taking the feedback and arranging the follow-up meeting.

(iii) Decisions that should be taken by lower level management are

- Interpretation of planned targets to the actual workforce and labourers.
- Helping and directing the workers regarding how to carry out the work.
- Maintaining standards, quality control and frequent checks.
- Minimisation of wastage and motivating the workers so that they can deliver upto their maximum potential.
- Communicating the grievances and feedback to the middle management and bringing in the changes, if required.
- Maintaining safety standards.

Case Study 19

Nalini has an online flower and gifts retail business. She has eight outlets in four cities of India. From November to February, during the wedding season, the demand shoots up. She coordinates the efforts of her staff in a conscious and deliberate manner and plans for the wedding season demand in the month of June itself.

She ensures that there is adequate workforce and continuously monitors whether work is proceeding according to plans. She also briefs the marketing department in time to prepare their promotional and advertising campaigns.

Thus, her coordination with all departments of the organisation begins at the planning stage and continues till controlling. This acts as a binding force between the departments and ensures that all action is aimed at achieving organisational goals. As a result, Nalini is able to give a common focus to group effort to ensure that the business is performing as planned, year after year.

Quoting lines from the above paragraph, identify and explain four features of an important concept of management highlighted in the above case. **CBSE 2024**

Ans. The concept of management highlighted in the case is coordination. Following are the four features of coordination

(i) **Coordination is a Continuous Process**

"She continuously monitors whether work is proceeding according to plans." Coordination is a never ending process whose need is felt at each and every step in the organisation. It starts with planning and continues till controlling.

(ii) **Coordination Ensures Unity of Action**

"She ensures that there is adequate workforce and continuously monitors whether work is proceeding according to plans."

Coordination aims to unite the efforts of every individual, departments and levels for the realisation of a common purpose.

It leads to action of all individuals in one common direction towards achieving organisational goals.

(iii) **Coordination Integrates Group Efforts**

"She coordinates the efforts of her staff in a conscious and deliberate manner." Coordination is always required where a group of people work towards a common goal. It binds unrelated or diverse interests into purposeful work activity. It gives a common focus to group effort to ensure that performance is as per plans.

(iv) **Coordination is an All Pervasive Function**

"Her coordination with all departments of the organisation begins at the planning stage and continues till controlling." Coordination is required at all levels, departments and functions of management due to the interdependent nature of various activities.

Absence of coordination at any level, gives rise to overlapping of activities and chaos.

SELF ASSESSMENT TEST

Objective Type Questions

1. Management is multidimensional because it manages ………. .
   (a) work (b) people
   (c) operations (d) All of these
2. ……… implies completing the work in hand irrespective of the cost.
   (a) Effectiveness (b) Efficiency
   (c) Planning (d) Controlling
3. To meet the objectives of the firm, the management of Mathura Ltd. offers employment to physically challenged persons. Identify the objective it is trying to achieve.
   (a) Organisational objective
   (b) Personal objective
   (c) Social objective
   (d) None of these
4. ……… highlights that every manager applies his knowledge of principles in his own way.
   (a) Ethical code of conduct
   (b) Existence of theoretical knowledge
   (c) Personalised application
   (d) Universal validity
5. Which of the following have no representative professional organisations available?
   (a) Law (b) Management
   (c) Medical (d) Accountancy
6. Supervisor is at which level of management?
   (a) All levels of management
   (b) Top level of management
   (c) Middle level of management
   (d) Lower level of management
7. Policy formulation is the function of
   (a) top level managers
   (b) middle level managers
   (c) operational management
   (d) All of the above

Answers 1. (d) 2. (a) 3. (c) 4. (c) 5. (b) 6. (d) 7. (a)

Short Answer Type Questions

8. Management is a complex activity that has three main dimensions. Explain these dimensions.
9. "Management is the process of designing and maintaining an environment in which individuals work together in groups to accomplish selected goals."
   In the light of this statement, explain any three features of management.
10. "Management is not visible, it can be felt." Explain.
11. List any three examples of social objectives of management.
12. Mayank, a post graduate in English, is successfully running his family business. All of a sudden, he thought of taking employment and got a job of finance manager in a company on the basis of his experience and efficiency.
    (i) Do you think his appointment is valid?
    (ii) Was it not necessary for him to be a part of professional association to attain the post?
13. Gagan, a manager of Telcom Ltd. believes that management is an art. Do you agree with the view point of Gagan? Give reasons in support of your answer.
14. Rohan is working as a Chief Executive Officer in Gagna Ltd. Identify the managerial level at which he is working and state any three functions that he will perform as Chief Executive Officer.
15. "Coordination is a systematic and orderly arrangement of individual and group efforts." In the light of the statement, state any four features of coordination.

Long Answer Type Questions

16. "Management is a comprehensive process that involves a series of functions to ensure the effective and efficient achievement of organisational goals." In the light of this statement, explain the five functions of management.
17. A firm plans in advance and has a sound organisational structure with efficient supervisory staff and control system, but on several occasions, it finds that plans are not adhered to. It leads to confusion and duplication of work. Advise remedies.

02

CHAPTER

Principles of Management

Management is required to perform a number of functions to achieve the organisational goals. These management functions can be effectively performed with the application of various principles of management.

▼ **YOUR STUDY GOALS**

2.1 Concept of Principles of Management
2.2 Fayol's Principles of Management
2.3 Principles of Scientific Management
2.4 Techniques of Scientific Management
2.5 Comparison of Contributions of Fayol and Taylor

▼ **YOUR PRACTICE GOAL**

- Objective Type Questions (76 Qs ; MCQs, A-R, Statements, Matching)
- Subjective Questions (16 SAs, 12 LAs)
- Case Study Based Questions (Short Case Studies-14, Long Case Studies-8)
- Self Assessment Test (6 MCQs, 7 SAs, 3 LAs)

2.1 Concept of Principles of Management

Principles of management are broad and general guidelines for decision-making and behaviour of managers. These are the statements of fundamental truth, which serve as general guidelines for a manager to make decisions, take appropriate steps to accomplish desired goals, etc.

Management Principles vs Principles of Pure Science

- Management principles are flexible, required to be applied creatively and have to keep pace with the changing environment while principles of pure science are rigid, applied in absolute or static manner and do not have to be adaptive to changing environment.

Management Principles vs Techniques of Management

- Management principles are flexible and act as guidelines for decision-making or taking actions while techniques are less flexible and are methods or procedures involving a series of steps to achieve desired goals.

Management Principles vs Values

- Management principles are guidelines, technical in nature and formed through research in work situations while values are ethical and general rules for individual behaviour which are formed through common practice.

Nature of Principles of Management

Following points characterise the nature of principles of management

Nature of Principles of Management

- Universal applicability
- General guidelines
- Formed by practice and experimentation
- Flexible
- Mainly behavioural
- Cause and effect relationship
- Contingent

1. **Universal Applicability** The principles can be applied in all types of organisations, business as well as non-business whether small or large, manufacturing or service sector.
2. **General Guidelines** The principles are general guidelines to action and decision-making, but they do not provide readymade solutions as the business situations are ever changing or dynamic and are a result of multiple factors.
3. **Formed by Practice and Experimentation** The principles are developed after thorough research work on the basis of experiences, observation and experimentation of managers.
4. **Flexible** The principles can be adapted and modified by the practicing managers as per the demands of the situations as they are man-made principles.
5. **Mainly Behavioural** Since the principles aim at influencing complex human behaviour, they are mainly behavioural in nature. They help in motivating and inspiring the human beings working in an organisation.
6. **Cause and Effect Relationship** The principles establish cause and effect relationship as they tell us if a particular principle is applied in a particular situation, which can be its likely effect.
7. **Contingent** Their applicability depends upon the prevailing situation at a particular point of time.

Significance of Principles of Management

1. Providing managers with useful insights into reality	• The application of these principles helps the managers to take the right decisions at the right time as they help managers to improve the knowledge, ability and understanding of managerial situations.
2. Optimum utilisation of resources and effective administration	• By applying the management principles, the managers can focus on optimum use of available resources at minimum costs and maximum profits.
3. Scientific decisions	• Management decisions taken on the basis of principles are free from bias and prejudice. They are based on objective assessment of situation.
4. Meeting changing environment requirements	• Principles are general guidelines, but they are dynamic, flexible and help the organisation to adapt environmental changes.
5. Fulfilling social responsibility	• Principles of management not only guide managers to achieve organisational goals but also guide them to perform social responsibilities.
6. Management training, education and research	• Principles provide basic groundwork for the development of management as a discipline. Thus, they act as a base for management training, education and research.

2.2 Fayol's Principles of Management

Henri Fayol, is also known as the father of general management. He introduced a general theory that can be applied to all levels of management and every department.

The 14 principles of management created by Henri Fayol are explained below

Name of Principle	Meaning
Division of Work	Dividing the work into small tasks and then assigning them to trained specialists would help in taking the advantage of specialisation. According to **Fayol**, "The intent of division of work is to produce more and better work for the same effort. Specialisation is the most efficient way to use human effort."
Authority and Responsibility	Authority is the right to give orders and obtain obedience while responsibility means obligation to complete the assigned tasks on time. There must be a balance between authority and responsibility. Authority can be formal as well as informal and it is of two types, i.e. official authority (authority to command) and personal authority (authority of individual manager).
Discipline	Discipline is the obedience to organisational rules and employment agreement which are necessary for the smooth working of the organisation. According to **Fayol**, discipline requires good superiors at all levels, clear and fair agreements and judicious application of penalties.
Unity of Command	Each subordinate should receive orders and be answerable to one superior only. If this principle is violated, then "Authority is undermined, discipline is in jeopardy, order disturbed and stability threatened."
Unity of Direction	There should be one head and one plan for a group of activities having the same objective. According to this principle, all units of an organisation should move towards the same objectives through coordinated and focused efforts.
Subordination of Individual Interest to General Interest	The interest and objectives of the company should supersede the interest of anyone individual.
Remuneration of Employees	Employees should be paid fair wages, which would give them a reasonable standard of living and at the same time, it must be within the paying capacity of an organisation.
Centralisation and Decentralisation	Centralisation refers to the concentration of decision-making authority at the top levels of management, whereas decentralisation, involves distributing decision-making authority to lower levels of management and even to individual employees. According to **Fayol**, "There is a need to balance subordinate involvement through decentralisation with managers' retention of final authority through centralisation."
Scalar Chain	The hierarchy steps should be from the top to the lowest. This is necessary so that every employee knows his/her immediate senior, and also he/she should be able to contact any, if needed. However, a shorter route is (available in case of emergency which is known as the **Gang Plank**. It refers to an arrangement in which two employees working at the same level can communicate with each other directly without following the scalar chain.
Order	There should be an orderly arrangement and specific place for everything and everyone in the organisation. According to **Fayol**, "People and materials must be in suitable places at appropriate time for maximum efficiency."
Equity	There should be no discrimination against anyone on account of sex, religion, language, caste, belief or nationality and equal opportunities should be available for all.

Name of Principle	Meaning
Stability of Personnel	Personnel should be selected and appointed after due and rigorous procedure. But once selected they should be kept at their post/position for a minimum fixed tenure. According to **Fayol**, "Employee turnover should be minimised to maintain organisational efficiency."
Initiative	Employees at all levels should be encouraged and given an opportunity to take some initiative in making and executing the plans.
Esprit De Corps	Management should promote a team spirit of unity and harmony among employees. A manager should replace 'I' with 'We' in all his conversations to foster team spirit.

Unity of Command

Employees were reporting to multiple supervisors, leading to conflicting instructions and confusion. The management implemented the unity of command principle, assigning each employee to a single supervisor.

This change clarified reporting lines, streamlined communication and improved overall productivity.

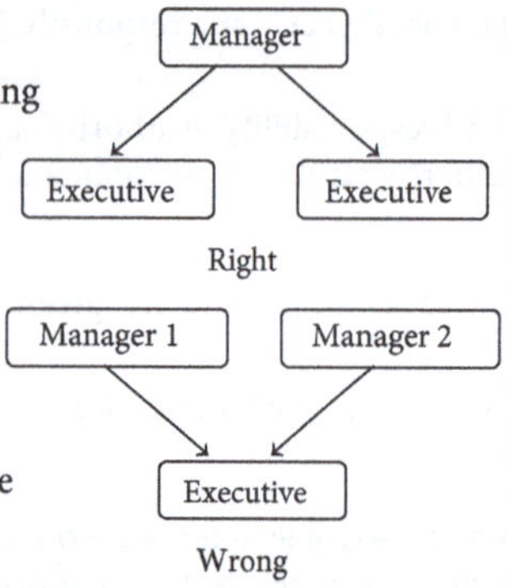

Unity of Command

Scalar Chain

In a bustling film studio, the scalar chain operates like a movie set: actors report to directors, directors update producers, producers brief the studio head and the studio head communicates with the CEO. This chain keeps everyone in sync, ensuring that every scene is shot on time and within budget.

Scalar Chain

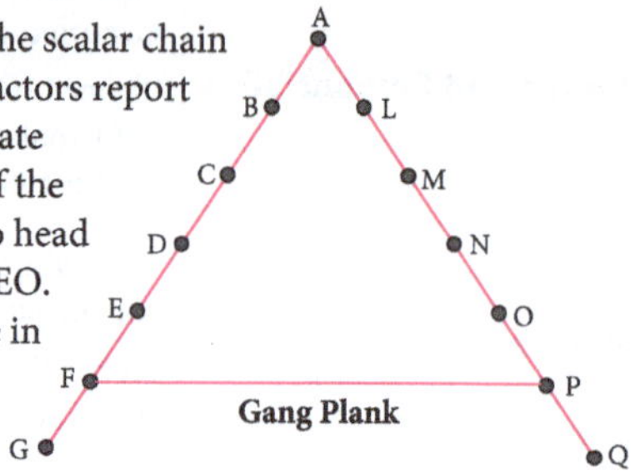

In a film studio, if an actor directly approaches the CEO with issues or suggestions without going through the director or producer, it disrupts the scalar chain. This bypass can lead to confusion, miscommunication and inefficiencies, as the proper channels and processes are not followed.

2.3 Principles of Scientific Management

FW Taylor is known as the father of scientific management. He made a significant contribution to the management of factory system. He gave following principles of scientific management

Science, Not Rule of Thumb

This means using scientific methods to find the best way to do tasks instead of relying on old habits or guesses. It involves studying work processes carefully and using data to make decisions. This approach helps to improve efficiency and productivity by finding the most effective methods.

Taylor believed that there was only one best method to maximise efficiency and this method should substitute 'rule of thumb' throughout the organisation.

Harmony, not Discord

There should be complete harmony between management and workers. For this, Taylor called for complete **mental revolution** which means a change in the mindset of both management and workers. It implies that management should share the gains with workers and workers should work hard for the betterment of the business.

Cooperation, not Individualism

There should be complete cooperation between the labour and the management instead of individualism.

This principle is an extension of principle of 'harmony, not discord'. According to this principle, competition should be replaced by cooperation.

Management and workers both should realise that they need each other.

According to Taylor, there should be an almost equal division of work and responsibility between workers and management.

Development of Each and Every Person to His or Her Greatest Efficiency and Prosperity

According to this principle, "Each person should be scientifically selected and then assigned work as per his specialisation and in any case, if training is required, then required training should be given as efficient employees would produce more and earn more."

Japanese Work Culture

Japanese work culture is a classic example of harmony, not discard. In Japanese companies, paternalistic style of management is in practice. There is complete openness between the management and workers. If at all workers go to strike, they wear a black badge but work more than normal working hours to gain the sympathy of the management.

2.4 Techniques of Scientific Management

Following techniques were deployed by FW Taylor

Name of Technique	Meaning
Functional Foremanship	It is an extension of principle of division of work and specialisation to the shop floor. Since, a single person cannot possess all the qualities (like intelligence, education, honesty, etc.), thus, he advocated the functional foremanship through eight foremen to guide workers, under planning and production departments. Under the **planning incharge**, there are four personnel • *Instruction Card Clerk*, responsible to give instructions to the workers. • *Route Clerk*, responsible to specify the route of production. • *Time and Cost Clerk*, responsible to prepare time and cost sheets. • *Disciplinarian*, responsible to maintain discipline among workers. Under the **production incharge**, there are four personnel • *Speed Boss*, responsible for timely and accurate completion of job. • *Gang Boss*, responsible for keeping machines and tools ready for work. • *Repair Boss*, responsible to keep machines and tools in proper working condition. • *Inspector*, responsible to maintain quality of work.
Standardisation and Simplification	Standardisation refers to the process of setting standards for every business activity; it can be standardisation of process, raw material, etc. The objectives of standardisation are to reduce a given line of product to fixed types, sizes and characteristics, to provide interchangeability of manufactured parts and products, to establish standards of excellence and quality in materials and to establish performance standards of men and machines. Simplification aims at eliminating unnecessary diversity of products, thereby reduce costs and implies fuller utilisation of equipment and increasing turnover.
Method Study	It aims to find the most efficient way to perform a job, i.e. find out one best way of doing the job and includes activity from raw material procurement to final delivery, reducing costs and enhancing customer satisfaction.

Name of Technique	Meaning
Motion Study	It involves analysing a worker's movements to eliminate unnecessary movements in doing a task and find the best job methods, often using cameras or stopwatches. Eliminating wasteful motions can increase productivity upto four times.
Time Study	It determines the standard time taken by a worker to perform a well-defined job. This type of study is helpful in deciding the standard time required to perform a job.
Fatigue Study	It determines the necessary rest intervals to prevent tiredness and maintain worker efficiency in completing a task. This would help the worker to regain his stamina and work again with the same capacity.
Differential Piece Wage System	It pays workers based on their productivity, with higher rates for exceeding a set standard and lower rates for underperformance. e.g. Standard output = 100 units/per day, Wage rate 1 = ₹ 10/unit for standard output or more, Wage rate 2 = ₹ 7/unit for below standard output Worker 1 = Output 99 units, Wages = 99 × 7 = ₹ 693 Worker 2 = Output 101 units , Wages = 101 × 10 = ₹ 1,010 Thus, a difference of ₹ 317 (1,010 — 693) because of difference of 2 units in output, is enough to motivate the inefficient worker to work for more output.

Techniques

- **Functional Foremanship** In a logistics company, the route clerk plans efficient delivery routes, the disciplinarian enforces company policies, the time and cost clerk manages expenses and monitors work hours and the instruction card clerk trains drivers on procedures.

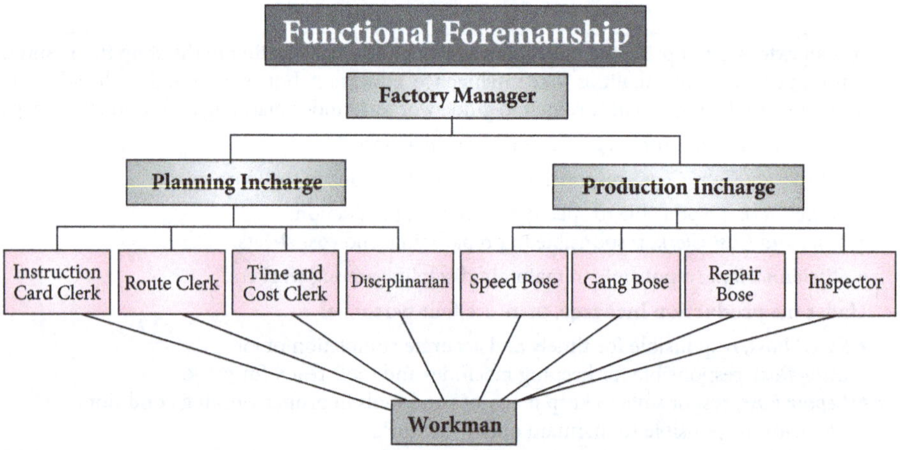

- **Standardisation** Think of a fast-food restaurant chain. To ensure that every burger tastes the same regardless of the location, the chain standardises the ingredients, cooking methods and even the order in which items are added to the burger.
- **Motion Study** In a warehouse, a motion study might reveal that workers are spending too much time walking back and forth to pick up items. By reorganising the layout so that frequently used items are closer together and optimising the paths that workers take, the warehouse can reduce wasted movement and increase efficiency.

2.5 Comparison of Contributions of Fayol and Taylor

Fayol and Taylor, both have contributed immensely to the knowledge of management which has formed a basis for further practice by managers. The following points lay down clear distinction between the two

Basis	Henri Fayol	FW Taylor
Perspective	Top level of management	Shop floor level of a factory
Applicability	Universally applicable	Applicable to specialised situations (factory situation)
Basis of Formation	Personal experience	Observations and experimentation
Focus	Improving overall administration	Increasing productivity of workers
Status	Father of general management	Father of scientific management
Personality	Practitioner	Scientist
Unity of Command	Strictly followed	Did not feel that it is important as under functional foremanship, a worker received orders from eight specialists
Expression	General theory of administration	Scientific management

Mind Map

1 Concept of Principles of Management

Principles of management are broad and general guidelines for decision-making and behaviour of managers

- Management principles are flexible in nature while principles of pure science are rigid in nature
- Management principles are guidelines for decision-making while techniques of management are methods involving a series of steps to achieve desired goals
- Management principles are technical in nature while values are ethical in nature

2 Nature of Principles of Management

- **Universal Applicability** Principles are universal and can be applied in all types of organisations
- **General Guidelines** Management principles do not provide readymade solutions to all problems. They are only general guidelines
- **Formed by Practice and Experimentation** Developed after research, observation, experimentation and experience
- **Flexible** Management principles can be modified by the managers
- **Mainly Behavioural** Management principles aim at influencing human behaviour
- **Cause and Effect Relationship** Management principles tell the likely effect in a particular situation
- **Contingent** Application of management principles is dependent upon prevailing situation

PRINCIPLES OF MANAGEMENT

3 Significance of Principles of Management

- Providing managers with useful insights into reality
- Optimum utilisation of resources and effective administration
- Scientific decisions
- Meeting changing environment requirements
- Fulfilling social responsibility
- Management training, education and research

4 Fayol's Principles of Management

- **Division of Work** Work divided into smaller tasks
- **Authority and Responsibility** There must be a balance between the two
- **Discipline** Sincerity and obedience towards organisational rules
- **Unity of Command** Each subordinate should receive orders and be answerable to one superior only
- **Unity of Direction** There should be one head and one plan
- **Subordination of Individual Interest to General Interest** Interest of organisation should supersede all other interests
- **Remuneration of Employees** Remuneration should be fair and reasonable
- **Centralisation and Decentralisation** Balance is required between the two
- **Scalar Chain** Formal lines of authority from highest to lowest ranks
- **Order** There should be a specific place for everyone and everything
- **Equity** There should be no discrimination and equal opportunities should be given
- **Stability of Personnel** Employee turnover should be minimised
- **Initiative** Employees should be encouraged to take initiative
- **Espirit De Corps** Team spirit should be promoted

6 Comparison of Fayol and Taylor

Basis	Henry Fayol	FW Taylor
Perspective	Top level of management	Shop floor level of a factory
Basis of Formation	Personal experience	Observations and experimentations
Focus	Improving overall administration	Increasing productivity of workers
Personality	Practitioner	Scientist
Expression	General theory of administration	Scientific management

Techniques of Scientific Management

- **Science, not Rule of Thumb** Each job should be performed as per the scientific approach
- **Harmony, Not Discord** There should be complete harmony between the management and workers
- **Cooperation, Not Individualism** There should be complete cooperation between the management and labour
- **Development of Workers to their Greatest Efficiency and Prosperity** Workers should be given training to learn the best method

5 Taylor's Scientific management

Scientific management means knowing exactly what you want men to do and seeing that they do it in the best and the cheapest way.

Techniques of Scientific Management

- **Functional Foremanship** Consists of planning and production incharge
- **Standardisation and Simplification of Work** Involves setting standards and elimination of unnecessary varieties of products
- **Method Study** Involves finding one best method
- **Motion Study** Involves study of movements or motions
- **Time Study** Determines the standard time taken by a worker
- **Fatigue Study** Determines the amount and frequency of rest intervals
- **Differential Piece Wage System** Helps in differentiating between efficient and inefficient workers

EXAM PATTERN QUESTIONS

Objective Type Questions

Multiple Choice Questions (MCQs)

1. Management principles and pure science principles are different because management principles are

(a) applied creatively (b) applied in static manner
(c) rigid (d) vague

2. Management principles are ...., whereas values are ethical.

(a) technical (b) common
(c) organised (d) Both (a) and (b)

3. Principles of management are not

(a) applicable only in large firms
(b) formed by practice and experience of managers
(c) flexible
(d) contingent

4. Which of the following is the statement of fundamental truth, which serves as guidelines for decisions and actions of managers?

(a) Values of management
(b) Principles of management
(c) Techniques of management
(d) None of the above

5. Principles of management are not

(a) universal (b) flexible
(c) absolute (d) behavioural

6. Which of the following statements about the principles of management is incorrect?

(a) Principles of management are universal in nature
(b) Principles of management are rigid and cannot be adapted to different situations
(c) Principles of management provide a guideline for managerial decision-making
(d) Principles of management are based on both empirical evidence and theoretical research

7. M/s JK Computers' is a small organisation engaged in assembling of computers. In this organisation, decision making rests with top management while the middle level is involved in only the implementation of plans.

On the other hand, 'Progressive Computers Ltd.' is a large company where a number of people from each level are involved in the decision-making process.

The application of the principle of 'centralisation and decentralisaton' is different in the two organisations as the situation in each enterprise is not same. From the following identify the nature of principles of management. CBSE 2023; Competency Based Que

(a) Mainly behavioural (b) Contingent
(c) Flexible (d) Universal

8. "Management principles focus on logic rather than blind faith." Which of the following points describe the significance of principles of management as indicated in the statement? Competency Based Que

(a) Fulfilling social responsibility
(b) Scientific decisions
(c) Meeting changing environment requirements
(d) Optimum utilisation of resources and effective administration

9. Which of the following statements about Fayol's principles of management is incorrect?

(a) The principle of unity of command suggests that an employee should receive orders from only one superior.
(b) The principle of division of work advocates for specialisation to increase efficiency.
(c) The principle of scalar chain emphasises the importance of a clear chain of command.
(d) The principle of esprit de corps means that individual goals should take precedence over organisational goals.

10. The principle of .... emphasises that each employee should have only one direct supervisor to avoid confusion and conflicting instructions, thereby improving efficiency.

(a) unity of command (b) unity of direction
(c) division of work (d) discipline

11. Amit, a purchasing manager, needs to acquire 35 tonnes of raw material. He decides to purchase it from a supplier who is a relative, but the price is above the market rate. Which principle of management is being violated in this scenario? Competency Based Que

(a) Discipline
(b) Equity
(c) Subordination of individual interest to general interest
(d) Remuneration to employees

12. **A company has recently implemented a new set of rules and procedures to standardise operations. However, employees are finding it challenging to follow these rules due to a lack of clear communication and support. Which Fayol's principles is being neglected in this situation?** Competency Based Que

(a) Authority and responsibility
(b) Discipline
(c) Initiative
(d) Subordination of individual interest to general interest

13. **Maya works as an executive assistant to the CEO of Tech Solutions, a research and development firm. She is assigned the task of obtaining test reports from the laboratory. However, she is unable to complete the task because only technicians, researchers and senior executives are permitted to access and collect the test reports.**

Which principle of management is likely being violated in this situation? Competency Based Que

(a) Unity of command
(b) Authority and responsibility
(c) Discipline
(d) Subordination of individual interest to general interest

14. **Sunflower Ltd. specialises in fruit juices and hair oils. To maintain coordinated efforts and ensure unity in action, the company has established two distinct divisions for each product category. Each division is managed by its own leader and is equipped with dedicated planning and execution resources. This organisational structure enables both divisions to work towards shared objectives through focused efforts.**

Identify the management principle being applied by Pioneer Ltd. in this scenario. Competency Based Que

(a) Esprit de corps
(b) Equity
(c) Unity of direction
(d) Authority and responsibility

15. **Identify the principle of management highlighted in the below picture.**

(a) Initiative
(b) Equity
(c) Remuneration of employees
(d) Subordination of individual interest to general interest

16. **'Vanguard Inc.', a company manufacturing footwear for men, women and children has been earning consistent profits for the last many years.**

It has a democratic style of working. Workers are encouraged to develop and carry out plans for improvement in the organisation. Varun who is working in the production department gave a suggestion which resulted in 10% reduction in the cost of production of shoes. He was rewarded for his suggestion.

Identify the principle of management followed by 'Vanguard Inc.' in the above case.
CBSE 2024; Competency Based Que

(a) Esprit de corps
(b) Subordination of individual interest to general interest
(c) Initiative
(d) Equity

17. **Identify the principle violated in the below picture.**

(a) Unity of command
(b) Unity of direction
(c) Discipline
(d) Equity

18. **Eminent Ltd. is a leading international consulting firm headquartered in London. The company is renowned for hiring talented young professionals from various countries. It is highly sought after due to its excellent work environment, competitive salaries and promising career growth.**

Eminent Global Ltd. fosters a culture of open communication and maintains a work atmosphere free from discrimination. Managers at Eminent Ltd. exhibit kindness and fairness, which enhances employee loyalty and dedication. The company promotes mutual trust and a sense of belonging among team members, which helps in achieving its objectives through effective teamwork. Identify the two management principles that the managers of Eminent Ltd. are following.
Competency Based Que

(a) Equity and espirit de corps
(b) Equity and discipline
(c) Remuneration and unity of command
(d) Unity of direction and equity

19. **Sangeeta visited Dental Clinic for treatment of toothache. She observed that the receptionist was seated at the reception desk, the place fixed for her. Dental instruments were laid neatly in dental instrument trays and the used instruments were placed in the sterilisation area.**

There was a fixed place for everything and it was present there. There was no hindrance in the work of the dentist and she was working with her maximum efficiency. The principle of management followed is **CBSE 2023; Competency Based Que**

(a) equity (b) discipline
(c) order (d) initiative

20. **Identify the principle of management highlighted in the below picture.**

(a) Equity (b) Remuneration
(c) Cooperation, not individualism
(d) Discipline

21. **Saarthi Enterprises, a growing IT firm in Bangalore, recently hired a new project manager, Rajesh, to oversee a major client project. The company decided to pay Rajesh a monthly salary of ₹ 80,000. However, Rajesh felt that this salary was not commensurate with his responsibilities and the industry standards. He discovered that similar positions at competing firms were paying ₹ 1,00,000 per month.**

Rajesh approached the HR department and expressed his concern, stating, "The compensation does not reflect the level of expertise and responsibility required for this role. Other firms are offering significantly higher salaries for similar positions."

Identify the management principle that Saarthi Enterprises has potentially overlooked in this situation. **Competency Based Que**

(a) Discipline (b) Remuneration of employees
(c) Equity (d) Unity of command

22. **Vikas Solutions, a tech startup, focused on maximising the efficiency and well-being of its employees by implementing several new initiatives. The company introduced regular training programmes to enhance skill sets and foster career growth. Additionally, they provided employees with opportunities to participate in decision-making processes and set clear career advancement paths.**

This approach aimed to not only improve individual performance but also ensure employees' overall job satisfaction and career development. Vikas Solutions believed that investing in their workforce would lead to higher productivity and employee retention.

Which principle of management is highlighted by 'Vikas Solutions' approach to employee development? **Competency Based Que**

(a) Unity of direction
(b) Cooperation, not individualism
(c) Initiative
(d) Development of workers to their greatest efficiency and prosperity

23. **The principle of management which aims at preventing overlapping of activities is**

(a) division of work (b) unity of command
(c) unity of direction (d) order

24. **Sharma Electric has divided its operations into various departments such as marketing, finance and production. Each department has specialised staff, allowing the company to enhance efficiency and output.**

Which principle of management is demonstrated by PQR Corporation's departmental structure? **Competency Based Que**

(a) Division of work (b) Unity of direction
(c) Discipline (d) Order

25. **ABC Manufacturing Company noticed that efficiency was decreasing and employees were overwhelmed by the workload. The management decided to restructure the work process. They divided the production tasks into smaller segments and assigned them to workers who had specialised training in each area. This approach quickly improved the company's productivity and quality of goods.**

Which principle of management is being applied by ABC Manufacturing Company? **Competency Based Que**

(a) Authority and responsibility
(b) Discipline
(c) Division of work
(d) Unity of command

26. **XYZ Ltd. experienced conflicts among employees as some subordinates were receiving instructions from more than one superior. This led to confusion, missed deadlines and a lack of accountability. To resolve the issue, the management ensured that every employee was assigned to report to only one manager.**

Which principle of management was violated at XYZ Ltd. before the corrective action? **Competency Based Que**

(a) Unity of command
(b) Stability of tenure
(c) Scalar chain
(d) Equity

27. **At Reliable Tech, the management observed that employees from different departments were working on similar projects without any coordination. To resolve this, the company introduced a unified plan for all departments working toward the same objective. This plan helped streamline efforts and avoid duplication of tasks.**

Which of Fayol's principles did Reliable Tech implement to resolve their coordination issue? **Competency Based Que**

(a) Unity of direction
(b) Unity of command
(c) Centralisation
(d) Esprit de corps

28. **Speedy Logistics faced dissatisfaction among its employees due to unfair wage policies. Some employees felt underpaid compared to others, leading to decreased morale.**

The company then reviewed its wage structure and ensured that wages were fair and reflected the employees' work contributions, while still remaining within the company's paying capacity.

Which principle of management is being referred to in this scenario? **Competency Based Que**

(a) Remuneration (b) Equity
(c) Order (d) Initiative

29. **At Global Enterprises, the CEO believed in delegating some decision-making power to lower levels of management while retaining key decision-making authority at the top level. This balance allowed the organisation to function smoothly, with both senior leaders and junior managers involved in decisions.**

Which principle of management is described in this situation? **Competency Based Que**

(a) Division of work
(b) Centralisation and decentralisation
(c) Authority and responsibility
(d) Scalar chain

30. **"If there is a fixed place for everything and it is present there, then there will be no hindrance in the activities of business/factory."**

The principle of management that is highlighted in the above statement is **CBSE 2024 C; Competency Based Que**

(a) Discipline (b) Order
(c) Unity of direction (d) Esprit de corps

31. **The purpose of the principle of 'unity of command' is that** **CBSE 2024 C**

(a) it avoids dual subordination
(b) it subordinates individual interests to organisational interests
(c) it promotes a team spirit of unity and harmony among employees
(d) it concentrates decision-making authority at the top level

32. **......... is known as the father of scientific management.**

(a) Henri Fayol (b) Frederick W Taylor
(c) Adam Smith (d) Max Weber

33. **"The management should not close its cars to any constructive suggestions made by the employees but reward them for their suggestions which results in substantial reduction in costs."**

Which principle of scientific management is discussed in the above statement?

CBSE 2024 C; Competency Based Que

(a) Science, not rule of thumb
(b) Harmony, not discord
(c) Cooperation, not individualism
(d) Development of each and every person to his or her greatest efficiency and prosperity

34. **Harmony, not discord principle is associated with ....**

(a) management sharing the gain of the company with workers
(b) investigation of task
(c) scientific inquiry
(d) observation and analysis

35. **Which of the following statements about Taylor's scientific management is incorrect?**

(a) Taylor's principles advocate for scientific study and analysis of work tasks.
(b) Taylor's scientific management focuses on the development of a standard method for performing tasks.
(c) Taylor's principles emphasise the importance of worker satisfaction over efficiency.
(d) Taylor's scientific management aims to increase productivity through time and motion studies.

36. **Identify the principle demonstrated in the below picture where the owner is giving bonus to the worker for making high profit.**

(a) Harmony, not discord
(b) Cooperation, not individualism
(c) Science, not rule of thumb
(d) Efficiency and prosperity

37. **Taylor called for complete mental revolution on the part of both management and workers. It meant that management and workers should transform their thinking. Management should share the gains of the company, if any, with the workers. At the same time, workers should work hard and be willing to embrace change for the good of the company.**

The principle of management highlighted above is **CBSE 2023; Competency Based Que**

(a) science, not the rule of thumb
(b) cooperation, not individualism
(c) harmony, not discord
(d) development of each and every person to his or her greatest efficiency and prosperity

38. **Raj works as a foreman in Disha Automatives Ltd. a company manufacturing cars. He is subordinate to Ramesh, who is the production incharge in the factory. Raj is the incharge of timely and accurate completion of job by workers working in the production department.**

There are three other foremen who work under the production incharge, while four other foremen work under Naresh, the planning incharge in the factory.

Each of the eight foremen are specialist in their area and give orders to the workers relating to them.

The technique of scientific management highlighted in the above case is **Competency Based Que**

(a) method study
(b) differential piece wage system
(c) functional foremanship
(d) standardisation and simplification of work

39. **The main objective of 'motion study' is**

(a) to save cost of labour and machines
(b) to determine and eliminate the unnecessary movements
(c) to represent a clear picture of management
(d) to plan and execute day-to-day work

40. **Analyse the below image. It highlights the need to conduct one of the techniques of scientific management. Identify the technique.**

(a) Time study
(b) Functional foremanship
(c) Method study
(d) Fatigue study

41. **"He keeps machines, materials, tools, etc. ready for operations by concerned workers." Whose work is described by this sentence under functional foremanship?**

(a) Instruction card clerk (b) Gang boss
(c) Repair boss (d) Route clerk

42. **TechMakers Ltd. a mid-sized electronics manufacturer, faced productivity and cost issues. To improve efficiency, the management introduced several changes**

(i) **They recorded the time taken for each production task to identify the most efficient methods.**
(ii) **Standard procedures were implemented to ensure consistency in tasks.**
(iii) **The hiring process was revamped to select workers based on specific skills and comprehensive training was introduced.**
(iv) **A new compensation system was adopted where employees were paid based on their output.**
(v) **Regular meetings were held to review progress and make necessary adjustments.**

Based on the case study of TechMakers Ltd. identify the principle or technique applied when the management recorded the time taken for each production task to identify the most efficient methods. **Competency Based Que**

(a) Scientific selection (b) Standardisation
(c) Time and motion study (d) Piece rate system

43. **Following are the objectives of standardisation technique of scientific management except**
(a) to ensure savings of cost of labour, machine and tools.
(b) to establish standards of excellence and quality in materials.
(c) to establish interchange ability of manufactured parts and products.
(d) to reduce a given line of product of fixed types, sizes and characteristics.

44. **The purpose of the motion study is to .... the movements made while doing some work.**
(a) maximise (b) minimise
(c) nil (d) stabilise

45. **Elegant Furniture manufactures wooden chairs, but the production process was inefficient as workers used different techniques to assemble the chairs. To resolve this, the company studied each worker's methods and implemented a uniform assembly process that all workers followed, improving consistency and reducing costs.**

Which technique is Elegant Furniture applying by finding the best method for assembling chairs? **Competency Based Que**

(a) Simplification (b) Standardisation
(c) Method study (d) Time study

46. **Tech Tools noticed that their workers often performed repetitive tasks with unnecessary steps, slowing down production. Management decided to observe and record each worker's movements to identify and eliminate wasteful actions, resulting in a significant boost in productivity.**

Which scientific management concept is Tech Tools employing to enhance productivity? **Competency Based Que**

(a) Motion study (b) Division of work
(c) Equity (d) Functional foremanship

47. **Ashok Industries Ltd. is a company manufacturing components for automobile industries. In this company, standards have been set for every manufacturing activity including standardisation of process, new material, time, product, machinery and methods which must be adhered to during production. This has been done to bring excellence in quality of the materials produced. The foreman of the company, Mehra, has designed the jobs of the workers in such a manner that unnecessary movements are eliminated and it takes less time to complete the jobs efficiently. He has also scientifically analysed the duration and frequency of rest intervals that should be provided to the workers in the factory so that they can regain stamina and work efficiently.**

Out of the following, which technique of scientific management has not been discussed in the above paragraph? **CBSE 2024 C; Competency Based Que**
(a) Fatigue study
(b) Method study
(c) Motion study
(d) Standardisation and simplification

Direction *Read the following case study and answer the questions 48 to 51 on the basis of the same*

Stellar Tech Solutions, a rapidly growing IT company founded by Jane Thompson, faced challenges as it expanded from a small team to over 200 employees. To enhance organisational efficiency and ensure sustainable growth, Jane implemented several management principles.

She focused on dividing work among employees based on their skills and expertise. This approach allowed the Research and Development (R&D) department to concentrate on technology development, while the sales and marketing teams handled market needs and product promotion.

To clarify roles and responsibilities, Jane established clear authority for managers, ensuring they were accountable for their teams. She also enforced a policy where employees reported to only one manager, preventing conflicting instructions and confusion.

Initially, Jane preferred centralised decision-making to retain control over strategic choices. However, as the company grew, she gradually decentralised some decision-making powers, enabling departmental managers to make operational decisions more efficiently.

To improve communication, Jane created a clear hierarchy within the organisation, defining reporting relationships and ensuring smooth information flow from top management to lower levels. She also introduced a code of conduct to maintain discipline, addressing behaviour expectations and grievance resolution.

As a result, Stellar Tech Solutions experienced significant improvements in productivity and employee satisfaction, effectively coordinating its departments and maintaining a strong market position.

48. **"Jane emphasised dividing work among employees based on their skills and expertise."**

Which principle is being followed in the given case?
(a) Authority and responsibility
(b) Unity of command
(c) Division of work
(d) Scalar chain

49. **"Jane enforced a policy where employees reported to only one manager to avoid conflicting instructions." Which principle is being highlighted in the given line?**
(a) Division of work
(b) Authority and responsibility
(c) Unity of command
(d) Discipline

50. **What was Jane Thompson's approach to decision-making initially and how did it evolve over time?**
(a) Centralisation, with no change over time
(b) Decentralisation, with no change over time
(c) Centralisation, gradually moving towards decentralisation
(d) Decentralisation, gradually moving towards centralisation

51. **"Jane created a clear hierarchy within the organisation, defining reporting relationships and ensuring smooth communication." Which principle is being highlighted in the given line?**
(a) Scalar chain (b) Unity of command
(c) Division of work
(d) Authority and responsibility

Assertion-Reason

Direction (Q.No. 52 to 61) *Read the following Assertion (A) and Reason (R) and choose the correct alternative from the following*

Alternatives
(a) Both Assertion (A) and Reason (R) are true and Reason (R) is the correct explanation of Assertion (A)
(b) Both Assertion (A) and Reason (R) are true, but Reason (R) is not the correct explanation of Assertion (A)
(c) Assertion (A) is true, but Reason (R) is false
(d) Assertion (A) is false, but Reason (R) is true

52. **Assertion** (A) The nature of management principles is prescriptive, meaning they provide specific instructions for managers to follow.
Reason (R) Management principles are more descriptive than prescriptive, offering general guidelines rather than detailed instructions.

53. **Assertion** (A) Principles of management make administration more effective.
Reason (R) Principles are flexible and can be modified to meet the dynamic business environment.

54. **Assertion** (A) The significance of management principles lies in their ability to provide a framework for managers to solve organisational problems.
Reason (R) Management principles offer a structured approach to addressing issues by applying well-established guidelines and methods.

55. **Assertion** (A) Henri Fayol's principle of division of work suggests that tasks should be divided among workers to improve efficiency.
Reason (R) By dividing work, employees can specialise in specific tasks, leading to increased expertise and productivity.

56. **Assertion** (A) Fayol's principle of centralisation refers to spreading decision-making authority across various levels of management.
Reason (R) Centralisation involves concentrating decision-making authority at the top levels of management.

57. **Assertion** (A) Unity of command with the objective of one head and one plan ensures unity of action and coordination.
Reason (R) As dual subordination is avoided through unity of command, there are no confusions regarding the task to be done.

58. **Assertion** (A) The principle of order states that to achieve maximum efficiency, everything and everyone should have a designated place.
Reason (R) Having a designated place for each item and person ensures that nothing is misplaced, preventing work disruptions.

59. **Assertion** (A) The principle of unity of direction suggests that activities aimed at achieving a common objective should be grouped together under one plan.
Reason (R) Unity of direction ensures that employees work in isolation on their respective tasks, leading to improved focus on individual responsibilities.

60. **Assertion** (A) Taylor advocated for fostering cooperation between management and workers rather than promoting individualism.
Reason (R) The principle of 'harmony, not discord' emphasises that effective collaboration between management and workers is essential for achieving organisational goals.

61. **Assertion** (A) Taylor's principle of scientific management involves using time studies to determine the most efficient way to perform tasks.
Reason (R) Time studies focus on improving workers' morale by providing them with better working conditions.

Two Statements Based MCQs

Direction (Q.No. 62 to 71) *Read the following statements carefully and choose the correct alternative*

Alternatives

(a) Statement I is correct and Statement II is incorrect
(b) Statement II is correct and Statement I is incorrect
(c) Both the statements are correct
(d) Both the statements are incorrect

62. **Statement I** The principle of division of work leads to increased specialisation and efficiency in performing tasks.

Statement II Fayol's principle of division of work is applicable only to technical tasks and not managerial tasks.

63. **Statement I** The principle of centralisation refers to the concentration of decision-making authority at the top levels of management.

Statement II Centralisation is the opposite of the principle of delegation, which involves distributing decision-making authority.

64. **Statement I** The principle of esprit de corps emphasises the importance of team spirit and harmony among employees.

Statement II Esprit de corps is a principle outlined by FW Taylor in his management theories.

65. **Statement I** Fayol's principle of equity focuses on fairness and justice in dealing with employees.

Statement II The principle of equity is related to the division of work and specialisation.

66. **Statement I** Fayol's principle of equity emphasises fairness and justice in treatment and compensation.

Statement II The principle of equity suggests that compensation should be determined by employee seniority alone.

67. **Statement I** The principle of remuneration ensures that employees are compensated fairly according to their roles and contributions.

Statement II Fair remuneration also considers market standards and cost of living adjustments to maintain employee satisfaction.

68. **Statement I** Scientific management emphasises the use of scientific methods to determine the best way to perform a job.

Statement II The principle of scientific management involves applying general management principles rather than specific techniques.

69. **Statement I** The principle of scientific management includes time studies to improve work efficiency.

Statement II Taylor's scientific management focuses on the development of a systematic approach to management.

70. **Statement I** Functional foremanship is a technique used in scientific management.

Statement II Functional foremanship is an extension of the principle of unity of direction.

71. **Statement I** Time study helps to establish standard times for tasks, which can be used for setting performance benchmarks.

Statement II Method study is primarily used to determine the optimal time required for completing a task.

Matching

72. **Match the following features of principles of management with their correct options given in Column II**

Column I	Column II
A. Flexibility	(i) Principles depend upon prevailing situations
B. Contingent	(ii) Principles are applied to all organisations
C. Mainly behavioural	(iii) Principles can be modified by the managers
D. Universal applicability	(iv) Management principles aim at influencing human behaviour

Codes

	A	B	C	D		A	B	C	D
(a)	(i)	(ii)	(iv)	(iii)	(b)	(ii)	(iii)	(iv)	(i)
(c)	(iii)	(i)	(iv)	(ii)	(d)	(ii)	(i)	(iii)	(iv)

73. **Match the following management principles with their correct options given in Column II**

Column I	Column II
A. Unity of command	(i) The chain of command from top to bottom should be clear and unbroken
B. Authority and responsibility	(ii) Work should be divided into specialised tasks for efficiency
C. Division of work	(iii) Managers must have the authority to give orders and the responsibility to ensure they are executed
D. Scalar chain	(iv) Each employee should receive orders from only one superior

Codes

	A	B	C	D		A	B	C	D
(a)	(i)	(ii)	(iii)	(iv)	(b)	(iv)	(iii)	(ii)	(i)
(c)	(ii)	(iii)	(i)	(iv)	(d)	(iii)	(ii)	(iv)	(i)

74. **Match the following techniques with their correct options given in Column II**

Column I	Column II
A. Order	(i) Management should promote a team spirit of unity
B. Stability of personnel	(ii) Employees at all levels should be encouraged to take the first step
C. Espirit de corps	(iii) Employee turnover should be minimised to maintain organisational efficiency
D. Initiative	(iv) There should be a place for everything and everyone

Codes

	A	B	C	D		A	B	C	D
(a)	(i)	(ii)	(iii)	(iv)	(b)	(ii)	(iii)	(iv)	(i)
(c)	(i)	(iii)	(iv)	(iii)	(d)	(iv)	(iii)	(i)	(ii)

75. **Match the following management principles and techniques with their correct options given in Column II**

Column I	Column II
A. Fayol's principle of unity of command	(i) A clear line of authority from top to bottom in the organisation
B. Taylor's technique of standardisation	(ii) Applying systematic analysis to improve work processes
C. Fayol's principle of scalar chain	(iii) Each employee should have only one superior
D. Taylor's technique of scientific management	(iv) Creating uniform procedures to increase efficiency

Codes

	A	B	C	D		A	B	C	D
(a)	(ii)	(i)	(iii)	(iv)	(b)	(iii)	(iv)	(i)	(ii)
(c)	(i)	(iii)	(ii)	(iv)	(d)	(iv)	(i)	(iii)	(ii)

76. **Match the techniques of scientific management given in Column I with their meaning given in Column II** **CBSE 2025**

Column I	Column II
A. Method study	(i) It refers tothe study of movements like lifting, putting objects, sitting and changing positions, etc. which are undertaken while doing a typical job.
B. Motion study	(ii) It determines the amount and frequency of rest intervals in completing a task.
C. Time study	(iii) It determines the standard time taken to perform a well defined job.
D. Fatigue study	(iv) It determines one best way of doing a job.

Codes

	A	B	C	D
(a)	(ii)	(iii)	(i)	(iv)
(b)	(i)	(iv)	(ii)	(iii)
(c)	(iv)	(i)	(iii)	(ii)
(d)	(iii)	(ii)	(iv)	(i)

Answers

1. (a) applied creatively
2. (a) technical
3. (a) Applicable only in large firms
4. (b) Principles of management
5. (c) absolute
6. (b) Principles of management are not rigid; they are flexible and can be adapted to different situations. They serve as guidelines for decision-making and are based on empirical evidence and theoretical research, making them applicable in various contexts.
7. (c) Flexible
8. (b) Scientific decisions
9. (d) The principle of esprit de corps emphasises the importance of teamwork and harmony among employees, not individual goals over organisational goals. It aims to build team spirit and unity within the organisation.
10. (a) unity of command
11. (c) Subordination of individual interest to general interest
12. (b) Discipline
13. (b) Authority and responsibility
14. (c) Unity of direction
15. (a) initiative
16. (c) Initiative
17. (a) Unity of command
18. (a) Equity and espirit de corps
19. (c) order
20. (d) Discipline
21. (b) Remuneration of employees
22. (d) Development of workers to their greatest efficiency and prosperity
23. (c) unity of direction
24. (a) Division of work
25. (c) Division of work
26. (a) Unity of command

27. (a) Unity of direction
28. (a) Remuneration
29. (b) Centralisation and decentralisation
30. (b) Order
31. (a) it avoids dual subordination
32. (b) Frederick W Taylor
33. (c) Cooperation, not individualism
34. (a) management sharing the gain of the company with workers
35. (c) Taylor's scientific management primarily focuses on increasing efficiency and productivity through scientific study, standard methods, and time and motion studies. While worker satisfaction is important, it is not the primary emphasis of Taylor's principles, which are centered on efficiency and productivity.
36. (a) Harmony, not discord
37. (c) harmony, not discord
38. (c) Functional foremanship
39. (b) to determine and eliminate the unnecessary movements
40. (d) Fatigue study
41. (b) Gang boss
42. (c) Time and motion study
43. (a) to ensure savings of cost of labour, machine and tools.
44. (b) minimise
45. (c) Method study
46. (a) Motion study
47. (b) Method study
48. (c) Division of work
49. (c) Unity of command
50. (c) Centralisation, gradually moving towards decentralisation
51. (a) Scalar chain
52. (d) Management principles are generally descriptive rather than prescriptive, providing broad guidelines rather than specific instructions.
53. (b) Both Assertion (A) and Reason (R) are true, but Reason (R) is not the correct explanation of Assertion (A)
54. (a) Both Assertion (A) and Reason (R) are true and Reason (R) is the correct explanation of Assertion (A)
55. (a) Both Assertion (A) and Reason (R) are true and Reason (R) is the correct explanation of Assertion (A)
56. (d) Fayol's principle of centralisation actually involves concentrating decision-making at the top levels, not spreading it.
57. (d) It is unity of direction and not the unity of command which ensures unity of action and coordination as its objective is one head and one plan. Unity of command talks about one person, one boss.
58. (a) Both Assertion (A) and Reason (R) are true and Reason (R) is the correct explanation of Assertion (A)
59. (c) Unity of direction is about ensuring coordination and alignment towards common objectives, not about having employees work in isolation.
60. (b) Both Assertion (A) and Reason (R) are true, but Reason (R) is not the correct explanation of Assertion (A)
61. (c) Taylor's use of time studies is aimed at optimising task performance, not specifically improving worker morale or conditions.
62. (a) The principle of division of work enhances specialisation and efficiency by dividing tasks according to skills and expertise. This principle is applicable to both technical and managerial tasks, not just technical ones.
63. (c) Both the statements are correct
64. (a) The principle of esprit de corps, which promotes team spirit and harmony, is indeed one of Fayol's principles of management.
65. (a) Fayol's principle of equity emphasises fairness and justice in management. It is not related to the division of work or specialisation, which are covered by other principles.
66. (a) Fayol's principle of equity emphasises fairness and justice in treatment, including compensation. It does not suggest that compensation should be based solely on seniority.
67. (c) Both the statements are correct
68. (a) Scientific management focuses on using scientific methods and techniques to improve work efficiency and productivity. It involves applying specific techniques.
69. (c) Both the statements are correct
70. (a) Functional foremanship is not an extension of the principle of unity of direction. The principle of unity of direction refers to directing all activities with the same objective by one manager using one plan.
71. (a) Method study focuses on analysing and improving work methods rather than determining the time required.
72. (c) (iii) (i) (iv) (ii)
73. (b) (iv) (iii) (ii) (i)
74. (d) (iv) (iii) (i) (ii)
75. (b) (iii) (iv) (i) (ii)
76. (c) (iv) (i) (iii) (ii)

Subjective Questions

Short Answer Type Questions

1. Briefly explain how management principles are different from principles of pure science, techniques and values.

Ans. Management principles are different from principles of pure science, techniques and values in the following ways

(i) **Management Principles vs Principles of Pure Science**
Management principles are flexible, required to be applied creatively and have to keep pace with the changing environment while principles of pure science are rigid, applied in absolute or static manner and do not have to be adaptive to changing environment.

(ii) **Management Principles vs Techniques of Management**
Management principles are flexible and act as guidelines while techniques are less flexible and are methods or procedures.

(iii) **Management Principles vs Values**
Management principles are guidelines, technical in nature while values are ethical and general rules for individual behaviour.

2. Explain the following as nature of principles of management
(i) Universal applicability (ii) General guidelines

Ans.

(i) **Universal Applicability**
The principles of management can be applied to all kinds of organisations, irrespective of size (small or large) and nature (business, government or social organisation). However, extent of application varies depending on nature and size of organisation.

(ii) **General Guidelines**
Management principles are guidelines to action and cannot be used as tailor made tools, i.e. they do not provide readymade, straitjacket solutions.
This is so because real business situations are very complex and dynamic. So, principles of management are general guidelines and cannot be applied strictly as the principles of physical sciences.

3. If an organisation does not provide the right place for physical and human resources in an organisation, which principle is violated? What are the consequences of it? NCERT; Competency Based Que

Ans. Principle of order is violated in this case. Its consequences are as follows

(i) Wastage of time and energy in search of men and material.
(ii) Productivity will suffer, as resources would not be available at the right time.
(iii) Obstacle in smooth working in the organisation.

4. Briefly explain the following principles of management
(i) Unity of direction (ii) Esprit de corps

Ans.

(i) **Unity of Direction**
It implies that there should be one head and one plan for a group of activities having the same objective. All the related activities should be put under one group and they should be in the control of one manager.

(ii) **Esprit De Corps**
It means union is strength. Fayol emphasised that management should promote a team spirit of unity and harmony among employees to achieve the targets of an organisation. For this, managers should replace 'I' with 'We' in all their conversations.

5. What do you understand by 'unity of command'? Differentiate between unity of command and unity of direction.

Or **How is the principle of 'unity of command' useful in management? Explain briefly.** NCERT

Ans. According to the principle of unity of command, an employee should receive orders from one superior at a time and that employee should be answerable only to that superior.

If this principle is violated, then authority is undermined, discipline is in jeopardy, order disturbed and stability threatened. If unity of command is maintained in organisation, it would help to avoid confusion among workers, conflict among superiors and create better relations between workers and managers.

Following are the differences between unity of command and unity of direction

Basis	Unity of Command	Unity of Direction
Meaning	One subordinate should receive orders from one boss only.	Each group of activities should have one head and one plan.
Aim	It avoids dual subordination.	It avoids overlapping of activities.
Implications	It affects individual employee.	It affects the entire organisation.

6. (i) Identify and explain the principle of management which requires imposing penalties by management in case of non-obedience.

(ii) **Identify and explain the principle of management which involves encouraging the workers to give their suggestions for the growth of the organisation.** Competency Based Que

Ans.

(i) The principle of discipline requires imposing penalties by management in case of non-obedience. It is the sincerity and obedience towards organisational rules and employment agreement, necessary, for the smooth functioning of an organisation.

According to Fayol, good superiors at all levels, clear and fair agreements and judicious application of penalties are required in maintaining discipline. It leads to healthy or better relations between workers and managers. It helps in smooth working and improves efficiency, as work is done as per the rules and standards.

(ii) The principle of initiative involves encouraging the workers to give their suggestions for the growth of the organisation. Initiative means taking the first step with self-motivation.

Fayol suggested that employees at all levels should be encouraged and given an opportunity to take some initiative in making and executing the plans. It develops a feeling of belongingness in employees and leads to improvements in operations.

7. Illustrate the principle of scalar chain through a suitable example. Competency Based Que

Ans. An organisation consists of superiors and subordinates. The formal lines of authority from highest to lowest ranks are known as scalar chain.

According to Fayol, organisations should have a chain of authority and communication that runs from top to bottom and should be followed by managers and the subordinates.

e.g. In a manufacturing company, the scalar chain starts with the CEO who sets the company's strategic goals. The CEO communicates these objectives to the vice-president of production, who is responsible for overseeing all production activities.

The vice-president then directs the production manager, who handles daily operations on the shop floor. The production manager supervises team leaders, each in charge of a specific production line. Finally, the workers on the production lines follow the instructions from their team leaders.

This clear hierarchy ensures that instructions flow smoothly from top management to the operational staff, maintaining order and accountability throughout the organisation.

8. "An organisation's success largely depends on its ability to maintain fairness among employees and ensure long-term stability in its workforce."

In the light of this, explain Fayol's principles of 'equity' and 'stability of personnel' with relevant examples. Competency Based Que

Ans. Equity

According to the principle of equity, there should not be any discrimination among the employees on the basis of religion, language, caste, sex, belief or nationality. This principle emphasises kindliness and justice in the behaviour of managers towards workers.

e.g. Raj and Rahul work in a company at the position of head clerk and both of them have same educational qualification. With the same job profile and nature of work, Raj gets a salary of ₹ 20,000 per month, while Rahul gets ₹ 23,000 per month as he a relative of manager. In the given case, principle of equity is violated. As per equity, employees performing similar jobs should be paid same salary.

Stability of Personnel

According to the principle of stability of personnel, there should be proper efforts to achieve stability and continuity of tenure of personnel. Fayol was of the view that employees should be selected and appointed after due and rigorous procedure. Once selected, they should be kept at their position for a minimum period and must be given reasonable time to show results.

Employee turnover should be minimised to maintain organisational efficiency. e.g. If a new employee is appointed, then the employee must be given time to settle down and to adapt to the new environment and working conditions.

9. Which principle involves concentration and dispersal of decision-making authority? Give two adverse effects if this principle if violated.

Ans. Centralisation refers to concentration of decision-making authority with few people, whereas decentralisation refers to evenly distribution of authority at all levels of management.

There is a need to balance subordinate involvement through decentralisation and managers' retention official authority through centralisation.

Following are the adverse effects if this principle if violated

(i) Complete centralisation leads to delay in decision-making and action.

(ii) Complete decentralisation leads to misuse of authority.

10. Explain briefly the principle of division of work. State two positive impact of following this principle.

Ans. According to the principle of division of work, dividing the work into small tasks and then assigning them to trained specialists would help in taking the advantage of specialisation. This principle is applicable to all kinds of technical and managerial work.

Following points indicate the positive impact of this principle is followed

(i) Repeated performance by an individual leads to specialisation.

(ii) There is less wastage of resources and increase in efficiency and effectiveness of work.

11. **"A key factor in maintaining employee motivation and reducing turnover is ensuring that employees are fairly compensated for their work." In the light of this, identify and explain the principle of management that involves fair payment of wages to employees.**

Competency Based Que

Ans. The principle which involves fair payment of wages to the employees is remuneration of employees. According to this principle, overall pay and compensation should be fair to both employees and organisation.

The remuneration should be just and fair to everybody. Employees should be paid fair wages, which should give them at least a reasonable standard of living. At the same time it should be within the paying capacity of the company.

12. **Explore the dynamic interplay between authority and responsibility within an organisation.**

Competency Based Que

Ans. According to this principle, there should be a proper balance between authority and responsibility. Authority is the right to give orders to subordinates and responsibility is the duty, which a subordinate is expected to perform by virtue of his position in organisation.

Authority and responsibility go hand in hand. An organisation should build safeguards against abuse of managerial power. At the same time, a manager should have necessary authority to carry out his responsibility.

13. **Explain how the principle of science in management goes beyond just being a rule of thumb.**

Ans. According to this principle, there should be scientific study and analysis of each element of a job, in order to replace the old rule of thumb approach or hit and trial method. Taylor believed that there was only one best method to maximise efficiency.

This method can be developed through study and analysis. Scientific method involves investigation of traditional methods through work study, unifying the best practices and developing a standard method of work. The method so developed should substitute rule of thumb throughout the organisation.

14. **Explain 'cooperation, not individualism' as the principle of scientific management given by Taylor.**

Ans. According to this principle, there should be cooperation between management and workers instead of individualism. This principle is an extension to 'harmony, not discord'.

Competition should be replaced by cooperation. Both management and workers should realise the need and importance of each other.

For this, management should encourage constructive suggestions by employees through proper rewards. Management should take workers into confidence before making any important decision.

At the same time, workers should avoid strikes and unreasonable demands.

15. **Explain the technique of scientific management, in which planning or production departments are segregated.**

Or **Explain in detail the technique of 'functional foremanship'.**

Ans. Functional foremanship is an extension of division of work and specialisation to the shop floor. Taylor advocated separation of planning and execution functions. This concept was extended to the lowest level of the shop floor. It was known as functional foremanship.

Under the factory manager there was a planning incharge and a production incharge.

Under the planning incharge, there are four personnel

(i) **Instruction Card Clerk**
He is responsible to give instructions to the workers.

(ii) **Route Clerk**
He is responsible to specify the route of production.

(iii) **Time and Cost Clerk**
He is responsible to prepare time and cost sheets.

(iv) **Disciplinarian**
He is responsible to maintain discipline among workers.

Under the production incharge, there are four personnel

(i) **Speed Boss**
He is responsible for timely and accurate completion of job.

(ii) **Gang Boss**
He is responsible for keeping machines and tools ready for work.

(iii) **Repair Boss**
He is responsible to keep machines and tools in proper working condition.

(iv) **Inspector**
He is responsible to maintain quality of work.

16. **Write short notes on the following**

(i) Method study

(ii) Development of workers to their greatest efficiency and prosperity

Ans.

(i) **Method Study**

There are various methods of doing the job. To determine the best way, there are several parameters.

The search for the best method starts from procurement of raw materials and continues till the final product is delivered to the customer.

For finding one best method of performing the job, critical analysis is made for plant layout, product design, material handling and work processes. The objective of method study is to minimise the cost of production and maximise quality and satisfaction of customers.

(ii) **Development of Workers to their Greatest Efficiency and Prosperity**
According to this principle, management should aim to develop workers to their greatest efficiency and prosperity.
The concern for efficiency should start from the selection process. Every organisation should follow a scientific system of selection.
The selected workers should be assigned job as per their physical, mental and intellectual abilities. To increase the efficiency and to achieve the maximum potential of workers, they should be provided scientific training.

Long Answer Type Questions

17. **Explain the following characteristics of principles of management**
(i) **Formed by practice and experimentation**
(ii) **Flexible**
(iii) **Mainly behavioural**

Ans.
(i) **Formed by Practice and Experimentation**
The principles of management are formed by experience and collective wisdom of managers as well as experimentation.
Management principles are evolutionary in nature, i.e. they have been developed through observations, experimentation and experience of the management thinkers.

(ii) **Flexible**
Management principles are not as rigid as in case of pure science principles.
They are flexible and can be modified by the manager as per changes in the business environment. These principles cannot be applied blindly, even in an identical situation.

(iii) **Mainly Behavioural**
Principles of management aim at influencing human behaviour because all work is done by human beings. Human behaviour is very complex and dynamic in nature.
Management principles aim to influence such unpredictable behaviour in order to achieve organisational goals. Therefore, principles of management are mainly behavioural in nature. Principles also enable a better understanding of relationship between human and material resources in accomplishing organisational purposes.

18. **"The application of sound management principles helps organisations achieve their goals more effectively while fostering a positive work environment."**
In the light of this, explain in detail why understanding management principles is important and beneficial for the organisation. **Competency Based Que**

Or **Explain the following points of significance of principles of management** **CBSE 2025**
(i) **Providing managers with useful insights into reality**
(ii) **Optimum utilisation of resources and effective administration**

Or **Explain the following points of significance of principles of management** **CBSE 2025**
(i) **Scientific decision**
(ii) **Fulfilling social responsibility**

Or **Explain the following points of significance of principles of management** **CBSE 2025**
(i) **Meeting changing environment requirements**
(ii) **Management training, education and research**

Ans. Understanding management principles is important and beneficial for the organisation in the following ways

(i) **Providing Managers with Useful Insights into Reality**
These principles provide the managers with useful insights into real world situations. Adherence to these principles help managers to improve the knowledge, ability and understanding of managerial situations. These principles enable managers to learn from past mistakes and conserve time by solving recurring problems quickly.

(ii) **Optimum Utilisation of Resources and Effective Administration**
Each company has limited availability of resources (human and material) and therefore, they are required to be put to optimum use. Optimum utilisation of resources emphasise that resources should be utilised in such a manner that it should give maximum benefit with minimum cost.

(iii) **Scientific Decisions**
Management principles help in thoughtful decision-making which should be based on facts and justifiable in terms of intended purposes. They emphasise logic and are based on objective assessment of the situation.

(iv) **Meeting Changing Environment Requirements**
Modern business environment is complex and ever-changing. In order to be successful, organisations have to adapt to these changes.
Though, principles are general guidelines, but they are dynamic, flexible and help the organisation to implement the changes.

(v) **Fulfilling Social Responsibility**
The increased awareness of public has forced business organisations to fulfill their social responsibilities.

Management principles are also evolved to serve these demands of society. These principles not only guide managers to achieve organisational goals but also guide them to perform social responsibilities.

(vi) **Management Training, Education and Research**
Management principles act as a base for management training, education and research. These principles provide basic groundwork for the development of management as a discipline. Therefore, professional courses like MBA and BBA also teach these principles as a part of their curriculum.

19. Explain 'cause and effect relationship' as a feature of principles of management, meeting changing environment requirements and management training, education and research as significance of principles of management. **CBSE 2023**

Ans. Following is the explanation of feature and significance of principles of management

(i) **Cause and Effect Relationships**
The principles of management are intended to establish relationship between cause and effect so that they can be used in similar situations in a large number of cases. It means, principles help in predicting the outcome of managerial actions.

(ii) **Meeting Changing Environment Requirements**
Modern business environment is complex and ever-changing. In order to be successful, organisations have to adapt to these changes. Though, principles are general guidelines, but they are dynamic, flexible and help the organisation to implement the changes.

(iii) **Management Training, Education and Research**
Management principles act as a base for management training, education and research. These principles provide basic groundwork for the development of management as a discipline. Therefore, professional courses like MBA and BBA also teach these principles as a part of their curriculum.

20. Explain the following principles of general management
(i) Unity of command
(ii) Subordination of individual interest to general interest
(iii) Initiative

Ans.

(i) **Unity of Command**
According to this principle, an individual employee should receive orders from only one superior at a time and that employee should be answerable only to that superior. If this principle is violated, then authority is undermined, discipline is in jeopardy, order disturbed and stability threatened.

(ii) **Subordination of Individual Interest to General Interest**
In an organisation, every individual has his own interest and company has its own objectives. According to this principle, in all situations, company's interest or objectives should supersede the interest of anyone individual.

This is so because the interests of various stakeholders, i.e. owners, shareholders, creditors, financers and the society at large cannot be sacrificed for one individual or small group of individuals.

The manager can assure this principle through his exemplary behaviour like he should avoid misuse of his powers for obtaining benefit at the cost of general interest of workers. There is a coordination between organisational and personal goals of employees. It facilitates achievement of organisational goals.

(iii) **Initiative**
The principle of initiative involves encouraging the workers to give their suggestions for the growth of the organisation. Initiative means taking the first step with self-motivation. Fayol suggested that employees at all levels should be encouraged and given an opportunity to take some initiative in making and executing the plans. It develops a feeling of belongingness in employees and leads to improvements in operations.

21. Explain the following principles of management.
(i) Authority and responsibility
(ii) Centralisation and decentralisation
(iii) Initiative **CBSE 2024 C**

Or **Explain the following principles of management given by Fayol** **CBSE 2025**
(i) Division of work
(ii) Authority and responsibility

Ans.

(i) **Authority and Responsibility**
- Authority is the right to give orders and responsibility is the corollary of authority. There should be a balance between authority and responsibility.
- An organisation should build safeguards against abuse of managerial power. At the same time a manager should have necessary authority to carry out his responsibility.

(ii) **Centralisation and Decentralisation**
- The concentration of decision-making authority is called centralisation whereas its dispersal among more than one person is known as decentralisation.
- There is a need to balance subordinate involvement through decentralisation with managers' retention of final authority through centralisation.

(iii) **Initiative**
Refer to Q.No. 20 (iii) of long answer type questions.

(iv) **Division of Work**
According to the principle of division of work, dividing the work into small tasks and then assigning them to trained specialists would help in taking the advantage of specialisation. This principle is applicable to all kinds of technical and managerial work.

22. Explain any three principles of scientific management. NCERT

Ans. Following are the three principles of scientific management

(i) **Harmony, not Discord**
There should be complete harmony between the management and workers. It implies that management should share the gains with workers and workers should work hard for the betterment of the business. This attitude will bring prosperity to both, the company as well as workers. Taylor also called for mental revolution which means that management and workers should transform their thinking.

(ii) **Science, not Rule of Thumb**
Taylor believed that there is only one best way of doing a work, which can be developed through scientific study and analysis. The method, so developed, should substitute 'rule of thumb' or 'trial and error' method in the organisation. By using scientific investigation and work study, the method so devised, will save effort and reduce wastage of resources.

(iii) **Development of Each and Every Person to His or Her Greatest Efficiency and Prosperity**
Scientific management advocates that the best method of doing a work should be developed through a scientific approach. This method should be taught to the workers through proper training. Taylor advocated that each person should be scientifically selected and then allotted work to suit his/her physical, mental and intellectual capabilities. Proper training should be imparted to increase the efficiency.

23. Principles of Taylor and Fayol are mutually complementary. One believed that the management should share the gains with the workers, while the other suggested that employees compensation should depend on the earning capacity of the company and should give them a reasonable standard of living. Identify and explain the principles of Fayol and Taylor referred to in the above para. Competency Based Que

Ans. Taylor believed, 'management should share the gains with workers'. This has been emphasised by the principle of 'harmony, not discord', which is also emphasised by 'mental revolution'.

Harmony, not Discord
The interests of the employer and employees should be fully harmonised, so as to create a good relationship.

Taylor emphasised that there should be complete harmony between the management and workers.

This requires a transformation in the thinking of both, which can be achieved through mental revolution.

Thus, management should share the gains of the company with the workers. At the same time, workers should work and embrace changes. Taylor believed, that prosperity for the employer cannot exist for a long time unless it is accompanied by prosperity of the employees and *vice-versa*.

In the same way, Fayol's principle of 'remuneration of employees' suggested that the employees compensation should depend on the earning capacity of the company and should give the employees a reasonable standard of living.

Remuneration of Employees
According to Fayol, the quantum and methods of remuneration payable to employees should be fair and reasonable.

It should be satisfactory to both employers and employees, which gives them a reasonable standard of living and should be within the paying capacity of the company.

Thus, we can say that Taylor's and Fayol's principles are mutually complementary.

24. Explain the following techniques of scientific management CBSE 2023
(i) Fatigue study (ii) Motion study (iii) Time study

Ans.

(i) **Fatigue Study**
This study seeks to find out the amount and frequency of rest intervals to be given to workers 'in completing a task'.

Fatigue refers to tiredness physically or mentally. A person feels tired when he does not rest while working. Thus, he must be provided with proper rest intervals. This would help the worker to regain his stamina and work again with the same capacity. This will result in increased productivity.

(ii) **Motion Study**
This study refers to an in-depth study of movements or motions of a worker like lifting, putting objects, changing positions, etc. while doing a task. Taylor recognised three types of movements productive, unproductive and incidental. The objective of motion study is to eliminate unproductive movements in doing a task to achieve efficiency and reduce the time required to do the task.

(iii) **Time Study**
It determines the standard time taken by a worker to perform a well-defined job. Time measuring devices are used to conduct this study.

This type of study is helpful in deciding the standard time required to perform a job.

The objective of time study is to determine the number of workers to be employed, to determine incentive schemes and labour costs and to set up the standard target for workers.

25. **Explain the following techniques of scientific management** CBSE 2024 C

(i) **Time study** (ii) **Differential piece wage system**

(iii) **Standardisation and simplification of work**

Or **Explain the following techniques of scientific management** CBSE 2023

(i) **Differential piece wage system**

(ii) **Standardisation and simplification of work**

Ans.

(i) **Time Study**

Refer to Q.No. 24 (iii) of long answer type questions.

(ii) **Differential Piece Wage System**

Taylor strongly advocated piece wage system. In order to differentiate between efficient and inefficient workers, he proposed a system of wage payment on the basis of work done. Under this system, higher rates are given to efficient workers who are producing standard product or more and lower rates are given to inefficient workers who are producing less.

(iii) **Standardisation and Simplification of Work**

Standardisation is the process of setting standards for every business activity, process, raw materials, time, machinery and methods, to achieve efficiency. These standards should be the benchmarks, which must be adhered to during production.

The objectives of standardisation are to reduce a given line or product to fixed types, sises and characteristics, to provide interchangeability of manufactured parts and products, to establish standards of excellence and quality in materials, to establish performance standards of men and machines.

Simplification means eliminating superfluous sizes, varieties and dimensions of products. Its aim is to eliminate unnecessary diversity of products and thereby reduce costs.

26. **"Effective management practices can significantly enhance productivity by dividing responsibilities and fostering a mindset of cooperation between workers and management."**

In the light of this, explain the technique of 'functional foremanship' and the concept of 'mental revolution' as enunciated by Taylor. Competency Based Que

Or **Explain the technique of 'functional foremanship' and the concept of 'mental revolution' as enunciated by Taylor.** NCERT

Ans. **Functional Foremanship**

It is an extension of principle of division of work and specialisation to the shop floor.

Since, a single person cannot possess all these qualities, thus, he advocated the functional foremanship through eight foremen to guide workers, under planning and production departments.

Under the planning incharge, there are four personnel

(i) **Instruction Card Clerk**

He is responsible to give instructions to the workers.

(ii) **Route Clerk**

He is responsible to specify the route of production.

(iii) **Time and Cost Clerk**

He is responsible to prepare time and cost sheets.

(iv) **Disciplinarian**

He is responsible to maintain discipline among workers.

Under the production incharge, there are four personnel

(i) **Speed Boss**

He is responsible for timely and accurate completion of job.

(ii) **Gang Boss**

He is responsible for keeping machines and tools ready for work.

(iii) **Repair Boss**

He is responsible to keep machines and tools in proper working condition.

(iv) **Inspector**

He is responsible to maintain quality of work.

Mental Revolution

It involves change in the attitude of workers and management. Both should realise the importance of the other and should cooperate with each other. Both should aim to increase the size of surplus.

Managers should share their gains with workers, while workers should contribute to increase profits. This attitude will bring prosperity to both, the company as well as the workers.

27. **Explain 'cooperation, not individualism' as a principle and 'fatigue study' as a technique of scientific management.**

Ans. **Cooperation, not Individualism**

According to this principle, there should be cooperation between management and workers instead of individualism. This principle is an extension to 'harmony, not discord'. Competition should be replaced by cooperation.

Both management and workers should realise the need and importance of each other. For this, management should encourage constructive suggestions by employees through proper rewards. Management should take workers into confidence before making any important decision. At the same time, workers should avoid strikes and unreasonable demands.

Fatigue Study
This study seeks to find out the amount and frequency of rest intervals to be given to workers in completing a task. Fatigue refers to tiredness physically or mentally. A person feels tired when he does not rest while working.

Thus, he must be provided with proper rest intervals. This would help the worker to regain his stamina and work again with the same capacity. This will result in increased productivity.

28. **Differentiate between the contributions of Taylor and Fayol.**

Or **Discuss the difference between the contributions of Taylor and Fayol.** NCERT

Ans. Following are the differences between the contributions of Taylor and Fayol

Basis	Henri Fayol	FW Taylor
Perspective	Top level of management	Shop floor level of a factory
Applicability	Universally applicable	Applicable to specialised situations (factory situation)
Basis of Formation	Personal experience	Observations and experimentation
Focus	Improving overall administration	Increasing productivity of workers
Status	Father of general management	Father of scientific management
Personality	Practitioner	Scientist
Unity of Command	Strictly followed	Did not feel that it is important as under functional foremanship, a worker received orders from eight specialists
Expression	General theory of administration	Scientific management

Case Study Based Questions

Short Case Studies

Case Study 1

ABC Corporation, a leading technology firm, faced a significant challenge when its production line experienced frequent delays and quality issues. The management team decided to implement a series of changes to improve efficiency.

They introduced new quality control measures and adjusted the production schedule to better match demand fluctuations.

The changes were based on the principle that adjusting operations according to the specific circumstances and understanding the impact of these changes on production and quality would lead to better outcomes.

Identify and explain the two features of management principles illustrated in the case.

Ans. Following are the two features of management principles illustrated in the case

(i) **Contingent**
The case mentions that changes were based on the principle that adjusting operations according to the specific circumstances would be better. The application of management principles is dependent or contingent upon the prevailing conditions at a particular point of time. They have to be suitably amended as per the situation.

(ii) **Cause and Effect Relationships**
The principles of management are intended to establish relationship between cause and effect so that they can be used in similar situations in a large number of cases. It means, principles help in predicting the outcome of managerial actions.

Case Study 2

Mr. Kapoor, the chief financial officer at Bright Tech Industries, was responsible for selecting the auditing firm for the company's financial statements for the fiscal year 2023-24. During this process, he chose to award the contract to a firm owned by his close friend, despite the fact that a more reputable and cost effective firm offered to provide the same services at a lower price. Mr. Kapoor's decision was influenced by personal relationships rather than the best interests of the company.

(i) Which principle of management was violated by Mr. Kapoor?

(ii) State two positive and negative effects if the principle is followed and violated.

Ans.

(i) The principle of management that was violated by Mr. Kapoor was subordination of individual interest to general interest.
According to this principle, interest of the organisation as a whole must prevail over the interest of the individuals or employees.

(ii) Following are the positive effects if the principle is followed

- There is coordination between organisational and personal goals of employees.
- It facilitates achievement of organisational goals.

Following are the negative effects if the principle is violated

- There is lack of coordination between personal and organisational goals.
- Achievement of organisational goals becomes difficult.

Case Study 3

EcoSolutions introduced a new eco-friendly water bottle called the 'EcoHydrate Bottle' aimed at reducing plastic waste. Mrs. Mehta, the marketing manager, was given the task to ensure the product reaches 1,000 units sold within two months. She quickly created a marketing strategy without involving her team, who had previously managed successful campaigns.

Mrs. Mehta also dismissed any feedback or ideas from her team members, instructing them to strictly adhere to her plan. The lack of team input and the rigid enforcement of her plan led to a lower than expected sales figure and missed the target.

(i) Identify and state the management principle overlooked in the given case.

(ii) State how the company would have benefitted if the principle would have been followed.

Ans.

(i) The management principle overlooked in the given case is initiative. Fayol suggested that employees at all levels should be encouraged and given an opportunity to take some initiative in making and executing the plans. It develops a feeling of belongingness in employees and leads to improvements in operations.

(ii) The company would have benefitted in the form of development of feeling of belongingness in the employees and improvement in operations.

Case Study 4

A production supervisor was authorised to approve overtime hours for employees up to a maximum of 10 hours per week. The company's workload increased significantly and a major client requested urgent delivery. The supervisor recognised that approving overtime beyond the 10-hours limit would be necessary to meet the deadline.

However, since the supervisor's authority did not extend beyond the 10-hours limit, the request for additional overtime could not be approved.

This limitation in authority led to delays and jeopardised the client relationship. Discuss the principle of management that is being overlooked in the case of the production supervisor.

Ans. The principle of management that is being overlooked in the case of the production supervisor is authority and responsibility.

The supervisor could not extend the limit because of lack of authority. According to this principle, there should be a proper balance between authority and responsibility.

Authority is the right to give orders to subordinates and responsibility is the duty, which a subordinate is expected to perform by virtue of his position in organisation.

Authority and responsibility go hand in hand. An organisation should build safeguards against abuse of managerial power. At the same time, a manager should have necessary authority to carry out his responsibility.

Case Study 5

Ravi owns a small restaurant in Jaipur specialising in local cuisine. Despite having a steady stream of customers, Ravi faces a persistent challenge with employee retention. His approach to management is quite informal; he often changes employees' roles based on immediate needs rather than assigning them specific responsibilities. This inconsistency creates confusion and dissatisfaction among the staff, leading many to leave for more stable job opportunities.

Although Ravi is known for his generous nature and offers competitive salaries, his lack of structured management practices is affecting his business's stability.

(i) Identify and explain the principle of management that Ravi is failing to apply, which is causing him to face ongoing difficulties with employee retention.

(ii) Identify and explain the principle of management which is followed in the case.

Ans.

(i) Stability of personnel is principle of management which Ravi is unable to apply. According to Fayol, "Employee turnover should be minimised to maintain organisational efficiency."

Personnel should be selected and appointed after due and rigorous procedure. After placement, they should be kept at their post for a minimum fixed tenure so that they get time to show results.

(ii) The principle of management which is followed in the case is 'remuneration of employees'. According to Fayol, the overall pay and compensation should be fair and equitable to both employees and the organisation. The employees should be paid fair wages so that they are able to maintain at least a reasonable standard of living.

At the same time, it should be within the paying capacity of the company. This will ensure pleasant working atmosphere and good relations between workers and management.

Case Study 6

Hedo Vehicles is a vehicle manufacturing company. The company has started facing some major difficulties which is affecting its pace of operations and completion of work. The company has the same unit producing both scooters and cars.

This leads to confusion among the employees regarding the reporting as well as differentiation of work.

(i) Identify and explain the principle of Fayol which is violated here.

(ii) State the negative effects of violation of this principle.

Ans.

(i) The principle of Fayol which is violated here is 'unity of direction'. This principle says that there should be one boss and one plan.

The related activities should be placed in one department. So, there should be separate departments for the production of cars and the scooters.

(ii) Following are the negative effects of violation of this principle

- Lack of coordination and failure in achievement of organisational goals.
- Duplication of efforts and wastage of resources.

Case Study 7

Electrola India Ltd. has a large-scale business of manufacturing and distribution of home appliances. It has a good reputation in the market because of its good quality products.

There are separate departments for manufacturing, finance, sales, maintainance and technical services. The company is planning to modify the existing principle of management to meet the changing requirements of the environment. There has been an increase in the area of operations and customer demands have increased.

(i) State the general principle of management which the company wants to modify to meet the changing requirements.

(ii) Also explain briefly two more principles of management.

Ans.

(i) The general principle of management which the company wants to modify is the principle of division of work which states that the work should be divided into small tasks/jobs each performed by a specialist.

(ii) Following are two more principles of management

- **Remuneration of Employees**
  Employees should be paid fair wages, which would give them a reasonable standard of living and at the same time, it must be within the paying capacity of an organisation.
- **Unity of Command**
  Each subordinate should receive orders and be answerable to one superior only.

  If this principle is violated, then authority is undermined, discipline is in jeopardy, order disturbed and stability threatened.

Case Study 8

A production manager at top level in a reputed corporate, Mr. Rathore holds the responsibility for ordering raw material for the firm.

While deciding on the supplier for the financial year 2017-18, he gave the order to his cousin at a higher price per unit instead of the firm's usual supplier who was willing to lower the rates for the order. **NCERT**

(i) Which principle of management was violated by Mr. Rathore?

(ii) What are the positive impacts of following the above identified principle?

Ans.

(i) Principle of management violated by Mr. Rathore is 'subordination of individual interest to general interest'.

(ii) Following can be the positive impacts of the above identified principle

- It brings a coordination between organisational and personal goals, as employees are more focused towards group goals, in order to get personal benefits.
- It facilitates achievement of organisational goals.

Case Study 9

Shreejee Ltd. is engaged in producing electricity from domestic garbage. There is almost equal division of work and responsibility between workers and management. The management even takes workers into confidence before taking important decisions. All the workers are satisfied as the behaviour of the management is very good. State and explain the principle of scientific management described in the above para.

Ans. Principle of management discussed is 'cooperation, not individualism'. This principle given by FW Taylor suggests that any form of competition should be replaced by cooperation. He also suggested that there should be equal division of work and responsibility between workers and management.

According to this principle, there should be cooperation between management and workers instead of individualism. This principle is an extension to 'harmony, not discord'.

Both management and workers should realise the need and importance of each other. For this, management should encourage constructive suggestions by employees through proper rewards. Management should take workers into confidence before making any important decision. At the same time, workers should avoid strikes and unreasonable demands.

Case Study 10

Dhiren Patel is the chief executive officer of a milk processing company. He is a very effective manager. He is quite organised in his work and exhibits exemplary behaviour. Dhiren Patel insists that all managers and subordinates in the organisation should follow a chain of authority that runs from top to bottom for all communication purposes.

Identify and explain the general principle of management highlighted in the above case. **CBSE 2024 C**

Ans. The general principle of management highlighted in Dhiren Patel's case in 'scalar chain'.

(i) The formal lines of authority i.e. a chain of authority and communication that runs from top to bottom is known as scalar chain.

(ii) The scalar chain should not be violated in the normal course of formal communication. However, if there is an emergency, a shorter route known as gang plank may be used so that communication may not be delayed.

Case Study 11

The production supervisor at Delta Corp. noticed that workers were often reluctant to help each other, cope up with management and preferred to work individually.

This lack of cooperation with the management and peer group led to inefficiencies and delays in completing tasks.

To address this, the supervisor implemented team based tasks and encouraged workers to collaborate and support each other. Additionally, the supervisor observed that workers seemed exhausted and their performance was declining.

To combat this, scheduled breaks were introduced to allow workers to rest and regain their energy during their shifts.

(i) State the principle of management emphasised in the case study. Explain why this principle was important in the given context.

(ii) Identify and state the scientific management technique used to address the issue of workers getting exhausted.

Ans.

(i) The principle of management emphasised in the case study is 'cooperation, not individualism'. The supervisor encouraged teamwork and mutual support among workers, which improved efficiency and productivity compared to working in isolation. According to this principle, there should be complete cooperation between the management and workers.

In this case, workers were reluctant to cooperate with each other and preferred to work individually, which led to inefficiencies and delays in task completion.

The lack of teamwork and support between workers created a disjointed work environment, resulting in reduced productivity. Hence, the principle of "cooperation, not individualism" was crucial.

(ii) The scientific management technique used is fatigue study. Scheduled breaks were introduced to alleviate worker fatigue, helping them maintain their energy levels and improving their overall productivity.

Case Study 12

'Furniture Ltd.' is the manufacturer of leather products. It is producing on large scale and its organisational structure is functional. In the production department various foremen have been employed. Each foreman has been made responsible for production, planning, implementation and control. This has led to a situation of confusion and uncertainty. Suggest a technique of scientific management to Furniture Ltd. which may help it to effectively organise planning and its execution.

Ans. The technique of scientific management which may help Furniture Ltd. to effectively organise planning and its execution is functional foremanship. Following are its important elements

(i) It is a technique which aims to improve the quality of supervision at shop floor. Taylor identified a list of qualities of a good foreman or a supervisor.

Since all the qualities could not be found in a single person, Taylor proposed eight specialists.

(ii) In this technique, planning is separated from execution. Taylor suggested four foremen for planning and four foremen for execution. It is an extension of the principle of division of work and specialisation.

(iii) The four foremen for planning were route clerk, instruction card clerk, time and cost clerk and disciplinarian. The four foremen for planning would draft instructions for the workers, specify the route of production, prepare time and cost sheet and ensure discipline respectively.

(iv) The four foremen for execution were gang boss, speed boss, repair boss and inspector. The four foremen for execution were responsible for timely and accurate completion of the job, keeping machines and tools ready for operation by the workers, ensuring proper working conditions of machines and tools and checking the quality of work.

Case Study 13

Rajesh is employed at a company that manufactures light bulbs. The bulbs produced are of uniform size and quality. If a particular type of bulb becomes obsolete or unnecessary, its production is halted. For instance, when the company learned that 20-watt bulbs were no longer in demand, they discontinued their production.

Rajesh is responsible for purchasing the filaments used in bulb manufacturing. Recently, when acquiring filaments, the supplier informed him that special care was needed during the first hour of assembling the filaments into the bulbs.

Rajesh realises this critical information must reach the production team before assembly starts. However, the company's policy requires him to pass the message to his immediate supervisor, who will relay it to their superior and so on, until it eventually reaches the right person in the production department.

(i) Which technique of management is being used?

(ii) What principle of management is being followed by the company?

Ans.

(i) The technique of management which is followed here is standardisation (each bulb which is manufactured is of standard size and quality) and simplification (further if there is any unrequired type of bulb manufactured then its production is stopped).

(ii) The principle of management which is followed here is scalar chain.

Case Study 14

Peer Jeans hires workers in their factory to stitch jeans. Each worker is assigned a target of 100 jeans per week, with a fixed rate of ₹ 50 per piece. To incentivise higher productivity, the company announced that workers who stitch more than 100 jeans in a week will receive ₹ 55 per piece for all the jeans they complete.

Jogi, who stitches at a faster pace than his colleagues, worked an extra hour and managed to complete 120 jeans. As a result, he earned ₹ 55 per piece for all 120 jeans, totaling ₹ 6,600 for the week.

In contrast, his colleague Jack stitched only 90 jeans, earning ₹ 50 per piece and a total of ₹ 4,500. Name and explain the technique of management which is applied here to motivate the workers.

Ans. The technique of management which is applied to motivate the workers is differential piece wage system. Differential piece wage refers to a system in which efficient and inefficient workers are paid at different rates. According to Taylor, financial incentives act as motivators and scope of extra earnings motivates the worker to put extra efforts.

So, Taylor developed the concept of 'differential piece wage system'. In this technique, incentive is directly linked with productivity.

First of all, a standard task is established with the help of time and motion study. Then, two rates are fixed: Higher wage rate for workers who produce equal to or more than the standard output.

Low wage rate for workers who do not reach the standard. The basic purpose of fixing two rates is to differentiate efficient and inefficient workers and to suitably reward the efficient workers.

Long Case Studies

Case Study 15

Neha Patel was the general manager of 'Eco Apparel,' a company specialising in sustainable fashion. Under Neha's leadership, the company gained a reputation for its commitment to eco-friendly and high quality garments. Neha was renowned for her strategic use of management principles, which guided the company's operations and decision-making.

Before launching new product lines, EcoTrends Apparel meticulously followed the principles of management to ensure effective planning, organisation and execution. They regularly assessed market trends, evaluated resource availability and aligned their objectives with the company's vision. This strategic approach allowed the company to efficiently utilise resources and remain adaptable to market changes.

However, during a particular fiscal year, the company faced unexpected challenges due to a sudden rise in raw material costs. EcoTrends Apparel struggled to adjust their budget and production schedules promptly in accordance with the market. As a result, they experienced a temporary setback in their production capacity. However, they soon adapted to the changing environmental conditions.

Quoting lines from the above paragraph, identify and explain three ways in which management principles play an important role as discussed in the above case.

Ans. Following are the three ways in which management principles play an important role as discussed in the above case

(i) **Optimum Utilisation of Resources**
"They regularly assessed market trends, evaluated resource availability and aligned their objectives with the company's vision." Management principles emphasise the effective use of available resources (both human and material).

In EcoTrends Apparel's case, the application of these principles helped in planning and utilising resources optimally, aiming to achieve maximum benefit with minimal cost.

(ii) **Scientific Decisions**
"The company gained a reputation for its commitment to eco-friendly and high quality garments." By adhering to management principles, EcoTrends Apparel made thoughtful decisions based on facts and strategic planning. These principles guided the company to make logical, well-informed decisions about product lines and market strategy.

(iii) **Meeting Changing Environment Requirements**
"EcoTrends Apparel struggled to adjust their budget and production schedules promptly in accordance with the market."

Management principles are dynamic and flexible, helping organisations adapt to changes in the business environment. While EcoTrends Apparel initially faced challenges, the principles provided a framework for adapting to market changes and adjusting strategies to overcome setbacks.

Case Study 16

Ravi Kapoor was the general manager of 'GreenTech Electronics,' a company specialising in the production of eco-friendly electronic devices. GreenTech Electronics was renowned for its commitment to innovation and environmental sustainability.

Ravi Kapoor emphasised the importance of a structured approach to management to ensure smooth operations and achieve organisational goals.

Under Ravi's leadership, GreenTech Electronics implemented a systematic approach where tasks were divided into specialised departments and each department had clear roles and responsibilities. This division of work allowed employees to focus on their areas of expertise, enhancing efficiency and productivity.

Additionally, Ravi ensured that there is no discrimination on the basis of gender, caste, etc. Each manager had the authority to make decisions within their department and was held accountable for their actions.

This clear reporting structure helped in maintaining order and reducing confusion within the organisation.

However, despite these well-structured processes, GreenTech Electronics encountered difficulties when the market rapidly shifted towards smart technology. The rigid adherence to established processes and hierarchical structure, including strict adherence to unity of command, made it challenging for the company to adapt quickly to the new market demands.

Competitors who were more flexible and responsive gained a significant advantage.

Quoting lines from the above paragraph, identify and explain the three principles of management that have been followed in the case.

Ans. Following are the three principles of management that have been followed in the case

(i) "Under Ravi's leadership, GreenTech Electronics implemented a systematic approach where tasks were divided into specialised departments and each department had clear roles and responsibilities." This statement depicts the principle of division of work. Dividing the work into small tasks and then assigning them to trained specialists would help in taking the advantage of specialisation. This is applicable to all kinds of managerial and technical work.

(ii) "Additionally, Ravi ensured that there is no discrimination on the basis of gender, caste, etc." This statement depicts the principle of equity.

According to the principle of equity, there should not be any discrimination among the employees on the basis of religion, language, caste, sex, belief or nationality. This principle emphasises kindliness and justice in the behaviour of managers towards workers.

(iii) "Each manager had the authority to make decisions within their department and was held accountable for their actions." This statement depicts the principle of authority and responsibility. Authority is the right to give orders to subordinates and responsibility is the duty, which a subordinate is expected to perform by virtue of his position in organisation. Authority and responsibility go hand in hand. An organisation should build safeguards against abuse of managerial power. At the same time, a manager should have necessary authority to carry out his responsibility.

Case Study 17

A famous cricket coach, Alam Raza was hired by Sports College, Indore to coach the college Cricket team for a National level competition. In the first meeting itself, the principal of the college announced that the players would enter into an agreement with the college.

The agreement would state the reporting time for players on the field and other rules and regulations. Failure to obey the agreement and rules would lead to judicious application of penalties.

It was also announced by the college principal that the players would receive orders from the coach and they would all be responsible only to the coach, to prevent confusion regarding tasks to be done. The coach was very determined to train the players to win, as the entire responsibility was on his shoulders. He promoted the spirit of mutual trust and belongingness among the team members without which he felt it would be difficult to win.

The players were also enthusiastic and the training started in full swing. Identify and explain the three principles of management discussed in the above case. **CBSE 2023**

Ans. Following are the three principles of management discussed in the case

(i) **Discipline**
According to this principle, the organisational rule and employment agreement should be obeyed by both the superiors and subordinates which are necessary for the successful working of the organisation.

(ii) **Unity of Command**
According to this principle, an individual employee should receive orders from only one superior at a time and that employee should be answerable only to that superior. If this principle is violated, then authority is undermined, discipline is in jeopardy, order disturbed and stability threatened.

(iii) **Esprit De Corps**
According to this principle, management should promote a team spirit of unity and harmony among employees. A manager should replace 'I' with 'We' in all the conversations with workers to foster team spirit.

Case Study 18

'Bhasin' Limited was engaged in the business of food processing and selling its products under a popular brand. Lately the business was expanding due to good quality and reasonable prices. Also with more people working the market for processed food was increasing. New players were also coming to cash in on the new trend. In order to keep its market share in the short-run the company directed its existing workforce to work overtime. But this resulted in many problems.

Due to increased pressure of work the efficiency of the workers declined. Sometimes the subordinates had to work for more than one superior resulting in declining efficiency.

The divisions that were previously working on one product were also made to work on two or more products. This resulted in a lot of overlapping and wastage. The workers were becoming indisciplined. The spirit of teamwork, which had characterised the company, previously was beginning to wane.

Workers were feeling cheated and initiative was declining. The quality of the products was beginning to decline and market share was on the verge of decrease. Actually the company had implemented changes without creating the required infrastructure. **NCERT**

(i) Identify the principles of management (out of 14 given by Henry Fayol) that were being violated by the company.
(ii) Explain these principles in brief.
(iii) What steps should the company management take in relation to the above principles to restore the company to its past glory?

Ans.

(i) Company violated following principles

- Division of work
- Unity of command
- Unity of direction
- Discipline
- Remuneration of personnel
- Order
- Initiative
- Esprit de corps

(ii) Following is the explanation of the principles that have been violated in the case

- **Division of Work**
Dividing the work into small tasks and then assigning them to trained specialists would help in taking the advantage of specialisation.
- **Unity of Command**
Each subordinate should receive orders and be answerable to one superior only. If this principle is violated, then authority is undermined, discipline is in jeopardy, order disturbed and stability threatened.
- **Unity of Direction**
There should be one head and one plan for a group of activities having the same objective.
- **Discipline**
Discipline is the obedience to organisational rules and employment agreement which are necessary for the smooth working of the organisation.
- **Remuneration of Personnel**
Employees should be paid fair wages, which would give them a reasonable standard of living and at the same time, it must be within the paying capacity of an organisation.
- **Order**
There should be an orderly arrangement and specific place for everything and everyone in the organisation.
- **Initiative**
Employees at all levels should be encouraged and given an opportunity to take some initiative in making and executing the plans.

- **Espirit de Corps**
  Management should promote a team spirit of unity and harmony among employees. A manager should replace 'I' with 'We' in all his conversations with workers to foster team spirit.

(iii) The following steps should be taken by the company management in relation to the principles to restore the company to its past glory

- The existing capacity of the company is not able to cope-up with the increased work load in the short-run. So, the company must increase capital investments or outsource its production.
- It must ensure unity of command, by making subordinate responsible to only one superior.
- Clearly define authority-responsibility relationships in context of expansion of production activity.
- To ensure division of work and unity of direction, one division for one product should be followed.
- With unity of direction and proper authority-responsibility relationship, there will be reduction in overlapping and wastages.
- Financial and non-financial incentives should be given to motivate the employees. Motivated staff will lead to restored discipline, initiative and esprit de corps.
- Fair remuneration should be given, according to increase in work of employees, after due negotiation with them.

Case Study 19

(Further information related to the above question 17) The management of company Bhasin Limited now realised its folly. In order to rectify the situation, it appointed a management consultant-Mukti Consultants – to recommend a restructure plan to bring the company back on the rails. Mukti Consultants undertook a study of the production process at the plant of the company Bhasin Limited and recommended the following changes

- The company should introduce scientific management with regard to production.
- Production planning including routing, scheduling, dispatching and feedback should be implemented.
- In order to separate planning from operational management 'functional foremanship' should be introduced.
- 'Work study' should be undertaken to optimise the use of resources.
- 'Standardisation' of all activities should be implemented to increase efficiency and accountability.
- To motivate the workers 'differential piece rate system' should be implemented.

It was expected that the changes will bring about a radical transformation in the working of the company and it will regain its pristine glory. **NCERT**

(i) Do you think that introduction of scientific management as recommended by M consultants will result in intended outcome?

(ii) What precautions should the company undertake to implement the changes?

Ans.

(i) I think that introduction of scientific management humanely after due consultations with all stakeholders and obtaining their motivated willingness will result in improvement of company's fortunes. However, all the changes should not neglect the human factor. The concept of lean manufacturing which is an offshoot of scientific management can be adopted. So, the form of scientific management introduced should be the latest like

- Lean manufacturing
- Just-in-time manufacturing
- Kanban
- Kaizen
- Six sigma, etc.

(ii) The company should introduce the latest form of scientific management, as pointed above with due consideration to human factor in mind and by obtaining their motivated willingness.

It should undertake following precautions

- Production planning including routing, scheduling, dispatching and feedback should be implemented keeping in mind the human factor for better compliance.
- Functional foremanship will be good but it neglects unity of command. It might not be useful for the company, so it should be avoided.
- Standardisation should be implemented in the right earnest. It will improve productivity and also reduce quality variations. But right training and willingness must be obtained.
- 'Differential piece rate system', if introduced, should be done with extreme caution. It must not result in unhealthy competition. However, monetary and non-monetary incentives can be introduced in place of differential piece rate system.

Case Study 20

Anita Sharma recently assumed the role of CEO at 'Tech Wave Solutions,' a company that had struggled with inefficiency and declining performance for several years. Anita was committed to turning the company around. She noted that the existing methods of production and employee selection were outdated and lacked scientific rigor.

Anita was convinced that there was a single optimal method to enhance productivity. She also believed that once this method was identified, it was crucial to train employees to master it.

She instructed the operations manager to devise this optimal method and implement a comprehensive training programme.

The operations manager devised a new method by meticulously analysing various aspects, such as the order of tasks, the arrangement of personnel, machinery and raw materials, up to the final delivery of products.

This standardised method was applied across the company. As a result, the company experienced a significant boost in productivity, improved product quality and reduced operational costs and waste.

(i) Identify and explain one principle of scientific management followed by the operation manager in the above case.

(ii) Identify and explain the techniques of scientific management followed by the operation manager in the above case.

Ans.

(i) Following is the principle of scientific management followed by the operation manager in the above case

Science, not Rule of Thumb

Taylor believed that there is only one best way of doing a work, which can be developed through scientific study and analysis. The method, so developed, should substitute 'rule of thumb' or 'trial and error' method in the organisation. By using scientific investigation and work study, the method so devised, will save effort and reduce wastage of resources.

(ii) Following are the techniques of scientific management followed by the operation manager in the above case

- **Development of Each and Every Person to His or Her Greatest Efficiency and Prosperity**
  Scientific management advocates that the best method of doing a work should be developed through a scientific approach. This method should be taught to the workers through proper training. Taylor advocated that each person should be scientifically selected and then allotted work to suit his/her physical, mental and intellectual capabilities. Proper training should be imparted to increase the efficiency.
- **Method Study**
  This study determines the best way of doing a job. Right from procurement of raw materials to the delivery of final product, every activity is studied carefully. The best method is devised to minimise the cost of production and maximise the quality to the satisfaction of the customer.

Case Study 21

Disha Work Ltd. a manufacturing company, had been struggling with frequent conflicts between management and workers. The tension had led to several strikes and a decrease in overall productivity.

The management decided to address the issue by implementing principles inspired by Frederick Taylor's scientific management.

The company organised a series of workshops aimed at fostering better relationships between the management and the workforce. These workshops focused on creating a 'mental revolution', where both parties were encouraged to change their attitudes towards one another. The objective was to eliminate the existing discord and build a spirit of cooperation.

Management and workers participated in team building exercises, open forums for discussion and regular feedback sessions. The goal was to align everyone's efforts towards the organisational goals and eliminate the negative feelings and opposition that had previously characterised their interactions.

Additionally, Harmony at Work Ltd. employed techniques to optimise their work processes. This involved analysing the time required for various tasks and identifying the obstacles and unnecessary movements that are leading to delays in completion of work.

The data collected helped streamline operations, reduce wastage and improve overall productivity.

(i) Identify and explain the management principle which has been followed by the company.

(ii) State the meaning of mental revolution.

(iii) Identify the two techniques of scientific management that have helped the company to improve the productivity.

Ans.

(i) The management principle that has been followed by the company is harmony, not discord. According to this principle, there should be complete harmony and proper understanding between management and workers and they should work together for organisational goals.

To get such harmonious relations, Taylor stressed on 'mental revolution', i.e. complete change in their mental outlook for each other.

Both should give up their attitude of opposition and enmity towards each other and should have a positive feeling for each other.

It means that management and workers should transform their thinking. In such a situation, even trade unions will not think of going on strike.

According to Taylor, true interests of the management and workers are one and the same and prosperity of organisation depends upon prosperity of employer as well as employees.

(ii) Mental revolution means that both management and workers should give up their attitude of opposition and enmity towards each other and should have a positive feeling for each other. It means that management and workers should transform their thinking.

In such a situation, even trade unions will not think of going on strike. According to Taylor, true interests of the management and workers are one and the same and prosperity of organisation depends upon prosperity of employer as well as employees.

(iii) The two techniques of scientific management that have helped the company to improve the productivity are as follows

- **Motion study** refers to making thorough analysis of various motions being performed by a worker while he is doing a particular task. Motion study involves study of movements like lifting, putting objects, sitting and changing positions, etc. which are undertaken while doing a typical job.

  The purpose is to detect and eliminate unnecessary movements or motions and to find out the best method of doing a particular job.

- **Time study** refers to a technique, which is used to determine the standard time taken by a workman of reasonable skills and ability to perform a well defined job.

  It helps in determining how much work an employee should be able to do in a given period of time.

  Under time study, the job is divided into a series of elements and time taken to perform each element of work is recorded with time measuring devices (like stopwatch).

  The standard time is fixed for the whole of the task by taking several readings. The method of time study depends on volume and frequency of the task, the cycle time of the operation and time measurement costs.

Case Study 22

Leena has been appointed as the operations manager in a small trading company dealing in garments, with growing online sales.

The company has recently rented space in a warehouse to store garments and mail out orders.

In order to take over the responsibilities of order fulfilment, Leena promotes an associate, Kushagra to the post of inventory and order fulfilment supervisor. Kushagra has been given the task to assess whether it is best to process orders as they come in or let them accumulate and then to process them in batches.

He concludes that accumulating and then processing them in batches is the best way of fulfilling orders, in order to minimise cost and maximise customer satisfaction.

Through several readings Leena finds that the standard time taken from the placement of order to the delivery of garments for a batch of 100 pieces is 72 hours. This helped her to determine the labour cost.

On the basis of the understanding of concepts of scientific management, identify and explain the techniques used by Leena and Kushagra to improve the performance of the employees. **CBSE SQP 2025**

Ans. The techniques used by Leena and Kushagra to improve the performance of the employees are

(i) **Method Study**
Refer to case study 20.

(ii) **Time Study**
Refer to case study 21.

SELF ASSESSMENT TEST

Objective Type Questions

1. What is the meaning of the universality of the principles of management?
   (a) Applicable to all the fields
   (b) Applicable no where
   (c) Applicable only to business
   (d) Applicable only to non-business field
2. Which of the following indicate positive effect of principle of equity?
   (a) It ensures loyalty among the workers
   (b) Cordial relation between workers and managers
   (c) Congenial atmosphere within the organisation
   (d) All of the above
3. Rajesh, the manager of a company does not give his employees parameters or rules for reporting to work and completion of assignments. Which principle of management is being overlooked?
   (a) Division of work (b) Discipline
   (c) Scalar chain (d) Initiative
4. Rahul, a manger, expects his subordinates to work for the happiness and pleasure of being in the organisation. Which principle of management is being overlooked?
   (a) Subordination of individual to general interest
   (b) Remuneration to employees
   (c) Espirit de corps
   (d) Centralisation and decentralisation
5. What did Taylor want to standardise?
   (a) Material (b) Machine and tools
   (c) Methods (d) All of these
6. Mohan keeps machines, materials, tools, etc. ready for operations by concerned workers. Whose work is described by this sentence under functional foremanship?
   (a) Instruction card clerk (b) Repair boss
   (c) Gang boss (d) Route clerk

Answers 1. (a) 2. (d) 3. (b) 4. (b) 5. (d) 6. (c)

Short Answer Type Questions

7. Explain the principle of 'stability of tenure' through a suitable example.
8. Explain the principle of 'scalar chain' and 'gang plank'.
9. Which principle of management emphasises that employees should remain with the organisation for a long period? Mention two negative consequences if this principle is not followed.
10. Which principle of management states that each group of activities with the same objective should have one head and one plan? Illustrate this principle with an appropriate example.
11. Mahesh, a manager of Meraki Ltd. has given the work on the basis of favouritism. Which principle is overlooked? Give some of its violating effects.
12. Distinguish between unity of command and unity of direction.
13. Which technique of Taylor suggests that each worker should be supervised by specialists? Briefly discuss any two of its designations suggested by Taylor.

Long Answer Type Questions

14. Explain briefly the nature of principles of management with suitable examples.
15. Mahesh and Ramesh are two employees in a company having same experience and samed educational background. But Mahesh is getting ₹ 6,000 per month for his work and Ramesh is getting ₹ 3,000 per month. Which principle of management is violated? Discuss it briefly and state some of its consequences.
16. Discuss in brief the two studies given by Taylor which aim to determine standard time and eliminate unnecessary movements. Support your explanation with a suitable example.

03 CHAPTER

Business environment consists of forces like social, political, economic, legal, technological and other forces which operate outside the business enterprise. It also includes individual, consumer, competitor, government, court, media, etc. working outside an enterprise.

Business Environment

▼ **YOUR STUDY GOALS**

3.1 Concept of Business Environment
3.2 Dimensions of Business Environment
3.3 Demonetisation

▼ **YOUR PRACTICE GOAL**

- Objective Type Questions (65 Qs ; MCQs, A-R, Statements, Matching)
- Subjective Type Questions (13 SAs, 4 LAs)
- Case Study Based Questions (Short Case Studies-14, Long Case Studies-5)
- Self Assessment Test (6 MCQs, 7 SAs, 3 LAs)

3.1 Concept of Business Evironment

The term business environment means the sum total of all individuals, institutions and other forces that are outside the control of a business enterprise but may affect its performance.

Features of Business Environment

Features	Explanation
Totality of External Forces	The business environment is the sum total of all external factors, including social, political, economic, legal and technological influences on a business.
Specific and General Forces	Specific forces like investors, customers, competitors and suppliers affect individual enterprises directly, while general forces such as economic, social, political, legal and technological conditions impact all enterprises indirectly.
Inter-relatedness	Elements of the business environment are interconnected, such as increased healthcare awareness driving demand for health-related products or rising income enhancing living standards.
Dynamic Nature	The business environment is constantly evolving due to technological advancements, shifting consumer preferences, new market entrants, policy changes or evolving trends.

Features	Explanation
Uncertainty	The business environment is unpredictable, with challenges in forecasting changes like technological advancements and policy shifts, especially in rapidly evolving sectors like information technology or fashion industry.
Complexity	Since business environment consists of numerous interrelated and dynamic conditions or forces which arise from different sources. So, it becomes difficult to comprehend at once what exactly constitutes a given environment. Thus, it is easier to understand its components in parts, but difficult to grasp in totality.
Relativity	Business environment is a relative concept as it differs from country to country and region to region.

Importance of Business Environment

1. **It enables the Firm to Identify Opportunities and Getting the First Mover Advantage** Knowledge of the business environment helps managers spot positive trends and take first-mover advantages.

   e.g. Maruti Udyog was the first automobile company in India to recognise the opportunity to develop small cars, due to which, it is still one of the market leaders in that segment.

2. **It helps the Firm to Identify Threats and Early Warning Signals** Understanding the environment allows managers to recognise possible threats early and act on them, serving as an early warning signal.

   e.g. If an Indian firm finds that a foreign MNC is entering the Indian market with new substitutes, it should act as a warning signal and the Indian firms should prepare themselves to meet the threat by adopting such measures as improving the product quality, reducing production cost and so on.

Business Environment Helps

- → To identify opportunities and getting first mover advantage
- → To identify threats and early warning signals
- → In tapping useful resources
- → In coping with rapid changes
- → In assisting in planning and policy formulation
- → In improving performance

3. **It helps in Tapping Useful Resources** A good understanding of the environment helps businesses access essential resources like finance and raw materials, and effectively convert them into outputs for the society.
4. **It helps in Coping with Rapid Changes** Rapid changes in the business environment, such as technology shifts and market turbulence, etc. require managers to stay informed and adapt strategies suitable courses accordingly.
5. **It helps in Assisting in Planning and Policy Formulation** Proper analysis of the business environment helps in identifying opportunities and threats, providing a foundation for effective planning and guides in policy formulation.

   e.g. Entry of new players in the market, which means more competition, may make an enterprise think afresh about how to deal with the situation.

6. **It helps in Improving Performance** Monitoring the environment helps in improving both present as well as future performance of the business.

Importance of Business Environment

- **Identifying Threats** Nokia, once a dominant player in the mobile phone industry, failed to recognise the threat posed by the smartphone revolution and the rise of touchscreen technology. Despite its strong market position, Nokia's inability to swiftly adapt to the changing environment and the increasing importance of software and apps led to its decline.
- **Coping with Rapid Changes** Netflix's ability to cope with rapid changes in technology and consumer behaviour is a prime example. Initially a DVD rental service, Netflix recognised the shift towards digital streaming and invested heavily in this new technology.
- **Tapping Useful Resources** Amazon has excelled in tapping and optimising its resources, particularly in its supply chain. By leveraging advanced technology, data analytics and a vast network of warehouses, Amazon has been able to efficiently source, store and deliver products.

3.2 Dimensions of Business Environment

Dimensions of business environment consists of factors like economic, social, political, legal and technological environment. These factors needs to be thoroughly analysed for decision-making and improving a business performance. The business environment is made up of five dimensions that can affect a business's performance.

These are as follows

1. Economic Environment

It consists of the factors and forces concerning with means of production and distribution of wealth in the country. It comprises of interest rate, rate of inflation, value of GDP, per capita inomce, tax rates, change in disposable income, etc.

Example With an increase in the inflation rates, there is a rise in the cost of production. This affects the profit of the business adversely.

Components of Economic Environment

- Structure of economy
- Rate of growth of GNP and per capita income at current and constant prices
- Rates of savings and investments
- Balance of payments and changes in foreign exchange reserves
- Value of exports and imports
- Agricultural and industrial production
- Money supply in the economy
- Public debt (internal and external)
- Planned outlay in private and public sectors

2. Social Environment

It consists of all the social and cultural forces within which the business firm operate. It comprises of customs and traditions, values, social trends, etc.

Traditions refer to such social practices that are followed since decades, values are the concepts that a society holds in high esteem like freedom, social justice, etc and social trends include changes as well as inclination towards new products.

Example Emerging trends of health and fitness provide opportunities to businesses like gyms, diet drinks, food supplements, etc. Celebration of festivals provides opportunities for sweets, gifts, etc.

Components of Social Environment

- Concern with quality of life
- Expectations from workforce
- Population shifts
- Shifts in the presence of women in workforce
- Educational system and literacy rates
- Consumption habits
- Composition of family
- Attitude towards product innovations, lifestyles, occupational distribution and consumer preferences
- Life expectancy
- Birth and death rates

3. Technological Environment

It includes forces relating to scientific improvements and innovations which provide new ways of producing goods and services and new methods and techniques of operating a business. Some of the components include import and export of technology, innovations, new equipment, etc.

Example Shifts in demand from vaccum tubes to transistors, from steam locomotives to diesel and electric engines, from fountain pens to ballpoint pens, from propeller airplanes to jets and from typewriters to computer based word processors, etc.

4. Political Environment

Political environment includes political conditions such as general stability and peace in the country and attitude of the elected government representatives towards businesses and business policy.

Example In 1977, Janta Government followed a strict policy against MNCs and forced companies like Coca-cola and IBM to move out of India. Change in government policies in 1991 allowed Pepsico and other MNCs to enter into Indian market.

Components of Political Environment

- The Constitution of the country
- The degree of politicalisation of business and economic issues
- Dominant ideologies and values of major political parties
- Nature and profile of political leadership and thinking of political personalities
- The level of political morality
- Political institutions like the government and allied agencies
- Political ideology and practices of the ruling party
- The extent and nature of government intervention in business
- The nature of relationship of our country with foreign countries

5. Legal Environment

It consists of various legislations passed by the government, administrative orders issued by government authorities, court judgements as well as the decisions rendered by various commissions and agencies at every level of the government. It is necessary for business enterprises to have adequate knowledge of these legislations and are required to comply with these laws. Non-compliance of laws can land the business enterprise into legal problems.

Example The advertisement of alcoholic beverages is prohibited. Advertisements of cigarettes carry the statutory warning 'Cigarette smoking is injurious to health'.

3.3 Demonetisation

Demonetisation is the act of removing a currency unit of its status as legal tender. The Government of India, made an announcement on 8th November, 2016, wherein the two largest denomination notes, ₹ 500, ₹ 1,000, were 'demonetised' with immediate effect, ceasing to be legal tender except for a few specified purposes such as paying utility bills. This led to 86% of the money in circulation, invalid.

The aim of demonestation was to

- curb corruption
- counterfeit the use of high denomination in notes for all illegal activities
- accumulate black money generated by income that has not been declared to tax authorities.

Legal Tender Money

Legal tender money is the money which can be legally used to make payments.

Features of Demonetisation

- Demonetisation is viewed as a **tax administration measure.** Cash holdings arising from declared income was readily deposited in banks and exchanged for new notes. But those with black money had to declare their unaccounted wealth and pay taxes at a penalty rate.
- It is also interpreted as a shift on the part of the government indicating **no tolerance of tax evasion**.
- It also led to tax administration, **channelising savings into formal financial system**. Though, much of the cash that has been deposited in the banking system is bound to be withdrawn but some of the new deposits schemes offered by the banks will continue to provide a base loans, at lower interest rates.
- It also aimed to create a **less-cash** or **cash-lite economy**, i.e. channelising more savings through the formal financial system and improving tax compliance.

Impact of Demonetisation

1. **Money/Interest Rates** It led to decline in cash transactions and increase in banks deposits as well as financial savings.
2. **Private Wealth** It led to decline in private wealth since some high demonetised notes were not returned and real estate prices fell.
3. **Public Sector Wealth** It had no effect on public sector wealth.
4. **Digitisation** It led to increase in digital transactions amongst new users (RuPay/AEPS).
5. **Real Estate** It led to decline in prices.
6. **Tax Collection** It led to rise in income tax collection because of increased disclosure.

Mind Map

BUSINESS ENVIRONMENT

1 Concept of Business Environment

Business environment means the sum total of all individuals, institutions and other forces that are outside the control of a business enterprise but may affect its performance.

2 Features of Business Environment

- **Totality of External Forces** Business environment is the sum total of all external factors, including social, political, economic, legal and technological factors
- **Includes both Specific and General Forces** Specific forces such as suppliers, investors and general forces such as economic, social, etc.
- **Inter-relatedness** Different elements are inter-related
- **Dynamic Nature** Business environment keeps on changing
- **Uncertainity** It is difficult to predict future events
- **Complexity** Business environment consists of several inter-related and dynamic forces
- **Relative Concept** Business environment differs from country to country and region to region

5 Demonetisation

Demonetisation can be defined as the act of removing a currency unit of its status as legal tender. It aims to curb corruption, counterfeit the use of high denomination notes for illegal activities and accumulate black money.

Features of Demonetisation

- Viewed as a tax administration measure
- Helps in channelising savings into formal financial system
- Shift on part of the government indicating that tax evasion will no longer be tolerated
- Aims to create a less-cash economy

3 Importance of Business Environment

- It enables the firm to identify opportunities and getting first mover advantage
- It helps the firm to identify threats and early warning signals
- It helps in tapping useful resources
- It helps in coping with rapid changes
- It helps in assisting in planning and policy formulation
- It helps in improving performance

4 Dimensions of Business Environment

- **Economic Environment** It comprises of interest rates, inflation, tax rates, etc.
- **Social Environment** It consists of values, traditions, social trends, etc.
- **Technological Environment** It consists of innovation, research & development, import and export of technology
- **Political Environment** It involves political forces, stability, ideology, political institutions, etc.
- **Legal Environment** It consists of rules, legislations, orders passed by government, court judgements, etc

EXAM PATTERN QUESTIONS

Objective Type Questions

Multiple Choice Questions (MCQs)

1. Business environment consists of numerous inter-related and dynamic conditions or forces which arise from different sources. Identify the characteristic of business environment being highlighted here.

(a) Inter-relatedness (b) Dynamic nature
(c) Complexity (d) Relativity

2. Which of the following statements is incorrect?

(a) The business environment is the sum total of external factors, including social, political, economic, legal and technological influences on a business

(b) Specific forces like investors and customers affect all enterprises indirectly, while general forces such as economic conditions impact individual enterprises directly

(c) Elements of the business environment are inter-connected, such as increased healthcare awareness driving demand for health-related products

(d) The business environment is constantly evolving due to technological advancements, shifting consumer preferences and policy changes

3. In 2016, the government of India implemented demonetisation, aiming to eliminate black money and reduce corruption by invalidating ₹ 500 and ₹ 1,000 currency notes. This sudden move impacted various businesses, forcing them to rely more on digital transactions.

Companies like Paytm and other digital payment platforms experienced a surge in users, while those heavily dependent on cash transactions faced significant disruptions.

Which feature of the business environment is highlighted by the impact of demonetisation on companies like Paytm? **Competency Based Que**

(a) Dynamic nature (b) Interrelatedness
(c) Complexity (d) Specific and general forces

4. TechNova Solutions, a leading software development company, has experienced significant growth over the past few years. The company has adapted to various external factors impacting their business environment, including rapid technological advancements and shifting consumer preferences.

Recently, TechNova faced challenges due to new data privacy regulations, which required significant adjustments to their software products.

The rise in healthcare awareness has also increased demand for their health-related software solutions. Despite these challenges, TechNova Solutions has successfully navigated the dynamic and complex business environment by integrating new technologies and responding proactively to regulatory changes.

Which aspect of the business environment is illustrated by TechNova Solutions adapting to new data privacy regulations and shifting consumer preferences? **Competency Based Que**

(a) Uncertainty
(b) Complexity
(c) Inter-relatedness
(d) Dynamic nature

5. Which of the following statements best reflects a benefit of being aware of the business environment?

(a) Businesses can avoid any form of competition
(b) Managers can better anticipate and respond to market changes
(c) Understanding the environment ensures maximum profits at all times
(d) Companies will not need to adapt their strategies

6. The study of environment makes available .... resources.

(a) costly (b) cheap
(c) inferior (d) useful

7. Which of the following statements is incorrect?

(a) Knowledge of the business environment helps managers spot positive trends and seize first-mover advantages, as seen with Maruti Udyog's early entry into the small car market

(b) Understanding the environment allows managers to recognise potential threats early and act on them, serving as an early warning system

(c) A good grasp of the environment is unnecessary for businesses to access essential resources like finance and raw materials

(d) Rapid changes in the business environment require managers to stay informed and adapt strategies accordingly

8. **A financial services company has adjusted its strategy to leverage new economic policies that favour investment in the sector. This adjustment is part of a broader plan to enhance overall performance and strategic direction. Which importance of business environment is highlighted in this scenario?** Competency Based Que

(a) Planning and policy formulation
(b) Improvement in performance
(c) Identifying opportunities (d) Tapping resources

9. **Mohan and Raj are working as general managers in XYZ and ABC Limited, respectively. Mohan's approach involves closely monitoring the business environment, paying attention to both significant and minor market changes and preparing proactively. In contrast, Raj is indifferent to the business environment, believing he can dictate its course rather than adapt to it.**

As time passed, XYZ emerged as a market leader among its competitors, while ABC began to lose relevance and became obsolete. Identify the point of 'importance of business environment' which is referred to by the incident stated above. Competency Based Que

(a) It helps in assisting in planning and policy formulation
(b) It helps in identifying threats
(c) It helps in tapping useful resources
(d) It helps in coping with rapid changes

10. **SK Builders' became the market leader in the designer house segment as it was the first to recognise the need of using artificial intelligence in designing houses in the changing environment of technological advancement. This highlights the following point of importance of business environment.** CBSE 2024; Competency Based Que

(a) It helps to identify threats and early warning signals
(b) It enables the firm to identify opportunities and getting the first mover advantage
(c) It helps in tapping useful resources
(d) It helps in improving performance

11. **Maruti Udyog's entry into the small car market was influenced by its ability to anticipate changes in the market environment. The business environment provided signals about consumer preferences shifting toward more fuel-efficient vehicles, allowing Maruti to launch its small car segment at the right time. This move gave Maruti a competitive edge over other players who entered the market later.**

What importance of business environment is best illustrated by Maruti Udyog's early entry into the small car market? Competency Based Que

(a) Coping with changes (b) Identifying threats
(c) Planning and policy formulation
(d) Identifying opportunities

12. **"Understanding the business environment helps managers to identify both opportunities and threats, allowing for effective planning and resource allocation." Based on the statement, which of the following is a correct implication?** Competency Based Que

(a) Businesses can ignore the external environment while planning
(b) Identifying threats is irrelevant to business performance
(c) Knowledge of the business environment aids in strategic decision-making
(d) Effective planning does not require understanding consumer preferences

13. **.............. environment refers to all those forces that have economic impact on the business activities.**

(a) Legal
(b) Economic
(c) Political
(d) Technological

14. **The Government of India has recently come up with an amendment to Section 6 of the Payment of Wages Act, 1936, to allow employees of certain industries to make payment through various electronic modes of payments.**

The amendment will be applicable to all the public sector enterprises for wages disbursement using e-payment options. This is another milestone in the direction to further push to cashless economy. Identify the dimension of business environment which relate to the above mentioned case. Competency Based Que

(a) Political environment
(b) Legal environment
(c) Technological environment
(d) All of the above

15. **A fashion retailer sees a shift in customer preferences towards sustainable and eco-friendly products, leading to changes in its product lines. This trend represents the impact of which environment?** Competency Based Que

(a) Economic environment (b) Technological environment
(c) Social environment (d) Political environment

16. **Due to increasing presence of women in the workforce, 'Kisan Mart' comes out every Friday with big discount offers on daily use items to attract office going women to shop on weekends.**
Which dimension of business environment is being highlighted in the above case?
CBSE 2024; Competency Based Que

(a) Social environment
(b) Legal environment
(c) Political environment
(d) Technological environment

17. **Identify the dimension of business environment illustrated by the given picture.** **CBSE 2025**

(a) Social (b) Political
(c) Technological (d) Economic

18. **In response to a recent global health crisis, a pharmaceutical company accelerates its research and development efforts to create a vaccine. This rush to develop new products and enhance existing ones is influenced by recent advancements in medical research and technology. This scenario exemplifies the effect of which environment?** **Competency Based Que**

(a) Technological environment
(b) Political environment
(c) Economic environment (d) Social environment

19. **Digilocker is a flagship initiative of 'Ministry of Electronics and IT', Government of India. It aims at digital empowerment of the citizens by providing access to authentic digital documents such as academic certificates issued by different examination boards, driving licenses, vehicle registrations, etc. in a digital format.**

The above para discusses a few dimensions of business environment. Identify the correct dimensions from the following. **CBSE 2023; Competency Based Que**

(a) Economic environment and technological environment
(b) Social environment and economic environment
(c) Social environment and political environment
(d) Political environment and technological environment

20. **Shift towards packaged food industry as represented in below picture is related to which dimension of business environment?**

(a) Social environment (b) Legal environment
(c) Political environment
(d) Technological environment

21. **Following a new policy introduced by the government to promote entrepreneurship, a start-up receives various incentives such as tax breaks, funding support and simplified regulatory procedures. This change in the startup's business environment is a result of which type of environment dimension?**

(a) Economic environment (b) Political environment
(c) Technological environment (d) Social environment

22. **'Online booking of rail and air tickets instead of going to Reservation Office' is an example of .... environment.**

(a) technological (b) political
(c) legal (d) economic

23. **Which of the following is not a part of social environment of business?** **CBSE 2023**

(a) Life expectancy
(b) Education system and literacy rates
(c) Consumption habits
(d) Money supply in the economy

24. **The image given below shows mandatory information on the label of Baby Food. Which dimension of business environment is depicted?**

(a) Legal environment (b) Political environment
(c) Social environment (d) Economic environment

25. **In a recent ruling, the Supreme Court of India has ordered an immediate stop on commercial activities in a 500-metre radius of the Taj Mahal and asked Agra Development Authority to ensure compliance of its directive. Which dimension of business environment is reflected here?** **CBSE 2023; Competency Based Que**

(a) Social (b) Technological
(c) Legal (d) Political

26. **Social and cultural forces, including factors such as life expectancy, birth and death rates and the presence of women in the workforce, significantly influence business operations. For instance, emerging trends in health and fitness create opportunities for businesses like gyms and dietary products, while the celebration of festivals boosts demand for sweets and gifts.**

Which of the following conclusions can be drawn from the statement? **Competency Based Que**

(a) Social elements have no impact on business opportunities
(b) Understanding social trends is irrelevant for businesses aiming to grow
(c) Businesses can leverage social and cultural trends to identify new market opportunities
(d) Only demographic factors are important for business success

27. **"The attitude of the government officials towards business may have either positive or negative impact upon business." Which factor of general environment is highlighted in the above statement?** **Competency Based Que**

(a) Technological environment
(b) Political environment
(c) Social environment (d) Legal environment

28. **Which of the following is a component of the economic environment?**

(a) Social trends (b) Inflation rates
(c) Cultural values (d) Consumer preferences

29. **Techpack Ltd. is a company in Hyderabad that produces and sells packaging material to various industries across the nation in a B2B e-business form. It is a dynamic company. Over the years, due to rising concerns for climate change and shift of preferences of Indian customers towards environment-friendly products, the company has shifted to the production of biodegradable packaging material. Moreover, due to its digital transformation, the company has tremendously benefitted as its customers could place orders and make cashless payments in various online modes.**

The dimensions of business environment discussed in the above case are **CBSE 2024 C; Competency Based Que**

(a) economic and social environments
(b) social and technological environments
(c) technological and economic environments
(d) social and political environments

30. **Goodwill Enterprises is a large-scale automobile manufacturer, who fulfills the needs of both industrial users and consumers. The company is providing easy finance facilities at a low rate of interest, which has considerably increased the demand for the product. The company has installed a new branch management software to efficiently manage and coordinate activities across their multiple branches and locations.**

Identify the components of the business environment from the above case study.
CBSE SQP 2025; Competency Based Que

(a) Political and economic environment
(b) Economic and social environment
(c) Technological and legal environment
(d) Economic and technological environment

31. **Demonetisation is viewed as a ……… measure.**

(a) tax administration
(b) tax evasion
(c) economic (d) financial

32. **Post-demonetisation, banks saw a large influx of cash deposits as people scrambled to exchange old currency notes. Many banks began offering new savings schemes and loans became available at lower interest rates. This measure was a result of the government's initiative to channelise informal savings into the formal banking system, promoting tax compliance and enhancing financial transparency.**

Which feature of demonetisation is reflected in the increased cash deposits and lower interest rates for loans? **Competency Based Que**

(a) Shift towards a cash-lite economy
(b) Reduction in tax evasion
(c) Channelising savings into the formal financial system
(d) Black money disclosure

33. **Which of the following statements is incorrect?**

(a) Demonetisation is viewed as a tax administration measure where cash holdings from declared income were readily deposited in banks and exchanged for new notes
(b) Demonetisation is interpreted as a government shift indicating no tolerance for tax evasion and aims to create a less-cash or cash-lite economy
(c) Demonetisation led to channeling savings into the formal financial system and improving tax compliance, with most of the deposited cash likely to be withdrawn
(d) Demonetisation primarily focused on increasing the amount of physical cash in circulation to encourage spending

34. **Which of the following is not a benefit of demonetisation in India?**

(a) Control over corruption
(b) Counterfeiting the use of high denomination notes for illegal activities
(c) Control on black money
(d) More demanding customers

35. **Demonetisation in India aimed to create a cash-lite economy, channelising savings through formal financial systems and improving tax compliance among citizens.**

Which of the following is a consequence of this statement? **Competency Based Que**

(a) Increase in black money circulation
(b) Growth of informal lending systems
(c) Enhanced transparency in financial transactions
(d) Decline in digital payment adoption

Direction *Read the following case study and answer the questions 36 to 39 on the basis of the same*

FreshBi, a prominent player in the FMCG industry, is renowned for its wide range of consumer products, including snacks, beverages and personal care items. The company has successfully expanded its market presence by adapting to evolving consumer preferences and leveraging technological advancements. By closely monitoring changes in consumer behaviour and market trends, FreshBi has been able to introduce innovative products that cater to emerging demands.

Additionally, the company's strategic use of market research has allowed it to identify and mitigate potential threats, ensuring that it remains competitive in a dynamic and uncertain market environment.

36. How did FreshBi utilise market research to maintain its market position?
(a) By ignoring consumer preferences
(b) By introducing outdated products
(c) By identifying and mitigating potential threats
(d) By limiting product innovation

37. In the context of the above case, identify one valid importance of business environment.
(a) Identifying opportunities (b) Increasing complexity
(c) Reducing inter-relatedness (d) Decreasing uncertainty

38. Which dimension of the business environment would be most relevant to FreshBi's decision to introduce innovative products?
(a) Economic (b) Technological
(c) Legal (d) Social

39. How does the 'legal' dimension of the business environment impact companies like FreshBi in the FMCG sector?
(a) By regulating product quality standards
(b) By influencing consumer preferences directly
(c) By determining the economic conditions of the market
(d) By driving technological advancements

Assertion-Reason

Direction (Q.No. 40 to 49) *Read the following Assertion (A) and Reason (R) and choose the correct alternative from the following*

Alternatives
(a) Both Assertion (A) and Reason (R) are true and Reason (R) is the correct explanation of Assertion (A)
(b) Both Assertion (A) and Reason (R) are true, but Reason (R) is not the correct explanation of Assertion (A)
(c) Assertion (A) is true, but Reason (R) is false
(d) Assertion (A) is false, but Reason (R) is true

40. **Assertion** (A) It is important for management to be highly cautious, alert and adaptable.
Reason (R) The business environment is dynamic in nature.

41. **Assertion** (A) One of the important features of business environment is totality of external forces.
Reason (R) Business environment is the sum total of all things external to business organisations and as such, is aggregative in nature.

42. **Assertion** (A) Element of uncertainty exists in business environment.
Reason (R) Predicting future happenings is difficult especially when environment changes are taking place too frequently.

43. **Assertion** (A) Understanding of business environment in a timely manner helps in making appropriate changes in the organisation.
Reason (R) Business environment provides various resources or inputs to the firm.

44. **Assertion** (A) Equal payment for equal work to male and female employees is an example of social environment.
Reason (R) Analysis of social environment is vital as it helps in determining the products, services and standards of conduct that are acceptable to society.

45. **Assertion** (A) The legal framework in a country can significantly impact the operational efficiency of businesses.
Reason (R) Legal frameworks dictate the rules and regulations that businesses must follow, affecting their operational practices.

46. **Assertion** (A) Demand for sarees may be fairly high in India whereas it may be almost non-existent in France.
Reason (R) Business environment consists of numerous inter-related and dynamic conditions of forces which arise from different sources.

47. **Assertion** (A) Nokia's decline in the mobile phone industry was due to its failure to recognise the threat of the smartphone revolution.
Reason (R) Nokia's strong market position prevented it from swiftly adapting to the changing environment and the importance of software and apps.

48. **Assertion** (A) Political stability is essential for creating a favourable business environment.
Reason (R) Political stability ensures consistent policies and reduces uncertainty for businesses.

49. **Assertion** (A) Demonetisation led to an increase in digital transactions among new users.

Reason (R) The decline in cash transactions encouraged more people to adopt digital payment methods such as RuPay and AEPS.

Two Statements Based MCQs

Direction (Q.No. 50 to 59) *Read the following statements carefully and choose the correct alternative*

Alternatives

(a) Statement I is correct and Statement II is incorrect
(b) Statement II is correct and Statement I is incorrect
(c) Both the statements are correct
(d) Both the statements are incorrect

50. **Statement I** The business environment is predictable, especially in sectors like information technology.

Statement II Uncertainty in the business environment makes forecasting challenging.

51. **Statement I** Business environment is a combination of both specific and general forces.

Statement II It is easy to predict the business environment.

52. **Statement I** Specific forces like investors and suppliers affect individual enterprises directly.

Statement II General forces, such as economic conditions, impact individual enterprises directly.

53. **Statement I** Studying business environment helps the firm in identifying opportunities and getting the first mover advantage.

Statement II Business environment is different for different business firms.

54. **Statement I** Environment is a complex phenomenon that is relatively easier to understand in parts but difficult to grasp in its totality.

Statement II Frequent environmental changes in the field of technology and fashion industry are related with uncertainty of business environment.

55. **Statement I** Rising income levels lead to enhanced living standards, which impacts consumer behaviour.

Statement II The elements of the business environment are independent of each other and do not affect one another.

56. **Statement I** Technological advancements like the transition from typewriters to computers revolutionised office work.

Statement II The technological environment includes innovations such as new equipment and methods.

57. **Statement I** The decline in cash transactions post-demonetisation led to increased financial savings in banks.

Statement II Demonetisation had a noticeable impact on real estate prices, leading to a decrease in demand and a subsequent reduction in prices across various segments of the real estate market.

58. **Statement I** Demonetisation led to an increase in digital transactions due to greater adoption of technology.

Statement II Demonetisation contributed to a rise in tax collection through improved disclosure and transparency.

59. **Statement I** Demonetisation led to a significant portion of money in circulation ceasing to be legal tender.

Statement II Demonetisation had no impact on the formal financial system or on the public's use of cash.

Matching

60. **Match the statements given in Column I with the characteristic of business environment given in Column II**

	Column I		Column II
A.	Increased demand of Khakhra and Thepla in the region of Gujarat as compared to Delhi region.	(i)	Uncertainty
B.	Digital academic certificates are issued to students accessible in a secured manner to eliminate undesirable practices like corruption and manipulation of records under digital India initiative. Such technological improvements are happening at a very fast pace.	(ii)	Dynamic
C.	Fashion market is facing both opportunities and challenges. Therefore, it is difficult to predict the future of the fashion market.	(iii)	Relativity
D.	A new government will result in changing. government rules, fiscal policies, market conditions, etc.	(iv)	Interrelatedness

Codes **CBSE SQP 2025**

	A	B	C	D
(a)	(iii)	(ii)	(i)	(iv)
(b)	(ii)	(i)	(iii)	(iv)
(c)	(iv)	(ii)	(i)	(iii)
(d)	(iii)	(i)	(ii)	(iv)

61. **Match the following features of business environment with their correct options given in Column II**

Column I	Column II
A. Inter-relatedness	(i) Political, legal, social and technological conditions
B. Relativity	(ii) Business environment has a connection with local conditions
C. Specific forces	(iii) Customers, competition, investors and suppliers
D. General forces	(iv) Change in one force may lead to changes in other forces

Codes

	A	B	C	D		A	B	C	D
(a)	(iii)	(i)	(iv)	(ii)	(b)	(iii)	(iv)	(i)	(ii)
(c)	(i)	(iii)	(ii)	(iv)	(d)	(iv)	(ii)	(iii)	(i)

62. **Match the following management actions with their correct options given in Column II**

Column I	Column II
A. Identifying opportunities	(i) This benefit allows businesses to effectively secure necessary inputs and convert them into valuable products or services.
B. Identifying threats	(ii) Managers can gain insights into potential risks and implement measures before they escalate into significant problems.
C. Tapping resources	(iii) This approach helps companies anticipate and take advantage of new market trends, similar to a company's strategic move into a new market segment.
D. Coping with repaid changes	(iv) This benefit equips organisations with the agility to modify their strategies in response to evolving market conditions or technological innovations.

Codes

	A	B	C	D		A	B	C	D
(a)	(ii)	(i)	(iv)	(iii)	(b)	(iii)	(iv)	(i)	(ii)
(c)	(i)	(iii)	(ii)	(iv)	(d)	(iii)	(ii)	(i)	(iv)

63. **Match the following points of importance of business environment with their correct options in Column II**

Column I	Column II
A. First mover advantage	(i) The environment presents various threats along with opportunities.
B. Early warning signal	(ii) The environment offers numerous opportunities.
C. Planning and policy formulation	(iii) The market is characterised by turbulence and rapid changes.
D. Coping with rapid changes	(iv) It serves as a foundation for future actions and helps develop decision-making guidelines.

Codes

	A	B	C	D		A	B	C	D
(a)	(ii)	(i)	(iv)	(iii)	(b)	(iii)	(iv)	(i)	(ii)
(c)	(i)	(iii)	(ii)	(iv)	(d)	(iv)	(ii)	(iii)	(i)

64. **Match the following dimensions of business environment with their correct options given in Column II**

Column I	Column II
A. Technological	(i) Decrease in bank interest rates increases the demand of products and *vice-versa*
B. Economic	(ii) Shift in demand from typewriter to computers
C. Political	(iii) It is important for Baby food companies to mention on their product that 'Mother food is the best'
D. Legal	(iv) Unstable political environment creates uncertainty in business activities

Codes

	A	B	C	D		A	B	C	D
(a)	(ii)	(i)	(iv)	(iii)	(b)	(iii)	(iv)	(i)	(ii)
(c)	(i)	(iii)	(ii)	(iv)	(d)	(ii)	(i)	(iii)	(iv)

65. **Match the following dimensions of business environment with their correct options in Column II**

Column I	Column II
A. Social environment	(i) This aspect involves regulations and rules established by the government to ensure fair practices and protect the rights of businesses and individuals
B. Legal environment	(ii) Research and development activities
	(iii) This aspect influences business operations through social values, cultural norms and demographic changes that affect consumer behaviour and market demand.

Codes

	A	B		A	B
(a)	(iii)	(i)	(b)	(iii)	(ii)
(c)	(i)	(iii)	(d)	(i)	(ii)

Answers

1. (a) Inter-relatedness
2. (b) Specific forces like investors and customers directly impact individual enterprises, while general forces like economic conditions impact all enterprises indirectly.
3. (b) Interrelatedness
4. (d) Dynamic nature
5. (b) Managers can better anticipate and respond to market changes
6. (d) useful
7. (c) A good understanding of the business environment is crucial for accessing resources and making informed decisions
8. (b) Improvement in performance
9. (d) It helps in coping with rapid changes
10. (b) It enables the firm to identify opportunities and getting the first mover advantage
11. (d) Identifying opportunities
12. (c) Knowledge of the business environment aids in strategic decision-making
13. (b) Economic
14. (c) Technological environment
15. (c) Social environment 16. (a) Social environment
17. (c) Technological
18. (a) Technological environment
19. (d) Political environment and technological environment
20. (a) Social environment 21. (b) Political environment
22. (a) technological
23. (d) Money supply in the economy
24. (a) Legal environment 25. (c) Legal
26. (c) Businesses can leverage social and cultural trends to identify new market opportunities
27. (b) Political environment
28. (b) Inflation rates
29. (b) social and technological environments
30. (d) Economic and technological environment
31. (a) tax administration
32. (c) Channelising savings into the formal financial system
33. (d) The primary goal of demonetisation was not to increase the amount of physical cash but to reduce black money and promote digital transactions.
34. (d) More demanding customers
35. (c) Enhanced transparency in financial transactions
36. (c) By identifying and mitigating potential threats
37. (a) Identifying opportunities
38. (b) Technological
39. (a) By regulating product quality standards
40. (a) Both Assertion (A) and Reason (R) are true and Reason (R) is the correct explanation of Assertion (A)
41. (a) Both Assertion (A) and Reason (R) are true and Reason (R) is the correct explanation of Assertion (A)
42. (a) Both Assertion (A) and Reason (R) are true and Reason (R) is the correct explanation of Assertion (A)
43. (b) Both Assertion (A) and Reason (R) are true, but Reason (R) is not the correct explanation of Assertion (A)
44. (b) Analysis of social environment discusses the broader importance of analysing the social environment for understanding acceptable societal conduct, which is a different aspect of the social environment and not directly related to equal payment to employees.
45. (a) Both Assertion (A) and Reason (R) are true and Reason (R) is the correct explanation of Assertion (A)
46. (b) Business environment is a relative concept as it differs from country to country.
47. (b) Nokia's strong market position did not prevent it from adapting; rather, it was more about the lack of innovation and strategic change.
48. (a) Both Assertion (A) and Reason (R) are true and Reason (R) is the correct explanation of Assertion (A)
49. (a) Both Assertion (A) and Reason (R) are true and Reason (R) is the correct explanation of Assertion (A)
50. (b) Business environment, particularly in sectors like information technology, is often unpredictable.
51. (a) Predicting the business environment is often challenging due to its dynamic and complex nature.
52. (a) General forces impact enterprises indirectly, affecting all businesses broadly rather than individually.
53. (c) Both the statements are correct
54. (c) Both the statements are correct
55. (a) Elements of the business environment are inter-connected and influence each other.
56. (c) Both the statements are correct
57. (c) Both the statements are correct
58. (c) Both the statements are correct
59. (a) Demonetisation had a major impact on both the financial system and cash usage due to ceasing of legal tender money.
60. (a) (iii) (ii) (i) (iv)
61. (d) (iv) (ii) (iii) (i) 62. (d) (iii) (ii) (i) (iv)
63. (a) (ii) (i) (iv) (iii) 64. (a) (ii) (i) (iv) (iii)
65. (a) (iii) (i)

Subjective Questions

Short Answer Type Questions

1. **"The business environment is defined as the combination of internal and external factors that influence an organisation's operations and decision-making processes."**
In light of this statement, define business environment. Explain how it is a relative concept? **Competency Based Que**

Or **What is meant by business environment?** **NCERT**

Ans. The term business environment means the sum total of all individuals, institutions and other forces that are outside the control of a business enterprise but may affect its performance. Business environment is a relative concept as it differs from country to country and region to region.

e.g. Demand for sarees is quite high in India but in foreign countries, it almost has no existence. Similarly, regulations, government policies, consumers' preference, etc all differ from one region to another.

2. **Explain the following features of business environment.**
(i) Inter-relatedness (ii) Dynamic nature

Ans.

(i) **Inter-relatedness**
The different elements of business environment are closely inter-related. e.g. Increased awareness for healthcare have increased the demand of many healthcare products like sugar free, diet coke, cholestrol free oil, etc. Similarly, an increase in the income of consumer (economic environment) will help in improving his standard of living (social environment).

(ii) **Dynamic Nature**
Business environment is dynamic in nature as it keeps on changing whether in terms of upgradation of technologies, shifts in consumer preference, entry of new competition in the market, change in government policy or changes in trends and traditions.

3. **"The business environment can be categorised into general and specific environments, each impacting organisations differently." In the light of the given statement, explain with examples, the difference between general and specific environment.** **Competency Based Que**

Ans. Following are the differences between general and specific environment

Basis	General Environment	Specific Environment
Meaning	It refers to all those factors of the environment which influence all enterprises almost in the same way.	It refers to all those factors of the environment which influence each business unit differently.
Examples	Economic, social, technological, political and legal conditions.	Customers, suppliers, competitors, public, market intermediaries, etc.
Impact	These forces affect a particular organisation indirectly.	These forces are specific to a particular organisation or a company.

4. **Does study of business environment help in maintaining image in market?**

Ans. Yes, by understanding the business environment, it becomes easy for a company to maintain good image in the market as the company produces goods according to the need of the customer.

After proper scanning of the environment, they are able to adapt the changes as per the requirement, which help them in improving performances also.

5. **"Business environment or environmental scanning helps in the identification of threats and early warning signals." Explain.** **Competency Based Que**

Ans. Environmental scanning helps an enterprise to recognise qualitative information in advance, which can be used to prepare it for facing likely challenges.

e.g. If any new multinational company is entering in Indian market, the manager of an Indian firm dealing with same product, as that of the multinational company, should take it as a warning signal.

He should take measures like improving the quality of his product, heavy advertisement, etc. to face the challenge.

6. **State the various ways in which managers respond to changes in business environment.**

Ans. Following are the ways in which managers respond to changes in business environment.

(i) Strategic alliances, mergers and acquisitions of businesses
(ii) Diversification
(iii) Collaboration with multinationals
(iv) Brand building
(v) Restructuring of business activities
(vi) Capital restructures
(vii) Customer focus
(viii) Latest technology
(ix) Compensation levels and incentive schemes

7. What do you understand by 'political environment' of business?

Ans. Political environment consists of the forces concerning management of public affairs and their impact on business. It includes political conditions like general stability and peace in the country and attitude of the elected government representatives towards businesses and business policy.

e.g. The attitude of government officials toward business may have either positive or negative impact on business. Some of the components political institution, level of political morality, nature and profile of political leadership and thinking of political personalities, political ideology, etc.

8. State any three impact of technological environment on business.

Ans. The following are the examples of impact of technological environment on business

(i) With the advent of television in the market, the cinema and radio industry were adversely affected.

(ii) With the arrival of photostate machines in the market, the carbon paper industry suffered a setback.

(iii) With the entry of synthetic cloth in the market, the cotton cloth industry was badly affected.

9. "Changes in the economic environment can have a significant impact on business organisations in various ways".

Give any three examples of the impact on business organisations due to change in economic environment. Competency Based Que

Ans. Three examples of the impact of changes in economic environment are as follows

(i) Due to improvements in the banking sector, bank loans are now easily available on easy terms. This has led to an increase in production, investment and expenditure.

(ii) Changes in economic environment has resulted in establishment of mutual funds and venture capital business.

(iii) Economic downturns or global recessions reduce consumer demand, leading to lower sales and profits. This often forces businesses to cut costs, downsize or delay expansion plans.

10. Explain why there is a need to study economic environment?

Ans. Economic environment consists of the factors and forces concerning with means of production and distribution of wealth in the country.

It comprises of interest rate, rate of inflation, value of GDP, per capita income, tax rates, change in disposable income, etc. 'Short and long-term interest rates' affect the demand for the product and services significantly.

Knowledge of economic conditions aids in planning and forecasting. Businesses can anticipate changes in demand, costs and economic conditions, allowing for better strategic planning and risk management.

Economic policies, such as taxation, interest rates and trade policies, have significant effects on businesses and consumers. Understanding these policies helps in assessing their potential impact on financial stability and business operations.

11. What do you understand by legal environment? Give example.

Ans. Legal environment consists of legislations passed by the government, administrative orders issued by government authorities, court judgements as well as the decisions rendered by various commissions and agencies at every level of the government. In India, these laws and legislations have been implemented by the government through Companies Act, Factories Act, Competition Act, Consumer Protection Act, etc.

Thus, it is necessary for business enterprises to have adequate knowledge of rules and regulations and are required to comply with these laws. Non-compliance of laws can land the business enterprise into legal problems.

e.g. The advertisement of alcoholic beverages is prohibited, which affects the marketing of such products. Products like tobacco and cigarettes are required to carry a statutory warning on their packages, 'Smoking is injurious to health'.

12. "The social environment as a dimension of the business environment includes the customs, values, beliefs, lifestyle and demographic characteristics of society."

In the light of the given statement, discuss in brief the social environment as the dimension of business environment. Competency Based Que

Ans. Social environment consists of all the social and cultural forces within which the business firms operate. It comprises of customs and traditions, values, social trends, society's expectations from business, etc.

Traditions refers to such social practices that are followed since decades. e.g. Celebrations of festivals like Diwali, Eid, etc. provide greater opportunities to businesses like confectionary, sweets, greeting cards, gift galleries, etc.

Values refer to concepts that a society holds in high esteem, such as freedom, social justice, equality of opportunity and national integration, etc. Social trends refers to changes and inclination towards new products. They provide various opportunities and threats to business enterprises.

13. State any three features of demonetisation. CBSE 2024

Ans. Following are the features of demonetisation

(i) **Change in Currency**

Demonetisation is viewed as a tax administration measure.

It is the act of removing or discontinuing a currency unit of its legal status by government.

(ii) **Contingent**
Success or failure of demonetisation is dependent upon various factors.

(iii) **Objective**
The objective of demonetisation can be curbing corruption, fake currency, illegal activity and making cashless economy. It also aimed to create a less-cash or cash-lite economy, i.e. channelising more savings through the formal financial system and improving tax compliance.

Long Answer Type Questions

14. **Explain the following features of business environment.**
(i) Totality of external forces
(ii) Complexity
(iii) Uncertainty

Ans.
(i) **Totality of External Forces**
The business environment is the sum total of external factors, including social, political, economic, legal and technological influences on a business. Business environment is aggregative in nature.

(ii) **Complexity**
Business environment is complex, as it consists of numerous inter-related and dynamic factors which affects business enterprises at the same time.
This makes it difficult to comprehend at once what exactly constitutes a given environment. Thus, it is easier to understand its components in parts, but difficult to grasp in totality.
e.g. It may be difficult to know the extent of the relative impact of the social, economic, political, technological or legal factors on change in demand of a product in the market.

(iii) **Uncertainty**
Business environment is largely uncertain as it is very difficult to predict future events such as technological changes, change in government policies, etc. especially, when changes are taking place at a fast pace like in case of information technology or fashion industries.

15. **"Understanding of business environment plays a crucial role for managers."**
Explain why it is important to study business environment? **Competency Based Que**

Or **How would you argue that the success of a business enterprise is significantly influenced by its environment?** **NCERT**

Or **Explain any four points that highlight the significance of business environment.** **CBSE 2024 C**

Ans. It is important to study business environment due to following reasons

(i) **It enables the Firm to Identify Opportunities and Getting the First Mover Advantage**
Opportunities are the positive trends that help firms to improve their performance. A good knowledge of business environment helps a manager to identify such opportunities earlier to take its benefit, rather than losing it to other competing enterprises. e.g. Maruti Udyog was the first automobile company in India to recognise the opportunity to develop small cars, due to which, it is still one of the market leaders in that segment.

(ii) **It helps the Firm to Identify Threats and Early Warning Signals**
Threats refer to the external environment trends and changes, which will hinder the performance of the enterprise. Proper knowledge and understanding of the environment helps the managers to identify the possible threats on time and act as an early warning signal.
e.g. If an Indian firm finds that a foreign MNC is entering the Indian market with new subsititutes, it should act as a warning signal and the Indian firms should prepare themselves to meet the threat by adopting such measures as improving the product quality, reducing production cost and so on.

(iii) **It helps in Tapping Useful Resources**
Environment is a source of various resources for business like finance, machinery, raw materials, etc. including financiers, government and suppliers. In return, business provides its output to the environment in the form of goods and services for customers, payment of taxes to government, return on financial investment to investors, etc.
Thus, a good understanding of environment helps the firm to convert such resources into output required by the environment and society.

(iv) **It helps in Coping with Rapid Changes**
Business environment is changing at a fast pace due to turbulent market conditions, less brand loyalty, divisions and sub-divisions of markets, more demanding customers, changing technology and increasing global competition.
In order to effectively cope up with such changes, managers must understand and examine their environment and develop suitable courses of action.

(v) **It helps in Assisting in Planning and Policy Formulation**
Since, business environment is a source of identifying both opportunities and threats, its proper analysis and understanding provides the base for planning (deciding the future course of action) and guides in framing policies.

e.g. Entry of new players in the market, which means more competition, may make an enterprise think a fresh about how to deal with the situation.

(vi) **It helps in Improving Performance**
An enterprise that monitors its environment continuously, is in a position to improve not only its present performance, but also improve its future performance. This ensures success of the business in the market for a longer period.

16. Explain with examples, the various dimensions of business environment. **NCERT**

Ans. Following are the various dimensions of business environment

(i) **Economic Environment**
It comprises of the economic variables such as interest rates, income, stock market indices that affect the functioning of the enterprises.

e.g. An increase in the income of the consumers increases the demand for goods and services of the enterprises. Similarly, a fall in the interest rates for loans for consumer durables increases the spending capacity and thereby, increases the demand for such products.

(ii) **Social Environment**
Social environment refers to the social forces such as customs, traditions, social values, social trend, etc.

e.g. Religious celebrations provide business opportunities to many enterprises such as those producing sweets, decoration items, etc. Similarly, in India a change in social trend towards western lifestyle has increased the demand for western wear, fast food, etc.

(iii) **Technological Environment**
Technological environment comprises of the technological changes and improvements.

e.g. Introduction of computers, internet, have changed the way organisations work today. Similarly, continuous improvement and innovations in the technology used in the production improves the quality of production. While on one hand, improvement in technology provides new business opportunities for the enterprises, on the other hand, it is a threat for the enterprises using outdated technology.

(iv) **Legal Environment**
It refers to the legislation and rules passed by the government such as the Companies Act, Factories Act, Competition Act, Trade Union Act, etc. Knowledge of these legislation is essential for enterprises as their non-compliance can lead to legal trouble for them.
e.g. An export-import company in India has to follow the rules and regulations as stated under the EXIM policy and the Foreign Trade (Development and Regulation) Act, 1992.

Similarly, the refining, processing, distribution, sale of petroleum, petroleum products is governed by the Petroleum and Natural Gas Regulatory Board Act, 2006.

(v) **Political Environment**

Political environment comprises of political conditions such as peace and stability, law and order, etc.

e.g. A situation of political unrest such as frequent change in the ruling government implies a change in the rules and policies of the government regarding production and manufacturing.

Such a frequent change in the regulations regarding production discourages investment. Similarly, the opening up of our economy under the New Economic Policy in 1991, provided business opportunity to many foreign companies.

17. What do you understand by demonetisation? Explain briefly the impact of demonetisation.

Ans. Demonetisation is the act of removing a currency unit of its status as legal tender. The Government of India, made an announcement on 8th November, 2016.

The two largest denomination notes, ₹ 500, ₹ 1,000, were 'demonetised' with immediate effect, ceasing to be legal tender except for a few specified purposes such as paying utility bills. This led to 86% of the money in circulation invalid.

The purpose of demonetisation was to accumulate black money generated by income that has not been declared to tax authorities, etc.
Following is the impact of demonetisation

(i) **Money/Interest Rates**
It led to decline in cash transactions and increase in bank deposits as well as financial savings.

(ii) **Private Wealth**
It led to decline in private wealth since some high demonetised notes were not returned and real estate prices fell.

(iii) **Public Sector Wealth**
It had no effect on public sector wealth.

(iv) **Digitisation**
It led to increase in digital transactions amongst new users (RuPay/AEPS).

(v) **Real Estate**
It led to decline in prices.

(vi) **Tax Collection**
It led to rise in income tax collection because of increased disclosure.

Case Study Based Questions

Short Case Studies

Case Study 1

Mr. Vivek Vaswani, a foodpreneur combined his passion for food with his entrepreneurial skills and started his innovative fast food outlet OH CHILLI! in 2021. He had started his career as a food blogger and had noticed that numerous Indian consumers were looking for reasonable and pure vegetarian fast food options for dining out. The high end restaurants were not opted by many as they were exorbitantly priced. Though many global fast food chains were running across the country, yet not many outlets offered reasonable and healthy pure vegetarian fast food options to consumers. OH CHILLI! became a pioneer in offering a healthy and delicious variety of food.

What came as a surprise for consumers was that even without using onion or garlic in the pasta sauce, marinade and ketchup, the food could actually taste great. The company witnessed an increase in net profit of 26% in its second financial year and became a market leader.

(i) State the concept of business environment.

(ii) Identify and explain in what way, a good understanding of business environment enabled Mr. Vivek Vaswani to improve the performance of the enterprise.

CBSE SQP 2025

Ans.

(i) Business environment means the sum total of all individuals, institutions and other forces that are outside the control of a business enterprise but that may affect its performance.

(ii) It enables the firm to identify opportunities and getting the first mover advantage. Opportunities are the positive trends that help firms to improve their performance. A good knowledge of business environment helps a manager to identify such opportunities earlier to take its benefit, rather than losing it to other competing enterprises.

Case Study 2

ABCDE Ltd. has opened a customised shoe business in 23 cities. The organisation has done a lot of research on the nature of business environment in which it is doing business.

The market has fragmented as there are many players, brand loyalties of the customers keep on changing, customers are more demanding and there is intense competition in the market. Every week on Saturday, the board of directors sits for a meeting and decides the future course of action. They rely on their surveys and past performances of other companies to achieve policy making and deciding future course of action. The company devotes its lot of time in understanding the external environment.

With all the research, the company has realised that the business environment does tend to have a lot of impact on the organisation, so it is necessary to continuously monitor it.

Quoting the lines from the case, name the various importance of management highlighted above.

Ans. The various points of importance of business environment highlighted above

(i) It helps in coping with rapid changes. "The market has fragmented as there are many players, brand loyalties of the customers keep on changing, customers are more demanding and there is intense competition in the market."

(ii) It helps in planning and policy formulation. "They rely on their surveys and past performances of other companies to achieve policy making and deciding future course of action."

(iii) It helps in improving performance. "With all the research, the company has realised that the business environment does tend to have a lot of impact on the organisation so it is necessary to continuously monitor it."

Case Study 3

Mrs Renu Garg is the divisional manager of the export division of 'Swarag Tea Limited'. For some time since past a restriction has been imposed on export of tea. It is evident that the company's export business depends on the government's policy. Recently there has been a change of government in the centre.

As soon as the new government took over, it removed the restriction imposed on export of tea. With the coming of this news, the division under Mrs Garg heaved a sigh of relief.

(i) The change of government is having its impact on the two dimensions of business environment. Identify them.

(ii) Identify one of the characteristic of 'business environment' described.

Ans.

(i) Following are the two dimensions of business environment that have been impacted

- A new government coming into power – Political environment
- Change in the policy of import-export – Economic environment

(ii) The characteristic of 'business environment' described is inter-relatedness. Elements of the business environment are inter-connected, such as increased healthcare awareness driving demand for health-related products or rising income enhancing living standards.

Case Study 4

Tech Innovations Inc., a leading player in the technology sector, has recently embarked on a new project to develop an advanced Artificial Intelligence (AI) system. The company is investing heavily in research and development to stay ahead in the rapidly evolving tech industry. However, Tech Innovations Inc. faces significant challenges due to the rapid pace of technological advancements and the constant introduction of new technologies by competitors.

The company's management must continuously adapt to these technological changes to remain competitive and meet the growing demands of consumers. The company also regularly collaborates with tech startups and research institutions to gain insights and innovative solutions. Despite these efforts, the uncertainty surrounding future technological developments and the unpredictability of market trends pose ongoing risks to the company's strategic planning and operations.

(i) Identify and state the component of the business environment highlighted in the above case.

(ii) State two features of the business environment as indicated in the case.

Ans.

(i) The component of the business environment highlighted in the above case is 'technological environment'.

It includes forces relating to scientific improvements and innovations which provide new ways of producing goods and services and new methods and techniques of operating a business.

e.g. Recent technological advances in computers and electronics have modified the ways in which companies advertise their products.

(ii) The two features of the business environment as indicated in the case are

- **Dynamic Nature**
  The business environment is constantly evolving due to technological advancements, shifting consumer preferences, new market entrants, policy changes and evolving trends.
- **Uncertainty**
  The business environment is unpredictable, with challenges in forecasting changes like technological advancements and policy shifts, especially in rapidly evolving sectors like information technology or fashion industry.

Case Study 5

A company, 'GreenTech Industries,' is an integral part of the market, utilising various resources such as raw materials, labour, human resources, power, water and other inputs. These resources are essential for the production process. The raw materials and other inputs go through multiple operations, transforming them into final products which are then sold in the market.

Despite the seamless conversion of inputs into outputs, 'GreenTech Industries' must navigate various challenges and opportunities influenced by the business environment. For instance, regulatory changes regarding resource usage and environmental standards directly impact how the company sources and utilises raw materials and energy. Adapting to these regulations is crucial for maintaining compliance and achieving operational efficiency.

(i) Identify the dimension of business environment that has been highlighted in the case.

(ii) Identify and explain the point of importance of business environment mentioned in the case.

Ans.

(i) The dimension of business environment highlighted in the case is 'legal environment'.

(ii) The point of importance of the business environment mentioned in the case is that it helps in coping with rapid changes.

The case mentions that GreenTech Industries must adapt to regulatory changes regarding resource usage and environmental standards.

By understanding and responding to the legal environment, the company can ensure compliance and maintain operational efficiency, which is essential for developing in a dynamic market.

Business environment is changing at a fast pace due to turbulent market conditions, less brand loyalty, divisions and sub-divisions of markets, more demanding customers, changing technology and increasing global competition.

In order to effectively cope up with such changes, managers must understand and examine their environment and develop suitable courses of action.

Case Study 6

VBR Cinema an Indian multiplex cinema hall was the first to recognise the change in consumption habits of people. It changed its food menu from burgers, pizza, soft drinks, etc. and switched over to healthier options like salads and smoothies, soups and anjeer-based sweets. Within a month, the revenue of the multiplex from sale of food items doubled.

VBR Cinema, by continuously monitoring the environment and adopting suitable business practices, was able to improve its revenues and profits and was hopeful that it will continue to succeed in the market in the long-run too. Identify and explain one dimension of business environment and one point of importance of understanding the business environment highlighted in the above case.

CBSE 2024

Ans. The dimension of business environment is 'social environment'. This dimension includes the changes in consumer preferences and lifestyle trends. In this case, VBR Cinema identified the shift towards healthier eating habits among consumers and adapted its food menu to align with these new preferences.

The point of importance of understanding the business environment is identifying opportunities. VBR Cinema recognised a positive trend in consumer preferences for healthier food options, which allowed it to seize the opportunity to update its menu. This aligns with how understanding the business environment helps managers spot positive trends and act on them to gain a competitive advantage.

Case Study 7

The Covid-19 pandemic accelerated the adoption of remote work as companies worldwide adapted to new ways of operating. Many businesses have now embraced hybrid work models as a long-term strategy, driven by technological advancements and changing employee expectations.

Recent reports show a surge in investments in digital collaboration tools and flexible workspace solutions. Identify and explain the dimension of the business environment illustrated in the case above.

Ans. The dimension of business environment illustrated in the case above is 'technological environment'. It includes forces relating to scientific improvements and innovations which provide new ways of producing goods and services and new methods and techniques of operating a business. e.g. Recent technological advances in computers and electronics have modified the ways in which companies advertise their products.

Case Study 8

With increasing concerns about data privacy, several countries have introduced stringent regulations to protect consumer information. e.g. The European Union's General Data Protection Regulation (GDPR) has set new standards for data handling and privacy. Companies operating globally are required to comply with these regulations, impacting their data management practices.

Identify and explain the dimension of the business environment illustrated in the case above.

Ans. The dimension of business environment illustrated in the above case is 'legal environment'. It consists of various legislations passed by the government administrative orders issued by government authorities, court judgements as well as the decisions rendered by various commissions and agencies at every level.

The advertisement of alcoholic beverages is prohibited. Advertisements, of cigarettes carry the statutory warning 'Cigarette smoking is injurious to health'.

Case Study 9

Recent studies show that consumers are increasingly prioritising sustainability when making purchasing decisions. Brands that promote eco-friendly practices and products are seeing a rise in customer loyalty and sales. This shift in consumer behaviour is driving companies to adopt sustainable practices and transparent sourcing to appeal to environmentally conscious customers.

(i) Identify and explain the dimension of the business environment illustrated in the case above.

(ii) Explain why this dimension is important for businesses.

Ans.

(i) The dimension of business environment illustrated in the case above is 'social environment'. Social environment consists of all the social and cultural forces within which the business firms operate.
It comprises of customs and traditions, values, social trends, society's expectations from business, etc.

(ii) The dimension of social environment is important because understanding and responding to social trends can help businesses align their products and services with consumer values, enhancing brand reputation and customer loyalty. Analysis and understanding of social environment is important as it determines the products, services and standards of conduct that are acceptable to society.

Case Study 10

Identify and explain the dimension of business environment in following cases

(i) At the time of holi, a large number of manufacturing firms get involved in making colours which are used in the celebration of this colourful festival.

(ii) It is not advisable to open a luxury car showroom in the middle of an economy where per capita income is very low.

Ans.

(i) **Social Environment**
It consists of all the social forces within which business operates such as trends, customs and traditions. This dimension encompasses societal factors such as cultural norms, demographics, lifestyle trends and social attitudes, influencing consumer behaviour, workforce expectations and business practices.

(ii) **Economic Environment**
It includes economic factors like inflation, interest rates, tax rates, GDP, that affect business enterprises. This dimension refers to the financial aspects affecting businesses, including economic growth, inflation, interest rates and exchange rates, which impact purchasing power, cost structures and overall business profitability.

Case Study 11

A recent rate cut in the interest on loans announced by the banks encouraged Amit, a science student of Progressive School to take a loan from State Bank of India to experiment and develop cars to be powered by fuel produced from garbage. He developed such a car and exhibited it in the Science Fair organised by Directorate of Education. He was awarded first prize for his invention.

Identify and explain the dimensions of business environment discussed in the above case.

Ans. Following are the dimensions of business environment discussed in the above case are

(i) **Economic Environment**
Economic dimension of business environment includes various economic factors like inflation, interest rates, currency value, income of people, etc. Both short and long-term interest rates affect the demand for various goods and services in the economy. Lower interest rates lead to higher demand while higher interest rates lead to less spending by consumers leading to reduced demand.

(ii) **Technological Environment**
Scientific improvements and innovations are included in the technological dimension of business environment. It provides new ways and methods of producing goods and services. e.g. Technological developments in the field of computers and information technology have changed the ways in which companies promote their goods and services.

Case Study 12

National Digital Library of India (NDL India) is a pilot project initiated by the HRD Ministry. It works towards developing a framework of virtual repository of learning resources with a single-window search facility.

It provides support to all academic levels including researchers, life-long learners and differently-abled learners free of cost. State the dimensions of business environment highlighted above. **NCERT**

Ans. The dimensions highlighted in the given case are social and technological environment.

Social environment consists of all the social and cultural forces within which the business firms operate. It comprises of customs and traditions, values, social trends, society's expectations from business, etc.

Traditions refers to such social practices that are followed since decades.
e.g. Celebrations of festivals like Diwali, Eid, etc. provide greater opportunities to businesses like confectionary, sweets, greeting cards, gift galleries, etc.
Technological environment comprises of the technological changes and improvements. For example, introduction of computers, internet, have changed the way organisations work today. Similarly, continuous improvement and innovations in the technology used in the production improves the quality of production. While on one hand, improvement in technology provides new business opportunities for the enterprises, on the other hand, is a threat for the enterprises using outdated technology.

Case Study 13

Long Drive Manufacturers is a leading vehicle manufacturing company. It claims that it can create a fuel in its laboratory which can run the newly designed car. The company is ready to provide this fuel to its customers for free for one year provided they buy the car. Which dimension of business environment is affected here by the company's innovative solution? Explain.

Ans. The dimension of business which is affected here by the company's innovation is the 'technological' environment. The case mentions the creation of fuel which can run the newly designed car. It indicates a technological change.
Technological environment comprises of the technological changes and improvements. For example, introduction of computers, internet, have changed the way organisations work today. Similarly, continuous improvement and innovations in the technology used in the production improves the quality of production. While on one hand, improvement in technology provides new business opportunities for the enterprises, on the other hand, is a threat for the enterprises using outdated technology.

Case Study 14

Amaira is a seven years old girl. She planned with her father to give a gift on her mother's birthday. She took her piggy bank to shopkeeper with her father.

She selected a purse for her mother and when she took out one note of ₹ 1,000 from the piggy bank the shopkeeper refused to take that note saying that it is no longer a valid currency.

Her father explained her that shopkeeper is saying right.

(i) Identify the concept discussed in above case.
(ii) State three impacts of that concept.

Ans.

(i) The concept discussed in above case is demonetisation. Demonetisation is the act of removing a currency unit of its status as legal tender.

(ii) Following are the three impacts of demonetisation

- **Money/Interest Rates**
  It led to decline in cash transactions and increase in banks deposits as well as financial savings.
- **Private Wealth**
  It led to decline in private wealth since some high demonetised notes were not returned and real estate prices fell.
- **Digitisation**
  It led to increase in digital transactions amongst new users (RuPay/AEPS).

Long Case Studies

Case Study 15

After completing his MBA from the USA, Mr. Vikram Patel returned to India to launch his new enterprise, GreenTech Innovations Pvt. Ltd. The company focuses on developing sustainable energy solutions tailored to the Indian market, which has been experiencing rapid growth in renewable energy demand. Upon entering the market, Mr. Patel encountered several aspects of the business environment that influenced his operations.

The Indian government had recently introduced supportive policies and incentives for renewable energy projects, creating a favourable legal and economic environment. However, the market also faced unpredictable fluctuations due to changing political scenarios and global energy prices. The technology in renewable energy was advancing swiftly and Mr. Patel had to stay updated with the latest innovations to remain competitive.

Moreover, GreenTech Innovations had to navigate through complex regulations and establish relationships with various stakeholders, including investors, local communities and environmental groups. The company also experienced the effects of rising consumer awareness about sustainability, which drove demand for eco-friendly products.

Quoting lines from the above paragraph, identify and explain the three features of the business environment that have been indicated in the case.

Ans. Following are the three features of business environment that have been indicated in the case

(i) **Totality of External Forces**
"The Indian government had recently introduced supportive policies and incentives for renewable energy projects, creating a favourable legal and economic environment."
The business environment is the sum total of external factors, including social, political, economic, legal and technological influences on a business. Business environment is aggregative in nature.

(ii) **Dynamic Nature**
"The technology in renewable energy was advancing swiftly and Mr. Patel had to stay updated with the latest innovations to remain competitive."
Business environment is dynamic in nature as it keeps on changing whether in terms of upgradation of technologies, shifts in consumer preference, entry of new competition in the market, change in government policy or changes in trends and traditions.

(iii) **Complexity**
"GreenTech Innovations had to navigate through complex regulations and establish relationships with various stakeholders, including investors, local communities and environmental groups."
Business environment is complex, as it consists of numerous inter-related and dynamic factors which affects business enterprises at the same time. This makes it difficult to understand at once what exactly constitutes a given environment. Thus, it is easier to understand its components in parts, but difficult to grasp in totality.
e.g. It may be difficult to know the extent of the relative impact of the social, economic, political, technological or legal factors on change in demand of a product in the market.

Case Study 16

Vort Ltd. is a textile manufacturing company based in Jaipur, Rajasthan. Despite having a wide range of products and a skilled workforce, Vort Ltd. is experiencing declining sales compared to its rival, Eclipse Ltd., which operates in Delhi.

Both Vort and Eclipse are influenced by various local factors, such as the availability of raw materials, customer preferences and market competition.

Additionally, both companies are indirectly affected by broader factors like government policies, economic conditions and advancements in textile technology.

(i) Identify and state the feature of the concept discussed in the above paragraph.

(ii) Also, state any four points of importance of this concept.

Ans.

(i) The concept discussed in the case is 'business environment' and the feature is 'relativity'. Business environment is a relative concept as it differs from country to country and region to region.
e.g. Demand for sarees is quite high in India but in foreign countries, it almost has no existence.
Similarly, regulations, government policies, consumers' preference, etc all differ from one region to another.

(ii) For importance, refer to Q.No. 15 of long answer type questions.

Case Study 17

GlobalTech Solutions, a technology company specialising in innovative software solutions, decided to expand its operations into several new international markets. As they ventured into these new territories, they faced a series of challenges related to various aspects of the business environment.

In Country A, the company encountered a complex regulatory landscape. The local government imposed strict regulations concerning data privacy and the use of technology. GlobalTech Solutions had to meticulously comply with these regulations to avoid hefty fines and potential legal issues. Additionally, the political climate in Country A was somewhat unstable, which posed a risk to their business continuity and required careful strategic planning.

In Country B, the social environment played a significant role in shaping the company's approach. The local community highly valued corporate social responsibility and ethical business practices. To gain acceptance and foster goodwill, GlobalTech Solutions decided to invest in local social initiatives.

They supported educational programmes and focused on promoting diversity and inclusion within their workforce, aligning with the societal expectations of the region.

In Country C, the legal framework presented another set of challenges. The country's labour laws were stringent, requiring companies to adhere to comprehensive standards for employment practices. GlobalTech Solutions needed to overhaul their HR policies to meet these requirements, ensuring fair wages, safe working conditions and ample employee benefits. This adaptation was crucial for maintaining compliance and fostering a positive working environment.

Quoting lines from the above paragraph, identify and explain the three key aspects of the business environment that GlobalTech Solutions had to navigate.

Ans. Following are the three key aspects of the business environment that GlobalTech Solutions had to navigate

(i) **Political Environment**

"The local government imposed strict regulations concerning data privacy and the .... political climate in Country A was somewhat unstable, which posed a risk to their business continuity and required careful strategic planning."

Political environment consists of the forces concerning management of public affairs and their impact on business. It includes political conditions like general stability and peace in the country and attitude of the elected government representatives towards businesses and business policy.

e.g. The attitude of government officials toward business may have either positive or negative impact on business. Some of the components political institution, level of political morality, nature and profile of political leadership and thinking of political personalities, political ideology, etc.

(ii) **Social Environment**

"The local community highly valued corporate .... on promoting diversity and inclusion within their workforce."

Social environment refers to the social forces such as customs, traditions, social values, social trend, etc.

e.g. Religious celebrations provide business opportunities to many enterprises such as those producing sweets, decoration items, etc. Similarly, in India a change in social trend towards western lifestyle has increased the demand for western wear, fast food, etc.

(iii) **Legal Environment**

"The country's labour laws were stringent, requiring companies to adhere to .... ensuring fair wages, safe working conditions and ample employee benefits."

It consists of various legislations passed by the government administrative orders issued by government authorities, court judgements as well as the decisions rendered by various commissions and agencies at every level. The advertisement of alcoholic beverages is prohibited. Advertisements of cigarettes carry the statutory warning 'Cigarette smoking is injurious to health'.

Case Study 18

Rakesh and Gaurav after finishing their graduation under vocational stream decided to start their own travel agency which will book Rail Tickets and Air Tickets on commission basis.

They also thought of providing tickets within ten minutes through the use of internet. They discussed the idea with their Professor Mr. Mehta who liked the idea and suggested them to first analyse the business environment which consists of investors', competitors and other forces like social, political etc. that may affect their business directly or indirectly.

He further told them about the technological improvements and shifts in consumer preferences that were taking place and hence they should be aware of the environmental trends and changes which may hinder their business performance.

He emphasised on making plans keeping in mind the threat posed by the competitors, so that they can deal with the situation effectively. This alignment of business operations with the business environment will result in better performance.

(i) Identify and state the component of business environment highlighted in the above para.
(ii) State any two features of business environment as discussed by Professor Mehta with Rakesh and Gaurav.
(iii) Also, state any two points of importance of business environment as stated by Professor Mehta in the above situation.

Ans.

(i) Technological environment is the component of business environment highlighted in the above para. It includes forces relating to scientific improvements and innovations which provide new ways of producing goods and services and new methods and techniques of operating a business.

(ii) The two features of business environment as discussed by Professor Mehta with Rakesh and Gaurav are as follows

- **Dynamic Nature** It is dynamic in nature and keeps on changing due to technological up gradations, shifts in consumer preferences or increase in competition in the market.
- **Inter-relatedness** All the elements of business environment are closely interrelated. Therefore, any change in one element may necessitate corresponding changes in the other elements as well.

(iii) The two points of importance of business environment as stated by Professor Mehta in the above situation are described below

- **It enables the Firm to Identify Opportunities and Getting the First Mover Advantage**
  Opportunities are the positive trends that help firms to improve their performance. A good knowledge of business environment helps a manager to identify such opportunities earlier to take its benefit, rather than losing it to other competing enterprises.

  e.g. Maruti Udyog was the first automobile company in India to recognise the opportunity to develop small cars, due to which, it is still one of the market leaders in that segment.
- **It helps the Firm to Identify Threats and Early Warning Signals**
  Threats refer to the external environment trends and changes, which will hinder the performance of the enterprise.
  Proper knowledge and understanding of the environment helps the managers to identify the possible threats on time and act as an early warning signal.
  e.g. If an Indian firm finds that a foreign MNC is entering the Indian market with new subsititutes, it should act as a warning signal and the Indian firms should prepare themselves to meet the threat by adopting such measures as improving the product quality, reducing production cost and so on.

Case Study 19

The Government of India announced demonetisation of ₹ 500 and ₹ 1,000 currency notes with effect from the midnight of 8th November, 2016. As a result, the existing ₹ 500 and ₹ 1,000 currency notes ceased to be legal tender from that date.

New currency notes of the denomination of ₹ 500 and ₹ 2,000 were issued by Reserve Bank of India after the announcement. This step resulted in a substantial increase in the awareness about and use of Point of Sale machines, e-wallets, digital cash and other modes of cashless transactions. Also, increased transparency in monetary transactions and disclosure led to a rise in government revenue in the form of tax collection. **NCERT**

(i) Enumerate the dimensions of business environment highlighted above.
(ii) State the features of demonetisation.

Ans.

(i) Following are the dimensions of business environment highlighted in the case

- **Political Dimension**
  The government's decision to demonetise currency is a political move aimed at curbing black money and counterfeit currency.
- **Economic Dimension**
  The demonetisation impacted the economy by invalidating a large portion of the currency in circulation, influencing cashless transactions and affecting liquidity.
- **Technological Dimension**
  The increase in awareness and use of Point of Sale machines, e-wallets and digital cash reflects the technological advancements and shifts in payment methods.

(ii) Following are the features of demonetisation

- **Change in Currency**
  Demonetisation is viewed as a tax administration measure. It is the act of removing or discontinuing a currency unit of its legal status by government.
- **Contingent**
  Success or failure of demonetisation is dependent upon various factors.
- **Objective**
  The objective of demonetisation can be curbing corruption, fake currency, illegal activity and making cashless economy. It also aimed to create a less-cash or cash-lite economy, i.e. channelising more savings through the formal financial system and improving tax compliance.
- **Crunches**
  Generally after demonetisation, people face cash crunches for a shorter period.

SELF ASSESSMENT TEST

Objective Type Questions

1. Business environment is ……… as it is difficult to predict the future environment changes and their impact with full accuracy.
   (a) uncertain (b) complex
   (c) simple (d) inter-related
2. ……… forces have impact on all business enterprises.
   (a) General (b) Specific
   (c) Both (a) and (b) (d) None of these
3. Which of the following does not characterise the business environment?
   (a) Uncertainty
   (b) Employees
   (c) Relativity
   (d) Complexity
4. Which of the following is a component of social environment?
   (a) Expectations from the workforce
   (b) Educational system and literacy rates
   (c) Birth and death rates
   (d) All of the above
5. Which of the following components of business environment focus on the nature of the relationship of our country with foreign countries?
   (a) Social environment
   (b) Legal environment
   (c) Political environment
   (d) Economic environment
6. The government has recently implemented a law requiring companies to provide clear labelling of nutritional information on all packaged food products. Which aspect of the business environment is highlighted in the above statement?
   (a) Social environment
   (b) Economic environment
   (c) Legal environment
   (d) Technological environment

Answers 1. (a) 2. (a) 3. (b) 4. (d) 5. (c) 6. (c)

Short Answer Type Questions

7. "Environment provides both constraints and opportunities". Comment.
8. The success of a business largely depends on its ability to understand and adapt to various external factors such as economic policies, technological advancements, social trends and legal regulations. Based on the above statement, explain the concept of business environment and state any three features of it.
9. How first mover advantage is made available by the business environment? Give an example.
10. How do political stability and attitude of government affect business enterprises?
11. Discuss in brief the social environment as the dimension of business environment.
12. In November 2016, the Indian government made a sudden announcement that ₹ 500 and ₹ 1,000 currency notes would no longer be legal tender. Which economic measure is being described in the above statement? Explain its concept briefly.
13. What were the objectives of demonetisation in India?

Long Answer Type Questions

14. Why is the understanding of business environment important for managers? Explain with the help of any four points.
15. The business environment is composed of various dimensions that impact the way companies operate. Based on the above statement, explain any three dimensions of the business environment, providing examples for each.
16. Recently, many companies have planned for major investment in retail business. Increasing incomes, rise in living standards, government policy of liberalisation and its favourable attitude towards modernisation has favoured their decision. Identify the various dimensions of business environment and explain their effect on businesses.

04 CHAPTER

> "Planning is the thinking process, the organised foresight, the vision based on facts and experience that is required for intelligent action." — *Alfred and Beatty*

▼ YOUR STUDY GOALS

▼ YOUR PRACTICE GOAL

- Objective Type Questions (60 Qs ; MCQs, A-R, Statements, Matching)
- Subjective Type Questions (17 SAs, 6 LAs)
- Case Study Based Questions (Short Case Studies-14, Long Case Studies-6)
- Self Assessment (7 MCQs, 6 SAs, 3 LAs)

Planning

4.1 Concept of Planning

Planning is deciding in advance what is to be done, when it is to be and by whom it is to be done. It bridges the gap between where we are and where we want to go.

Planning can be defined as setting objectives to be achieved during a given period, formulating alternative courses of action to achieve them and selecting the best possible alternative from among the various courses of action available.

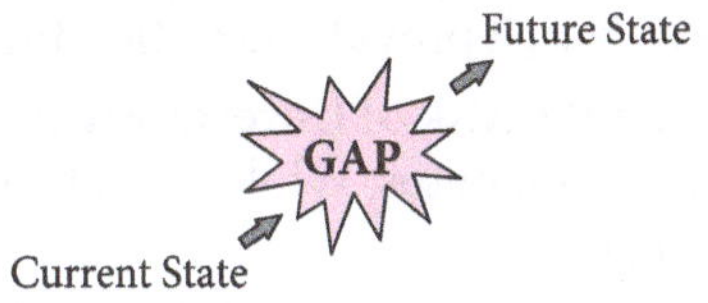

Features of Planning

Following are the features of planning

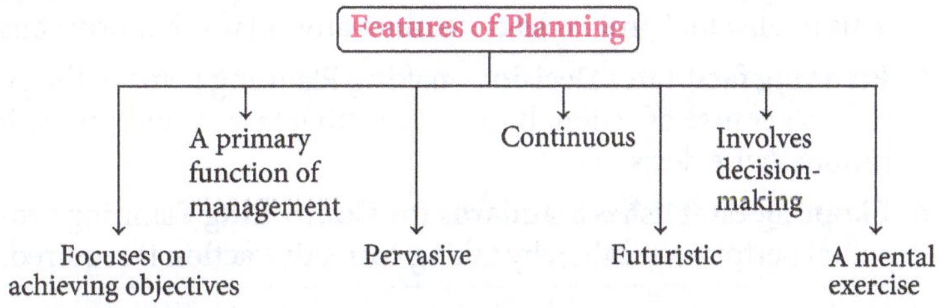

1. **Planning focuses on Achieving Objectives** Every organisation is set-up with a predetermined purpose or goal to achieve. Planning helps to set out specific goals and activities to be undertaken to achieve them.

2. **Planning is a Primary Function of Management** It lays down the base for all other functions of management. Thus, it can be said that planning precedes other functions. This is also referred to as the primacy of planning.
3. **Planning is Pervasive** It is required at all levels of management as well as in all the departments of the organisation.
4. **Planning is Continuous** Plans are made for a specific time period. At the end of such time period, new plans have to be drawn. Also, planning is required to be modified according to the changing requirements and future conditions.
5. **Planning is Futuristic** Planning involves looking ahead, analysing and predicting future events to prepare effectively. Thus, it is regarded as a forward looking function based on forecasting.
6. **Planning involves Decision-making** Planning requires choosing from among various alternatives and presupposes their existence.
7. **Planning is a Mental Exercise** Planning is a mental process requiring foresight, creativity, imagination and logical thinking, rather than doing as it determines the action to be taken.

4.2 Importance of Planning

Planning is certainly important as it tells us where to go.

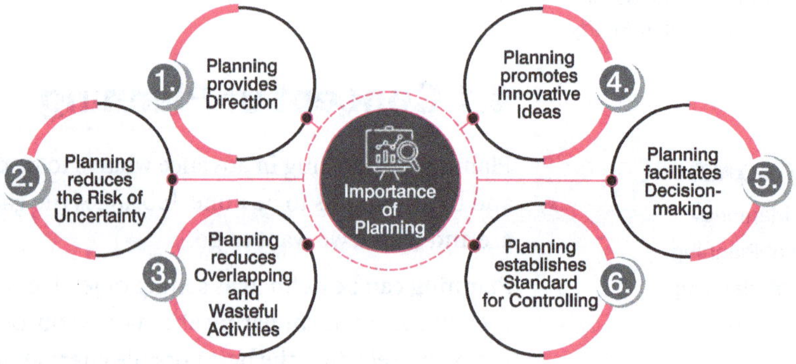

1. **Planning provides Direction** Planning states in advance how work is to be done, defining tasks, timelines and responsibilities. Thus, it provides direction for action.
2. **Planning reduces the Risk of Uncertainty** Planning allows managers to anticipate changes and uncertainties, enabling proactive responses. While it can't eliminate risks altogether, it prepares the organisation to handle potential challenges.
3. **Planning reduces Overlapping and Wasteful Activities** Planning coordinates activities across divisions and departments, eliminating redundant and wasteful actions. It also helps to identify inefficiencies and implement corrective measures to deal with them.
4. **Planning promotes Innovative Ideas** Planning involves generating new ideas through creativity and foresight. This intellectual process leads to innovative plans that drive business growth and success.
5. **Planning facilitates Decision-making** Planning helps in the evaluation of various alternatives and then choosing the best course of action. It involves setting targets and predicting future conditions which helps in taking rational/wise decisions.
6. **Planning establishes Standards for Controlling** Planning provides the standards which helps in measurement of actual performance thereby taking corrective action if required. Thus, it provides the basis of control.

Planning Importance

When opening a new cafe, the team plans each step i.e. menu design, supplier choice and marketing, to avoid overlapping tasks. They anticipate risks like supplier delays and plan accordingly. This planning encourages creative ideas, such as a unique cafe theme, helps in deciding the best location and sets standards like tracking customer reviews to measure success.

4.3 Limitations of Planning

Planning has both internal and external limitations

Limitation	Meaning
I. Internal	
Planning leads to Rigidity	Specific plans set clear objectives and timelines, potentially limiting flexibility. Adhering to rigid plans despite changing circumstances can harm organisational interests.
Planning may not Work in a Dynamic Environment	The business environment is dynamic, involving economic, political, physical, legal and social dimensions. Adapting to constant changes makes it challenging to predict future trends accurately. Planning cannot foresee everything and there may be obstacles to effective planning.
Planning reduces Creativity	Top management makes plans while others merely implement them, limiting initiative and creativity. This lack of flexibility can lead to a lack of innovation and there will be nothing new or innovative in the organisation.
Planning involves Huge Costs	Formulating plans requires significant time, effort and expense. Costs for data collection, meetings and expert consultations may not always justify the benefits.
Planning is a Time Consuming Process	Drawing up plans can consume so much time that there's little left for implementation, often leading to planning failures.
Planning does not Guarantee Success	Plans must be effectively implemented to succeed. Relying on past tested successful plans may create a false sense of security and may lead to failure.
II. External	
Unforeseen Events	Nature calamities like floods, earthquakes, etc. are beyond the control of managers and may cause failure of plans.
Change in Government Policy	Industrial or economic policy of government can impact business activities and lead to failure of planning.
Environmental Changes	Changes in social, economic, legal and technological environment may also affect forecasting and planning.
Competitors' Strategy	Change in the strategy of competitor may lead to failure in planning.
Change in Consumers Preference	Unexpected change in taste, fashion and preferences of customers may cause failure of plans.

4.4 Process of Planning

The planning process involves a sequence of certain logical steps performed by managers.

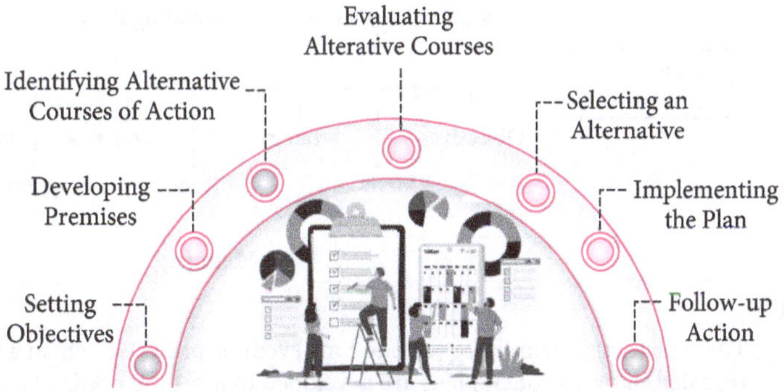

Planning Process

1. **Setting Objectives** Every organisation has certain objectives which specify what the organisation wants to achieve. Objectives should be achievable, they should not be too high or too low. They should be stated clearly for all departments, units and employees.

2. **Developing Premises** Premises are the assumptions that we make today about the future. Premises are the base on which plans are made and may be in the form of forecasts, existing plans or any past information about policies.
3. **Identifying Alternative Courses of Action** Once the objectives are set and assumptions are made, the next step would be to act upon them. The managers should make a list of alternatives through which an organisation can achieve its objectives. The course of action which may be taken could be either routine or innovative.
4. **Evaluating Alternative Courses** After making the list of various alternatives, the next step is to weigh the pros and cons of each alternative. All alternatives should be evaluated in the light of their feasibility and consequences.
5. **Selecting an Alternative** This is the real point of decision-making. A plan has to be adopted and implemented which is the most feasible, profitable and has the least negative consequences.
6. **Implementing the Plan** This step is concerned with putting the plan into action i.e. doing what is required. This is the step where other managerial functions come into existence.
7. **Follow-up Action** It is equally important to see whether the plans are being implemented and activities are performed according to the schedule. It helps to verify whether the predictions are holding true or not.

Planning Process

To launch a new energy drink, a company first sets the objective of capturing 10% of the market within six months. They base their plans on the assumption that consumer interest in health drinks will rise. They explore alternatives such as unique flavours, organic ingredients or a budget-friendly version.

After evaluating, they decide on a unique flavour strategy to stand out. They implement this plan by developing the product, marketing it aggressively and then monitor sales and feedback to ensure that it meets their target.

4.5 Plan

A plan is a specific action proposed to help the organisation in achieving its objective.

Types of Plan

Plans can be classified on the following basis

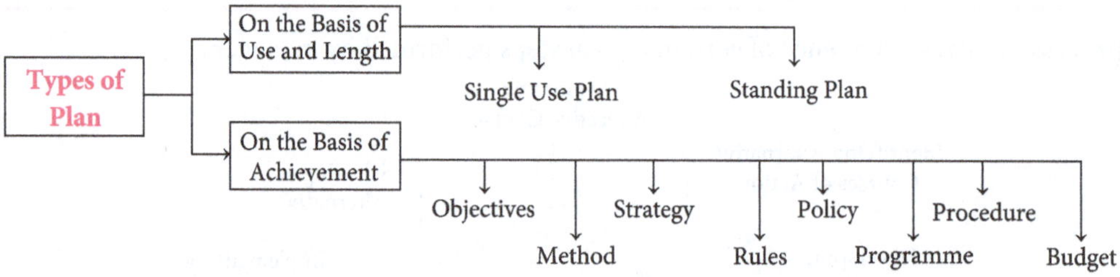

Type	Meaning
I. On the Basis of Use and Length	
Single Use Plan	These plans are formulated for one time event or project. Such an action is not expected to be repeated in future. Such plans are developed to meet the needs of a unique situation. Types of such plans are budgets and programmes. It is also known as specific plan.
Standing Plan	These plans are formed for the activities which occur regularly over a period of time. It is formed, so the operations of the organisation can run smoothly. Types of such plans are policies, procedures, methods and rules. It is also known as repeated use plan.

Type	Meaning
II. On the Basis of Achievement	
Objectives	Objectives are the desired future position that an organisation aims to achieve. Set by top management, they guide all managerial activities and overall planning. They should be specific and measurable, such as a 10% increase in sales or a 15% rise in profits.
Strategy	It is a comprehensive plan for achieving organisational goals by setting long-term objectives, adopting particular course of action and allocating resources. It serves as a blueprint, outlining the organisation's direction and scope and is formulated considering the environmental changes. Major strategic decisions involve whether to stay in the current business, add new activities or seek market dominance.
Policy (Standing Plan)	It is a general statement guiding responses to specific problems or situations, with major policies visible to all stakeholders and minor policies for internal use. Policies are based on organisational objectives and provide a framework for interpreting strategy. They define the broad parameters within which a manager may function.
Procedure (Standing Plan)	It outlines the specific sequence of steps for performing an activity, addressing routine problems and executing policies. Procedures are detailed steps, meant for internal use and align with broader policy frameworks to achieve objectives.
Method (Standing Plan)	It describes standardised ways to perform specific tasks, often part of a procedure. Methods are formalised to accomplish repetitive and routine jobs efficiently, varying by task and helps to save time and resources.
Rule (Standing Plan)	Rules are strict, specific directives or statement on what must be done, with no flexibility allowed. They represent firm managerial decisions and are the simplest form of plans, requiring strict adherence.
Programme (Single Use Plan)	Programmes are comprehensive plans detailing objectives, policies, procedures, rules and budgets for a specific project. They cover all aspects of the project within a broad policy framework.
Budget (Single Use Plan)	A budget projects expected results and costs in numerical terms for a project. It quantifies future facts and figures in numbers which makes it easier to compares actual figures with expected figures and take corrective actions.

Types of Plan

Imagine a bakery, "Sweet Treats," aiming to boost sales. The owner sets an *objective* to increase sales by 10% in one year. To achieve this, they create a *strategic* plan outlining steps like introducing new flavours and launching a marketing campaign.

They also develop *policies* for staff, such as maintaining high-quality ingredients. *Procedures* are established for daily operations, like the exact recipe for each cake.

Methods are used to ensure tasks like frosting are done consistently. *Rules* dictate that all cakes must be decorated within 30 minutes.

A programme might be created for a special holiday promotion, detailing every step from planning to execution. Finally, the bakery prepares a budget to estimate the costs of new ingredients and expected sales.

Mind Map

PLANNING

1 Concept of Planning

Planning is deciding in advance what is to be done, when it is to be done, how it is to be done and by whom it is to be done.

2 Features of Planning

- Planning focuses on achieving objectives
- Planning is a primary function of management
- Planning is pervasive
- Planning is continuous
- Planning is futuristic
- Planning involves decision-making
- Planning is a mental exercise

3 Importance of Planning

- Planning provides direction
- Planning reduces the risk of uncertainty
- Planning reduces overlapping and wasteful activities
- Planning promotes innovative ideas
- Planning facilitates decision-making
- Planning establishes standards for controlling

4 Limitations of Planning

Internal Limitations

- Planning leads to rigidity
- Planning may not work in a dynamic environment
- Planning reduces creativity
- Planning involves huge costs
- Planning is a time consuming process
- Planning does not guarantee success

External Limitations

- Unforeseen events (Natural calamities like floods, earthquakes, etc.)
- Change in government policy (This includes industrial or economic policy)
- Environmental changes (Changes in social, economic, political environment)
- Competitor's strategy (This involves failure of planning due to change in competitor's strategy)
- Change in consumer preference (Changes in taste, fashion, preference of consumers)

5 Process of Planning

- **Setting Objectives** Objectives are set for organisation and departments
- **Developing Premises** Premises are the base upon which plans are drawn
- **Identifying Alternative Courses of Action** It involves discovering the various courses of action
- **Evaluating Alternative Courses** It involves weighing the pros and cons of each alternative
- **Selecting an Alternative** It involves selecting the best profitable and feasible plan
- **Implement the Plan** It involves putting the plan into action
- **Follow-up Action** It involves following up the plan to see whether the plans are properly implemented and are as per the schedule

6 Types of Plan

A plan is a specific action proposed to help the organisation in achieving its objective.

On the Basis of Achievement

- **Budget** It is statement of expected results expressed in numerical terms
- **Programme** These are detailed statements about a project
- **Objective** Desired future position that an organisation seeks to achieve
- **Strategy** It is a comprehensive plan and includes dimensions for attaining goals
- **Policy** General statement that guides thinking or channelise energies towards a particular direction
- **Rule** Specific statements that inform what is to be done
- **Method** Provides the prescribed ways or manner in which a task has to be performed
- **Procedure** Describes the exact manner in which a certain activity is to be performed

On the Basis of Use and Length

- **Single-use Plan** It is formulated to achieve a specific target or for a one-time event
- **Standing Plan** It is formulated by companies to deal with situations that occur regularly over a period of time

EXAM PATTERN QUESTIONS

Objective Type Questions

Multiple Choice Questions (MCQs)

1. **"Planning involves looking ahead, analysing and predicting future events to prepare effectively."**

Identify the feature of planning discussed in the above statement. **Competency Based Que**

(a) Planning is continuous
(b) Planning is futuristic
(c) Planning is pervasive
(d) Planning is a mental exercise

2. **Which of the following statements is incorrect?**

(a) Planning is an exclusive function of top management
(b) If there are no alternatives, there is no need for planning function of management
(c) Planning helps in maintaining cooperation between different departments, divisions and individuals
(d) Planning is closely connected with creativity and innovation

3. **......... is the essence of planning.**

(a) Forecasting (b) Controlling
(c) Staffing (d) Organising

4. **Which of the following statements is incorrect?**

(a) Planning is a pre-requisite for controlling
(b) Planning does not lead to rigidity
(c) Planning enables a manager to look ahead and anticipate changes
(d) Planning facilitates coordination among departments and individuals in the organisation

5. **"Organisations aim to increase their sales and earn profits to be successful. All managers dream of this. Managers need to work hard in thinking about future, in making predictions and achieving business targets."**

The above lines describe one of the functions of management. Identify that function. **Competency Based Que**

(a) Planning (b) Organising
(c) Staffing (d) Directing

6. **Plans are prepared for a specific period of time, may be for a month, a quarter or a year. At the end of that period, there is a need for a new plan to be drawn on the basis of new requirements and future conditions.**

The feature of planning reflected in the above lines is **CBSE 2024; Competency Based Que**

(a) planning is futuristic
(b) planning is continuous
(c) planning is pervasive
(d) planning is a mental exercise

7. **XYZ Ltd. is a leading electronics company that has set ambitious targets for the upcoming year. The company aims to achieve a 20% increase in market share by introducing new product lines and expanding its presence in untapped markets. These targets have been set by the top management and are intended to guide the company's strategic planning and operational activities.**

Every department has been instructed to align their efforts with this goal, which is expected to be specific, measurable and time-bound.

Which feature of planning is highlighted in the case of XYZ Ltd.? **Competency Based Que**

(a) Planning is pervasive
(b) Planning is futuristic
(c) Planning focuses on achieving objectives
(d) Planning reduces risk

8. **Identify the feature of planning from the picture below in which top level managers are discussing about their next project.**

(a) Planning is pervasive
(b) Planning is continuous
(c) Planning involves decision-making
(d) Planning is a mental exercise

9. **Which of the following statements is incorrect?**

(a) Planning focuses on achieving objectives
(b) Planning is required at all levels of management
(c) Planning reduces the risk of uncertainty
(d) Planning eliminates the need for making future decisions

10. **Nihar Naturals Ltd. is a renowned Indian company known for its range of herbal skincare products. The company had set a goal to launch a new line of herbal sunscreen lotions and capture a 35% market share by the end of the financial year. However, midway through the year, a global health crisis led to an unexpected shift in consumer priorities towards basic hygiene products rather than skincare.**

As a result, despite their meticulous planning and heavy investments in marketing and production, the sales of the new sunscreen line were much lower than anticipated, causing the market share to drop to 20%.

Identify the limitation of planning highlighted in the above case. **Competency Based Que**

(a) Planning may not work in dynamic environment
(b) Planning is time consuming
(c) Planning involves huge costs
(d) Planning reduces overlapping and wasteful activities

11. **Mr. Kapil, an educationist found that the teachers have to travel long to attend the workshops and they lose the opportunity to gain the knowledge on updates. He listed various alternatives and finally developed an app which could work on mobile and laptops to launch online sessions.**

Suggest which next step should he follow? **Competency Based Que**

(a) Developing premises
(b) Identifying that alternatives course of action
(c) Implementation of plan
(d) Follow-up action

12. **Which step in the process of 'planning' function of management involves weighing pros and cons of each alternative?**

(a) Developing premises
(b) Identifying alternative courses of action
(c) Evaluating alternative courses
(d) Selecting an alternative

13. **Name the most critical step in the process of planning.**

(a) Implementing the plan
(b) Developing the plan
(c) Selecting the best possible course of action
(d) None of the above

14. **Priya Sharma has launched a handcrafted jewelry brand, 'Glimmer & Shine,' in Mumbai. She primarily sells her products through social media platforms and aims to expand her customer base across the city. Priya set a goal to achieve a profit of ₹ 3,00,000 in the first six months. She shared this objective with her team and encouraged them to brainstorm strategies to reach the target.**

Priya Sharma has completed the initial step in the process of one of the management functions. The next step to be undertaken is **Competency Based Que**

(a) identifying alternative courses of action
(b) setting objectives
(c) developing premises
(d) follow-up action

15. **……… is not a standing plan.**

(a) Policy
(b) Procedure
(c) Programme
(d) Rule

16. **Identify the type of plan indicated in the below picture.**

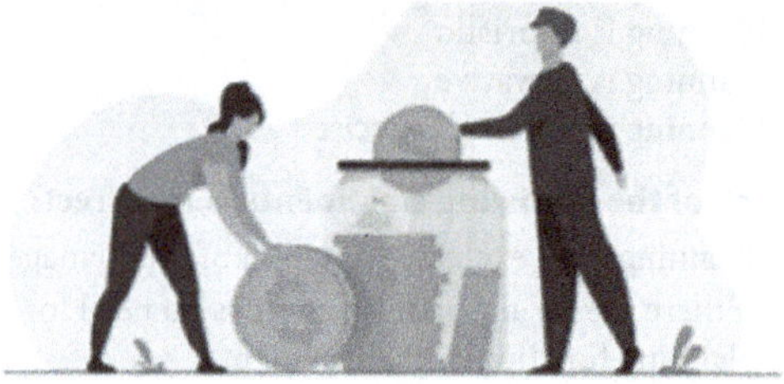

(a) Method (b) Rule
(c) Policy (d) Budget

17. **Micromax was India's largest seller of mobile handsets. It launched low-cost Chinese manufacturing with some smart packaging and features like long-lasting batteries and dual-sim functionality to garner 20% market share in India's value-conscious mobile handset market.**

Identify the two types of plans being described in the above lines. **Competency Based Que**

(a) Strategy and objective
(b) Rule and programme
(c) Programme and objective
(d) Method and objective

18. **According to a survey, these days the young children have more power in purchasing decisions than ever before. The parents seek their kids' opinions about all kinds of once-adult decisions, including where to go for dinner, what kind of car to buy, even what to wear.**

Therefore, the retailers are adapting to this by enhancing their kids' sections. If the children want to shop in the store for their clothes, then there's a greater chance the parent will also see something they want to buy as well.

Identify the type of plan being described in the above lines. **Competency Based Que**

(a) Programme
(b) Method
(c) Strategy
(d) Rule

19. The government has been doubling down on its efforts to switch to 100% electric vehicles by 2030. Many companies such as Tata Motors, Kinetic Motors, Maruti Suzuki and Hyundai Motors are all readying their EV models for a 2020 launch in order to support the plan.

Identify the type of plan being described in the above lines. **Competency Based Que**

(a) Method (b) Strategy
(c) Programme (d) Objective

20. Rama Stationery Mart has made a decision to make all the payments by e-transfers only. Identify the type of plan adopted by Rama Stationery Mart. **NCERT Modified**

(a) Policy (b) Programme
(c) Method (d) Rule

21. .... is usually the simplest type of plan as there is no compromise unless a policy decision is taken.

(a) Programme (b) Policy
(c) Method (d) Rule

22. A company having 'No smoking' as shown below, is an example of which type of plan?

(a) Rule (b) Policy
(c) Objective (d) Method

23. Identify the type of plan illustrated in the given picture.

(a) Budget (b) Method
(c) Rule (d) Programme

24. To meet the increased demand of internet due to online classes all over the world, the Indian companies decided to use 5G network. This is an example of which type of plan?

(a) Policy (b) Strategy
(c) Programme (d) Objective

25. Identify the type of plan depicted in the picture.

(a) Policy (b) Rule
(c) Budget (d) Programme

26. Kavi works as a marketing manager in stationery mart. It deals in various types of stationery items for many schools across the country. When new session starts in schools, Kavi forecasts the sales of different stationery products for each school for every month. All items are represented in numbers so that it becomes easier for him to compare the actual sales with expected sales.

The type of plan discussed above is

CBSE 2025; Competency Based Que

(a) strategy (b) policy
(c) programme (d) budget

27. ABC Corp. a global manufacturing company, has formulated a detailed plan to achieve its long-term growth. The top management has decided to expand into international markets and diversify its product line to include eco-friendly products. This plan outlines specific goals for the next five years and allocates significant resources for research, marketing and production.

The management has also considered the impact of global environmental regulations and market trends while developing this plan. The plan serves as a blueprint for the company's future direction and key decisions on whether to remain in the current business or expand.

Which type of plan is ABC Corp. implementing?

Competency Based Que

(a) Policy
(b) Strategy
(c) Procedure
(d) Method

28. Reena Lahoti after completing her fashion designing course from NIFT planned to enter into designer clothing venture. She had to address issues like her target customers, channel of distribution to be used, pricing policy, etc. Identify the type of plan that Reena needs to develop to provide direction and scope to her organisation in the long-run. **Competency Based Que**

(a) Policy (b) Method
(c) Strategy (d) Objective

29. **At Zenith Enterprises, employees are required to adhere strictly to certain workplace guidelines. For instance, all employees must wear safety helmets in the production area at all times. Failure to comply with this directive results in immediate disciplinary action, with no exceptions. This strict guideline is non-negotiable and must be followed by every employee, ensuring workplace safety and preventing accidents.**

What type of plan is being followed by Zenith Enterprises in the above case? **Competency Based Que**

(a) Policy (b) Method (c) Rule (d) Procedure

30. **The basic role of strategy is to provide**

(a) setting procedures (b) direction for action
(c) direction for motivation (d) direction for control

31. **In T-pex Ltd, a company trading in stationery items, it was decided that all purchases would be made from AK Ltd. on credit basis with credit period of at least 7 days. This was done because no other company was offering credit facility. Which type of plan has been referred to in the above paragraph?** **CBSE 2024 C**

(a) Rule (b) Policy
(c) Method (d) Strategy

Direction *Read the following case study and answer the questions 32 to 35 on the basis of the same*

Verma Limited had been taken over by Gupta Group immediately following India's independence. Since then it enjoys a rich record of industry presence and experience. In 2005, with the aim to accelerate growth, the company had gone through several rounds of meetings and discussions before launching ERP system to attract large projects.

The management had done effective forecast and critical thinking regarding allocation resources to reduce wastage. For this purpose, the company had laid down multiple courses of action to meet the challenge of adverse situations.

In 2008, the company suffered loss in many projects due to the great recession despite taking many cost cutting measures. The management had taken utmost care regarding the possible outcome and timely review of the plans to achieve the set target during that hard time.

In 2010, the system implemented successfully which subsequently helped the company to execute numerous projects with precision and timeliness.

32. **"In 2005, with the aim to accelerate growth, the company had gone through several rounds of meetings and discussions." What is the objective mentioned here according to the process stated here?**

(a) Developing premises (b) Growth and development
(c) Launching IT enabled system
(d) Cost cutting

33. **"In 2008, the company suffered loss in many projects due to the great recession despite taking many cost cutting measures." Which limitation of the management process is indicated here?**

(a) It fails to cope with sudden changes
(b) It involves huge cost
(c) It requires critical thinking
(d) Economic environment

34. **Verma Limited implemented an ERP system in 2010 after going through several rounds of discussions and forecasts.**
This was part of their planning process aimed at accelerating growth and improving project execution. Which of the following aspects of planning is most evident from Verma Limited's approach?

(a) Planning is a continuous process
(b) Planning is a mental exercise
(c) Planning involves decision-making
(d) Planning is a primary function of management

35. **"The management had taken utmost care regarding the possible outcome and timely review of the plans to achieve the set target during that hard time." Which is the last step of the process mentioned here?**

(a) Implementation of plan
(b) Timely execution of projects
(c) Follow-up
(d) To prepare alternative course of action

Assertion-Reason

Direction (Q.No. 36 to 45) *Read the following Assertion (A) and Reason (R) and choose the correct alternative from the following*

Alternatives

(a) Both Assertion (A) and Reason (R) are true and Reason (R) is the correct explanation of Assertion (A)
(b) Both Assertion (A) and Reason (R) are true, but Reason (R) is not the correct explanation of Assertion (A)
(c) Assertion (A) is true, but Reason (R) is false
(d) Assertion (A) is false, but Reason (R) is true

36. **Assertion** (A) Planning is a primary function of management that lays the foundation for all other management functions.

Reason (R) Planning occurs after organising, leading and controlling functions.

37. **Assertion** (A) Planning involves setting objectives and selecting the most appropriate course of action.

Reason (R) Objectives should be flexible and not specific.

38. **Assertion** (A) Planning involves looking ahead and preparing for the future.

Reason (R) The purpose of planning is to meet future events effectively to the best advantage of an organisation.

CBSE 2025

39. **Assertion** (A) Planning is futuristic.

Reason (R) Planning is concerned with the future which is certain and does not require forecast.

40. **Assertion** (A) Planning provides the base for controlling.

Reason (R) Planning establishes the standards against which the actual performance is evaluated.

41. **Assertion** (A) Planning is pervasive.

Reason (R) Planning is required at all levels and in all departments of the organisation.

42. **Assertion** (A) Planning is a choice making activity.

Reason (R) Planning involves selecting the best alternative out of various available options.

43. **Assertion** (A) Planning increases the risk of uncertainty.

Reason (R) Planning is an activity which enables a manager to look ahead and anticipate changes.

44. **Assertion** (A) Forecasting is important in developing premises.

Reason (R) Forecasting is a technique of gathering information.

45. **Assertion** (A) Planning helps in avoiding confusion and misunderstanding.

Reason (R) Planning ensures clarity in thoughts and action, work is carried on smoothly without interruptions.

Two Statements Based MCQs

Direction (Q.No. 46 to 55) *Read the following statements carefully and choose the correct alternative*

Alternatives

(a) Statement I is correct and Statement II is incorrect
(b) Statement II is correct and Statement I is incorrect
(c) Both the statements are correct
(d) Both the statements are incorrect

46. **Statement I** Planning focuses on achieving organisational objectives through detailed and specific steps.

Statement II Planning is a one time activity that does not need to be revisited once established.

47. **Statement I** Planning is only required at the top level of management.

Statement II Planning is a pervasive function that is required at all levels of management.

48. **Statement I** Planning can reduce overlapping and redundancy in organisational activities.

Statement II Planning typically creates inefficiencies and redundancies.

49. **Statement I** Plans are static and do not need modifications once they are created.

Statement II Planning is continuous and may require modifications according to changing needs.

50. **Statement I** Planning works perfectly in a dynamic environment.

Statement II Planning guarantee success for an organisation.

51. **Statement I** Planning requires application of the mind involving foresight, intelligent, imagination and sound judgement.

Statement II Monitoring the plans is equally important to ensure that objectives are achieved.

52. **Statement I** Planning seeks to bridge the gap between where we are and where we want to go.

Statement II Planning is basically an intellectual activity of thinking.

53. **Statement I** Single use plans are designed for events or projects that are expected to recur in the future.

Statement II Single use plans are formulated for unique, one time events or projects.

54. **Statement I** Standing plans are used for activities that are recurring and ongoing.

Statement II Standing plans are formulated for one time projects or events.

55. **Statement I** Procedure is an example of single use plan.

Statement II Objectives should be measurable in qualitative terms.

Matching

56. **Match the importance of planning in Column I with their respective statements in Column II**

Column I	Column II
A. Planning provides direction.	(i) Planning shows the ways to deal with changes.
B. Planning establishes standard for controlling.	(ii) Planning helps in avoiding confusions and misunderstanding.
C. Planning reduces the risk of uncertainty.	(iii) Planning clarifies how work is to be done.
D. Planning reduces overlapping and wasteful activities.	(iv) Planning provides the basis for controlling.

Codes

	A	B	C	D
(a)	(ii)	(i)	(iii)	(iv)
(b)	(iii)	(iv)	(i)	(ii)
(c)	(i)	(iii)	(iv)	(ii)
(d)	(ii)	(i)	(iv)	(iii)

57. **Match the limitations of planning in Column I with their respective statements in Column II**

Column I	Column II
A. Planning leads to rigidity	(i) Usually, managers rely on previously tried and tested successfully plans.
B. Planning reduces creativity	(ii) Plans are drawn by top management and rest of the members just implement them.
C. Planning does not guarantee success	(iii) Detailed plans require scientific calculations to ascertain facts and figures.
D. Planning involves huge costs	(iv) Managers are not in a position to change planning.

Codes

	A	B	C	D
(a)	(iv)	(ii)	(i)	(iii)
(b)	(ii)	(iii)	(i)	(iv)
(c)	(i)	(iii)	(iv)	(ii)
(d)	(ii)	(i)	(iv)	(iii)

58. **Match the various stages of planning process in Column I with their respective statements in Column II**

Column I	Column II
A. Selecting an alternative	(i) This is the point of real decision making.
B. Evaluating alternative course	(ii) At this stage, pros and cons of each alternative is to be analysed.
C. Setting objectives	(iii) Assumptions are the base material upon which plans are to be drawn.
D. Developing premises	(iv) It is the first and foremost step of planning process.

Codes

	A	B	C	D		A	B	C	D
(a)	(iii)	(i)	(ii)	(iv)	(b)	(iii)	(ii)	(i)	(iv)
(c)	(i)	(iii)	(iv)	(ii)	(d)	(i)	(ii)	(iv)	(iii)

59. **Match the following**

Column I	Column II
A. Comprehensive plan to achieve objective	(i) Policy
B. Strategy and objective	(ii) Strategy
C. Provides basis for interpreting strategies	(iii) Procedure
D. Exact manner how work is to be performed	(iv) Neither single use nor standing plans

Codes

	A	B	C	D		A	B	C	D
(a)	(ii)	(i)	(iii)	(iv)	(b)	(ii)	(iv)	(i)	(iii)
(c)	(ii)	(iii)	(iv)	(i)	(d)	(i)	(ii)	(iv)	(iii)

60. **Match the following**

Column I	Column II
A. Reporting progress in production	(i) Objective
B. Reporting for work at a particular time	(ii) Strategy
C. Guide for overall planning	(iii) Rule
D. General plan prepared by top management outliving resource allocation	(iv) Procedure

Codes

	A	B	C	D		A	B	C	D
(a)	(iii)	(i)	(ii)	(iv)	(b)	(iii)	(iv)	(i)	(ii)
(c)	(ii)	(iii)	(iv)	(i)	(d)	(iv)	(iii)	(i)	(ii)

Answers

1. (b) Planning is futuristic
2. (c) Planning helps in maintaining coordination.
3. (a) Forecasting
4. (b) Planning leads to rigidity because of already developed plans
5. (a) Planning
6. (b) planning is continuous
7. (c) Planning focuses on achieving objectives
8. (d) Planning is a mental exercise
9. (d) Planning does not eliminate the need for making future decisions; rather, it provides a framework for making them.
10. (a) Planning may not work in dynamic environment
11. (c) Implementation of plan
12. (c) Evaluating alternative courses
13. (c) Selecting the best possible course of action
14. (c) developing premises
15. (c) Programme
16. (d) Budget
17. (a) Strategy and objective
18. (c) Strategy
19. (b) Strategy
20. (a) Policy
21. (d) Rule
22. (a) Rule
23. (a) Budget
24. (d) Objective
25. (a) Policy
26. (d) Budget
27. (b) Strategy
28. (c) Strategy
29. (c) Rule
30. (b) direction for action
31. (b) Policy
32. (b) Growth and development
33. (a) It fails to cope with sudden changes
34. (a) Planning is a continuous process
35. (c) Follow-up
36. (c) Planning is indeed a primary function of management, but it precedes other functions, not follows them.
37. (c) Planning involves setting specific objectives and selecting courses of action, objectives should be specific and measurable.
38. (a) Both Assertion (A) and Reason (R) are true and Reason (R) is the correct explanation of Assertion (A)
39. (c) Planning indeed focuses on the future, but the future is uncertain and planning involves forecasting to deal with this uncertainty.
40. (a) Both Assertion (A) and Reason (R) are true and Reason (R) is the correct explanation of Assertion (A)
41. (a) Both Assertion (A) and Reason (R) are true and Reason (R) is the correct explanation of Assertion (A)
42. (a) Both Assertion (A) and Reason (R) are true and Reason (R) is the correct explanation of Assertion (A)
43. (d) Planning actually helps to reduce the risk of uncertainty by allowing managers to anticipate potential changes and prepare for them.
44. (a) Both Assertion (A) and Reason (R) are true and Reason (R) is the correct explanation of Assertion (A)
45. (a) Both Assertion (A) and Reason (R) are true and Reason (R) is the correct explanation of Assertion (A)
46. (a) Planning is indeed focused on achieving objectives and is not a one time activity; it requires ongoing revision and adjustment.
47. (b) Planning is required at all levels of management, not just at the top level.
48. (a) Effective planning reduces overlapping and redundancy rather than creating it.
49. (b) Planning is a continuous process and requires modifications to adapt to changes.
50. (d) Planning is often challenging in a dynamic environment because of the frequent changes and unpredictability. Planning does not guarantee success; it only provides a framework and direction.
51. (c) Both the statements are correct
52. (c) Both the statements are correct
53. (b) Single use plans are intended for unique, one time events, not recurring ones.
54. (a) Standing plans are designed for recurring activities, not one time events.
55. (d) A procedure is a standing plan, not a single use plan. It is used repeatedly to guide actions in recurring situations. Objectives should be measurable, but they are typically quantified in numerical or quantitative terms rather than qualitative terms.
56. (b) (iii) (iv) (i) (ii)
57. (a) (iv) (ii) (i) (iii)
58. (d) (i) (ii) (iv) (iii)
59. (b) (ii) (iv) (i) (iii)
60. (d) (iv) (iii) (i) (ii)

Subjective Questions

Short Answer Type Questions

1. "Planning is an important function of management." In the light of the given statement, define planning and state any four features of planning.

Ans. Planning is deciding in advance what to do, how to do it, when and who is to do it. It is the process of thinking before doing.

Following are the features of planning

(i) **Planning is Goal-oriented**
Planning seeks to achieve certain objectives and all plans are linked with the goals of the organisation. Planning identifies the action that would lead to the desired results quickly and economically.

(ii) **Planning is a Primary Function**
Planning serves as the basis for all other functions of management. It precedes organising, staffing, directing and controlling. All these functions are performed within the framework of plans.

(iii) **Planning is Pervasive**
Planning is required at all levels of management as well as in all departments of the organisation. It is not only for top management, but it differs at different levels and among different departments.

(iv) **Planning involves Decision-making**
The need of planning arises because of the availability of various alternatives to achieve specified objectives. It considers or evaluates the various alternatives to find out the best choice which serves the purpose. Thus, planning involves decision-making.

2. Briefly explain the following characteristics of planning
(i) Planning is futuristic
(ii) Planning is a mental exercise

Ans.

(i) **Planning is Futuristic**
It is essentially looking ahead and preparing for the future. It implies looking into the future, analysing it and predicting it to meet future events effectively. Therefore, planning is regarded as a forward looking function based on forecasting. Through forecasting, future events are anticipated and plans are drawn accordingly.

(ii) **Planning is a Mental Exercise**
It is a mental exercise as it requires foresight, creativity, imagination and higher thinking skills with sound judgement. It is an intellectual activity of thinking rather than doing as it determines the action to be taken.

3. Briefly discuss the following significance of planning
(i) Planning establishes standards for controlling
(ii) Planning provides direction

Ans.

(i) **Planning establishes Standards for Controlling**
Planning provides the standards against which actual performance is measured. By comparing actual performance with standards, managers can know whether they have actually been able to attain the goals or not.

(ii) **Planning provides Direction**
By stating in advance how work is to be done, planning provides direction for action. It clearly defines what the employees have to do, when to do, how to do and for whom to do.

When employees are aware of what they have to do, departments and individuals are able to work in coordination.

4. "Planning leads to increased efficiency." Justify.
Competency Based Que

Ans. Planning determines in advance, what is to be done in future. It helps us in knowing as to what we will have to perform in order to achieve the objectives. Various activities of different departments and divisions are carried out in an effective manner, thereby, reducing overlapping and wasteful activities.
It results in timely completion of motives, reduces wastage and leads to increase in efficiency.

5. "Planning reduces creativity." Critically comment.
NCERT; Competency Based Que

Ans. No doubt, planning reduces creativity, but at the same time it promotes innovative ideas too.

(i) **Planning promotes Innovative Ideas**
- While planning selects the best alternative out of many, many new ideas emerge.
- Since planning is the first function of management new ideas can take the shape of concrete plans.

(ii) **Planning reduces Creativity**
- Plans are drawn by the top management and rest of the members just implement them.
- They are neither allowed to deviate from plans nor are permitted to act on their own.

6. State how planning
(i) Reduce creativity
(ii) Leads to rigidity
CBSE SQP 2025

Ans.

(i) **Planning reduces Creativity**
Planning is an activity, which is done by the top management and the rest of the members just implement these plans. Middle management and other decision makers are neither allowed to deviate from plans nor are permitted to act on their own. Due to this, much of the initiative or creativity inherent in them gets lost or reduced and there is nothing new or innovative in the organisation.

(ii) **Planning leads to Rigidity**
A specific plan is made in an organisation which clearly indicates the objective to be achieved within a specific time frame.

These plans decide the future course of action, which the manager may not be in a position to change. This kind of rigidity in plans may create difficulty. Following a pre-decided plan in case of change in circumstances may not turn out to be in the organisation's interest.

7. Explain the following limitations of planning
(i) Planning may not work in dynamic environment
(ii) Planning involves huge costs.

Or **Can planning work in a changing environment? Give a reason to justify your answer.**

NCERT; Competency Based Que

Ans.

(i) **Planning may not Work in a Dynamic Environment**
Business environment is dynamic. It consists of number of dimensions like economic, political, physical, legal and social dimensions.

The organisation has to constantly adapt itself to changes. Changes in economic policy, instability of political conditions or natural calamity makes it difficult to accurately assess future trends in the environment.

(ii) **Planning involves Huge Costs**
Plans usually involve a lot of time, effort and cost in their formulation. e.g. Checking accuracy of facts may involve lot of time. Collection of data, boardroom meetings, investigations and discussions with professional experts involve a lot of expenditure of the organisation. Sometimes, the cost incurred may not justify the benefit derived from the plans.

8. "Planning involves working out details for future, still it does not guarantee success." Comment.

Competency Based Que

Ans. The success of an enterprise is possible only when the plans are properly made and then implemented. In order to achieve goals, plans need to be translated into action otherwise they become meaningless.

Managers usually rely on previously tried and tested successful plans and like to use them in every similar condition/situation because of the view that the plan has worked before too.

But, business environment is dynamic and rigid plan is not a guarantee of success.

9. Explain the first three steps in the process of planning.

Ans. The first three steps of planning or steps to be followed by a manager before performing the step of evaluation of alternatives are as follows

(i) **Setting Objectives**
Objectives specify what an organisation wants to achieve. Therefore, the first step in planning is to set-up clear objectives for the organisation as well as all the departments of the organisation.

(ii) **Developing Premises**
Premises are the base upon which plans are drawn. They may be forecasts, existing plans or past information. Therefore, the manager is required to make certain assumptions about the future, called premises.

(iii) **Identifying Alternative Courses of Action**
After the setting up of objectives, the managers make a list of alternatives through which the organisation can achieve its objectives as there can be many ways to achieve the objectives and managers must know all those ways to reach these objectives.

10. What are derivative plans and why they are formulated?

Ans. Derivative plans are the supporting plans, which are formulated for executing the primary plan. When the primary plan is decided, the next logical step is to formulate the derivative plans.

e.g. If the basic plan is to increase the sale of a product, the derivative plans would be to recruit and train employees, launch an advertising campaign, procure funds, etc.

11. State the meaning of single use plans and standing plans. **CBSE SQP 2025**

Ans. **Single Use Plans**
These plans are formulated for one time event or project. Such an action is not expected to be repeated in figure. Such plans are developed to meet the needs of a unique situation. Types of such plans are budgets and programmes. It is also known as specific plan.

Standing Plans
These plans are formed for the activities which occur regularly over a period of time. It is formed, so the operations of the organisation can run smoothly. Types of such plans are policies, procedures, methods and rules. It is also known as repeated-use plan.

12. **What are the distinct characteristics that differentiate standing plans from single use plans?**

Ans. Following are the differences between standing plans and single use plans

Basis	Standing Plans	Single Use Plans
Period	They are formed for a long period.	They are formed for a short period and discarded when the assignment/project is over.
Scope	They have a wide scope as they involve the whole organisation in its scope.	They have a narrow scope and they are formulated for a specific project/ assignment/situation.
Frequency of Use	These are repetitive in nature.	They are one time plan, not used for recurring situations.
Examples	Policies, procedures, methods, etc.	Objectives, budgets, etc.

13. **What is a 'procedure'? Give an example for the same.**

Ans. Procedure is a sequence of steps undertaken to complete a certain activity. It describes the exact manner in which an activity is performed. e.g. In the process of staffing of employees, following steps are followed

(i) Estimating manpower (ii) Recruitment
(iii) Selection (iv) Placement/Orientation
(v) Training (vi) Performance appraisal
(vii) Career planning (viii) Remuneration

14. **Explain 'objective' and 'strategy' as types of plan.**

Ans. **Objective**

It refers to the desired future positions that an organisation seeks to reach. It is usually framed by the top management. They are the end results of managerial activities, set in specific, quantitative terms for all the departments and units of the organisation.

e.g. To achieve 10% increase in sales in the next quarter.

Strategy

A comprehensive plan for achieving organisational goals by setting long-term objectives, choosing actions and allocating resources. It serves as a blueprint, outlining the organisation's direction and scope, and is formulated considering environmental changes. Major strategic decisions involve whether to stay in the current business, add new activities or seek market dominance.

15. **What are 'programmes'? Support it with an example.**

Ans. Programmes are the detailed statements stating the objectives, policies, procedures and budgets related to an activity to be undertaken. They clearly state how, when and by whom work is to be done.

Since they are developed for a particular project, they are considered as single use plan. e.g. Programme developed for construction of a shopping mall.

16. **Explain 'budget' as a type of plan.**

Ans. Budget is a significant component of planning wherein expected results are expressed in numerical terms for a definite period of time in the future. A budget is monetary and quantitative expression of business plans and policies to be pursued in the future.

Budget may be prepared for production, sales, material, cash, income, expenditure, etc. Normally, budgets are prepared by all organisations of varying sizes. They are used for exercising control on business activities.

17. **State the type of plan and state whether they are single use or standing plan.** NCERT; Competency Based Que

(i) A type of plan which serves as controlling device as well.

(ii) A plan based on research and analysis and is concerned with physical and technical tasks.

Ans.

(i) It is 'budget'. It is a single use plan which is developed for a one time project or event and it serves as a controlling device also.

(ii) It is 'method'. It is a standing plan as it is used for activities which occur regularly over a period of time.

Long Answer Type Questions

18. **Explain with the help of any four points why planning is important in an organisation.** CBSE 2024 C

Or **Explain the following as importance of planning function of management** CBSE 2023

(i) Planning reduces overlapping and wasteful activities

(ii) Planning reduces the risks of uncertainty

Ans.

(i) **Planning reduces Overlapping and Wasteful Activities**
Planning serves as the basis of coordinating the activities and efforts of different divisions, departments and individuals. It ensures clarity in thought and action and work is carried on smoothly by minimising or eliminating useless and redundant activities. Planning also makes it easier to detect inefficiencies and take corrective measures to deal with them.

(ii) **Planning reduces the Risks of Uncertainty**
Planning is an activity which enables a manager to look ahead and anticipate changes. By deciding in advance, planning shows the way to deal with changes and uncertain events.

Such changes or uncertain events cannot be eliminated altogether, but they can be anticipated and managerial responses to them can be developed.

(iii) **Planning facilitates Decision-making**
Planning helps in the evaluation of various alternatives and then choosing the best course of action. It involves setting targets and predicting future conditions which helps in taking rational/wise decisions.

(iv) **Planning establishes Standards for Controlling**
Planning provides the standards which helps in measurement of actual performance thereby taking corrective action if required. Thus, it provides the basis of control.

19. "Planning is a continuous process, helps in decision-making but is time consuming." Explain. Competency Based Que

Ans. Plans are made for a specific time period. At the end of such time period, new plans have to be drawn. When plans are objective based and goals are achieved, new plans are drawn with new objectives.

Also, due to ever changing environment, planning is required to be modified according to the requirements and future conditions. Thus, planning is a continuous process.

Planning helps the manager to look into the future and choose amongst the various alternative courses of action. The manager should evaluate each alternative and select the most viable plan.

Planning involves setting targets and predicting future conditions which helps in taking rational decisions. Thus, it helps in decision-making.

Sometimes, plans to be drawn up take so much of time that there is not much time left for their implementation. This leads to failure of planning.

20. Explain any four limitations of planning. CBSE 2024 C

Or **Briefly explain the external factors that can limit the effectiveness of planning.**

Ans. Following are the external factors that can limit the effectiveness of planning

(i) **Unforeseen Events**
Natural calamities like floods, earthquakes, etc. are beyond the control of managers and may cause failure of plans.

(ii) **Change in Government Policy**
Government's industrial or economic policies have significant influence on the activities of business. Managers have no control on these policies. An unfavourable policy may cause failure of plans.

(iii) **Environmental Changes**
Changes in social, economic, legal and technological environment may also affect forecasting and planning.

(iv) **Competitors' Strategy**
Sometimes, a change in the strategy of competitor may lead to failure of planning.

(v) **Change in Consumers' Preference**
Unexpected changes in consumers' preferences, taste and fashion, may also cause failure of plans.

21. Give the meaning of 'planning'. State the first five steps in the process of planning. CBSE 2024 C

Or

What are the various steps taken by management in the planning process? NCERT

Ans. Planning is deciding in advance what is to be done, when it is to be done and by whom, it is to be done. It bridges the gap between where we are and where we want to go.

Planning can be defined as setting objective to be achieved during a given period, formulating alternative courses of action to achieve them and selecting the best possible alternative from among the various courses of action available.

Following are the various steps taken by management in the planning process

(i) **Setting Objectives**
Objectives specify what an organisation wants to achieve. Therefore, the first step in planning is to set-up clear objectives for the organisation as well as all the departments of the organisation.

(ii) **Developing Premises**
Premises are the base upon which plans are drawn. They may be forecasts, existing plans or past information. Therefore, the manager is required to make certain assumptions about the future, called premises.

(iii) **Identifying Alternative Courses of Action**
After the setting up of objectives, the managers make a list of alternatives through which the organisation can achieve its objectives as there can be many ways to achieve the objectives and managers must know all those ways to reach these objectives.

(iv) **Evaluating Alternative Courses**
The next step is to weigh the pros and cons of each alternative. It is necessary to evaluate the positive and negative aspect of each alternative in the light of the objectives to be achieved. This might involve a number of calculations to measure the cost and benefits related to an alternative.

(v) **Selecting an Alternative**
This is the real point of decision-making. The best plan has to be adopted and implemented.

An ideal plan would be the one which is most profitable, most feasible and has the least negative consequences.

(vi) **Implementing the Plan**
This is the step where other managerial functions also come into the picture. This step is concerned with putting the plan into action, i.e. doing what is required. The managers start communicating the plans to employees and initiate them to carry out the activities according to the specifications of plans.

e.g. If there is a plan to increase production, then more labour, more machinery will be required. This step would also involve organising for labour and purchase of machinery.

(vii) **Follow-up Action**
Planning is a continuous process, so the managers keep on following up the plans to see whether plans are being implemented and activities are performed as per the schedule or not. Monitoring the plans is important to ensure the achievement of objectives.

22. Explain 'policy' and 'method' as type of plans. CBSE 2023

Ans. Policy
A general statement guiding responses to specific problems or situations, with major policies visible to all stakeholders and minor policies for internal use.

Policies are based on organisational objectives and provide a framework for interpreting strategy. e.g. Sale on cash basis only.

Method
It describes standardised ways to perform specific tasks, often part of a procedure. Methods are formalised to accomplish routine jobs efficiently, varying by task and helping save time and resources. e.g. Methods of training, methods of recruitment, etc.

23. Distinguish between policy and rule.

Ans. Following are the differences between policy and rule

Basis	Policy	Rule
Meaning	A broad plan laying down the limits within which discretion can be exercised in decision-making.	A specific plan indicating what is to be done or not done in a given situation.
Nature	A general statement.	A specific statement.
Purpose	To guide decision-making.	To guide behaviour and ensure discipline.
Flexibility	It is flexible as it provides scope for discretion and judgement.	It is rigid as it leaves no scope for discretion and judgement.
Penalty	Penalty for violation is not specified.	Penalty for violation is generally specified.
Source	Based on objectives.	Based on policies and procedures.

Case Study Based Questions

Short Case Studies

Case Study 1

When Chandrashekhar Shukla returned to India after completing a certificate course in Food Quality Assurance and Quality Control from the Netherlands, he was convinced that he would fulfil his grandfather's dream of converting their 58 acre land into a fertile farm. He started by setting out specific goals and laid down related activities to be performed to achieve the goals. Soon he launched his own company 'Food and Agribusiness Solutions Private Limited'.

He sought to ensure that the future events effectively meet the best interest of the company. He prepared an annual statement for production and sales, based on sales forecasting. He noticed that the farmers grew only paddy due to which land remained idle for the subsequent 8 to 9 months of the year. He identified and assessed various alternatives through which farms could be utilised for the remaining months of the year.

Through his accurate vision, judgement and systematic thinking based on analysis of the facts, he presented a scheme to the farmers where both paddy and vegetables could be grown.

Identify and explain the features of one of the functions of management highlighted above. CBSE SQP 2025

Ans. Function of management highlighted here is planning.

Feature of Planning

- **Planning is Goal-oriented**
Planning seeks to achieve certain objectives and all plans are linked with the goals of the organisation. Planning identifies the action that would lead to the desired results quickly and economically.
- **Planning is a Primary Function**
Planning serves as the basis for all other functions of management. It precedes organising, staffing, directing and controlling. All these functions are performed within the framework of plans.
- **Planning is Pervasive**
Planning is required at all levels of management as well as in all departments of the organisation. It is not only for top management, but it differs at different levels and among different departments.

- **Planning is Continuous**
  They prepare plans for short-term as well as long-term where it can be seen that throughout the year the plans are prepared one after the other.

Case Study 2

Prachi is working as an academic counsellor for specially abled students at one of the top school to provide special support and guidance to these students. She clearly states in advance the methods of teaching and tackling the students. She ensures that the goals are clearly stated for each and every teacher so that they act as a guide for deciding what action should be taken and in which direction. Her well laid plans will serve as a basis for coordinating the activities and efforts of teachers teaching different subjects to these students. It helps the teachers in bringing clarity of thought and action to their work. Identify and explain the two points of importance of 'planning' function of management highlighted in the above para. **CBSE 2025**

Ans. The two points of importance of planning function of management highlighted in the above para are as follows

(i) **Planning provides Direction**
By stating in advance how work is to be done, planning provides direction for action. It clearly defines what the employees have to do, when to do, how to do and for whom to do. When employees are aware of what they have to do, departments and individuals are able to work in coordination.

(ii) **Planning reduces Overlapping and Wasteful Activities**
Planning serves as the basis of coordinating the activities and efforts of different divisions, departments and individuals. It ensures clarity in thought and action and work is carried on smoothly by minimising or eliminating useless and redundant activities. Planning also makes it easier to detect inefficiencies and take corrective measures to deal with them.

Case Study 3

'Serious Business' is a balloon manufacturing firm. With the arrival of foreign firms, it is feeling the pressure of improving its business strategy. Because of the firm's advance planning, it could not suddenly bring changes in its plans as the whole organisation had started implementing the decided plan. But this year, the organisation wants to ensure success. However, the firm knows that the external environment is changeable and continues to vary in a fast manner.

The organisation wants to prepare in advance for a better future. It has decided to allocate a portion of its budget specifically for proper planning as it knows there are going to be expenses like expert's fee, survey charges, etc.

Which limitations of planning have been identified in the above case?

Ans. The limitations of planning highlighted in the above case are

(i) **Planning may not Work in a Dynamic Environment**
Business environment is dynamic. It consists of number of dimensions like economic, political, physical, legal and social dimensions. The organisation has to constantly adapt itself to changes. Changes in economic policy, instability of political conditions or natural calamity makes it difficult to accurately assess future trends in the environment.

(ii) **Planning involves Huge Costs**
Plans usually involve a lot of time, effort and cost in their formulation.
e.g. Checking accuracy of facts may involve lot of time. Collection of data, boardroom meetings, investigations and discussions with professional experts involve a lot of expenditure of the organisation. Sometimes, the cost incurred may not justify the benefit derived from the plans.

(iii) **Planning leads to Rigidity**
Planning leads to rigidity. A specific plan is made in an organisation which clearly indicates the objective to be achieved within a specific time frame. These plans decide the future course of action, which the manager may not be in a position to change. This kind of rigidity in plans may create difficulty. Following a pre-decided plan in case of change in circumstances may not turn out to be in the organisation's interest.

Case Study 4

It is deciding in advance what to do and how to do. It is one of the basic managerial functions. It requires that before doing something, the manager must formulate an idea of how to work on a particular task.

This function is closely connected with creativity and innovation. It seeks to bridge the gap between where we are and where we want to go and is performed at all levels of management.

In spite of this the function of management referred above has a number of limitations. Explain any two such limitations.

Ans. Planning function of management has been referred above. Two limitations of the planning function of management are

(i) **Planning leads to Rigidity**
A specific plan is made in an organisation which clearly indicates the objective to be achieved within a specific time frame.

These plans decide the future course of action, which the manager may not be in a position to change. This kind of rigidity in plans may create difficulty.

Following a pre-decided plan in case of change in circumstances may not turn out to be in the organisation's interest.

(ii) **Planning reduces Creativity**
Planning is an activity, which is done by the top management and the rest of the members just implement these plans. Middle management and other decision makers are neither allowed to deviate from plans nor are permitted to act on their own. Due to this, much of the initiative or creativity inherent in them gets lost or reduced and there is nothing new or innovative in the organisation.

Case Study 5

You are a strategic analyst in XYZ Ltd. while developing the planning premises, list out certain assumptions regarding

(i) Tangible and intangible premises.
(ii) Controllable and uncontrollable premises.

Ans. Following are the assumptions, which should be considered

(i) Tangible premises are units of production, capital investment, etc. while intangible premises include employee morale, goodwill, etc.
(ii) Controllable premises are policies, procedures, etc. while uncontrollable premises include trade cycle, political changes, etc.

Case Study 6

Mohan decided to start a desert cooler manufacturing business. He sets the target of earning 20% profit on sales in the first year. He was very much concerned about the future prospects of the business, which were uncertain.

For this, he gathered information from the potential market and analysed that the demand for wall mounted coolers is increasing day by day. He used this information as the base for future planning.

On the basis of the gathered information, he called a meeting in the following week to find new methods to achieve the objective.

(i) Identify the function of management involved in the above case.
(ii) Enumerate the next two steps, which have been followed by Rahul that are related to the process of one of the functions of management.

Ans.

(i) The function of management involved in the above case is planning.
(ii) Following are the next two steps, which have been followed by Rahul

- **Identifying Alternative Courses of Action**
After the setting up of objectives, the managers make a list of alternatives through which the organisation can achieve its objectives as there can be many ways to achieve the objectives and managers must know all those ways to reach these objectives.
- **Evaluating Alternative Courses**
The next step is to weigh the pros and cons of each alternative. It is necessary to evaluate the positive and negative aspect of each alternative in the light of the objectives to be achieved. This might involve a number of calculations to measure the cost and benefits related to an alternative.

Case Study 7

An established firm has fifty years of experience in shipping industry. The company time and again proves itself as one of the dominant figures in the market. The plan for the whole year is given a lot of importance. According to the owner of the company their plans are the basic structures upon which other important functions of management rest. It is important that the plans are communicated to the employees.

The top management ensures that the plans are communicated and implemented at all levels and in all departments.

To learn from past mistakes is a habit of this successful company. They prepare plans for short-term as well as long-term where it can be seen that throughout the year the plans are prepared one after another. Shipping industry needs such dedicated companies.

The goals are specific and the activities to achieve these specific goals are undertaken.

The company has planned a growth of 20% in revenue this year. Let's see how much it's possible for it to achieve it by the end of the year.

(i) In the above case, identify the various features of planning highlighted.
(ii) Which type of plan is indicated in the above case?

Ans.

(i) The features of planning highlighted above are
- Planning is goal-oriented
- Planning is a primary function
- Planning is pervasive
- Planning is continuous

For explanation, refer to case study 1.

(ii) The type of plan which is indicated in the above case is 'objective'.
The company has planned a growth of 20% in revenue this year. Here the plan is precise and quantified. When a goal is quantified it becomes an objective.

Case Study 8

In an attempt to cope with Reliance Jio's onslaught in 2018, market leader Bharti Airtel has reafreshed its ₹ 149 prepaid plan to offer 2GB of 3G/4G data per day, twice the amount it offered earlier.

Name the type of plan is highlighted in the given example. State its three dimensions also. **NCERT**

Ans. 'Strategy' is a plan which is highlighted above. Three dimensions are as follows

(i) Determining long-term objective.
(ii) Allocating resources necessary to achieve the objectives.
(iii) Adopting a particular course of action.

Case Study 9

Identify and state the type of plan in the following cases

(i) On the wall of 'Health is Wealth' hospital a board is hanging. On this board. It is written 'We care for the health of senior citizens as our topmost priority'. This hospital is known for treating people aged more than 60 years.

(ii) Rakesh calls his new subordinates for a meeting. He is a top level manager. He arranges for a power point presentation to train his subordinates who are all middle level managers.

He tells them the way of doing task of treating suppliers through a new software system to be installed within next 30 days.

(iii) Dinesh takes a meeting and guides his employees in a type of plan which is chronological in nature and is situation specific. It is a collection of various methods in a step wise sequence.

Ans.

(i) It is a type of policy. Policies are guidelines which facilitate the achievement of the pre-determined objective.

(ii) It is a type of method. It describes standardised ways to perform specific tasks, often part of a procedure. Methods are formalised to accomplish routine jobs efficiently, varying by task and helping save time and resources.

(iii) It is a type of procedure. Procedure is a sequence of steps undertaken to complete a certain activity. It describes the exact manner in which an activity is performed.

Case Study 10

The human resource manager of Ajanta Ltd. adopted a special process for the selection of employees. Its main stages includes preliminary screening, selection tests, employment interview, medical examination and job offer.

Identify the type of plan described above and explain its two features.

Ans. The type of plan is procedure. It describes the exact manner, in which a certain activity is to be performed. It is a chronological sequence of steps to be taken. It prescribes ways to handle routine problems and execute policies. e.g. Procedure of selection of employees, procedure of issuing materials from stores, etc.

Following are the features of procedure

(i) It includes routine steps on how to carry out activities.
(ii) It is to be followed in particular circumstances.

Case Study 11

RapidTech Solutions is introducing a new customer onboarding process to ensure a seamless experience for its clients.

The management has designed a detailed plan that specifies the exact sequence of steps that employees must follow when onboarding a new client.

This plan addresses all routine activities involved in the process, ensuring consistency across the organisation.

Additionally, the company has established standardised ways to carry out specific tasks within this process, such as how to verify client information and how to set up their accounts in the system.

(i) Identify the two types of plans being implemented by RapidTech Solutions in this scenario.
(ii) Distinguish between the two types of plans on any three basis identified in (i).

Ans.

(i) The two types of plans implemented by RapidTech Solutions are procedure and method.
(ii) Following are the differences between procedure and method

Basis	Procedure	Method
Meaning	It is a guide to action. It contains steps to be taken in a chronological order.	It provides formalised and standardised ways to perform routine and repetitive tasks.
Scope	These are broader in scope as they determine a sequence of all activities to be performed to do a particular work.	Its scope is limited as they are related to a particular step of a procedure.
Importance	It creates coordination among different departments.	It helps in reducing costs as they help in performing an activity efficiently.

Case Study 12

Identify and explain the types of plans in the following

(i) Hitesh is a senior middle level manager. He is busy in allocating resources to his staff, he has also finalised the objectives and decided the course of action to be followed. He is expecting energy in his staff for the whole season but he will have to be cautious.

(ii) Suresh is giving a speech to the workers of his factory. He is the owner of a toy manufacturing factory and has 123 workers. He tells them that this year's target of production is 7.5 lakh toys.

Ans.

(i) The type of plan is strategy. A comprehensive plan for achieving organisational goals by setting long-term objectives, choosing actions and allocating resources. It serves as a blueprint, outlining the organisation's direction and scope and is formulated considering environmental changes. Major strategic decisions involve whether to stay in the current business, add new activities or seek market dominance.

(ii) The type of plan is objective. Objectives are the desired future positions an organisation aims to achieve. Set by top management, they guide all managerial activities and overall planning. They should be specific and measurable, such as a 10% increase in sales or a 15% rise in profits.

Case Study 13

Ramesh is a supervisor in a company. He works at the lower level of management. He teaches 'on-the-job training' the ways in which a task is to be done by the workers at the shop floor level. He meets his boss on ce a week day and gives him a numerical statement quantifying the numbers needed in various activities at the shop floor for next 6 months. The boss approves his requirements and gives him a job to set targets in figures about the next plan he thinks is good for the manufacturing unit.

Ramesh's dedication is noticed by all.

(i) In the above case which types of plans have been highlighted?

(ii) Which step of planning process is highlighted in the above case?

Ans.

(i) The types of plans which have been highlighted above are

- **Method**
  It describes standardised ways to perform specific tasks, often part of a procedure. Methods are formalised to accomplish routine jobs efficiently, varying by task and helping save time and resources
- **Budget**
  A budget projects expected results and costs in numerical terms for a project. It quantifies future facts and figures.

(ii) The step of planning process highlighted in the above case is 'setting objectives'. Objectives specify what an organisation wants to achieve. Therefore, the first step in planning is to set-up clear objectives for the organisation as well as all the departments of the organisation.

Case Study 14

Three years ago, Rakesh completed his MBA in finance and decided to start his own financial consultancy firm. His main objective was to secure a 30% market share in the first two years of operation by providing exceptional financial advisory services to Small and Medium-sized Enterprises (SMEs). To achieve this, Rakesh set clear goals and developed an action plan.

One of the policies he implemented was to offer flexible payment options to clients, allowing them to pay for services in installments over six months. This policy was intended to attract more clients who might otherwise find it difficult to afford upfront payments. Rakesh also decided to focus on providing personalised financial solutions tailored to each client's needs.

(i) Identify the two types of plans discussed in the case.

(ii) Differentiate between the two types of plan identified in (i) on any three basis.

Ans.

(i) The two types of plans discussed in the case are policy and objective.

(ii) Following are the differences between policy and objective

Basis	Policy	Objective
Meaning	Policies are guidelines which facilitate the achievement of the pre-determined objective.	Objectives are the end results towards which all activities of an enterprise are directed.
Purpose	Policies determines how the work is to be done.	Objectives determine what is to be done.
Function	Policies prescribe the mode and manner in which objectives can be achieved.	Objectives are the end-points of planning.

Long Case Studies

Case Study 15

An auto company C Ltd. is facing a problem of declining market share due to increased competition from other new and existing players in the market. Its competitors are introducing lower priced models for mass consumers who are price sensitive. C Ltd. realised that it needs to take steps immediately to improve its market standing in the future.

For quality conscious consumers, C Ltd. plans to introduce new models with added features and new technological advancements. The company has formed a team with representatives from all the levels of management. This team will brainstorm and will determine the steps that will be adopted by the organisation for implementing the above strategy.

Explain the features of planning highlighted in the situation. **NCERT**

Ans. Following are the features of planning highlighted in the situation

(i) **Planning is Futuristic**
It is essentially looking ahead, as it is based on forecasting and is prepared for the future. Planning is regarded as a forward-looking function based on forecasting. It implies looking into the future, analysing it and predicting it to meet future events effectively.

(ii) **Planning is a Mental Exercise**
It is a mental exercise as it requires creativity, imagination and higher thinking skills with sound judgement. It is an intellectual activity of thinking rather than doing. It requires logical and systematic thinking rather than guesswork or wishful thinking.

(iii) **Planning is Pervasive**
Planning is required at all levels of management as well as in all departments of the organisation. It is not only for top management, but it differs at different levels and among different departments. It is performed by managers at all the levels.

Case Study 16

Arjun is the operations manager at 'NutriDelight', a company that manufactures organic health snacks. Recently, the company received a special order to produce 500 boxes of energy bars for a renowned sports event, with a cost price of ₹ 300 per box and a planned profit margin of 25%. The order was to be completed within 15 days.

To ensure smooth execution, Arjun meticulously prepared a detailed plan outlining the required raw materials, production schedule, labour allocation and delivery timelines. He allocated resources based on his plan and ensured that every step was followed precisely. However, after the order was completed, Arjun noticed that the actual cost of producing each box was ₹ 450, significantly higher than the estimate. Concerned about this discrepancy, he reported the matter to the managing director.

The managing director appointed Meera, an experienced business analyst, to investigate the issue. Meera found that the initial plan had underestimated the cost of raw materials and there were unforeseen delays in production due to equipment downtime that had not been accounted for in the plan.

As a result, the company faced higher costs than anticipated.

The case above highlights an important function of management.

(i) Identify the function of management discussed above.

(ii) State any five points of importance of the function identified in (i).

Ans.

(i) The function of management discussed in the case is planning.

(ii) Following are the five points of importance of planning

- **Planning reduces Overlapping and Wasteful Activities**
Planning serves as the basis of coordinating the activities and efforts of different divisions, departments and individuals.
It ensures clarity in thought and action and work is carried on smoothly by minimising or eliminating useless and redundant activities. Planning also makes it easier to detect inefficiencies and take corrective measures to deal with them.
- **Planning reduces the Risks of Uncertainty**
Planning is an activity which enables a manager to look ahead and anticipate changes. By deciding in advance, planning shows the way to deal with changes and uncertain events.
Such changes or uncertain events cannot be eliminated altogether, but they can be anticipated and managerial responses to them can be developed.
- **Planning promotes Innovative Ideas**
It is an intellectual process, which involves finding better ideas and better methods to perform a particular job. In planning, new ideas can take the shape of concrete plans.
- **Planning provides Directions**
By stating in advance how work is to be done, planning provides direction for action. It clearly defines what the employees have to do, when to do, how to do and for whom to do.
When employees are aware of what they have to do, departments and individuals are able to work in coordination. In the absence of planning employees would be working in different directions and the organisation would not be able to achieve its desired goals.
- **Planning establishes Standards for Controlling**
Planning provides the standards against which actual performance is measured. By comparing actual performance with standards, managers can know whether they have actually been able to attain the goals or not.

Case Study 17

Suhasini, a home science graduate from a reputed college, has recently done a cookery course. She wished to start her own venture with a goal to provide 'health food' at reasonable prices. She discussed her idea with her teacher (mentor) who encouraged her.

After analysing various options for starting her business venture, they shortlisted the option to sell readymade and 'ready to make' vegetable shakes and sattu milk shakes. Then, they weighed the pros and cons of both the shortlisted options.

On the basis of above para, answer the following

(i) Name the function of management being discussed above.

(ii) Give any one of its characteristics.

(iii) Also briefly discuss any three limitations of the function discussed in the case.

Ans.

(i) Planning is the function of management which is being discussed above.

(ii) **Planning involves Decision-making**
Planning essentially involves application of rational thinking to choose the best alternative among the various available alternatives in order to achieve the desired goals efficiently and effectively.

(iii) The limitations of planning are described below

- **Planning may not Work in a Dynamic Environment**
The business environment is dynamic in nature. Every organisation has to constantly adapt itself to changes in its environment in order to survive and grow. However, it is difficult to anticipate all the likely future changes in the environment with utmost accuracy.
Hence, even with planning, everything cannot be foreseen.
- **Planning reduces Creativity**
The top management undertakes planning of various activities whereas the other members are expected to merely implement these plans. This restricts the creativity of the middle level managers as they are neither allowed to deviate from plans nor are permitted to act on their own.
- **Planning involves Huge Costs**
The process of planning involves huge cost in terms of time and money as detailed planning is based on a series of scientific calculations. Moreover, it may include a number of related costs as well, like expenses on boardroom meetings, discussions with professional experts and preliminary investigations to find out the viability of the plan. As a result, the expenses on planning may turn out to be much more than benefits derived from it.

Case Study 18

Atul Sharma was the chief executive officer of a footwear company, 'Stepone Footwear'. The company manufactured innovative and comfortable footwear for all age groups. Atul Sharma was known for meticulous planning.

He ensured that the goals and objectives of the company are clearly stated so that they act as a guide for deciding what action should be taken and in which direction. Before each season, Stepone Footwear carefully analysed market trends, customer preferences and production schedules.

This analysis enabled the company to look ahead and anticipate changes and develop managerial responses, wherever necessary.

As a result, they were able to consistently deliver innovative and comfortable shoes to the market. During one season, there was a sudden surge in demand for eco-friendly shoes.

Stepone Footwear had already planned their production for the year with specific goals to be achieved within a specific time frame.

The managers of Stepone Footwear did not have the flexibility to change the plan to cope with the changed circumstances.

Another shoe company, Eco Step quickly adapted and started manufacturing comfortable eco-friendly shoes. By not being able to adjust to the rapidly changing market, Stepone Footwear faced inventory surplus while Eco Step emerged as a market leader in sustainable eco-friendly footwear.

Quoting lines from the above paragraph, identify and explain two benefits and two limitations of planning function of management discussed in the above case.

CBSE 2024

Ans. The benefits of 'planning' function of management are

(i) He ensured that the goals......... in which direction.

Planning provides Directions
By stating in advance how work is to be done, planning provides direction for action.
It clearly defines what the employees have to do, when to do, how to do and for whom to do. When employees are aware of what they have to do, departments and individuals are able to work in coordination.

(ii) This analysis enabled .... shoes to the market.

Planning promotes Innovative Ideas
Planning is an intellectual process, which involves generation of new ideas through creativity, innovation and foresightedness. These new ideas can take the shape of concrete plans. Planning is the most challenging activity for the management as it guides all future actions leading to growth and prosperity of the business.

The limitations of planning function of management are

(i) The manager of 'Stepone Footwear' .... circumstances.

Planning leads to Rigidity
A specific plan is made in an organisation which clearly indicates the objective to be achieved within a specific time frame. These plans decide the future course of action, which the manager may not be in a position to change. This kind of rigidity in plans may create difficulty. Following a pre-decided plan in case of change in circumstances may not turn out to be in the organisation's interest.

(ii) Another shoe company ...... eco-friendly footwear.

Planning may not Work in a Dynamic Environment
Business environment is dynamic. It consists of number of dimensions like economic, political, physical, legal and social dimensions. The organisation has to constantly adapt itself to changes. Changes in economic policy, instability of political conditions or natural calamity makes it difficult to accurately assess future trends in the environment. Further, market competition can also upset the financial plan, sale targets as well as cash budgets. Planning cannot foresee everything and there may be obstacles to effective planning.

Case Study 19

Indian Drugs and Pharmaceuticals Ltd.' is engaged in the manufacturing and distribution of medicines. The company has set-up an objective of increasing its sales turnover by 20%.

To achieve this objective, the company has decided to diversify into baby health care products. Since the company has already set its objectives and developed the premises based on the same, it wants your help for the remaining steps to be taken in this process.

Explain briefly these steps.

Ans. Following are the remaining steps in planning process

(i) **Developing Premises**
Premises are the base upon which plans are drawn. They may be forecasts, existing plans or past information. Therefore, the manager is required to make certain assumptions about the future, called premises.

(ii) **Identifying Alternative Courses of Action**
After the setting up of objectives, the managers make a list of alternatives through which the organisation can achieve its objectives as there can be many ways to achieve the objectives and managers must know all those ways to reach these objectives.

(iii) **Evaluating Alternative Courses**
The next step is to weigh the pros and cons of each alternative. It is necessary to evaluate the positive and negative aspect of each alternative in the light of the objectives to be achieved. This might involve a number of calculations to measure the cost and benefits related to an alternative.

(iv) **Selecting an Alternative**
This is the real point of decision-making. The best plan has to be adopted and implemented. An ideal plan would be the one which is most profitable, most feasible and has the least negative consequences.

(v) **Implementing the Plan**
This is the step where other managerial functions also come into the picture. This step is concerned with putting the plan into action, i.e. doing what is required. The managers start communicating the plans to employees and initiate them to carry out the activities according to the specifications of plans. e.g. If there is a plan to increase production, then more labour, more machinery will be required. This step would also involve organising for labour and purchase of machinery.

(vi) **Follow-up Action**
Planning is a continuous process, so the managers keep on following up the plans to see whether plans are being implemented and activities are performed as per the schedule or not. Monitoring the plans is important to ensure the achievement of objectives.

Case Study 20

Two years ago, Naina completed her degree in culinary arts. Initially, she worked for a well-known restaurant chain, but she soon realised that she wanted to start her own venture in gourmet desserts. Motivated by this desire, she set clear goals and formulated a detailed action plan to establish her own dessert boutique. One of her main objectives was to achieve a 40% return on investment in the first year.

She decided that high-quality ingredients like cocoa, vanilla and cream would be sourced from local suppliers on a three month credit basis.

Naina also made plans to market her products through premium retail outlets. She hired Rohan as the operations manager, who devised the specific procedures for producing the desserts.

Rohan also developed a schedule outlining the workforce requirements for the boutique throughout the year. Naina shared her quarterly sales targets with Rohan, broken down by product and region. Additionally, a fine of ₹ 200 per day was imposed on employees who failed to adhere to the hygiene standards, including wearing hairnets, gloves and aprons.

Quoting lines from the above case, identify and explain the different types of plans discussed.

Ans. Following are the different types of plans discussed in the case

(i) **Objective**

"One of her main objectives was to achieve a 40% return on investment in the first year." Objectives are the desired future positions an organisation aims to achieve. Set by top management, they guide all managerial activities and overall planning. They should be specific and measurable, such as a 10% increase in sales or a 15% rise in profits.

(ii) **Policy**

"She decided that high-quality ingredients like cocoa, vanilla and cream would be sourced from local suppliers on a three-month credit basis."

A general statement guiding responses to specific problems or situations, with major policies visible to all stakeholders and minor policies for internal use. Policies are based on organisational objectives and provide a framework for interpreting strategy.

(iii) **Procedure**

"Rohan devised the specific procedures for producing the desserts."

It outlines the specific sequence of steps for performing an activity, addressing routine problems and executing policies. Procedures are detailed, meant for internal use and align with broader policy frameworks to achieve objectives.

(iv) **Rule**

"A fine of ₹ 200 per day was imposed on employees who failed to adhere to the hygiene standards, including wearing hairnets, gloves and aprons."

Rules are strict, specific directives on what must be done, with no flexibility allowed. They represent firm managerial decisions and are the simplest form of plans, requiring strict adherence.

(v) **Budget**

"Naina shared her quarterly sales targets with Rohan, broken down by product and region." Budget is a significant component of planning wherein expected results are expressed in numerical terms for a definite period of time in the future. A budget is monetary and quantitative expression of business plans and policies to be pursued in the future. Budget may be prepared for production, sales, material, cash, income, expenditure, etc.

SELF ASSESSMENT TEST

Objective Type Questions

1. The step in the process of planning which is concerned with putting the plan into action i.e. doing what is required is called
   (a) implementing the plan
   (b) follow-up action
   (c) developing premises
   (d) selecting an alternative

2. "Following a pre-decided plan, when circumstances have changed, may not turn out to be in the organisation's interest." The limitation of planning being referred to in the above statement is ....
   (a) planning does not guarantee success
   (b) planning may not work in a dynamic environment
   (c) planning leads to rigidity
   (d) planning is a time consuming process

3. 'Dos' and 'Don't' are prescribed by
   (a) rules
   (b) policies
   (c) methods
   (d) budgets

4. Library will issue the books for 5 days. Identify the type of plan in the given statement.
   (a) Policy (b) Rule
   (c) Programme (d) Method

5. Anhay Ltd. prepares budget in its annual general meeting for the year 2023-24. What kind of plan is it?
   (a) Single use plan
   (b) Standing plan
   (c) Objective plan
   (d) None of the above

6. A company wants to introduce a new product. What type of plan it should prepare?
   (a) Objective
   (b) Strategy
   (c) Policy
   (d) None of the above

7. Name the type of plan in which the move of competitors is considered.
   (a) Budget (b) Rule
   (c) Strategy (d) Method

Answers 1. (a) 2. (c) 3. (a) 4. (a) 5. (a) 6. (b) 7. (c)

Short Answer Type Questions

8. "Planning is an important function of management." Give any three reasons in favour of the statement.
9. State two examples of limitations of planning, which are beyond the control of an organisation.
10. How does planning lead to rigidity and not guarantee success? Explain.
11. Being a management consultant, you observe that adopted plan is not appropriate for your company. Suggest an ideal plan and state its characteristics.
12. Distinguish between procedures and methods as type of plan.
13. "No smoking in the factory is a rule." In the light of the given statement, explain rule as a type of plan.

Long Answer Type Questions

14. "Planning is important as it provides directions for action, reduces the risks of uncertainty and facilitates decision-making." Explain.
15. Why is that organisations are not always able to accomplish all their objectives?
16. A company is manufacturing baby garments. The manager wants to increase the profits by purchasing new high speed machines or increasing the sale price or using waste material in manufacturing soft toys.
    He decided that using waste material to increase the profit is the best solution for him. Explain the steps involved in the above process by quoting the lines from the question.

05
CHAPTER

"Organising is the process of defining and grouping the activities of the enterprise and establising authority relationships among them."
— *Theo Haimman*

YOUR STUDY GOALS

YOUR PRACTICE GOAL

- Objective Type Questions (68 Qs ; MCQs, A-R, Statements, Matching)
- Subjective Type Questions (18 SAs, 9 LAs)
- Case Study Based Questions (Short Case Studies-13, Long Case Studies-8)
- Self Assessment Test (7 MCQs, 7 SAs, 3 LAs)

Organising

5.1 Concept of Organising

Organising involves identifying and grouping activities within an organisation and bringing together physical, financial and human resources to create most productive relationships for achieving specific goals.

This function leads to the development of an **organisational structure** that includes designing roles for suitably skilled individuals and defining their inter-relationships to eliminate ambiguity in job performance.

Organising can also be defined as the **process** of implementing plans by clarifying jobs and working relationships and effectively deploying resources to meet organisational objectives.

Process of Organising

The following steps are to be undertaken in the organising process

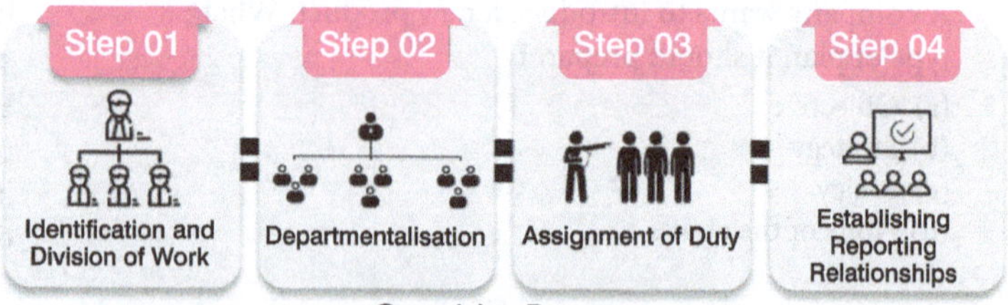

Organising Process

Step 1 **Identification and Division of Work** The first step in organising is to identify the tasks that need to be performed based on the plans. These tasks are then divided into smaller, manageable activities to avoid duplication and ensure that the workload is distributed effectively among the employees.

Step 2 **Departmentalisation** Once tasks are divided, similar activities are grouped together into departments. This grouping facilitates specialisation and can be based on criteria like territory, product type or functions.

Step 3 **Assignment of Duties** After departments are formed, each department is placed under the charge of an individual, called departmental head. Then, specific jobs are assigned to individuals based on their skills and competencies. It is essential to match the job requirements with the individual's abilities for optimal performance.

Step 4 **Establishing Authority and Reporting Relationships** Clear authority and reporting lines are established to ensure that everyone knows whom they have to report to and who they supervise. This helps to create a hierarchical structure and helps in coordinating various activities in the organisation.

Case Study
Process of Organising

Decors Ltd. is preparing for a **corporate product launch**. For this, they followed on organising process

- **Identification and Division of Work** First, they identified tasks like venue selection, marketing, guest invitations and product demos.
- **Departmentalisation** Next, they created departments for *event planning, marketing* and *logistics*.
- **Assignment of Duties** They assigned Sarah to lead event planning, John to handle marketing and Emily for logistics, ensuring roles match their strengths.
- **Establishing Authority and Reporting Relationships** Finally, they established that all department heads report to the project manager, keeping communication clear and efficient for a successful launch.

Importance of Organising

Following points highlight the importance of organising

Importance of Organising
- Benefits of Specialisation
- Clarity in Working Relationship
- Optimum Utilisation of Resources
- Adaptation to Change
- Effective Administration
- Development of Personnel
- Expansion and Growth

1. **Benefits of Specialisation** Organising allocates jobs systematically, enhancing productivity through specialisation and reducing the workload.
2. **Clarity in Working Relationships** Organising establishes a clear communication and hierarchy specifying who is to report to whom. This removes doubtfulness and enables fixation of responsibility.
3. **Optimum Utilisation of Resources** Organising ensures proper use of resources, avoiding duplication of work and minimising wastage.
4. **Adaptation to Change** Organising enables smooth transitions through modification in organisational structure and stability despite business environment changes. This helps organisation to continue to survive and grow.
5. **Effective Administration** It gives a clear description of jobs and duties as well as responsibilities of each individual. This helps to avoid confusion and duplication of activities.
6. **Development of Personnel** Effective delegation reduces the workload of managers, allowing them to foster creativity and develop way of performing tasks. This also helps subordinates to develop new skills and help them to realise their full potential.
7. **Expansion and Growth** Organising supports growth by adding new positions, departments and diversifying operations of an enterprise by enabling it to deviate from existing norms and taking up new challenges.

Organising Importance

- A rapidly growing technology firm restructured its organisation into specialised departments i.e. software development, quality assurance, customer support and marketing. This clear division of roles improved productivity and resource utilisation by minimising duplication and enhancing expertise.
- The new structure facilitated smooth adaptation to industry changes and supported company growth through the addition of new units like AI Research and Development. Additionally, delegating tasks allowed managers to mentor their teams, fostering personal development and creativity.

5.2 Organisation Structure

Organisation structure is the outcome of the organising process. It can be defined as the framework within which managerial and operating tasks are performed. The **need** for an adequate organisation structure is felt by an enterprise whenever it grows in size or complexity.

Types of Organisation Structure

The type of structure adopted by an organisation will vary with the nature and types of activities performed by an organisation. The organisation structure can be classified under two categories which are as follows

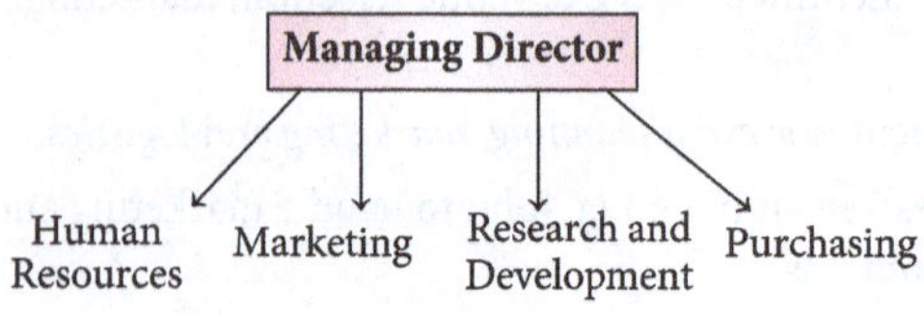

Functional Structure

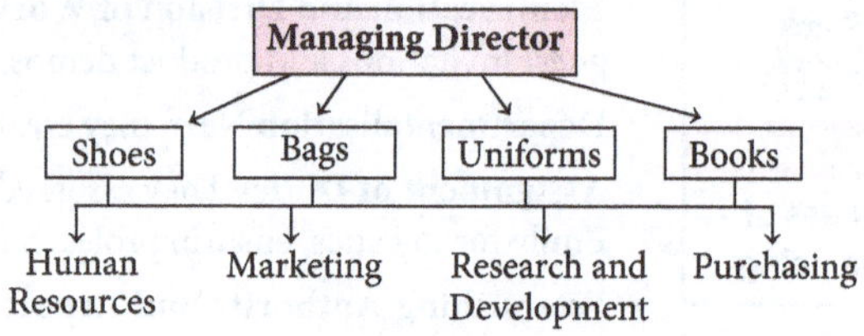

Divisional Structure

Structure	Advantages	Disadvantages
Functional Structure Under this structure, jobs of similar nature are grouped under one department. In other words, departments are created on the basis of different functions performed in the organisation. All departments in such organisations, report to a coordinating head. **Suitability** Best for large organisations with diversified activities requiring high degree of specialisation.	• Promotes occupational specialisation. • Facilitates better control and coordination. • Increases managerial and operational efficiency. • Minimises duplication of effort, achieving economies of scale. • Simplifies employee training. • Ensures that all functions receive appropriate attention.	• May overemphasise departmental objectives over overall enterprise goals, leading to functional empires. It can lead to hinder interaction between two or more departments. • Can cause coordination issues due to the need for exchanging information across departments. • Difficult to hold a particular department responsible for any problem. • Potential for inter-departmental conflicts. • Can lead to inflexibility and a narrow perspective.
Divisional Structure In a divisional structure, the organisation structure comprises of separate business units or divisions on the basis of products, territory or region. Each unit has a divisional manager responsible for performance and who has authority over the unit. **Suitability** Ideal for businesses with a wide product range or needing separate divisions for different products or when growth prospects are high.	• Product specialisation develops diverse skills in divisional heads, preparing them for higher roles. • Divisional heads are accountable for profits, as revenue and costs are easily identifiable. Thus, fixation of responsibility and accountability is easy. • It promotes flexibility and initiative. • It facilitates growth by allowing new divisions to be added without disrupting existing operations.	• Conflicts may arise among divisions over fund allocation and one division may prioritise its profits over others. • Costs may increase due to duplication of activities, as each division may require separate similar functions. • Managers gain authority over all division related activities, which can lead to issues over time. • Managers may focus on their own division's objectives, without thinking of organisational goals.

Span of Management

- To a great extent, span of management gives shape to the organisational structure. It refers to the number of subordinates that can be effectively managed by a superior.
- Larger the span, lesser the number of levels in the organisation structure, leading to a flat organisation while narrow span results in tall structure.

Formal Organisation

This organisation refers to the organisation structure which is designed by the management to accomplish a particular task. It specifies the relationships among various job positions and the nature of their interrelationship. This clarifies who has to report to whom.

According to **Chester Barnand**, "Formal organisation is a system of consciously coordinated activities of two or more persons towards a common objective."

Features of Formal Organisation

- It specifies the relationships among various job positions and the nature of their inter-relationships. This clarifies who has to report to whom.
- It is a means to achieve objectives specified in the plans.
- It helps to coordinate, interlink and integrate the efforts of various departments.
- It is deliberately designed by the top management.
- It places more emphasis on work rather than interpersonal relations among the employees.

Advantages and Disadvantages of Formal Organisation

Advantages	Disadvantages
• Easier to fix responsibility due to clearly defined relationships. • No ambiguity in roles and duties, avoiding confusion and duplication of effort. • Unity of command is maintained with a clear chain of command. • Effective goal accomplishment through structured operations. • Provides stability to organisation.	• Formal communication can cause procedural delays and delayed decision-making. • Rigid policies may hinder recognition of creative talent. • Emphasises structure over human relationships, as well as social needs of the employees.

Informal Organisation

An informal organisation originates from within the formal organisation as a result of personal interaction among employees. Informal organisation has no prescribed rules and does not have fixed lines of communication.

According to **Chester Barnand**, "An informal organisation is an aggregate of interpersonal relationships without any conscious purpose but which may contribute to joint results."

Features of Informal Organisation

- It originates from within the formal organisation, due to interaction among employees.
- The standard of behaviour evolve from group norms rather than officially laid down rules and regulations.
- Communication is free and independent.
- It emerges spontaneously and not deliberately created by the management.
- It has no definite structure or form as it is a complex network of social relationships among members.

Advantages and Disadvantages of Informal Organisation

Advantages	Disadvantages
• Faster communication and quick feedback bypassing formal lines. • Fulfills social and psychological needs, enhancing job satisfaction and belongingness. • Compensates for formal organisation gaps by testing employee reactions. Thus, contributes towards fulfillment of organisational objectives.	• Spreads rumors, potentially harming formal organisation interests. • Can resist change, hindering management's efforts and growth. • Pressurises conformity to group norms, which may conflict with organisational goals.

5.3 Concept of Delegation

Delegation refers to the downward transfer of authority from a superior to subordinate. It is a pre-requisite to the efficient functioning of an organisation because it enables a manager to use his time on high priority activities.

According to **Theo Haimman**, "Delegation of authority merely means the granting of authority to subordinates to operate within prescribed limits."

Elements of Delegation

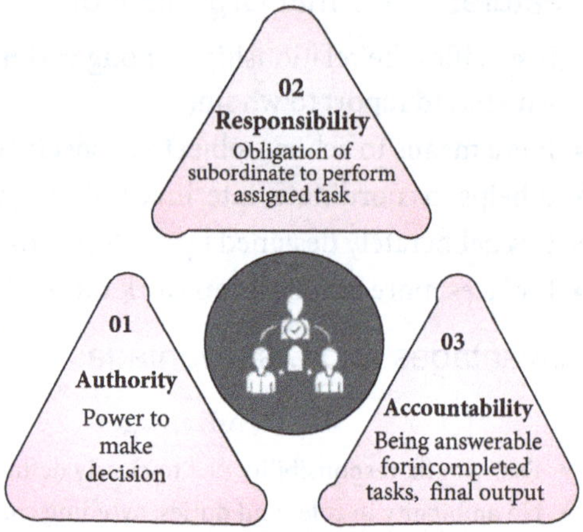

1. **Authority** It determines the superior-subordinate relationship wherein the superior communicates his decision to the subordinate and the subordinate executes it as per the guidelines of the superior. Authority is restricted by laws, and the rules and regulation of the organisation, which limit its scope. However, as we go up in the management hierarchy, the scope of authority increases.
2. **Responsibility** It arises from a superior-subordinate relationships because the subordinate is bound to perform the duty assigned to him. Thus, it flows upward i.e. a subordinate is always responsible to his superior. When an employee is given responsibility for a job, he must also be given the degree of authority necessary to carry it out.
3. **Accountability** It is the obligation to carry out responsibility and exercise authority. It flows upwards i.e. a subordinate will be accountable to his superior. Though, delegation of authority empowers an employee to act for his superior but the superior would still be accountable for the outcome. It indicates that the manager has to ensure the proper discharge of duties by his subordinates. It is generally enforced through regular feedback on the extent of work accomplished.

To sum up, it can be stated that while authority is delegated, responsibility is assumed, accountability is imposed. Responsibility is derived from authority and accountability is derived from responsibility.

Importance of Delegation

Importance	Explanation
Effective Management	Delegation frees managers from routine tasks, allowing them to focus on important matters.
Employee Development	Delegation provides employees with opportunities to enhance their skills and career prospects. It helps to make them better leaders and decision maker, thus, creating better future managers.
Motivation of Employees	Entrusting tasks build employees, self-esteem and confidence, encouraging better performance. It also involves trust of the superior on his/her subordinate.
Facilitation of Growth	Delegation enables organisational expansion by preparing a skilled workforce for new ventures.
Basis of Management Hierarchy	Delegation defines superior-subordinate relationships, establishing organisational hierarchy. It is the degree and flow of authority which determines who has to report to whom.
Better Coordination	Delegation helps to define the powers, duties and answerability related to various positions, which helps in reducing overlapping and duplication of effort.

5.4 Concept of Decentralisation

Decentralisation refers to dispersal of authority throughout all the departments and at all levels of the organisation. Decision-making authority is shared with lower levels and is consequently placed nearest to the points of action.

According to **Henri Fayol**, "Everything which goes to increase the importance of subordinate's role is decentralisation, everything that goes to reduce, it is centralisation."

Centralisation and Decentralisation

An organisation is centralised when decision-making authority is retained by higher management levels whereas it is decentralised when such authority is delegated. Complete centralisation would imply concentration of all decision-making functions at the apex of the management hierarchy. Such a scenario would prevent the need for a management hierarchy. On the other hand, complete decentralisation would imply the delegation of all decision- making functions to the lower level of the hierarchy and this would prevent the need for higher managerial positions.

Importance of Decentralisation

Following points highlight the importance of decentralisation

Importance of Decentralisation

- Develops Initiative among Subordinates
- Develops Managerial Talent for the Future
- Quick Decision-making
- Relief to Top Management
- Facilitates Growth
- Better Control

1. **Develops Initiative among Subordinates** Decentralisation promotes self-reliance and confidence in subordinates by allowing them to make decisions independently.
2. **Develops Managerial Talent for the Future** It provides opportunities for subordinates to gain experience and prove their abilities, creating a talent pool for higher roles. It also helps to identify those who may not be successful in assuming greater responsibility.
3. **Quick Decision-making** Decisions are made faster as they occur at levels closest to the action, reducing communication delays. There are also less chances of information getting distorted as it does not have to go through long channels.
4. **Relief to Top Management** It helps to reduce direct supervision over subordinates. Thus, top management can focus on policy decisions rather than being trapped by routine operational tasks.
5. **Facilitates Growth** Greater autonomy and competition among departments enhance productivity and support expansion through more returns.
6. **Better Control** Decentralisation allows for individual departmental accountability and improved performance evaluation. Feedback from all levels helps to analyse variances and improve operations.

Decentralisation Significance

Imagine a tech company that recently adopted a decentralised structure, giving its regional managers the autonomy to make decisions about local marketing strategies. This shift led to a surge in innovative campaigns tailored to diverse regional markets, such as a viral social media push in one region and a local influencer partnership in another. As a result, the company saw a 30% increase in regional sales and empowered its managers to develop valuable leadership skills. The top executives were then able to concentrate on strategic expansions, knowing that the day-to-day decisions were in capable hands.

Delegation vs Decentralisation

Delegation	Decentralisation
• **Delegation** happens when a manager assigns tasks within their team while maintaining oversight.	• **Decentralisation** involves giving entire departments the autonomy to make decisions independently.
• **Scenario 1 : Delegation** Sarah, the production manager, delegates the task of quality inspection and inventory management to her team members but closely monitors their work to ensure everything runs smoothly. This approach helps Sarah manage her workload while keeping control over the production process.	• **Scenario 2 : Decentralisation** The company implements decentralisation by creating separate departments for research and development, marketing and customer service, each with its own decision-making authority. This shift allows each department to operate independently, fostering innovation and agility as they tailor strategies to their specific needs and goals.

Mind Map

ORGANISING

1 Concept of Organising

Organising can be defined as identifying and grouping different activities in the organisation and bringing together the physical, financial and human resources to establish the most productive relations for the achievement of specific goals.

2 Process of Organising

- **Identification and Division of Work** Identifying and dividing the work that has to be done in accordance with previously determined plans
- **Departmentalisation** Similar activities are grouped together
- **Assignment of Duties** Job is allocated to individuals as per their skill and knowledge
- **Establishing Authority and Reporting Relationships** Creates superior-subordinate relationship, which helps to create a hierarchical structure

3 Importance of Organising

- **Benefits of Specialisation** Repetitive performance helps in gaining specialisation
- **Clarity in Working Relationships** Helps in fixation of responsibility
- **Optimum Utilisation of Resources** Leads to proper usage of materials, financial and human resources
- **Adaptation to Change** Facilitates modification in organisational structure and inter-relationships
- **Effective Administration** Gives a clear description of jobs, duties and responsibilities
- **Development of Personnel** Stimulates creativity amongst the managers
- **Expansion and Growth** Helps in the growth and diversification of an enterprise

4 Organisational Structure

It can be defined as the framework within which managerial and operating tasks are performed.

Functional Structure
(Grouping of jobs of similar nature under one department)

Advantages
- Occupational specialisation
- Effective control and coordination
- Improves efficiency
- Avoids duplication of functions
- Ease in training
- Proper attention

Disadvantages
- Functional empire
- Difficulty in coordination between different departments
- Conflict of interest
- Inflexibility
- Difficult to hold accountable

Divisional Structure
(Grouping of jobs related to one product under one department)

Advantages
- Product specialisation
- Greater accountability
- Flexibility
- Expansion and growth

Disadvantages
- Departmental conflicts
- Costly
- Ignore organisational interests

5 Formal Organisation

It is the organisation structure designed by the management to accomplish a particular task.

Features
- Clearly defined reporting relationships
- Created to achieve organisational objectives
- Coordinates efforts of various departments
- Intentionally created
- Places more emphasis on work

Advantages
- It makes fixation of responsibility easy
- Roles and duties are clearly specified
- Unity of command is maintained
- It helps in accomplishment of goals
- It provides stability to the organisation

Disadvantages
- Delay in action leads to procedural delays
- Lack of initiative reduces creativity
- Ignores human element as it places more emphasis on structure and work

6 Informal Organisation

It originates from within the formal organisation as a result of personal interaction among employees.

Features
- Originates from within formal organisation
- Standards of behaviour evolve from group norms
- Follows independent channels of communication
- Emerges spontaneously
- No definite structure

Advantages
- Faster communication as prescribed lines of communication not followed
- Fulfill social needs by providing sense of belongingness
- Helps in achieving organisational objectives

Disadvantages
- Spread of rumours which acts as destructive force
- Resistance to change leads to delays or restricts growth
- Pressurises members to conform to group expectations

7 Delegation

Delegation refers to the downward transfer of authority from a superior to subordinate.

Elements
- **Authority** Right of an individual to take decisions
- **Responsibility** Obligation of a subordinate to properly perform the assigned duty
- **Accountability** Being answerable for the final outcome

Importance
- It leads to effective management
- It helps in the employee development
- It helps in motivating the employees
- It leads to facilitation of growth
- It serves as basis of management hierarchy
- It helps in better coordination

8 Decentralisation

It refers to dispersal of authority throughout all the departments and at all levels of organisation.

Importance
- It helps in promoting self-reliance and confidence
- It leads to quick decision-making
- It facilitates growth
- It helps in developing managerial talent
- It gives relief to top management
- It leads to better control

EXAM PATTERN QUESTIONS

Objective Type Questions

Multiple Choice Questions (MCQs)

1. Which of the following statements is incorrect about the organising function in management?
(a) Organising ensures effective and efficient use of resources
(b) Organising defines the roles and responsibilities of employees
(c) Organising focuses on setting long-term strategic goals
(d) Organising helps in establishing a structure for coordinating activities

2. The process that initiates implementation of plans by clarifying jobs and working relationships and effectively deploying resources for attainment of identified and desired results is known as CBSE 2023
(a) organising (b) controlling
(c) staffing (d) planning

3. Which of the following statements does not correctly describe the impact of organising on an organisation?
(a) Organising helps in achieving the organisation's goals through systematic division of work
(b) Organising enhances the clarity of authority and reporting relationships
(c) Organising eliminates the need for formal communication channels
(d) Organising facilitates better resource utilisation by avoiding duplication of work

4. A school principle believes in proper organising. He tells his staff to be organised as he believes that through proper organising they can move away from present norms and accept new challenges with success. They will be able to add more activities and projects in their yearly plan. Which importance of organising has been indicated in the above paragraph? Competency Based Que
(a) Expansion and growth
(b) Benefits of specialisation
(c) Clarity in working relationships
(d) Optimum utilisation of resources

5. "The process of organising allows a business enterprise to accommodate changes in the business environment. It allows the organisation structure to be suitably modified to pave the way for a smooth transition."

The point of importance of organising function of management highlighted in the above lines is CBSE 2025
(a) benefits of specialisation
(b) clarity in working relationships
(c) optimum utilisation of resources
(d) adaptation to change

6. Neha has recently taken up the role of operations manager at GreenTech Innovations. One of her key responsibilities is to ensure that the operational activities are structured and managed effectively. After she has established the tasks and grouped them according to the overall operational plans, her next step in the organising process would be to Competency Based Que
(a) establishing reporting relationships
(b) delegate authority
(c) coordinate activities
(d) proceed for departmentalisation

7. Jasmine Ahluwalia is the manager of an artefacts museum's marketing team, responsible for promoting exhibitions and events. In the previous season, she defined the total work of managing the events into graphic designing, registration inquiries, bill payments, etc, in order to facilitate specialisation. However, instead of allocating work, she had assigned each team member the full responsibility of managing the promotion of an entire event.

Inspite of holding regular team meetings to take feedback, Jasmine found problems throughout the events season in the quality of graphic design, registration inquiry, bill payments, etc.

For the upcoming events season, Jasmine has decided to divide these responsibilities on the basis of her observation of the areas in which the individual team members have excelled in the previous season and allocate the roles based on their skills and competencies. Identify the step in the organising process which was not properly performed in the previous season but has been duly performed for the upcoming season. CBSE SQP 2025; Competency Based Que
(a) Identification and division of work
(b) Establishing reporting relationships
(c) Departmentalisation
(d) Assignment of duties

8. **Which of the following options denotes the correct sequence of steps in the process of 'organising' function of management?** CBSE 2024 C

(a) Departmentalisation → Identification and division of work → Establishing authority and reporting relationships → Assignment of duties
(b) Departmentalisation → Identification and division of work → Assignment of duties → Establishing authority and reporting relationships
(c) Identification and division of work → Establishing authority and reporting relationships → Assignment of duties → Departmentalisation
(d) Identification and division of work → Departmentalisation → Assignment of duties → Establishing authority and reporting relationships

9. **Span of management refers to**

(a) number of subordinates at lower level
(b) total number of managers
(c) number of subordinates under a superior
(d) number of levels in the organisation

10. **Name the outcome of the function of management which includes designing of roles to be filled by suitably skilled people and defining the inter-relationship between rules so that ambiguity in performance of duties can be eliminated.**

(a) Organisation structure (b) Delegation of authority
(c) Decentralisation (d) Controlling

11. **......... gives shape to the organisation structure.**

(a) Extent of delegation
(b) Span of management
(c) Number of employees
(d) Planning

12. **Which of the following incorrectly describes the characteristic of a well-organised structure?**

(a) Clearly defined roles and responsibilities
(b) Hierarchical levels of authority
(c) Spontaneous and unstructured communication channels
(d) Effective coordination among departments

13. **TechSavvy Inc. is a technology company that specialises in developing software solutions. As the company has grown, it has decided to create separate divisions for its various product lines, including mobile apps, cloud services and cybersecurity.**

Each division operates independently with its own management team and resources. Based on this description, what type of organisational structure is TechSavvy Inc. using? Competency Based Que

(a) Functional structure (b) Divisional structure
(c) Matrix structure (d) Flat structure

14. **Online retailer 'Bizen' has grown to be the biggest provider worldwide in the field of e-commerce. Its revenues are growing steadily year after year. It owes its success to the rapid rate of digitisation and its organisational structure. 'Bizen's managing director, Mohit makes strategic decisions and has control over the entire organisation.**

In 'Bizen', jobs of similar nature are grouped together into human resource department, marketing department, purchase department and research and development department. These departments are further divided into sections and all departmental heads report to Mohit who is the coordinating head.

This ensures efficiency in the utilisation of manpower and minimises duplication of efforts. The type of organisational structure of 'Bizen' is CBSE 2024; Competency Based Que

(a) informal organisational structure
(b) divisional organisational structure
(c) functional organisational structure
(d) Both (b) and (c)

15. **Ms. Patel started working at a firm called Creative Solutions Ltd. She found that the firm has created separate teams for different geographic regions, such as North America, Europe and Asia. Each team operates with its own budget and makes decisions independently, focusing on the specific needs of its region.**

What can be inferred about the organisational structure of Creative Solutions Ltd. based on Ms. Patel's observations? Competency Based Que

(a) It is a matrix structure
(b) Divisional structure is being used
(c) The company follows a functional structure
(d) The firm has a line structure

16. **Identify the type of organisation structure from the organisational chart given below.**

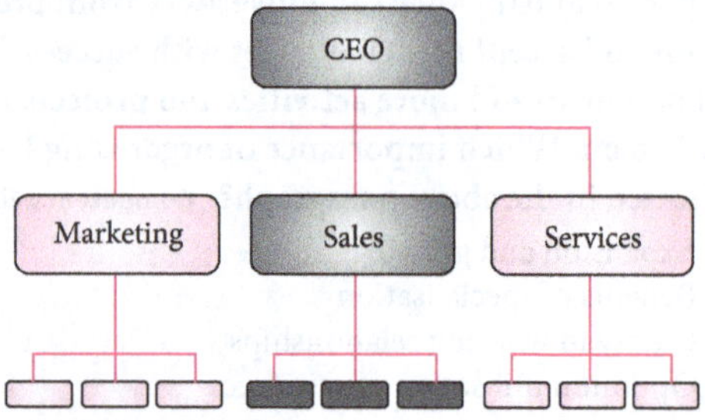

(a) Functional structure
(b) Divisional structure
(c) Formal structure
(d) Matrix structure

17. TechFusion Ltd. is a technology company that recently divided its business into different departments based on functions like Research and Development (R & D), marketing, finance and human resources. Each department is responsible for specialised tasks, ensuring smooth operations and efficiency in their respective areas.

Which type of organisational structure has TechFusion Ltd. adopted? **Competency Based Que**

(a) Divisional structure (b) Functional structure
(c) Matrix structure (d) Network structure

18. Under this type of organisational structure, manpower is grouped on the basis of different products manufactured.

(a) Divisional structure (b) Functional structure
(c) Network structure (d) Matrix structure

19. Indigo Limited has a staff of 300 people which is grouped into different departments. The organisational structure depicts that 100 people work in production department, 150 in finance department, 20 in technology department and 30 in human resource department. Identify the type of organisational structure being followed by the company. **Competency Based Que**

(a) Functional structure (b) Divisional structure
(c) Informal structure (d) None of these

20. Which of the following is an advantage of divisional structure?

(a) Duplicity of functions
(b) Quick decision-making
(c) Selfish attitude
(d) Conflicts

21. An organisation is working by clubbing similar related jobs under different departments. The HR department is not in direct touch with the marketing department and this has created problems. The HR head feels that he only knows about the HR department and similar is the case with the marketing department. However the truth is both of them have limited and specific skills.

Which type of organisation structure does this organisation has? **Competency Based Que**

(a) Divisional structure (b) Matrix structure
(c) Functional structure (d) Project structure

22. A company has been registered under the Companies Act with an authorised share capital of ₹ 20,000 crores. Its registered office is situated in Delhi and manufacturing unit in a backward district of Rajasthan. Its marketing department is situated in Bhopal. The company is manufacturing Fast Moving Consumer Goods (FMCG).

Identify a suitable organisation structure for the company. **Competency Based Que**

(a) Functional structure (b) Divisional structure
(c) Matrix structure (d) Formal structure

23. Organisational structure that is based on rules and procedures is known as

(a) formal (b) informal
(c) Both (a) and (b) (d) Neither (a) nor (b)

24. Lalit has joined a manufacturing firm as a worker. He has recently started working on the shop floor. The management is quite liberal and has allowed the workers to form a hockey club. The workers assemble and play hockey in the evening after the completion of their work. However, the management is little worried about the outcomes.

The management is trying to change the schedule of the workers but they are unsure about the reaction of the workers. Though majority of the workers are sincere, like Lalit, yet the management is concerned about their companions in the hockey club. Which type of organisation is the hockey club? **Competency Based Que**

(a) Formal organisation (b) Informal organisation
(c) Matrix organisation (d) Project organisation

25. Which type of organisation is created as a result of the group indicated in below image?

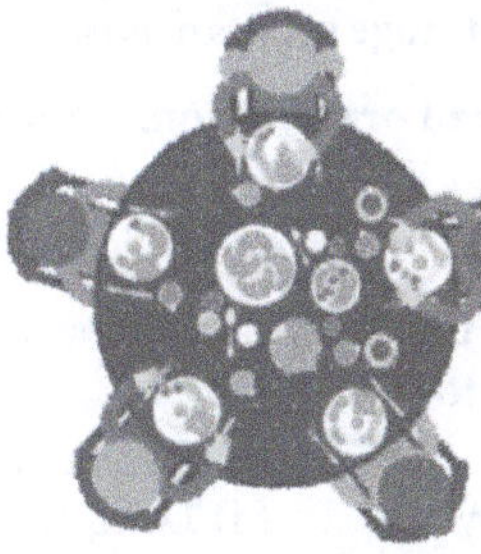

(a) Formal organisation (b) Informal organisation
(c) Divisional organisation (d) Functional organisation

26. ABC Corporation has a well-structured hierarchy where each employee knows their role, responsibilities and whom they report to. The company strictly follows established procedures for decision-making. However, lately, the management has noticed that while this system ensures clarity and accountability, it often results in significant delays when decisions need to be made.

Employees feel that the time taken to follow the procedural steps slows down the decision-making process, especially in urgent situations.

What is the likely cause of the delays in decision-making at ABC Corporation? **Competency Based Que**

(a) Freedom and independence
(b) Procedural delays and delayed decision-making
(c) More emphasis on interpersonal relations
(d) Faster spreading of information

27. **In XYZ Enterprises, employees tend to rely heavily on personal relationships and informal networks to get work done. While this informal set-up allows for flexibility and quick communication, it also leads to a preference for maintaining the status-quo. Employees often resist changes to their routine, resulting in a lack of innovation and productivity in the workplace.**
What is one of the disadvantages of the informal organisation at XYZ Enterprises? **Competency Based Que**
(a) Deviance (b) Status quo
(c) Disruptiveness (d) Disorderliness

28. **Which of the following is not a feature of informal organisation?**
(a) It has no written rules and procedures
(b) It clearly defines the authority and responsibility of every individual
(c) It is not deliberately created by the management
(d) It is personal means the feelings of individuals are kept in mind

29. **Realit Drinks is an organisation which helps quench the thirst of people sitting on roadside and parks on sundays. This organisation has originated from mountain cold storage spontaneously.**
Identify the type of organisation. **Competency Based Que**
(a) Informal (b) Formal
(c) Matrix (d) Functional

30. **......... refers to the downward transfer of authority from a superior to subordinate.** **CBSE 2023**
(a) Organising (b) Decentralisation
(c) Accountability (d) Delegation

31. **Identify the process illustrated by the picture in which the superior is providing a part of his authority to his subordinate for making decisions.**

(a) Authority (b) Delegation
(c) Responsibility (d) Centralisation

32. **The right of an individual to command his subordinates and to take action within the scope of his position is called** **CBSE 2025**
(a) decentralisation (b) authority
(c) responsibility (d) accountability

33. **Identify the essential concept of organising which is missing as depicted in the below picture.**

(a) Delegation of authority (b) Span of control
(c) Decentralisation (d) Accountability

34. **What is the key to managerial post?**
(a) Responsibility (b) Authority
(c) Accountability (d) None of these

35. **Identify the importance of delegation of authority that can be interpreted from the picture below in which the manager of company is worried to approve all the files while candidates are waiting for the interview outside his office.**

(a) Delegation of authority leads to effective management
(b) Delegation of authority leads to employee development
(c) Delegation of authority leads to better coordination
(d) None of the above

36. **"It refers to concentration of authority at higher management levels." Name it.**
(a) Centralisation (b) Decentralisation
(c) Both (a) and (b) (d) Neither (a) nor (b)

37. **"It is a process that assigns specific authority and responsibility to various managers, allowing decisions to be made closer to the point of action, improving efficiency and responsiveness." Identify the process.**

(a) Centralisation (b) Organising
(c) Decentralisation (d) Staffing

38. **The marketing manager of AD Ltd. an organisation manufacturing generators, has been asked to achieve a target sale of 100 generators per day. He delegates the task to 15 sales managers and 5 subordinates working under him. Identify the concept used in the case.** **Competency Based Que**

(a) Decentralisation (b) Span of control
(c) Authority (d) Responsibility

39. **NeoTech Ltd. has given its department heads the authority to make decisions regarding their areas. However, the heads must regularly report to top management and work according to the overall company guidelines. This approach ensures faster decision-making and flexibility in operations.**

Which concept of organising is highlighted by NeoTech Ltd.? **Competency Based Que**

(a) Centralisation (b) Decentralisation
(c) Formalisation (d) Span of control

Direction *Read the following case study and answer the questions 40 to 43 on the basis of the same*

Delta Solutions, a leading software development firm, initially operated with a functional organisational structure. This structure worked well for the company's early stages, focusing on core functions like development, marketing and support. However, as the company expanded its product lines and entered new markets, it faced difficulties in managing these diverse operations effectively.

In 2020, Delta Solutions decided to adopt a divisional organisational structure. This new structure divided the company into distinct divisions based on product lines and geographical regions. Each division had its own management team responsible for all aspects of its operations, including product development, marketing and customer support. This restructuring aimed to improve focus and responsiveness.

In 2022, the company reviewed its organising process and delegation practices to ensure that responsibilities were clearly defined and aligned with its strategic goals.

40. **"Delta Solutions initially operated with an organisational structure focusing on core functions like development, marketing and support." Which type of organisational structure is described here?**

(a) Divisional (b) Matrix
(c) Functional (d) Line and staff

41. **"In 2020, Delta Solutions decided to adopt a divisional organisational structure, dividing the company into distinct divisions based on product lines and geographical regions."**

What is the main benefit of adopting a divisional structure mentioned here?

(a) Improved centralisation
(b) Enhanced coordination
(c) Better focus on products and markets
(d) Simplified management hierarchy

42. **"Each division had its own management team responsible for all aspects of its operations, including product development, marketing and customer support." Which aspect of organising is highlighted by this statement?**

(a) Establishment of reporting relationships
(b) Division of work
(c) Delegation of authority
(d) Coordination across departments

43. **"In 2022, the company reviewed its organising process and delegation practices to ensure that responsibilities were clearly defined and aligned with its strategic goals." What is the primary objective of reviewing the organising process as described here?**

(a) To enhance employee morale
(b) To ensure effective resource allocation
(c) To align responsibilities with strategic goals
(d) To simplify communication channels

Assertion-Reason

Direction (Q. No. 44 to 53) *Read the following Assertion (A) and Reason (R) and choose the correct alternative from the following*

Alternatives

(a) Both Assertion (A) and Reason (R) are true and Reason (R) is the correct explanation of Assertion (A)
(b) Both Assertion (A) and Reason (R) are true, but Reason (R) is not the correct explanation of Assertion (A)
(c) Assertion (A) is true, but Reason (R) is false
(d) Assertion (A) is false, but Reason (R) is true

44. **Assertion** (A) Organising helps in establishing working relationships, which clarifies the lines of communication and specifies who is to report to whom.

Reason (R) Repetitive performance of a particular work also leads to specialisation.

45. **Assertion** (A) Organising leads to the optimum utilisation of resources.

Reason (R) Organising helps in establishing authority relationships among employees.

46. Assertion (A) The organising function is crucial for the smooth running of an organisation.

Reason (R) Organising ensures that every department works in isolation without interfering with others.

47. Assertion (A) Organising function helps in adapting to changes in the environment.

Reason (R) Organising provides a framework for creating formal communication channels.

48. Assertion (A) The first step of organising is concerned with dividing the work into manageable activities.

Reason (R) With the help of this, duplication cannot be avoided.

49. Assertion (A) Functional structure allows for functional specialisation.

Reason (R) Functional structure does not allow grouping based on specific functions.

50. Assertion (A) Coordination is easy in a divisional structure.

Reason (R) All functions related to a particular product are integrated in one department in a divisional structure.

51. Assertion (A) Delegation helps in the efficient functioning of an organisation.

Reason (R) Delegation helps the manager to use his time on high priority activities.

52. Assertion (A) In centralised organisation, decision making is very slow.

Reason (R) In a centralised organisation, every decision is taken by top management and information has to pass through many levels.

53. Assertion (A) There are more chances of getting the information distorted in decentralisation.

Reason (R) Information does not have to go through long channels in decentralisation.

Two Statements Based MCQs

Direction (Q. No. 54 to 63) *Read the following statements carefully and choose the correct alternative*

Alternatives

(a) Statement I is correct and Statement II is incorrect
(b) Statement II is correct and Statement I is incorrect
(c) Both the statements are correct
(d) Both the statements are incorrect

54. Statement I Organising is a process that identifies and groups the work to be performed.

Statement II Organising creates authority relationships and communication channels within the organisation.

55. Statement I Organising ensures the coordination of various activities and resources within the organisation.

Statement II Organising is unrelated to the accomplishment of organisational goals.

56. Statement I Organising function helps in establishing clear reporting relationships in an organisation.

Statement II Organising results in duplication of work and overlapping of duties.

57. Statement I Organising results in the optimum utilisation of resources.

Statement II Organising leads to the fragmentation of work, causing inefficiency.

58. Statement I Span of control refers to the number of subordinates that a manager can effectively control.

Statement II Wider span of control leads to a tall organisational structure.

59. Statement I Divisional structure groups employees based on their specialised functions.

Statement II Functional structure is more suitable for large organisations with diverse products.

60. Statement I Formal organisation is based on the established hierarchy within the organisation.

Statement II Informal organisation is created deliberately by the management to ensure efficient task completion.

61. Statement I Delegation of authority refers to the retention of all decision-making power by top management.

Statement II In organising, decentralisation involves systematically retaining authority at higher levels.

62. Statement I Accountability can be delegated.

Statement II Responsibility can be delegated completely.

63. Statement I Centralisation refers to the concentration of decision-making authority at the top level of management.

Statement II Decentralisation leads to quicker decision-making and greater flexibility within the organisation.

Matching

64. Match the importance of organising in Column I with their respective statements in Column II

Column I	Column II
A. Growth and expansion	(i) Organising stimulates creativity amongst managers.
B. Specialisation benefits	(ii) Repetitive performance of a particular task allows workers to gain experience in that area.
C. Optimum utilisation of resources	(iii) It helps to increase customer base.
D. Personnel development	(iv) Proper assignment of jobs avoids overlapping.

Codes

	A	B	C	D
(a)	(iii)	(ii)	(iv)	(i)
(b)	(iii)	(iv)	(i)	(ii)
(c)	(i)	(iii)	(iv)	(ii)
(d)	(ii)	(i)	(iv)	(iii)

65. Match the stages of organising process in Column I with their respective statements in Column II

Column I	Column II
A. Departmentalisation	(i) The work to be completed at each point is clearly defined.
B. Assignment of duties	(ii) It is made clear that from whom each individual takes orders and to whom he/she is accountable.
C. Identification and division of work	(iii) The activities of the same nature are grouped together and assigned to a particular department.
D. Establishing reporting relationships	(iv) It helps to avoid duplication of work.

Codes

	A	B	C	D
(a)	(iii)	(i)	(iv)	(ii)
(b)	(ii)	(iv)	(i)	(iii)
(c)	(iii)	(ii)	(iv)	(i)
(d)	(ii)	(i)	(iv)	(iii)

66. Match the organisational structure in Column I with their respective statements in Column II

Column I	Column II
A. Functional structure	(i) It is costly as all resources are required in each department.
B. Divisional structure	(ii) It leads to functional specialisation.
C. Formal organisation	(iii) It specifies the reporting relationships among various job positions.
D. Informal organisation	(iv) It emerges spontaneously and is not created deliberately.

Codes

	A	B	C	D		A	B	C	D
(a)	(ii)	(i)	(iii)	(iv)	(b)	(ii)	(iv)	(i)	(iii)
(c)	(iii)	(i)	(iv)	(ii)	(d)	(ii)	(i)	(iv)	(iii)

67. Match the type of organisation in Column I with their respective statements in Column II

Column I	Column II
A. Formal organisation	(i) It arises out of personal qualities.
B. Informal organisation	(ii) Groups similar or related jobs together.
C. Functional structure	(iii) It arises by virtue of position in management.

Codes

	A	B	C		A	B	C
(a)	(ii)	(i)	(iii)	(b)	(iii)	(i)	(ii)
(c)	(i)	(iii)	(ii)	(d)	(ii)	(iii)	(i)

68. Match the elements of delegation in Column I with their respective statements in Column II

Column I	Column II
A. Authority	(i) Answerability for the results of the task assigned.
B. Responsibility	(ii) Obligation of a subordinate to complete the assigned task.
C. Accountability	(iii) Right given to an individual to direct or command others.

Codes

	A	B	C		A	B	C
(a)	(iii)	(ii)	(i)	(b)	(iii)	(i)	(ii)
(c)	(i)	(iii)	(ii)	(d)	(ii)	(iii)	(i)

Answers

1. (c) Organising is concerned with arranging resources and defining roles to achieve goals efficiently. Setting long-term strategic goals is part of planning, not organising.
2. (a) organising
3. (c) Organising involves establishing formal communication channels to ensure effective information flow. It does not eliminate the need for these channels but rather structures them.
4. (a) Expansion and growth
5. (d) Adaptation to change
6. (d) proceed for departmentalisation
7. (d) Assignment of duties
8. (d) Identification and division of work → Departmentalisation → Assignment of duties → Establishing authority and reporting relationships
9. (c) number of subordinates under a superior
10. (a) Organisation structure
11. (b) Span of management
12. (c) A well-organised structure involves clearly defined roles, hierarchical authority and effective coordination. Spontaneous and unstructured communication can lead to confusion and inefficiency.
13. (b) Divisional structure
14. (c) functional organisational structure
15. (b) Divisional structure is being used
16. (a) Functional structure
17. (b) Functional structure
18. (a) Divisional structure
19. (a) Functional structure
20. (b) Quick decision-making
21. (c) Functional structure
22. (b) Divisional structure
23. (a) formal
24. (b) Informal organisation
25. (b) Informal organisation
26. (b) Procedural delays and delayed decision-making
27. (b) Status quo
28. (b) It clearly defines the authority and responsibility of every individual
29. (a) informal
30. (d) Delegation
31. (b) Delegation
32. (b) authority
33. (a) Delegation of authority
34. (b) Authority
35. (a) Delegation of authority leads to effective management
36. (a) Centralisation
37. (c) Decentralisation
38. (a) Decentralisation
39. (b) Decentralisation
40. (c) Functional
41. (c) Better focus on products and markets
42. (c) Delegation of authority
43. (c) To align responsibilities with strategic goals
44. (b) Both Assertion (A) and Reason (R) are true, but Reason (R) is not the correct explanation of Assertion (A)
45. (b) Both Assertion (A) and Reason (R) are true, but Reason (R) is not the correct explanation of Assertion (A)
46. (c) Organising does not ensure that departments should work in isolation, rather, it facilitates collaboration and coordination among them.
47. (b) Both Assertion (A) and Reason (R) are true, but Reason (R) is not the correct explanation of Assertion (A)
48. (c) Proper division of work in the organising process helps in avoiding duplication of efforts.
49. (c) A functional structure is indeed based on functions and allows grouping according to specific functions.
50. (a) Both Assertion (A) and Reason (R) are true and Reason (R) is the correct explanation of Assertion (A)
51. (a) Both Assertion (A) and Reason (R) are true and Reason (R) is the correct explanation of Assertion (A)
52. (a) Both Assertion (A) and Reason (R) are true and Reason (R) is the correct explanation of Assertion (A)
53. (d) In decentralisation, there are fewer chances of information getting distorted because decisions are made at various levels without needing to pass through many hierarchical levels.
54. (c) Both the statements are correct
55. (a) Organising is directly related to achieving organisational goals.
56. (b) Effective organising prevents duplication and overlapping by clearly defining roles and responsibilities.
57. (a) Effective organising avoids fragmentation of work by properly allocating tasks and resources.
58. (a) A wider span of control actually leads to a flatter organisational structure, not a tall one.
59. (d) Divisional structure groups employees based on products, geography or markets, not functions. Functional structure groups employees based on specialised functions and is more suited for organisations with a single product line.
60. (a) Informal organisation emerges naturally among employees and is not created by management.

61. (d) Delegation of authority involves assigning decision-making power to subordinates and decentralisation means distributing authority to lower levels.

62. (d) Accountability cannot be delegated, while responsibility and authority can be delegated, the person who delegated the task remains accountable for the outcome.
Responsibility can be delegated, but the original person delegating the task still holds some level of responsibility, especially in ensuring that the task is done correctly.

63. (c) Both the statements are correct

64. (a) (iii) (ii) (iv) (i)

65. (a) (iii) (i) (iv) (ii)

66. (a) (ii) (i) (iii) (iv)

67. (b) (iii) (i) (ii)

68. (a) (iii) (ii) (i)

Subjective Questions

Short Answer Type Questions

1. Define organising both as a structure and as a process.

Ans. Organising can be defined as identifying and grouping different activities in the organisation and bringing together the physical, financial and human resources to establish the most productive relations for the achievement of specific goals.

The organising function of management leads to the creation of an **organisational structure** which includes the following

(i) Designing of roles to be filled by suitably skilled people and

(ii) Defining the inter-relationship between these roles so that ambiguity in performance of duties can be eliminated.

Organising can also be defined as a **process** that initiates implementation of plans by clarifying jobs and working relationships and effectively deploying resources for the attainment of organisational objectives.

2. Explain how

(i) Adaptation to change and

(ii) Expansion and growth make organising important

Ans.

(i) **Adaptation to Change**
It facilitates modification in organisational structure and revision of inter-relationships among people in order to adapt to environmental changes.
It also helps to provide stability to the enterprise, so that it can continue to survive and grow inspite of changes.

(ii) **Expansion and Growth**
It helps in the growth and diversification of an enterprise by enabling it to deviate from existing norms and taking up new challenges.
It allows a business enterprise to add more job positions, departments and new lines of product. This helps in increasing customer base, sales volume and profits of the enterprise.

3. What are the steps in the process of organising? NCERT

Ans. The following steps are to be undertaken in the organising process

(i) **Identification and Division of Work**
The first step in the process of organising involves identifying and dividing the work that has to be done in accordance with previously determined plans. Work is divided into manageable tasks, so that duplication can be avoided and workload can be shared among employees.

(ii) **Departmentalisation**
Once work has been divided into small and manageable activities, then those activities which are similar in nature, are grouped together. This process is called departmentalisation. Departments can be created on the basis of products, functions and territory.

(iii) **Assignment of Duties**
Once the departments are created, each department is placed under the charge of an individual, called departmental head. Then, each job is allocated to an individual, according to his knowledge and skill. There should be a proper match between the nature of jobs and the ability of an individual.

(iv) **Establishing Reporting Relationships**
In the organisation, each employee has some authority as well as responsibility. It is necessary that every individual must know whom he has to take orders from and to whom he is answerable. This creates superior-subordinate hierarchy and helps in coordinating various activities in the organisation.

4. Explain the concept of functional organisational structure. Also, explain four advantages of functional organisational structure.

Or **State any six advantages of functional structure of organisation.** CBSE 2025

Ans. Under functional organisational structure, jobs of similar nature are grouped under one department. An organisation structure in which departments are created on the basis of different functions performed in the organisation is called a functional structure.

All departments in such organisations, report to a coordinating head.

Functional structure has the following advantages

(i) It leads to occupational specialisation, since emphasis is placed on specific functions and repeated performance of similar tasks by employees leads to efficient functioning.

(ii) It promotes control and coordination within a department because of similarity in the tasks performed.

(iii) It leads to increased managerial and operational efficiency which results in increased profits.

(iv) It leads to minimal duplication of efforts, which results in economies of scale and lower costs.

(v) It makes training of employees easier as the focus is only on a limited range of skills.

(vi) It ensures that all functions get due attention.

5. Explain any four advantages that divisional structure offers to the organisation.

Ans. Divisional structure has the following advantages

(i) It helps the managers to develop varied skills related to a product and prepares him for higher positions. This is because he gains experience in all functions related to a particular product.

(ii) Fixation of responsibility and accountability is easy, as divisional heads are responsible for the profits and losses of their divisions. This provides a proper basis for performance measurement and helps to take appropriate remedial action in case of poor performance of the division.

(iii) It promotes flexibility and initiative because each division functions as an autonomous unit which leads to faster decision-making.

(iv) It facilitates expansion and growth as new division can be added without interrupting the existing operations.

6. "The divisional organisational structure can enhance flexibility and responsiveness in large organisations. However, it also comes with certain drawbacks that can impact overall efficiency and coordination."

In light of the above statement, discuss three disadvantages of the divisional organisational structure. **Competency Based Que**

Ans. Divisional structure suffers from the following disadvantages

(i) Conflict may arise between different divisions on allocation of funds and other resources.

(ii) There is a duplication of physical facilities and functions, which leads to increase in cost.

(iii) Greater autonomy to divisional heads may lead to misuse of authority.

7. State four disadvantages of functional organisational structure.

Ans. Following are the disadvantages of functional organisational structure

(i) This structure places less emphasis on overall enterprise objectives than the objectives pursued by a functional head. Pursuing departmental interests at the cost of organisational interests can also hinder the interaction between two or more departments.

(ii) It may lead to problems in coordination as information has to be exchanged across functionally differentiated departments.

(iii) It becomes difficult to hold a particular department responsible for any problem.

(iv) Conflict often arises when the interests of two or more departments are not compatible.

8. Explain the concept of divisional structure. When it is suitable to use a divisional structure for an organisation.

Ans. An organisational structure in which various departments are created on the basis of products, territory or region, is called a divisional structure. Following are the situations when it is advisable to use a divisional structure

(i) It is most suitable when organisation deals in large variety of products using different productive resources.

(ii) Growth prospects are high.

(iii) Organisation wants to add more departments or diversify into different products and even expand to different territories.

9. State the features of formal organisation.

Ans. Some features of formal organisation are

(i) It specifies the relationships among various job positions and the nature of their inter-relationships. This clarifies who has to report to whom.

(ii) It is a means to achieve objectives specified in the plans.

(iii) It helps to coordinate, interlink and integrate the efforts of various departments.

(iv) It is deliberately designed by the top management.

(v) It places more emphasis on work rather than interpersonal relations among the employees.

10. The employee of Manav Ltd. have formed a dramatic group for their recreation. Explain the type of organisation so created and state its features.

Or **"Informal organisation plays a crucial role in facilitating communication and enhancing relationships within a workplace. Without it, the flow of information may become restricted, leading to misunderstandings and a lack of collaboration."**

In light of the above statement, explain informal organisation and state its features. Competency Based Que

Ans. Interaction among people at work gives rise to a network of social relationships among employees. This is called informal organisation.

Following are the features of informal organisation

(i) It originates from within the formal organisation, due to interaction among employees.

(ii) The standard of behaviour evolve from group norms rather than officially laid down rules and regulations.

(iii) Communication is free and independent.

(iv) It emerges spontaneously and not deliberately created by the management.

(v) It has no definite structure or form as it is a complex network of social relationships among members.

11. In a formal organisation with strict rules and clear roles, what are some drawbacks that may arise? Competency Based Que

Ans. Formal organisation has the following drawbacks

(i) It may lead to procedural delays and delayed decision-making as the established chain of command has to be followed.

(ii) Creativity gets reduced, as it does not allow any deviations from the rigidly laid down policies.

(iii) It places more emphasis on structure and work and ignores human relationships as well as social needs of the employees.

12. While informal organisations are known to foster close-knit relationships and a sense of camaraderie among employees, they can sometimes lead to challenges in maintaining official communication channels and decision-making authority.

Identify and explain any three potential drawbacks that may arise from such informal networks within an organisation. Competency Based Que

Ans. Informal organisation has the following drawbacks

(i) When an informal organisation spreads rumours, it becomes a destructive force and goes against the interest of the formal organisation.

(ii) The management may not be able to implement changes successfully if the informal organisation opposes them. Such resistance to change may delay or restrict growth.

(iii) It pressurises members to conform to group expectations which can be harmful to the organisation if the norms set by the group are against organisational interest.

13. What do you understand by the term 'formal organisation'? State any three advantages of formal organisation.

Ans. Formal organisation refers to the organisation structure which is designed by the management to accomplish a particular task.

In formal organisation, job description, rules and procedures related to work processes are laid down so as to enable smooth functioning of the enterprise.

Formal organisation has the following advantages

(i) Unity of command is maintained through an established chain of command.

(ii) Role and duties of each member are clearly specified which avoids confusion and duplication of effort.

(iii) It helps in effective accomplishment of goals by providing a framework for the operations to be performed.

14. How does informal organisation support the formal organisation? NCERT; Competency Based Que

Ans. Informal organisation support formal organisation in the following ways

(i) **Quick Feedback**
Prescribed lines of communication are not followed. Thus, the informal organisation leads to faster spread of information as well as quick feedback.

(ii) **Social Needs**
It helps to fulfill social needs of the members. This enhances their job satisfaction, since it gives them a sense of belongingness in the organisation.

(iii) **Flexibility**
In formal organisation, rules and policies are fixed, thus it is rigid in nature. On the other hand, in informal organisation, no such rules are there, thus leads to flexibility.

15. Discuss the elements of delegation. NCERT

Ans. Following are the various elements of delegation

(i) **Authority**
It is the power granted to an individual to facilitate the performance of the assigned work. When a manager assigns some of his responsibility to his subordinate, it means he has also granted some authority to his subordinate.

The subordinate needs authority to make the right decision and to carry out the responsibility given by the superior. Authority flows downwards because the superior has authority over the subordinates.

Authority determines the superior and subordinate relationship, where the subordinate has to execute the order of the superior.

(ii) **Responsibility**
The delegation process begins when the manager passes on some of his responsibility to his subordinate. Responsibility is the obligation of an individual to carry out assigned duties properly. Responsibility flows upward, i.e. a subordinate will always be responsible to his superior. This is because every subordinate has to execute the order of a superior.

When responsibility is given to an employee for a particular job, there is a consideration that is to be kept in view. The employee must be given the degree of authority to carry out his assigned job. The authority provided must be commensurate to the responsibility for an effective delegation.

(iii) **Accountability**
It is the third and final step in the process of delegation. Accountability means being answerable to the superior for the final result. Once authority has been delegated and responsibilities have been accepted, then a person cannot deny accountability because the subordinate is accountable to his superior.
Accountability flows upward, i.e. subordinates are accountable to their superiors for their assigned jobs. Therefore, managers have to make sure that there is a proper discharge of duties by the subordinates.

16. State any four points that highlight the importance of delegation for an organisation.

Or **"Effective delegation of authority leads to many benefits." Explain the above statement with the help of any four points.** **CBSE 2024 C**

Or **"Delegation helps a manager to extend his area of operations as without it, his activities would be restricted to only what he himself can do."**
In light of the above statement, explain how effective delegation helps the organisation in achieving objectives. **CBSE SQP 2025**

Ans. The importance of delegation can be explained with the help of the following points

(i) **Motivation of Employees**
Delegation provides a feeling of status and recognition to subordinates, as it is not only a process of sharing workload, but also involves trust of the superior on his/her subordinate. Responsibility for work builds the self-esteem of an employee and improves his/her confidence. He/She feels encouraged and tries to improve his/her performance further.

(ii) **Facilitation of Growth**
Delegation helps in the expansion of an organisation by providing a ready workforce to take up leading positions in new ventures. Trained and experienced employees are able to play significant role in the launch of new projects of the organisation.

(iii) **Basis of Management Hierarchy**
Delegation of authority establishes superior-subordinate relationships, which are the basis of hierarchy of management. It is the degree and flow of authority which determines who has to report to whom.
The extent of delegated authority also decides the power that each job position enjoys in the organisation.

(iv) **Better Coordination**
The elements of delegation namely authority, responsibility and accountability helps to define the powers, duties and answerability related to various positions in an organisation. This helps to avoid overlapping and duplication of work. Such clarity in reporting relationships help in developing and maintaning effective coordination amongst the departments, levels and functions of management.

17. Can a large sized organisation be totally centralised or decentralised? Give your opinion. **NCERT; Competency Based Que**

Ans. No, an organisation cannot be completely centralised or decentralised. It is because complete centralisation implies concentration of authority in a few hands while complete decentralisation implies greater autonomy to the lower levels of management. Therefore, every organisation must have a blend of centralisation and decentralisation. As an organisation grows, there is a tendency to move towards decentralisation. At the same time, decisions need to be centralised in priority and Key Result Areas (KRAs).

18. "If we delegate authority, we multiply it by two; if we decentralise it, we multiply it by many." How? **Competency Based Que**

Ans. Delegation of authority refers to granting authority by one individual (superior) to another (subordinate). Therefore, its scope is confined to a manager and his immediate subordinate. When we delegate authority, we multiply it by two i.e. the delegator and his subordinate, to whom authority is delegated. Delegation is a process of sharing of task and authority between a manager and his subordinate.

Decentralisation of authority is not restricted to two individuals. It involves systematic delegation of authority at all levels and in all functions of the organisation.

In case of decentralisation, managers at middle and lower levels are granted the authority for taking decisions on tasks assigned to them. Therefore, the scope of decentralisation is wider than that of delegation. When we decentralise authority, we multiply it by many.

Long Answer Type Questions

19. Explain the following points of 'importance of organising's function of management.
(i) **Optimum utilisation of resources**
(ii) **Effective administration**
(iii) **Benefits of specialisation**

Ans.

(i) **Optimum Utilisation of Resources**
It leads to proper usage of all materials, financial and human resources. Proper assignment of jobs to workers reduces duplication of work which helps to prevent confusion, minimises wastages and allows the best possible use of resources.

(ii) **Effective Administration**
It gives a clear description of jobs and duties as well as responsibilities of each individual. This helps to avoid confusion and duplication of activities. Clarity in working relationships enables proper execution of work and brings effectiveness in administration.

(iii) **Benefits of Specialisation**
Organising leads to a systematic allocation of job amongst the workforce. This reduces the work load as well as enhances productivity.

Repetitive performance of a particular task by a worker helps him to gain experience and attain specialisation.

20. What is a divisional structure? Discuss its advantages and limitations.

Or **State any three advantages and any three disadvantages of divisional structure of an organisation.** CBSE 2025

Ans. An organisation structure in which various departments are created on the basis of products, territory or region, is called a divisional structure. Each unit has a divisional manager, who is responsible for performance and has authority over their division. Each division is further divided into functional units like production, sales, finance, etc. The divisional head is solely responsible for the profit or loss of their division.

Divisional structure has the following advantages

(i) It helps the managers to develop varied skills related to a product and facilitates managerial development.

(ii) Fixation of responsibility and accountability is easy, as divisional heads are responsible for the profits and losses of their divisions.

(iii) With more initiative and flexibility, decisions are taken much faster in divisional structure.

Divisional structure suffers from the following disadvantages

(i) Conflict may arise between different divisions on allocation of funds and other resources.

(ii) There is a duplication of physical facilities and functions, which leads to increase in cost.

(iii) Greater autonomy to divisional heads may lead to misuse of authority.

21. Differentiate between functional structure and divisional structure on the basis of

(i) Formation **(ii) Specialisation**
(iii) Responsibility **(iv) Managerial development**
(v) Cost **(vi) Coordination**

CBSE SQP 2025

Or **Differentiate between 'functional structure' and 'divisional structure' of organisation on any six basis.** CBSE 2025

Ans. Difference between functional and divisional structure

Basis	Functional Structure	Divisional Structure
Formation	Formation is based on functions.	Formation is based on product lines and is supported by functions.
Specialisation	Functional specialisation.	Product specialisation.
Responsibility	Difficult of fix on a department.	Easy to fix responsibility for performance.
Managerial Development	Difficult, as each functional manager has to report to the top management.	Easier, autonomy as well as the chance to preform multiple functions helps in managerial development.
Cost	Functions are not duplicated hence economical.	Duplication of resources in various departments, hence costly.
Coordination	Difficult for a multiproduct company.	Easy, because all functions related to a particular product are integrated in one department.

22. What is meant by 'formal organisation'? State any four advantages of formal organisation. CBSE 2023

Or **Give the meaning of formal organisation. State any five features of formal organisation.** CBSE 2025; 2024 C

Ans. Formal organisation refers to the organisation structure which is designed by the management to accomplish a particular task. In formal organisation, job description, rules and procedures related to work processes are laid down so as to enable smooth functioning of the enterprise.

Features of Formal Organisation

(i) It specifies the relationships among various job positions and the nature of their inter-relationships.
This clarifies who has to report to whom.

(ii) It is a means to achieve objectives specified in the plans.

(iii) It helps to coordinate, interlink and integrate the efforts of various departments.

(iv) It is deliberately designed by the top management.

(v) It places more emphasis on work rather than interpersonal relations among the employees.

Formal organisation has the following advantages

(i) Unity of command is maintained through an established chain of command.

(ii) Role and duties of each member are clearly specified which avoids confusion and duplication of effort.

(iii) It helps in effective accomplishment of goals by providing a framework for the operations to be performed.
(iv) It makes fixation of responsibility easy since mutual relationships are clearly defined.

23. What do you understand by informal organisation? State any three advantages and two limitations of informal organisation.

Or **State any three advantages and any three limitations of informal organisation.** **CBSE 2025**

Ans. Interaction among people at work gives rise to a network of social relationships among employees, this is called informal organisation.

Following are the advantages of informal organisation

(i) **Quick Feedback**
Prescribed lines of communication are not followed. Thus, the informal organisation leads to faster spread of information as well as quick feedback.

(ii) **Social Needs**
It helps to fulfill social needs of the members. This enhances their job satisfaction, since it gives them a sense of belongingness in the organisation.

(iii) **Flexibility**
In formal organisation, rules and policies are fixed, thus it is rigid in nature. On the other hand, in informal organisation, no such rules are there, thus leads to flexibility.

Following are the limitations of informal organisation

(i) When an informal organisation spreads rumours, it becomes a destructive force and goes against the interest of the formal organisation.
(ii) The management may not be able to implement changes successfully if the informal organisation opposes them. Such resistance to change may delay or restrict growth.
(iii) It pressurises members to conform to group expectations which can be harmful to the organisation if the norms set by the group are against organisational interest.

24. Distinguish between formal and informal organisation by giving any four points. **CBSE 2024 C**

Or **Distinguish between formal and informal organisation on the basis of the following**
(i) Origin (ii) Authority
(iii) Flow of communication
(iv) Nature (v) Behaviour (vi) Stability

Ans. Following are the differences between formal and informal organisation

Basis	Formal Organisation	Informal Organisation
Origin	It arises as a result of company rules and policies.	It arises as a result of social interactions among members.
Authority	It arises by virtue of position in management.	It arises out of personal qualities.
Flow of Communication	Members are required to use the scalar chain of communication.	There is no planned route of communication. It can take place in any direction.
Nature	It is rigid in nature.	It is flexible in nature.
Behaviour	It is directed by rules.	There is no set behaviour pattern.
Stability	It is more stable as it exists till survival of the organisation.	It is less stable as employees can change their social group according to their desire.

25. Within the fabric of organisational dynamics, responsibility, accountability and authority intertwine to shape roles and decision-making. Yet, these concepts, while interconnected, serve distinct purposes in defining who does what, who answers for it and who has the power to decide.

In the light of the given statement, explain the differences between the three elements of delegation.

Competency Based Que

Ans. Following are the differences between three elements of delegation

Basis	Authority	Responsibility	Accountability
Meaning	It means power to take decisions.	It means obligation to perform a task.	It means answerability for the outcome of assigned task.
Delegation	It can be delegated.	It cannot be entirely delegated.	It cannot be delegated at all.
Origin	It arises due to formal position in an organisation.	It arises from delegated authority.	It arises from responsibility.
Flow	It flows downward from superior to subordinate.	It flows upward from subordinate to superior.	It flows upward from subordinate to superior.

26. What is meant by decentralisation? State any four points that highlight the importance of decentralisation. **CBSE 2023**

Ans. Decentralisation means systematic dispersal of authority among all departments and at all levels of management for taking decisions and actions appropriate at the respective levels.

It explains the manner in which decision-making responsibilities are divided among hierarchical levels.

Following points highlight the importance of decentralisation

(i) **Facilitates Growth**
Decentralisation provides greater autonomy to lower level managers and departmental heads. This encourages them to function in a manner best suited to their department and a sense of competition amongst the departments. Consequently, each department puts in best efforts, which helps to increase productivity level and the organisation is able to generate more returns which can be used for expansion purposes.

(ii) **Develops Initiative among Subordinates**
Decentralisation helps to promote self-reliance and confidence amongst the subordinates. This is because, when lower managerial levels are given freedom to take their own decisions, they learn to depend on their own judgement. Decentralisation policy helps to identify those executives who have the necessary potential to become dynamic leaders.

(iii) **Develops Managerial Talent for the Future**
Formal training along with experience of handling assignments independently helps to create a reservoir of qualified and capable manpower, who can take up more challenging positions through promotions.

(iv) **Relief to Top Management**
Decentralisation helps to reduce the need of direct supervision over subordinates by giving them freedom to take decision and act on their own within the limits set by the superior. Personal supervision is generally replaced by other forms of control such as return on investment, etc. Decentralisation enables top management to devote more time to important policy decisions rather than occupying their time with both policy as well as operational decisions.

27. Though both delegation and decentralisation empower employees and distribute authority within an organisation, they differ in meaning, purpose, freedom of action, scope, nature and status.

In the light of this statement, discuss the key differences between delegation and decentralisation.

Competency Based Que

Ans.

Basis	Delegation	Decentralisation
Meaning	It means granting of authority by superiors to their subordinates.	It means systematic dispersal of authority among all departments and at all levels of management.
Scope	It has narrow scope as it is limited to superior and his immediate subordinate.	It has wide scope as it implies extension of delegation to the lowest level of management.
Status	It is a process followed to share tasks.	It is the result of the policy decision of the top management.
Nature	Delegation is a compulsory act because no individual can perform all tasks on his own.	Decentralisation is an optional policy decision. It is done at the discretion of the top management.
Freedom of Action	More control by superiors hence less freedom to take own decisions.	Less control over executives hence greater freedom of action.
Purpose	To lessen the burden of the manager.	To increase the role of the subordinates in the organisation by giving them more autonomy.

Case Study Based Questions

Short Case Studies

Case Study 1

A company named Mahi Cycles has decided to start a new branch in the Middle East. The company has recognised the amount of work to be done in number of hours. The company has found out that it will take 25,000 hours of man work and has subsequently divided the number of hours for different operations. The real challenges of the company begin here. Very methodically responsibility of the recognised amount of work has been given to different individuals according to their capabilities.

(i) Which function of management is highlighted above? State its meaning.

(ii) Identify and explain the two steps of this function indicated above.

Ans.

(i) The function of management which is highlighted above is 'organising'.

Organising involves identifying and grouping activities within an organisation and bringing together physical, financial and human resources to create productive relationships for achieving specific goals.

(ii) The two steps of organising which are indicated in the above case are

- **Identification and Division of Work**
The first step in the process of organising involves identifying and dividing the work that has to be done in accordance with previously determined plans. Work is divided into manageable tasks, so that duplication can be avoided and workload can be shared among employees. In the case, the company has found out that it will take 25,000 hours of man work and has subsequently divided the number of hours for different operations.
- **Assignment of Duties**
Once the departments are created, each department is placed under the charge of an individual, called departmental head. Then, each job is allocated to an individual, according to his knowledge and skill. There should be a proper match between the nature of jobs and the ability of an individual. In the case, very methodically responsibility of the recognised amount of work has been given to different individuals according to their capabilities.

Case Study 2

Rakesh and Mannana Ltd. is manufacturing baby bottles and has separate departments of production, sales and finance. Which type of structure you would suggest to them and state some of its advantages?

Ans. I would suggest functional structure to them, because of its following advantages

(i) It leads to occupational specialisation.

(ii) It makes training of employees easier.

(iii) It leads to increased efficiency and profits.

(iv) It ensures that all the functions get due attention.

Case Study 3

Reena Industries is a company, manufacturing office furniture. The company chose to diversify its operations to improve its growth potential and increase market share. As the project was important, many alternatives were generated for the purpose and were thoroughly discussed amongst the members of the organisation.

After evaluating the various alternatives Sukhvinder, the Managing Director of the company decided that they should add 'Home Interiors and Furnishings' as a new line of business activity.

(i) Name the framework, which the diversified organisation should adopt. Give one reason in support of your answer.

(ii) State any two limitations of this framework.

Ans.

(i) Divisional structure should be adopted by the company. It is because the organisation wants to add more departments or diversify into different products.

(ii) Following are the limitations of 'divisional structure'

- Conflict may arise between different divisions on allocation of funds and other resources.
- There is a duplication of physical facilities and functions, which leads to increase in cost.

Case Study 4

Neha runs a factory wherein she manufactures shoes. The business has been doing well and she intends to expand by diversifying into leather bags as well as western formal wear thereby making her company a complete provider of corporate wear. This will enable her to market her business unit as the one stop for working women.

Which type of structure would you recommend for her expanded organisation and why? **NCERT**

Ans. Neha must adopt divisional structure for her organisation, as it is formed on the basis of different products.

Divisional structure is suitable because of the following reasons

(i) The organisation deals in more than one product.

(ii) Growth prospects are high.

(iii) There is a scope of diversification into different products and expansion to different territories.

Case Study 5

Some college friends together set-up a multi-product company. Their company makes five different products. Three products of the company have been successfully launched in market.

But the company has not succeeded to launch the fourth and fifth product in market.

(i) What sort of organisational structure, in your view, might have been adopted by the company?

(ii) Explain any two advantages of the structure identified in (i).

Ans.

(i) Divisional organisational structure has been adopted by the company. An organisation structure in which various departments are created on the basis of products, territory or region, is called a divisional structure. Each unit has a divisional manager, who is responsible for performance and has authority over their division. Each division is further divided into functional units like sales, finance, production, etc.

(ii) Following are the two advantages of divisional organisational structure
- It helps the managers to develop varied skills related to a product and prepares him for higher positions. This is because he gains experience in all functions related to a particular product.
- Fixation of responsibility and accountability is easy, as divisional heads are responsible for the profits and losses of their divisions. This provides a proper basis for performance measurement and helps to take appropriate remedial action in case of poor performance of the division.

Case Study 6

DEF Ltd., a leading manufacturing company, has a strict hierarchy where every employee has a clear set of duties and responsibilities.

The company follows a formal structure, where communication flows through established channels and everyone knows their role within the organisation. This formal structure has led to a high degree of discipline and clarity in operations, with well-defined rules and procedures guiding every action.

(i) Identify the type of organisation being used by DEF Ltd.

(ii) State three benefits of this organisation.

Ans.

(i) The type of organisation being used by DEF Ltd. is 'formal organisation'.

(ii) Following are the benefits of formal organisation
- Unity of command is maintained through an established chain of command.
- Role and duties of each member are clearly specified which avoids confusion and duplication of effort.
- It helps in effective accomplishment of goals by providing a framework for the operations to be performed.

Case Study 7

Mr. Atul is the owner of a garment manufacturing company. He finds the spreading of message in his organisation a problem as a lot of time is taken. On many occasions he tried to bring different equipments and software systems to increase the speed of spreading of message. In the month of February this year a new type of machine was installed in the production department.

He wanted to have a candid opinion about the utility of the machine from the employees but no one had the courage to tell him about the flaws of the machine on his face. After three months, when there were shortcomings in the production of garments he realised his limitation.

With passage of time he found the motivation level of employees too low. Many of the employees and workers were new and found the place unfamiliar and didn't have friends which resulted in the lowering of production.

(i) What would you suggest to Mr. Atul in this scenario?

(ii) Identify the three problems in the above case and give the outcomes of your solution given in the point (i) above on these problems.

Ans.

(i) Mr. Atul should promote the growth of an informal organisation like cricket club, hockey club, etc. within his organisation for the workers.

(ii) The three problems which are highlighted in the above case and the outcomes of the respective solutions are
- The spreading of message in his organisation is a problem as a lot of time is taken. An informal organisation results in faster spread of information as the prescribe lines of communication are not followed.
- Employees' reaction towards plans and steps of the organisation are not clear to the management. Through the informal organisation a candid opinion of the employees can be found.
- The social needs of the employees are not fulfilled. An informal organisation helps in the fulfillment of social needs which increases the confidence and satisfaction level of employees.

Case Study 8

Manoj Ghai was the managing director of a restaurant in Lucknow called 'Kitchen Hues'. The restaurant was doing well and the volume of work started increasing slowly and steadily. Manoj Ghai was not able to manage all the work on his own. The increasing magnitude of work made it impractical for him to handle it all by himself. Moreover, his objective is to open more branches of this restaurant at different places. He appointed Nikhil Gupta as a general manager of 'Kitchen Hues' and gave him the right to command his subordinates and to take action within the scope of his position.

For smooth running of the restaurant, he also gave him authority to hire and train the staff as per the requirements. Manoj Ghai was satisfied with the work of Nikhil Gupta and was able to open other branches of the restaurant in Agra and Kanpur also.

(i) Identify the concept followed by Manoj Ghai which helped him to open the new branches of the restaurant.

(ii) Also, explain briefly the two points of importance of this concept identified in (i).

Ans.

(i) The concept followed by Manoj Ghai which helped him to open the new branches of the restaurant is 'delegation of authority'.

(ii) Following are the two points of importance of this concept

- **Effective Management**
  By empowering the employees, the managers are able to function more efficiently as they get more time to concentrate on important matters.
- **Employee Development**
  Delegation provides more opportunities to the employees to utilise their talent and develop latent abilities. It allows them to develop those skills which will enable them to perform complex tasks and assume those responsibilities which will improve their career prospects. It helps to make them better leaders and decision makers, thus, creating better future managers.

Case Study 9

The production head of Ahanya Limited, an organisation that manufactures generators has been asked to achieve a target of 100 generators per day. He delegates the task to 12 production managers working under him. Seven of the production managers could not achieve their respective targets. Is the production head responsible? Explain in brief the relevant principle in support of your answer.

Ans. Yes, the production head is responsible for it.

Here, the principle of absoluteness of responsibility will apply (By responsibility, we mean responsibility to/ultimate responsibility/accountability). As per this principle, authority can be delegated but accountability is absolute and cannot be delegated. The person who delegates authority remains accountable to his own boss for the work he has delegated to his subordinate. In brief, it can be said that the process of delegation of authority does not relieve the production head of his own accountability.

Case Study 10

The directors of Alfa Ltd. an organisation manufacturing computers, have asked their production manager to achieve a production target of 150 computers per day. The production manager has asked his foreman to achieve this target, but he did not give him the authority for the requisition of tools and materials from the stores department. The foreman could not achieve the desired target.

Can the directors blame the production manager and can the production manager blame his foreman for not achieving target? Discuss.

Ans. The production manager cannot blame the foreman, if he is not able to achieve the desired target, as the authority delegated to a subordinate should be equal to his responsibility. Authority and responsibility of a subordinate should go hand in hand.

This principle suggests that if a subordinate is given the responsibility to do a particular task in a proper manner, he should be given adequate authority to perform the task. Similarly, if a subordinate is given authority to do a particular task, he should be equally held responsible for doing the task in the proper manner.

In this case, the production manager has not given authority to the foreman for the requisition of tools and materials from the stores department. Therefore, foreman cannot be held responsible for not achieving the desired result. But, the director can blame the production manager for not achieving the target.

Case Study 11

Team Leader : "I have so many tasks piling up and it feels like there's no end to it."

Team Member : "Maybe I can assist you with some of the tasks. It might ease your burden."

Team Leader : "I appreciate the offer, but I prefer to handle everything myself. I'm not sure it anyone else can do it the way I need it done."

Team Member : "I understand, but I'm confident I can complete the tasks efficiently."

Team Leader : "I'm sorry, but I'd rather manage it all on my own. Thanks, though."

(i) Which element is missing in the above conversation, as reflected by the team leader's attitude?

(ii) Do you think this element is important? Give any three reasons.

Ans.

(i) Delegation is missing, as the team leader is unwilling to distribute tasks and authority among the team members.

(ii) Delegation is important because of the following reasons

- **Motivation of Employees**
  Delegation provides a feeling of status and recognition to subordinates, as it is not only a process of sharing workload, but also involves trust of the superior on his/her subordinate. Responsibility for work builds the self-esteem of an employee and improves his/her confidence. He/She feels encouraged and tries to improve his/her performance further.
- **Facilitation of Growth**
  Delegation helps in the expansion of an organisation by providing a ready workforce to take up leading positions in new ventures. Trained and experienced employees are able to play significant role in the launch of new projects of the organisation.
- **Basis of Management Hierarchy**
  Delegation of authority establishes superior-subordinate relationships, which are the basis of hierarchy of management. It is the degree and flow of authority which determines who has to report to whom. The extent of delegated authority also decides the power that each job position enjoys in the organisation.

Case Study 12

Rahul Gupta started a telecommunication company, 'Essence Ltd.' to manufacture economical mobile phones for the Indian rural market with 15 employees. The company did very well in its initial years. As the product was good and marketed well, the demand of its products went up. To increase production the company decided to recruit additional employees. Rahul Gupta, who was earlier taking all decisions for the company had to selectively disperse the authority.

He believed that subordinates are competent, capable and resourceful and can assume responsibility for effective implementation of their decisions. This paid-off and the company was not only able to increase its production but also expanded its product range.

(i) Identify the concept used by Rahul Gupta through which he was able to steer his company to greater heights.

(ii) Also, explain any three points of importance of this concept.

Ans.

(i) The concept used by Rahul Gupta through which he was able to steer his company to greater heights is 'decentralisation'.

(ii) Following are the points of importance of decentralisation

- **Quick Decision-making**
  Under decentralisation, decisions are taken at levels which are nearest to the points of action and there is no requirement for approval from many levels. This makes process much faster and facilitates quick decision-making. There are also less chances of information getting distorted because it does not have to go through long channels.
- **Relief to Top Management**
  Decentralisation helps to reduce the need of direct supervision over subordinates by giving them freedom to take decision and act on their own within the limits set by the superior. Personal supervision is generally replaced by other forms of control such as return on investment, etc. Decentralisation enables top management to devote more time to important policy decisions rather than occupying their time with both policy as well as operational decisions.
- **Facilitates Growth**
  Decentralisation provides greater autonomy to lower level managers and departmental heads. This encourages them to function in a manner best suited to their department and a sense of competition amongst the departments. Consequently, each department puts in best efforts, which helps to increase productivity level and the organisation is able to generate more returns which can be used for expansion purposes.

Case Study 13

Arnav Electricals is a company, which has in recent years adopted the decentralised method of running the organisation. The company has grown dynamically and the decisions taken by the lower level management are implemented which saves time as people taking decisions are near the point of action. However, recently chairman of another manufacturing firm who is also a good friend of Arnav, chairman of Arnav Electricals, met him and asked him how he could evaluate performance of employees in case he goes for a decentralised approach.

A few hours later, Arnav's secretary calls him and asks for the list of works to be done the next day.

He narrates him all the important tasks to be executed.

(i) Which importance of decentralisation has been highlighted in the above case?

(ii) What advice do you think Arnav should give to have better control in a decentralised organisation?

Ans.

(i) The importance of decentralisation which is highlighted above is quick decision-making. The company has grown dynamically and the decisions taken by the lower level management are implemented which saves time as people taking decisions are near the point of action.

(ii) The advice that Arnav should give in order to get a better control is to make the departments answerable for the final outcomes. Better control systems like balance score card, management information system and observation through CCTV cameras to be adopted to keep track of the employees' performance.

Long Case Studies

Case Study 14

Priya works as a project manager in an event planning company. She has been assigned the responsibility of overseeing a large-scale fashion show for one of the firm's prestigious clients.

To ensure the event's success, Priya carefully analyses the different tasks involved and then organises the work into specific task groups, such as the logistics team, design team and hospitality team.

To ensure smooth coordination both within and among these teams, she appoints a leader for each group. Every team member is instructed to report to their respective leader and all team leaders are expected to follow Priya's overall directions.

(i) Identify the management function Priya is performing.

(ii) Briefly describe the various steps involved in the performance of the management function identified in point (i) of the question.

Ans.

(i) The management function which Priya is performing is organising.

(ii) Various steps involved in the performance of 'organising' function are as follows
- Identification and division of work
- Departmentalisation
- Assignment of duties
- Establishing reporting relationships

For explanation, refer to Q.No. 3 of short answer type questions.

Case Study 15

Riya Kapoor was the Chief Operating Officer of 'Fresh Organics', a company specialising in organic food products. Fresh Organics offered a wide range of organic fruits, vegetables and other food items. Riya Kapoor ensured that the company's operations were efficient and organised by dividing the work according to specific functions such as production, marketing, finance and human resources. Each department had specialised tasks and was headed by an expert in that particular area.

This structure helped Fresh Organics streamline its operations, resulting in high productivity and efficiency. The marketing department, for example, was able to focus entirely on market research and promotional activities, leading to an increase in brand awareness. The production department, on the other hand, ensured that the quality of the products remained top-notch, as they could focus solely on manufacturing processes.

However, as Fresh Organics grew, the company faced some challenges. The departments started working in silos, leading to communication breakdowns. The production and marketing teams often had conflicting priorities, which resulted in delays in launching new products. Additionally, the rigid departmental boundaries made it difficult for the company to adapt quickly to market changes, such as the sudden demand for ready-to-eat organic meals.

(i) Quoting lines from the above paragraph, identify the type of organisational structure adopted by Fresh Organics.

(ii) Explain three benefits of this structure as discussed in the case.

(iii) Explain two drawbacks of this structure as discussed in the case.

Ans.

(i) The type of organisational structure adopted by Fresh Organics is 'functional organisational structure'.

Quoting Lines "Riya Kapoor ensured that the company's operations were efficient and organised by dividing the work according to specific functions such as production, marketing, finance and human resources. Each department had specialised tasks and was headed by an expert in that particular area."

(ii) Following are the benefits of functional organisational structure
- It leads to increased managerial and operational efficiency which results in increased profits.
- It leads to minimal duplication of efforts, which results in economies of scale and lower costs.
- It makes training of employees easier as the focus is only on a limited range of skills. It ensures that all functions get due attention.

(iii) Following are the drawbacks of functional organisational structure
- This structure places less emphasis on overall enterprise objectives than the objectives pursued by a functional head.

  Pursuing departmental interests at the cost of organisational interests can also hinder the, interaction between two or more departments.
- It may lead to problems in coordination as information has to be exchanged across functionally differentiated departments.

Case Study 16

'Health Relax Ltd.' is one of India's leading consumer healthcare brands in diagnostic services. It has an integrated nationwide network of diagnostic centers. The company was exploring new avenues for its expansion. The top level managers analysed the business environment and found that since the year 2023 was the international year of millets, it was expected that the global demand for millets will grow by around 5% annually.

India being one of the leading producer and exporter of millets, it was realised that there was a great business opportunity in the millet industry. The board of directors approved the idea of venturing into the business of selling bread, noodles and dosa mix made of millets.

The company had to restructure itself. It diversified into varied product categories and created a structure comprising of separate business units. Each unit had a manager responsible for performance who had authority over the unit.

Manpower was grouped on the basis of different products manufactured.

(i) Identify the type of organisational structure of Health Relax Ltd. after restructuring and give its meaning.

(ii) Explain any two advantages and two disadvantages of the type of organisational structure identified in the above case. **CBSE 2024 C**

Ans.

(i) **Divisional Structure**

Divisional structure is an organisation structure which comprises of separate business units or divisions when the organisation has more than one category of products to offer.

(ii) **Advantages of Divisional Structure**

- Product specialisation helps in the development of varied skills in the divisional heads and prepare him for higher positions.
- It helps in fixation of responsibility as divisional heads are accountable for profits as revenues and costs related to different departments can be easily identified and assigned to them.

Disadvantages of Divisional Structure

- Conflicts may arise among different divisions with reference to allocation of funds.
- It may increase the cost of operations since there may be duplication of activities across products.

Case Study 17

ABC Corporation, a multinational company operating in the technology sector, specialises in developing software solutions for various industries including finance, healthcare and retail. With a global presence, the company has grown rapidly over the past decade, expanding its operations into multiple countries.

In response to its increasing complexity and the need for more efficient management of diverse product lines, ABC Corporation adopted a suitable organisational structure. This structure is characterised by the creation of separate divisions based on product lines and geographic regions. Each division operates as an independent entity with its own set of functions, including marketing, sales, R&D and customer service.

The company's organisational chart shows several key divisions

- **North American Division** Responsible for the company's operations in the United States and Canada. This division handles all aspects of product development, marketing and sales specific to North American clients.
- **European Division Manages** The company's operations across European countries. It tailors products and marketing strategies to meet the needs of the diverse European market.
- **Asia-Pacific Division** Focuses on the Asia-Pacific region, which includes countries like China, Japan and India. This division addresses regional market demands and coordinates local operations.
- **Healthcare Solutions Division** Specialises in software products tailored specifically for the healthcare industry. This division is responsible for developing industry-specific solutions and managing relationships with healthcare clients globally.
- **Financial Services Division** Dedicated to providing software solutions for the financial sector. This division manages client relationships and product development for financial institutions worldwide.

Each division has its own head who reports directly to the company's CEO. This set-up allows each division to operate with a degree of autonomy, making decisions that best suit their specific market or product line.

It facilitates a more focused approach to managing diverse product lines and regions, enabling quicker decision-making and more effective responses to market changes.

However, this structure also presents challenges. Each division operates somewhat independently, which can lead to duplication of efforts and a lack of standardisation across the company.

Coordination between divisions can sometimes be complex, as each division prioritises its own goals and objectives.

(i) Identify the organisational structure of ABC Corporation.

(ii) State the meaning of the organisational structure identified in (i).

(iii) How does this structure differ from a functional structure?

Ans.

(i) The organisational structure of ABC Corporation is 'divisional organisational structure'.

(ii) An organisation structure in which various departments are created on the basis of products, territory or region, is called a divisional structure.

Each unit has a divisional manager, who is responsible for performance and has authority over their division. Each division is further divided into functional units like sales, finance, production, etc.

(iii) Following are the differences between functional and divisional organisational structure

Basis	Functional Structure	Divisional Structure
Formation	It is formed on the basis of the basis of functions performed in the organisation.	It is formed on the basis of product line, territory or region.
Specialisation	It leads to functional specialisation.	It leads to product specialisation.

Basis	Functional Structure	Divisional Structure
Managerial Development	It does not help in managerial development as functional manager lacks autonomy.	It helps in managerial development, as they have autonomy and knowledge of various aspects of a product.
Cost	It is economical as there is no duplication.	It is costlier, as there is duplication of resources.
Responsibility	It is difficult to fix responsibility on one department.	It is easier to fix responsibility on each division.

Case Study 18

A company manufacturing sewing machines, set-up in 1945 by the British promoters, follows formal organisation culture in totality. It is facing lot of problems in delays in decision-making.

As the result, it is not able to adapt to changing business environment. The workforce is also not motivated, since they cannot vent their grievances except through formal channels, which involve red tape. Employee turnover is high.

Its market share is also declining due to changed circumstances and business environment. **NCERT**

(i) You are to advise the company with regard to change it should bring about in its organisation structure to overcome the problems faced by it.

(ii) Give reasons in terms of benefits, it will I derive from the changes suggested by you.

Ans.

(i) The suggestions are

- To overcome the limitations of formal organisation, the management should encourage workers to interact and socialise with each other through get togethers and outings. In this way, everyone will interact and like minded people will come closer. The net result will be more satisfied workforce.
- The management should also introduce employee suggestion systems so that good suggestions can be implemented and rewarded.

  The communication channels should be open so that a sense of belongingness is created in the company.
- The management should try to decentralise organisation structure.
- The suggested area where the business can be diversified is textile machineries like embroidery units, sequencing units, buttoning units.

(ii) Benefits the company will derive from these changes

- Introduction of informal interaction between employees will help in fulfilling social needs of the employees. It will enhance their job satisfaction and give them a sense of belongingness in the organisation.
- Quick decision-making will also take place since prescribed lines of communication will not be followed and faster spread of information will give quick feedback.
- Introduction of employee suggestion systems will result in increased motivation for those employees who make good suggestions. This also helps in reduction of labour turnover. Introduction of decentralisation will also I help in this.
- All of the above will help in fulfilling , organisational objectives and eliminate the inadequacies of formal structure.

Case Study 19

Rewton Ltd., was a reputed computer software company providing unique software all over India. The turnover of the company was very high resulting in good profits. The chief executive officer, Vihaan, was very strict and disciplined. He specified the boundaries of authority and responsibility for achieving organisational goals. There was systematic coordination among the various activities and specific relationships among various job positions.

The company provided facilities like a canteen, a gym, a library, a music room and a rest area for its employees, which they could use during rest intervals. Using these facilities, the employees developed friendships and discussed not only their personal, social and emotional issues, but also the official ones.

The general manager was of a different view. He told the chief executive officer that there was no use providing these facilities to the employees as it is an extra financial burden on the organisation on one hand and on the other hand, it encourages groupism and whenever any change is required in the organisation, they all resist.

He suggested that they should do away with these facilities. But the chief executive officer, Vihaan, explained to the general manager that this type of social interaction is necessary and is in the best interest of the organisation. These interactions among people at work give rise to a network of social relationships among employees and have many benefits. **CBSE 2024**

(i) Identify and explain the type of organisation whose existence the chief executive officer felt was necessary.

(ii) State any two advantages and two disadvantages of the type of organisation identified in (i) point above.

Ans.

(i) The type of organisation whose existence is necessary as specified by chief executive officer is 'informal organisation'. Interaction among people at work gives rise to a network of social relationships among employees. This is called informal organisation.

(ii) Following are the advantages of informal organisation

- **Quick Feedback**
  Prescribed lines of communication are not followed. Thus, the informal organisation leads to faster spread of information as well as quick feedback.
- **Social Needs**
  It helps to fulfill social needs of the members. This enhances their job satisfaction, since it gives them a sense of belongingness in the organisation.

  Following are the disadvantages of informal organisation
- When an informal organisation spreads rumours, it becomes a destructive force and goes against the interest of the formal organisation.
- The management may not be able to implement changes successfully if the informal organisation opposes them. Such resistance to change may delay or restrict growth.

Case Study 20

Nisha and Arjun had always been passionate about eco-friendly fashion and wanted to create a business that promoted sustainable clothing. They founded 'EcoThreads', a company dedicated to selling clothing made from organic and recycled materials. Initially, they handled all the operations from their small office, making decisions about design, production, marketing and sales.

However, as their business grew, they realised that centralising all the decision-making was slowing down their operations. They needed to respond quickly to market demands and it became clear that they couldn't manage everything on their own. Recognising this, they decided to decentralise the decision-making process by empowering different departments within the company.

They appointed a design team to independently create new clothing lines based on market trends, a production team to manage manufacturing and a marketing team to handle customer engagement and sales strategies.

This allowed each department to make quick decisions without waiting for approval from the founders. As a result, 'EcoThreads' was able to release new collections faster, improve their supply chain efficiency and tailor their marketing strategies to specific customer segments.

In just a few months, their sales increased significantly and they expanded their market reach to include international customers.

Quoting lines from the above paragraph, identify and explain the concept discussed in the case.

Also, state reasons why it is important to adopt this concept.

Ans. The concept discussed in the case is 'decentralisation'.

Quoting Lines "They decided to decentralise the decision-making process by empowering different departments within the company."

It is important to adopt 'decentralisation' because of the following reasons

(i) **Quick Decision-making**
Under decentralisation, decisions are taken at levels which are nearest to the points of action and there is no requirement for approval from many levels. This makes process much faster and facilitates quick decision-making. There are also less chances of information getting distorted because it does not have to go through long channels.

(ii) **Relief to Top Management**
Decentralisation helps to reduce the need of direct supervision over subordinates by giving them freedom to take decision and act on their own within the limits set by the superior. Personal supervision is generally replaced by other forms of control such as return on investment, etc. Decentralisation enables top management to devote more time to important policy decisions rather than occupying their time with both policy as well as operational decisions.

(iii) **Develops Initiative among Subordinates**
Decentralisation helps to promote self-reliance and confidence amongst the subordinates. This is because, when lower managerial levels are given freedom to take their own decisions, they learn to depend on their own judgement. Decentralisation policy helps to identify those executives who have the necessary potential to become dynamic leaders.

(iv) **Facilitates Growth**
Decentralisation provides greater autonomy to lower level managers and departmental heads. This encourages them to function in a manner best suited to their department and a sense of competition amongst the departments.

Consequently, each department puts in best efforts, which helps to increase productivity level and the organisation is able to generate more returns which can be used for expansion purposes.

(v) **Better Control**

Decentralisation makes it possible to evaluate performance at each level and held the departments accountable for their results.

Feedback from all levels helps to analyse variances and improve operations.

To meet the challenges of accountability of performance, various better control systems are being evolved such as Balance Scorecard and Management Information System (MIS).

Case Study 21

A company X Ltd. manufacturing cosmetics, which has enjoyed a pre-eminent position in business, has grown in size. Its business was very good till 1991.

But after that, new liberalised environment has seen entry of many MNC's in the sector. With the result, the market share of X Ltd. has declined.

The company had followed a very centralised business model with directors and divisional heads making even minor decisions.

Before 1991, this business model had served the company very well as consumers has no choice. But now, the company is under pressure to reform. **NCERT**

(i) What organisation structure changes should the company bring about in order to retain its market share?

(ii) How will the changes suggested by you help the firm? (Keep in mind that the sector in which the company is FMCG).

Ans.

(i) In view of increased competition and constant changes in market dynamics and consumer preferences, following changes are advised

- The company should increase delegation and decentralisation of authority to allow decision-making at all levels.
- Since, the company is dealing in FMCG (Fast Moving Consumer Goods Sector), the lower level staff should be given more power to clinch deals like giving them authority to give customers more discounts on bulk orders, etc. This is done because FMCG sector characterise dynamic customer preferences and frequent change in taste which can be judged easily by people at action points.
- Development of good communication system from lower levels to top level, to help top management take strategic decisions on changing situations.
- Suggestion system should be initiated and good suggestions should be rewarded.
- Maximum participation in decision-making should be ensured to motivate staff and achieve good results for the company.

(ii) Benefits that the company would derive from these changes are

- Developing initiative among subordinates.
- Development of managerial talent for future.
- Quick decision-making.
- Relief to the top management.
- Better control, since each department or individual can be held accountable for his/her results.

SELF ASSESSMENT TEST

Objective Type Questions

1. When managers are made responsible for coordinating a particular number of jobs effectively, it is called
(a) adaptation (b) span of control
(c) coordination (d) job design

2. Under this type of organisational structure, manpower is grouped on the basis of different products manufactured.
(a) Divisional structure (b) Functional structure
(c) Network structure (d) Matrix structure

3. Identify the type of organisational structure which facilitates occupational specialisation.
(a) Functional structure (b) Horizontal structure
(c) Network structure (d) Divisional structure

4. Nexa Limited is a company dealing in metal products. The work is mainly divided into functions including production, purchase, marketing, accounts and personnel. Identify the type of organisational structure followed by the organisation.
(a) Functional structure (b) Relational structure
(c) Divisional structure (d) None of these

5. "I refer to a network of personal and social relationships which spontaneously originates within the formal set up." Who is 'I' in the given statement?
(a) Informal organisation (b) Party organisation
(c) Social organisation (d) Formal organisation

6. The basis of delegation of authority is
(a) centralisation (b) decentralisation
(c) Both (a) and (b) (d) division of labour

7. .... refers to retention of decision-making authority by higher management levels.
(a) Decentralisation (b) Departmentalisation
(c) Span of control (d) Centralisation

Answers 1. (b) 2. (a) 3. (a) 4. (a) 5. (a) 6. (d) 7. (d)

Short Answer Type Questions

8. A company is manufacturing a wide range of electronic items. Suggest a suitable organisational structure and state its three advantages.

9. A multinational company operating in diverse product lines, such as electronics, textiles and pharmaceuticals, allows each division to function independently with its own set of managers for production, marketing and finance. In light of the above statement, explain the disadvantages of using a divisional organisational structure.

10. How does formal organisation benefit from informal organisation?

11. You are working in HR department. Day-by-day you are facing problems due to the existence of informal groups.

    What steps would you take to manage such informal groups?

12. Explain the three important things which an overburdened manager should keep in mind while taking help from his subordinates.

13. Delegation of authority 'develops employees' and 'motivates them'. Explain how.

14. Give any three reasons why an organisation would choose to be decentralised.

Long Answer Type Questions

15. The employees of Label AJ, an apparel brand, have formed a dramatic group for their recreation. Name the type of organisation so formed. State three advantages and two disadvantages of such organisation.

16. "Effective organising requires proper delegation." Comment.

17. What is decentralisation? State any four points that highlight its advantages.

06

CHAPTER

Staffing

"The managerial function of staffing involves the organisational structure through proper and effective selection, appraisal and development of personnel to fill the roles designed into the structure." *–Koontz and O' Donnell*

YOUR STUDY GOALS

YOUR PRACTICE GOAL

- Objective Type Questions (72 Qs ; MCQs, A-R, Statements, Matching)
- Subjective Type Questions (20 SAs, 5 LAs)
- Case Study Based Questions (Short Case Studies-11, Long Case Studies-7)
- Self Assessment Test (8 MCQs, 7 SAs, 2 LAs)

6.1 Concept of Staffing

Staffing is that part of the management process which is concerned with obtaining, utilising and maintaining a satisfactory and satisfied workforce. It has been described as the managerial function of filling and keeping filled the positions in the organisation structure.

Importance of Staffing

1. **Obtaining Competent Personnel** It helps in finding and hiring skilled individuals for various roles.
2. **Higher Performance** It ensures better performance by placing the right person on the right job.
3. **Continuous Survival and Growth** It supports the enterprise's continuous survival and growth by successive planning for managers.
4. **Optimum Utilisation of Human Resources** It prevents over-staffing, high labour cost and underutilisation, ensuring efficient workforce management. It also prevents work disruption by indicating the likely shortage of employees in advance.
5. **Job Satisfaction and Morale** It enhances employee satisfaction and morale through fair evaluation and rewards for their contribution.

Staffing as a Part of Human Resource Management

Staffing function deals with the human element of management. It is important because the performance of an organisation depends upon its human resource, its competence and motivation. In small organisations, HR duties may be performed by managers but as organisations grow, a separate department called Human Resource Department (HRD) is formed.

HRM includes many specialised activities to be performed by HR personnel, which are as follows

- Recruitment, i.e. search for qualified people.
- Analysing jobs, collecting information about jobs to prepare job descriptions.
- Developing compensation and incentive plans.
- Training and development of employees.
- Maintaining labour relations and union management relations.
- Handling grievances and complaints.
- Providing social security and welfare of employees.
- Defending the company in law suits and avoiding legal complications.

Evolution of HRM

Human resource management has emerged from number of significant inter-related developments

- **Labour Welfare Officer** During the industrial revolution, emergence of trade unions necessitated a mediator between workers and owners, leading to the creation of the labour welfare officer. His role was focused on basic employee welfare but was undervalued by both parties.
- **Personnel Officer and Personnel Manager** As the factory system expanded, a dedicated individual was assigned the responsibility of hiring and maintaining staff, evolving into the roles of personnel officer and later personnel manager to oversee recruitment, selection and placement.
- **Human Resource Manager** Human relations approach emphasised the importance of the human factor in organisational success, leading to the transition from personnel manager to human resource manager, reflecting a broader scope that included skill development and training.

Staffing Process

Following steps are followed in the staffing process

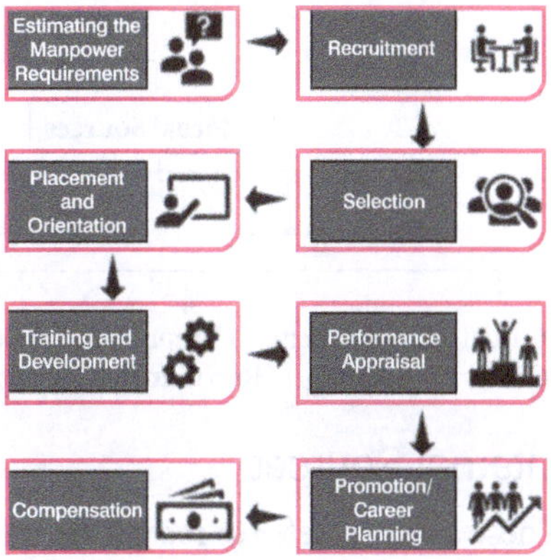

1. **Estimating the Manpower Requirements** Understanding manpower requirements involve not just the number but the type (skills, experience, personality, etc.) of people required, considering diversity in gender, community and abilities.

   Manpower requirements necessitate two kinds of analysis

   (i) **Workload Analysis** It helps a manager to assess the number and type of human resources necessary to perform various jobs in the organisation.

   (ii) **Workforce Analysis** It helps to know the number and type of human resource already available in the organisation.
2. **Recruitment** It is the process of searching for and attracting potential employees to apply for jobs in the organisation. The objective is to create a pool of prospective job candidates.
3. **Selection** Selection involves choosing the best candidate from the pool, ensuring that organisation gets the best talent while boosting the selected candidates' self-esteem and prestige.
4. **Placement and Orientation** Placement relates to occupying position for which candidate is selected while under orientation, new employees are familiarised with the workplace, colleagues and company policies, impacting their decision to stay and perform.

5. **Training and Development** Ongoing employee learning is essential for career growth and organisational effectiveness, often facilitated by in-house training centers or partnerships with educational institutes.
6. **Performance Appraisal** It involves evaluating employees' performance against set standards, providing feedback and identifying areas for improvement.
7. **Promotion and Career Planning** Promotion involves placing employees in positions of greater responsibility, offering higher pay and job satisfaction.
8. **Compensation** Compensation includes direct (wages, salaries, etc.) and indirect (insurance, vacations, etc.) payments or rewards given to an employee, influenced by performance, legal factors and company policies.

Types of Direct Payment

Direct payment can be of two types

- **Time Based Payment** It means salary and wages are paid either daily, weekly or monthly or anually.
- **Performance Based Payment** It means salary and wages are paid according to piece work.

Certain pay plans can be created which are a combination of time based pay plus incentives for higher performance.

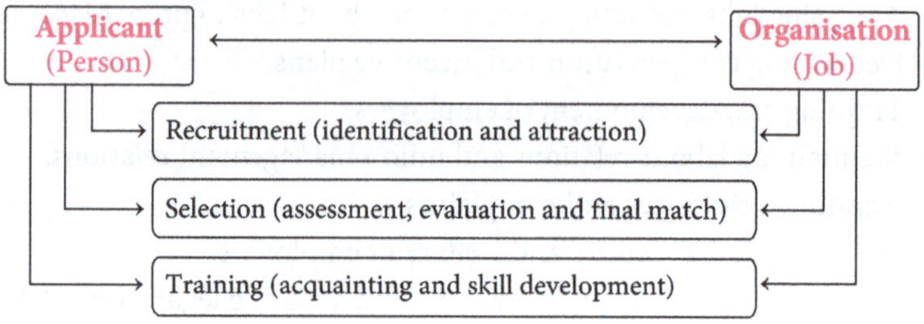

Aspects of Staffing

6.2 Recruitment

It may be defined as the process of searching for prospective employees and stimulating them to apply for jobs in the organisation.

It is considered as a **positive process** as it invites a large number of candidates towards the organisation.

Sources of Recruitment

There are two sources of recruitment i.e. internal and external.

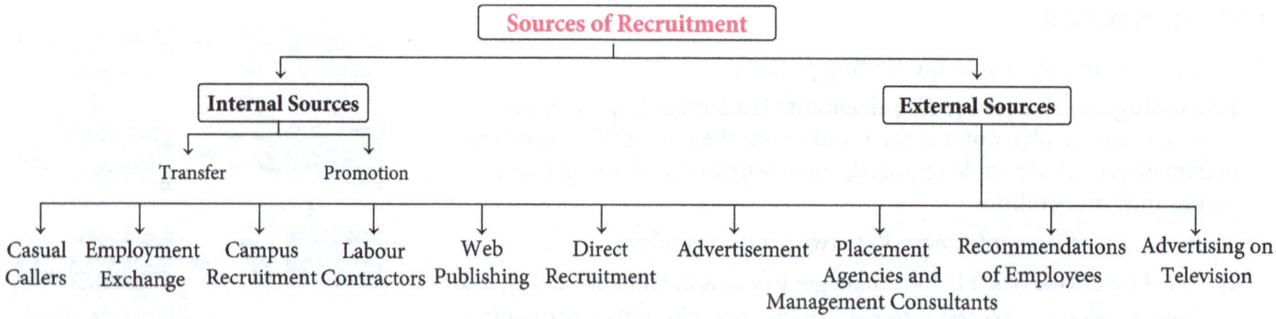

Internal Sources

These sources refer to recruitment from within the organisation, from the existing staff and employees.

These sources include the following

1. **Transfer** It refers to shifting of an employee from one job or department to another without a significant change in salary, responsibilities or status. It is a horizontal movement that can address staffing imbalances and help to avoid terminations and removing individual problems and grievances.
2. **Promotions** It means shifting an employee to a higher position with increased responsibilities, status and pay. This vertical shift boosts motivation and loyalty among employees.

External Sources

These sources refer to the recruitment of employees from outside the organisation. These sources include the following

1. **Direct Recruitment** Jobs are posted on the company noticeboard specifying the job details. Job seekers assemble outside the organisation and selection happens on the spot. This type of recruitment is mainly for casual vacancies.
2. **Casual Callers** Companies keep a database of unsolicited applicants which can be recalled for filling of vacancies.
3. **Advertisement** Job vacancies are advertised in newspapers for a wider choice of candidates, often for senior positions. Advertising provides lot of information about job and gives management a wider range of candidates for selection.
4. **Employment Exchange** These exchanges are run by government and help to match demand and supply between job seekers and employers often used for unskilled or skilled jobs.
5. **Placement Agencies and Management Consultants** Agencies provide nationwide services, screening and recruiting for technical, managerial and professional roles. Such agencies charge fee for their services and specialise in middle and top level executive placements.
6. **Campus Recruitment** Organisations recruit from colleges and management institutes for technical, professional and managerial roles. This method provides a fresh talent and qualified personnel to the organisation.
7. **Recommendations of Employees** Current employees recommend potential candidates such as their friends, relatives or neighbours. This method also offers a form of preliminary screening.
8. **Labour Contractors** Contractors can supply unskilled workers at short notice. But, in case of conflict with contractor, the entire workforce quits from work.
9. **Advertising on Television** Job vacancies and company profiles are advertised *via.* television broadcasts detailing the job requirements and the qualities required to do it.
10. **Web Publishing** Job vacancies and applicant profiles are posted on dedicated recruitment websites like Naukri.com. These websites are visited both by the prospective employees as well as organisations.

Merits and Demerits of Sources of Recruitment

Source	Merits	Demerits
Internal Source	• Promotion motivates employees to enhance their performance. • Internal recruitment simplifies selection, offering a reliable and economical process. • Transfers serve as training for higher roles, eliminating the need for induction training for internal hires. • Transfers help balance workforce by shifting staff from surplus to shortage areas. • Internal hiring is more cost and time effective than recruiting externally.	• Internal promotions reduce opportunities for new talent. • Employees may become lethargic with assured promotions. • New enterprises can't avail the benefit of this source. • Internal hiring might hamper competition among employees. • Frequent employee transfers can lower productivity of the organisation.
External Source	• **Qualified Personnel** External recruitment attracts qualified and trained candidates for job vacancies. • **Wider Choice** Advertising vacancies widely offers a broader pool of applicants for selection. • **Fresh Talent** External recruitment brings new talent in the organisation. • **Competitive Spirit** Existing staff works harder for better performance due to creation of competitive spirit by new entrants.	• **Dissatisfaction among Existing Staff** External recruitment may frustrate and dissatisfy existing employees, reducing their promotion chances. • **Lengthy Process** External recruitment takes time, requiring vacancy notifications and a lengthy selection process. • **Costly Process** Recruiting externally is expensive, involving significant costs for advertising and processing applications.

6.3 Selection

Selection is the process of identifying and choosing the best person out of a number of prospective candidates for a job. It involves a series of tests, interviews and examination. It is regarded as a **negative process** as it involves elimination of candidates at every step.

Process of Selection

Following steps are followed in the process of selection

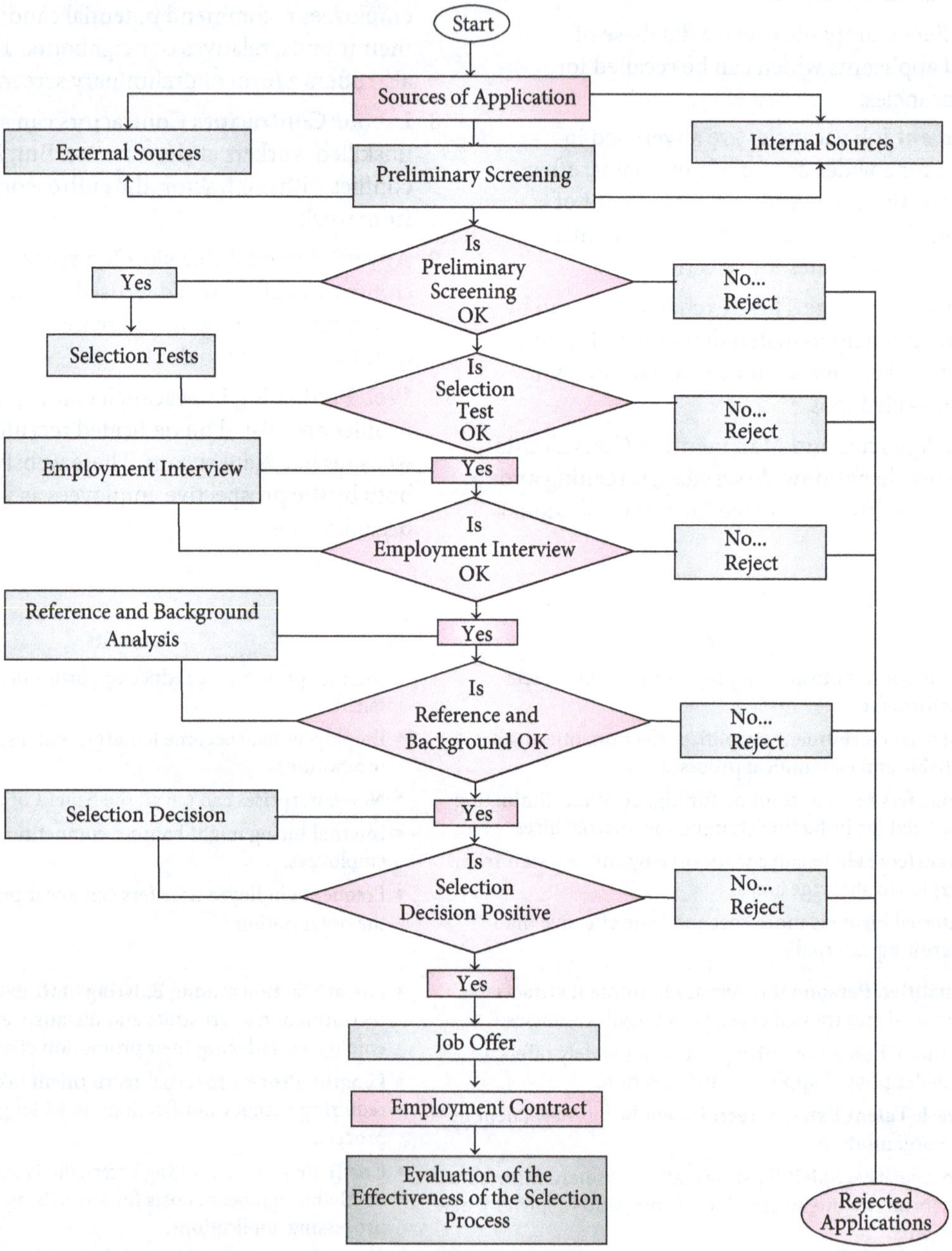

Selection Process

***Step* 1** **Preliminary Screening** At this step, recruiter eliminates unqualified candidates based on information provided in application form. Preliminary interview help reject misfits for reasons, that did not appear in application.

***Step* 2** **Selection Tests** These tests measure characteristics like aptitudes, intelligence and personality of individuals. These include the following

(i) **Intelligence Tests** Assess intelligence, learning ability and decision-making abilities of an individual.

(ii) **Aptitude Tests** Evaluate potential for learning new skills.

(iii) **Personality Tests** Provide insights into emotional and behavioural traits like reaction, maturity, etc.

(iv) **Trade Tests** Measure current technical or professional skills of an individual to perform a job.

(v) **Interest Tests** Identify job preferences and interests of a person that will satisfy him/her.

***Step* 3** **Employment Interview** It is a formal, in-depth conversation to assess the applicant's suitability for the job.

***Step* 4** **Reference and Background Checks** Many employers verify applicant's information through previous employers and other references like teachers, lecturers, etc.

***Step* 5** **Selection Decision** Final choice is made based on test results, interviews and reference checks. The views of the concerned manager are also considered in the final selection.

***Step* 6** **Medical Examination** The candidate is required to undergo a medical fitness test. The job offer is given to the candidate, who is declared fit after the medical examination.

***Step* 7** **Job Offer** Official offer is made through an appointment letter to confirm his acceptance. The letter contains joining date, terms and conditions of job, etc.

***Step* 8** **Contract of Employment** After the acceptance of job offer, a signed document detailing job terms, duties and conditions is made. This form serves as a valid record for future reference.

6.4 Training and Development

Training is a process by which the aptitudes, skills and abilities of employees to perform specific jobs are increased.

Development refers to the learning opportunities designed to help employees grow and enhance their personality. Training and development improve the present and future performance of employees by increasing employee's ability to perform through learning, by changing the employee's attitude and increasing his/her skills and knowledge.

Importance (Benefits) of Training and Development

Training and development help both the organisation and the individual in the following ways

Benefits to the Organisation	Benefits to the Employee
• Training provides systematic learning, avoiding wastage of efforts and money. • Training enhances employee productivity, leading to higher profits. • Training prepares future managers for emergencies. • Training boosts employee morale, reducing absenteeism and turnover. • Training helps in adapting to technological and economical environment changes.	• Improved skills and knowledge leads to a better career prospects. • Increased performance by individual leads to higher earnings. • Enhanced efficiency to handle machines reduces the risk of accidents. • Increases job satisfaction and morale of employees.

Training Importance

A tech company faced frequent project delays due to coding errors, frustrating clients and harming profits.

After implementing a targeted training programme, error rates dropped, delivery times improved and client satisfaction increased. Employees, now more skilled and confident, enjoyed greater job satisfaction, while the company saw a boost in productivity and profits. Training turned a major problem into a win-win solution.

Methods of Training

There are various methods of training which can be broadly categorised into two groups, which are as follows

1. **On-the-Job Methods** These methods are applied to the workplace, while the employee is actually working. The concept underlying this method is 'learning while doing'.
2. **Off-the-Job Methods** These methods are used away from the workplace. It means 'learning before doing'.

Various Methods of Training

1. **Apprenticeship Programmes** Trainees work with a master or experienced worker (such as plumber, electricians, carpenters, etc.) to gain high-level skills, with training adjusted based on learning speed.
2. **Internship Training** Educational institutions and businesses collaborate to impart training to selected candidates alongside their regular studies.
3. **Vestibule Training** Employees train on equipment similar to what they'll use, but in a simulated environment away from the actual work floor. This is usually done when employees are required to handle sophisticated machinery and equipment.
4. **Induction Training** It is a type of training given to help a new employee in settling down quickly into the job by becoming familiar with the people, the surrounding, the job and the business. The duration of such type of training may be from a few hours to a few days.

Vestibule Training

In a luxury car manufacturing company, new technicians are trained in a simulated workshop where they practice assembling and testing high-end car engines.

They work with similar tools and components but on non-operational models, ensuring they gain experience without the risk of damaging expensive equipment.

Training vs Development

Training is a process of increasing knowledge and skills while development is a process of learning and growth.

Example Imagine an employee learning to operate a new machine (training), while another is attending workshops to improve leadership and communication skills (development). Training focuses on immediate job skills, whereas development enhances broader capabilities for future roles.

Mind Map

STAFFING

1 Concept of Staffing

Staffing is that part of the management process which is concerned with obtaining, utilising and maintaining a satisfactory and satisfied work force.

2 Importance of Staffing

- Helps in discovering and obtaining competent personnel
- Placing the right person on the right job ensures higher performance
- Helps in continuous survival and growth by successive planning for managers
- Helps in optimum utilisation of human resource
- Helps in improving morale of employees

3 Staffing and HRM

Specialised activities by HR personnel
- Recruitment, i.e. searching for qualified people
- Analysing jobs, collecting information about jobs
- Developing compensation and incentive plans
- Training and development of employees
- Maintaining labour relations and union management relations
- Handling grievances and complaints
- Providing social security and welfare of employees
- Defending the company in lawsuits

4 Staffing Process

- Estimating the manpower requirements, using workload and workforce analysis
- Recruitment, searching for prospective employees
- Selection, choosing the right candidate for the right job
- Placement and orientation, occupying the position and making the employee familiar
- Training and development, improving job knowledge, skills and attitude
- Performance appraisal, evaluating performance of employees
- Promotion and career planning, address the career related concerns
- Compensation, all forms of pay and reward given to employee

5 Recruitment

It is the process of searching for prospective employees and stimulating them to apply for jobs in company.

Internal Sources
- Promotion
- Transfer

Merits
- Motivates the employees
- Simple process
- Facilitate training
- Filling deficiencies
- Inexpensive

Demerits
- No fresh talent
- Lethargic employees
- Not available to new enterprises
- No competitive spirit
- Reduce productivity

External Sources
- Direct recruitment
- Casual callers
- Advertisement
- Employment exchange
- Placement agencies and management consultants
- Campus recruitment
- Recommendations of employees
- Labour contractors
- Advertising on television
- Web publishing

Merits
- Qualified personnel
- Wider choice
- Fresh talent
- Competitive spirit

Demerits
- Dissatisfaction among existing staff
- Lengthy process
- Costly process

6 Selection Process

- **Preliminary Screening** Eliminating unfit or unqualified job seekers
- **Selection Tests** Measure characteristics of individuals using intelligence, aptitude, trade, personality and interest test
- **Employment Interview** In-depth conversation to evaluate suitability
- **Reference and Background Checks** Helps in gaining more information
- **Selection Decision** Final decision is made
- **Medical Examination** Medical fitness test is conducted
- **Job Offer** Letter of appointment is given
- **Contract of Employment** Given after acceptance of job offer

7 Methods of Training

On-the-job Applied to workplace while the employee is actually working. It includes
- **Apprenticeship** Put the trainee under the guidance of a master worker
- **Internship** Educational institutions and business firms cooperate to impart training
- **Induction** Given to new employee in settling down quickly

Off-the-job Learning before doing. It includes
- **Vestibule** Training is conducted away from the actual work floor

8 Benefits of Training

Benefits to Organisation
- Systematic learning
- Increased productivity
- Prepare future managers
- Boost morale of employees
- Better response to fast changing environment

Benefits to Employees
- Career growth
- Increased earnings
- Safety of employees
- High morale

EXAM PATTERN QUESTIONS

Objective Type Questions

Multiple Choice Questions (MCQs)

1. Which of the following functions of management is helpful in finding out a competent employee?

(a) Planning (b) Organising
(c) Staffing (d) Directing

2. Which of the following statements is incorrect?

(a) The staffing process involves selecting the best candidates from a pool of applicants.
(b) Internal recruitment may limit the influx of new ideas into the organisation.
(c) Effective staffing contributes to the overall success and growth of the organisation.
(d) The staffing function is not affected by the organisation's strategic goals.

3. The function of staffing is performed by

(a) top level management
(b) operational level management
(c) middle level management
(d) All of the above

4. "It assists the organisation in finding and bringing in capable individuals for various job roles."

Identify the importance of staffing highlighted here. Competency Based Que

(a) Higher performance
(b) Obtaining competent personnel
(c) Continuous survival and growth
(d) Optimum utilisation of human resources

5. .... reveal the number and type of employees available in the organisation.

(a) Training (b) Workforce analysis
(c) Interview
(d) Selection

6. Which of the following statements is incorrect?

(a) Training and development are part of the staffing function.
(b) Staffing does not include activities related to employee compensation.
(c) Recruitment can be conducted through various methods, including online job portals and job fairs.
(d) Staffing helps in ensuring that the organisation has the required skills to achieve its goals.

7. Bharat Enterprises was a company manufacturing refrigerators. The company had a functional structure with four main functions i.e. production, marketing, finance and human resource. As the demand for the products grew, the company decided to hire more employees.

Identify the concept which will help the human resource manager in identifying the type of human resources necessary for the performance of various jobs and accomplishment of organisational objectives. Competency Based Que

(a) Workload analysis (b) Staffing
(c) Workforce analysis (d) Both (b) and (c)

8. ABC Manufacturing is expanding its operations to a new location. To ensure a smooth transition and meet production targets, the company needs to hire skilled workers and managerial staff. The HR Manager begins by analysing the number and types of employees required for the new location. Following this, job descriptions are prepared and recruitment processes are initiated to attract suitable candidates.

Finally, after a series of interviews and assessments, the selected candidates are given job offers and onboarded. Which step of the staffing process is being described when the HR Manager is analysing the number and types of employees required for the new location? Competency Based Que

(a) Recruitment
(b) Selection
(c) Placement
(d) Estimating manpower requirements

9. Reena Enterprises is a company engaged in the marketing of washing machines. The company has a functional structure with four main functions i.e. purchase, sales, finance and staffing. The company decided to hire more employees.

Identify the concept which will help the HR manager to find out the number and type of personnel available, so that he could decide and recruit the required number of persons for each department. Competency Based Que

(a) Workload analysis (b) Workforce analysis
(c) Both (a) and (b) (d) None of these

10. Which step in the staffing process considers the aspect as depicted in the image given below?

Overstaffing : More play, less work

(a) Selection (b) Recruitment
(c) Placement and orientation
(d) Estimating the manpower requirements

11. Goel Industries Pvt Ltd. is a renowned company manufacturing different kinds of gifts. The company is in the need of some employees. Mr. Subhu Kedar, HR manager, is keen to select such people who are well equipped with the latest knowledge. He also desires that the area of selection should be extensive.

In your opinion, which source of recruitment should be used by the HR manager? **Competency Based Que**

(a) External (b) Internal
(c) Promotion (d) Transfer

12. Tech Solutions, a rapidly expanding logistics company, has secured a major delivery contract with a tight deadline. To meet the urgent demand, the company needs additional delivery workers who can start immediately, without going through a lengthy hiring process. The most suitable source of recruitment for this situation is **Competency Based Que**

(a) campus recruitment (b) employment agencies
(c) direct recruitment (d) web portals

13. Identify the external source of recruitment illustrated by the picture given below **CBSE 2023**

(a) Direct recruitment (b) Casual callers
(c) Advertisement (d) Labour contractor

14. It is the custom of a company to avoid to say 'No' to any person who approaches for a job. The application is collected and the company tells him that he would be called on requirement of his services. As a result, the company builds the database.

It is beneficial when a suitable applicant is required. This helps in saving expenses on advertisement. Identify the source of recruitment referred to in the above paragraph. **Competency Based Que**

(a) Direct recruitment
(b) Casual callers
(c) Campus recruitment
(d) Web publishing

15. Arun Nandan, Chairman of Mehta Group of Companies founded Arun University for undergraduate and postgraduate courses in diverse disciplines.

The Information Technology Department of the Mehta Power Ltd. had few vacancies related to cyber security.

The human resource department of the company decided to recruit fresh engineering graduates from Arun University for the same. Identify the type of source of recruitment. **Competency Based Que**

(a) Advertisement
(b) Direct recruitment
(c) Campus recruitment
(d) Casual callers

16. Casual employees can be recruited from which of the following source?

(a) Direct recruitment
(b) Casual callers
(c) Media advertisement
(d) Employment exchange

17. Choose the statement that correctly highlights the benefit of using internal sources of recruitment. **CBSE 2025**

(a) It helps in simplifying the process of selection.
(b) It provides wider choice while selecting the employees.
(c) It brings new blood in the organisation.
(d) It is an expensive and time consuming source.

18. "This drawback of internal recruitment may limit the organisation's ability to bring in new perspectives and ideas, leading to a lack of innovation."

Identify the drawback of internal recruitment being referred to. **Competency Based Que**

(a) Reduced competition among employees
(b) Lethargic attitude due to assured promotions
(c) Danger of inbreeding and lack of fresh talent
(d) Lower productivity due to frequent transfers

19. **"Used primarily for filling senior positions, this method allows the organisation to reach a larger audience by providing detailed information about the job and the company."**

Which recruitment method is described here? **Competency Based Que**

(a) Direct recruitment
(b) Employment exchange
(c) Advertisement
(d) Campus recruitment

20. **Promotion is the .... shifting of an employee.**

(a) horizontal (b) vertical
(c) lateral (d) diagonal

21.

Identify the method of staffing illustrated in the picture in which Wipro Ltd. is taking interview.

(a) Direct recruitment
(b) Placement agencies and management consultants
(c) Campus recruitment
(d) Employment exchange

22. **Recruitment of employees from external sources increases dissatisfaction among the present employees as their chances of .... are reduced.**

(a) promotion
(b) voluntary retirement
(c) salary increment
(d) None of the above

23. **Choose the statement that correctly highlights the benefit of using external sources of recruitment.** **CBSE SQP 2025**

(a) Competitive spirit among the existing staff
(b) Reduction in employees turnover
(c) Helps in increasing employees satisfaction
(d) Develops a sense of security amongst employees

24. **Which of the following is a managerial decision-making process to predict which job applicants will be successful if hired?**

(a) Selection (b) Recruitment
(c) Training (d) Compensation

25. **Identify the stage of selection process illustrated by the picture given here.**

Time Left : 20 min

(a) Employment interview (b) Selection decision
(c) Selection test (d) None of these

26. **The image given summarises the IQ test result interpretations. This test will fall under which type of test in the selection process?**

Wechsler (WAIS-III) 1997 IQ Test Classification

IQ Range ('Deviation IQ')	IQ Classification
130 and above	Very superior
120-129	Superior
110-119	High average
90-109	Average
80-89	Low average
70-79	Borderline
69 and below	Extremely low

(a) Aptitude test (b) Interest test
(c) Intelligence test (d) Personality test

27. **.............. test is a measure of an individual's potential for learning new skills.**

(a) Personality (b) Aptitude
(c) Intelligence (d) Interest

28. **Mr. Rahul is the HR manager of Savan Store Pvt. Ltd. He has to appoint some salespersons for the store. As the customers come to the store of different nature, he wants to find out salesperson's maturity and emotions in dealing with the customers. Identify the selection test required in the above case.** **Competency Based Que**

(a) Intelligence test (b) Aptitude test
(c) Personality test (d) Trade test

29. **'VK Public School' had a vacancy for an English teacher for Class XII. After preliminary screening of the applications, they shortlisted 10 candidates. Now, the school management asked the candidates to give a demonstration lesson related to the curriculum of Class XII. The purpose of these demonstration lessons was to measure the existing teaching skills of the candidates and proficiency in the area of profession. Identify the type of selection test used by 'VK Public School' in the above case.** **CBSE 2024 C; Competency Based Que**

(a) Aptitude test (b) Intelligence test
(c) Trade test (d) Personality test

30. The next step in the process of selection after job offer is **CBSE 2023**

(a) medical examination
(b) selection decision
(c) employment interview
(d) contract of employment

31. The next step in the 'selection process' after 'selection decision' is **CBSE 2023**

(a) job offer
(b) medical examination
(c) selection test
(d) contract of employment

32. Which of the following step of selection process helps in eliminating unqualified applicants on the basis of information supplied in the application form?

(a) Preliminary screening
(b) Interview
(c) Medical examination
(d) Intelligence test

33. .... is the last step in the process of selection.

(a) Selection decision
(b) Job offer
(c) Contract of employment
(d) Selection tests

34. .... is a long-term process that takes place throughout the life of a person.

(a) Development (b) Education
(c) Training (d) Induction

35. It is a career-oriented process designed to help the employees in the progress towards maturity and actualisation of their potential capabilities. Identify the process. **CBSE 2024**

(a) Staffing (b) Selection
(c) Development (d) Training

36. Which of the following statements is incorrect?

(a) Development programmes are designed to improve long-term capabilities and leadership skills.
(b) Training and development should align with organisational goals and objectives.
(c) Training is primarily focused on immediate job performance and tasks.
(d) Development programmes should only focus on technical skills relevant to the current job role.

37. The workers of a factory are unable to work on new machines and always demand for help of supervisor. The supervisor is overburdened with their frequent calls. Which of the following can be a remedy to solve the problem? **NCERT Modified**

(a) Training (b) Development
(c) Recruitment (d) Counselling

38. XYZ Corporation noticed a decline in employee productivity over the past quarter. The HR department conducted a survey and found that employees felt they were not equipped with the latest skills required to perform their tasks effectively.

To address this issue, the company decided to implement a new training and development programme focused on upskilling employees in emerging technologies and improving their soft skills. What is the most likely objective of XYZ Corporation's new training and development programme? **Competency Based Que**

(a) To reduce employee turnover
(b) To improve employee satisfaction
(c) To increase productivity by enhancing employee skills
(d) To decrease the workload of the HR department

39. "Joining a job marks the beginning of socialisation of employees at the workplace. The employee should be given a post for which he has been selected."

Place the subsequent steps of staffing in a small organisation in the correct order.

CBSE SQP 2025; Competency Based Que

(a) Training and development, promotion and career planning, performance appraisal, compensation
(b) Performance appraisal, training and development, promotion and career planning, compensation
(c) Training and development, performance appraisal, promotion and career planning, compensation
(d) Training and development, performance appraisal, compensation, promotion and career planning

40. Shiwakumar runs a legal consultancy firm in Chhattisgarh. Whenever the firm hires new employees, on the first day of joining, they are welcomed to the organisation and are given details about the dress code, lunch timings, introduction to daily operations and fellow colleagues. They are also familiarised with the organisational policies and procedures, emergency exits, evacuation procedure, etc. Name the type of training which is provided by Shiwakumar in his firm.

CBSE SQP 2025; Competency Based Que

(a) Apprenticeship training (b) Vestibule training
(c) Induction training (d) Internship training

41. Identify the type of training method from the image given below

(a) Vestibule training (b) Internship training
(c) Apprenticeship training (d) Induction training

42. **The workers of a factory remain idle because of lack of knowledge of hi-tech machines. Frequent visit of engineer is made which causes high overhead charges. Which of the following method can be useful to remove the problem?** **NCERT Modified; Competency Based Que**

(a) Induction training (b) Vestibule training
(c) Internship training (d) Promotion

43. **Kundan Lai joined a food processing unit as a factory worker. Since he was expected to work on sophisticated machinery, he was asked to undergo special training. Identify the training method with reference to the above lines.** **Competency Based Que**

(a) Vestibule training (b) Apprenticeship training
(c) Internship training (d) Induction training

Direction *Read the following text and answer the 44 to 47 on the basis of the same*

EcoGreen Solutions, a company specialising in eco-friendly products, has recently expanded its operations due to increased demand for sustainable goods.

The company has grown from a small start-up to a medium-sized enterprise, necessitating a more structured approach to staffing. With this expansion, the management realised that effective staffing was crucial to support the company's growth and maintain its high standards of product quality and customer service.

To address staffing needs, EcoGreen Solutions implemented a comprehensive recruitment and selection process. They established a dedicated HR team responsible for hiring skilled professionals across various departments, including production, marketing and customer service. The HR team focused on identifying the right talent through a series of interviews, skill assessments and background checks.

They also introduced training programmes to ensure that new employees were well-integrated into the company culture and understood their roles and responsibilities. Additionally, EcoGreen Solutions introduced performance appraisal systems to regularly evaluate employee performance and identify areas for improvement.

This approach not only helped in maintaining high performance standards but also facilitated career development and growth opportunities for employees.

The management's efforts in effective staffing have resulted in improved operational efficiency, higher employee satisfaction and enhanced company performance.

44. **What was the primary reason for EcoGreen Solutions to enhance its staffing function?**

(a) To increase the number of products sold
(b) To support the company's expansion and maintain product quality
(c) To reduce the company's operational costs
(d) To improve the company's financial performance

45. **Which aspect of staffing did EcoGreen Solutions focus on to ensure new employees were well-integrated?**

(a) Offering higher salaries to attract talent
(b) Introducing training programmes
(c) Reducing the number of employees
(d) Increasing the number of promotions

46. **How did EcoGreen Solutions evaluate employee performance?**

(a) Through annual financial reports
(b) By conducting performance appraisals
(c) By increasing work hours
(d) Through customer feedback only

47. **What was one of the outcomes of the effective staffing practices at EcoGreen Solutions?**

(a) Increased number of product defects
(b) Decreased employee satisfaction
(c) Improved operational efficiency and employee satisfaction
(d) Reduced training programmes

Assertion-Reason

Direction (Q.No. 48 to 57) *Read the following Assertion (A) and Reason (R) and choose the correct alternative from the following*

Alternatives

(a) Both Assertion (A) and Reason (R) are true and Reason (R) is the correct explanation of Assertion (A)
(b) Both Assertion (A) and Reason (R) are true, but Reason (R) is not the correct explanation of Assertion (A)
(c) Assertion (A) is true, but Reason (R) is false
(d) Assertion (A) is false, but Reason (R) is true

48. **Assertion** (A) Staffing contributes to higher productivity in an organisation.

Reason (R) Staffing ensures that each employee is placed in a role that matches their skills and capabilities.

49. **Assertion** (A) The staffing process is limited to the hiring of new employees.

Reason (R) The staffing process includes training, development and promotion of employees.

50. **Assertion** (A) Staffing help in optimum utilisation of human resources.

Reason (R) Staffing helps in avoiding overstaffing and understaffing.

51. **Assertion** (A) The nature of staffing function is pervasive.
Reason (R) Staffing function is required only at top level.

52. **Assertion** (A) Internal recruitment provides limited choice.

Reason (R) Recruitment from internal sources is less time consuming.

53. **Assertion** (A) Promotion leaves a positive psychological impact on the employees.

Reason (R) Promotion at the higher level may lead to a chain of promotions at the lower levels in the organisation.

54. **Assertion** (A) Advertisements gives the managers a wider range of candidates to choose from.

Reason (R) Advertisements helps in giving more information about the job and the organisation.

55. **Assertion** (A) Aptitude tests are good indices of a person's future success score.

Reason (R) These tests measure the existing skills of the individual.

56. **Assertion** (A) Training and development are essential components of the staffing process.

Reason (R) Training helps employees acquire skills, while development focuses on enhancing overall growth.

57. **Assertion** (A) Training is a job-oriented process.

Reason (R) Training is essential to enable the overall growth of the employee.

Two Statements Based MCQs

Direction (Q.No. 58 to 67) *Read the following statements carefully and choose the correct alternative*

Alternatives

(a) Statement I is correct and Statement II is incorrect
(b) Statement II is correct and Statement I is incorrect
(c) Both the statements are correct
(d) Both the statements are incorrect

58. **Statement I** Staffing is that part of the process of management which is concerned with obtaining, utilising and maintaining a satisfied and satisfactory workforce.

Statement II Staffing is a continuous process. **CBSE 2025**

59. **Statement I** Staffing is needed in both new and existing organisations.

Statement II Staffing is both a line as well as staff activity.

60. **Statement I** Compensation includes both financial and non-financial rewards.

Statement II Only financial rewards are effective in retaining employees.

61. **Statement I** Orientation is the process of introducing new employees to the organisation's policies, culture, and expectations.

Statement II Orientation is not necessary if employees have prior experience in similar organisations.

62. **Statement I** Recruitment is the process of identifying and attracting potential candidates.

Statement II Selection involves rejecting unsuitable candidates from the pool of applicants.

63. **Statement I** Internal sources of recruitment involve promoting employees from within the organisation.

Statement II Internal recruitment leads to employee motivation and retention.

64. **Statement I** Transfer is a vertical shifting of employees.

Statement II Labour contractors can provide the required number of unskilled workers at short notice.

65. **Statement I** External sources of recruitment bring new ideas and perspectives to the organisation.

Statement II External recruitment can be more expensive and time-consuming than internal recruitment.

66. **Statement I** Trade test helps in measuring the potential to acquire skills.

Statement II Medical examination of the candidate is done after giving the appointment letter.

67. **Statement I** Training increases the job skill while development shapes the attitude.

Statement II Training is a short-term process while development is a long-term process.

Matching

68. **Match the items in Column I with their respective statements in Column II**

Column I	Column II
A. Placement	(i) Evaluates an employee's performance against certain pre-determined standards.
B. Training	(ii) Refers to assigning the post to the employee for which he has been selected.
C. Performance appraisal	(iii) Familiarising the selected employee to other employees and with the rules of the organisation.
D. Orientation	(iv) Skills and abilities of employees to perform specific jobs are increased.

Codes

	A	B	C	D
(a)	(ii)	(iv)	(i)	(iii)
(b)	(iii)	(iv)	(i)	(ii)
(c)	(iii)	(ii)	(iv)	(i)
(d)	(i)	(ii)	(iv)	(iii)

69. **Match the external sources of recruitment in Column I with their respective statements in Column II**

Column I	Column II
A. Direct recruitment	(i) Recruitment from educational institutions.
B. Casual callers	(ii) Organisation keep a database of unsolicited applicants to fill the vacancies easily as they arise.
C. Management consultants	(iii) Firms help various organisations to fill vacancies of middle level and top level executives.
D. Campus recruitment	(iv) Job seekers assemble outside the premises of the organisation.

Codes

	A	B	C	D
(a)	(iii)	(i)	(iv)	(ii)
(b)	(ii)	(iv)	(i)	(iii)
(c)	(iv)	(ii)	(iii)	(i)
(d)	(iii)	(ii)	(iv)	(i)

70. **Match the explanation of different sources of external recruitment given in Column I with the sources given in Column II** **CBSE 2024 C**

Column I	Column II
A. Websites designed and dedicated for the purpose of providing information about both, job seekers and job openings	(i) Casual callers
B. Liaison of business houses with the educational institutes to recruit qualified personnel for various jobs	(ii) Web publishing
C. Notice placed on the notice-board of the enterprise specifying the details of the jobs available	(iii) Campus recruitment
D. Database of unsolicited applicants in the office, prepared and screened to fill vacancies	(iv) Direct recruitment

Codes

	A	B	C	D
(a)	(iii)	(i)	(iv)	(ii)
(b)	(i)	(iii)	(iv)	(ii)
(c)	(ii)	(iv)	(i)	(iii)
(d)	(ii)	(iii)	(iv)	(i)

71. **Match the types of selection tests in Column I with their respective statements in Column II**

Column I	Column II
A. Aptitude test	(i) Individual's capacity to develop
B. Trade test	(ii) Measures the existing skills of an individual
C. Personality test	(iii) Described as an indicator of individual's learning ability or the ability to make decisions and judgement
D. Intelligence test	(iv) Helps in knowing clues to a person's emotions

Codes

	A	B	C	D
(a)	(ii)	(i)	(iv)	(iii)
(b)	(ii)	(iv)	(i)	(iii)
(c)	(iii)	(ii)	(iv)	(i)
(d)	(i)	(ii)	(iv)	(iii)

72. **Match the various training methods in Column I with their respective statements in Column II**

Column I	Column II
A. Induction training	(i) Helps when the employees are required to handle sophisticated machinery.
B. Internship training	(ii) Helps when people want to enter skilled trades, e.g. Plumbers, electrician.
C. Apprenticeship programme	(iii) Helps in accommodating new employees in the new environment expeditiously.
D. Vestibule training	(iv) Helps in creating a balance between theoretical and practical knowledge.

Codes

	A	B	C	D
(a)	(iii)	(iv)	(ii)	(i)
(b)	(iii)	(i)	(ii)	(iv)
(c)	(i)	(ii)	(iv)	(iii)
(d)	(ii)	(i)	(iv)	(iii)

Answers

1. (c) Staffing
2. (d) The staffing function is closely linked to the organisation's strategic goals. Effective staffing ensures that the organisation has the right people to achieve its strategic objectives, making it highly influenced by those goals.
3. (d) All of the above
4. (b) Obtaining competent personnel
5. (b) Workforce analysis
6. (b) While staffing primarily involves recruiting, selecting and training employees, it is closely linked with employee compensation and benefits, which are also part of managing human resources.
7. (a) Workload analysis
8. (d) Estimating manpower requirements
9. (b) Workforce analysis
10. (d) Estimating the manpower requirements
11. (a) External
12. (c) direct recruitment
13. (a) Direct recruitment
14. (b) Casual callers
15. (c) Campus recruitment
16. (a) Direct recruitment
17. (a) It helps in simplifying the process of selection
18. (c) Danger of inbreeding and lack of fresh talent
19. (c) Advertisement
20. (b) vertical
21. (c) campus recruitment
22. (a) promotion
23. (a) Competitive spirit among the existing staff
24. (a) Selection
25. (c) Selection test
26. (c) Intelligence test
27. (b) Aptitude
28. (c) Personality test
29. (c) Trade test
30. (d) contract of employment
31. (b) medical examination
32. (a) Preliminary screening
33. (c) Contract of employment
34. (a) Development
35. (c) Development
36. (d) Development programmes should focus not only on technical skills but also on broader competencies such as leadership, communication and strategic thinking, which prepare employees for future roles and responsibilities.
37. (a) Training
38. (c) To increase productivity by enhancing employee skills
39. (c) Training and development, performance appraisal, promotion and career planning, compensation
40. (c) Induction training
41. (c) Apprenticeship training
42. (b) Vestibule training
43. (a) Vestibule training
44. (b) To support the company's expansion and maintain product quality
45. (b) Introducing training programmes
46. (b) By conducting performance appraisals
47. (c) Improved operational efficiency and employee satisfaction
48. (a) Both Assertion (A) and Reason (R) are true and Reason (R) is the correct explanation of Assertion (A)
49. (d) The staffing process is not limited to hiring new employees; it also encompasses training, development and promotion of employees to ensure that the organisation has a competent workforce capable of achieving its objectives.
50. (a) Both Assertion (A) and Reason (R) are true and Reason (R) is the correct explanation of Assertion (A)
51. (c) Staffing is necessary at every level of the organisation, including lower, middle and top levels, to ensure that the right people are in the right positions.
52. (b) Both Assertion (A) and Reason (R) are true, but Reason (R) is not the correct explanation of Assertion (A)
53. (b) Both Assertion (A) and Reason (R) are true, but Reason (R) is not the correct explanation of Assertion (A)
54. (b) Both Assertion (A) and Reason (R) are true, but Reason (R) is not the correct explanation of Assertion (A)
55. (c) Aptitude tests are designed to measure potential and ability, not existing skills.
56. (a) Both Assertion (A) and Reason (R) are true and Reason (R) is the correct explanation of Assertion (A)
57. (c) Training is primarily aimed at improving job-specific skills not necessarily the overall growth of the employee.
58. (c) Both the statements are correct
59. (c) Both the statements are correct
60. (a) Compensation packages should include both financial rewards (salary, bonuses) and non-financial rewards (recognition, work-life balance) to effectively retain employees.
61. (a) Orientation is essential for all new employees, regardless of their prior experience, to help them understand the specific policies and culture of the new organisation.
62. (c) Both the statements are correct
63. (c) Both the statements are correct
64. (b) Transfer usually involves a horizontal shift of employees within the organisation to a different department or location.

65. (c) Both the statements are correct

66. (d) Trade test helps in measuring existing skills of an individual. Medical examinations are usually conducted before an appointment letter is issued to ensure the candidate is fit for the role.

67. (c) Both the statements are correct

68. (a) (ii) (iv) (i) (iii)

69. (c) (iv) (ii) (iii) (i)

70. (d) (ii) (iii) (iv) (i)

71. (d) (i) (ii) (iv) (iii)

72. (a) (iii) (iv) (ii) (i)

Subjective Questions

Short Answer Type Questions

1. Explain any four points highlighting the importance of staffing.

Ans. Following are the points of importance of staffing

(i) **Obtaining Competent Personnel**
It helps in discovering and obtaining competent personnel for various jobs.

(ii) **Higher Performance**
By placing the right person on the right job, it ensures higher performance.

(iii) **Continuous Survival and Growth**
It ensures the continuous survival and growth of the enterprise, through the successive planning for managers.

(iv) **Optimum Utilisation of Human Resource**
It helps in avoiding overmanning, under utilisation of manpower and high labour cost.
It also helps in preventing the disruption of work by indicating in advance about the likely shortage of employees.

2. "No organisation can be successful unless it fills and keeps the various positions filled with the right kind of people for the right job." Elucidate. NCERT; Competency Based Que

Ans. For an organisation to run successfully, it needs to have all type of skilled persons assigned to that portion of the job. Different people have different type of skills. If the type of job and their skills doesn't match, then the work can't be done successfully.
So the organisation should assign those jobs to the persons who have that particular skills. In this way, the productivity will be good and the organisation will run smoothly and efficiently.

3. "Human resource management includes many specialised activities and duties." Explain. Competency Based Que

Ans. Human resources is the foundation of any business. The right people can take the business to a greater height whereas the wrong people can break the business.
Human resource management includes many specialised activities and duties, which are as follows

(i) Recruitment, i.e. search for qualified people.

(ii) Analysing jobs, collecting information about jobs to prepare job descriptions.

(iii) Developing compensation and incentive plans.

(iv) Training and development of employees for efficient performance and career growth.

(v) Maintaining labour relations and union management relations.

(vi) Handling grievances and complaints.

(vii) Providing for social security and welfare of employees.

(viii) Defending the company in law suits and avoiding legal complications.

4. Identify and explain the following as steps in the process of 'staffing'. CBSE 2023; Competency Based Que

(i) Evaluating an employee's current and/or past performance against certain predetermined standards.

(ii) Placing an employee in a position of increased responsibility usually with more pay and job satisfaction.

Ans.

(i) It is performance appraisal. After training and job experience, employee performance is evaluated against set standards. The appraisal process includes defining job expectations, assessing performance and providing feedback, crucial for employee development.

(ii) It is promotion and carrer planning. Organisations must address career growth and promotional opportunities to help employees realise their full potential. Promotions involve increased responsibility and satisfaction, integral to long-term employee motivation.

5. What is meant by recruitment? How it is different from selection? NCERT

Ans. Recruitment can be defined as the process of searching for prospective employees and stimulating them to apply for jobs in an organisation.

Following are the differences between recruitment and selection (any three)

Basis	Recruitment	Selection
Meaning	It is the process of stimulating people to apply for vacant job position in the organisation.	It is the process of selecting the best candidate from those who have applied for the job.
Objective	The objective of recruitment is to create a pool of eligible candidates for the purpose of selection.	The objective of selection is to get the best candidate selected for the job.
Nature	It is a positive process as it attracts people towards the organisation.	It is a negative process as it involves rejection of candidates at every stage of it.
Sequence	It takes place before selection.	It takes place after recruitment.

6. Identify and explain the sources of recruitment which cannot be utilised when there is shortage of existing staff or it does not fulfill the eligibility criteria of the jobs to be filled. Competency Based Que

Or **Identify and explain the two sources of recruitment which reduce the induction of fresh talent in the organisation and cannot be used to fill all vacancies.** CBSE 2023

Ans. Internal sources of recruitment cannot be utilised when there is shortage of existing staff or it does not fulfill the eligibility criteria of the jobs to be filled.

Following are the types of such sources

(i) **Transfer**
It refers to shifting an employee to a similar job with no change in salary, status and responsibility. Since, it involves shifting the employee from one job to another, one shift to another or one department to another, it may lead to changes in duties and working conditions. It is a horizontal movement of employees, which also helps in the training of employees and filling deficiency of one department with the surplus of another. Job transfer is also helpful in avoiding termination and removing individual problems and grievances. e.g. Transfer of a college professor from one branch to another branch.

(ii) **Promotion**
It means shifting an employee to a higher post carrying higher salary, status and responsibility. It is a vertical shifting of employees, which helps to increase the motivation, loyalty and satisfaction level of employees. It has a great psychological impact over the employees because a promotion at the higher level may lead to a chain of promotions at lower levels in the organisation. e.g. Promotion of a supervisor to the post of a assistant manager.

7. Explain 'direct recruitment' and 'advertisement' as external sources of recruitment.

Ans. Direct Recruitment
Under the direct recruitment, a notice is placed on the noticeboard of the enterprise specifying the details of the jobs available. Job seekers assemble outside the premises of the organisation on the specified date and selection is done on the spot. The practice of direct recruitment is followed usually for casual vacancies of unskilled or semi-skilled jobs.

Advertisement
Advertisement in newspapers or trade and professional journals is generally used when a wider choice is required. Most of the senior positions of industry as well as commerce are filled by this method. The advantage of advertising vacancies is that more information about the organisation and job can be given in the advertisement. Advertisement gives the management a wider range of candidates from which to choose.

8. How does recruitment takes place through recommendations of employees and employment exchange?

Ans. Recruitment takes place through recommendations of employees and employment exchange in the following ways

Recommendations of Employees
Applicants introduced by present employees, or their friends and relatives may prove to be a good source of recruitment. Such applicants are likely to be good employees because their background is sufficiently known.

A type of preliminary screening takes place because the present employees know both the company and the candidates and they would try to satisfy both.

Employment Exchange
Employment exchanges run by the government are regarded as a good source of recruitment for unskilled and skilled operative jobs. In some cases, compulsory notification of vacancies to employment exchange is required by law. Thus, employment exchanges help to match personnel demand and supply by serving as link between job seekers and employers.

9. "Campus recruitment and web publishing serve as vital external sources of recruitment for organisations." Discuss these methods in the recruitment process. Competency Based Que

Ans. Following are the external sources of recruitment

Campus Recruitment
Colleges and institutes of management and technology have become a popular source of recruitment for technical, professional and managerial jobs. Many big organisations maintain a close liaison with the universities, vocational schools and management institutes to recruit qualified personnel for various jobs.

Recruitment from educational institutions is a well established practice of businesses. This is referred to as campus recruitment.

Web Publishing

There are certain websites specifically designed and dedicated for the purpose of providing information about both job seekers and job opening. In fact, websites are very commonly visited both by the prospective employees and the organisations searching for suitable people.

10. "An organisation can reap numerous benefits by prioritising internal sources of recruitment for filling job vacancies."

Explain how employing internal recruitment methods can be advantageous for an organisation.

Competency Based Que

Ans. Following are the benefits of internal source of recruitment (any four)

(i) Employees are motivated to improve their performance. A promotion at a higher level may lead to a chain of promotion at lower levels in the organisation. This motivates the employees to improve their performance through learning and practice. Employees work with commitment and loyalty and remain satisfied with their jobs.

(ii) Internal recruitment also simplifies the process of selection and placement. The candidates that are already working in the enterprise can be evaluated more accurately and economically. This is a more reliable way of recruitment since the candidates are already known to the organisation.

(iii) Transfer is a tool of training the employees to prepare them for higher jobs. Also people recruited from within the organisation do not need induction training.

(iv) Transfer has the benefit of shifting workforce from the surplus departments to those where there is shortage of staff.

(v) Filling of jobs internally is cheaper as compared to getting candidates from external sources.

11. Highlight the potential drawbacks of relying on existing employees as the primary source for filling vacancies within an organisation. **Competency Based Que**

Ans. Following are the potential drawbacks of relying on existing employees as the primary source for filling vacancies within an organisation (any four)

(i) When vacancies are filled through internal promotions, the scope for induction of fresh talent is reduced. Hence, complete reliance on internal recruitment involves danger of 'inbreeding' by stopping 'infusion of new blood' into the organisation.

(ii) The employees may become lethargic if they are sure of time bound promotions.

(iii) A new enterprise cannot use internal sources of recruitment. No organisation can fill all its vacancies from internal sources.

(iv) The spirit of competition among the employees may be hampered.

(v) Frequent transfers of employees may often reduce the productivity of the organisation.

12. "Tapping external sources for various job positions has many benefits." State any four such benefits. **CBSE 2023**

Ans. Following are the benefits of external sources of recruitment

(i) **Qualified Personnel**
By using external sources of recruitment, the management can attract qualified and trained people to apply for vacant jobs in the organisation.

(ii) **Wider Choice**
When vacancies are advertised widely, a large number of applicants from outside the organisation apply. The management has a wider choice while selecting the people for employment.

(iii) **Fresh Talent**
The present employees may be insufficient or they may not fulfill the specifications of the jobs to be filled. External recruitment provide wider choice and brings new blood in the organisation. However, it is expensive and time consuming.

(iv) **Competitive Spirit**
If a company taps external sources, the existing staff will have to compete with the outsiders. They will work harder to show better performance.

13. While external sources of recruitment introduce fresh perspectives into an organisation, what drawbacks might arise from relying on this approach when it comes to employee selection?

Ans. Following are the drawbacks of external sources of recruitment

(i) **Dissatisfaction among Existing Staff**
External recruitment may lead to dissatisfaction and frustration among existing employees. They may feel that their chances of promotion are reduced.

(ii) **Lengthy Process**
Recruitment from external sources takes a long time. The business has to notify the vacancies and wait for applications to initiate the selection process.

(iii) **Costly Process**
It is very costly to recruit staff from external sources. A lot of money has to be spent on advertisement and processing of applications.

14. What are the various types of tests that may be used for selection of employees? Explain any four tests.

Or **In order to streamline the selection procedure, so as to minimise the margin of errors, certain tests are carried out that attempt to measure the characteristics of individuals. Explain any four such tests.** CBSE SQP 2025

Ans. Following are the various types of tests that may be used for selection of employees

(i) **Intelligence Test**
It is a psychological test used to measure the level of intelligence of an individual. It indicates a person's learning ability or the ability to make decisions and judgements.

(ii) **Aptitude Test**
It is used to measure the potential of an individual to learn new skills. It indicates person's capacity to develop and helps to know how he/she will perform in future.

(iii) **Personality Test**
It is a test that provides clues regarding a person's emotions, reactions, maturity and value system, etc.
It aims to explore the overall personality. This test is difficult to design and implement.

(iv) **Trade Test**
It is a test used to measure the existing skills of an individual to perform a job. It is different from aptitude test in the sense it measures the actual skills possessed by an individual while aptitude test measures the potential of an individual to acquire skills.

(v) **Interest Test**
It is a test used to know the interests or involvement of a person in a job that will satisfy him/her.

15. Differentiate between on-the-job training and off-the-job training.

Ans. Following are the differences between on-the-job training and off-the-job training (any four)

Basis	On-the-job Training	Off-the-job Training
Principle	It is based on the principle of learning while doing.	It is based on the principle of learning before doing.
Place of Training	The training is conducted at workplace.	The training is conducted away from the workplace.
Instructor	Superiors are the instructors.	Experts are the instructors.
Contribution	Employees contribute towards work.	Employees do not contribute towards work.
Examples	Apprenticeship training, internship training.	Vestibule training, films, etc.

16. Explain how the provision of training can be beneficial for the organisation.

Ans. Provision of training can be beneficial for the organisation in the following ways (any four)

(i) Training is a systematic learning, always better than hit and trial methods which lead to wastage of efforts and money.
(ii) It enhances employee productivity both in terms of quantity and quality, leading to higher profits.
(iii) Training equips the future manager who can take over in case of emergency.
(iv) Training increases employee morale and reduces absenteeism and employee turnover.
(v) It helps in obtaining effective response to fast changing environment whether technological and economic.

17. Due to rapid technological changes, jobs have become more complex and importance of training has increased for employees. State any four such benefits.
CBSE 2023; Competency Based Que

Or **Since jobs have become more complex, the importance of employee training has increased. Training programmes provide numerous benefits to workers. Explain any four points that support this statement.**
CBSE SQP 2025

Ans. Following are the benefits of training for the employees

(i) Improved skills and knowledge due to training lead to better career of the individual.
(ii) Increased performance by the individual help him to earn more.
(iii) Training makes the employee more efficient to handle machines. Thus, less prone to accidents.
(iv) Training increases the satisfaction and morale of employees.

18. Explain the following methods of training CBSE 2024 C

(i) Vestibule training (ii) Internship training

Ans.

(i) **Vestibule Training**
Employees learn their jobs on the equipment they will be using, but the training is conducted away from the actual work floor. Actual work environments are created in a class room and employees use the same materials, files and equipment. This is usually done when employees are required to handle sophisticated machinery and equipment.

(ii) **Internship Training**
It is a joint programme of training in which educational institutions and business firms cooperate. Selected candidates carry on regular studies for the prescribed period. They also work in some factory or office to acquire practical knowledge and skills.

19. Distinguish between training and development. NCERT

Ans. Following are the differences between training and development (any four)

Basis	Training	Development
Concept	It is the process of imparting technical knowledge and skills for doing a particular job.	It is a learning process aimed at maturity and growth of managerial personnel.
Initiative in Learning	The initiative of providing training is taken by employer.	The initiative is mainly taken by the employee.
Orientation	It is a job-oriented process.	It is a career-oriented process.
Duration	It is a short-term process, for a fixed duration.	It is a long-term process.
Objective	It enables the employee to perform the job better.	It ensures the overall growth of the employee.
Focus	It focuses on technical skills.	It focuses on conceptual and human ideas.

20. Explain the following methods of training.
(i) Induction training
(ii) Apprenticeship training CBSE 2024 C

Ans.

(i) **Induction Training**
It is a type of training given to introduce the selected employee to other employees. It helps to familiarise the new employee with the rules and policies of the organisation.

(ii) **Apprenticeship Training**
Apprenticeship programmes put the trainee under the guidance of a master worker for a prescribed time to acquire a higher level of skill.
People seeking to enter skilled jobs like plumbers, electricians, etc. are often required to undergo apprenticeship training.

Long Answer Type Questions

21. Outline the various steps that are involved in the process of staffing.

Or **Explain the following steps in the process of staffing** CBSE 2025

(i) Placement and orientation
(ii) Training and development
(iii) Performance appraisal
(iv) Promotion and career planning

Ans. Following are the various steps involved in the process of staffing

(i) **Estimating Manpower Requirements**
Analysing decisions, activities and relationships is crucial for defining organisational structure and job positions. Each job requires specific qualifications, skills and experience.
Understanding manpower needs involves knowing both the quantity and type of required personnel, with emphasis on diversity. Workload analysis assesses the human resources needed to meet organisational goals. Workforce analysis determines the current staffing levels. This process identifies if the organisation is understaffed, overstaffed or optimally staffed, guiding subsequent staffing actions.

(ii) **Recruitment**
Recruitment is the process of finding and encouraging prospective employees to apply for jobs. It involves creating a pool of candidates using internal and external sources. The objective is to find the best fit for the job roles based on job descriptions and candidate profiles.

(iii) **Selection**
Selection involves choosing the best candidate from the recruitment pool. The process includes tests and interviews to ensure the organisation hires the best available talent. Successful candidates are offered an employment contract outlining terms and conditions.

(iv) **Placement and Orientation**
Upon joining, the new employee is introduced to the organisation, colleagues and job responsibilities. This familiarisation process, including orientation to company policies, is crucial for long-term job satisfaction and performance.

(v) **Training and Development**
Employees seek career growth and organisations benefit from providing continuous learning opportunities. Training enhances employee motivation, strengthens competencies and improves organisational effectiveness, making career development essential.

(vi) **Performance Appraisal**
After training and job experience, employee performance is evaluated against set standards. The appraisal process includes defining job expectations, assessing performance and providing feedback, crucial for employee development.

(vii) **Promotion and Career Planning**
Organisations must address career growth and promotional opportunities to help employees realise their full potential. Promotions involve increased responsibility and satisfaction, integral to long-term employee motivation.

(viii) **Compensation**
Compensation includes all forms of pay and rewards given to employees, such as wages, salaries and benefits. Establishing a fair and competitive pay plan is essential for attracting and retaining talent, based on the job's worth.

22. Define the term 'recruitment'. Explain any five external sources of recruitment of employees.

Ans. Recruitment is the process of searching prospective employees and stimulating them to apply for jobs in the organisation. Thus, it is also called a positive process. Following are the external sources of recruitment of employees

(i) **Direct Recruitment**
Under the direct recruitment, a notice is placed on the noticeboard of the enterprise specifying the details of the jobs available. Job seekers assemble outside the premises of the organisation on the specified date and selection is done on the spot. The practice of direct recruitment is followed usually for casual vacancies of unskilled or semiskilled jobs.

(ii) **Advertisement**
Advertisement in newspapers or trade and professional journals is generally used when a wider choice is required. Most of the senior positions of industry as well as commerce are filled by this method. The advantage of advertising vacancies is that more information about the organisation and job can be given in the advertisement. Advertisement gives the management a wider range of candidates from which to choose.

(iii) **Placement Agencies and Management Consultants**
Placement agencies provide a nationwide service in matching personnel demand and supply. They compile the bio-data of large number of candidates and provide them to organisation on demand. Such agencies charge fee for their services and are useful where extensive screening is required.

Management consultancy firms help the organisations to recruit technical, professional and managerial personnel. They specialise in middle level and top level executive placements. They maintain data bank of persons with different qualifications and skills and even advertise the jobs on behalf of their clients to recruit right type of personnel.

(iv) **Campus Recruitment**
Many organisations maintain a close link with universities, vocational schools and management institutes, in order to recruit fresh talent and qualified personnel. On one hand, it gives good opportunities to freshers to be employed in reputed firms and on the other hand, it provide qualified manpower in a cost effective way.

It has become a popular source of recrui- tment for technical, professional and managerial jobs.

(v) **Recommendations of Employees**
Employees of an organisation recommend the names of their friends, relatives and neighbours, which may prove to be a good external source of recruitment.

It is a reliable source as the background of the suggested candidate is well known. A type of preliminary screening also takes place because the present employees know both the company and the candidates and they would try to satisfy both.

23. Explain the following external sources of recruitment.
(i) Casual callers
(ii) Labour contractors
(iii) Placement agencies and management consultants

Ans.

(i) **Casual Callers**
Many reputed business organisations keep a database of unsolicited applicants in their offices. Such jobseekers can be a valuable source of man power. A list of such jobseekers can be prepared and can be screened to fill the vacancies as they arise.

(ii) **Labour Contractors**
Labour contractors maintain close contacts with labourers and they can provide the required number of unskilled workers at short notice. Workers are recruited through labour contractors who are themselves employees of the organisation.

The disadvantages of this system are that if the contractor himself decides to leave the organisation, all the workers employed through him will follow suit.

(iii) **Placement Agencies and Management Consultants**
Placement agencies provide a nationwide service in matching personnel demand and supply. These agencies compile bio-data of a large number of candidates and recommend suitable names to their clients. Such agencies charge fee for their services and they are useful where extensive screening is required. Management consultancy firms help the organisations to recruit technical, professional and managerial personnel. They specialise in middle level and top level executive placements.

24. External sources are valuable sources of recruitment. However, there are certain drawbacks that restrict the success of external sources.

In the light of the given statement, state any three advantages and two disadvantages of external source of recruitment. **Competency Based Que**

Ans. Following are the advantages of external source of recruitment

(i) **Qualified Personnel**
By using external sources of recruitment, the management can attract qualified and trained people to apply for vacant jobs in the organisation.

(ii) **Wider Choice**
When vacancies are advertised widely, a large number of applicants from outside the organisation apply. The management has a wider choice while selecting the people for employment.

(iii) **Fresh Talent**
The present employees may be insufficient or they may not fulfill the specifications of the jobs to be filled. External recruitment provides wider choice and brings new blood in the organisation. However, it is expensive and time consuming.

Following are the disadvantages of external source of recruitment

(i) **Dissatisfaction among Existing Staff**
External recruitment may lead to dissatisfaction and frustration among existing employees. They may feel that their chances of promotion are reduced.

(ii) **Lengthy Process**
Recruitment from external sources takes a long time. The business has to notify the vacancies and wait for applications to initiate the selection process.

25. **Describe the essential stages involved in filtering and choosing the right candidate from a group of applicants.**

Or **Explain the following steps in the process of selection.** **CBSE 2025**

(i) **Preliminary screening**
(ii) **Selection tests** (iii) **Employment interview**
(iv) **Reference and background checks**

Ans. A well-organised selection process of personnel involves the following steps

(i) **Preliminary Screening**
It helps the manager to eliminate unqualified or unfit jobseekers, based on the information supplied in the application forms.

(ii) **Selection Tests**
An employment test is a mechanism (either a paper and pencil test or an exercise) that attempts to measure certain characteristics of individuals.
These characteristics range from aptitudes, such as manual dexterity, to intelligence, to personality, etc.

(iii) **Employment Interview**
Interview is a formal, indepth conversation, conducted to evaluate the applicant's suitability for the job. Through an interview, an interviewer seeks to obtain maximum information about the interviewee and the interviewee seeks information about the job and the company.

(iv) **Reference and Background Checks**
Many employers request names, addresses and telephone numbers of references for the purpose of verifying information and gaining additional information of an applicant.

(v) **Selection Decision**
The final decision has to be made from among the candidates, who pass the tests, interviews and reference checks.

(vi) **Medical Examination**
After the selection decision and before the job offer, the candidate is required to undergo a medical fitness test. The job offer is given to the candidate, who is declared fit after the medical examination.

(vii) **Job Offer**
The next step in the selection process is issuing job offer to those applicants, who have passed all the previous hurdles.
It is made through a letter of appointment to confirm his acceptance and communicating to him the reporting date and time.

(viii) **Contract of Employment**
When a candidate accepts the job offer, the contract of employment is made, which is in a written form and includes job title, duties, responsibilities, date when continuous employment starts and the basis for calculating service, rates of pay, allowances, hours of work, leave rules, sickness, grievance procedure, etc.

Case Study Based Questions

Short Case Studies

Case Study 1

Human resources are the most important asset of an organisation. The ability of an organisation to achieve its goal depends upon the quality of its human resources. The general manager of 'Allied and Sons' appointed an IIM graduate, Pawan Rai, specialised in finance as marketing manager. On monthly evaluation, it was found that Pawan Rai's performance was not up to expectations and he was not able to meet the monthly targets of the organisation. The Chief Executive Officer (CEO) of the company asked for investigation into the matter. The CEO was told that Pawan Rai has a specialisation in finance but was appointed as a marketing manager.

The CEO discussed this matter with the general manager and explained to him the importance of putting the right person at the right job.

He further explained that it would not only lead to higher performance but would also provide many other benefits.

Besides the benefits of putting the right man at the right job, state the three other benefits which the CEO might have explained to the general manager that are not given in the above para. **CBSE 2023**

Ans. Following are the benefits of staffing which the CEO might have explained to the general manager

(i) **Obtaining Competent Personnel**
It helps in discovering and obtaining competent personnel for various jobs.

(ii) **Continuous Survival and Growth**
It ensures the continuous survival and growth of the enterprise, through the successive planning for managers.

(iii) **Optimum Utilisation of Human Resource**
It helps in avoiding overmanning, under utilisation of manpower and high labour cost.
It also helps in preventing the disruption of work by indicating in advance about the likely shortage of employees.

Case Study 2

Alpha Enterprises is a company manufacturing water geysers. The company has a functional structure with four main functions i.e. production, marketing, finance and human resource.

As the demand for the product grew, the company decided to hire more employees.

(i) Identify and explain the concept which will help the human resource manager in deciding the actual number of persons required in each department.

(ii) Explain the step of the staffing process in which the concept identified in (i) exists.

Ans.

(i) Workload analysis will help the human resource manager in deciding the actual number of persons required in each department.
Workload analysis assesses the human resources needed to meet organisational goals. Workforce analysis determines the current staffing levels.
This process identifies if the organisation is understaffed, overstaffed, or optimally staffed, guiding subsequent staffing actions.

(ii) Workload analysis is a part of estimating manpower requirements. Analysing decisions, activities and relationships is crucial for defining organisational structure and job positions. Each job requires specific qualifications, skills and experience. Understanding manpower needs involves knowing both the quantity and type of required personnel, with emphasis on diversity.

Case Study 3

A greeting card manufacturing company has established itself as a reliable supplier of high-quality cards, printing an impressive 1,00,000 cards each day. As the festive season approaches, the company receives an urgent order for an additional 50,000 cards to meet the growing demand for Christmas and New Year greetings.

Given the time constraints and the need for immediate hiring, the company is faced with the challenge of efficiently recruiting additional workers to fulfill the order without compromising on quality or efficiency. Which method of recruitment do you suggest?

Ans. In order to complete the order in time, more people are required at short notice. Thus, labour contractor should be approached.

Labour contractors maintain close contacts with labourers and they can provide large number of workers at short notice. A drawback of this method is that if a conflict occurs with the contractor, the entire workforce quits from work.

Case Study 4

Ashish, the marketing head, Raman, the assistant manager and Jyoti, the human resource manager of 'Senor Enterprises Ltd. decided to leave the company. The chief executive officer of the company called Jyoti, the human resource manager and requested her to fill up the vacancies before leaving the organisation. Informing that her subordinate Miss Alka Pandit was very competent and trustworthy, Jyoti suggested that if she could be moved up in the hierarchy, she would do the needful.

The chief executive officer agreed for the same. Miss Alka Pandit contacted 'Keith Recruiters' who advertised for the post of marketing head for 'Senor Enterprises Ltd. They were able to recruit a suitable candidate for the company.

Raman's vacancy was filled up by screening the database of unsolicited applications lying in the office.

(i) Name the internal/external sources of recruitment used by 'Senor Enterprises Ltd.' to fill up the above stated vacancies.

(ii) Also, state any one merit of each of the above identified source of recruitment.

Ans.

(i) Sources of recruitment used by 'Senor Enterprises Ltd' are as follows

- **Promotion**
  For the post of human resource manager.
- **Placement Agencies and Management Consultants**
  For the post of marketing head.
- **Casual Callers**
  For the post of assistant manager.

(ii) One merit of each source of recruitment is as follows

- **Promotion**
  Promotion of employees helps in improving their motivation, loyalty and satisfaction level.
- **Management Consultants**
  Management consultancy firms help the organisation to recruit technical, professional and managerial personnel. They recommend suitable names to their clients.
- **Casual Callers**
  Maintaining a database of unsolicited applicants in their offices helps the organisation in reducing the cost of recruiting workforce. It is the cheapest source of recruitment.

Case Study 5

Anjana Chemicals is looking for qualified and talented people to apply for vacant jobs in the organisation. With the passage of time the organisation has learned a lot with its experience.

It knows when it goes for final selection of candidates, if will have to design different tests. They want to test the employees on the basis of their learning and decision-making ability. The company wants to ensure proper testing of the recruited candidates. After this the candidates will be judged on the basis of in-depth formal conversation.

After the selection the candidates are placed and trained. Employees have to be trained on the equipment they will be using but this training will take place away from the workplace.

(i) Which type of recruitment should the company depend upon?

(ii) Which type of test should be done by the organisation to suit their need?

Ans.

(i) The company should depend upon external recruitment to meet its needs. Anjana chemicals is looking for qualified and talented people to apply for vacant jobs in the organisation.

(ii) The type of test needed by the organisation to suit their need is intelligence test. They want to test the employees on the basis of their learning and decision-making ability.

Case Study 6

Ashish Steel Makers' has decided to include a team of dynamic managers in the company. For this, they want to judge the pattern of interests of the potential managers. After giving this test they want to further know how much the candidate is useful for organisation.

They decide to take another test which can measure the existing skills of the candidates. Rajeev, an exceptional candidate, is given certain document which contains information like job title, pay, allowances, responsibilities, etc. After the employees join they are given a very good training.

The company doesn't want to stop at 'training' which is a job related process. They want to bring a concept which is a career related process.

(i) Which two type of selection tests are highlighted in the above case?

(ii) Which document is given to Rajeev?

Ans.

(i) The two types of selection tests highlighted in the above case are

- **Interest Test**
  Every individual has fascination for some job than the other. Interest tests are used to know the pattern of interests or involvement of a person.
- **Trade Test**
  These tests measure the existing skills of the individual.

They measure the level of knowledge and proficiency in the area of professions or technical training.

(ii) The document which is given to Rajeev is contract of employment.

Basic information that should be included in a written contract of employment will vary according to the level of the job, but the following checklists sets out the typical headings – Job title, duties, responsibilities, date when continuous employment starts and the basis for calculating service, rates of pay, allowances, hours of work, leave rules, sickness, grievance procedure, disciplinary procedure, work rules, termination of employment.

Case Study 7

An organisation provides security services. It requires such candidates who are reliable and don't leak out the secrets of their clients. What step should be incorporated in selection process? **NCERT**

Ans. The organisation should include 'reference and background checks' in the selection process. The purpose of this step is to verify the information and gaining additional information about an applicant. Previous employers, known persons, teachers and professors can act as references and ensure that the candidate is reliable and trustworthy.

Case Study 8

Bharti Enterprises is a company having a very good HR department. It provides learning opportunities that are designed to assist the employees to achieve career growth.

With the passage of time the organisation has learned several methods of training. In one of the methods the trainee is put under the guidance of a master worker for skilled jobs. Moreover, things are not easy for the organisation at the stage of selection process. The recruitment process followed is very lengthy and costly for the firm. Secondly, a very large number of candidates appear for the different posts after recruitment is started.

However, at the first stage of the selection process the managers eliminate unqualified and unsuitable applicants on the basis of the reasons which are not found in their application forms as they are not fit to meet basic requirements.

(i) Which type of 'on-the-job' training is provided by the organisation to its employees?

(ii) At which stage of the selection process do the managers get rid of unqualified candidates?

Ans.

(i) The type of training provided by the organisation to its employees is apprenticeship training. Under this training the trainee is put under the guidance of a master worker.

(ii) The stage of the selection process at which the managers get rid of unqualified and unsuitable candidates is preliminary screening. At the first stage of the selection process the managers eliminate unqualified and unsuitable applicants on the basis of the reasons which were not found in their application forms.

Case Study 9

Identify and state the type of training involved and also categorise whether it is 'on-the-job' training or 'off-the-job training' in the following cases

(i) In a shoe manufacturing company a group of new recruits are being trained. They are trained under an experienced trainer Mr. Arun.

He is training them skills which will require atleast six months of dedication under real work environment.

(ii) A student of ABC MBA College is having a combined training analysis where he is having two mentors.

One mentor is from the college and the other is from the company. The idea is to give real knowledge about the corporate functioning.

Ans.

(i) The type of training is apprentice programme (On-the-job training). Apprenticeship programmes put the trainee under the guidance of a master worker. These are designed to acquire a higher level of skill. People seeking to enter skilled jobs, to become, for example, plumbers, electricians or ironworkers, are often required to undergo apprenticeship training. These apprentices are trainees who spend a prescribed amount of time working with an experienced guide or trainer.

(ii) The type of training is internship training (On-the-job training). It is a joint programme of training in which educational institutions and business firms cooperate. Selected candidates carry on regular studies for the prescribed period. They also work in some factory or office to acquire practical knowledge and skills.

Case Study 10

Rahul has been dedicatedly working under the guidance of Raju, an experienced electrician, for the past two years. Eager to master the intricacies of electrical work, Rahul views this opportunity as a crucial step in his career development. Under Raju's mentorship, he has been exposed to various aspects of thc job, including wiring, circuit installation, troubleshooting electrical issues and understanding safety protocols.

This hands-on experience is integral to Rahul's learning process, as he not only observes Raju's techniques but also engages in practical tasks that allow him to apply theoretical knowledge in real-world scenarios.

Identify and explain the method of training Rahul is undergoing.

Ans. The method of training which Rahul is undergoing is apprenticeship programme. Apprenticeship programmes put the trainee under the guidance of a master worker. These are designed to acquire a higher level of skill. People seeking to enter skilled jobs, to become, for example, plumbers, electricians or ironworkers, are often required to undergo apprenticeship training.

These apprentices are trainees who spend a prescribed amount of time working with an experienced guide or trainer.

A uniform period of training is offered to trainees, in which both fast and slow learn here, are placed together.

Case Study 11

A renowned car company named 'BB Motors' was known for producing high performance cars. They were committed to ensure that its employees had the skills and knowledge to build these innovative high-performance cars. To achieve this, they implemented a unique approach for training. The company transformed a section of its factory into what they called the 'Learning Floor'. Actual work environment was created by allotting a specialised space.

The space was equipped with a range of car components, tools and sophisticated car equipment identical to those used on the factory floor, where the company's employees would undergo their training. Identify and explain the method of training used by 'BB Motors' to ensure that its employees had the skills and knowledge to build innovative high-performance cars. **CBSE 2024**

Ans. The method of training used by 'BB Motors' to ensure that its employees had the skills and knowledge to build innovative high performance cars is 'vestibule training' Vestibule training employees learn their jobs on the equipment they will be using, but the training is conducted away from the actual work floor.

Actual work environments are created in a class room and employees use the same materials, files and equipment. This is usually done when employees are required to handle sophisticated machinery and equipment.

Long Case Studies

Case Study 12

Shyam Mehta is the founder of 'Good Beans Coffee' a famous chain of 11 outlets in South India, selling high quality filter coffee. He is known for his leadership and vision. He believes that human resources are the most important assets of an organisation.

He often quotes, "The right people can help you take your business to the top and the wrong people can break your business". This is the reason he considers the function of management that fills the various positions in the organisation structure to be the most critical and fundamental to organisational performance.

(i) Identify and state the function of management that has been emphasised by Shyam Mehta.

(ii) State any four points of importance of function identified in (i) above.

Ans.

(i) The function of management that has been emphasised by Shyam Mehta is staffing. Staffing has been described as the managerial function of filling and keeping filled the positions in the organisation structure.

(ii) Following are the points of importance of staffing functions

- **Obtaining Competent Personnel**
  It helps in discovering and obtaining competent personnel for various jobs.
- **Higher Performance**
  By placing the right person on the right job, it ensures higher performance.
- **Continuous Survival and Growth**
  It ensures the continuous survival and growth of the enterprise, through the successive planning for managers.
- **Job Satisfaction and Morale**
  It improves job satisfaction and morale of employees through objective assessment and fair reward for their contribution.

Case Study 13

Ms Jayshree recently completed her post graduate diploma in human resource management. A few months from now a large steel manufacturing company appointed her as its human resource manager. As of now, the company employs 800 persons and has an expansion plan in hand, which may require another 200 persons for various types of additional requirements. Ms Jayshree has been given complete charge of the company's human resource department. **NCERT**

(i) Point out, what functions is she supposed perform?

(ii) What problems do you foresee in her job?

(iii) What steps is she going to take to perform her job efficiently?

(iv) How significant is her role in the organisation?

Ans.

(i) Ms Jayshree as HR Manager is required to perform the following functions

- Recruitment
- Prepare job description

- Preparing compensation and incentive plans
- Arranging training programmes
- Making welfare schemes for employees
- Handling grievances of employees
- Handling labour disputes

(ii) She may face the following problems
- Properly qualified candidates may not bell available.
- Demand for wages may go higher.
- After providing training, the workers may leave the organisation.
- Trade unions may bring unreasonable demands.

(iii) Following steps can be taken by her to perform her job efficiently
- She should make use of all the possible sources of recruitment.
- She should frequently consult the experts and also observe the policies followed by competitors to recruit and retain the workforce.
- She should maintain cordial relationship with trade unions and encourage them to act as one big family.

(iv) Her role is very significant in the organisation.

She is a human resource manager and concerned with timely procurement of competent manpower and ensuring its effective and efficient utilisation, so as to survive along with the three main objectives i.e. organisational, individual and societal objective.

Case Study 14

ABC Ltd., an IT company known for its innovative solutions and strong market presence, has been experiencing rapid growth over the past few years. As part of its expansion strategy, the company recently opened a new branch in Pune, a city with a burgeoning tech industry. The management at ABC Ltd. was keen on ensuring that the new branch would be fully operational within a short span of time to capitalise on the growing opportunities in the region.

To quickly staff the new office with skilled professionals, the HR manager, Mr. Singh, decided to explore different recruitment strategies. Given the need for immediate and reliable talent, Mr. Singh chose to rely on the applicants introduced by present employees or their friends and relatives.

(i) Identify the external source of recruitment used by ABC Ltd. in this case.

(ii) Explain the benefits of using this recruitment method.

Ans.

(i) The external source of recruitment used by ABC Ltd. in this case is recommendation of employees.

(ii) Following are the benefits of using this recruitment method

- **Qualified Personnel**
  By using external sources of recruitment, the management can attract qualified and trained people to apply for vacant jobs in the organisation.
- **Wider Choice**
  When vacancies are advertised widely, a large number of applicants from outside the organisation apply. The management has a wider choice while selecting the people for employment.
- **Fresh Talent**
  The present employees may be insufficient or they may not fulfill the specifications of the jobs to be filled. xternal recruitment provide wider choice and brings new blood in the organisation. However, it is expensive and time consuming.
- **Competitive Spirit**
  If a company taps external sources, the existing staff will have to compete with the outsiders. They will work harder to show better performance.

Case Study 15

Rajat Verma was the human resources manager at 'GreenLife Products', a company known for its innovative range of eco-friendly household items. GreenLife Products had experienced rapid growth over the past few years and the company was now looking to expand its workforce to meet increasing production demands.

Rajat believed in bringing fresh talent into the organisation to foster innovation and maintain a competitive edge. He decided to use external sources of recruitment to fill several key positions. Rajat ensured that the job vacancies were advertised widely through various online job portals and recruitment agencies. This strategy attracted a large pool of qualified candidates from diverse backgrounds, offering the company a wider choice when selecting the most suitable candidates.

After a rigorous selection process, GreenLife Products successfully hired several highly qualified professionals, bringing fresh perspectives and innovative ideas into the company.

However, the decision to recruit externally did not come without challenges. The existing employees at GreenLife Products felt demotivated and frustrated as they believed their chances of promotion were diminished by the influx of new talent from outside the company.

Additionally, the recruitment process proved to be lengthy and expensive. The company had to invest significant resources in advertising the vacancies and processing the numerous applications received.

Quoting lines from the above paragraph, identify and explain two benefits and two limitations of external sources of recruitment discussed in the above case.

Ans. Benefits of external sources of recruitment are as follows

(i) **Qualified Personnel**

"This strategy attracted a large pool of qualified candidates from diverse backgrounds, offering the company a wider choice when selecting the most suitable candidates."

By using external sources of recruitment, GreenLife Products was able to attract a wide range of qualified and trained individuals.

This provided the company with the opportunity to select from a diverse pool of talent, ensuring that the best candidates were chosen for the job.

(ii) **Fresh Talent**

"GreenLife Products successfully hired several highly qualified professionals, bringing fresh perspectives and innovative ideas into the company."

External recruitment brought in new employees with fresh ideas and perspectives, which can be crucial for driving innovation and growth within the company.

This fresh talent helped GreenLife Products maintain its competitive edge in the market.

Limitations of external sources of recruitment are as follows

(i) **Dissatisfaction among Existing Staff**

"The existing employees at GreenLife Products felt demotivated and frustrated as they believed their chances of promotion were diminished by the influx of new talent from outside the company."

External recruitment can lead to dissatisfaction among current employees who may feel that their opportunities for advancement within the company are being reduced. This can result in decreased morale and motivation among the existing staff.

(ii) **Lengthy and Costly Process**

"Additionally, the recruitment process proved to be lengthy and expensive. The company had to invest significant resources in advertising the vacancies and processing the numerous applications received."

The external recruitment process is often time consuming and expensive.

GreenLife Products had to allocate substantial resources for advertising and processing applications, which could have been used elsewhere in the organisation.

Case Study 16

A company, Xylo Ltd., is setting up a new plant in India for manufacturing auto components. India is a highly competitive and cost effective production base in this sector. Many reputed car manufacturers source their auto components from here. Xylo Ltd. is planning to capture about 40% of the market share in India and also export to the tune of atleast 50 crore in about 2 years of its planned operations.

To achieve these targets it requires a highly trained and motivated workforce. You have been retained by the company to advise it in this matter. While giving answer, keep in mind the sector the company is operating. **NCERT**

(i) Outline the process of staffing the company should follow.

(ii) Which sources of recruitment the company should rely upon? Give reasons for your recommendation.

(iii) Outline the process of selection the company should follow with reasons.

Ans.

(i) Xylo Ltd. is planning to set-up new plant in India for manufacturing auto components. The prime concern of the company is to hire the manpower, who are highly trained and motivated. In order to achieve the targets, the company should follow the staffing process in this manner

- Estimating manpower requirements
- Recruitment
- Selection
- Placement and orientation
- Training and development
- Performance appraisal
- Promotion and career planning
- Compensation of employees

(ii) The company is establishing a new unit in India. Thus, they should rely on external sources of recruitment. They should adopt this source and through employment exchange, placement agencies and labour contractors, they will able to get good staff in the company.

This recommendation is fruitful because through these sources the company will have a wide choice of candidates. They can get the qualified personnel and bring new blood in the organisation who are highly competitive and will work harder to show better performance.

(iii) Through recruitment process, organisation receive large number of applications. In order to select the most suitable candidate to perform the job, selection process is to be considered.

Following steps are to be taken in series

First step, preliminary screening, helps the manager to select from among those candidates who have applied.

Second step is selection test, it is to be conducted to check the practical knowledge of the candidate.

Third step, interview, is to be taken of those candidates, who qualify the test. A panel of experts is called for, to identify the best among hundreds.

Fourth step is selection decision. The candidates who pass the test and interview, are included in selection list and critically examined that they are best or not.

Fifth step is examining their medical fitness whether they are physically and mentally fit or not.

Sixth step is to offer the job, providing them a letter of appointment, in which terms and conditions are mentioned.

Final step is a contract of employment. When candidate accepts the job offer, they sign the contract of employment. The employer and candidate exchange certain documents as the final process of selection.

Case Study 17

Mohan, the director of an apparels company decides to manufacture bags in order to utilise the waste material from one of his apparels units. The decision is taken to establish the manufacturing unit in rural area of Jharkhand where less job opportunities are available and the benefit of cheap labour can be availed. He decides to give equal job opportunities and refrain from discriminating between men and women. He decides to recruit four different heads for sales, accounts, purchase, marketing.

He gives an advertisement and shortlists fifteen candidates per post after conducting selection tests.

Identify and state the next four steps for choosing the best candidate from the shortlisted candidates.

Ans. Following are the next four steps of selection process

(i) **Employment Interview**
Interview is a formal, in-depth conversation, conducted to evaluate the applicant's suitability for the job. Through an interview, an interviewer seeks to obtain maximum information about the interviewee and the interviewee seeks information about the job and the company.

(ii) **Reference and Background Checks**
Many employers request names, addresses and telephone numbers of references for the purpose of verifying information and gaining additional information of an applicant.

(iii) **Selection Decision**
The final decision has to be made from among the candidates, who pass the tests, interviews and reference checks.

(iv) **Medical Examination**
After the selection decision and before the job offer, the candidate is required to undergo a medical fitness test. The job offer is given to the candidate, who is declared fit after the medical examination.

Case Study 18

Ritika Mehta was recently appointed as the Chief Operating Officer (COO) of a clothing brand, 'FashionForward'. The company specialises in producing trendy and affordable fashion apparel for young adults. Ritika is known for her structured approach to management, ensuring that new employees are well-integrated into the company culture and are equipped with the necessary knowledge to perform their roles effectively.

Before each fashion season, FashionForward carefully selects new hires who are then introduced to the company through a systematic training process. The new employees are given a comprehensive overview of the company's history, values and product lines. This helps them understand their roles and responsibilities within the larger organisational structure.

One day, a newly hired employee mentioned that the training they received provided them with clarity on the company's expectations, making them feel more confident in their new position.

FashionForward continued to grow, with employees generally feeling well-prepared and supported in their roles.

(i) Quoting lines from the above paragraph, identify and explain the type of training method adopted by the organisation.

(ii) State any four benefits of training for the employees.

Ans.

(i) The type of training method adopted by the organisation is induction training. "The new employees are given a comprehensive overview of the company's history, values and product lines." It is a type of training given to help a new employee in settling down quickly into the job by becoming familiar with the people, the surrounding, the job and the business. The duration of such type of training may be from a few hours to a few days.

(ii) Following are the benefits of training for the employees

- Improved skills and knowledge due to training lead to better career of the individual.
- Increased performance by the individual help him to earn more.
- Training makes the employee more efficient to handle machines. Thus, less prone to accidents.
- Training increases the satisfaction and morale of employees.

SELF ASSESSMENT TEST

Objective Type Questions

1. Our assets walk out of the door each evening. We have to make sure that they come back the next morning. Here the assets refer to ....
   (a) vehicles (b) goods
   (c) employees (d) machines
2. Workforce analysis is a part of
   (a) recruitment process
   (b) selection process
   (c) training and development process
   (d) estimation of manpower requirement
3. An analysis that enables an assessment of the number and type of human resources available in the organisation is
   (a) development
   (b) promotion
   (c) workload analysis
   (d) workforce analysis
4. TCS recruits candidate from Gargi College is an example of .... method of one of the sources of recruitment.
   (a) campus recruitment
   (b) direct recruitment
   (c) employment exchange
   (d) labour contractors
5. The organisations which are established recently and are new cannot enjoy the benefits of which of the following source of recruitment?
   (a) Internal (b) External
   (c) Both (a) and (b) (d) Direct recruitment
6. Which test is helpful in assessing the individual's capacity for learning new skills?
   (a) Aptitute test (b) Personality test
   (c) Interest test (d) Trade test
7. "It is conducted to strike a balance between the theoretical and practical knowledge". Identify the method of training from the above objective.
   (a) Induction training
   (b) Apprenticeship training
   (c) Internship training
   (d) Vestibule training
8. "A trainee is put under the guidance of a master work." Identify the method of on the job training.
   (a) Apprenticeship programme
   (b) Internship training
   (c) Vestibule training
   (d) Induction training

Answers 1. (c) 2. (d) 3. (d) 4. (a) 5. (a) 6. (a) 7. (c) 8. (a)

Short Answer Type Questions

9. "Staffing is an essential part of human resource management." Discuss.
10. "Promotion stops infusion of new blood in the organisation. However it is still being used as a good source of filling the vacancies internally."
    State any three reasons for the same.
11. Explain briefly 'transfers' and 'promotions' as internal sources of recruitment.
12. What is meant by recruitment? How is it different from selection?
13. Mahesh visits one of the prestigious colleges in Delhi to carry out the recruitment process. Identify the source and type of recruitment. State any two types of the same source of recruitment.
14. Mohan, an HR professional conducted interview and selection tests of 100 candidates for filling one of the vacancies in the organisation. State any four types of tests that Mohan would have used for the selection.
15. Rajesh is working under the guidance of Harish, a carpenter to learn different skills of the job. Name and explain the method of training Rajesh is undergoing.

Long Answer Type Questions

16. Explain the steps involved in the staffing process.
17. A public transport corporation advertised in the newspaper in order to fill vacancies. The company has to now undertake the process of selection. Explain the first six steps involved in the process.

07

CHAPTER

Directing aims to ensure that activities of all employees are mobilised towards organisational goals. It is the connecting link between planning, organising, staffing and the function of controlling.

▼ **YOUR STUDY GOALS**

7.1 Concept of Directing
7.2 Supervision
7.3 Motivation
7.4 Leadership
7.5 Communication

▼ **YOUR PRACTICE GOAL**

- Objective Type Questions (70 Qs ; MCQs, A-R, Statements, Matching)
- Subjective Type Questions (24 SAs, 6 LAs)
- Case Study Based Questions (Short Case Studies-23, Long Case Studies-7)
- Self Assessment Test (6 MCQs, 7 SAs, 3 LAs)

Directing

7.1 Concept of Directing

Directing refers to the process of instructing, guiding, counselling, motivating and leading people in the organisation to achieve its pre-determined objectives.

Features of Directing

1. **Directing initiates Action** Directing is an execution function of management i.e. while other functions prepare a setting for action, directing initiates action.
2. **Directing takes Place at Every Level of Management** Directing is a pervasive function which takes place wherever a superior-subordinate relationship exists.
3. **Directing is a Continuous Process** Directing is an ongoing process that persists throughout the life of the organisation irrespective of people occupying managerial positions.
4. **Directing Flows from Top to Bottom** Directing is initiated at top level and flows downward in the hierarchy.

Importance of Directing

Following points highlight the importance of directing

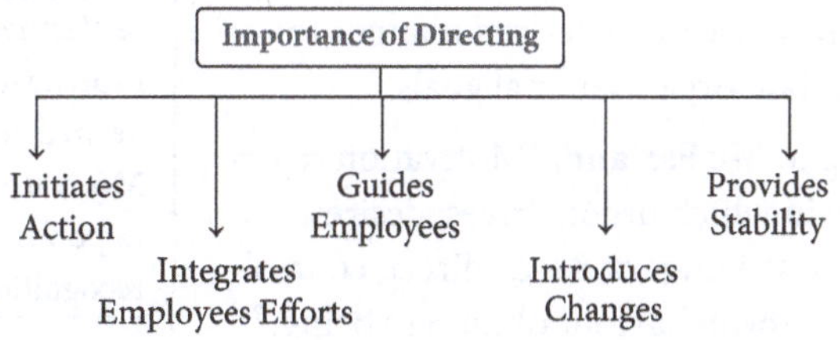

1. **Initiates Action** Directing initiates action by guiding and clarifying tasks to employees, helping them to achieve pre-determined goals.
2. **Integrates Employees Efforts** It integrates individual efforts towards the achievement of organisational goals, ensuring collective performance.
3. **Guides Employees** Directing helps employees realise their full potential and latent capabilities through motivation and effective leadership.
4. **Introduces Changes** It facilitates change by reducing resistance and developing required cooperation through motivation, communication and leadership.
5. **Provides Stability** Effective directing fosters cooperation and commitment, bringing stability and balance in the organisation.

Directing Importance

If a supervisor guides his subordinates and clarifies their doubts in performing a task, it will help the worker to achieve work targets given to him.

If a manager wants to introduce new system of accounting, there may be initial resistance from accounting staff. But, if manager explains the purpose, provides training and motivates with additional rewards, the employees may accept change and cooperate with manager.

Elements of Directing

A manager directs his subordinates by guiding, leading, motivating and instructing them to achieve organisational goals, as per the needs of the individual.

Therefore, the elements of directing include

- Supervision
- Motivation
- Leadership
- Communication

7.2 Supervision

Supervision refers to instructing, guiding and observing the subordinates while they are performing jobs in the organisation.

Supervision as an Element of Directing and as Function of Supervisor

Supervision, a key element of directing, involves guiding and overseeing employees to ensure optimum utilisation of resources and goal achievement. It also refers to the role of a supervisor, positioned directly above workers in the organisational hierarchy. The supervisors' role is vital as they maintain direct contact with workers, unlike other managers, ensuring effective implementation of tasks.

7.3 Motivation

Motivation means incitement or inducement to act or move. In the context of an organisation, it means the process of making subordinates to act in a desired manner to achieve certain organisational goals.

According to **Mc Farland**, "Motivation refers to the way in which urges, drives, desires, aspirations, strivings or needs direct, control and explain the behaviour of human being."

Interrelated Terms

Motive A motive is an inner drive that energises and directs behaviour toward achieving goals. It arises from individuals' needs and causes restlessness, prompting action to alleviate it.

Motivation It is the process of encouraging people to take action to achieve desired goals. It involves satisfying individuals' needs to inspire their efforts.

Motivators These are the techniques used by managers to inspire employees to perform at their best. Examples include financial rewards, promotions, recognition and additional responsibilities.

Features of Motivation

1. **Motivation is a Psychological Phenomenon** It is a personal and internal feeling, such as desires and aspirations, that drives human behaviour, like the urge for a motorbike or a comfortable house.
2. **Motivation Produces Goal Directed Behaviour** Motivation leads to actions aimed at achieving specific goals, such as improved performance to earn a job promotion.
3. **Motivation may be Positive or Negative** Positive motivation offers rewards like pay increases and promotions, while negative motivation involves penalties or threats to induce a person to act in the desired way.
4. **Motivation is a Complex Process** Motivation is complex because individuals vary in their expectations, perceptions and reactions, leading to different effects for each person.

Motivation Process

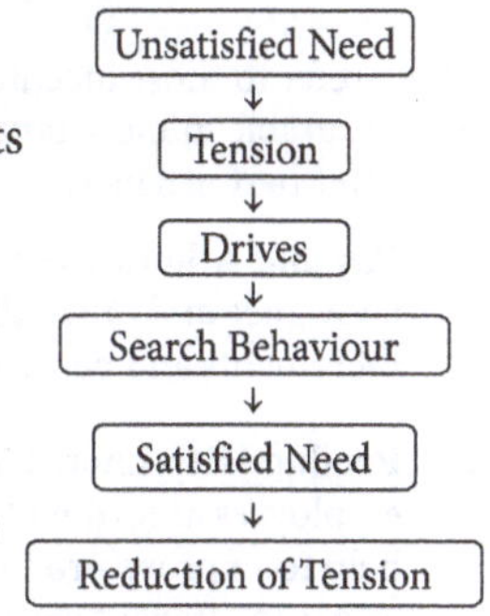

Motivation process is based on human needs. It can be understood through the following points

- An unsatisfied need of an individual creates tension, which stimulates his drives.
- These drives generate a search behaviour to satisfy such need.
- When the need is satisfied, the individual is relieved of tension.

e.g. Akash is very hungry, due to which he became restless and started walking on the road in search for different options to satisfy his need. Once his need is satisfied after having a meal, he is relieved of his tension.

Maslow's Need Hierarchy Theory of Motivation

Maslow's theory was based on human needs. He felt that within every human being, there exists a hierarchy of five needs. These are given below

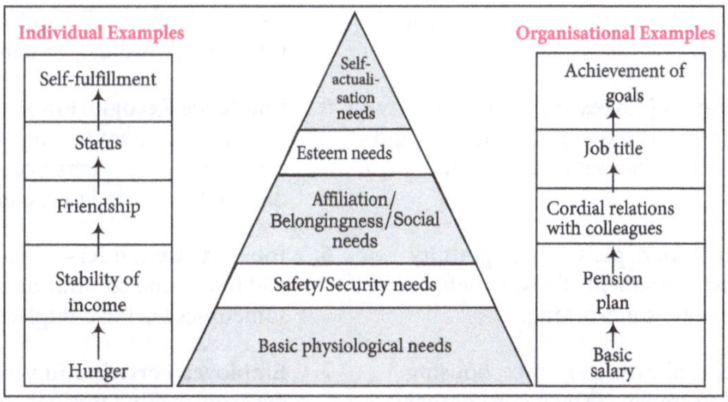

1. **Basic Physiological Needs** These needs are essential for survival, such as hunger, thirst, shelter and sleep. In organisations, a basic salary helps to meet these needs.
2. **Safety/Security Needs** These needs involve protection from physical and emotional harm, such as job security, stable income and pension plans.
3. **Affiliation/Belonging Needs** These needs focus on affection, acceptance and a sense of belonging within social and work environments.
4. **Esteem Needs** These needs include self-respect, recognition, autonomy status and attention.
5. **Self-Actualisation Needs** It is the highest level of need, involving personal growth, self-fulfillment and achieving one's potential.

Assumptions of Maslow's Need Hierarchy Theory

- People's behaviour is based on their needs. Satisfaction of such needs influences their behaviour.
- People's needs are in hierarchical order, starting from basic physiological needs to other higher level needs.
- A satisfied need can no longer motivate a person; only next higher level need can motivate him.
- A person moves to the next higher level of the hierarchy only when the lower need is satisfied.

Financial and Non-financial Incentives

Incentive means all measures which are used to motivate people to improve performance. These incentives may be broadly classified as financial and non-financial.

Financial Incentives	Non-financial Incentives
These refer to those incentives which are in direct monetary form or measurable in monetary term and serve to motivate employees for better performance. 1. **Pay and Allowances** Salary includes basic pay, dearness allowance and other allowances. It often features regular increments and performance-linked pay hikes.	The incentives which cannot be calculated in terms of money are known as non-financial or non-monetary incentives. 1. **Status** Status in an organisation refers to the ranking of positions, including authority, rewards and recognition, satisfying psychological, social and esteem needs.
2. **Productivity-Linked Wage Incentives** Wages are given to employees according to their performance. These incentives help to improve productivity of employees by paying higher wages to efficient workers.	2. **Organisational Climate** Organisational climate includes characteristics like autonomy, reward orientation, risk taking, etc. that affect employee behaviour and distinguish one organisation from another.
3. **Bonus** Bonus is an additional reward beyond regular wages or salary. It serves as an extra motivation for employees. It may be paid in cash or kind.	3. **Career Advancement Opportunity** Providing skill development and promotion opportunities helps employees to grow and enhances their performance.
4. **Profit Sharing** Employees receive a share in the company's profits. This system motivates them to enhance performance and contribute to profit growth.	4. **Job Enrichment** It involves designing roles with varied content, higher skill requirements and more autonomy as well as responsibility to enhance motivation and growth.
5. **Co-partnership/Stock Option** Employees are given company's shares at reduced prices. This fosters a sense of ownership and encourages their commitment to organisational growth.	5. **Employee Recognition Programmes** Recognition means acknowledgement of work with a show of appreciation. e.g. Giving award/certificate for best performance, distributing momentos, complementaries, etc.
6. **Retirement Benefits** Provident fund, pension and gratuity provide financial security post-retirement. These benefits serve as motivation while employees are still working.	6. **Job Security** It offers employees stability, reducing worry and increasing commitment towards work, though it can sometimes lead to complacency (self-contented).
7. **Perquisites** Additional benefits like car allowance, housing and medical aid are provided to employees by many companies. These perks enhance motivation and job satisfaction.	7. **Employee Participation** Involving employees in decision-making through committees fosters engagement and collaboration.
	8. **Employee Empowerment** Empowering subordinates by granting more autonomy and responsibility enhances job importance and performance.

7.4 Leadership

Leadership may be defined as the process of influencing the behaviour of people by making them strive voluntarily towards the achievement of organisational goals.

According to **George Terry**, "Leadership is the activity of influencing people to strive willingly for group objectives."

Features of Leadership

- Leadership indicates ability of an individual to influence others.
- Leadership tries to bring change in the behaviour of others.
- Leadership indicates interpersonal relations between leaders and followers.
- Leadership is exercised to achieve common goals of the organisation.
- Leadership is a continuous process.

Leadership Styles

Leadership style refers to a leader's behavioural pattern reflected by him/her in his/her role. There are several bases for classifying leadership styles. The most popular classification is based on use of authority, according to which different leadership styles are

1. Autocratic or Authoritarian Leadership

An autocratic leader makes all the decisions and expects everyone to follow orders without question. Under this style, there is only one way communication, as the subordinate acts according to the command given by manager. This leadership style is very effective in getting productivity in many situations like in a factory where supervisor is responsible for production on time and has to ensure labour productivity. It also facilitates quick decision-making.

2. Democratic or Participative Leadership

A democratic leader involves the team in making decisions and values their opinions. This style is more common and popular now-a-days, as it ensures achievement of goals, when they are set with acceptance of subordinates themselves.

A democratic leader provides freedom of thinking and listens to suggestions, grievances and opinions of subordinates. This improves the attitude of employees towards their jobs and the organisation, thereby increasing their morale.

This style is of mutual benefit which helps subordinates to become part of team and help leaders (seniors) to make better decisions. A democratic leader exercises more control by using forces within the group.

3. Laissez Faire or Free-rein Leadership

It involves complete delegation of authority, so that subordinates themselves take decisions. Group members work on their own tasks resolving issues themselves. The manager is there only to support them and supply them required information to complete the task assigned. At the same time, subordinate assumes responsibility for work to be performed.

This style of leadership is appropriate when the subordinates are well trained, knowledgeable, self-motivated and ready to assume responsibility.

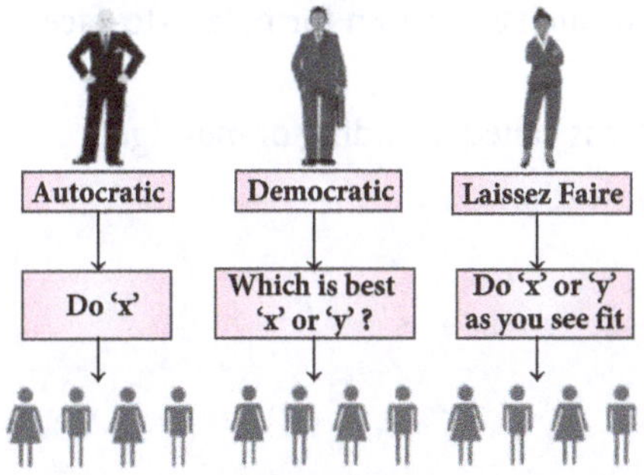

Types of Leadership Styles

Rahul, a factory manager, tells workers exactly what to do and when to do, it indicates autocratic style. This style helps get things done quickly but can make workers feel left out.

Mohan, a team leader, asks for everyone's ideas before deciding on a new project, it indicates democratic style. This style helps build teamwork and makes people feel more engaged.

Raj, a project leader, lets the team decide how to complete a task and only steps in when needed, it indicates laissez faire style. This approach encourages creativity but can sometimes lead to a lack of direction.

7.5 Communication

Communication can be defined as a process of exchange of ideas, views, facts, feelings, etc., between two or more people to create common understanding.

According to **Rogers**, "Communication is a process by which people create and share information with one another in order to reach common understanding."

Features of Communication

- It is a two-way process in which sender sends the message to receiver.
- It is a continuous process.
- It aims to create understanding between sender and receiver.
- It is all pervasive, as information is exchanged at all levels and all departments.
- It is a social process.

Elements of Communication Process

Following are the elements of communication process

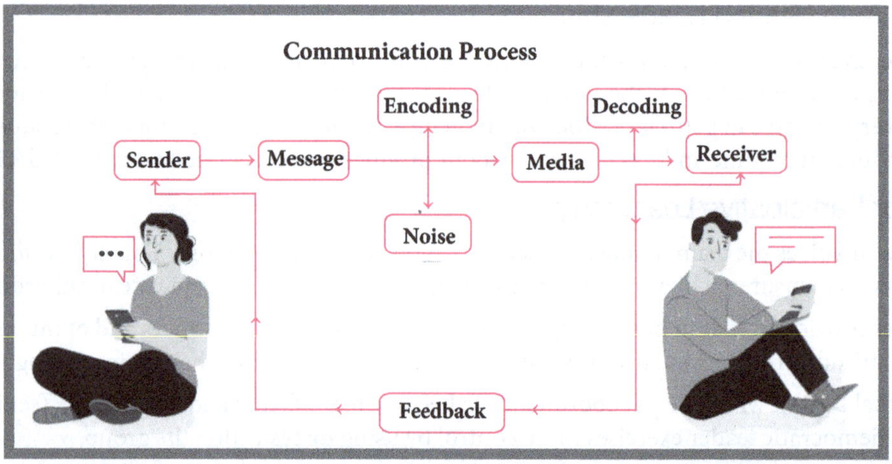

1. **Sender** He/She is the person who conveys his/her thoughts or ideas to the receiver, representing the source of communication.
2. **Message** It is the subject matter of communication which consists of ideas, feelings or instructions intended to be communicated.
3. **Encoding** The process of converting the message into symbols like words or gestures understandable by the receiver is called encoding of message.
4. **Media** It is the path through which the encoded message is transmitted, such as written form, face-to-face or phone call.
5. **Decoding** The process of converting the encoded symbols of the sender is called decoding of message.
6. **Receiver** The person who receives and interprets the sender's communication.

7. **Feedback** It includes the receiver's response indicating that the message has been received and understood. When the feedback is received by the sender, the process of communication is complete.
8. **Noise** It means any obstruction or hindrance to communication affecting the sender, message or receiver.

Some Examples of Noise

- Ambiguous symbols that lead to faulty encoding.
- A poor telephone connection.
- An inattentive receiver.
- Faulty decoding (attaching wrong meanings to message).
- Prejudices obstructing the poor understanding of message.
- Gestures and postures that may distort the message.

Formal and Informal Communication

Communication taking place within the organisation may be classified as formal communication and informal communication.

I. Formal Communication

It refers to the communication taking place through official channels in an organisation.

Features of Formal Communication

- It follows scalar chain i.e. it takes place through formal lines of communication.
- It may be oral or written, but is generally recorded for future reference.
- It is easy to fix responsibility as source of information can be located.
- It is used for communicating official matters like order, instruction, notice, etc.

Types of Formal Communication

1. **Vertical Communication** It takes place between two levels in the organisation. It may take place in two forms
   (i) **Upward Communication** It refers to flow of communication from subordinate to superior.
   (ii) **Downward Communication** It indicates flow of communication from a superior to subordinate.
2. **Horizontal or Lateral Communication** It takes place between individuals working at the same level.
3. **Diagonal Communication** It is a flow of information between the persons working in different departments and holding different levels of authority.

Networks of Formal Communication

1. **Single Chain** Communication flows from every superior to his subordinate through a single chain in a hierarchical structure.
2. **Wheel Network** All subordinates communicate, through their superior only who acts as the central hub. Subordinates are not allowed to talk among themselves.
3. **Circular Network** Communication moves in a circle where each person can communicate with his two adjoining colleagues, leading to a slower flow.
4. **Free Flow** Everyone can communicate freely with others, resulting in a fast flow of communication.
5. **Inverted V** A subordinate can communicate with his immediate superior and also with his superior's superior, but only for prescribed communication.

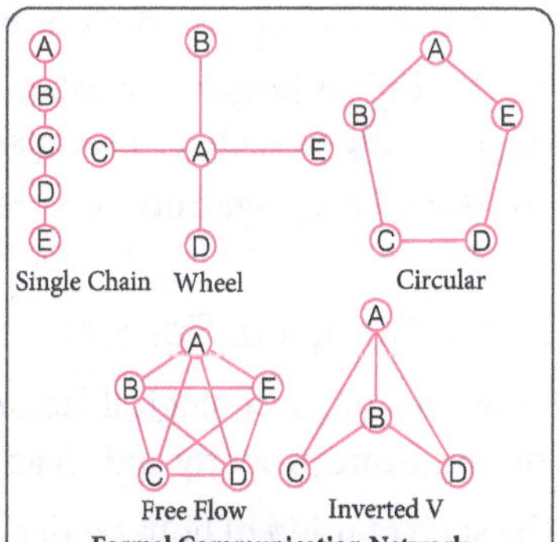

Formal Communication Network

II. Informal Communication/Grapevine

It takes place in an organisation without following the formal lines of communication.

The network of communication followed in this communication is referred to as grapevine network, as it spreads throughout the organisation with its branches going out in all directions, irrespective of the levels of authority.

Features of Informal Communication

- It takes place without following formal lines of communication.
- It helps in developing friendly relationships and gets social satisfaction.
- The flow of communication is very fast.
- It leads to rumours as it is difficult to find the source of such communication.

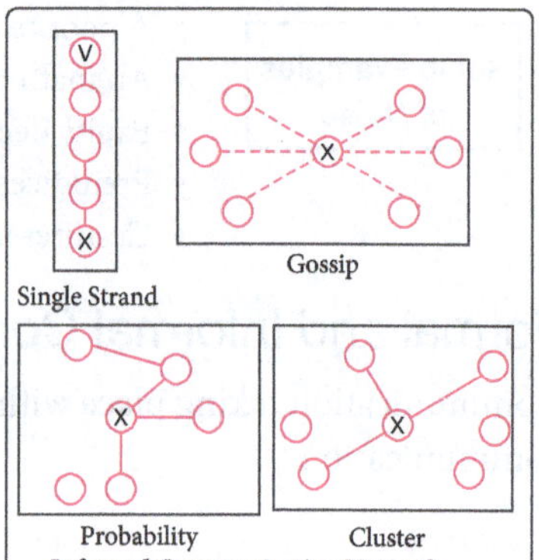

Informal Communication Network

Networks of Informal Communication

1. **Single Strand Network** Each person communicate with another in a sequence.
2. **Gossip Network** One person communicates with all, on non-selective basis.
3. **Probability Network** Any person communicate with anyone else randomly.
4. **Cluster Network** An individual communicates with only those people whom he trusts. This network is most popular in organisations.

Barriers to Effective Communication

The barriers to communication can be categorised as

I. Semantic Barriers

Semantics is the branch of linguistics dealing with the meaning of words and sentences. Semantic barriers are concerned with problems and obstructions in the process of encoding and decoding of message into words or impressions. These barriers are as follows

1. **Badly Expressed Messages** Miscommunication may arise due to inadequate vocabulary, incorrect word usage or omission of necessary words.
2. **Symbols with Different Meanings** The same word or symbol may carry different meanings to different people. e.g. Words like 'value' can have multiple meanings depending on the context, leading to confusion if misinterpreted by receiver.
3. **Faulty Translations** Errors in translating messages between languages can result in miscommunication if the translator is not proficient in both languages involved in translation.
4. **Unclarified Assumptions** Assumptions in communication can lead to misunderstandings if the sender does not clarify his/her assumptions behind message.
5. **Technical Jargon** Specialists often use technical terms which can confuse non-experts to understand the actual meaning of such terms, causing miscommunication.
6. **Body Language and Gesture Decoding** Discrepancies between verbal messages and body language can lead to misinterpretation of the message.

II. Psychological Barriers

Emotional or psychological factors act as barriers to communicators. For example, a worried person cannot communicate properly and an angry receiver cannot understand the real meaning of message.

The state of mind of both sender and receiver affect the process of communication. Some of them are given below

1. **Premature Evaluation** Evaluating a message before it is completely sent or conveyed by the sender due to biases or preconceived notions can lead to misinterpretation.

2. **Lack of Attention** Distractions or preoccupation of receiver's mind can prevent proper listening and understanding of the message.
3. **Loss by Transmission and Poor Retention** When communication passes through various levels, it may result in loss of, or transmission of inaccurate information. Sometimes, poor retention is also due to lack of interest and attention which leads to miscommunication.
4. **Distrust** Lack of trust between sender and receiver can hinder accurate understanding of the message.

III. Organisational Barriers

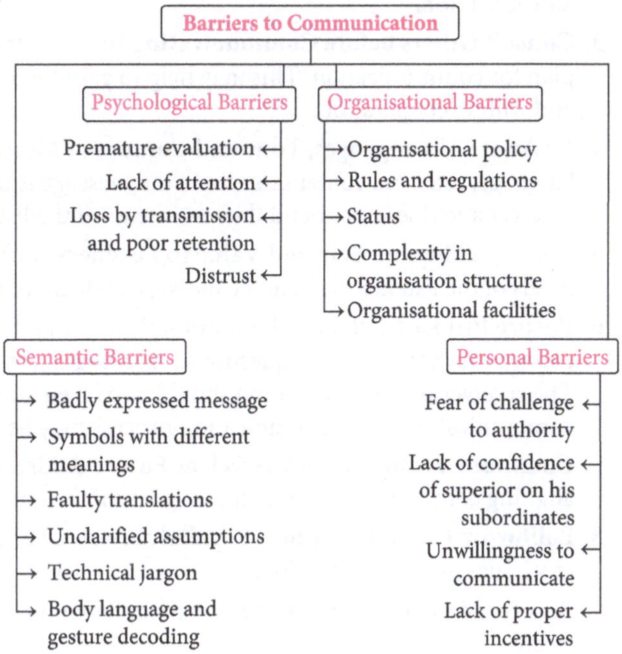

The factors related to organisation structure, authority relationships, rules and regulations may, sometimes, act as barriers to effective communication.

Some of them are as follows

1. **Organisational Policy** Policies that restrict communication flow can hinder effective communication, as seen in highly centralised organisations.
2. **Rules and Regulations** Rigid rules and cumbersome procedures can obstruct communication and cause delays.
3. **Status** High status of managers may create a psychological barrier between him and his subordinates. A status conscious manager may not allow his subordinates to express their feelings freely.
4. **Complexity in Organisation Structure** Multiple managerial levels can delay and distort communication due to numerous filtering points.
5. **Organisational Facilities** Absence of proper communication facilities, like meetings, suggestion boxes, social and cultural gatherings, etc. can hamper effective communication.

IV. Personal Barriers

The personal characteristics of both sender and receiver may exert influence on effective communication. Some of them are as follows

1. **Fear of Challenge to Authority** Superiors may suppress communications that could adversely affect their authority.
2. **Lack of Confidence of Superior on his Subordinates** If superiors doubt their subordinates' abilities, they may avoid seeking their advice and suggestions.
3. **Unwillingness to Communicate** Subordinates might avoid communicating with their superiors, if they fear that it could adversely affect their interests.
4. **Lack of Proper Incentives** Without motivation or rewards, subordinates may lack initiative to communicate or offer suggestions.

Improving Communication Effectiveness

1. **Clarify the Ideas before Communication** The message to be conveyed should be clear in all aspects to the executive himself/herself. It should be studied in depth, analysed and stated in such a manner that it is clearly conveyed to subordinates.
2. **Communicate According to the Needs of Receiver** Sender should communicate with receiver according to his/her level of understanding and education.
3. **Consult Others before Communicating** Involve others in developing a plan for communication. This may help to gain their ready acceptance and willing cooperation.
4. **Be Aware of Languages, Tone and Content of Message** Use appropriate language, tone and content to ensure the message is understandable to the receiver and does not offend the sentiments of the listener.
5. **Convey Things of Help and Value to Listeners** Address the interests and needs of the listener to make the message relevant and engaging.
6. **Ensure Proper Feedback** The communicator may ensure the success of communication by asking questions regarding the message conveyed. The receiver of communication should also be encouraged to respond to communication. So, communication process may be improved by the feedback.
7. **Communicate for Present as well as Future** Address current issues or meet present commitments, while also aligning communication with future goals of the enterprise.
8. **Follow-up Communications** Regularly review and follow-up on instructions given to subordinates, to address any issues in implementation.
9. **Be a Good Listener** Attentive and patient listening by management will encourage employees to communicate freely.

Measures to Improve Communication Effectiveness

- → Clarify the ideas before communication
- → Communicate according to the needs of receiver
- → Consult others before communicating
- → Be aware of languages, tone and content of message
- → Convey things of help and value to listeners
- → Ensure proper feedback
- → Communicate for present as well as future
- → Follow up communication
- → Be a good listener

Mind Map

DIRECTING

1 Concept of Directing

Directing refers to the process of instructing, guiding, leading, counselling and motivating people in an organisation to achieve pre-determined objectives.

It's features are

- Directing initiates action in the organisation
- Directing is pervasive and takes place at all levels in the organisation
- Directing is a continuous function and takes place throughout the life of the organisation
- Directing is initiated at the top level and flows to the bottom, i.e. it flows from top to bottom

2 Importance of Directing

- Directing helps to initiate action by people in the organisation
- Directing helps a manager to integrate individual efforts towards the achievement of organisational goals
- Effective directing provides motivation and leadership to the employees
- Directing helps to reduce resistance and introduces changes
- Directing develops cooperation & commitment and helps to bring stability and balance in the organisation

3 Elements of Directing

- **Supervision** Refers to instructing, guiding and observing the subordinates while they are performing jobs in the organisation
- **Motivation** Process of making subordinates to act in a desired manner to achieve certain organisational goals
- **Leadership** Process of influencing the behaviour of people by making them strive voluntarily towards the achievement of organisational goals
- **Communication** Process of exchange of ideas, facts, feelings, etc between two or more people to create common understanding

4 Maslow's Need Hierarchy Theory of Motivation

- Basic physiological needs (Hunger, thirst, shelter)
- Safety needs (Job security, stability of income)
- Social needs (Affection, acceptance, friendship)
- Esteem needs (Self-respect, status, autonomy)
- Self-actualisation needs (Growth, self-fulfillment)

Financial Incentives

- Pay and allowances
- Productivity linked wage incentives
- Bonus
- Profit sharing
- Co-partnership
- Retirement benefits
- Perquisites

Non-financial Incentives

- Status
- Organisational climate
- Career advancement opportunities
- Job enrichment
- Employee recognition programmes
- Job security
- Employee participation
- Employee empowerment

5 Leadership Styles

- **Autocratic** An autocratic leader exercises complete control over the subordinates
- **Democratic** A democratic leader develops action plan and takes decision in consultation with the subordinates
- **Laissez Faire** It involves complete delegation of authority so that subordinates themselves take decisions

6 Elements of Communication

- **Sender** Conveys his/her thoughts and ideas to the receiver
- **Message** Subject matter of communication
- **Encoding** Process of converting the message into symbols
- **Media** Path through which encoded message is transmitted
- **Decoding** Process of converting the encoded symbols of the sender
- **Receiver** Person who receives and interprets the sender's communication
- **Feedback** Includes receiver's response indicating that message has been received
- **Noise** Obstruction or hindrance to communication

7 Formal and Informal Communication

Formal Communication Communication taking place through official channels in an organisation.

Types

- Vertical
  - Upward
  - Downward
- Horizontal
- Diagonal

Networks

- Single chain
- Wheel
- Circular
- Free flow
- Inverted V

Informal Communication Takes place without following the formal lines.

Networks

- Single strand
- Probability
- Gossip
- Cluster

8 Barriers to Communication

Semantic Barriers

- Badly expressed message
- Symbols with different meanings
- Faulty translations
- Unclarified assumptions
- Technical jargon
- Body language and gesture decoding

Psychological Barriers

- Premature evaluation
- Lack of attention
- Loss by transmission and poor retention
- Distrust

Organisational Barriers

- Organisational policy
- Rules and regulations
- Status
- Complexity in organisation structure
- Organisational facilities

Personal Barriers

- Fear of challenge to authority
- Lack of confidence of superior on his subordinates
- Unwillingness to communicate
- Lack of proper incentives

9 Improving Communication Effectiveness

- Clarify ideas before communication
- Communicate according to the needs of receiver
- Consult others communicating
- Be aware of languages, tone and content of message
- Follow up communications
- Convey things of help and value to listeners
- Ensure proper feedback
- Communicate for present as well as future
- Be a good listener

EXAM PATTERN QUESTIONS

Objective Type Questions

Multiple Choice Questions (MCQs)

1. "It takes place throughout the life of the organisation." Identify the feature of directing in the given statement. Competency Based Que

(a) Directing initiates action
(b) Directing takes place at every level of management
(c) Directing is a continuous process
(d) Directing flows from top to bottom

2. Function of directing is performed at which of the following levels?

(a) Top level (b) Middle level
(c) Operational level (d) All of these

3. Which of the following is not an advantage of directing?

(a) Initiates action
(b) Integrates employee efforts
(c) Provides leadership
(d) Restricts changes

4. Rahul who works as a manager in Satvik Enterprises decides to introduce updated system of customer relationship management. Out of 100, 15 employees were able to work on the new system comfortably. However, other employees were resistant to change. Rahul decides to communicate the benefits, provide training and motivate the staff with additional rewards. This resulted in acceptance of the accounting system. Identify the point of 'importance of directing' to which the above paragraph is related. Competency Based Que

(a) Directing initiates action
(b) Directing integrates employees' efforts
(c) Directing attempts to get maximum out of employees
(d) Directing facilitates implementing changes

5. The workers show their inability whenever a new task is given to them. They are not willing to take up any new tasks. Due to excess orders, the manager is finding it difficult to cope up with the situation. Identify the element of directing that can help the manager in handling the problem. Competency Based Que

(a) Motivation (b) Leadership
(c) Communication (d) Supervision

6. Which of the following is not an assumption of Maslow's Need Hierarchy Theory?

(a) People's behaviour is based on their needs
(b) People's needs are in hierarchial order
(c) People are motivated by unfulfilled needs
(d) A person moves to next higher level need even if lower need is not satisfied

7. To satisfy esteem needs, which type of incentives are needed?

(a) Financial incentives
(b) Non-financial incentives
(c) Additional incentives
(d) None of the above

8. The production head of a publishing company has no autonomy to sign bills for any amount and he has to approach the owner of the company. So, he feels demotivated. Which of his need is not fulfilled as per Maslow's need hierarchy? Competency Based Que

(a) Self-actualisation need (b) Belonging need
(c) Safety need (d) Esteem need

9. Which process is indicated in the image given below?

(a) Supervision (b) Leadership
(c) Motivation (d) Communication

10. Fill in the blank with appropriate need of motivation as given by Maslow in the given image.

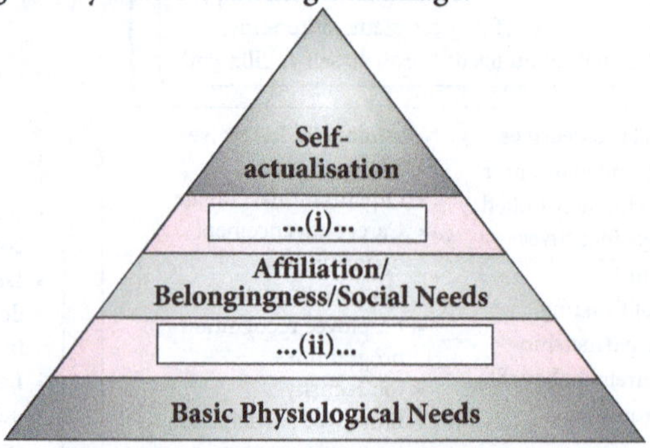

(a) Safety Need, Esteem Need
(b) Personal Need, Safety Need
(c) Esteem Need, Safety Need
(d) Safety Need, Personal Need

11. **Which of the following statements is incorrect?**
(a) Copartnership/stock options offer shares at a lower price than market value, promoting ownership and growth.
(b) Retirement benefits like provident fund and pension act as incentives while employees are still in service.
(c) Perquisites and fringe benefits include items like car allowances for employees.
(d) Status in an organisation is determined solely by the physical location of the job.

12. **Analyse the below picture and identify the non-financial incentive where the employee is awarded for achieving the sales target.**

(a) Employee recognition programme
(b) Career advancement opportunity
(c) Perquisites
(d) Bonus

13. **Gitanjali Makan is a successful business leader. She believes that if jobs are made interesting by including greater variety of work content and providing a meaningful work experience, the jobs themselves become a source of motivation to individuals. The non-financial incentive that has been discussed in the above case is** CBSE 2023; Competency Based Que
(a) employee participation
(b) job enrichment
(c) career advancement opportunity
(d) job security

14. **At ABC Ltd., management recently implemented a programme aimed at motivating employees through various non-financial incentives. In a recent event, the company congratulated several team members for their outstanding performance and recognised an employee who contributed a valuable suggestion that improved workplace efficiency.**

These actions were designed to make employees feel appreciated and valued for their efforts.

Which type of non-financial incentive is illustrated by the actions taken by ABC Ltd. to recognise and reward employees for their contributions? Competency Based Que
(a) Status
(b) Employee recognition programmes
(c) Job security
(d) Organisational climate

15. **ABC Corporation provides its employees with opportunities to attend international conferences, receive higher education and participate in advanced training programmes, in addition to their regular salary.**

What type of incentive is the company offering? Competency Based Que
(a) Job rotation
(b) Perquisites
(c) Career advancement programmes
(d) Job security

16. **"Inspite of recession, no worker will be retrenched from the job."**

Identify the type of incentive offered to the employees in the given statement. Competency Based Que
(a) Job security (b) Perquisites
(c) Job enrichment (d) Bonus

17. **XYZ Ltd., a leading technology firm, has been implementing several financial incentives to boost employee motivation and productivity. Recently, Mrs. Rani, the HR Manager, proposed a co-partnership/stock option plan. Under this plan, employees would receive a share in the company's profits or be allowed to purchase shares at a discounted rate, encouraging them to feel a sense of ownership in the company.**

Alongside this, XYZ Ltd. also introduced productivity linked wage incentives, where employees are paid based on their performance, as well as bonuses for outstanding achievements, such as a 100% attendance bonus or a performance bonus. These initiatives aim to inspire employees to work efficiently and contribute to the company's growth.

Which of the following financial incentives introduced by XYZ Ltd. specifically provides employees with a sense of ownership in the company? Competency Based Que
(a) Productivity linked wage incentives
(b) Co-partnership/stock option
(c) Attendance bonus
(d) Differential piece wage system

18. **ABC Corp. values employee motivation through non-financial incentives. To meet employees' psychological and social needs, it emphasises status, offering recognition and authority in their roles.**

The company also fosters a positive organisational climate by encouraging autonomy and rewarding achievements.

Additionally, career advancement opportunities are provided through promotion policies, allowing employees to grow and remain committed to the organisation's goals.

Which non-financial incentive at ABC Corp. meets the psychological and social needs of employees by recognising their position in the organisation? **Competency Based Que**

(a) Career advancement opportunity
(b) Organisational climate
(c) Status
(d) Skill development programme

19. Which of the following statements is incorrect?

(a) Directing is a wider concept than management
(b) Leadership and motivation are the two elements of directing
(c) Motivation creates goal directed behaviour
(d) All managers are leaders but all leaders are not managers

20. Ms. Priya, the founder and CEO of TechVision Inc., decided to retire and selected Mr. Vikram, her long-time colleague, as her successor. Mr. Vikram was chosen because of his ability to inspire and guide the team effectively, ensuring a smooth transition and continued success for the company. Which management concept explains why Ms. Priya chose Mr. Vikram as her successor? **Competency Based Que**

(a) Motivation (b) Leadership
(c) Communication (d) Staffing

21. Rajesh is the manager of a mid-sized tech company that values innovation and teamwork. Recently, the team was assigned a challenging project with a tight deadline. Instead of dictating specific tasks, Rajesh gathered his team for an open discussion, where everyone shared ideas on how best to approach the project. He encouraged each member to contribute suggestions and voiced his belief in shared responsibility.

Decisions on task allocation were made collectively and Rajesh ensured that everyone's input was considered before finalising the plan. Throughout the project, he continued to seek feedback and made adjustments based on the team's ideas.

What type of leadership style does Rajesh demonstrate? **Competency Based Que**

(a) Autocratic (b) Democratic
(c) Laissez-faire (d) Bureaucratic

22. Identify the leadership style depicted in the below picture

(a) Democratic (b) Autocratic
(c) Laissez faire (d) All of these

23. Atul was working as an employee in a readymade garments factory. He was very sincere and dedicated and always completed his work in time. It pained him to see that his colleaguesm were reluctant to do the work even though they had the ability to do it. Due to his good behaviour and willingness to work, he was promoted to the post of the supervisor of the same team in which he was a worker earlier.

He understood very well that it was not always possible to get the best of work from employees merely by exercising formal authority. He had insights into the causes of behaviour of people.

He knew how to get the work done by the workers in a desired manner to achieve the organisational objectives. Under his supervision even the workers who were reluctant to work started working efficiently and effectively. From the following, identify the concept used by Atul, as a supervisor to get the work completed. **CBSE 2025; Competency Based Que**

(a) Leadership (b) Financial incentives
(c) Motivation (d) Non-financial incentives

24. Obedience of order and discipline is found in

(a) autocratic leadership (b) democratic leadership
(c) free-rein leadership (d) paternalistic leadership

25. Alok is view supervisor of Ram, Rahim and Khan. He consults all his subordinates while framing work schedules, they provide suggestions and Alok consider such suggestions if they are productive. Which leadership style is followed by Alok? **Competency Based Que**

(a) Democratic style (b) Autocratic style
(c) Free rein style (d) None of these

26. Democratic style of leadership helps in

(a) improving morale of subordinates
(b) developing positive attitude among subordinates
(c) developing self-confidence in subordinates
(d) All of the above

27. **"Set the goal and makes plans accordingly." Identify the leadership style in the given statement.** **Competency Based Que**

(a) Democratic (b) Authoritative
(c) Laissez faire (d) None of these

28. **In which element of directing does a manager need to ensure that subordinates understand instructions properly and give feedback?**

(a) Communication (b) Supervision
(c) Leadership (d) Motivation

29. **Which of the following statements is incorrect regarding the elements involved in the communication process?**

(a) Encoding is the process of converting the message into communication symbols such as words, pictures or gestures.
(b) Feedback includes actions by the receiver indicating that they have received and understood the message.
(c) Decoding is the process of converting encoded symbols of the sender back into understandable content.
(d) Noise refers to the content of ideas and feelings that disrupt communication.

30. **The process of converting the message into communication symbols is known as**

(a) media (b) encoding
(c) feedback (d) decoding

31. **"It is the process of converting encoded symbols of the sender back into understandable content." Identify the element of communication process in the given statement.** **Competency Based Que**

(a) Encoding (b) Decoding
(c) Media (d) Message

32. **Loss of email is the example of ....**

(a) decoding (b) message
(c) encoding (d) noise

33. **In a Marketing Department, Ms. Anita is the team leader and there are five team members reporting directly to her. She communicates with each team member individually in a structured manner. This communication pattern where Ms. Anita directly communicates with each team member is known as** **Competency Based Que**

(a) single chain (b) inverted V
(c) wheel network (d) free flow

34. **Communication that spreads quicky is**

(a) formal (b) informal (c) written (d) All of these

35. **Informal communication tries to fulfil**

(a) safety need (b) basic physiological need
(c) social need (d) Self-actualisation need

36. **Which of the following communication barrier is depicted by 'Presence of more managerial levels'?**

(a) Personal barrier (b) Organisational barrier
(c) Psychological barrier (d) Semantic barrier

37. **Which type of communication barrier is depicted in the conversation between boss and employee in the picture?**

(a) Personal barrier (b) Semantic barrier
(c) Organisational barrier (d) Psychological barrier

38. **If there is no match between 'what is said' and 'what is expressed' in body movements, communication may be wrongly perceived. Name the type of semantic barrier highlighted here.**

(a) Badly expressed messages
(b) Body language and gesture decoding
(c) Technical jargon
(d) Faulty translation

39. **Nimesh was working as a production manager in HL Ltd., an electrical wire manufacturing company. One of the vendors who was supplying copper to HL Ltd. wanted to close down his business within 15 days as he had to go abroad to live with his son. The vendor was selling all his stocks at 60% discount. Nimesh wrote a letter to the general manager to seek approval for procurement of this material. But due to rigid rules and cumbersome procedures there was delay in getting sanction and order could not be placed. The type of communication barrier that led to procedural delay was** **CBSE 2025; Competency Based Que**

(a) semantic barrier (b) psychological barrier
(c) organisational barrier (d) personal barrier

40. **Mahesh Sha works in a logistics company as a manager. He works in Punjab and all the communication from other departments takes place in Punjabi language. However, he understands English and Hindi language. He is not comfortable with Punjabi language. This results in increased difficulty in interpreting the messages. Which of the following semantic barriers is indicated in the above paragraph?** **Competency Based Que**

(a) Badly expressed messages
(b) Unclarified assumptions
(c) Technical jargon
(d) Faulty translation

41. **Mohan works in the marketing department of Bizfisita Limited. The employees who work under Mohan are not satisfied. As a result, the company decided to appoint a specialist who can observe and analyse the cause behind dissatisfaction among the employees. Upon research, it was found that Mohan likes to keep a distance from his subordinates. As a result, subordinates are not able to express their emotions and opinions. Which of the following organisational barriers is discussed in the paragraph?** **Competency Based Que**

(a) Organisational policies (b) Status
(c) Organisational facilities (d) Rules and regulations

Direction *Read the following case study and answer the questions 42 to 45 on the basis of the same*

Zenith Manufacturing Ltd. is a leading company in the electronics industry. The company recently launched a new product line of smart home devices. To ensure the success of this new line, the company has focused heavily on the directing function of management. The CEO, Mr. Sharma, believes that effective leadership, motivation and communication are essential to achieve the company's goals.

To implement the directing function effectively, Mr. Sharma appointed Mr. Ahuja as the head of the new product line.

Mr. Ahuja involves team members in decision-making processes. He regularly communicates with his team to understand their concerns and provides feedback to help them improve. To keep the team motivated, Mr. Ahuja introduced a reward system where employees are recognised for their contributions with bonuses and public acknowledgment.

Additionally, Mr. Ahuja has emphasised the importance of coordination among different departments, ensuring that the marketing, production and sales teams work together seamlessly. He also organised training programmes to help employees develop the necessary skills for handling the new product line effectively. As a result of these efforts, the team has been working efficiently and the new product line has received positive feedback from the market.

42. **Which of the following aspects of the directing function is most evident in Mr. Ahuja's leadership approach?**

(a) Supervision (b) Motivation
(c) Communication (d) Coordination

43. **Which leadership style is Mr. Ahuja known for, as mentioned in the case study?**

(a) Autocratic (b) Democratic
(c) Laissez-faire (d) Transformational

44. **The reward system introduced by Mr. Ahuja primarily focuses on which element of directing?**

(a) Supervision (b) Communication
(c) Motivation (d) Leadership

45. **Which function of management does Mr. Ahuja emphasise to ensure different departments work together efficiently?**

(a) Planning (b) Organising
(c) Staffing (d) Coordination

Assertion-Reason

Direction (Q.No. 46 to 55) *Read the following Assertion (A) and Reason (R) and choose the correct alternative from the following*

Alternatives

(a) Both Assertion (A) and Reason (R) are true and Reason (R) is the correct explanation of Assertion (A)
(b) Both Assertion (A) and Reason (R) are true, but Reason (R) is not the correct explanation of Assertion (A)
(c) Assertion (A) is true, but Reason (R) is false
(d) Assertion (A) is false, but Reason (R) is true

46. **Assertion** (A) Directing facilitates introduction of needed changes in the organisation.

Reason (R) Directing increases resistance to changes in the organisation. **CBSE 2025**

47. **Assertion** (A) One of the key aspects of directing is that it takes place at every level of management.

Reason (R) At times there can be changes in managers, but the directing process continues as organisational activities cannot continue further without direction.

48. **Assertion** (A) Effective directing ensures that employees are motivated and their potential is fully utilised in achieving organisational goals.

Reason (R) Directing involves only instructing employees to perform specific tasks assigned by their managers.

49. **Assertion** (A) Motivation is a complex process.

Reason (R) Any type of motivation may not have uniform effect on all the members.

50. **Assertion** (A) Motivation is crucial in directing because it helps in boosting the morale of employees.

Reason (R) Motivation only involves offering financial incentives to employees.

51. **Assertion** (A) Money is important to satisfy the physical needs of daily life.

Reason (R) Money has the purchasing power.

52. **Assertion** (A) Leadership is an integral part of the directing function in management.

Reason (R) Leadership involves commanding and controlling subordinates strictly to ensure compliance.

53. **Assertion** (A) Autocratic leadership helps in facilitating quick decision-making.

Reason (R) Decisions are made by autocratic leaders in consultation with their subordinates.

54. **Assertion** (A) Communication is a critical aspect of directing because it facilitates understanding between managers and employees.

Reason (R) Effective communication ensures that the employees are aware of what is expected of them.

55. **Assertion** (A) Informal communication spreads rapidly.

Reason (R) It is very difficult to detect the source of informal communication.

Two Statement MCQs

Direction (Q.No. 56 to 65) *Read the following statements carefully and choose the correct alternative*

Alternatives

(a) Statement I is correct and Statement II is incorrect
(b) Statement II is correct and Statement I is incorrect
(c) Both the statements are correct
(d) Both the statements are incorrect

56. **Statement I** Directing is required only at the top level of management.

Statement II Effective directing helps in reducing resistance in introducing changes in the organisation.

57. **Statement I** Directing involves issuing instructions and supervising subordinates.

Statement II Directing is solely about planning and does not include supervision.

58. **Statement I** Motivation is a simple process because people are of homogeneous nature.

Statement II Motivation is an external feeling and can be easily forced on employees.

59. **Statement I** According to Maslow's hierarchy, physiological needs are the most basic and must be satisfied first.

Statement II Safety needs are the highest level needs in Maslow's hierarchy of needs.

60. **Statement I** Self-actualisation is the highest level need in Maslow's hierarchy of needs.

Statement II Belongingness needs are satisfied after achieving self-actualisation.

61. **Statement I** Leadership is a key component of the directing function.

Statement II Leadership does not influence employee performance or productivity.

62. **Statement I** Leader helps in changing possibility into reality.

Statement II Laissez-faire is a self directed leadership style.

63. **Statement I** Decoding involves converting encoded symbols into understandable form.

Statement II Formal communication is created keeping in view the organisational objectives.

64. **Statement I** Formal communication takes place in an impersonal manner.

Statement II Formal communication helps in fixing responsibility.

65. **Statement I** Organisational barriers arise because of emotional status of sender and receiver of the message.

Statement II Semantic barriers arise because of use of wrong words, faulty translations, etc.

Matching

66. **Match the elements of directing in Column I with their respective statements given in Column II**

Column I	Column II
A. Supervision	(i) Exchange of information
B. Motivation	(ii) Influencing people to take up job voluntarily
C. Leadership	(iii) Stimulating people to act in a desired manner
D. Communication	(iv) Overseeing the activities of employees

Codes

	A	B	C	D		A	B	C	D
(a)	(i)	(ii)	(iii)	(iv)	(b)	(ii)	(iii)	(iv)	(i)
(c)	(iii)	(iv)	(i)	(ii)	(d)	(iv)	(iii)	(ii)	(i)

67. **Match the various Maslow's needs in Column I with their respective statements given in Column II**

Column I	Column II
A. Self-actualisation needs	(i) Needs which have to be satisfied for the survival
B. Basic physiological needs	(ii) Need for respect, status, recognition and autonomy
C. Affiliation needs	(iii) Need for acceptance, friendship and affection
D. Esteem needs	(iv) Need for growth, achievement of goals, etc.

Codes

	A	B	C	D		A	B	C	D
(a)	(iv)	(i)	(iii)	(ii)	(b)	(iii)	(iv)	(i)	(ii)
(c)	(ii)	(i)	(iv)	(iii)	(d)	(iii)	(i)	(iv)	(ii)

68. **Match the various financial and non-financial incentives in Column I with their respective statements given in Column II**

Column I		Column II
A. Status	(i)	Employees are offered company shares at a price less than market price.
B. Job enrichment	(ii)	Fringe benefits like car allowance, medical aid, etc.
C. Co-partnership	(iii)	Designing jobs that include greater variety of work content, require higher level of knowledge and skill, etc.
D. Perquisites	(iv)	Refers to ranking of positions in the organisation.

Codes

	A	B	C	D
(a)	(i)	(ii)	(iii)	(iv)
(b)	(iv)	(iii)	(i)	(ii)
(c)	(iii)	(i)	(iv)	(ii)
(d)	(iii)	(ii)	(iv)	(i)

69. **Match the various leadership style in Column I with their respective statements given in Column II**

Column I		Column II
A. Autocratic leadership style	(i)	Helps in faster decision-making
B. Democratic leadership style	(ii)	Manager is there only to support the subordinates.
C. Laissez-faire leadership style	(iii)	Manager encourages subordinates to participate in decision-making.

Codes

	A	B	C
(a)	(i)	(iii)	(ii)
(b)	(ii)	(iii)	(i)
(c)	(iii)	(i)	(ii)
(d)	(iii)	(ii)	(i)

70. **Match the various communication barriers in Column I with their respective categories given in Column II** **CBSE 2023**

Column I		Column II
A. Semantic barriers	(i)	Distrust
B. Psychological barriers	(ii)	Lack of proper incentives
C. Organisational barriers	(iii)	Symbols with different meanings
D. Personal barriers	(iv)	Status

Codes

	A	B	C	D
(a)	(i)	(ii)	(iii)	(iv)
(b)	(iv)	(iii)	(i)	(ii)
(c)	(iii)	(i)	(iv)	(ii)
(d)	(iii)	(ii)	(iv)	(i)

Answers

1. (c) Directing is a continuous process
2. (d) All of these
3. (d) Restricts changes
4. (d) Directing facilitates implementing changes
5. (a) Motivation
6. (d) A person moves to next higher level need even if lower need is not satisfied
7. (b) Non-financial incentives
8. (d) Esteem need relates to the self-respect, autonomy status, recognition and attention.
9. (c) Motivation
10. (c) Esteem Need, Safety Need
11. (d) Status in an organisation is determined by factors like authority, rewards and recognition, not merely by the physical location of the job.
12. (a) Employee recognition programme
13. (b) job enrichment
14. (b) Employee recognition programmes
15. (c) Career advancement programmes
16. (a) Job security
17. (b) Co-partnership/stock option
18. (c) Status
19. (a) Directing is a part of management. So, it is a narrow concept than management.
20. (b) Leadership
21. (b) Democratic
22. (b) Autocratic
23. (a) Leadership
24. (a) autocratic leadership
25. (a) Democratic style
26. (d) All of the above
27. (c) Laissez faire
28. (a) Communication

29. (d) Noise refers to obstructions or hindrances that disrupt the communication process, not the content of ideas and feelings.
30. (b) encoding
31. (b) Decoding
32. (d) noise
33. (c) wheel network
34. (b) informal
35. (c) social need
36. (b) Organisational barrier
37. (a) Personal barrier
38. (b) Body language and gesture decoding
39. (c) organisational barrier
40. (d) Faulty translation
41. (b) Status
42. (c) Communication
43. (b) Democratic
44. (c) Motivation
45. (d) Coordination
46. (c) Directing does not increase resistance to change; instead, it helps in overcoming resistance by providing proper communication, motivation and leadership.
47. (b) Both Assertion (A) and Reason (R) are true, but Reason (R) is not the correct explanation of Assertion (A)
48. (c) Directing is not limited to merely instructing employees to perform tasks; it encompasses a range of activities including motivation, leadership, communication and supervision. These elements collectively enable employees to work towards organisational goals effectively.
49. (a) Both Assertion (A) and Reason (R) are true and Reason (R) is the correct explanation of Assertion (A)
50. (c) Motivation is not limited to financial incentives; it also includes non-financial incentives like recognition, career development opportunities and a positive work environment.
51. (a) Both Assertion (A) and Reason (R) are true and Reason (R) is the correct explanation of Assertion (A)
52. (c) Effective leadership is not just about commanding and controlling; it also involves inspiring, influencing and empowering employees to perform their best.
53. (b) Both Assertion (A) and Reason (R) are true, but Reason (R) is not the correct explanation of Assertion (A)
54. (a) Both Assertion (A) and Reason (R) are true and Reason (R) is the correct explanation of Assertion (A)
55. (b) Informal communication takes place without following the formal lines of communication.
56. (b) Directing is not limited to the top level of management. It is required at all levels of management i.e. top, middle and lower because it involves guiding and overseeing employees to ensure that organisational goals are achieved.
57. (a) Directing includes issuing instructions and supervising subordinates to ensure that tasks are performed effectively. It is not limited to planning alone.
58. (d) Motivation is not a simple process. People are not of homogenous nature; they have diverse needs, desires and goals. Motivation is an internal feeling. It is driven by internal needs and desires and cannot be easily forced on employees.
59. (a) Safety needs are not the highest; they come after physiological needs but before belongingness and esteem needs.
60. (a) Self-actualisation need is indeed the highest level need in Maslow's hierarchy. Belongingness needs are satisfied before reaching self-actualisation.
61. (a) Leadership plays a significant role in directing by influencing and motivating employees, which directly impacts their performance and productivity. Effective leadership is essential for achieving organisational goals.
62. (c) Both the statements are correct
63. (c) Both the statements are correct
64. (c) Both the statements are correct
65. (b) Psychological barriers arise because of emotional status of sender and receiver of the message.
66. (d) (iv) (iii) (ii) (i)
67. (a) (iv) (i) (iii) (ii)
68. (b) (iv) (iii) (i) (ii)
69. (a) (i) (iii) (ii)
70. (c) (iii) (i) (iv) (ii)

Subjective Questions

Short Answer Type Questions

1. Explain any two features of directing function of management. CBSE 2023

Or **Explain any four features of 'directing' function of management.** CBSE 2024 C

Ans. Following are the features of directing function of management

(i) **Directing Initiates Action**
Directing is an execution function of management. While the other functions prepare a setting for action, directing initiates action in the organisation. Therefore, a manager has to perform this function along with planning, organising, staffing and controlling.

(ii) **Directing Takes Place at Every Level**
Directing is a pervasive function as every manager from top to bottom performs this function. It takes place wherever superior-subordinate relationship exists.

(iii) **Directing is Continuous Process**
Directing is an ongoing process that persists throughout the life of the organisation irrespective of people occupying managerial positions.

(iv) **Directing Flows from Top to Bottom**
Directing is initiated at top level and flows downward in the hierarchy.

2. What is meant by directing function of management? State any three points highlighting the importance of directing function. CBSE 2023

Ans. Directing refers to the principle of instructing, guiding, counselling, motivating and leading people in the organisation to achieve its pre-determined objectives.
Following points indicate the importance of directing

(i) **Guides Employees**
Effective directing provides motivation and leadership to the employees, which helps them to identify their potential and realise their latent capabilities, leading to growth. A good leader can always identify the potential of his employees and motivate them to extract work up to their full potential.

(ii) **Introduces Changes**
Changes in an organisation are usually resisted by employees. Effective directing through motivation, communication and leadership helps to reduce such resistance and develop required cooperation in introducing changes in the organisation.

(iii) **Provides Stability**
Effective directing helps to develop cooperation and commitment on part of subordinates. This provides stability to the organisation and helps to achieve balance among various groups, activities and departments.

3. Identify and state any three features of the process of stimulating people to action to accomplish desired goals. CBSE 2023

Or

Explain any four features of 'motivation' as an element of the directing function of management. CBSE 2024 C

Ans. The process of stimulating people to action to accomplish desired goals is known as motivation.
Following are the features of motivation

(i) **Motivation is a Psychological Phenomenon**
It is a personal and internal feeling like an urge, drives, desires and aspirations of human being, which influence human behaviour.
e.g. Desire or urge for possessing a motorbike, comfortable house, etc.

(ii) **Motivation Produces Goal Directed Behaviour**
Motivation inspires an employee to achieve goals. Thus, it encourages goal directed behaviour. e.g. A person who desires to get promoted, will work efficiently to achieve this goal.

(iii) **Motivation may be Positive or Negative**
Motivation can be either positive or negative. Positive motivation provides positive rewards like increase in pay, promotion, recognition, etc.

(iv) **Motivation is a Complex Process**
Motivation is complex because individuals vary in their expectations, perceptions and reactions, leading to different effects for each person.

4. "It is important to motivate the employees so that they can contribute their efforts towards organisational goals."

In the light of this statement, state three reasons why it is essential to motivate employees. Competency Based Que

Ans. Motivation is necessary for the following reasons

(i) It helps to improve the performance level of employees.

(ii) It helps to change negative attitude of employees to positive attitude.

(iii) It helps to reduce employee turnover and absenteeism.

5. Explain the process of motivation with the help of a diagram. NCERT

Ans. The process of motivation is explained below

(i) An unsatisfied need of an individual creates tension, which stimulates his drives.

(ii) These drives generate a search behaviour to satisfy such need.

(iii) When the need is satisfied, the individual is relieved of tension.

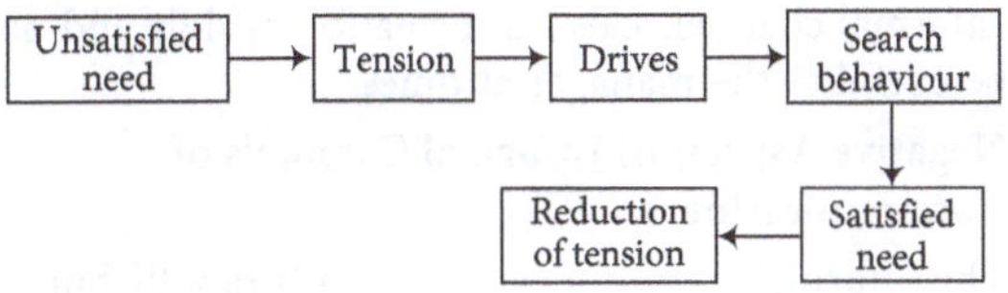

6. Maslow's need hierarchy theory is based on certain assumption. Discuss.

Ans. The main assumptions of Maslow's need hierarchy theory are as follows

(i) People's behaviour is based on their needs. Satisfaction of such needs influences their behaviour.

(ii) People's needs are in hierarchical order. They start from basic physiological needs and reach to high level needs.

(iii) A satisfied need can no longer motivate a person, only next higher level need can motivate a person.

(iv) A person moves to the next higher level need, only when the lower level need is satisfied.

7. State four incentives which are in direct monetary form or measurable in monetary terms and serve to motivate people for better performance. CBSE 2023

Or **Explain any four financial incentives used to motivate employees.** CBSE 2024 C

Ans. Following are the various financial incentives which are in direct monetary form or measurable in monetary terms

(i) **Pay and Allowances**
For every employee, salary is the basic monetary incentive. It includes basic pay, dearness allowance, house rent allowance, pay hikes and increments. These incentives induce employees to improve performance.

(ii) **Productivity Linked Wage Incentives**
In this incentive, wages are given to employees according to their performance. These incentives help to improve productivity of employees by paying higher wages to efficient workers. e.g. Differential piece wage system.

(iii) **Bonus**
It is a one time reward for high performance. Bonus may be paid in cash or kind over and above the salary. e.g. Performance bonus, 100% attendance bonus, festive bonus, etc.

(iv) **Profit Sharing**
It means to provide employees, a share in the profits of the enterprise.
This is in addition to their wages/salaries, which motivates them to improve performance and contribute to increase profits in future.

8. Distinguish between financial and non-financial incentives.

Ans. Following are the differences between financial and non-financial incentives

Basis	Financial Incentives	Non-financial Incentives
Meaning	The rewards or incentives which can be calculated in terms of money.	The rewards or incentives which are not in monetary terms.
Satisfaction	It satisfies lower level needs.	It satisfies higher level needs.
Effective	They are effective in case of lower level employees.	They are effective in case of higher level employees.
Examples	Pays and allowances, bonus, profit sharing, etc.	Status, organisational climate, job enrichment, etc.

9. What is meant by non-monetary incentives? State any two non-monetary incentives.

Ans. Non-monetary incentives are those which satisfy social, psychological and emotional needs of individuals. Following are the two non-monetary incentives

(i) **Job Enrichment**
It is concerned with designing jobs that include greater variety of work content, require higher level of knowledge and skill, etc.

(ii) **Employee Recognition Programmes**
Recognition means acknowledgment of work with a show of appreciation. With such appreciation, employees feel motivated.

10. Explain the concept of leadership. Give two situations in which autocratic leadership style is most effective. CBSE SQP 2025

Ans. Leadership is the process of influencing the behaviour of people by making them strive voluntarily towards achievement of organisational goals.

Two situations is which autocratic leadership is most effective

(i) This leadership style is effective in getting productivity in many situations like in a factory where the supervisor is responsible for production on time and the supervisor has to ensure labour productivity.

(ii) Quick decision-making is facilitated.

11. State any four features of leadership.

Ans. Following are the features of leadership

(i) It is the ability of an individual to influence people.
(ii) It tries to bring change in the behaviour of others.
(iii) It is exercised to achieve common goals of the organisation.
(iv) It explains the interpersonal relationship between leaders and followers.

12. Explain the concept of communication. Give the meaning of formal and informal communication.
CBSE SQP 2025

Ans. Communication

It is the process of exchange of information on between two or more persons to reach common understanding.

Formal Communication

Formal communication flows through official channels designed in the organisation chart.

Informal Communication

Communication that takes place without following the formal lines of communication is said to be informal communication.

13. State any four features of communication.

Ans. Following are the features of communication

(i) It is a two-way process in which sender sends the message to receiver.
(ii) It is a continuous process.
(iii) It aims to create understanding between sender and receiver.
(iv) It is a social process

14. Differentiate between formal and informal communication.

Ans. Following are the differences between formal and informal communication (any four)

Basis	Formal Communication	Informal Communication
Mutual Relationship among Members	Based on formal superior-subordinate relationship.	Based on interpersonal contacts.
Nature	Systematic and orderly.	Unsystematic and irregular.
Speed of Communication	It is slow and time consuming.	It is fast and time saving.
Authenticity	Official and well planned messages are authentic.	Unofficial and unplanned messages may not be authentic.
Contents or Subject Matter	Work related matters, e.g. Orders and instructions are communicated.	Personal matters are discussed.

15. "An intelligent manager should make use of positive aspects of informal channels and minimise the use of negative aspects of this channel of communication."

In the light of the above statement, explain any one positive and any two negative aspects of informal channels of communication.
CBSE 2024 C; Competency Based Que

Ans. Positive Aspects of Informal Channels of Communication

- Informal channels carry information rapidly and may be useful to the manager at times.

Negative Aspects of Informal Channels of Communication

- The informal communication spreads rapidly but sometimes gets distorted.
- It is very difficult to detect the source of such communication.

16. Distinguish between upward and downward communication.

Ans. Following are the differences between upward and downward communication

Basis	Upward Communication	Downward Communication
Meaning	It refers to the flow of information from the lower level to the top level.	It refers to the flow of information from the top level to the lower level.
Authority	It is non-authoritative.	It is authoritative.
Speed	It is slow in speed.	It is fast in speed.
Purpose	Its main purpose is to provide feedback.	Its main purpose is to get work done.

17. "While working in a project team, employees often share ideas, concerns and updates through casual conversations and social interactions rather than official channels."

Based on the above statement, identify and state any four feature of informal communication.
Competency Based Que

Ans. Following are the features of informal communication

(i) It takes place without following the formal lines of communication.
(ii) It enables employees to develop friendly relationship and get social satisfaction.
(iii) The flow of communication is very fast.
(iv) It leads to rumours as it is difficult to find the source of such communication.

18. Discuss the different types of networks of grapevine communication. NCERT

Ans. The network of informal communication is called 'grapevine'. This is because it spreads throughout organisation with its branches going out in all directions.

Some popular grapevine networks are as follows

(i) **Single Strand Network**
In this network, each person communicate with another in a sequence.

(ii) **Gossip Network**
In this network, one person communicates with all on non-selective basis.

(iii) **Probability Network**
In this network, any person can communicate with anyone else randomly.

(iv) **Cluster Network**
An individual communicates with only those people whom he trusts.

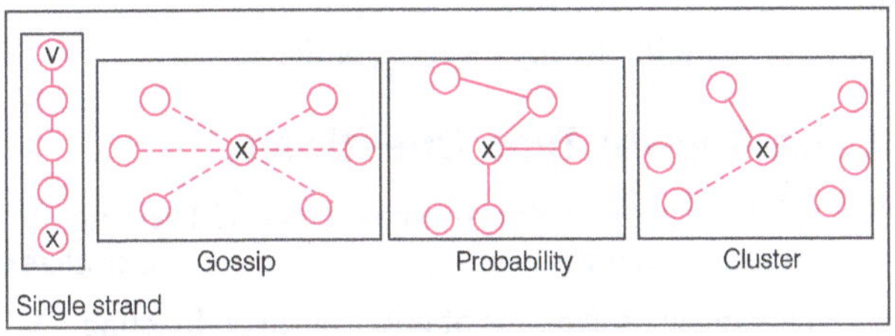

19. "In a multinational corporation, information flows systematically from top management down to employees at various levels. This structured approach ensures that everyone receives consistent information and follows a clear chain of command."

Based on the above statement, identify and state the types of formal communication network.

Competency Based Que

Ans. Following are the types of formal communication networks

(i) **Single Chain**
Communication flows from every superior to their subordinate through a single chain in a hierarchical structure.

(ii) **Wheel**
All subordinates communicate only through their superior, who acts as the central hub, with no direct communication among them.

(iii) **Circular**
Communication moves in a circle where each person can only communicate with their two adjoining colleagues, leading to a slower flow.

(iv) **Free Flow**
Everyone can communicate freely with others, resulting in a fast flow of communication.

(v) **Inverted V**
A subordinate can communicate with their immediate superior and also with their superior's superior, but only for prescribed communication.

20. "Misunderstandings often arise from the subtle nuances of language used in communication." In the light of this statement, discuss any four semantic barriers to communication. Competency Based Que

Or **Explain any four semantic barriers to communication.**

CBSE 2024 C

Ans. Following are the four semantic barriers to communication

(i) **Faulty Translations**
Sometimes, the communication originally drafted in one language (e.g. English) need to be translated to the language understandable to workers (e.g. Hindi). When the translator is not proficient in both the languages involved in translation, the meaning of the message may get distorted.

(ii) **Unclarified Assumptions**
Some communications may have certain assumptions which are subject to different interpretations. A message may be misunderstood, when the sender does not clarify the assumptions behind it.

e.g. A boss may instruct his subordinate, 'take care of our guest'. Here, boss may mean that subordinate should take care of transport, food, accommodation of guest, etc. But the subordinate may interpret that guest should be taken to hotel with care. In this case, guest suffers due to the unclarified assumptions.

(iii) **Technical Jargon**
Specialists often use technical language while explaining to persons who are not specialists in the concerned field. Therefore, they may not understand the actual meaning of many such words.

(iv) **Body Language and Gesture Decoding**
Sometimes, the body language and gestures of the individual does not match with his communication. Thus, it leads to miscommunication.

21. "Communication barriers act as hindrances in the effectiveness of transmission of message." State any four organisational barriers of communication that can distort the information. Competency Based Que

Ans. Following are the four organisational barriers of communication

(i) **Status**
Status of a superior may create a psychological distance between him and his subordinates. A status conscious manager also may not allow his subordinates to express their feelings freely.

(ii) **Complexity in Organisation Structure**
When there are several managerial levels, communication gets delayed and distorted as number of filtering points are more. There is loss of information as the message is transmitted again and again before it reaches the receiver.

(iii) **Organisational Facilities**
If facilities for smooth, clear and timely communication are not provided, communication may be hampered. Facilities like frequent meetings, suggestion box, complaint box, social and cultural gatherings, etc. will encourage free flow of communication. Lack of these facilities may create communication problems.

(iv) **Rules and Regulations**
Rigid rules and cumbersome procedures act as a barrier to effective communication.

Similarly, communication through the prescribed channels may result in delays.

22. **Discuss any three personal barriers to communication.**

Ans. Following are the three personal barriers to communication

(i) **Fear of Challenge to Authority**
A superior is likely to withhold or suppress a message, if he perceives that it will adversely affect his authority.

(ii) **Lack of Confidence of Superior on His Subordinates**
A superior, who does not have confidence on the competency of his subordinates, is not likely to seek their advice and suggestions.

(iii) **Unwillingness to Communicate**
A subordinate may not communicate with his superiors, if he perceives that it will adversely affect his interests.

23. **Explain any four psychological barriers to communication.** CBSE 2024 C

Ans. Following are the four psychological barriers to communication

(i) **Premature Evaluation**
Evaluating a message before it is completely sent or conveyed by the sender due to biases or preconceived notions can lead to misinterpretation.

(ii) **Lack of Attention**
Distractions or preoccupation of receiver's mind can prevent proper listening and understanding of the message.

(iii) **Loss by Transmission and Poor Retention**
When communication passes through various levels, it may result in loss of or transmission of inaccurate information. Sometimes poor retention is also due to lack of interest and attention which leads to miscommunication.

(iv) **Distrust**
Lack of trust between sender and receiver can hinder accurate understanding of the message.

24. **"In the communication process, various barriers can disrupt the clarity and effectiveness of the message being conveyed. These disruptions often lead to misunderstandings or incomplete communication between the sender and receiver."**

Based on the above statement, explain the concept of 'noise' in the communication process and provide four examples of such disruptions. Competency Based Que

Ans. Noise is the hindrance in the process of communication. It creates hurdle in the way of conversation. It can take place at any step in the communication process.

Its main examples are

(i) Use of ambiguous symbols in encoding
(ii) Telephone line going dead
(iii) An inattentive receiver
(iv) Understanding wrong meaning of the message

Long Answer Type Questions

25. **Explain any four points of importance of directing function of management.** CBSE 2024 C

Ans. Following are the points of importance of directing function of management

(i) **Initiates Action**
Directing helps to initiate action by people in the organisation for the achievement of predetermined goals.

e.g. If a supervisor guides his subordinates and clarifies their doubts while performing a task, it will help the worker to achieve work targets given to him.

(ii) **Integrates Employees Efforts**
Directing helps a manager to integrate individual efforts towards the achievement of organisational goals. It ensures that all individuals work for the benefit of the organisation, by establishing harmony between organisational and personal goals.

e.g. Manager with good leadership abilities will be in a position to convince the employees that individual efforts and team effort will lead to achievement of goals.

(iii) **Guides Employees**
Effective directing provides motivation and leadership to the employees, which helps them to identify their potential and realise their latent capabilities, leading to growth.

A good leader can always identify the potential of his employees and motivate them to extract work up to their full potential.

(iv) **Introduces Changes**
Changes in an organisation are usually resisted by employees. Effective directing through motivation, communication and leadership helps to reduce such resistance and develop required cooperation in introducing changes in the organisation.

26. **"Maslow's need hierarchy is considered fundamental to understand motivation." Explain the role of need hierarchy in motivation.** **Competency Based Que**

Or **Discuss Maslow's need hierarchy theory of motivation.** **NCERT**

Ans. Maslow's need hierarchy is based on human needs. It plays an important role by helping the managers to understand the level of needs of an individual. Following are the five needs

(i) **Basic Physiological Needs**
These are the most basic needs, which a person is required to satisfy in order to survive. Hunger, thirst, shelter, sleep are some of the examples of these needs. In an organisation, basic salary helps to satisfy these needs.

(ii) **Safety/Security Needs**
These needs provide security and protection from physical and emotional harm. e.g. Job security, stability of income, etc. These needs include two types of securities, i.e. physical security and financial security.

(iii) **Affiliation/Belongingness/Social Needs**
These needs are concerned with affection, sense of belongingness, acceptance and friendship. It is fulfilled when employees have cordial relations with colleagues.

(iv) **Esteem Needs**
These needs include factors such as self-respect, autonomy status, recognition and attention. When these needs are fulfilled through job title, it enhances self-confidence and prestige of employees.

(v) **Self-actualisation Needs**
It is the highest level of need in the hierarchy. It refers to the drive to become what one is capable of becoming. It includes growth, self-fulfillment and achievement of goals.

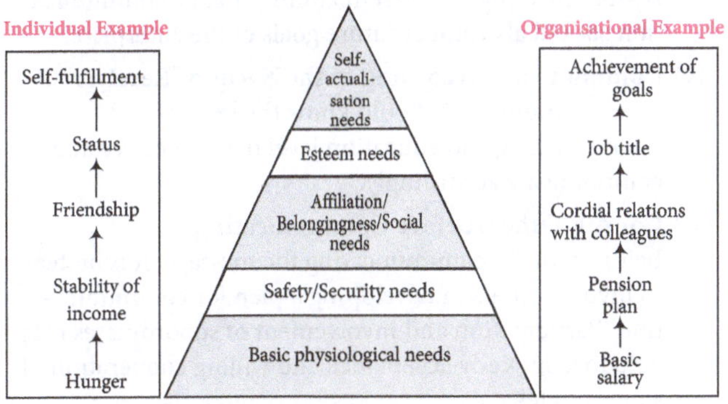

Maslow's Need Hierarchy Theory

27. **Explain the following non-financial incentives** **CBSE 2025**

(i) **Status** (ii) **Organisational climate**
(iii) **Job enrichment** (iv) **Employee participation**

Ans.

(i) **Status**
In business terms, status means ranking of positions in the organisation.
The authority, responsibility, rewards, recognition, perquisites and prestige of job indicate the status given to a person holding a managerial position. Psychological, social and esteem needs of an individual are satisfied by status given to their job.

(ii) **Organisational Climate**
It indicates the characteristics that describe an organisation and distinguish it from the other.
e.g. Individual autonomy, reward orientation, consideration to employees, risk-taking, etc. These characteristics influence the behaviour of individuals in the organisation. Positive measures by managers help to develop better organisational climate.

(iii) **Job Enrichment**
It is concerned with designing jobs that include greater variety of work content, require higher level of knowledge and skill, etc.

(iv) **Employee Participation**
It means involving employees in decision-making regarding the issues related to them. These programmes are in practice in many companies in the form of joint management committees, work committees, canteen committees, etc.

28. **"In guiding teams towards success, leaders adopt different approaches that shape the dynamics and outcomes of their interactions."**

Define leadership and explain three distinct leadership styles that influence how leaders manage and inspire their teams. **Competency Based Que**

Or **Explain 'democratic (participative) style of leadership'.** **CBSE 2024 C**

Or **Explain 'autocratic' and 'laissez faire' style of leadership.** **CBSE 2024 C**

Ans. Leadership is the process of influencing the behaviour of other people so that they work willingly for the attainment of goals in a given situation.

The leadership styles are as follows

(i) **Authoritarian or Autocratic Leadership**
An autocratic leader exercises complete control over the subordinates. He centralises power in himself and takes all decisions without consulting the subordinates.

(ii) **Democratic or Participative Leadership**
A democratic leader takes decisions after consultation and encourages the participation of subordinates. He decentralises authority and allows the subordinates to share his power.

(iii) **Laissez Faire or Free-rein Leadership**
It involves complete delegation of authority, so that subordinates themselves take decisions. The free-rein leader does not believe in the use of power unless it is absolutely essential. This is also known as 'laissez-faire' which means 'no interference' in the affairs of others. The group members work on their own tasks resolving issues themselves.

29. **"Effective collaboration in an organisation hinges on a seamless exchange of ideas and information."**

Explain the elements of process of communication that helps in effective collaboration. **Competency Based Que**

Ans. Communication has been defined as process which involves various elements. These elements are as follows

(i) **Sender**
The person who conveys his thoughts or ideas to the receiver, is known as the sender or communicator. He initiates the process of communication.

(ii) **Message**
It is the subject matter of communication. It may consist of facts, information, ideas, opinions, feelings, etc., which sender wants to share with receiver.

(iii) **Encoding**
The sender translates the message into communication symbols like words, gestures or other symbols, which he feels will make the receiver understand the message. This process is known as encoding of message.

(iv) **Channel or Media**
The encoded message is transmitted to receiver through some medium, which is known as the communication channel. e.g. Writing, phone call, internet, face to face, etc.

(v) **Decoding**
It is the process of conversion of encoded symbols into the effective language that can be understood by the receiver.

(vi) **Receiver**
The person, who receives the message, is called the receiver.

(vii) **Feedback**
It includes all those actions of receiver indicating that he/she has received and understood message of sender. When the feedback is received by the sender, the process of communication is complete.

(viii) **Noise**
It means an obstruction or hindrance in the communication process. This hindrance may be caused to sender, message or receiver.

Some examples of noise are Ambiguous symbols, poor telephone connection etc.

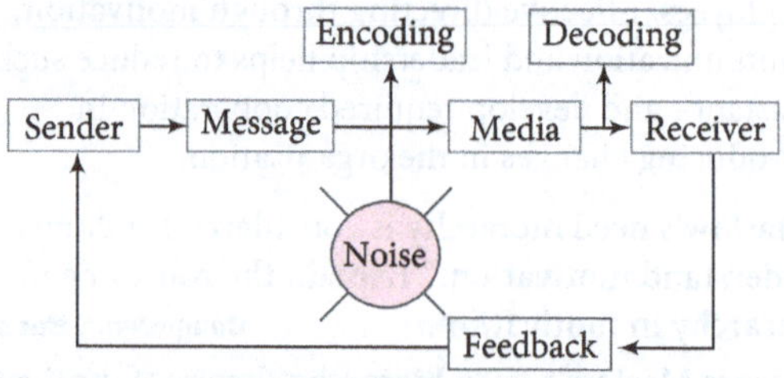

Communication Process

30. **"The barriers to effective communication exist in all organisations to a greater or lesser degree." State any six measures to overcome these barriers.**
Competency Based Que

Or

Explain any four measures to overcome the barriers to communication. **CBSE 2024 C**

Ans. Following are the measures to overcome barriers to effective communication

(i) **Be Aware of Languages, Tone and Content of Message**
The language, tone and content used for conveying the message must be understandable to the receiver and should not offend the sentiments of the listener.

(ii) **Convey Things of Help and Value to Listeners**
While conveying the message, it is better to know the interests and needs of the receiver. If the message relates directly or indirectly to such interests and needs, it certainly evokes response from communicatee.

(iii) **Ensure Proper Feedback**
The communicator may ensure the success of communication by asking questions regarding the message conveyed.
The receiver of communication should also be encouraged to respond to communica- tion. The communication process may be improved by the feedback received to make it more responsive.

(iv) **Communicate for Present as well as Future**
Besides meeting the present commitments, communication should also aim at future goals of the enterprise.

(v) **Communicate According to the Needs of Receiver**
The communicator should know the level of understanding and education level of the receiver and communicate accordingly.

(vi) **Consult Others before Communicating**
Before actually communicating the message, it is better to involve others in developing a plan for communication. Participation and involvement of subordinates may help to gain ready acceptance and willing cooperation of subordinates.

Case Study Based Questions

Short Case Studies

Case Study 1

Classic Rocks' is a pioneering advertisement making company. Mr. Anuj is a dynamic manager who has recently joined the organisation. He receives complete support from the management. There is proper infrastructure, planning mechanism and subordinate support. He gives orders and starts the actual working of a new unit from the 1st of May. His schedule becomes very hectic.

The demanding work involves him almost throughout the day. He is busy giving messages, talking to his subordinates or seniors, etc. throughout the day. One day he meets his friend Vijay who is working at the lower level management though he himself is a part of middle level management. He finds that even Vijay is involved in communicating and supervising his employees throughout the year though he works at the lower level management. Similar is the case with his seniors working at the higher level management. He feels relaxed after knowing this and continues his work with even more dedication.

(i) Which function of management is highlighted in the above case?

(ii) Identify any two features of this function of management highlighted in the above case.

Ans.

(i) Directing is highlighted in the above case.

(ii) The features of directing highlighted in the above case are

- **Directing takes Place at Every Level of Management**
  Directing is a pervasive function as every manager from top to bottom performs this function. It takes place wherever superior-subordinate relationship exists.
- **Directing is a Continuous Process**
  It is an ongoing process. It takes place throughout the life of the organisation irrespective of people occupying managerial positions.

Case Study 2

Manav wanted to bring some changes in his company. One of those changes was the establishment of new software in the organisation. The software has the capability to judge the performance of all the employees. Thus it makes them more accountable.

However, recently it so happened that the employees resisted Manav's decision. After a lot of thinking on the issue he decided to call a meeting to address their needs and performance.

He told them that with the installation of the new software their needs would be fulfilled and the best performing employee would be rewarded. Thus he was able to bring down the resistance level of the employees.

(i) Which concept of directing is applied by Manav in the above case?

(ii) Which one benefit of this concept has been highlighted in the above case?

Ans.

(i) The concept of directing applied by Manav in the above case is motivation. It means incitement or inducement to act or move.

(ii) The benefit of motivation highlighted in the above case is that it is able to introduce changes in the organisation by putting down the resistance of the employees.

Case Study 3

A company has a number of employees who don't harbour good feelings for the organisation. They don't care whether the organisation is progressing or not.

Some of them are even having negative attitude towards the management. When a local newspaper wanted to find out the reason for the declining productivity of the organisation it was found that it was mainly due to the lack of any incentives in the organisation.

Employees were not awarded for increasing the output of the organisation.

(i) What do you think needs to be done in such circumstances?

(ii) What could be the positive outcome of your step?

Ans.

(i) The organisation should apply the process of motivation here. They should identify the needs of the employees and satisfy them. There should be a proper reward/award system for the better performers.

(ii) By applying the process of motivation it can be expected that the neutral or negative attitude of the employees will be turned into positive. This will bring progress for the organisation.

Case Study 4

Identify and state the Maslow's needs applicable in the following cases of organisational set-up

(i) Virendra works in an organisation. He is part of the organisation for last 20 years. During all these years inspite of his best performance in the organisation he hasn't yet reached the post of Vice-President.

(ii) Vandana works in a software firm. She goes to office which is situated at a distance of 20 kms from her house. Her husband earns very well and is a pilot with a leading Airline. Though, she belongs to a good earning family yet she has decided to keep on going to her job which she feels helps her gain acceptance in her social circle.

Ans.

(i) The need referred in the statement is esteem need. These needs include factors such as self-respect, autonomy status, recognition and attention. When these needs are fulfilled through job title, it enhances self-confidence and prestige of employees.

(ii) The need referred in the statement is affiliation need. These needs are concerned with affection, sense of belongingness, acceptance and friendship. It is fulfilled when employees have cordial relations with colleagues.

Case Study 5

Shyam Malik, the CEO of Care Hospitals, a leading chain of hospitals, decide to reward the good work of the doctors of this organisation. For this, he instituted two running trophies.

A Healthcare Achievers Trophy to acknowledge and appreciate the tireless efforts of the doctors who rendered selfless services to the patients and another Beti Bachao Trophy to recognise the outstanding work done by the doctors in saving girl child. He decided that all doctors must work in rural areas for atleast six months to improve health services.

(i) Identify the incentive provided by Care Hospitals to its doctors through running trophies.

(ii) Which need of the doctors will be satisfied through the incentive identified in (i)? State.

Ans.

(i) The incentive provided by Care Hospitals to its doctors through running trophies is employee recognition.

(ii) The need of the doctors that will be satisfied through this incentive is Esteem need. It refers to the need for self-respect, autonomy, status, recognition and attention.

Case Study 6

Mrs. Rani is working as the Human Resource Consultant in a firm manufacturing cosmetic, which is facing a problem with high employee turnover.

The CEO of the company has invited suggestions from her for retaining the talented employees and reducing the employee turnover.

Mrs. Rani recommends that the good employees be rewarded in a way that it creates a feeling of ownership among the employees and at the same time makes them contribute towards the growth of the organisation.

(i) Identify the incentive and explain its type, which has been suggested by Mrs. Rani to the CEO of the company.

(ii) Also explain any two incentives of the same type.

Ans.

(i) The incentive suggested by Mrs. Rani is **copartnership/ stock option.** It is a financial incentive. In co-partnership or stock option, employees are given a share in the profits of the company or are allowed to purchase company shares at a lower price than the market price. This creates a sense of ownership among employees, motivating them to work towards the organisation's growth.

(ii) Two financial incentives are as follows

- **Retirement Benefits**
  Several retirement benefits such as provident fund, pension, gratuity are provided to the employees as a financial security after retirement. This acts as an incentive when they are in service in the organisation.
- **Perquisites**
  Apart from basic salary, some companies offer fringe benefits and perquisites to employees, e.g. Rent free accommodation, education of children, medical allowance, car allowance, etc. These measures help to provide motivation to the employees.

Case Study 7

Manoj, a highly dedicated sales manager at Stellar Enterprises, consistently worked toward his sales targets with strategic planning and an enthusiastic approach. Recognised for his commitment and motivation, Manoj exceeded expectations by achieving his sales target one full month before the deadline.

This impressive accomplishment not only highlighted his dedication but also inspired his team and colleagues.

To honour his achievement, the company's CEO decided to make an example of Manoj's hardwork. Manoj's success story was proudly displayed on the company noticeboard, celebrating him as a role model for other employees. Additionally, he was awarded a 'Best Performance' certificate in a formal ceremony, which boosted his morale and reinforced the company's culture of appreciating excellence.

(i) Name the incentive provided to Manoj and identify the type of incentive.

(ii) List two other incentives of the type identified in (i).

Ans.

(i) The incentive provided to Manoj is employee-recognition programme. It is a type of non-financial incentive.

(ii) Two other incentives of this type are as follows

- **Employee Participation**
  It means involving employees in decision-making regarding the issues related to them. These programmes are in practice in many companies in the form of joint management committees, work committees, canteen committees, etc.
- **Employee Empowerment**
  It means giving more autonomy and power to subordinates. It makes people feel that their jobs are important, as a result of which, they contribute positively to the use of skills and talents in the job performance.

Case Study 8

When Bhaanupriya joined as technical head of Logic Lotus Innovators, she was keen on increasing the productivity and profitability of the company. However, she observed that the employees were demotivated as no attention was given to their work. Also, the workers were given little freedom to make decisions.

Bhaanupriya decided to stimulate the employees by giving each worker T-shirts with their name on it. She also decided to include workers in work committees. This helped in improving the performance of the workers. **CBSE SQP 2025**

(i) On the basis of the understanding of Maslow's Need Hierarchy Theory of motivation, identify the human need that Bhaanupriya has recognised in order to make the subordinates act towards achievement of organisational goals.

(ii) Identify and explain two incentives that have been provided by Bhaanupriya to improve the performance of the employees.

Ans.

(i) Bhaanupriya has recognised 'esteen needs'.

(ii)

- Employee participation
- Employee empowerment

For explanation, refer to case study 7.

Case Study 9

Avni Enterprises organised a function for the employees. There were managers, supervisors, foremen and others. Some of the employees were engaged in having conversations related to personal experiences while others were discussing about company experiences.

One of the supervisor wanted to give a suggestion to the manager of his department. But he could not do it because of official fear. In the function, the supervisor got an opportunity to give his suggestion which was appreciated by the manager. As a result, appreciation letter was given to supervisor. This motivated other employees as well.

(i) Name the motivational method applied here.

(ii) List two more motivational methods of the same category.

Ans.

(i) The motivational method applied in the case is employee recognition programmes. Recognition means acknowledgement of work with a show of appreciation. When such appreciation is given to the work performed by employees, they feel motivated.

(ii) Two other motivational methods of the same category are as follows

- **Job Security**
  Employees want their job to be secure. They want certain stability of income and work, which will motivate them to work with greater zeal.
  However, it has one negative aspect i.e. when individuals feel that they are not likely to lose their jobs, they may become complacent and careless.
- **Employee Participation**
  It means involving employees in decision-making regarding the issues related to them. These programmes are in practice in many companies in the form of joint management committees, work committees, canteen committees, etc.

Case Study 10

A reputed hostel, GyanPradan provides medical aid and free education to children of its employees. Which incentive is being highlighted here? State its category and name any two more incentives of the same category. **NCERT**

Ans. GyanPradan has given perquisites and fringe benefits to the employees in the form of free education to children and medical aid. Perquisites and fringe benefits are a type of financial incentives. Financial incentives refer to those incentives which are in direct monetary form or measurable in monetary terms and used to motivate employees for better performance.

Some other financial incentives are

(i) Bonus
(ii) Stock option
(iii) Profit sharing
(iv) Retirement benefits

Case Study 11

In a renowned hospital having 300 beds, the CEO of the hospital congratulates the exceptionally performing employees by meeting in person. Sometimes the name of the employee of the month is displayed on the notice board at the main entrance along with his/her photograph.

Recently the company went a step ahead and distributed t-shirts to the employees who have been among the top 3 performers.

On the Employee Day every year employees who contribute a lot are either rewarded or awarded.

(i) In the above case, which type of incentive has been used by the company to improve employee performance?

(ii) Which type of incentive is this? Also, give the definition of this type of incentive.

Ans.

(i) The type of incentive used to improve performance in the above case is employee recognition. Recognition means acknowledgement of work with a show of appreciation.

When such appreciation is given to the work performed by employees, they feel motivated.

(ii) Employee recognition is a non-financial incentive. Non-financial incentives are the incentives which are given to improve the psychological and emotional satisfaction of an employee. So, the needs of the employees which are not satisfied by monetary means are satisfied by non-financial incentives.

Case Study 12

A popular magazine published an article on job cuts across the globe. It stated that due to reasons like cost cutting, market conditions and technological advancement, almost two lakh people in the IT sector have lost their jobs during the last year.

This was read and discussed by employees of Techwire Ltd. a software development company in India. It created a lot of unrest among them and their morale came down. The productivity of the employees started declining. The chief executive officer of the company observed the insecurity among the staff about their jobs.

Understanding his role as the leader, he wrote an e-mail to all the employees assuring them about the stability of their future income and job.

This communication gave the employees psychological and emotional satisfaction and showed positive results in terms of their performance. The chief executive officer was able to make the subordinates act in a desired manner to achieve the organisational goals, without giving them any monetary incentives. **CBSE 2024 C**

(i) Identify and explain the incentive used by the chief executive officer to improve the performance of the employees.

(ii) State the need of the employees as per Maslow's Hierarchy of Needs Theory which was satisfied in the above case.

Ans.

(i) **Job Security**

It is a non-monetary incentive in which employees are given certain stability about the future income and work so that they do not feel worried on these aspects and work with greater zeal.

(ii) As per Maslow's Need Hierarchy Theory, safety and security needs of the employees were satisfied in the above case which include providing security and protection from physical and emotional harm.

Case Study 13

Ravi, the operations manager at Jindal Tea Company in Assam, is known for his firm, directive approach. He gives clear orders to his team without involving them in decision-making, expecting compliance to maintain efficiency and meet production targets.

Ravi believes that consulting with his subordinates may slow down operations and prefers to make decisions independently to ensure swift execution and productivity.

(i) Identify and state the leadership style adopted by Ravi.

(ii) When can this style be useful for a manager? State.

Ans.

(i) The leadership style adopted by Ravi is autocratic or authoritarian style. An autocratic leader gives orders and expects his subordinates to obey those orders.

(ii) Autocratic style can be effectively used by a manager in the following situations

- Where the supervisor is responsible for production on time and has to ensure labour productivity.
- Where quick-decision making is needed.

Case Study 14

Pramod was a supervisor at 'Annapurna Atta' factory. The factory was producing 200 quintals of atta every day. His job was to make sure that the work goes on smoothly and there was no interruption in production. He was a good leader who would give orders only after consulting his subordinates and work out the policies with the acceptance of the group.

Identify and describe the leadership style being adopted by Pramod.

Ans. Participative or democratic leadership style is being followed by Pramod. In such a style of leadership, a leader consults the group and works out the policies with the acceptance of the group.

Participation of employees in decision-making is the main feature of such a leadership style.

The leader invites opinions and suggestions from the employees which increases their morale. It aims at improving the attitude of the employees towards their jobs as well as the organisation.

Using this style of leadership, is of mutual benefit as it allows subordinates to become part of the team and helps leaders make better decisions.

Case Study 15

In an organisation, one of the departmental manager is inflexible and once he takes a decision, he does not like to be contradicted. As a result, employees always feel they are under stress and they take least initiative and fear to express their opinions and problems before the manager.

What is the problem in the way authority is being used by the manager? **NCERT**

Ans. In the given situation, there is absence of free flow of communication. The style of leadership used by the departmental manager is autocratic style. This results in demotivation of the subordinates and they get uncomfortable in sharing their views with the superiors. The manager must involve his subordinates in the decision-making process and encourage them to actively give their feedback and suggestions.

Case Study 16

Balvinder is the production manager of 'Pramod Tea Company' in Guwahati. He gives orders to his subordinates and expects that they obey those orders. He does not consult them nor encourage them to participate in decision-making. **CBSE 2023**

(i) Identify and state the leadership style adopted by Balvinder.

(ii) When can this style be effectively used by a manager? State.

Ans.

(i) The leadership style adopted by Balvinder is autocratic leadership style. An autocratic leader exercises complete control over the subordinates. He gives orders and expects his subordinates to follow them. Under this style, there is only one way communication as the subordinate acts according to the command given by manager.

(ii) Autocratic style can be effectively used by manager in the following situations

- Where the supervisor is responsible for production on time and has to ensure labour productivity.
- Where quick decision-making is needed.

Case Study 17

Identify and state the type of leadership displayed in the following cases

(i) Mr. Umang Patel is the CEO of a leading software company. He is least concerned about the managerial development of his subordinates. The communication flows only from top to bottom in his organisation.

(ii) Ravish is the head of marketing department of his company. Recently he organised a series of meetings to know the suggestions of his team members on various issues.

His subordinates appreciate his habit of consulting his team before he takes any major decisions.

Ans.

(i) Autocratic/Authoritarian leadership style is indicated in the case. An autocratic leader exercises complete control over the subordinates.

He gives orders and expects his subordinates to follow them. Under this style, there is only one way communication as the subordinate acts according to the command given by the manager. The leader is dogmatic and does not wish to be changed or opposed. According to him, reward or punishment both can be given depending upon the result.

(ii) Democratic leadership style is indicated in the case. A democratic leader develops action plan and takes decisions in consultation with his subordinates. He encourages the participation of subordinates in decision-making.

This leadership style is more common and popular nowadays, as it ensures achievement of goals, when they are set with the acceptance of the subordinates themselves.

Case Study 18

Radhika started a business of supplying high class facial kits to beauty parlours in various cities of the country. Initially, the business was doing well and her products were popular. Despite the high quality of the products. Radhika faced difficulties in certain parlours, especially in Kagpur city, where her products failed to gain a strong market presence. To understand the cause, she appointed a qualified marketing manager.

The marketing manager discovered that there was no proper exchange of facts, ideas and views, etc. between the incharge of Kagpur city and the employees at different parlours at Kagpur. Vicky, who was the incharge and responsible for overseeing all parlours in Kagpur, was unable to effectively foster a common understanding of the product among the employees. As a result, the employees did not grasp the key benefits and features of the high class facial kits.

In turn, the employees were not able to convince potential clients about the product's value. **CBSE 2025**

(i) Identify the concept discussed in the above case.

(ii) The concept identified in (i) above can be defined as a process having various elements. State first five elements of this process.

Ans.

(i) The concept discussed in the above case is communication.

(ii) Following are the first five elements of the communication process

- **Sender**
  The person who conveys his thoughts or ideas to the receiver, is known as the sender or communicator.
- **Message**
  It is the subject matter of communication. It may consist of facts, information, ideas, opinions, feelings, etc. which sender wants to share with receiver.
- **Encoding**
  The sender translates the message into communication symbols like words, gestures or other symbols, which he feels will make the receiver understand the message.
- **Channel or Media**
  The encoded message is transmitted to receiver through some medium, which is known as the communication channel. e.g. Writing, phone call, internet, face to face, etc.
- **Decoding**
  It is the process of conversion of encoded symbols into the effective language that can be understood by the receiver.

Case Study 19

Rajesh and Suresh are working in the same company but in different departments. They often meet during coffee breaks to catch up on the latest news. One day, Rajesh tells Suresh that there is a rumor going around about the company planning to restructure, which might lead to some job cuts.

(i) Which type of communication is this?

(ii) State any four features of the type of communication identified in (i).

Ans.

(i) Communication between Rajesh and Suresh is informal communication.

(ii) Following are the features of informal communication

- It takes place without following the formal lines of communication.
- It enables employees to develop friendly relationship and get social satisfaction.
- The flow of communication is very fast.
- It leads to rumours as it is difficult to find the source of such communication.

Case Study 20

Neeraj, a Sales Representative of 'Omida Ltd.' has changed seven jobs in the last one year. He is a hard working person but not able to finalise deals with the customers due to his inadequate vocabulary and omission of needed words. Sometimes, he uses wrong words because of which intended meaning is not conveyed.

All this created a misunderstanding between him and his clients.

(i) Identify the communication barrier discussed above and state the category of this communication barrier.

(ii) Explain any other communication barrier of the same category.

Ans.

(i) Communication barrier discussed in the above case is badly expressed message. It is a type of semantic barrier. Such barriers are concerned with problems and obstructions in the process of coding and decoding of a message into words and expression.

(ii) Other communication barrier of the same category is Technical Jargon. These are words used by experts and specialists and are difficult to understand by people belonging to some other field. Use of such words can act as a barrier to effective communication.

Case Study 21

Mr. Fernandes is the owner of Unibie Enterprises, carrying on the business of manufacturing electrical appliances. There is a lot of discontentment in the organisation and targets are not being met. He asked his son, Michel, who has recently completed his MBA, to find out the reason. Michel found that all decision-making of the enterprise were in the hands of his father. Moreover, his father did not have confidence in the competency of the employees. Thus, the employees were not happy.

(i) Identify any two communication bafflers because of which 'Unibie Enterprise' was not able to achieve its target.

(ii) State one more barrier each of the types identified in part (i) above.

Ans.

(i) The two communication barriers because of which Unibie Enterprises was not able to achieve its target, were

- **Organisational Barrier** In the form of 'organisational policy', as it is indicated that it was the policy of the company that all the decisions were taken by Mr. Fernandes.
- **Personal Barrier** In the form of 'lack of confidence of superior on his subordinates', as it is indicated that Mr. Fernandes did not have confidence in the competency of his employees'.

(ii) Following are the barriers of each type identified in (i)

- **Organisational Barrier** Complexity in organisation structure.
- **Personal Barrier** Fear of challenge to authority.

Case Study 22

Jaideep recently joined as the managing director of Tivori Ltd, an apparel designing company. He observed that the company had a number of experienced fashion designers on its payroll. They regularly offered useful suggestions which were neither appreciated nor rewarded by the company.

Instead the company outsourced its services to some renowned fashion designers and paid them a good compensation for their services. Because of this the employees felt disheartened and stopped giving useful suggestions.

(i) Identify the communication barrier discussed above and state the category of this communication barrier.

(ii) Explain any two other communication barrier of the same category.

Ans.

(i) Communication barrier discussed in the case is lack of proper incentives. It is a type of personal barrier. Personal characteristics of both sender and receiver may influence the effective communication.

(ii) Communication barrier of the same category are as follows

- **Fear of Challenge to Authority**
  A superior is likely to withhold or suppress a message, if he perceives that it will adversely affect his authority.
- **Lack of Confidence of Superior on His Subordinates**
  A superior, who does not have confidence on the competency of his subordinates, is not likely to seek their advice and suggestions.

Case Study 23

Rajeev started working in an MNC. He was very devoted towards his job. However, whenever he used to communicate with his subordinates they were unable to understand him. The reason behind this problem was that he himself was unsure about the concept he used to explain to the subordinates. This problem was taking place on a daily basis. One day he got an order from his senior to fly to Goa for a project meeting. There he started explaining his concept to others but there were many aspects which the team of Goa wanted to explain to him.

He was more concerned about speaking than listening. This resulted in the failure of the meeting which was very important.

In this hopelessness he forgot to review the instructions he had given to his subordinates about a very important programme to be organised in his home town.

What measures would you suggest to Rajeev so that he could improve his communication effectiveness?

Ans. The measures we would suggest him to adopt to improve his communication effectiveness are

(i) **Rajeev should clarify his ideas before communication**
The message to be conveyed should be clear in all aspects to the executive himself/herself. It should be studied in depth, analysed and stated in such a manner that it is clearly conveyed to subordinates.

(ii) **Rajeev should become a good listener**
Attentive and patient listening on the part of the management will encourage employees to communicate freely. It solves half of the problems.

(iii) **He should try to follow-up communication**
Regular follow-up and review on the instructions given to subordinates, help in removing hurdles, if any, in implementing the instructions.

Long Case Studies

Case Study 24

Sunrise Manufacturing Pvt. Ltd., a medium-sized company based in Pune, has been a leading player in the automotive parts industry for over two decades. Founded by Mr. Raghav Mehra, the company started with a modest production unit and a team of 50 employees. Over the years, through hard work and dedication, Sunrise Manufacturing expanded its operations, now employing over 500 workers and supplying automotive components to major car manufacturers across India.

In 2022, Sunrise Manufacturing secured a large contract with one of the top automobile manufacturers in the country. This contract required the company to increase its production capacity significantly within a short period. To meet the growing demand, the management decided to install new machinery and hire additional workers. While the expansion was a positive development, it also brought challenges in managing the larger workforce and ensuring that production targets were met without compromising quality.

Mr. Mehra, the managing director, was aware that simply increasing the workforce and upgrading technology would not be sufficient to meet the new challenges. He understood that the company needed strong leadership and clear communication to guide the employees effectively.

Mr. Mehra appointed Ms. Priya Kapoor, a seasoned manager with a strong track record in team leadership, as the Head of Operations. Her primary responsibility was to oversee the expansion and ensure that the production targets were achieved.

Upon taking charge, Ms. Kapoor noticed that the rapid expansion had led to confusion among the workers.

The employees were unsure about their new roles, responsibilities and how the new machinery worked. There was a lack of coordination among different departments, and the production process was becoming inefficient. Recognising the urgency of the situation, Ms. Kapoor decided to take immediate action.

She started by organising a series of meetings with department heads to communicate the company's goals and the importance of each department's role in achieving these goals.

She then, held training sessions for the workers to familiarise them with the new machinery and production processes. During these sessions, Ms. Kapoor encouraged open communication, allowing workers to express their concerns and ask questions. This approach helped in building trust and ensuring that everyone was on the same page. To further enhance productivity, Ms. Kapoor introduced a system of regular feedback and performance reviews.

She set clear expectations for each team and provided guidance on how to meet these expectations.

Ms. Kapoor also recognised and rewarded employees who performed exceptionally well, motivating others to follow suit. Under her leadership, the workers began to feel more confident and engaged in their roles, leading to improved coordination and a significant increase in production efficiency.

As the company's production ramped up, Ms. Kapoor continued to monitor the progress closely.

She maintained regular communication with the teams, addressing any issues that arose and providing the necessary support to keep operations running smoothly. Her ability to direct the workforce effectively played a crucial role in Sunrise Manufacturing's ability to meet the demands of the new contract without any major disruptions.

By the end of the year, Sunrise Manufacturing had successfully fulfilled the contract, exceeding the client's expectations in terms of both quality and delivery time. The company's success was largely attributed to Ms. Kapoor's leadership and her ability to guide the employees towards achieving common goals. The experience also reinforced the importance of effective leadership and communication in managing a large and diverse workforce.

(i) Identify the management function that Ms. Priya Kapoor primarily utilised to address the challenges at Sunrise Manufacturing.

(ii) Discuss the importance of the management function identified in the case.

Ans.

(i) The management function that Ms. Priya Kapoor primarily utilised to address the challenges at Sunrise Manufacturing is 'directing'.

(ii) Following are the points of importance of directing function of management

- **Initiates Action**
  Directing helps to initiate action by people in the organisation for the achievement of pre-determined goals. e.g. If a supervisor guides his subordinates and clarifies their doubts while performing a task, it will help the worker to achieve work targets given to him.
- **Integrates Employees Efforts**
  Directing helps a manager to integrate individual efforts towards the achievement of organisational goals. It ensures that all individuals work for the benefit of the organisation, by establishing harmony between organisational and personal goals. e.g. Manager with good leadership abilities will be in a position to convince the employees that individual efforts and team effort will lead to achievement of goals.
- **Guides Employees**
  Effective directing provides motivation and leadership to the employees, which helps them to identify their potential and realise their latent capabilities, leading to growth. A good leader can always identify the potential of his employees and motivate them to extract work up to their full potential.
- **Introduces Changes**
  Changes in an organisation are usually resisted by employees.
  Effective directing through motivation, communication and leadership helps to reduce such resistance and develop required cooperation in introducing changes in the organisation.
- **Provides Stability**
  Effective directing helps to develop cooperation and commitment on part of subordinates. This provides stability to the organisation and helps to achieve balance among various groups, activities and departments.

Case Study 25

Riya Sharma was the Operations Manager at "FitGear Sportswear," a company known for its high-quality athletic apparel. The company was recognised for its dynamic work culture, where employees felt motivated and aligned with the company's goals.

Riya Sharma ensured that every employee clearly understood their role and responsibilities, creating a structured work environment.

To maintain high levels of productivity, Riya frequently communicated the company's vision and objectives to her team, making sure that everyone was on the same page. She was also known for providing timely feedback to her team members, praising their accomplishments and guiding them to improve when necessary.

Riya believed that encouraging her employees and recognising their achievements not only boosted their morale but also enhanced their commitment to the company's objectives.

Moreover, Riya delegated tasks efficiently, ensuring that work was distributed based on individual strengths and capabilities. This allowed the team to work cohesively and achieve their targets effectively. As a result, FitGear Sportswear consistently delivered high-quality products and maintained a strong market position.

However, during a crucial project, one of the team leaders faced difficulties in executing the assigned tasks. Riya provided guidance and additional training to help the team leader overcome the challenges. This support not only helped in the completion of the project but also strengthened the team leader's confidence and competence.

Quoting lines from the above case, identify and explain the three elements of the directing function of management discussed in the case.

Ans. Following are the four elements of the directing function of management

(i) **Supervision**

"Riya Sharma ensured that every employee clearly understood their role and responsibilities, creating a structured work environment."

Supervision refers to instructing, guiding and observing the subordinates at work by their superiors. It involves overseeing the work of subordinates to ensure that tasks are performed as per the plans.

In this case, Riya supervises her team by making sure that every employee understands their role and responsibilities, which helps in maintaining a structured and productive work environment.

(ii) **Communication**

"Riya frequently communicated the company's vision and objectives to her team, making sure that everyone was on the same page."

Communication is the process of sharing information, ideas, and instructions between managers and employees. Riya regularly communicates the company's vision and objectives to her team, ensuring that everyone is aligned with the company's goals, which is crucial for effective coordination and execution of tasks.

(iii) **Motivation**

"She was also known for providing timely feedback to her team members, praising their accomplishments and guiding them to improve when necessary."

Motivation means a process of stimulating people to action to accomplish desired goals. Motivation involves encouraging employees to perform at their best by recognising their achievements and providing necessary support. Riya motivates her team by giving timely feedback, praising their accomplishments and guiding them when needed, which boosts their morale and commitment to the company's objectives.

Case Study 26

Smita had been working as an assistant manager with 'Johnson Enterprises' for the last ten years. She was very popular amongst her colleagues because of her commitment and dedication towards the work. When the manager senior to her retired, all her colleagues thought that now Smita would be promoted. But to everyone's surprise the vacant post was filled by an outsider, Mrs. Rita. Smita felt demoralised and her performance started declining. She would abstain herself often and could not meet her targets.

Mrs. Rita was a good leader, who would not only instruct her subordinates but would also guide and inspire them. She noticed Smita's behaviour and felt that her performance could be improved. She started involving Smita in decision making issues related to the organisation and made her a part of high level joint management committee.

Smita was now punctual in office and her performance started improving.

(i) Identify and state the function of management being performed by Rita.

(ii) Name the element of the above function of management which helped Rita to improve Smita's behaviour.

(iii) State any four features of the element identified in (ii) above.

Ans.

(i) The function of management performed by Rita is directing. It refers to the process of instructing, guiding, leading, counselling and motivating people in an organisation to achieve pre-determined objectives.

(ii) The element of directing which helped Rita to improve Smita's behaviour is motivation. It means incitement or inducement to act or move.

(iii) Following are the features of motivation

- **Motivation is a Psychological Phenomenon**
  It is a personal and internal feeling like an urge, drives, desires and aspirations of human being, which influence human behaviour. e.g. Desire or urge for possessing a motorbike, comfortable house, etc.
- **Motivation Produces Goal Directed Behaviour**
  Motivation inspires an employee to achieve goals. Thus, it encourages goal directed behaviour. e.g. A person who desires to get promoted, will work efficiently to achieve this goal.

- **Motivation may be Positive or Negative**
  Motivation can be either positive or negative. Positive motivation provides positive rewards like increase in pay, promotion, recognition, etc. Negative motivation uses negative means such as punishment, stopping increments, threatening, etc. which also may induce a person to act in the desired way.
- **Motivation is a Complex Process**
  It is a complex process as all individuals are heterogeneous in their expectations, perceptions and reactions. Any type of motivation may not have uniform effect on all the members.

Case Study 27

Inaya Ltd. is a multinational technology company focusing on artificial intelligence, online advertising and search engine technology. The company is generating good profits and takes care of the well-being of its staff. The company offers benefits like car allowance, medical aid and allowance for childrens education to all employees above the manager level.

It regularly contributes towards the Employees Provident Fund and pays gratuity on retirement to its employees.

Under a special incentive scheme, the employees are offered shares of Inaya Ltd. at a set price which is lower than the market price. Each year, the company keeps aside funds to pay 1% percent of base salary as bonus to its employees. No wonder 90% of the employees would recommend working at Ltd. to a friend. Explain four incentives being provided by Inaya Ltd. to motivate their employees for better performance. **CBSE 2024**

Ans. Following incentives are provided by Inaya Ltd. to motivate their employees for better performance

(i) **Bonus**
It is a one time reward for high performance. Bonus may be paid in cash or kind over and above the salary.
e.g. Performance bonus, 100% attendance bonus, festive bonus, etc.

(ii) **Perquisites**
Apart from basic salary, some companies offer fringe benefits and perquisites to employees, e.g. Rent free accommodation, education of children, medical allowance, car allowance, etc. These measures help to provide motivation to the employees.

(iii) **Retirement Benefits**
Several retirement benefits such as provident fund, pension, gratuity are provided to the employees as a financial security after retirement. This acts as an incentive when they are in service in the organisation.

(iv) **Copartnership/Stock Option**
In this system, employees are offered shares of the company at a price lower than the market price. Sometimes, management may allot shares in line of various incentives payable in cash. This gives a feeling of ownership to the employees, which motivates them to improve performance and contribute for the growth of the company. e.g. In Infosys, the scheme of stock option has been implemented as a part of managerial compensation.

Case Study 28

Ramesh is a manager in a company engaged in production of electrical appliances. He has been on this position for quite a long time. He is liked by his subordinates as he encourages their participation whenever he takes an important decision. Being an experienced manager he believes that only money is not sufficient to motivate the employees.

Therefore, he uses the following non-financial incentives to motivate the employees

- Ramesh has set up a suggestion box system in order to involve his subordinates in decision-making. This has resulted in an increased involvement of the employees in issues related to the organisation.
- Ramesh has given more autonomy to the employees working under him with an assurance of greater responsibility from them. Since workers take part in the process of decision-making hence they feel that their job is important.
- Ramesh has made arrangements at the work place for the employees to make their work more meaningful. The outcome has been an increase in motivation for the employees at the place of work itself.
- Ramesh often makes arrangements for appropriate skill development programmes. He has chalked out a sound promotion policy to give more growth opportunities to the employees.

(i) Identify and explain the leadership style followed by Ramesh.
(ii) State the meaning of leadership.
(iii) Also identify and explain the various non-financial incentives used by Ramesh to motivate the employees.

Ans.

(i) The leadership style followed by Ramesh is participative or democratic. Under such a leadership style, a leader develops action plans and makes decisions in consultation with the subordinates. He encourages participation of workers in decision-making process.

(ii) Leadership may be defined as the process of influencing the behaviour of people by making them strive voluntarily towards the achievement of organisational goals.

(iii) Following are the non-financial incentives used by Ramesh to motivate the employees

- **Employee Participation**
  It means involving employees in decision-making regarding the issues related to them. These programmes are in practice in many companies in the form of joint management committees, work committees, canteen committees, etc.

- **Employee Empowerment**
  It means giving more autonomy and power to subordinates. It makes people feel that their jobs are important, as a result of which, they contribute positively to the use of skills and talents in the job performance.
- **Career Advancement Opportunity**
  Every individual wants to grow to the higher level in the organisation. When employees are provided opportunities to grow in status and responsibility, they are satisfied and are committed to organisational goals. Appropriate skill development programmes and sound promotion policy help employees to exhibit improved performance.
- **Job Enrichment**
  It is concerned with designing of jobs that include greater variety of work content, requiring higher level of knowledge and skill.

  This provides opportunity for growth and development of an employee on one hand and more autonomy and responsibility on the other, which becomes a source of motivation to the individual.

Case Study 29

In an organisation all the employees take things easy and are free to approach anyone for minor queries and problems.

This has resulted in everyone talking to each other and thus resulting in inefficiency in the office. It has also resulted in loss of secrecy and confidential information being leaked out. What system do you think the manager should adopt to improve communication? **NCERT**

Ans. The manager should adopt formal communication system in the organisation. It refers to the communication taking place through official channels in an organisation. Such type of communication takes place between 'superior and subordinate, or managers working at the same cadre, or employees working at the same cadre. Though, such communication may be oral or written, but it is recorded and filed in the office.

Following are the features of formal communication

(i) It follows scalar chain i.e. it takes place through formal lines of communication.

(ii) It may be oral or written, but is is generally recorded for future reference.

(iii) It is easy to fix responsibility as source of information can be located.

(iv) It is used for communicating official matters like order, instruction, notice, etc.

Case Study 30

Rajat Verma was the Marketing Head of a leading FMCG company, 'FreshPure Products'. The company was known for its wide range of organic and healthy food items.

Rajat was a skilled communicator who ensured that his team was well-informed about the latest market trends and customer preferences. He conducted regular meetings with his team to discuss sales strategies and new product launches.

During one of the meetings, Rajat introduced a new product line that required immediate attention and a strategic marketing push. However, during the discussion, several team members were distracted by their phones and didn't pay full attention to Rajat's presentation. Some members prematurely evaluated the strategy without fully understanding the details, which led to misunderstandings. When Rajat followed up on the actions discussed, he noticed that the team members had different interpretations of the plan, resulting in a poorly executed marketing campaign.

Additionally, many subordinates did not actively participate in the discussion as they felt that their suggestions wouldn't be rewarded or recognised, leading to a lack of initiative to communicate.

Meanwhile, a competitor, 'NutriFoods', launched a similar product but with a highly effective marketing strategy, capturing a significant market share. FreshPure Products failed to communicate their unique selling proposition effectively, which led to a drop in sales and loss of market position.

Quoting lines from the above paragraph, identify and explain three barriers to communication and state their category.

Ans. Following are the barriers to communication along with their category that have been discussed in the case

(i) **Premature Evaluation** (Psychological Barrier)
"Some members prematurely evaluated the strategy without fully understanding the details," which led to misinterpretation and misunderstandings. Communication is likely to fail, if the receiver evaluates the meaning of message before the sender completes the message.

Such premature evaluation may occur due to pre-conceived notions or prejudices against the communication.

(ii) **Loss by Transmission and Poor Retention** (Psychological Barrier)
"The team members had different interpretations of the plan," indicating that the message was distorted and poorly remembered. When communication passes through various levels, it may result in loss of or transmission of inaccurate information. Sometimes, poor retention of people due to lack of interest and attention leads to miscommunication.

(iii) **Lack of Proper Incentives** (Personal Barrier)
"Many subordinates did not actively participate in the discussion as they felt that their suggestions wouldn't be rewarded or recognised", leading to a lack of initiative to communicate or offer suggestions. Employees may not take initiative to communicate in the absence of proper incentives or motivation.

SELF ASSESSMENT TEST

Objective Type Questions

1. "Presence of more managerial levels." Identify the communication barrier highlighted in the statement.
   (a) Personal barrier (b) Organisational barrier
   (c) Psychological barrier (d) Semantic barrier
2. .... developed the theory which classifies needs in hierarchical order.
   (a) Fred Luthans (b) Abraham Maslow
   (c) Peter Drucker (d) Scott
3. Which of the following needs include factors such as growth, achievement of goals and self-fulfillment?
   (a) Self-actualisation needs
   (b) Esteem needs
   (c) Safety needs
   (d) Basic physiological needs
4. .... refers to ranking of positions in the organisation.
   (a) Job rotation
   (b) Status
   (c) Co-partnership
   (d) Job enrichment
5. .... is the process of converting encoded symbols of the sender.
   (a) Encoding (b) Decoding
   (c) Feedback (d) Receiver
6. The need of the employees which is satisfied by the non-financial incentive is/are
   (a) social (b) esteem
   (c) self-actualisation (d) All of these

Answers 1. (b) 2. (b) 3. (a) 4. (b) 5. (b) 6. (d)

Short Answer Type Questions

7. Explain briefly any three personal barriers to communication.
8. Managers in Nexa Ltd. faced lot of issues because of barriers in communication that led to an environment of distrust and misunderstanding. State any four measures that can help in improving the effectiveness of communication in Nexa Ltd.
9. State any four assumption of the theory developed by Maslow for classifying the needs in a hierarchical order.
10. State any four psychological barriers of communication.
11. Explain the process of motivation with the help of a diagram.
12. Directing is important as it helps to maintain balance in the organisation. Support your answer with any three points.
13. "Poorly motivated people can nullify the soundest organisation." Comment.

Long Answer Type Questions

14. "Incentives in direct monetary form play an important role in motivating people for better performance." In the light of the given statement, discuss any six such incentives.
15. Maheshwari textiles is facing a lot of problems in communication among the employees. After careful analysis, it was found that semantic barriers are the main cause behind miscommunication. State four such semantic barriers and list two possible measures to improve communication.
16. Identify and explain the various non-financial incentives used by managers to motivate people in an organisation.

08

CHAPTER

"Managerial control implies the measurement of accomplishment against the standard and the correction of deviations to assure attainment of objectives according to plans."

— Koontz and O'Donnel

▼ **YOUR STUDY GOALS**

8.1 Concept of Controlling
8.2 Importance of Controlling
8.3 Limitations of Controlling
8.4 Relationship between Planning and Controlling
8.5 Process of Controlling

▼ **YOUR PRACTICE GOAL**

- Objective Type Questions (53 Qs ; MCQs, A-R, Statements, Matching)
- Subjective Type Questions (11 SAs, 5 LAs)
- Case Study Based Questions (Short Case Studies-9, Long Case Studies-6)
- Self Assessment Test (6 MCQs, 7 SAs, 3 LAs)

Controlling

8.1 Concept of Controlling

Controlling refers to the process of comparing the actual performance with the standards, measuring deviations and taking corrective action to achieve pre-determined goals.

Features of Controlling

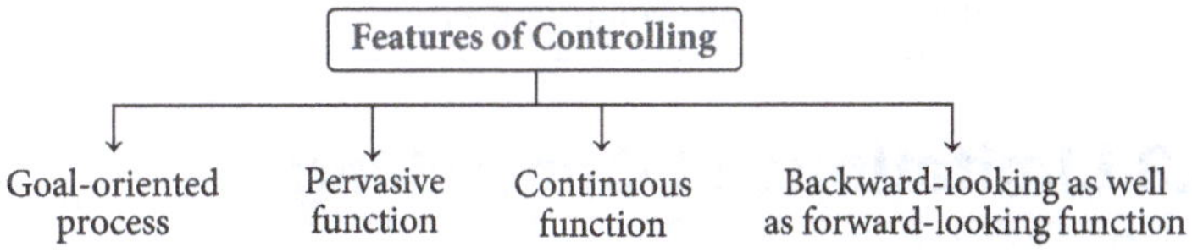

1. **Goal-oriented Process** Controlling ensures effective and efficient use of organisation's resources to achieve organisational goals, making it a goal-oriented process.
2. **Pervasive Function** Controlling is essential for all managers across all levels to check the activities of subordinates. It is equally required in both business as well as non-business organisations.
3. **Continuous Function** By analysing deviations and taking corrective action, controlling helps in formulating better plans for future. It brings back the management cycle to planning and is regarded as continuous function.
4. **Both a Backward-looking as well as Forward-looking Function** It is a backward-looking function as it reviews past actions to find deviations and it is also forward-looking function as it improves future outcomes by implementing corrective measures.

8.2 Importance of Controlling

1. **Accomplishing Organisational Goals** Controlling measures progress towards goals, identifies deviations and guides corrective actions, thus, it ensures that activities align with organisational plans.
2. **Judging Accuracy of Standards** Effective control helps managers to evaluate the accuracy and objectivity of standards. It also helps to revise standards according to the changes taking place in the organisation and environment.
3. **Making Efficient Use of Resources** Controlling reduces resource wastage and its spoilage by ensuring activities are performed according to pre-determined standards, promoting efficiency and effectiveness.
4. **Improving Employee Motivation** Controlling clarifies performance expectations to employees, on the basis of which they will be evaluated. This motivates them to meet set standards and perform better.
5. **Ensuring Order and Discipline** Control fosters order and discipline by monitoring employee activities and also helps to minimise their dishonest or undesirable behaviour.
6. **Facilitating Coordination in Action** It provides direction to all activities and efforts for achieving organisational goals. Each department and employee is governed by pre-determined standards which are well coordinated with one another.

Controlling Importance

Imagine you're baking a cake with your friends for a party. You have a recipe (*plan*) that you all follow. One friend acts as the leader (*manager*) and checks each step i.e. measuring ingredients, mixing and baking (*control*).

If someone adds too much sugar (*deviation*), the leader adjusts by adding more flour (*corrective action*) to keep the cake tasty (*achieving goals*).

This ensures everyone uses ingredients wisely (*resource use*), stays excited to see the final cake (*motivation*) and works together smoothly (*coordination*), resulting in a delicious cake ready for the party (*accomplishing the goal*).

8.3 Limitations of Controlling

Controlling process suffers due to the following reasons

Limitations of Controlling
- Difficulty in setting quantitative standards
- Little control on external factors
- Resistance from employees
- Costly affair

1. **Difficulty in Setting Quantitative Standards** In areas like employee morale and job satisfaction, it is not possible to define quantitative standards, which makes measurement and comparison difficult.
2. **Little Control on External Factors** External factors such as government policies, technological changes and competition are beyond the organisation's control, making it difficult to manage their impact.
3. **Resistance from Employees** Employees may resist control measures, viewing them as restriction or boundation on their freedom, such as close supervision through CCTV.
4. **Costly Affair** Control systems are expensive, requires significant time and effort. A small firm cannot afford to install an expensive control system. Also, managers must ensure that cost of installing control system should not exceed the benefits derived from it.

8.4 Relationship between Planning and Controlling

Planning and controlling are inseparable twins of management. They are mutually inter-related and inter-dependent activities. Following points highlight their relationship

1. **Controlling is Based on Standards Developed by Planning** Controlling relies on performance standards set by planning. Without these standards, controlling would lack direction, making planning a prerequisite for effective controlling.
2. **Planning without Controlling is Meaningless** Once plans are in action, controlling is essential to monitor progress measure it, discover deviations and take corrective measures to ensure alignment with the plans. Thus, planning is meaningless without controlling.
3. **Planning is Prescriptive while Controlling is Evaluative** Planning is an intellectual process which involves thinking, articulation and determining actions to achieve objectives, while controlling evaluates if those decisions are successfully implemented and aligned with the plan.
4. **Planning and Controlling are Forward-looking as well as Backward-looking**
   - *Planning* involves setting objectives and deciding the course of action based on forecasts about future conditions. Thus, it is regarded as a *forward-looking* function.
   - *Controlling* involves a post-mortem of the past activities of an enterprise and finding out deviations from the targetted standard. Thus, it is regarded as a *backward-looking* function.
   - *Planning* is guided by past experiences and corrective actions taken in the controlling process. Thus, it is regarded as a *backward-looking* function.
   - The process of control necessarily involves analysing deviations and taking corrective action, which aims to improve future performance and achieve pre-determined goals. Thus, *controlling* is regarded as a *forward-looking function.*

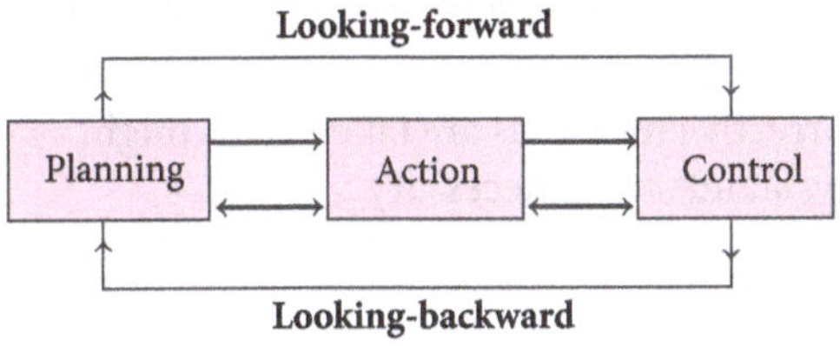

Planning-Controlling Relationship

Imagine students preparing for an important exam. They create a detailed study plan, setting goals for each week (planning). As they progress, they regularly check their understanding by taking practice tests to see if they're on track (controlling).

If the scores show they're struggling in a particular subject, they adjust their study plan to focus more on that area, ensuring their preparation remains effective and aligned with their goals. This illustrates how planning and controlling work together, with planning setting the path and controlling ensuring they stay on course.

8.5 Process of Controlling

The main steps in controlling process are

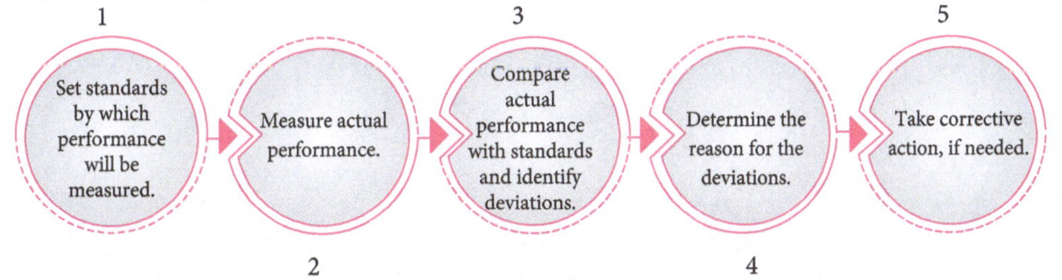

Controlling Process

1. **Setting Performance Standards** The first step in controlling involves setting benchmarks (quantitative or qualitative) against which actual performance is measured. e.g. Reduction of defects from 20 in every 1,500 pieces produced to 10 by end of the quarter (quantitative) or time taken by a customer to wait for a table (qualitative), etc. These standards should be precise and flexible, i.e. adaptable to changes.

Standards used in Functional Areas to Gauge Performance

Production	Marketing	Human Resource Management	Finance and Accounting
• Quantity • Quality • Cost • Individual job performance	• Sales volume • Sales expense • Advertising expenditures • Sales person's performance	• Labour relations • Labour turnover • Labour absenteeism	• Capital expenditures • Inventories • Flow of capital • Liquidity

2. **Measurement of Actual Performance** Performance is measured in an objective and reliable manner using techniques like personal observation, performance reports, etc. It's best to measure performance in the same units in which standards are set, for easy comparison.
3. **Comparing Actual Performance with Standards** This step involves comparing actual results with set standards to identify deviations. Quantitative standards make comparison easier and help in spotting significant deviations.
4. **Analysing Deviations** Deviations in key areas of business need to be attended on urgent basis as compared to deviations in insignificant areas. There is a need to determine the acceptable range of deviations in all operational areas. Techniques like critical point control and management by exception help in analysing deviations.
   (i) **Critical Point Control** Control system should first focus on Key Result Areas (KRAs) critical to the organisation's success. It is because, it is neither economical nor easy to keep a check on all the activities of the enterprise. Thus, monitoring KRA's prevents major issues, as problems here can severely impact the entire organisation.
   (ii) **Management by Exception** It is based on the belief that, if manager tries to control everything, he may end up in controlling nothing. Thus, control efforts should target only significant deviations that exceed set limits. This approach ensures management attention is directed where it is most needed, avoiding unnecessary focus on minor issues.
5. **Taking Corrective Action** If deviations exceed acceptable limits, corrective measures are taken. This might involve employee training, resource allocation or sometimes revising standards, if necessary.

Advantages of Critical Point Control and Management by Exception

- It saves the time and efforts of managers as they deal with only significant deviations.
- It focuses managerial attention on important areas. Thus, there is better utilisation of managerial talent.
- The routine problems are left to the subordinates. Management by exception, thus, facilitates delegation of authority and increases morale of the employees.
- It identifies critical problems which need timely action to keep the organisation in right track.

Mind Map

CONTROLLING

1 Concept of Controlling

Controlling refers to the process of comparing the actual performance with the standards, measuring deviations and taking corrective action to achieve pre-determined goals.

2 Features of Controlling

- Controlling ensures that organisation's resources are utilised for achievement of goals
- Controlling is pervasive, i.e. performed by all managers at all levels
- Controlling is a continuous function
- Controlling is both backward-looking as well as forward-looking function

3 Importance of Controlling

- **Accomplishing Organisational Goals** Measures progress towards organisational goals
- **Judging Accuracy of Standards** Careful check on changes and revision of standards
- **Making Efficient Use of Resources** Reduces wastage and spoilage of resources
- **Improving Employee Motivation** Helps in making employees realise about their potential and standards
- **Ensuring Order and Discipline** Keeps a check on all the activities
- **Facilitating Coordination in Action** Provides direction to all activities and efforts

4 Limitations of Controlling

- **Difficulty in Setting Quantitative Standards** Leads to absence of standard which makes comparison and measurement difficult
- **Little Control on External Factors** Controlling the factors, which are beyond the control, is difficult
- **Resistance from Employees** Employees resist control as they consider it as restriction
- **Costly Affair** Lot of expenditure, time and effort is required

5 Relationship between Planning and Controlling

- Controlling takes place on the basis of certain standards developed by planning
- Planning without controlling is meaningless
- Planning is prescriptive while controlling is evaluative
- Planning and controlling are forward-looking as well as backward-looking functions

6 Process of Controlling

Step-1

Setting Performance Standards
Standards are the criteria against which actual performance is measured

Step-2

Measurement of Actual Performance
Performance is measured in an objective and reliable manner

Step-3

Comparing Actual Performance with Standards
It involves comparison of actual performance with the established standards

Step-4

Analysing Deviation
Following points should be kept in mind
- **Critical Point Control** Control system should focus on the key result areas
- **Management by Exception** Significant deviations, which go beyond acceptable limit, should be handled

Step-5

Taking Corrective Action
When the deviations go beyond the acceptable range, corrective action is taken

EXAM PATTERN QUESTIONS

Objective Type Questions

Multiple Choice Questions (MCQs)

1. Which of the following function helps in measuring the progress of objectives and guiding the organisation to keep it on the right track so that organisational goals can be achieved?

(a) Planning (b) Staffing
(c) Directing (d) Controlling

2. Controlling is related to

(a) results (b) individuals
(c) things (d) managers

3. An efficient control system is useful for

(a) achieving objectives
(b) boosting the morale of employees
(c) efficient utilisation of resources
(d) All of the above

4. Umang was working as a 'production manager' at 'LG Paper Ltd.' The company had launched new eco-friendly paper straws in the market. He was given a target of producing 5,000 straws a day, by the general manager. Inspite of making the employees work overtime, Umang could not meet the target.

On investigation, it was found that the employees had not received the right training to manufacture these eco-friendly paper straws. So the employees were sent for special training. The function of management which helped Umang in identifying that he could not meet the target is **CBSE 2023; Competency Based Que**

(a) planning (b) organising
(c) directing (d) controlling

5. Meenakshi and Bhavya are working in two different organisations. Meenakshi is the principal of a school. Bhavya is working on the post of the production manager of one of the apparel companies. Both of them are performing the controlling function of management in their respective organisations in the similar manner.

In order to do this work successfully, they often take the advice of each other. To which feature of the controlling function of management is the above paragraph related? **Competency Based Que**

(a) Controlling is a fundamental function of management
(b) Controlling is a goal-oriented function
(c) Controlling is a pervasive function
(d) None of the above

6. Aman started a handcrafted jewellery business from home. His sister, who has a talent for designing, decided to assist him. Initially, they relied on social media to promote their products and gradually built a customer base through online platforms. To ensure that their business grows and meets customer expectations, Aman decided to set specific targets related to the quality of products, timely delivery and customer satisfaction.

He regularly monitors the progress and makes necessary adjustments to achieve these goals. The function of management being discussed in the above scenario is crucial for the success of Aman's business. An important characteristic of this function of management is **Competency Based Que**

(a) it is the first function of management
(b) it is the last function of management
(c) it is both forward-looking and backward-looking
(d) it is required only in manufacturing organisations

7. Which of the following statements is incorrect?

(a) A control system is effective only when it is flexible and adaptable to changes
(b) Controlling is irrelevant in small organisations and only important in large organisations
(c) Controlling helps in minimising errors by comparing actual performance with standards
(d) Controlling ensures that all activities conform to the plans laid down

8. Which of the following statements is incorrect?

(a) Controlling guides the organisation to keep everything on right track
(b) An accurate control system revises standards from time-to-time to match them with environmental changes
(c) The controlling function is performed only by top level management
(d) Controlling improves future planning by providing information derived from the past experience

9. **Mr. Tushar Goyal looks after the sale and production, both the departments of his own firm. At the beginning of the year, he determined the standards of both the departments. For the sale department, he fixed the objective of sale of 5,00,000 units. At the time of fixing this objective, he noticed that the normal production capacity of the production department was of 4,00,000 units.**

After making a deep study, it was decided that 1,00,000 units of goods would be purchased from the market. In this way, Mr. Goyal established the balance of both the departments. To which of the importance of controlling points, the given case is related? Competency Based Que

(a) Facilitating coordination in action
(b) Ensuring order and discipline
(c) Improving employee motivation
(d) Making efficient use of resources

10. **Bright Technologies, an IT company, recently faced challenges in meeting its targets. To address this, management introduced a control system to monitor activities, set clear standards and correct deviations from goals. This system motivated employees by clarifying expectations, reduced resource wastage and maintained order and discipline within the team. As a result, the company improved efficiency and stayed on track to achieve its goals.**

Which of the following reasons best explains why controlling is considered a pivotal function of management in Bright Technologies?

Competency Based Que

(a) It helps in forming teams with specific skills
(b) It allows for setting clear standards and checking deviations from goals
(c) It ensures employees work without any supervision
(d) It reduces the importance of planning

11. **"Controlling helps employees understand what is expected of them and the standards they must meet, which motivates them to perform better." This statement refers to which benefit of controlling?**

(a) Ensuring discipline Competency Based Que
(b) Improving employee motivation
(c) Efficient resource use
(d) Enhancing coordination

12. **Spiceworks, a company providing financial services to its clients is keeping a close check on the employee's activities by using biometric and retina scanning as modes of accessing the office premises, in order to ensure greater security of information in the organisation.** CBSE SQP 2025; Competency Based Que

Choose the correct point of significance of controlling highlighted above.

(a) Controlling helps in achievement of organisational goals
(b) Controlling helps in ensuring order and discipline
(c) Controlling helps in improving employees motivation
(d) Controlling enables optimum utilisation of resources

13. **XYZ Tech Solutions recently introduced a comprehensive quality control system to enhance the standard of their software products. The system includes regular performance evaluations, employee monitoring tools and frequent updates to quality standards. While the management expects this system to improve product quality and overall performance, they have encountered a few challenges.**

Unexpected changes in technology and market demands have made it difficult to maintain control over the quality standards. Which limitation of the controlling function is most evident in the case?

Competency Based Que

(a) Costly affair
(b) Resistance from employees
(c) Lack of flexibility
(d) Little control on external factors

14. **At Elite Manufacturing Ltd., the management decided to implement a new control system to enhance productivity and monitor operations closely. However, the system proved costly due to high installation and operational expenses, which strained the company's budget.**

Many employees also felt restricted by the constant monitoring, resisting the perceived loss of freedom. Furthermore, despite the control measures, external factors like changing government regulations and increasing competition continued to affect the company, limiting the system's effectiveness.

Which of the following is a limitation of controlling observed at Elite Manufacturing Ltd.?

Competency Based Que

(a) Ensures all employees perform efficiently
(b) Complete control over external factors
(c) High operational costs and employee resistance
(d) Enhances the freedom of employees

15. **Global Enterprises recently developed a comprehensive strategic plan for the upcoming year, outlining objectives and standards to achieve them. However, the management understood that without a control system in place, these plans would be ineffective.**

By implementing controlling measures, they could evaluate their progress against the standards set, identify deviations and take corrective actions.

The planning team also used past data to make forecasts, ensuring that both planning and controlling looked at past performance and aimed to improve future results. This interdependency between planning and controlling helped align the company's direction with its goals.

Which of the following statements best describes the relationship between planning and controlling at Global Enterprises? **Competency Based Que**

(a) Controlling is independent of planning and does not require pre-set standards
(b) Planning is prescriptive, while controlling evaluates whether actions meet objectives
(c) Planning and controlling are strictly forward-looking functions
(d) Controlling replaces planning in the management process

16. Cost at 100 per unit is an example of .... standard.

(a) quantitative (b) qualitative
(c) Both (a) and (b) (d) None of these

17. .... standard is associated with production.

(a) Quality (b) Quantity
(c) Quality and quantity (d) Labour

18. The below picture depicts employee turnover. It is associated with which of the following functional area?

Employee Turnover

(a) Quality (b) Production
(c) Human resource management
(d) Marketing

19. Which of the following is not a step in the process of 'controlling' function of management? **CBSE 2023**

(a) Setting performance standards
(b) Assignment of duties
(c) Taking corrective action
(d) Comparing actual performance with standards

20. Esha Sweets is a renowned name for quality sweets since 1948. Rohan, the owner of Esha Sweets, was worried as the sales had declined during the last three months. When he enquired from the sales manager, the sales manager reported that there were some complaints about the quality of sweets. Therefore, Rohan ordered for sample checking of sweets.

Identify the step taken by Rohan that is related to one of the functions of management. **Competency Based Que**

(a) Setting performance standards
(b) Measurement of actual performance
(c) Analysing deviations
(d) Taking corrective action

21. "In the process of controlling, setting performance standards acts as a guidepost for measuring actual performance." Therefore, it is referred to as **Competency Based Que**

(a) a criterion for control
(b) a benchmark function
(c) a performance indicator
(d) None of the above

22. "The principle of management by exception states that a manager should address only significant deviations beyond the acceptable limit."

This means that managers should **Competency Based Que**

(a) control each minor deviation equally
(b) only focus on permissible deviations
(c) give attention to deviations that exceed acceptable levels
(d) ignore all significant deviations

23. Which step of the controlling process is been depicted in the following image?

(a) Measurement of actual performance
(b) Analysing deviations
(c) Comparing actual performance with standards
(d) Setting standards

24. Mr. Ramesh, the manager of XYZ Manufacturing Ltd., regularly reviews the production reports to ensure that the output meets the company's quality standards. He closely examines the reports to assess the performance of the production team.

Identify the step involved in the controlling process being described in the above lines. **Competency Based Que**

(a) Setting of standards
(b) Measurement of actual performance
(c) Taking corrective action
(d) Analysing the deviations

25. Which of the following statements is incorrect?
- (a) Controlling helps in evaluating the performance against the standards set during planning
- (b) Controlling is not concerned with the correction of deviations; it only identifies them
- (c) Effective controlling requires setting both quantitative and qualitative standards
- (d) Controlling is an ongoing process that continues throughout the management cycle

26. In a manufacturing company, the production manager focuses more on a 2% decline in the quality of raw materials supplied than on a 10% increase in labour costs. He believes that maintaining the quality of raw materials is crucial for the final product. Identify the concept being used by the manager.

Competency Based Que

- (a) Management by exception
- (b) Critical point control
- (c) Corrective action
- (d) None of the above

27. Which step of the controlling process is highlighted in the given image?

- (a) Measurement of actual performance
- (b) Analysing deviations
- (c) Comparing actual performance with standards
- (d) Taking corrective action

28. Corrective action is a part of
- (a) planning
- (b) organising
- (c) controlling
- (d) All of the above

Direction *Read the following case study and answer the questions 29 to 32 on the basis of the same*

Mrs. Priya Sharma is the production manager at Star Electronics Ltd. a company specialising in the manufacturing of electronic gadgets. Recently, the company introduced a new assembly line to boost production. However, after a few weeks, Mrs. Sharma noticed that the production targets were consistently not being met and there was an increase in the number of defective products.

To address the issue, Mrs. Sharma decided to implement a detailed control process. She first reviewed the set production standards and compared them with the actual output. During the analysis, she discovered that several workers were taking longer breaks than allowed, which was affecting the overall productivity.

Mrs. Sharma immediately called a meeting with the team supervisors to discuss these discrepancies. She emphasised the importance of adhering to the set standards and instructed the supervisors to monitor break times closely. Additionally, she introduced regular inspections to ensure that the production process was followed correctly and that any issues could be identified and addressed promptly.

As a result of these control measures, the production quality improved and the targets were met consistently in the subsequent weeks. The management recognised Mrs. Sharma's effective use of the controlling function in addressing the issues and maintaining high production standards.

29. Which step in the controlling process did Mrs. Sharma perform by comparing the actual output with the set production standards?
- (a) Setting performance standards
- (b) Measuring actual performance
- (c) Analysing deviations
- (d) Taking corrective action

30. When Mrs. Sharma found that workers were taking longer breaks than allowed, which step should be taken after receiving this report from the supervisors?
- (a) Identify various alternatives
- (b) Setting-up standards
- (c) Taking corrective measures
- (d) Follow-up

31. Which final step in the controlling process did Mrs. Sharma execute by instructing supervisors to closely monitor break times and take necessary actions?
- (a) Setting objectives
- (b) Measuring performance
- (c) Analysing deviations
- (d) Taking corrective action

32. What role did Mrs. Sharma's meeting with the team supervisors play in the controlling process?
- (a) To set new performance standards for the team
- (b) To analyse performance feedback and identify deviations
- (c) To emphasise corrective actions needed to meet standards
- (d) To establish new inspection processes for production

Assertion-Reason

Direction (Q.No. 33 to 41) *Read the following Assertion (A) and Reason (R) and choose the correct alternative from the following*

Alternatives

(a) Both Assertion (A) and Reason (R) are true and Reason (R) is the correct explanation of Assertion (A)
(b) Both Assertion (A) and Reason (R) are true, but Reason (R) is not the correct explanation of Assertion (A)
(c) Assertion (A) is true, but Reason (R) is false
(d) Assertion (A) is false, but Reason (R) is true

33. **Assertion** (A) Controlling takes place at all levels of management.
Reason (R) Controlling is a pervasive function.

34. **Assertion** (A) Controlling helps in ensuring that there is effective and efficient utilisation of resources to achieve pre-determined goals.
Reason (R) Controlling is both a backward-looking as well as forward-looking function.

35. **Assertion** (A) Controlling ensures that resources are used in the most effective and efficient manner.
Reason (R) In controlling, each activity is performed in accordance with pre-determined standards and norms to reduce wastage and spoilage of resources.

36. **Assertion** (A) Controlling should not be misunderstood as the last function of management.
Reason (R) It is a function that brings back the management cycle to the planning function.

37. **Assertion** (A) Planning is considered a pre-requisite for controlling.
Reason (R) Planning provides standards against which actual performance is compared under controlling.

38. **Assertion** (A) Controlling is regarded as goal oriented process.
Reason (R) Controlling ensures that an organisation's resources are effectively and efficiently utilised for achievement of goal.

39. **Assertion** (A) Only significant deviations should be brought to the notice of management.
Reason (R) An attempt to control everything results in controlling nothing.

40. **Assertion** (A) Critical point control system should first focus on key result areas.
Reason (R) It is not possible to keep a check on all the activities of the enterprise.

41. **Assertion** (A) Controlling can prevent deviations.
Reason (R) Controlling helps in minimising deviations by taking actions and decisions that reduce their recurrence. **CBSE SQP 2025**

Two Statements Based MCQs

Direction (Q.No. 42 to 49) *Read the following statements carefully and choose the correct alternative*

Alternatives

(a) Statement I is correct and Statement II is incorrect
(b) Statement II is correct and Statement I is incorrect
(c) Both the statements are correct
(d) Both the statements are incorrect

42. **Statement I** Controlling is required in both business and non-business organisations.
Statement II When there is no plan, there is no basis of controlling.

43. **Statement I** Controlling ensures that activities conform to the plans.
Statement II Controlling focuses only on the current period and does not influence future planning.

44. **Statement I** Controlling involves setting standards, measuring performance and taking corrective actions.
Statement II Controlling is only necessary when deviations from standards are significant.

45. **Statement I** Planning is considered as prescriptive while controlling is considered as evaluative.
Statement II Third step of controlling process involves comparison of actual performance with the standards.

46. **Statement I** Critical point control focuses on key areas where deviations from standards will lead to significant impact.
Statement II Critical point control involves monitoring every activity within the organisation equally.

47. **Statement I** Corrective action is taken after comparing actual performance with standards in controlling.
Statement II Controlling is unrelated to the other management functions.

48. **Statement I** Deviations in key areas of business need to be attended more urgently as compared to deviations in certain insignificant areas.
Statement II Deviation can be positive, when actual performance is better than the standard performance.

49. **Statement I** Management by exception facilitates delegation of authority and increases the morale of the employees.
Statement II It saves the time and effort of managers as they deal with only significant deviations.

Matching

50. Match the following

Column I	Column II
A. Prescriptive	(i) Pervasive function
B. Evaluative	(ii) Judging accuracy of standards
C. Feature of controlling	(iii) Planning
D. Importance of controlling	(iv) Controlling

Codes

	A	B	C	D		A	B	C	D
(a)	(i)	(ii)	(iii)	(iv)	(b)	(ii)	(iii)	(iv)	(i)
(c)	(iii)	(iv)	(i)	(ii)	(d)	(iv)	(iii)	(ii)	(i)

51. Match the following

Column I	Column II
A. Measuring actual performance	(i) Only significant deviations which go beyond the permissible limit should be brought to the notice of management.
B. Setting performance standards	(ii) Comparison reveals the deviation between actual and desired results.
C. Management by exception	(iii) Performance should be measured in the same units in which standards are set.
D. Comparison of actual performance with standards	(iv) Standards can be set in both quantitative as well as qualitative terms.

Codes

	A	B	C	D		A	B	C	D
(a)	(ii)	(i)	(iii)	(iv)	(b)	(i)	(iii)	(iv)	(ii)
(c)	(iii)	(iv)	(i)	(ii)	(d)	(iv)	(iii)	(ii)	(i)

52. Match the following

Column I	Column II
A. Sales volume	(i) Production
B. Labour relations	(ii) Marketing
C. Flow of capital	(iii) Human resource management
D. Cost	(iv) Finance and accounting

Codes

	A	B	C	D		A	B	C	D
(a)	(i)	(iii)	(ii)	(iv)	(b)	(ii)	(iii)	(iv)	(i)
(c)	(iii)	(iv)	(i)	(ii)	(d)	(iv)	(ii)	(iii)	(i)

53. Match the following

Column I	Column II
A. Critical point control	(i) Unrealistic standards and defective process may be the reason for occurrence of deviations.
B. Taking corrective action	(ii) Control system should focus on key result areas.
C. Analysing deviations	(iii) If deviation cannot be corrected through managerial action, the standards may have to be revised.
D. Management by exception	(iv) Manager should give attention to significant deviations, which go beyond the permissible limit.

Codes

	A	B	C	D
(a)	(ii)	(iii)	(i)	(iv)
(b)	(ii)	(iii)	(iv)	(i)
(c)	(iii)	(iv)	(i)	(ii)
(d)	(iv)	(iii)	(ii)	(i)

Answers

1. (d) Controlling **2.** (a) results
3. (d) All of the above **4.** (d) controlling
5. (c) Controlling is a pervasive function
6. (c) it is both forward-looking and backward-looking
7. (b) Controlling is relevant and important in organisations of all sizes.
8. (c) It is performed by all levels of management.
9. (a) Facilitating coordination in action
10. (b) It allows for setting clear standards and checking deviations from goals
11. (b) Controlling improves employee motivation by clearly setting performance expectations.
12. (b) Controlling helps in ensuring order and discipline
13. (d) Little control on external factors
14. (c) High operational costs and employee resistance
15. (b) Planning is prescriptive, while controlling evaluates whether actions meet objectives
16. (a) quantitative **17.** (c) Quality and quantity
18. (c) Human resource management
19. (b) Assignment of duties

20. (b) Measurement of actual performance
21. (b) a benchmark function
22. (c) give attention to deviations that exceed acceptable levels
23. (c) Comparing actual performance with standards
24. (b) Measurement of actual performance
25. (b) Controlling is concerned with both identifying and correcting deviations.
26. (b) Critical point control
27. (d) Taking corrective action
28. (c) controlling
29. (c) Analysing deviations
30. (c) Taking corrective measures
31. (d) Taking corrective action
32. (c) To emphasise corrective actions needed to meet standards
33. (a) Both Assertion (A) and Reason (R) are true and Reason (R) is the correct explanation of Assertion (A)
34. (b) Both Assertion (A) and Reason (R) are true, but Reason (R) is not the correct explanation of Assertion (A)
35. (a) Both Assertion (A) and Reason (R) are true and Reason (R) is the correct explanation of Assertion (A)
36. (a) Both Assertion (A) and Reason (R) are true and Reason (R) is the correct explanation of Assertion (A)
37. (a) Both Assertion (A) and Reason (R) are true and Reason (R) is the correct explanation of Assertion (A)
38. (a) Both Assertion (A) and Reason (R) are true and Reason (R) is the correct explanation of Assertion (A)
39. (a) Both Assertion (A) and Reason (R) are true and Reason (R) is the correct explanation of Assertion (A)
40. (a) Both Assertion (A) and Reason (R) are true and Reason (R) is the correct explanation of Assertion (A)
41. (d) Assertion (A) is false, but Reason (R) is true
42. (c) Both the statements are correct
43. (a) Controlling ensures that activities conform to the plans, but it also influences future planning by identifying deviations and areas for improvement.
44. (a) Controlling is necessary even for minor deviations, not just significant ones.
45. (c) Both the statements are correct
46. (a) Critical point control focuses on key areas that have the most significant impact on organisational goals, not on monitoring every activity equally.
47. (a) Controlling is closely related to other management functions like planning, organising and directing.
48. (c) Both the statements are correct
49. (c) Both the statements are correct
50. (c) (iii) (iv) (i) (ii)
51. (c) (iii) (iv) (i) (ii)
52. (b) (ii) (iii) (iv) (i)
53. (a) (ii) (iii) (i) (iv)

Subjective Questions

Short Answer Type Questions

1. Identify and state the function which helps in ensuring that actual performance is as per the established standards.

Ans. Controlling is the function that helps in ensuring that actual performance is as per the established standards. Controlling refers to the process of measurement of actual performance against the standards, measuring deviations and taking corrective action to achieve pre-determined goals. In order to seek planned results, manager must exercise effective control over the activities of subordinates. Controlling means ensuring that activities in an organisation are performed as per the plans.

2. Which function of management ensures a manager that activities in an organisation are performed as per plans? Name and state some points of its importance.

Or

Explain any four points of importance of 'controlling' function of management. CBSE 2024 C

Ans. Controlling ensures that the activities in an organisation are performed as per plans.

Importance of controlling can be highlighted by the following points

(i) It helps in achieving the organisational goals.
(ii) It helps in judging the accuracy of standards.
(iii) It facilitates efficient use of resources.
(iv) It provides direction to all activities and thus, it facilitates coordination.

3. "Planning is looking ahead and controlling is looking back." Comment. NCERT; Competency Based Que

Or **Explain how planning and controlling are both backward-looking, as well as forward looking functions.** CBSE SQP 2025

Ans. Planning involves setting objectives and deciding the future course of action to achieve them. Thus, it is regarded as forward-looking. Controlling involves a post-mortem of the past activities of an enterprise and finding out deviations from the targeted standard. Thus, it is regarded as a backward-looking function.

However, planning is guided by past experiences and the corrective action initiated by the control function aims to improve future performance. Thus, planning and controlling are both backward-looking as well as forward-looking function.

4. "Controlling takes place at all levels of management." Explain. **Competency Based Que**

Ans. Controlling is performed by all managers, i.e. top, middle and lower, to keep a check on the activities of their subordinates. It is equally required in a business as well as non-business organisations such as a hospital, a club, an educational institution, etc.

5. "While controlling is crucial for guiding an organisation towards its goals, it is not without its challenges. One significant limitation lies is the difficulty of setting quantitative standards." Explain.

Ans. Difficulty in Setting Quantitative Standards
Control system is effective when standards are defined in quantitative terms.

But in some cases, like employee morale, job satisfaction, etc. it is not possible to set quantitative standards. In the absence of these standards, measurement and comparison becomes difficult.

6. Explain the following as steps in the process of controlling **CBSE 2023**
(i) Setting performance standards
(ii) Measurement of actual performance

Ans.

(i) **Setting Performance Standards**
The first step in the controlling process is setting-up of performance standards. Standards are the criteria against which actual performance would be measured.

Thus, standards serve as benchmarks towards which an organisation strives to work. Standards can be set in both quantitative as well as qualitative terms.

(ii) **Measurement of Actual Performance**
Once performance standards are set, the next step is measurement of actual performance. Performance should be measured in an objective and reliable manner. There are several techniques for measurement of performance.

These include personal observation, sample checking, performance reports, etc.

As far as possible, performance should be measured in the same units in which standards are set as this would make their comparison easier.

7. The first step in the controlling process is setting up performance standards. Explain the subsequent two steps in the process of controlling. **CBSE SQP 2025**

Ans. Subsequent two steps of controlling process are

(i) **Measurement of Actual Performance**
Refer to Q.No. 6 of short answer type questions.

(ii) **Comparing Actual Performance with Standards**
This step involves comparison of actual performance with the standard. Such comparison will reveal the deviation between actual and desired results.
Comparison becomes easier when standards are set in quantitative terms.

8. What are the various standards that are used in different functional areas?

Ans. Standards that are used in different functional areas are as follows

Functional Areas	Standards Used
Production	Quality, quantity, cost, individual job
Marketing	Sales volume, sales expenses, salesperson's performance, advertising expenditures
Human resource	Labour relations, labour turnover rate, absenteeism rate
Finance and accounting	Capital expenditure, flow of capital, liquidity, inventories

9. Critical point control is beneficial in a variety of ways. Explain. **Competency Based Que**

Ans. Critical point control is beneficial because of the following reasons

(i) It saves time and effort of the managers as they deal with significant deviations only.
(ii) There is better utilisation of managerial talent.
(iii) It facilitates delegation of authority and increases employees morale, when routine problems are left to the subordinates.
(iv) Timely action helps to keep the organisation on the right track.

10. Explain how 'management by exception' is useful in the controlling process. Justify with an example.

Or **"An effort to control everything may end up in controlling nothing." Explain.**

NCERT; Competency Based Que

Ans. Management by execption is an important principle of management. Control is based on the belief that an attempt to control everything results in controlling nothing.

Thus, only significant deviations which go beyond the permissible limit should be brought to the notice of management. e.g. If an organisation presupposes that there will be 2% defective product in the whole production then corrective action will be taken only when defective production will be more than 2%.

11. **Explain how 'critical point control' plays an important role in the controlling process. Justify with an example.**

Ans. According to the principle of critical point control, control should focus on Key Result Areas (KRAs), which are critical to the success of the organisation. When anything goes wrong in these areas, the entire organisation suffers. e.g. A 5% increase in the labour cost is much more harmful than a 20% increase in postal charges.

Long Answer Type Questions

12. **"Controlling is often considered as the backbone of effective management." Explain why controlling is considered to be a pivotal function of management.**

Competency Based Que

Ans. Controlling is considered to be a pivotal function of management because of the following reasons

(i) **Accomplishing Organisational Goals**
It measures progress towards the organisational goals, find out deviations, if any indicates corrective action. In the absence of control system, activities may not be carried out according to plans.

Thus, we can say, it guides the organisation and keeps it on the right track, so that it can attain its goals.

(ii) **Judging Accuracy of Standards**
Through an effective control system, managers can judge if the standards set are accurate and objective. It also keeps a careful check on the changes taking place in the organisation and in the environment, which facilitates the revision of standards, in the light of such changes.

(iii) **Making Efficient Use of Resources**
By exercising control, a manager seeks to reduce wastage and spoilage of resources. Each activity is performed in accordance with predetermined standards and norms, which helps in effective and efficient utilisation of resources.

(iv) **Improving Employee Motivation**
It helps employees in realising well in advance, what they are expected to do and what are the standards of performance, on the basis of which they will be appraised. This motivates them to perform better.

(v) **Ensuring Order and Discipline**
By keeping a check on the activities of the employees, controlling creates an atmosphere of order and discipline among them. It also helps to keep a check on the dishonest behaviour of employees and minimise undesirable activities.

(vi) **Facilitating Coordination in Action**
It provides direction to all activities and efforts for achieving organisational goals. Each department and employee is governed by predetermined standards which are well coordinated with one another. This ensures that overall organisational objectives are accomplished.

13. **Discuss the following limitations of controlling.**
(i) Costly affair
(ii) Resistance from employees
(iii) Little control on external factors

Ans.

(i) **Costly Affair**
Control is a costly affair as it involves a lot of expenditure, time and effort.
A small firm cannot afford to install an expensive control system. Managers must ensure that the costs of installing and operating a control system should not exceed the benefits derived from it.

(ii) **Resistance from Employees**
Employees often resist control as they consider it as restriction or boundation on their freedom.
e.g. Employees might resist working under close supervision of CCTV's and cameras.

(iii) **Little Control on External Factors**
There are certain external factors like change in government policies, technological changes, competition, etc. which are beyond the control of the organisation. Thus, controlling such factors becomes difficult.

14. **"Planning and controlling are considered to be inseparable twins of management." Explain.**

Competency Based Que

Or **Explain the relationship between 'planning' and 'controlling' with the help of any four points.**

CBSE 2024 C

Ans. Following are the reasons that depict why planning and controlling are inseparable twins of management

(i) **Controlling takes Place on the Basis of Certain Standards, Developed by Planning**
The standards of performance which serve as the basis of controlling are provided by planning. Planning is a pre-requisite for controlling.

(ii) **Planning without Controlling is Meaningless**
Once a plan becomes operational, controlling is necessary to monitor the progress, measure it, discover deviations and initiate corrective measures to ensure that events conform to plans. Thus, planning without controlling is meaningless.

(iii) **Planning is Prescriptive, whereas Controlling is Evaluative**
Planning is basically an intellectual process involving thinking, articulation and analysis to discover and prescribe an appropriate course of action for achieving objectives.

Controlling, on the other hand, checks whether decisions have been translated into desired action. Thus, controlling is evaluative.

(iv) **Planning and Controlling are Forward-looking as well as Backward-looking Functions**

It is often said that planning is looking ahead while controlling is looking back. However, the statement is only partially correct. Following points will help to understand this better

- Planning involves setting objectives and deciding the course of action based on forecasts about future conditions. Thus, it is regarded as a forward-looking function.
- Controlling involves a post-mortem of the past activities of an enterprise and finding out deviations from the targeted standard. Thus, it is regarded as a backward-looking function.
- Planning is guided by past experiences and corrective actions taken in the controlling process. Thus, it is regarded as a backward-looking function.
- The process of control necessarily involves analysing deviations and taking corrective action, which aims to improve future performance and achieve pre-determined goals.

Thus, controlling is regarded as a forward-looking function.

15. Bring out a comparison between planning and controlling.

Ans. A comparison of planning and controlling can be done in the following ways

Basis	Planning	Control
Emphasis	It emphasises more on non-personal, abstract and long-range problems.	It emphasises more on personal, concrete and immediate problems.
Premise	It is based on estimates.	It is based on actual facts.
Management Level involved	It is done by top level executives	It is done by operating and lower level executives
Ease of Evaluating Results	Under planning, the evaluation of results is very difficult.	Under control, the results are easily visible and are easily evaluated.
Time	The determination of results takes a very long time.	The determination of results takes comparatively less time.

16. Explain the various steps involved in the process of controlling. **NCERT**

Ans. Following are the steps involved in the process of controlling

(i) **Setting Performance Standards**

The first step in the controlling process is setting up of performance standards.

Standards are the criteria against which actual performance would be measured. Thus, standards serve as benchmarks towards which an organisation strives to work. Standards can be set in both quantitative as well as qualitative terms.

(ii) **Measurement of Actual Performance**

Once performance standards are set, the next step is measurement of actual performance.

Performance should be measured in an objective and reliable manner. There are several techniques for measurement of performance. These include personal observation, sample checking, performance reports, etc.

As far as possible, performance should be measured in the same units in which standards are set as this would make their comparison easier.

(iii) **Comparing Actual Performance with Standards**

This step involves comparison of actual performance with the standard. Such comparison will reveal the deviation between actual and desired results. Comparison becomes easier when standards are set in quantitative terms.

(iv) **Analysing Deviations**

Some deviation in performance can be expected in all activities. It is, therefore, important to determine the acceptable range of deviations. Also, deviations in key areas of business need to be attended more urgently as compared to deviations in certain insignificant areas.

(v) **Taking Corrective Action**

This is the final step in the controlling process. No corrective action is required when the deviations are within acceptable limits. However, when the deviations go beyond the acceptable range, especially in the important areas, it demands immediate managerial attention so that deviations do not occur again and standards are accomplished. Corrective action may involve training of employees, hiring labour for extra time, replacement of machinery, etc. Sometimes, if deviations cannot be corrected despite the best efforts of managers, standards may have to be revised.

Case Study Based Questions

Short Case Studies

Case Study 1

John is a sole proprietor in Assam. He started trade after getting MBA degree. He is fully familiar with all the functions of management. He starts his business with the planning function of management. He desires that all his activities should conform to planning. To this effect, he has adopted a system that keeps a constant watch on all activities of the business.

Consequently, there is zero possibility of adverse results. It can, therefore, be said that this method is directly related to the results. Mr. John also believes that this method applies not only to any one level of management but to all the levels as well.

(i) Identify the function of management referred to in the aforesaid paragraph.

(ii) Describe the above mentioned two features of the function of management as identified under point (i) above.

Ans.

(i) The function of management referred to in the paragraph is controlling.

(ii) Two features of controlling are as follows

- **Goal-oriented**
  Controlling keeps a close watch on the work-in-progress and constantly works towards the accomplishment of organisational goals.
- **Pervasive Function**
  Controlling is performed by all managers, i.e. top, middle and lower, to keep a check on the activities of their subordinates. It is equally required in a business as well as non- business organisations such as hospital, a club, an educational institution, etc.

Case Study 2

Suresh is trying to reduce wastage of resources in his company. He is trying to do it in the best possible manner. He has set standards for performance of different types of activities and is doing his level best to perform according to these set standards to minimise wastage of resources. Things are not going to be over for him as he will have to look into other aspects too.

He has set up a good monitoring system which helps him know how to employees are performing according to set standards as when the employees meet these standards they will be given incentives. He is hoping to pull out a good performance from his team this year.

(i) Which function of management has been referred to in the above case?

(ii) Which benefits of this function of management have been highlighted in the above case?

Ans.

(i) The function of management which has been referred to in the above case is controlling.

(ii) The benefits of controlling highlighted in the above case are

- **Controlling helps in Efficient Utilisation of Resources**
  By exercising control, a manager seeks to reduce wastage and spoilage of resources. Each activity is performed in accordance with pre-determined standards and norms, which helps in effective and efficient utilisation of resources.
- **Controlling helps in Improving Employee Motivation**
  It helps employees in realising well in advance, what they are expected to do and what are the standards of performance, on the basis of which they will be appraised. This motivates them to perform better.

Case Study 3

Saurabh is working in an MNC. He has created an atmosphere of proper controlling in his department. In order to do so, he keeps himself aware about any dishonest behaviour and takes a stern action immediately.

Recently he has installed CCTV cameras to keep vigil on the employees.

(i) In the above case, which importance of controlling has been implemented by Saurabh? State.

(ii) Name and explain one more importance of controlling other than the above highlighted.

Ans.

(i) The importance of controlling implemented in the above case by Saurabh is 'controlling ensures proper order and discipline' in the organisation.

By keeping a check on the activities of the employees, controlling creates an atmosphere of order and discipline among them. It also helps to keep a check on the dishonest behaviour of employees and minimise undesirable activities.

(ii) One more importance of controlling is that it helps in making efficient use of resources. By exercising control, a manager seeks to reduce wastage and spoilage of resources. Each activity is performed in accordance with pre-determined standards and norms, which helps in effective and efficient utilisation of resources.

Case Study 4

ABC Electronics Ltd. is a leading manufacturer of consumer electronics, known for its innovative products and efficient operations.

Recently, the company faced a decline in product quality, leading to an increase in customer complaints and returns. To address this issue, the management implemented a new system for regular quality checks and introduced performance metrics for the production team. They also started holding weekly meetings to review progress and ensure adherence to quality standards.

Despite these efforts, the company still faced challenges in meeting its quality targets and maintaining customer satisfaction.

(i) Identify the function of management discussed in the case.

(ii) State any three limitations of the function of management identified in (i).

Ans.

(i) The function of management discussed in the case is controlling.

(ii) Following are the limitations of controlling

- **Costly Affair**
  Control is a costly affair as it involves a lot of expenditure, time and effort. A small firm cannot afford to install an expensive control system. Managers must ensure that the costs of installing and operating a control system should not exceed the benefits derived from it.
- **Resistance from Employees**
  Employees often resist control as they consider it as restriction or boundation on their freedom.
  e.g. Employees might resist working under close supervision of CCTV's and cameras.
- **Little Control on External Factors**
  There are certain external factors like change in government policies, technological changes, competition, etc. which are beyond the control of the organisation. Thus, controlling such factors becomes difficult.

Case Study 5

Identify and state the step of controlling process applicable in the following cases

(i) Reena is keenly observing the quantity of capsules produced in a pharmaceutical company. She realises that there is no need for any action to be taken as the deviations are within the acceptable limits.

A day later when she comes to work she finds the situation opposite to that of the previous day. This lime the deviation was beyond the acceptable range and needed immediate action. She called her subordinates and told them that this should not happen again.

(ii) Ramesh who is the owner of a company has decided to focus only on a few activities of his business. He considers that the rest of all activities are not critical to the performance of his company. One such area he finds is of labour.

The labour cost recently went up by 4% sending signals of coming danger. Now he will put his efforts to control this variation by arranging labour at a cheaper rate.

Ans. Different steps in the controlling process are applicable as follows

(i) **Taking Corrective Action**
It is the step referred to in the case. This is the final step in the controlling process. No corrective action is required when the deviations are within acceptable limits. However, when the deviations go beyond the acceptable range, especially in the important areas, it demands immediate managerial attention so that deviations do not occur again and standards are accomplished.

(ii) **Analysing Deviations**
It is the step referred to in the case. Some deviation in performance can be expected in all activities. It is, therefore, important to determine the acceptable range of deviations. Also, deviations in key areas of business need to be attended more urgently as compared to deviations in certain insignificant areas.

Case Study 6

AS Ltd. is a large company engaged in assembly of air-conditioners. Recently the company had conducted the 'time' and 'motion' study and concluded that on an average a worker can assemble ten air-conditioners in a day. The target volume of the company in a day is assembling of 1,000 units of air-conditioners.

The company is providing attractive allowances to reduce labour turnover and absenteeism. All the workers are happy. Even then the assembly of air-conditioners per day is 800 units only. To find out the reason the company compared actual performance of each worker and observed through CCTV that some of the workers were busy in gossiping.

(i) Identify the function of management discussed above.

(ii) State those steps in the process of the function identified which are discussed in the above paragraph.

Ans.

(i) Function of management discussed in the case is controlling.

(ii) Following steps of controlling are identified in the given para

- Setting performance standards which are the criteria against which the actual performance would be measured.

The first step in the controlling process is setting up of performance standards. These, standards serve as benchmarks towards which an organisation strives to work. They can be set in both quantitative as well as qualitative terms.

- Measurement of actual performance with the standards in an objective and reliable manner. Performance should be measured in an objective and reliable manner. There are several techniques for measurement of performance personal observation, sample checking, performance reports, etc. As far as possible, performance should be measured in the same units in which standards are set as this would make their comparison easier.
- Comparing actual performance with standards to find out any deviations. Such comparison will reveal the deviation between actual and desired results. Comparison becomes easier when standards are set in quantitative terms.

Case Study 7

Anmol Pathak, a restaurant owner, observed that over a period of one year, the costs of raw material, transportation and packaging had increased. As a result the total cost had increased by 15%. He thought that it was not easy to keep a check on each and every activity in the organisation, so he decided to study deeply the increase in these three costs. He prepared a table of acceptable and actual increase in cost as given below

S.No.	Expense	Acceptable Increase in Cost	Actual Increase in Cost
1.	Raw Material	4%	7%
2.	Transportation	10%	8%
3.	Packaging	10%	20%

Explain the two concepts related to a function of management that will be used by Anmol Pathak to analyse the deviations. CBSE 2024 C

Ans. Anmol Pathak should follow the following principles of managerial control while analysing deviations

(i) **Critical Point Control**
According to this principle of managerial control a manager should focus on Key Result Areas (KRAs) that are critical to the success of an organisation.

A manager should not waste his precious time on checking each and every activity in the organisation.

He should focus on those areas which are critical to the success of the enterprise.

In the above case, Anmol should focus on improving the methods of packaging and managing raw material.

(ii) **Management by Exception**
As per this principle of managerial control a manager trying to control everything may end up controlling nothing.

Therefore, only significant deviations that go beyond the permissible limit should be brought to the notice of management. In the above case, increase in raw material and packaging cost needs immediate attention.

Case Study 8

Mr. Arfaaz had been heading the production department of Writewell Products Ltd., a firm manufacturing stationary items. The firm secured an export order that had to be completed on a priority basis and production targets were defined for all the employees.

One of the workers, Mr. Bhanu Prasad, fell short of his daily production target by 10 units for two days consecutively.

Mr. Arfaaz approached Ms. Vasundhara, the CEO of the company, to file a complaint against Mr. Bhanu Prasad and requested her to terminate his services. Explain the principle of management control that Ms. Vasundhara should consider while taking her decision. NCERT

Ans. The principle of management control that Ms. Vasundhara should consider while taking her decision is management by exception.

According to this technique, 'an effort to control everything may end up in controlling nothing'. Thus, only significant deviations which are beyond the permissible limit should be acknowledged. In this case, Mr. Bhanu had fallen short of only 10 units, thus, he should not be terminated for such a small deviation.

Case Study 9

You are the production manager of a garment manufacturing company. It has been reported that there is a 15% increase in electricity costs and a 3% increase in the cost of fabric. Which of the two deviations is more critical to you? Provide a reason for your answer.

Ans. A 3% increase in the cost of fabric is more critical, as this affects the Key Result Areas (KRAs) of the company. The cost of fabric is a major component in the production process and even a small increase can significantly impact the overall cost of goods sold, thereby affecting profitability. On the other hand, a 15% increase in electricity costs, though substantial, may not have as direct or significant an impact on profitability as the cost of fabric.

Long Case Studies

Case Study 10

Arjun and Meera started a tech company called 'Innovate Solutions' with the goal of providing cutting-edge software solutions to businesses. They were passionate about delivering high-quality, customised software that would help businesses optimise their operations.

However, as the company grew, they faced challenges in maintaining the consistency of their software's performance across different projects.

To address this issue, Arjun and Meera implemented a comprehensive monitoring system that tracked the progress of each software project from the initial coding phase to final deployment. This system included regular performance reviews and testing to ensure that every aspect of the software met the company's high standards.

They also set clear performance metrics and goals for their development teams, ensuring that every project aligned with the company's overall objectives. Regular team meetings were held to discuss progress, address any issues and make necessary adjustments. This ongoing process allowed them to continuously improve their software and stay competitive in the market.

As a result of their diligent efforts, Innovate Solutions quickly became known for its reliable and efficient software solutions.

The company's ability to consistently meet client expectations led to numerous contracts with top-tier businesses, significantly boosting their growth. Quoting lines from the above paragraph, identify and explain the three features of controlling discussed in the above case.

Ans. Following are the three features of controlling discussed in the above case

(i) **Pervasive**

"Arjun and Meera implemented a comprehensive monitoring system that tracked the progress of each software project from the initial coding phase to final deployment." Controlling is performed by all managers, i.e. top, middle and lower, to keep a check on the activities of their subordinates.

It is equally required in a business as well as a non-business organisations such as a hospital, a club, an educational institution, etc.

(ii) **Continuous**

"Regular team meetings were held to discuss progress, address any issues and make necessary adjustments." Controlling is an ongoing process as it involves a constant assessment and evaluation of the progress of current tasks and activities as against the set standards.

(iii) **Goal-oriented**

"They also set clear performance metrics and goals for their development teams, ensuring that every project aligned with the company's overall objectives."

Controlling keeps a close watch on the work-in-progress and constantly works towards the accomplishment of organisational goals.

Case Study 11

Asha was running a business of producing and selling pickles, murabbas and papad, etc. She was earning a good profit for the last many years. Now, she wanted to add some new products in her product line. Seeing the growing demand of millets, she decided to add some millet products. After doing a lot of market research, she found out that the demand for millet noodles, pasta and ready to eat millet cereals was increasing day-by-day.

To give a different taste and to have uniqueness in her products, she prepared a new tasty herb based sauce for cooking these products and decided to launch this along with millet products in the market. For this Asha hired 10 additional women workers specially trained for the same. However, despite adding more workers, to her surprise, production was not upto the mark. Concerned about this and to ensure that the activities were performed as per the plans and that the resources were being used effectively and efficiently for the achievement of predetermined goals, Asha appointed a supervisor Nabita. Nabita monitored the activities and discovered that two of the newly hired workers were spending their whole day gossiping and distracting the other workers. As a result the production was low. **CBSE 2025**

(i) Identify and state the function of management discussed above.

(ii) State any five points of importance of the function identified in (i) above.

Ans.

(i) The function of management discussed above is controlling. Controlling refers to the process of comparing the actual performance with the standards, measuring deviations and taking corrective action to achieve predetermined goals.

(ii) Following are the five points of importance of controlling

- **Accomplishing Organisational Goals**
  It measures progress towards the organisational goals, find out deviations, if any indicates corrective action. In the absence of control system, activities may not be carried out according to plans. Thus, we can say, it guides the organisation and keeps it on the right track, so that it can attain its goals.

- **Judging Accuracy of Standards**
Through an effective control system, managers can judge if the standards set are accurate and objective. It also keeps a careful check on the changes taking place in the organisation and in the environment, which facilitates the revision of standards, in the light of such changes.
- **Making Efficient Use of Resources**
By exercising control, a manager seeks to reduce wastage and spoilage of resources. Each activity is performed in accordance with predetermined standards and norms, which helps in effective and efficient utilisation of resources.
- **Improving Employee Motivation**
It helps employees in realising well in advance, what they are expected to do and what are the standards of performance, on the basis of which they will be appraised. This motivates them to perform better.
- **Ensuring Order and Discipline**
By keeping a check on the activities of the employees, controlling creates an atmosphere of order and discipline among them. It also helps to keep a check on the dishonest behaviour of employees and minimise undesirable activities.

Case Study 12

Mohan and Rohan are managers in the same organisation having different units. While discussing about the function of management, Mohan says "Planning is looking ahead whereas controlling is looking back." But Rohan says, "Planning is looking back whereas controlling is looking ahead."

Both are giving reasons in favour of their statements. Explain the possible reasons given by both and justify who is correct.

Ans. In the given case, both Mohan and Rohan are partially correct as planning and controlling both are forward as well as backward-looking functions.

(i) **Planning is a Forward-looking Function**
Planning involves setting objectives and deciding the future course of action to achieve them. Thus, it is regarded as a forward-looking function.

(ii) **Controlling is a Backward-looking Function**
Controlling involves a post-mortem of the past activities of an enterprise and finding out deviations from the targeted standard. Thus, it is regarded as a backward-looking function.

(iii) **Planning is a Backward-looking Function**
Planning is guided by past experiences and corrective actions taken in the controlling process. Thus, it is regarded as a backward-looking function.

(iv) **Controlling is a Forward-looking Function**
The process of control necessarily involves analysing deviations and taking corrective action, which aims to improve future performance and achievement of pre-determined goals. Thus, it is regarded as a forward-looking function.

Case Study 13

A company M Ltd. is manufacturing mobile phones both for domestic Indian market as well as for export. It had enjoyed a substantial market share and also had a loyal customer following.

But lately, it has been experiencing problems because its targets have not been met with regard to sales and customer satisfaction.

Also, mobile market in India has grown tremendously and new players have come with better technology and pricing. This is causing problems for the company. It is planning to revamp its controlling system and take other steps necessary to rectify the problems it is facing. **NCERT**

(i) Identify the benefits that the company will derive from a good control system.

(ii) How can the company relate its planning with control in this line of business to ensure that its plans are actually implemented and targets attained?

(iii) Give the steps in the control process that the company should follow to remove the problems it is facing.

Ans.

(i) When company starts following a good control on operations, it leads to certain benefits which are

- It helps in achieving desired goals.
- It helps in judging accuracy of operations and standards.
- It helps in making efficient and effective use of resources.
- It helps in improving employees morale.
- It helps in ensuring proper flow of orders and that the whole system is in discipline.
- It facilitates coordination and improves the performance of every individual.

(ii) Company relates its planning with control in this line of business by implementing effective control system. This will help in two aspects; planning makes controlling effective and efficient, whereas, controlling improves future planning because it is like a post-mortem of past activities to find out deviations from the standards and in order to ensure that its plans are actually implemented and targets are attained. They will take the help from controlling process as it is a systematic process and it leads to various benefits.

(iii) The company should follow these steps in a systematic manner
- Setting performance standards.
- Measurement of actual performance.
- Comparing actual performance with standards.
- Analysing deviations. • Taking corrective action.

Case Study 14

Amrita Textiles Limited is a company manufacturing plastic materials. Mr. Raj is the marketing manager and Mr. Rohan is the production manager. Both the managers have different working styles. Mr. Raj sets easy standards that can be achieved comfortably. Mr. Rohan sets difficult standards.

The marketing department was able to achieve the targets easily. Mr. Raj and his team were happy with the results. Mr. Rohan was far behind the targets. He and his team are disappointed.

(i) Which step of controlling process has been discussed in the above paragraph?

(ii) In your opinion, both the managers would have set standards for which activities, of their respective departments? Write two standards for each.

(iii) Of the two managers, one set easily achievable standards whereas the other set such standards as could be achieved with great difficulty. In your opinion, how the employees would be affected?

(iv) Mention in one word, what should be the type of standards?

Ans.

(i) The first step of the controlling process i.e. setting of performance standards, has been discussed. Standards are the criteria against which actual performance would be measured. Thus, standards serve as benchmarks towards which an organisation strives to work. Standards can be set in both quantitative as well as qualitative terms.

(ii) Main standards of marketing department
- Sales volume • Sales expenses

Main standards of production department
- Quality • Quantity

(iii) When standards are too easy, employees may lack motivation and become complacent, as they do not feel challenged. Conversely, setting overly difficult standards can lead to stress, disappointment and frustration if employees consistently fall short of expectations, potentially lowering morale and productivity.

(iv) The type of standards should be reasonable.

Case Study 15

Ananya and Rajat decided to open a bakery named 'Sweet Crumbs' in their hometown, offering a variety of gourmet cakes and pastries. They focused on using high-quality ingredients and ensuring every product was freshly baked. Initially, they had trouble managing the consistency of their products, as sometimes the cakes were either too dry or too moist. Recognising this issue, they realised the need for better control over their baking process. To address this, they established a system where the exact recipe and baking time were documented and strictly followed. Rajat, being the head baker, regularly monitored the baking process to ensure each batch met the desired quality standards. He checked the temperature, ingredients and mixing time to make sure everything was according to the set parameters.

Whenever Ananya noticed any deviation in the product quality, she would immediately investigate the cause and implement corrective actions, such as adjusting the baking time or changing the ingredient suppliers.

Within a few months, their consistent product quality earned them a reputation in the town. As a result, their customer base grew and they began receiving large orders from local events and parties. This success was attributed to their commitment to maintaining strict control over their production process.

Quoting lines from the above paragraph, identify and explain the three steps of the controlling process discussed in the case.

Ans. Following are the three steps of the controlling process discussed in the case

(i) **Setting Performance Standards**

"They established a system where the exact recipe and baking time were documented and strictly followed."

Standards are the criteria against which actual performance would be measured. Thus, standards serve as benchmarks towards which an organisation strives to work. Standards can be set in both quantitative as well as qualitative terms.

(ii) **Measuring Actual Performance**

"Rajat, being the head baker, regularly monitored the baking process to ensure each batch met the desired quality standards."

Once performance standards are set, the next step is measurement of actual performance. Performance should be measured in an objective and reliable manner. There are several techniques for measurement of performance. As far as possible, performance should be measured in the same units in which standards are set as this would make their comparison easier.

(iii) **Taking Corrective Action**

"Whenever Ananya noticed any deviation in the product quality, she would immediately investigate the cause and implement corrective actions, such as adjusting the baking time or changing the ingredient suppliers." No corrective action is required when the deviations are within acceptable limits. However, when the deviations go beyond the acceptable range, especially in the important areas, it demands immediate managerial attention so that deviations do not occur again and standards are accomplished.

SELF ASSESSMENT TEST

Objective Type Questions

1. Which of the following describes nature of controlling?
   (a) Goal-oriented process
   (b) Pervasive
   (c) Continuous process
   (d) All of the above
2. "Controlling in the absence of planning is blind". What does it indicate?
   (a) Only planning is essential
   (b) Only controlling is essential
   (c) Both are essential
   (d) Both are unnecessary
3. Principle of .... should be considered by a manager while dealing with deviations effectively.
   (a) management by exception
   (b) employees
   (c) future actions
   (d) past performance
4. The difference between standard and actual performance is
   (a) deviations (b) control
   (c) corrective action (d) standards
5. Which of the following factors is/are beyond the control of an organisation?
   (a) Change in government policies
   (b) Change in technology
   (c) Competition level
   (d) All of the above
6. Which of the following is a technique of measurement of performance?
   (a) Personal observation
   (b) Sample checking
   (c) Performance reports
   (d) All of the above

Answers 1. (d) 2. (c) 3. (a) 4. (a) 5. (d) 6. (d)

Short Answer Type Questions

7. State the nature of controlling with the help of any three points.
8. How does controlling help in decision-making? Support your answer with an example.
9. "If you try to control everything, you may end up in controlling nothing." Discuss.
10. "Controlling is looking back." Explain
11. "Planning and controlling are inseparable twins of management". Explain the relationship between planning and controlling.
12. Identify and state the standards that are used in various functional areas.
13. A manager of a manufacturing company comes across that postal expenses have increased by 20% and cost of raw materials by 3%. Which of the two deviations would be more critical to him? Explain.

Long Answer Type Questions

14. Raj works as a management consultant in one of the apparel companies them. He has been given the task to make the managers understand the importance of controlling. Explain what he would explain to the managers with respect to importance of controlling?
15. Identify and explain the steps in the process of control.
16. "Critical point control and management by exception are an important part of analysing deviations." In the light of the given statement, discuss their meaning and importance.

PART B Business Finance and Marketing

09

CHAPTER

Financial Management

Finance is central to running the day-to-day operations of business, like buying material, paying bills, salaries, collecting cash from customers, etc. So, it can be said that finance is the life blood of a business.

YOUR STUDY GOALS

9.1 Business Finance
9.2 Concept of Financial Management
9.3 Financial Decisions
9.4 Financial Planning
9.5 Capital Structure
9.6 Fixed Capital
9.7 Working Capital

YOUR PRACTICE GOAL

- Objective Type Questions (62 Qs ; MCQs, A-R, Statements, Matching)
- Subjective Questions (16 SAs, 9 LAs)
- Case Study Based Questions (Short Case Studies-17, Long Case Studies-8)
- Self Assessment Test (6 MCQs, 7 SAs, 3 LAs)

9.1 Business Finance

Money required for carrying out business activities is called business finance. Finance is needed to establish a business, to run it, to modernise it, to expand or diversify it. It is required for buying a variety of assets, which may be tangible like machinery, factories, buildings, offices or intangible such as trademarks, patents, technical expertise, etc.

9.2 Concept of Financial Management

Financial management is concerned with optimal procurement as well as usage of finance.

Here,

- **Optimal procurement** means to arrange the business finance in such a way that its cost and associated risks are minimum.
- **Optimal usage** means to invest the procured finance in such a way that its returns exceeds its cost.

In other words, financial management is the efficient acquisition and utilisation of finance as well as efficient distribution of profits to owners.

It aims to

- reduce the cost of funds procured,
- control risks,
- deploy funds effectively,
- ensure funds are available when needed,
- avoid idle finance.

Importance/Role of Financial Management

1. **Size and Composition of Fixed Assets** A capital budgeting decision impacts the fixed assets by increasing their size and value, i.e. the size of fixed assets depends on the amount which business decides to invest.
2. **Quantum of Current Assets** Financial management helps to decide the amount of current assets required as well as its break-up into cash, inventory and receivables required in the business.
3. **Amount of Long-term vs short-term Funds** Financial management helps to determine the amount required in business for long-term and short-term.
4. **Break-up of Long-term Financing** Financing decision helps to decide that how much part of long-term financing should be done from equity and how much from debt. Thus, the choice of debt vs equity effects financing, impacting the capital structure.
5. **Profit and Loss Items** Decisions on debt, equity and expansion influence future interest, dividends and other expenses.

Objectives of Financial Management

The primary aim of financial management is to maximise shareholders' wealth, which is referred to as the wealth maximisation concept. With the primary objective of wealth maximisation, following objectives are also achieved

- Funds should be deployed in such a way that returns from an investment exceed its cost.
- To raise funds at minimum cost and minimum risk, through effective financing decision.
- To maintain financial liquidity and profitability, through working capital decision.
- To ensure safety of funds by creating reserves, reinvestment of profits, etc.

9.3 Financial Decisions

Decisions related to financial operations of a firm *viz-a-viz* investment, financing and dividend are called financial decisions.

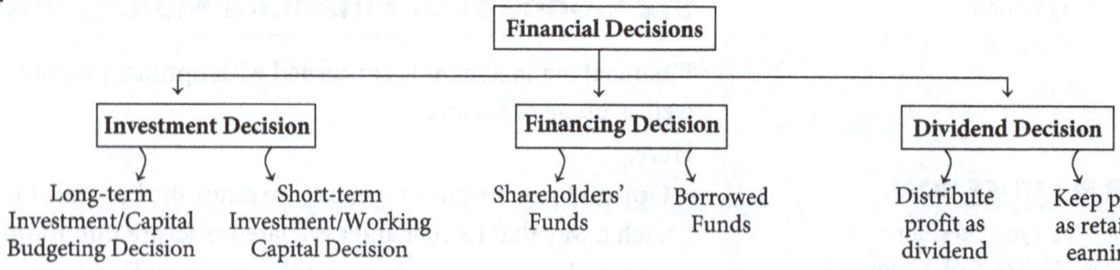

Investment Decision

Investment decision relates to how the firm's funds are invested in different assets. This decision involves careful selection of assets, so that they can earn highest possible return for their investors. Investment decision may be long-term or short-term.

1. **Long-term Investment/Capital Budgeting Decision**

   Long-term decisions involve committing the finance on a long-term basis. e.g. Investment in a new machine or opening new branch, etc.

   Since, these decisions are very crucial, involve huge amount of investment and are irreversible except at a huge cost, they need to be taken with utmost care.

2. **Short-term Investment/Working Capital Decision**
   Short-term decisions are concerned with the decisions about the levels of cash, inventory and receivables required to be held by the business for its smooth functioning.
   These decisions affect the day-to-day working and liquidity as well as profitability of business.

Factors affecting Capital Budgeting Decision

These are certain factors which affect capital budgeting decision

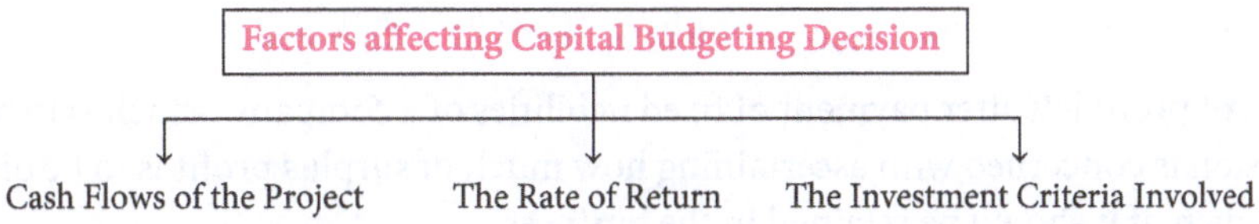

1. **Cash Flows of the Project** Investment decisions involve carefully analysing expected cash inflows and outflows over the desired project's life to ensure financial viability.
2. **The Rate of Return** Projects are evaluated based on their expected returns or income for the company and the degree of risk involved. Projects with higher return are typically preferred for wealth maximisation.
3. **The Investment Criteria Involved** Number of capital budgeting techniques evaluate investment proposals or factors like investment amount, interest rates, cash flows and rate of return to select a particular project.

Financing Decision

This decision relates to the amount of finance to be raised from various long-term sources.

The main sources of funds for a business are

1. **Shareholders' Funds** These funds include equity capital and retained earnings.
2. **Borrowed Funds** These funds include debentures, loans or other forms of debt.

Financing decision involves analysing risk and cost associated with each source and deciding a judicious mix of both debt and equity.

> ***Financial Risk and Floatation Cost***
> Borrowed funds are considered more risky as the interest on borrowed funds have to be paid regardless of whether or not, a firm has earned a profit. The risk of default of payment is called **financial risk**.
> The funds raising exercise also cost something, which is termed as **floatation cost**.

Factors affecting Financing Decision

1. **Cost** The cost of raising funds varies according to source. A prudent financial manager selects the source with the lowest cost to minimise financial burden.
2. **Risk** The risk associated with each of the source of finance is different. For instance, debt increases financial risk due to fixed interest obligations, while equity financing spreads risk among shareholders.

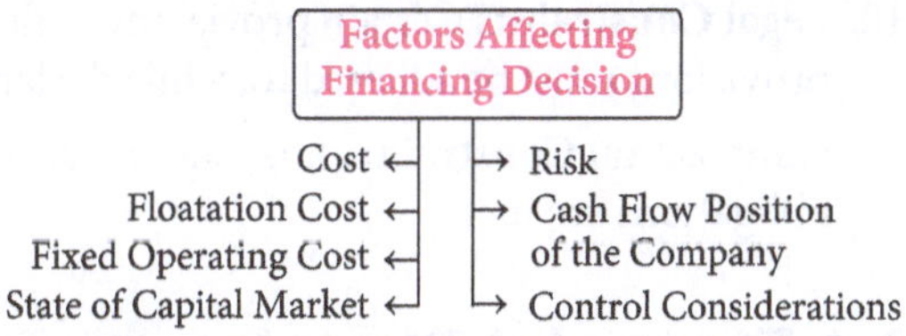

3. **Floatation Cost** It is the cost incurred while issuing securities, like underwriters fee, brokerage, legal fees, etc. Higher floatation cost makes a source, such as equity, less attractive compared to debt.
4. **Cash Flow Position of Company** A company with strong cash flow position can comfortably handle debt financing, as it has the liquidity to meet interest and principal payments.

5. **Fixed Operating Costs** Businesses with high fixed operating costs, such as rent and salaries, may prefer lower debt to avoid further fixed commitments. In contrast, firms with lower operating costs may take on more debt.
6. **Control Considerations** Issuing more equity can dilute existing shareholders' control over the company, making debt a more attractive option for those shareholders wishing to retain control over the business.
7. **State of Capital Market** When the stock market is performing well, issuing equity is easier as investors are more willing to buy shares. In a depressed capital market, raising funds through equity becomes difficult and companies have to opt for debt financing.

Dividend Decision

Dividend is that portion of profit left after payment of fixed liabilities of a company, which is to be distributed to the shareholders. This decision is concerned with ascertaining how much of surplus profit is to be distributed among shareholders and how much of it should be retained in the business.

Factors affecting Dividend Decision

1. **Amount of Earnings** Dividends are paid from current and past earnings, making earnings a key factor i.e. company earning more will declare higher dividend and *vice-versa*.
2. **Stability in Earnings** Companies with stable earnings are more likely to declare higher dividends as compared to companies with unstable earnings.
3. **Stability of Dividends** Generally, companies follow a policy of stabilising dividends per share and a steady dividend is given each year. It improves the company's reputation in the market and also satisfies the shareholders.
4. **Growth Opportunities** Firms with growth prospects retain more earnings for investment, leading to smaller dividends than that of the non-growth potential companies.

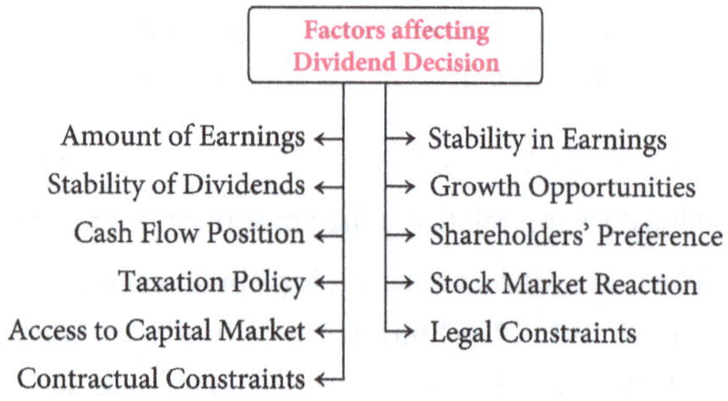

5. **Cash Flow Position** Sufficient cash is needed to pay dividends, even if profits of the company are high. Thus, company having surplus cash may declare higher dividend and *vice-versa*.
6. **Shareholders' Preference** Companies should consider shareholder preferences for consistent dividend payments.
7. **Taxation Policy** Rate of dividend also depends upon government's taxation policy. If the tax on dividend is higher, the company prefers to pay less by way of dividends and *vice-versa*.
8. **Stock Market Reaction** Rate of dividend and market value of shares are directly related to each other. So, increase in dividend usually boost stock prices and *vice-versa*.
9. **Access to Capital Market** Large and reputed companies with easier capital market access may pay higher dividends as compared to smaller companies having relatively low access to the market.
10. **Legal Constraints** Certain provisions of the Companies Act place restrictions on pay-outs as dividend. Such provisions must be adhered to, while declaring the dividend.
11. **Contractual Constraints** Loan agreements may impose certain restrictions on dividend payments to ensure debt obligations are met.

9.4 Financial Planning

Financial planning is the process of estimating the financial requirements of an organisation, specifying the sources of funds and ensuring that enough funds are available at the right time. It aims at providing smooth operations by forecasting activities and fund requirement on one hand and analysing the sources of funds generation, on the other.

Financial plans are made for both long-term as well as short-term

1. **Long-term Plans** These plans relate to long-term growth and investment matters and focus on capital expenditure programmes. They are made for 3-5 year time frames.
2. **Short-term Plans** They are also known as budgets and are made for a period of one year or less.

Financial Planning

Financial planning can be compared to preparing for a road trip.

Imagine you're driving to a new city, but you're unsure if it will rain, be sunny or snow. To be ready, you pack clothes for all types of weather.

Similarly, in business, financial planning involves creating plans for different scenarios, like predicting sales growth or drop. If the sales go up, the company can invest more; if they drop, it can cut unnecessary expenses. This way, the company is always prepared, just like you are for your trip!

Financial Planning vs Financial Management

It must be kept in mind that financial planning is not equivalent to, or a substitute for, financial management.

- Financial management aims at choosing the best investment and financing alternatives by focusing on their costs and benefits. It's objective is to increase the shareholder's wealth.
- On the other hand, financial planning aims at smooth operations by focusing on fund requirements and their availability in the light of financial decisions.

Objectives of Financial Planning

1. **To Ensure Availability of Funds Whenever Required** Financial planning estimates funds needed for various purposes and ensures that they are available in the company at right time, i.e. when required. It also tries to identify sources for these funds.
2. **To See that the Firm does not Raise Resources Unnecessary** Financial planning ensures that the firm doesn't raise unnecessary funds. It helps to use the surplus, if any, in best possible way to avoid idle financial resources and extra costs.

Importance of Financial Planning

- It **helps in forecasting** what may happen in future under different business situations. By doing this, it helps the firms to face the situation in a better way.
- It **helps in avoiding business shocks and surprises** and helps the company in preparing for the future.
- It **helps in coordinating various business functions** like production, sales, etc. by providing policies and procedures.
- It **tries to link the present with the future** by foreseeing the growth prospects, sales, etc.
- It **provides a link between investment and financing decisions** on a continuous basis.
- It **helps in reducing waste, duplication of efforts and gaps** in planning through detailed plans of action.
- It **makes the evaluation of actual performance easier** by spelling out the objectives of various business segments.

9.5 Capital Structure

Capital structure represents the proportion of debt capital and equity capital to make up the total capital of firm.

On the basis of ownership, the sources of business finance can be broadly classified into two categories, *viz*, owner's funds and borrowed funds.

- **Owners' funds** consist of equity share capital, preference share capital, reserves and surpluses or retained earnings.
- **Borrowed funds** can be in the form of long-term loans, debentures, public deposits, etc. These may be borrowed from banks, other financial institutions, debentureholders and public.

Capital structure can be calculated as debt-equity ratio, i.e. $\left(\frac{\text{Debt}}{\text{Equity}}\right)$ or as the proportion of debt out of total capital, i.e. $\left(\frac{\text{Debt}}{\text{Debt} + \text{Equity}}\right)$

Debt vs Equity

- The cost of debt is lower than the cost of equity for a business.
- Debt is cheaper but is more risky for a business. Any default in meeting interest payment and return of principal may force the business to go into liquidation.
- Equity is less risky as there is no compulsion of payment of dividend to equity shareholders.
- Thus, higher use of debt increases the financial risk.

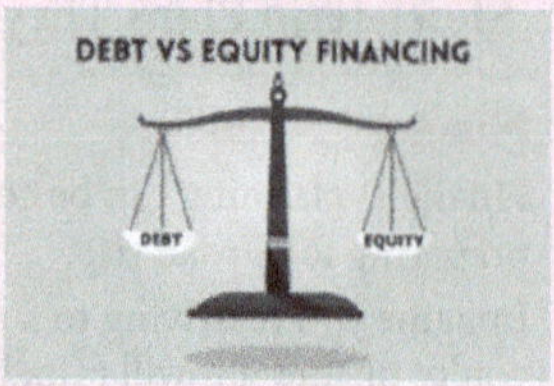

An **optimal capital structure** will be attained, when the proportion of debt and equity will result in increase in shareholders' wealth.

Normally, companies follow the concept of financial leverage to set-up capital structure.

Financial Leverage/Trading on Equity

The amount of total debt in the overall capital is called financial leverage. When financial leverage (i.e. debt) increases, the cost of funds decline but financial risk increases.

The use of debt along with equity increases Earnings Per Share (EPS). This use of fixed financial charge, i.e. interest, increases the profit earned by shareholders. This concept is known as **trading on equity**.

It should be remembered that excess use of debt will increase EPS only when Return on Investment (RoI) is more than the rate of interest on debt. The impact of financial leverage/trading on equity on the profitability of a business can be seen through Earning Before Interest and Taxes-Earning Per Share (EBIT-EPS) analysis.

Factors affecting Capital Structure

Factors affecting Capital Structure

Cash Flow Position	Interest Coverage Ratio
Debt Service Coverage Ratio	Return on Investment
Cost of Debt	Tax Rate
Cost of Equity	Floatation Cost
Risk Consideration	Flexibility
Control	Regulatory Framework
Stock Market Condition	Capital Structure of Other Companies

1. **Cash Flow Position** Company should ensure that cash flows cover normal operations, investments and debt payments, with an additional buffer. Thus, company having required cash flows can opt for more of debt in its capital structure and *vice-versa*.
2. **Interest Coverage Ratio** (ICR) It measures how well earnings before interest and tax cover interest payments. Higher ratio indicates that company can borrow more funds and *vice-versa*.

   It can be calculated as $\text{ICR} = \frac{\text{EBIT}}{\text{Interest}}$
3. **Debt Service Coverage Ratio** (DSCR) It compares cash profits to total debt and preference share payments. Higher ratio reflects better debt service capability and *vice-versa*.

   It is calculated as $\text{DSCR} = \frac{\text{Profit after Tax} + \text{Depreciation} + \text{Interest} + \text{Non-cash Expenses}}{\text{Preference Dividend} + \text{Interest} + \text{Repayment Obligation}}$
4. **Return on Investment** (RoI) RoI is the earnings of a company on its investments. Higher RoI allows more debt use to enhance EPS, but low RoI may reduce EPS despite higher debt.

   It can be calculated as $\text{RoI} = \frac{\text{EBIT}}{\text{Total Investment}} \times 100$
5. **Cost of Debt** Lower borrowing rates increase the firm's capacity to use debt in its capital structure and *vice-versa*.

6. **Tax Rate** Interest on debt is a deductible expense for company. Thus, higher tax rates reduce the effective cost of debt, making it more attractive.
7. **Cost of Equity** Higher debt increases equity risk, raising the desired rate of return. Thus, excessive debt may increase equity costs and lower share prices inspite of increased EPS.
8. **Floatation Costs** Issuing shares or debentures incurs costs like brokerage, stamp duty, etc. Higher floatation cost makes the source of finance less attractive and *vice-versa.*
9. **Risk Consideration** Debt increases financial risk, while business risk depends on operating costs. Total risk combines both. If a firm's business risk is lower, it can use more debt and *vice-versa.*
10. **Flexibility** Excess use of debt may reduce the future borrowing flexibility. Company should maintain some borrowing capacity to take care of unforeseen circumstances.
11. **Control** Debt doesn't dilute control over the business, unlike equity. Shareholders not wanting to loose control, can prefer more of debt and *vice-versa.*
12. **Regulatory Framework** The Companies Act and SEBI guidelines must be observed while raising funds from the public. Borrowings from banks and other financial institutions require fulfilment of certain norms, which has an impact on the choice of the source of finance.
13. **Stock Market Conditions** Bullish markets favour equity issuance, while bearish conditions make debt more attractive.
14. **Capital Structure of Other Companies** Industry norms provide guidance in capital structure planning but companies should not follow them blindly. They should adjust them based on their specific risk profile.

9.6 Fixed Capital

Fixed capital refers to investment in long-term assets or projects. The decision regarding investing in fixed assets must be taken very carefully as investment is quite. These decisions are also known as capital budgeting decisions. It involves allocation of firm's capital to different projects or assets with long-term implications for the business.

It is important due to following reasons

Importance	Explanation
Long-term Growth	These decisions impact the future as funds invested in long-term assets are likely to generate returns later, shaping future business prospects.
Large Amount of Funds Involved	Significant capital gets locked in long-term projects. Therefore, it requires careful analysis of funding sources and interest rates.
Risk Involved	Fixed capital decisions involve large investments. It affects long-term returns of the firm and influence the overall business risk.
Irreversible Decisions	These decisions, once made, are not reversible except at a huge loss. Thus, careful evaluation of each detail is essential to avoid financial losses.

Factors affecting Requirement of Fixed Capital

1. **Nature of Business** It has a great influence upon the fixed capital requirements. e.g. Trading firms need less fixed capital than manufacturing firms, as they don't require machinery.
2. **Scale of Operations** Larger firms operating at a larger scale need more fixed assets as compared to smaller firms.
3. **Choice of Technique** Capital intensive firms need more investment in fixed assets while labour intensive firms need less investment in fixed assets.
4. **Technology Upgradation** Industries with rapidly obsolete assets due to technology upgradation like computers, need more investment in fixed capital for replacements.

Factors Affecting Requirement of Fixed Capital

- Nature of Business
- Scale of Operations
- Choice of Technique
- Technology Upgradation
- Growth Prospects
- Diversification
- Financing Alternatives
- Level of Collaboration

5. **Growth Prospects** Firms with high growth expectations need more fixed capital to expand its production capacity for future demand.
6. **Diversification** When firms diversify, such as a textile company starting cement production, their fixed capital needs increase.
7. **Financing Alternatives** A developed financial market can provide leasing facilities as an alternative to outright purchase. If such alternatives are available with the company, the assets are not required to be purchased outrightly, but only rent or instalments have to be paid. This reduces the requirement of fixed capital.
8. **Level of Collaboration** The collaborations between the organisations to use one another's facilities and assets reduce the need for fixed capital. This is feasible if the scale of operations of each of them is not sufficient to make full use of the facility. This type of collaboration reduces the need of fixed assets for each one of the participating organisations.

Fixed Capital Requirement

A trading concern needs lower investment in fixed assets compared with a manufacturing organisation; since it does not require to purchase plant and machinery, etc. Computers become obsolete faster and are replaced much sooner than say, furniture. Thus, such organisations which use assets that are prone to obsolescence require higher fixed capital to purchase such assets.

9.7 Working Capital

Working capital means the portion of capital which is invested in current assets. This investment facilitates smooth day-to-day operations of the business.

The term 'working capital' may mean gross working capital or net working capital.

- **Gross working capital** means current assets.
- **Net working capital** may be defined as excess of current assets over current liabilities. Thus,

  Net Working Capital = Current Assets − Current Liabilities

  or NWC = CA − CL

Note Unless otherwise specified, working capital means NWC.

Current Assets and Current Liabilities

- The term current assets refer to those assets held in a business which can be converted in the form of cash within a period of one year. These assets are more liquid but contribute less to the profits fixed assets.
- The term current liabilites refer to those liabilities which are to be paid-off within a time span of one year. These are short-term sources of funds for acquisition of current assets.

Operating Cycle

- It is the time duration from procurement of raw materials to sales realisation.
- Working capital is required for this period to finance operations of the business.
- The operating cycle is different for different firms depending upon their size and nature of business.
- For example, manufacturing firm's operating cycle may be different from a trading concern.

Factors affecting Requirement of Working Capital

1. **Nature of Business** Trading and service firms need less working capital than manufacturing firms due to minimal inventory requirements.
2. **Scale of Operations** Larger firms require more working capital to manage higher inventory and debtor levels.

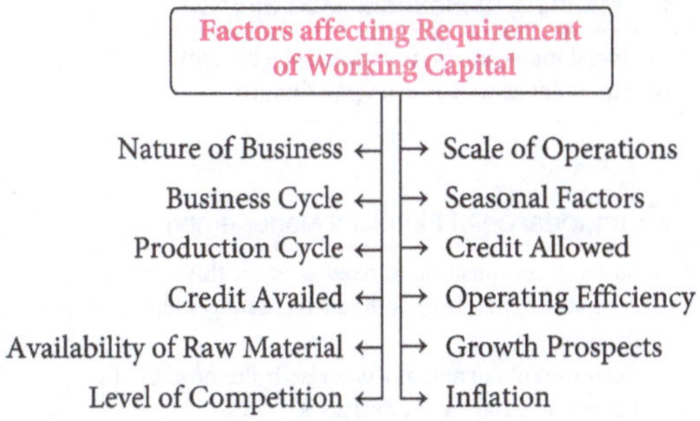

3. **Business Cycle** Different phases of business cycle affect working capital requirements. Boom period increases working capital needs due to higher sales and production while depression period lowers the working capital needs.
4. **Seasonal Factors** For businesses having seasonal operations, working capital requirement fluctuates with change in season. Peak seasons require more working capital due to higher activity while lean seasons need less working capital.
5. **Production Cycle** It is the time span between the receipt of raw material and their conversion into finished goods. Firms with longer production cycle need more working capital than those with shorter production cycle.
6. **Credit Allowed** Liberal credit policy of company increases debtors, thus raising working capital requirements and *vice-versa.*
7. **Credit Availed** Just as a firm allows credit to its customers, it also may get credit from its suppliers. To the extent, it avails the credit on purchases, the working capital requirement is reduced and *vice-versa.*
8. **Operating Efficiency** Companies manage their operations with varied degrees of efficiency. A firm that manages its raw materials efficiently may require less working capital. This is reflected in a higher inventory turnover ratio. Similarly, a better debtor turnover ratio can be achieved reducing the amount tied up in receivables.
9. **Availability of Raw Material** Easily and readily available raw material reduces stock levels thus requiring less working capital while irregular supply increases working capital.
10. **Growth Prospects** Firms with high growth potential need more working capital to meet future demand.
11. **Level of Competition** High competition increases working capital needs due to maintenance of higher inventory and liberal credit policies.
12. **Inflation** Price level changes also affect the working capital requirement. With rising prices, large amount is required even to maintain a constant volume of production and sales. Thus, working capital requirement becomes higher with higher rate of inflation.

Working Capital Requirement

Fresh Flavours Bakery, a popular bakery known for its custom cakes, needs careful working capital management to operate smoothly.

Since the bakery deals with perishable items like fresh cream and fruit, it requires significant working capital to maintain a steady supply of fresh ingredients daily. Additionally, during festival seasons like Christmas and Diwali, the demand for cakes surges, leading to a need for more raw materials and extra staff. This increases the working capital requirements, as Neha, the owner, must manage higher operational costs while awaiting customer payments.

Mind Map

FINANCIAL MANAGEMENT

1 Meaning of Financial Management

Financial management is concerned with optimal procurement as well as usage of finance.

2 Importance of Financial Management

- Size and composition of fixed assets of the company depends upon financial management decision
- Quantum of current assets is also influenced by financial management decisions
- Helps to determine the amount required on short-term and long-term basis
- Financial decision involves decision regarding procurement of finance
- Financial management decisions affect all the items in profit and loss account

3 Objectives of Financial Management

- Primary aim is to maximise wealth of shareholders
- Funds should be deployed in such a way that returns from an investment exceed its cost
- To raise funds at minimum cost and minimum risk, through effective financing decision
- To maintain financial liquidity and profitability
- To ensure safety of funds by creating reserves

4 Financial Decisions and Their Types

These decisions are related to financial operations of a firm *viz-a-viz* investment, financing and dividend.

Investment or Capital Budgeting Decision

Relates to how the firm's funds are invested in different assets.

Factors affecting Capital Budgeting Decision

- Cash flows of the project
- Rate of return
- Investment criteria

Financing Decision

Relates to the amount of finance to be raised from various long-term sources.

Factors affecting Financing Decision

- Cost
- Risk
- Floatation costs
- Cash flow position
- Fixed operating costs
- Control considerations
- State of capital markets

Dividend Decision

Ascertaining how much surplus profit is to be distributed among shareholders and how much of it should be retained.

Factors affecting Dividend Decision

- Amount of earnings
- Stability of earnings
- Stability of dividends
- Growth opportunities
- Cash flow position
- Shareholders' preference
- Taxation policy
- Stock market reaction
- Access to capital market
- Legal constraints
- Contractual constraints

5 Objectives of Financial Planning

- To ensure availability of funds whenever required
- To ensure unnecessarily finance is not raised

6 Importance of Financial Planning

- Helps to prepare for future
- Helps in avoiding business shocks and surprises
- Helps in achieving coordination between various functions
- Prevents duplication of efforts and gaps in planning
- Helps to link present with future
- Provides a link between investment and financing decisions
- Makes evaluation of actual performance easier

7 Capital Structure

It represents the proportion of debt capital and equity capital to make up the total capital of firm.

Factors affecting Choice of Capital Structure

- Cash flow position
- Interest coverage ratio
- Debt Service coverage ratio
- Return on investment
- Cost of debt
- Tax rate
- Cost of equity
- Floatation costs
- Risk consideration
- Flexibility
- Control
- Regulatory framework
- Stock market conditions
- Capital structure of other companies

8 Fixed Capital

Fixed capital involves allocation of firm's capital to long-term assets or projects.

Factors affecting Fixed Capital Requirements

- Nature of business
- Scale of operations
- Choice of technique
- Technology upgradation
- Growth prospects
- Diversification
- Financing alternatives
- Level of collaboration

9 Working Capital

It means the portion of capital which is invested in current assets

- Gross working capital means current assets
- Net working capital may be defined as excess of current assets over current liabilities

Factors affecting Working Capital Requirements

- Nature of business
- Scale of operations
- Business cycle
- Seasonal factors
- Production cycle
- Credit allowed
- Credit availed
- Availability of raw material
- Operating efficiency
- Growth prospects
- Level of competition
- Inflation

EXAM PATTERN QUESTIONS

Objective Type Questions

Multiple Choice Questions (MCQs)

1. Which of the following aspects is directly influenced by financial management decisions?

(a) The break-up of current assets into cash, inventory and receivables
(b) The increase in employee count
(c) The launch of new products
(d) The location of the company's headquarters

2. The main objective of financial management is

(a) wealth maximisation of shareholders
(b) increase rate of interest
(c) stabilisation of dividend
(d) decrease the financial risk

3. VNG Agro Food Ltd. is a famous multinational company. Mr. SK Nagi is its finance manager. He is trying to increase the market value of capital invested by the equity shareholders.

He already knew it could be possible only when the price of the shares increases and the price of shares increases only if financing, investment and dividend decisions are taken optimally.

He did the same and achieved success. Which objective of financial management has been referred to here? Competency Based Que

(a) Maximising the wealth of equity shareholders
(b) Effective utilisation of funds
(c) Ensures the safety of funds
(d) Avoiding idle finance

4. Identify the decision which is not taken under financial management. CBSE SQP 2025

(a) Dividend decision
(b) Capital budgeting decision
(c) Pricing decision
(d) Both (b) and (c)

5. Bharti Ltd. is a leading mobile company. It is planning to acquire Queen Ltd. (its close competitor) business worth ₹1,000 crore. Which financial decision is involved in it? Competency Based Que

(a) Investment
(b) Financing
(c) Dividend
(d) None of the above

6. Identify the concept of financial management illustrated in the below picture.

(a) Investment decision (b) Financing decision
(c) Dividend decision (d) None of these

7. Which of the following statements is correct for 'short-term investment decisions'? CBSE 2024 C

(a) They affect the earning capacity of a business in the long-run
(b) These decisions normally involve huge amounts of investment
(c) These decisions affect the liquidity as well as profitability of a business
(d) They are irreversible except at a huge cost

8. Identify the incorrect statement with respect to 'investment decision'. CBSE SQP 2025

(a) Net working capital refers to excess of current assets over current liabilities
(b) Current assets are those assets which get converted into cash within one year
(c) Capital budgeting decisions are irreversible
(d) Size of the assets, profitability and competitiveness are not affected by capital budgeting decisions

9. What are the factors that affect financing decisions?

(i) Cash flow position of the company
(ii) Stability of earnings
(iii) Degree of financial risk
(iv) Contractual constraints
(v) State of capital market
(vi) Level of competition CBSE SQP 2025

Codes

(a) (ii), (iii) and (vi) (b) (iv), (v) and (vi)
(c) (i), (iii) and (iv) (d) (i), (iii) and (v)

10. A company has decided to issue debentures as it knows that it will not lead to any additional costs. These debentures will be carrying a very low rate of return for the debentureholders but will be a surety for them to get their money back.

Investors who want financial safety would like to go for this option as there will be an assured definite return.

Identify the type of financial decision.

Competency Based Que

(a) Financing (b) Dividend
(c) Working capital (d) Fixed capital

11. Healthy Snacks Ltd. has been earning profits for several years consecutively. The company has to decide about the dividend to be declared this year. The company has enough goodwill in the capital market. As such, it is not at all difficult for it to arrange capital in the capital market.

Keeping in view all these factors, the company decided to increase last year's dividend by 15 percent. Which component affecting dividend decision has been highlighted in the above paragraph?

Competency Based Que

(a) Cash flow position (b) Taxation policy
(c) Access to capital market (d) Growth opportunity

12. Y Ltd. is looking forward to open its new branch. Which decision is depicted in picture below?

(a) Working capital decision
(b) Capital budgeting decision
(c) Dividend decision (d) Financing decision

13. Identify the financial decision highlighted in the picture in which manager has to take the decision regarding proportion of funds from each source.

(a) Investment decision (b) Financing decision
(c) Dividend decision (d) None of these

14. Identify the financial decision that is depicted in picture below.

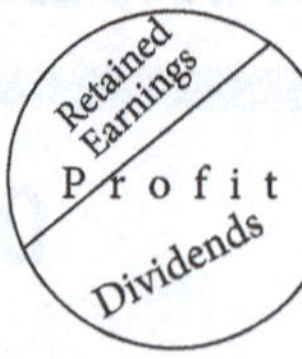

(a) Working capital decision (b) Capital budgeting decision
(c) Financing decision (d) Dividend decision

15. CVX Ltd. was a leading company, manufacturing home appliances like food processors, juicers and mixer grinders. The company was earning good profits and was paying high dividends to its shareholders consistently. The company now decided to manufacture soup-making machines, pop-up toasters and electric irons. The company wanted to enter into emerging markets out of India also. Entering these markets will require additional capital investment which will facilitate in production and distribution infrastructure etc.

For this, the management decided to retain money out of their earnings to finance the required investment and distribute smaller dividend to the shareholders. The factor affecting dividend decision which was kept in mind by the management of CVX Ltd. for entering into emerging markets and launching new products was

CBSE 2025; Competency Based Que

(a) amount of earnings (b) stability of earnings
(c) stability of dividends (d) growth opportunities

16. 'Dovex' was a large company with a renowned name in healthcare industry, specialising in the development and production of life saving medications and medical devices. With a strong reputation for ethical practices, 'Dovex' attracted a large number of investors who had great faith in the company's future. This allowed 'Dovex' to raise capital easily from the market whenever expansion or new projects were to be undertaken.

As a result, it could pay high dividends to the shareholders. The factor affecting dividend decision discussed above, which allowed 'Dovex' to pay high dividends to the shareholders is

CBSE 2024; Competency Based Que

(a) cash flow position (b) stock market reaction
(c) legal constraints (d) access to capital market

17. Avik is the finance manager of Mars Ltd. In the current year, the company earned high profits. However, Avik thinks that it is better to declare a smaller dividend as he is unsure about the earning potential of the company in the coming years. Avik's choice of dividend decision is based on which of the factor? **Competency Based Que**

(a) Amount of earnings (b) Stability in earnings
(c) Stability of dividends (d) Growth opportunities

18. Financial planning arrives at
(a) minimising external borrowing by resorting to equity issues
(b) entering that the firm always have significantly more fund than required so that there is no paucity of funds
(c) ensuring that the firm faces neither a shortage nor a glut of unusable funds
(d) doing only what is possible with the funds that the firm has at its disposal

19. To ensure that enough funds are available at 'right time to 'honour the commitments and to carry out the plans' is discussed in which of the following concepts? CBSE 2025
(a) Capital structure (b) Financial leverage
(c) Financial planning (d) Investment decision

20. Ravi, an entrepreneur from Karnataka, inherited a textile factory from his father. He is planning to modernise the factory and expand its production capacity to manufacture eco-friendly fabric. To achieve this, Ravi sought guidance from his cousin Priya, who is a financial advisor. Priya helped Ravi analyse his business's current financial position and create a detailed strategy for obtaining the necessary funds to finance the expansion. She also advised him on how to allocate resources effectively to meet both short-term and long-term business needs.

Identify the financial concept used by Priya while helping Ravi. Competency Based Que
(a) Capital structure (b) Financial planning
(c) Dividend decision (d) Investment decision

21. Which of the following statements is/are incorrect?
(a) Financial planning aims to help companies tackle uncertainties in the availability and timing of funds
(b) Financial planning helps in forecasting future business scenarios and prepares the firm for various situations
(c) Capital structure is the proportion of debt to equity in the overall capital of a business, but it is unrelated to the cost of capital
(d) Effective financial planning can help in avoiding business shocks and surprises

22. When the proportion of debt and equity is such that it results in an increase in the value of equity share, the ………… is/are said to be optimal. CBSE 2023
(a) working capital (b) fixed capital
(c) capital structure (d) Both (a) and (b)

23. Increase in the profit earned by the equity shareholders' due to the 'presence of fixed financial charges like interest' is called CBSE 2025
(a) financial planning (b) dividend decision
(c) financing decision (d) trading on equity

24. Company 'A' has profit after tax ₹ 1,50,000 and its number of equity shares are 10,000. Company 'B' has profit after tax, ₹ 1,20,000 and its number of shares are 12,000. Which company has better EPS and how much?
(a) Company 'A', ₹ 10
(b) Company 'A', ₹ 15
(c) Company 'B', ₹ 10
(d) Company 'B', ₹ 12

25. Which of the following is not a factor affecting capital structure of a company? CBSE 2023
(a) Cost of debt (b) Growth opportunities
(c) Cash flow position (d) Interest coverage ratio

26. Which of the following statements is/are incorrect?
(a) Business finance refers to the money required for carrying out business activities
(b) Dividend decision relates to the relative proportion of various sources of finance
(c) From the company point of view, the use of equity share capital results in more cost but less of risk
(d) Capital structure represents the proportion of debt capital and equity capital to make up the total capital of the firm

27. Debts financing is better than equity if
(a) company has a strong cash flow
(b) company has a weak cash flow
(c) cash flow position does not matter
(d) None of the above

28. Neelam has decided to consider debt as the source of raising finance. Her decision has come after considering the strong buffer of funds she already has. She has enough amount of funds to cover fixed cash payments. Her business unit has no problem in running normal business operation and it has low business risk. Further the financial risk is also low. Identify the factor affecting the choice of capital. Competency Based Que
(a) Cash flow position (b) Control
(c) Flexibility (d) Cost of debt

29. Mehul Bhattacharya, after leaving his job, wanted to start a Private Limited Company with his son. His son was keen that the company may start manufacturing of mobile phones with some unique features. Mehul Bhattacharya felt that the mobile phones are prone to quick obsolescence and a heavy fixed capital investment would be required regularly in this business. Therefore, he convinced his son to start a furniture business.

Identify the factor affecting fixed capital requirements which made Mehul Bhattacharya to choose furniture business over mobile phones. Competency Based Que
(a) Cash flow position
(b) Operating cycle
(c) Growth prospects
(d) Technology upgradation

30. Identify the concept of financial management depicted in the given picture.

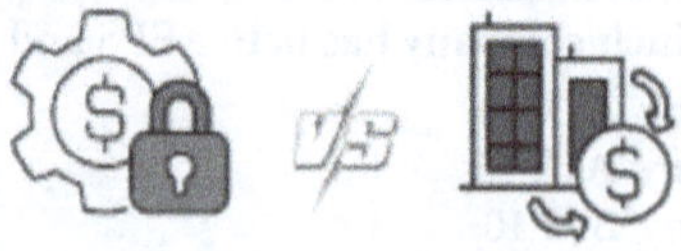

(a) Current assets vs Current liabilities
(b) Fixed capital vs Working capital
(c) Working capital vs Fixed capital
(d) Current liabilities vs Current assets

31. 'Isha Sweets' was set by Isha Sharma to prepare and sell organic, vegan and healthy sweets alternatives like hazelnuts date ladoos, dry fruit date burfi, stuffed mejdool date, etc. For the last many years, the demand for her products was very high as people these days prefer to buy healthier alternatives for consumption as well as gifting purposes.

But this year suddenly, the cost of dates, dry fruits and other ingredients used for preparing these healthy sweets had increased. With rising prices of raw materials, larger amounts of funds were required to maintain a constant volume of production and sales. As a result, the working capital requirement of 'Ish a Sweets' became higher.

The factor which led to an increase in the working capital requirements' of 'Isha Sweets' was

CBSE 2025; Competency Based Que

(a) availability of raw material (b) inflation
(c) scale of business (d) production cycle

32. Prashant started a grocery retail business. Due to increasing popularity of online shopping, the degree of competition is very high in this business. His requirement of working capital will be high as he would have to hold larger stocks of finished goods to meet urgent orders from customers. The factor affecting the requirement of working capital is

CBSE 2024 C; Competency Based Que

(a) availability of raw material (b) scale of operations
(c) level of competition (d) inflation

Direction *Read the following case study and answer the questions 33 to 36 on the basis of the same*

Ms. Neha Sharma is the owner of NS Electronics Pvt. Ltd. a successful company specialising in electronic gadgets. Ms. Sharma has decided to expand her business by investing in a new manufacturing plant. The total investment required is ₹ 80 crores. To make an informed decision, Ms. Sharma consulted her financial advisor, Mr. R. Mehta. Mr. Mehta recommended a financing mix of 50% equity and 50% debt. He advised that using a significant amount of debt might increase the return on equity, although it would also heighten financial risk.

Mr. Mehta suggested approaching a bank for the loan since the cost of borrowing from a bank is relatively low. Additionally, he informed Ms. Sharma that interest payments on the loan would be tax deductible, thus reducing the company's tax liability. However, he noted that while this approach would not dilute the control of existing shareholders, it would increase the financial risk due to higher leverage.

After considering Mr. Mehta's advice, Ms. Sharma decided to proceed with the proposed financing strategy.

33. In the case above, which concept of financial management is Mr. Mehta advising Ms. Sharma on?

(a) Capital budgeting (b) Capital structure
(c) Dividend decision (d) Working capital decision

34. According to Mr. Mehta's suggestion, if Ms. Sharma opts for a higher proportion of debt, it will result in

(a) lower financial risk
(b) higher degree of operating risk
(c) higher degree of financial risk
(d) higher earning of profit

35. "Mr. R. Mehta recommended a financing mix of 50% equity and 50% debt." The proportion of debt in the overall capital is referred to as …………… .

(a) working capital (b) financial leverage
(c) total assets (d) None of these

36. Using a significant amount of debt to increase the return on equity is known as

(a) equity trading (b) financial leverage
(c) investment decision (d) trading on equity

Assertion-Reason

Direction (Q.No. 37 to 46) *Read the following Assertion (A) and Reason (R) and choose the correct alternative from the following*

Alternatives

(a) Both Assertion (A) and Reason (R) are true and Reason (R) is the correct explanation of Assertion (A)
(b) Both Assertion (A) and Reason (R) are true, but Reason (R) is not the correct explanation of Assertion (A)
(c) Assertion (A) is true, but Reason (R) is false
(d) Assertion (A) is false, but Reason (R) is true

37. Assertion (A) Finance is the life blood of business.
Reason (R) Finance is very essential for the smooth running of the business.

38. Assertion (A) Capital budgeting decisions are important and must be taken carefully.
Reason (R) Investment decisions affect the earning capacity of firm over the long-run and are not reversible except at huge cost.

39. **Assertion** (A) While taking dividend decision, the extent of retained earnings also influences the financing decision of the firm.

Reason (R) The firm does not require funds to the extent of re-invested retained earnings. **CBSE 2024 C**

40. **Assertion** (A) Financial planning helps in the efficient allocation of resources and management of financial risks.

Reason (R) Financial planning involves forecasting future financial needs and preparing strategies to meet those needs.

41. **Assertion** (A) Financial planning aims at enabling the company to tackle the uncertainty in respect of the availability and timing of the funds.

Reason (R) Capital structure refers to the mix between owners' and borrowed funds. **CBSE SQP 2025**

42. **Assertion** (A) Maximising the wealth of equity shareholders is the primary objective of financial management.

Reason (R) Investment decision is associated with investment of firm's funds in different assets.

43. **Assertion** (A) Return of equity shareholders is increased because of trading on equity.

Reason (R) Cost of debt is lower than cost of equity and interest paid on debt is a deductible expense.

44. **Assertion** (A) Fixed capital refers to investments in long-term assets and involves careful allocation to projects with long-term implications.

Reason (R) The management of fixed capital is critical for ensuring that the firm's long-term assets are efficiently utilised to support the business's growth and operational stability.

45. **Assertion** (A) Lower investment is required in fixed assets by a trading concern.

Reason (R) Requirement to purchase plant and machinery does not exist for a trading concern.

46. **Assertion** (A) Working capital decisions play an important role in day-to-day working of a business.

Reason (R) Working capital decisions only affect the liquidity of the business.

Two Statements Based MCQs

Direction (Q.No. 47 to 57) *Read the following statements carefully and choose the correct alternative*

Alternatives

(a) Statement I is correct and Statement II is incorrect
(b) Statement II is correct and Statement I is incorrect
(c) Both the statements are correct
(d) Both the statements are incrorrect

47. **Statement I** Financial management involves managing finance to ensure that funds are procured at the lowest cost and used effectively.

Statement II The primary aim of financial management is to maximise shareholders' wealth.

48. **Statement I** Cost of debt is lower than cost of equity for a company.

Statement II The objective of financial management is to increase shareholder's wealth. **CBSE SQP 2025**

49. **Statement I** The cost of debt is more than the cost of equity.

Statement II Lenders risk is lower than the equity shareholders risk. **CBSE 2025**

50. **Statement I** Dividend can be paid only out of the earnings of current year.

Statement II A firm with limited access to capital market, is likely to declare high dividend.

51. **Statement I** Financial planning involves preparing a financial blueprint of an organisation's future operations.

Statement II Financial planning is the same as financial management.

52. **Statement I** Financial planning typically covers only short-term periods of one year or less, while long-term planning is not a part of financial planning.

Statement II Financial planning includes both short-term and long-term planning, such as budgets for short-term periods and capital expenditure programmes for long-term growth.

53. **Statement I** The cost of debt is lower than the cost of equity because debt offers a lower risk to lenders.

Statement II Increasing the proportion of debt in the capital structure will always decrease the financial risk of a company.

54. **Statement I** Shareholders' funds are considered more expensive than borrowed funds due to the lack of tax benefits.

Statement II Borrowed funds are less risky compared to shareholders' funds.

55. **Statement I** Shareholders' funds involve commitment regarding the payment of returns or the repayment of capital.

Statement II Debt is considered to be the cheapest of all the sources of funds and tax deductability of interest makes it still cheaper. **CBSE 2024 C**

56. **Statement I** Larger the spread of business activities, greater is the need for fixed capital.

Statement II Leasing facility avoids huge funds required to buy fixed assets.

57. Statement I More working capital is required in the lean season.

Statement II Liberal credit policy increases the need for working capital for the company.

Matching

58. Match the following

Column I	Column II
A. Financing decision	(i) It involves deciding how much of the profits to be distributed to shareholders and how much of it to be retained in the business.
B. Investment decision	(ii) Long-term investment decision.
C. Capital budgeting decision	(iii) Deciding investment of funds in long-term and short-term assets.
D. Dividend decision	(iv) Deciding sources of finance, i.e. ratio of debt and equity.

Codes

	A	B	C	D		A	B	C	D
(a)	(ii)	(i)	(iv)	(iii)	(b)	(iv)	(iii)	(ii)	(i)
(c)	(iii)	(ii)	(i)	(iv)	(d)	(iv)	(i)	(iii)	(ii)

59. Match the following

Column I	Column II
A. Investment decision	(i) Control consideration
B. Financing decision	(ii) Stability of earnings
C. Dividend decision	(iii) Investment criteria

Codes

	A	B	C		A	B	C
(a)	(ii)	(i)	(iii)	(b)	(iii)	(ii)	(i)
(c)	(iii)	(i)	(ii)	(d)	(i)	(ii)	(iii)

60. Match the following

Column I	Column II
A. Cost	(i) Companies afraid of a takeover bid would prefer debt to equity.
B. State of capital market	(ii) If fixed operating cost is less, more of debt financing may be preferred.
C. Fixed operating costs	(iii) During the period when stock market is rising, more people invest in equity.
D. Control consideration	(iv) A rational manager would choose debt being a cheaper source.

Codes

	A	B	C	D
(a)	(ii)	(i)	(iv)	(iii)
(b)	(iii)	(iv)	(ii)	(i)
(c)	(iii)	(ii)	(i)	(iv)
(d)	(iv)	(iii)	(ii)	(i)

61. Match the following

Column I	Column II
A. Capital structure	(i) It is concerned with optimal procurement as well as the usage of finance.
B. Financial management	(ii) It refers to the mix between owners and borrowed funds.
C. Financial planning	(iii) The proportion of debt in the overall capital.
D. Financial leverage	(iv) Its objective is to ensure that enough funds are available at right time.

Codes

	A	B	C	D		A	B	C	D
(a)	(ii)	(i)	(iv)	(iii)	(b)	(ii)	(iii)	(iv)	(i)
(c)	(iii)	(ii)	(i)	(iv)	(d)	(iv)	(i)	(iii)	(ii)

62. Match the following

Column I	Column II
A. Nature of business	(i) A trading organisation needs lower investments in fixed assets as compared to a manufacturing organisation.
B. Technology upgradation	(ii) A textile manufacturing company is installing a cement manufacturing plant and thus its investments in fixed assets is increasing.
C. Diversification	(iii) A capital intensive organisation requires higher investments in fixed assets as compared to labour intensive organisation.
D. Choice of technique	(iv) Mobile phones became obsolete faster and are replaced much sooner than furniture or many other assets. Hence these type of businesses require more fixed capital.

Codes

	A	B	C	D
(a)	(i)	(iv)	(ii)	(iii)
(b)	(ii)	(iii)	(iv)	(i)
(c)	(iii)	(ii)	(i)	(iv)
(d)	(iv)	(i)	(iii)	(ii)

Answers

1. (a) The break-up of current assets into cash, inventory and receivables
2. (a) wealth maximisation of shareholders
3. (a) Maximising the wealth of equity shareholders
4. (c) Pricing decision
5. (a) Investment
6. (a) Investment decision
7. (c) These decisions affect the liquidity as well as profitability of a business
8. (d) Size of the assets, profitability and competitiveness are not affected by capital budgeting decisions
9. (d) (i), (iii) and (v)
10. (a) Financing
11. (c) Access to capital market
12. (b) Capital budgeting decision
13. (b) Financing decision
14. (d) Dividend decision
15. (d) growth opportunities
16. (d) access to capital market
17. (b) Stability in earnings
18. (c) ensuring that the firm faces neither a shortage nor a glut of unusable funds
19. (c) Financial planning
20. (b) Financial planning
21. (c) Capital structure is related to the cost of capital, as the cost of debt is generally lower than the cost of equity.
22. (c) capital structure
23. (d) trading on equity
24. (b) Earning Per Share (EPS) = Profit after Tax/Number of Equity Shares

    EPS of Company 'A' = 1,50,000/10,000 = ₹ 15

    EPS of Company 'B' = 1,20,000/12,000 = ₹ 10

    Hence, EPS of Company 'A' is more than Company 'B'.
25. (b) Growth opportunities
26. (b) Financing decision relates to the relative proportion of various sources of finance.
27. (a) company has a strong cash flow
28. (a) Cash flow position
29. (d) Technology upgradation
30. (b) Fixed capital vs Working capital
31. (b) inflation
32. (c) level of competition
33. (b) Capital structure
34. (c) higher degree of financial risk
35. (b) financial leverage
36. (d) trading on equity
37. (a) Both Assertion (A) and Reason (R) are true and Reason (R) is the correct explanation of Assertion (A)
38. (a) Both Assertion (A) and Reason (R) are true and Reason (R) is the correct explanation of Assertion (A)
39. (a) Both Assertion (A) and Reason (R) are true and Reason (R) is the correct explanation of Assertion (A)
40. (a) Both Assertion (A) and Reason (R) are true and Reason (R) is the correct explanation of Assertion (A)
41. (b) Both Assertion (A) and Reason (R) are true, but Reason (R) is not the correct explanation of Assertion (A)
42. (b) Both Assertion (A) and Reason (R) are true, but Reason (R) is not the correct explanation of Assertion (A)
43. (a) Both Assertion (A) and Reason (R) are true and Reason (R) is the correct explanation of Assertion (A)
44. (a) Both Assertion (A) and Reason (R) are true and Reason (R) is the correct explanation of Assertion (A)
45. (a) Both Assertion (A) and Reason (R) are true and Reason (R) is the correct explanation of Assertion (A)
46. (c) While working capital decisions do affect liquidity, they also impact other aspects of the business, such as profitability and operational efficiency.
47. (c) Both the statements are correct
48. (c) Both the statements are correct
49. (b) The cost of debt is generally lower than the cost of equity. This is because interest payments on debt are tax deductible and debt holders have a fixed claim on assets, making it a lower risk investment compared to equity.
50. (d) Dividends can be paid out of retained earnings from previous years as well, not just from the current year's earnings. Firms with limited access to the capital market might actually prefer to retain earnings rather than pay out high dividends.
51. (a) While financial planning is a part of financial management, they are not the same. Financial management encompasses a broader range of activities, including financial planning, managing finances, analysing financial performance and making financial decisions.
52. (b) Financial planning encompasses both short-term and long-term planning.
53. (a) While increasing debt can initially lower the cost of capital, it increases the company's financial risk as debt obligations must be met regardless of the company's performance. Excessive debt can lead to higher financial risk and potential solvency issues.
54. (a) Shareholders' funds are more expensive due to the lack of tax benefits and borrowed funds carry financial risk due to the obligation of repayment.
55. (b) Statement II is correct and Statement I is incorrect
56. (c) Both the statements are correct
57. (b) More working capital is typically required during the peak season, not the lean season. During the lean season, businesses often have lower inventory and reduced sales, which means less working capital is needed.
58. (b) (iv) (iii) (ii) (i)
59. (c) (iii) (i) (ii)
60. (d) (iv) (iii) (ii) (i)
61. (a) (ii) (i) (iv) (iii)
62. (a) (i) (iv) (ii) (iii)

Subjective Questions

Short Answer Type Questions

1. State any four objectives of financial management.

Or **What are the main objective of financial management? Briefly explain.** NCERT

Ans. With the primary objective of wealth maximisation, following objectives are also achieved

(i) Funds should be deployed in such a way that returns from an investment exceed its cost.

(ii) To raise funds at minimum cost and minimum risk, through effective financing decision.

(iii) To maintain financial liquidity and profitability, through working capital decision.

(iv) To ensure safety of funds by creating reserves, reinvestment of profits, etc.

2. State any three factors affecting the dividend decision.

Ans. Following are the factors that affect the dividend decision

(i) **Cash Flow Position**
Payment of dividend involves an outflow of cash. A company may be earning profit but may be short on cash. Thus, company having surplus cash may declare higher dividend while during shortage of cash, company may declare low dividend.

(ii) **Shareholders' Preference**
While declaring dividends, management must keep in mind the preferences of the shareholders. If the shareholders in general, desire that atleast a certain amount is paid as dividend, the companies are likely to declare the same. There are always some shareholders' who depends upon a regular income from their investments like retired people, middle class shareholders, etc.

(iii) **Taxation Policy**
The rate of dividend also depends upon the taxation policy of the government. If the tax on dividends is higher, the company prefers to pay less by way of dividends.

But if the tax rates are lower, higher dividends may be declared by the company.

3. State any three factors affecting financing decision. CBSE 2024 C

Ans. Following are the factors affecting financing decision

(i) **Cost**
The cost of raising funds through different sources are different and a prudent financial manager would normally opt for a source which is the cheapest.

(ii) **Risk**
The risk associated with each of the source of finance is different. For instance, debt increases financial risk due to fixed interest obligations, while equity financing spreads risk among shareholders.

(iii) **Floatation Cost**
It is the cost incurred while issuing securities, like underwriters fee, brokerage, legal fees, etc. Higher floatation cost makes a source, such as equity, less attractive compared to debt.

4. Define financial planning. How it is different from financial management?

Ans. Financial planning is the process of estimating the financial requirements of an organisation, specifying the sources of funds and ensuring that enough funds are available at the right time.

Financial planning aims at smooth operations by focusing on fund requirements and their availability in the light of financial decisions. On the other hand, financial management aims at choosing the best investment and financing alternatives by focusing on their costs and benefits. Its objective is to increase the shareholder's wealth.

5. "Financial planning is a financial blueprint of an organisation's future operations." Explain the twin objectives of financial planning in the light of this statement. Competency Based Que

Or **State the two objectives of financial planning.** NCERT

Ans. Objectives of financial planning are

(i) **To ensure Availability of Funds whenever Required**
If adequate funds are not available, the business unit will not be able to honour its commitments and meet its day-to-day expenses of business.

(ii) **To see that the Firm does not Raise Funds Unnecessarily**
If excess of funds are available with the business unit, it will unnecessarily add to the cost and may encourage wasteful expenditure and misuse of funds.

6. "Financial management plays an important role in the financial health of a company." In the light of the above statement, discuss some aspects which affect the financial health of a company. Competency Based Que

Ans. Some of the factors which affect the financial health of a business are as follows

(i) **Size and Composition of Fixed Assets**
For instance, if a decision is taken to invest 200 crore in establishing plant and machinery, then this decision would raise the size of fixed assets blocked by this amount.

(ii) **Quantum of Current Assets**
With an increase in the investment in fixed assets, there is a commensurate increase in the working capital requirement. The quantum of current assets is also influenced by financial management decisions. It helps to determine the amount of current assets and its break-up into cash, inventory and receivables.

(iii) **The Amount of Long-term and Short-term Funds to be Raised**
Financial management involves decision related to the proportion of long-term and short-term funds. e.g. If an organisation wishes to have more liquid assets, it would raise relatively more amount on a long-term basis. Such cases create problem in choosing liquidity or profitability.

7. Choosing between debt and equity is a crucial decision. Differentiate between debt and equity on the basis of cost and risk that can help a finance manager to choose the better alternative.

Ans. Following are the differences between debt and equity

Basis	Debt	Equity
Cost	Debt is considered to be cheaper because (i) The risk assumed by debt capital holders is less than equity share-holders, thus they expect a low rate of return. (ii) Interest is a deductible expenditure for tax purposes and tax liability gets reduced.	Equity is considered to be costly because (i) Risk assumed by equity shareholders is more, thus they expect a higher rate of return. (ii) Dividend is an appropriation of profits and is not a deductible expense for tax purposes and does not affect tax liability of the company.
Risk	Debt is a risky form of capital, as it involves contractual obligations as to payment of interest and repayment of principle sum, irrespective of profits or losses of business.	Raising capital through equity shares involves least risk, as there is no obligation as to payment of dividend and repayment of capital.

8. How is shareholders' wealth maximisation linked with the market price of the shares of the company?
Competency Based Que

Ans. The main and foremost objective of financial management is to maximise the wealth of equity shareholders. The financial manager of a company takes this decision because the shareholders are the owners of the company. Financial decisions taken will determine the manner in which the funds are invested.

The return earned on investment will determine the value and price of the shares. The market price of the shares will increase if the benefit from the decision has exceeded its cost. Secondly, the objective of increase in value of equity shares automatically fulfils many other objectives like increasing the profitability, maintaining liquidity, effective utilisation of funds and growth of the company.

9. Smart Works Ltd. wants to raise funds of ₹ 40,00,000 for its new project.

The management is considering the following mix of debt and equity to raise this amount.

Capital Structure	Alternative		
	I (₹)	II (₹)	III (₹)
Equity	40,00,000	30,00,000	10,00,000
Debt	0	10,00,000	30,00,000

Other details are as follows

Interest Rate on Debt	9%
Face Value of Equity Shares	₹ 100 each
Tax Rate	30%
Earning Before Interest and Tax (EBIT)	₹ 8,00,000

(i) **Under which three alternatives will the company be able to take advantage of trading on equity?**
(ii) **Does Earning Per Share (EPS) always rise with increase in debt?** **Competency Based Que**

Ans.

(i) The company will be available to take advantage of trading on equity in Alternative (III). This is because of higher earning per share in Alternative (III).

Calculation of Earning Per Share (EPS)

Alternative

Particulars	I (₹)	II (₹)	III (₹)
EBIT	8,00,000	8,00,000	8,00,000
(–) Interest	—	(90,000)	(2,70,000)
	8,00,000	7,10,000	5,30,000
(–) Tax @ 30%	(2,40,000)	(2,13,000)	(1,59,000)
Profit After Tax	5,60,000	4,97,000	3,71,000
EPS	$\frac{5,60,000}{40,000}$ = ₹ 14	$\frac{4,97,000}{30,000}$ = ₹ 16.56	$\frac{3,71,000}{10,000}$ = ₹ 37.10

(ii) No, earning per share only rises with increase in debt when the rate of interest on debt is lower than the return on investment.

10. From the following information regarding Aditya Ltd. which is in the business of manufacturing green tea, calculate the return on investment and interest coverage ratio of the company. (Show working)

Earning before Interest and Tax	**₹ 15,00,000**
10% Debentures	**₹ 12,00,000**
Equity Share Capital (₹ 10 each)	**₹ 18,00,000**
Tax Rate	**40%**

CBSE SQP 2025; Competency Based Que

Ans. Calculation of Return on Investment (RoI)

$$\text{RoI} = \frac{\text{Earning before Interest and Tax}}{\text{Total Investment}} \times 100$$

$$\text{RoI} = \frac{15,00,000}{30,00,000\ (18,00,000 + 12,00,000)} \times 100 = 50\%$$

Calculation of Interest Coverage Ratio (ICR)

$$\text{Interest Coverage Ratio} = \frac{\text{Earning before Interest and Tax}}{\text{Interest}}$$

$$\text{ICR} = \frac{15,00,000}{1,20,000} = 12.5 \text{ times}$$

11. Silk Ltd. had an EPS of ₹ 1. It raised a loan of ₹ 10 lakh at an interest rate of 10% p.a. from a bank. After one year, the results were as follows

Details	Amt (₹)
Equity (Shareholders' funds) (2,00,000 shares of ₹ 10 each)	20 lakh
10% Loan	10 lakh
Earning Before Interest and Tax (EBIT)	6 lakh
Earning Per Share (EPS)	2

Tax rate 20%.

(i) Why did EPS in Silk Ltd. rise with the use of debt?

(ii) If EBIT of the company would have been ₹ 3 lakh, would using debt still be favourable for the company? Explain.

CBSE 2024 C; Competency Based Que

Ans.

(i) The EPS in Silk Ltd. rose with the use of debt because the cost of debt is lower than the return that the company is earning on funds employed (RoI) which is known as trading on equity/favourable financial leverage.

(ii) If EBIT of the company would have been ₹ 3 lakh, using debt would not been favourable for the company due to following reasons

- It is unfavourable for the company because the company's rate of Return on Investment (RoI) is not more than the cost of debt.
- The RoI of the company is (3/30) × 100 i.e. 10% and the interest rate on debt is also 10%.
- In such a case, the EPS will be reduced to ₹ 0.8. This is a situation of unfavourable financial leverage.

12. When can a capital structure be considered optimum and what kind of capital structure is best for a firm?

Ans. Capital structure refers to the composition of debt and equity.

A capital structure is said to be optimum when the proportion of debt and equity is such that, it results in increase in the wealth of shareholders.

If the capital structure results in increasing or maximising the wealth of shareholders, then it is considered best for a firm.

13. Differentiate between fixed capital and working capital.

Ans. Difference between fixed and working capital is as follows

Basis	Fixed Capital	Working Capital
Time period	Required for long-term.	Required for short-term.
Purpose	Money needed to buy fixed assets.	Money needed to buy current assets.
Nature	Remains sunk in business.	Revolves in business.
Source	Raised through shares, debentures and term loans.	Raised through banks, trade credit, shares and debentures.

14. State any four factors affecting the requirements of the fixed capital.

Ans. Following are the factors that affect the requirements of the fixed capital are as follows

(i) **Nature of Business**
The nature of business has a great influence upon the fixed capital requirements.
e.g. A trading company requires lower investment in fixed assets as compared to a manufacturing organisation, since it does not require to purchase plant and machinery, etc.

(ii) **Scale of Operations**
A larger organisation operating at a larger scale needs higher investment in fixed assets as compared to a small organisation.

(iii) **Choice of Technique**
Some organisations are capital intensive, whereas, others are labour intensive. A capital intensive organisation requires more investment in plant and machinery as it rely less on manual labour. On the other hand, labour intensive organisations require less investment in fixed assets.

(iv) **Technology Upgradation**
Industries in which assets becomes obsolete sooner due to technology upgradation, need higher investment in fixed assets to replace older assets. While companies whose assets are not or least affected by technology upgradation, needs lesser investment. e.g. Computers become obsolete faster and are replaced much sooner than say, furniture.

15. Explain how the following factors affect the working capital requirement of a business. CBSE 2024

(i) Operating efficiency (ii) Credit availed

Ans.

(i) **Operating Efficiency**
Companies manage their operations with varied degrees of efficiency. A firm that manages its raw materials efficiently may require less working capital. This is reflected in a higher inventory turnover ratio. Similarly, a better debtor turnover ratio can be achieved reducing the amount tied up in receivables.

(ii) **Credit Availed**
Just as a firm allows credit to its customers, it also may get credit from its suppliers. To the extent, it avails the credit on purchases, the working capital requirement is reduced and *vice-versa*.

16. "Financial management is concerned with inflow and outflow of money." Do you agree? If yes, How? Competency Based Que

Ans. Yes, financial management is concerned with inflow and outflow of money as it is concerned with taking decisions regarding optimal procurement and utilisation of funds.

For the effective procurement of funds, different available sources of finance are identified and compared in terms of cost and risk associated with them.

Procurement of funds is done for both long-term needs as well as short-term needs. For long-term financing needs, the funds can be sourced through debt and equity. Short-term financing involves management of working capital. Now, the funds so procured have to be invested in a manner that the returns are higher than the cost of funds. The outflow of money is through purchase of fixed assets, current assets, working capital needs, distribution of dividends, etc.

Long Answer Type Questions

17. Explain the role of financial management.

Ans. The role of financial management has a direct bearing on the financial health of a business. Almost all items in the financial statements of a business are affected directly or indirectly through some financial management decisions. Some prominent examples of the aspects being affected are as under

(i) The size and composition of fixed assets of the company depends on financial management decision, i.e. the size of fixed assets of the business depends on the amount that it decides to invest.
e.g. If the business decides to invest ₹ 500 crore in fixed assets, than size of fixed assets will increase by the equal amount.

(ii) The quantum of current assets is also influenced by financial management decisions.
Financial management helps to decide the amount of current assets required as well as its break-up into cash, inventory and receivables required in the business.

(iii) Financial management helps to determine the amount required in business for long-term and short-term basis. e.g. The organisation that requires more liquid assets will require more amount on long-term basis, but with this decision, the profitability will decrease as the organisation has to pay more interest.

(iv) Financing decision involves decision regarding procurement of finance, i.e. it helps to decide that how much part of long-term financing should be done from equity and how much from debt. Thus, financial management decision affects the proportion of equity and debt to make up the capital structure.

(v) Financial management decisions affect all the items in profit and loss account like interest, expense, depreciation, etc. Higher amount of debt means higher interest expense, use of higher equity means higher payment of dividends, expansion of fixed assets involve depreciation.

18. "Effective financial planning is essential for the success of any business enterprise." Explain this statement by giving any six reasons. Competency Based Que

Ans. Effective financial planning is essential for the success of any business enterprise because of the following reasons

(i) It helps in forecasting what may happen in future under different business situations. By doing this, it helps the firms to face the situation in a better way. e.g. A growth of 20% in sales is predicted. However, it may happen that the growth rate eventually turns out to be 10% or 30%. Many items of expenses shall be different in these three situations. By preparing a blueprint of these three situations, the management may decide what must be done in each of these situations.

(ii) It helps in avoiding business shocks and surprises and helps the company in preparing for the future.

(iii) It helps in coordinating various business functions like production, sales, etc. by providing policies and procedures.

(iv) It tries to link the present with the future by foreseeing the growth prospects, sales, etc.

(v) It provides a link between investment and financing decisions on a continuous basis.

(vi) It helps in reducing waste, duplication of efforts and gaps in planning through detailed plans of action.

19. Tara Ltd. is a company manufacturing textiles. It has a share capital of ₹ 60 lakh. In the previous year, its earning per share was 0.50. For diversification, the company requires additional capital of ₹ 40 lakh. The company raised funds by issuing 10% debentures for the same. During the year, the company earned profit of ₹ 8 lakh on capital employed.

It paid tax @ 40%.

(i) **State whether the shareholders gained or lost, in respect of earning per share on diversification. Show your calculations clearly.**

(ii) **Also, state any three factors that favour the issue of debentures by the company as part of its capital structure.** Competency Based Que

Ans. (i)

Particulars	Amt (₹)
Profit before Interest and Tax	8,00,000
(–) Debentures Interest $\left(40,00,000 \times \frac{10}{100}\right)$	(4,00,000)
Profit after Interest	4,00,000
(–) Tax $\left(4,00,000 \times \frac{40}{100}\right)$	(1,60,000)
Profit after Tax	2,40,000
Earning per Share	$\frac{\text{Profit After Tax}}{\text{Number of Shares}} = \frac{2,40,000}{6,00,000} = ₹\ 0.40$

Since earning per share has fallen from 0.50 to 0.40, therefore the shareholders stand to lose on diversification.

Note In the absence of any information, shares are assumed to be of ₹ 10 each.

$$\text{So, Number of Shares} = \frac{\text{Share Capital}}{\text{Face Value Per Share}} = \frac{60,00,000}{10}$$

$$= 6,00,000 \text{ shares}$$

(ii) Three factors that favour issue of debentures by the company as part of its capital structure are

- Debentures interest payable is a charge to the profits. Hence, a company stands to gain in terms of tax benefits.
- Issue of debentures help the shareholders of the company to gain through 'trading on equity'.
- Debenture is a cheaper source of finance as compared to equity.

20. Explain the term 'trading of equity'. Why, when and how it can be used by company? NCERT

Or **How are the shareholders likely to gain with loan components in capital employed? Explain with suitable example.** Competency Based Que

Ans. Trading on equity refers to the increase in profit earned by the equity shareholders due to the presence of fixed financial charges like interest. The use of more debt along with equity increases Earning Per Share (EPS). This is because, debt carry fixed amount of interest, which is a tax deductible expense. Trading on equity is beneficial only when RoI is greater than the rate of interest on debt. Let us take an example of companies A and B

Particulars	Company A (₹)	Company B (₹)
Share Capital (₹ 100 each)	10,00,000	4,00,000
Loan @ 15% p.a.	—	6,00,000
Total Capital	10,00,000	10,00,000
Profit Before Interest and Tax (30% RoI)	3,00,000	3,00,000
(–) Interest (15% of 6,00,000)	Nil	90,000
Profit Before Tax	3,00,000	2,10,000
(–) Tax @ 50%	1,50,000	1,05,000
Profit After Tax	1,50,000	1,05,000

Earning Per Share (EPS)

= Profit after Tax/Number of Equity Shares

A = 1,50,000/10,000 = 15; B = 1,05,000/4,000 = 26.25

Thus, from the above example, it is clear that shareholders of Company B receive higher EPS than the shareholders of Company A due to more debt in the total capital of Company B.

21. The determination of the overall cost of capital and financial risk of the enterprise is affected by several factors. Explain any six factors.

Ans. Following are the factors that affect the determination of the overall cost of capital and financial risk of the enterprise

(i) **Return on Investment** (RoI)

Return on Investment means the earnings of a company on its investments. It is calculated as

$$\text{RoI} = \frac{\text{EBIT}}{\text{Total Investment}} \times 100$$

When the RoI is more than the cost of debt (i.e. interest to be paid on debt), company should prefer more debt in its capital structure and *vice-versa*.

(ii) **Cost of Debt**

If the rate of interest on debt is high, the company should use less debt in its capital structure and *vice-versa*.

(iii) **Tax Rate**

If the tax rate is higher, it makes the debt cheaper because the interest paid on debt is a deductible expense from the taxable income of company, whereas companies are required to pay tax on dividend paid to shareholders. Thus, higher rate of tax makes debt financing more attractive and *vice-versa*.

(iv) **Cost of Equity**

When a company increases debt, the financial risk faced by equity shareholders increases. Increase in risk also increases the desired rate of return. Thus, debt can be used upto a limit.

If debt is used beyond that point, cost of equity may go up and share prices may decrease inspite of increased EPS.

(v) **Floatation Cost**
It is the cost involved in issue of securities such as underwriting fees, stamp duty, brokerage, etc. If the floatation cost is higher, the source of finance becomes less attractive and *vice-versa*.

(vi) **Flexibility**
If a company uses excess debt in its capital structure, it may lose flexibility to issue further debt. Financing should be done in such a way, that it should be able to cater to additional requirements of funds in future to take care of unforeseen circumstances.

22. Explain how the following factors affect the requirement of fixed capital.
(i) Level of collaboration
(ii) Financing alternatives (iii) Diversification

Ans.

(i) **Level of Collaboration**
The collaborations between the organisations to use one another's facilities and assets reduce the need for fixed capital.

This is feasible if the scale of operations of each of them is not sufficient to make full use of the facility. This type of collaboration reduces the need of fixed assets for each one of the participating organisations. e.g. Banks are using each other's ATMs, thus saving on individual setting of ATMs by each bank, which entails huge expenditures.

(ii) **Financing Alternatives**
A developed financial market can provide leasing facilities as an alternative to outright purchase. If such alternatives are available with the company, the assets are not required to be purchased outrightly, but only rent or instalments have to be paid. This reduces the requirement of fixed capital.

(iii) **Diversification**
When a company wants to diversify its operations or enter into a new business other than that of its current product, it requires more fixed capital. e.g. An apparel company diversifying into cosmetic business, will certainly require more fixed capital for investing into plant and machinery, building, etc.

23. What is working capital? Discuss five important determinants of working capital requirement. NCERT

Ans. Working capital means the portion of capital which is invested in current assets. This investment facilitates smooth day-to-day operations of the business. The term 'working capital' means gross working capital or net working capital.

(i) Gross working capital means current assets.

(ii) Net working capital may be defined as excess of current assets over current liabilities.

Factors Affecting Working Capital The main factors affecting the working capital requirements are given below

(i) **Nature of Business**
The basic nature of a business influences the amount of working capital required. A trading organisation and a service industry firm usually needs a smaller amount of working capital as compared to a manufacturing organisation.

(ii) **Scale of Operations**
Organisations which operate on a large scale, their quantum of inventory and debtors required is generally high. Such organisations, therefore, require large amount of working capital as compared to the organisations which operate on a lower scale.

(iii) **Business Cycle**
Different phases of business cycles affect the requirement of working capital by a firm. In case of a boom, the sales as well as production are likely to be larger and therefore, larger amount of working capital is required. As against this, the requirement for working capital will be lower during the period of depression, since the sales as well as production will be less.

(iv) **Seasonal Factors**
Some of the businesses have seasonal operations. During peak season, larger amount of working capital is required because of higher level of activity.

As against this, the level of activity as well as the requirement for working capital will be lower during the lean season.

(v) **Production Cycle**
Production cycle is the time span between the receipt of raw material and their conversion into finished goods. Some businesses have a longer production cycle while some have a shorter one.

Duration and the length of production cycle affects the amount of funds required for raw materials and expenses.

24. Explain how the following factors affect the working capital requirements of a company
(i) Business cycle
(ii) Nature of business
(iii) Seasonal factors

Ans.

(i) **Business Cycle**
Different phases of business cycles affect the requirement of working capital by a firm. In case of a boom, the sales as well as production are likely to be larger thus, larger amount of working capital is required. In case of depression, the requirement for working capital will be lower, since the sales as well as production will be less.

(ii) **Nature of Business**
The basic nature of a business influences the amount of working capital required.

A trading organisation and a service industry firm usually needs a smaller amount of working capital as compared to a manufacturing organisation.

This is because operating cycle of trading company is small in comparison to manufacturing company which have to convert raw material into finished goods before any sale become possible.

(iii) **Seasonal Factors**
Some of the businesses have seasonal operations, thus, there working capital requirement fluctuate with change in season.

25. Why is an adequate amount of working capital required in an enterprise? Competency Based Que

Ans. Adequate working capital is essential for smooth and efficient working of every business enterprise.

Adequate working capital provides the following advantages to a business enterprise

(i) A firm with adequate working capital can meet its liabilities promptly.

Prompt payment helps to raise the credit-standing or reputation of the enterprise.

(ii) Adequacy of working capital enables the firm to take advantage of any favourable business opportunity, e.g. To purchase raw materials at a discount or to execute a special order.

(iii) Financial soundness of business boosts the morale of employees.

(iv) Lack of adequate working capital may result in interruptions in operations and underutilisation of plant capacity.

(v) Adequate working capital permits timely and regular payment of cash dividends. This helps to maintain cordial relations with shareholders.

Case Study Based Questions

Short Case Studies

Case Study 1

Identify and state the type of decisions in the following cases

(i) Ravi wants to open a restaurant and is looking for a proper place to open it. He is also thinking of the amount of funds which will be required for some of the set-ups like food making and storing machineries.

(ii) Ravindra is running a toy manufacturing company. He thinks of expanding his business. He meets his uncle and asks him for a sum of ₹ 2 crore. His uncle asks for a high interest rate.

He agrees to it and promises to pay the money back within 2 years.

Ans.

(i) It is an investment decision. Investment decision relates to how the firm's funds are invested in different assets.

(ii) It is a financing decision. This decision relates to the amount of finance to be raised from various long-term sources.

Case Study 2

The demand for take away food business is increasing day-by-day. People working in multi-national companies have to work till night very often and they are reluctant to cook food.

Taking advantage of this opportunity, Amit and Bijoy started 'Langer', a take away food business. The food became famous because of its good quality and standards of hygiene followed by them. Over the years, the business became very profitable. They decided to expand the business by opening more branches in different cities. To ensure consistent food quality at all branches and to maintain the hygiene and quality they planned to import machines with advanced technology. The cost of each machine was ₹ 12 crores. They knew that this decision has to be taken very carefully, as it involves a huge cost and that the decision, once taken is irreversible. **CBSE 2025**

(i) Identify and state the financial decision discussed in the above para.

(ii) Explain any two factors affecting the decision identified in (i) above.

Ans.

(i) The financial decision discussed in the above paragraph is investment decision (capital budgeting decision). Investment decision relates to how the firm's funds are invested in different assets.

This decision involves careful selection of assets, so that they can earn highest possible return for their investors.

Long-term decisions involve committing the finance on a long-term basis. e.g. Investment in a new machine or opening new branch, etc.

(ii) Factors affecting long-term investment decision are

- **Cash Flows of the Project**
  When a business invests huge amount of money in a certain project, then it expects to generate some cash flows over a period. These cash flows are in the form of a series of cash receipts and payments over the life of an investment. These cash flows should be carefully analysed before selecting the desired project.
- **The Rate of Return**
  Each project is selected after comparing expected returns of different projects and the degree of risk involved in them.

Case Study 3

Hemant, the finance manager and Arun Chopra, the managing director of Ghokla Ltd. were discussing regarding the source of finance to be raised for modernisation of their existing plant.

Quoting that 'sensex has soared by 5078 points' in the last three years, Hemant suggests that equity should be preferred while Arun Chopra wanted to opt for debt.

(i) Keeping in mind the high operating costs of the company, suggest the source of finance that should be used for modernisation of existing plant.

(ii) Also, explain the two factors highlighted above which should be kept in mind for taking this decision.

Ans.

(i) The company should opt for equity as the source of finance to modernise the existing plant.

(ii) Following factors were taken into consideration for the decision

- **Stock Market Condition**
  In boom and favourable stock market conditions, equity should be preferred as the investors are ready to take risk.
- **Cash Flow Positions**
  If the costs are high and therefore cash flow position is weak, company should opt equity as there is permanent burden of payment of interest on debt.

Case Study 4

Sunrises Ltd. dealing in readymade garments, is planning to expand its business operations in order to cater to international market. For this purpose the company needs additional ₹ 80,00,000 for replacing machines with modern machinery of higher production capacity.

The company wishes to raise the required funds by issuing debentures. The debt can be issued at an estimated cost of 10%. The EBIT for the previous year of the company was ₹ 8,00,000 and total capital investment was ₹ 1,00,00,000.

Suggest whether issue of debenture would be considered a rational decision by the company. Give reason to justify your answer. **NCERT**

Ans. According to the given case, the debt can be issued at an estimated cost, i.e.

Cost of debt = 10% and Sunrises Ltd RoI as per the given information is

$$= (\text{Return}/\text{Investment}) \times 100$$
$$= (8{,}00{,}000/1{,}00{,}00{,}000) \times 100$$
$$= 8\%$$

Since the cost of debt is more than RoI, i.e. 10% > 8%, thus, it is advisable for a company not to issue debentures to raise the required funds.

Case Study 5

Sunflower Ltd. is a trusted name in diagnostic services with seven branches across the city of Mumbai. The directors of this company have projected that with the rise in health consciousness in the society and the rising burden of chronic diseases, the demand for tests is expected to grow in future. Considering this, they decided to open branches of their labs in Pune.

It was estimated that it will require 150 crore of additional funds. The directors have to take the decision about how much funds should be raised from equity capital and how much from debt.

It will affect the overall cost of capital and the financial risk of the company.

(i) Identify and state the financial decision discussed in the above paragraph.

(ii) State any three factors that should be kept in mind by the board of directors of Sunflower Ltd. while taking the decision identified in (i) above.

Ans.

(i) Financing decision is discussed in the above paragraph. This decision relates to the amount of finance to be raised from various long-term sources.

(ii) Factors that should be kept in mind by the board of directors of Sunflower Ltd. while taking the financing decision are

- **Cost**
  The cost of raising funds from different sources are different. A wise financial manager opts for the cheapest source of finance.
- **Risk**
  The risk associated with each of the source of finance is different. Borrowed funds involve more risk as compared to owner's funds. Thus, finance manager should analyse the risk involved and source with least risk should be preferred.

- **Floatation Cost**
  It is the cost involved in issue of securities like commission, brokerage, underwriters fee, etc. If the floatation cost is higher, the source of finance becomes less attractive.

Case Study 6

Chetanshi Ltd. is a company dealing in readymade garments from several years. Recently the profit of the company has started increasing. The finance manager decided to retain the profit instead of distributing it among the shareholders.

(i) Identify and state the financial decision taken by finance manager in the above case.

(ii) State any three factors affecting the decision identified in (i) above.

Ans.

(i) The financial decision taken by finance manager is dividend decision. This decision is concerned with ascertaining how much of surplus profit is to be distributed among shareholders and how much of it should be retained in the business.

(ii) Three factors affecting the dividend decision are as follows

- **Amount of Earnings**
  Dividends are paid out of current and past earnings. Thus, the company which is earning more will declare higher dividend where as low earning company will declare lower rate of dividend.
- **Stability in Earnings**
  A company having regular and stable earnings can declare higher dividends, while a company with unstable earnings is likely to pay smaller dividends.
- **Contractual Constraints**
  While granting loans to a company, sometimes, the lender may impose certain restrictions on the payment of dividends in future. The companies are required to ensure that the dividend payout does not violate the terms of the loan agreement in this regard.

Case Study 7

Gupta International Ltd. earned a net profit of ₹ 50 crore. Mahesh, the finance manager of Gupta International Ltd. wants to decide how to appropriate these profits.

(i) Identify and state the decision that Mahesh will have to take.

(ii) State any three factors which will help him in taking this decision.

Ans.

(i) The decision that Mahesh will have to take is dividend decision. This decision is concerned with ascertaining how much of surplus profit is to be distributed among shareholders and how much of it should be retained in the business.

(ii) Factors that will help Mahesh in taking this decision are

- **Stock Market Reaction**
  Rate of dividend and market value of the shares are directly related to each other. Investors view an increase in dividend as a good news and stock prices react positively to it and *vice-versa*. Thus, the management should consider the possible impact of dividend policy on the equity share price while taking a decision about it.
- **Access to Capital Market**
  Large and reputed companies having easy access to the capital market and whose securities are in demand, may depend less on retained earnings to finance their growth. These companies tend to pay higher dividends than the smaller companies which have relatively low access to the market.
- **Legal Constraints**
  Certain provisions of the Companies Act place restrictions on pay-outs as dividend. Such provisions must be adhered to, while declaring the dividend.

Case Study 8

Aval Ltd. is engaged in the business of export of canvas goods and bags. In the past, the performance of the company had been upto the expectations. In line with the latest demand in the market, the company decided to venture into leather goods for which it required specialised machinery.

For this, the finance manager Prabhu prepared a financial blueprint of the organisation's future operations to estimate the amount of funds required and the timings with the objective to ensure that enough funds are available at right time.

He also collected the relevant data about the profit estimates in the coming years. By doing this, he wanted to be sure about the availability of funds from the internal sources of the business. For the remaining funds, he is trying to find out alternative sources from outside.

(i) Identify the financial concept discussed in the above paragraph. Also, state the objectives to be achieved by the use of financial concept so identified.

(ii) "There is no restriction on payment of dividend by a company." Comment. **NCERT**

Ans.

(i) 'Financial planning' is the concept discussed in the above paragraph. The objectives to be achieved by the use of financial planning are

- To ensure availability of funds whenever these are required, in order to honour its commitments and meet day-to-day expenses of business, etc.
- To see that the firm does not raise resources unnecessarily, as idle funds raise the cost of finance as well as give way to wasteful expenditures.

(ii) The above said statement does not hold true, as there are certain restrictions on payment of dividend by a company which are imposed by following constraints

- **Legal Constraints**
  Certain provisions of the Companies Act place restrictions on payouts as dividend. Such provisions must be adhered to, while declaring the dividend.
- **Contractual Constraints**
  While granting loans to a company, sometimes, the lender may impose certain restrictions on the payment of dividends in future. The companies are required to ensure that the dividend payout does not violate the terms of the loan agreement in this regard.

Case Study 9

Gagneja Engineering Ltd, a leading manufacturer of rods wants to manufacture trucks. It is important for finance manager to ensure the availability of funds whenever required and its possible sources.

It is also important to ensure that the company does not raise funds unnecessarily. The fund requirement and the availability has to be matched.

(i) Identify and give the meaning of the concept discussed in the case which will help the finance manager to achieve his objectives.

(ii) Also, state any three points of importance of the concept identified in (i) above.

Ans.

(i) The concept discussed in the case is financial planning. It is the preparation of a financial blueprint of an organisation's future operations.

(ii) Financial planning is important because of the following reasons

- It helps in forecasting what may happen in future under different business situations. By doing this, it helps the firms to face the situation in a better way. e.g. A growth of 20% in sales is predicted. However, it may happen that the growth rate eventually turns out to be 10% or 30%. Many items of expenses shall be different in these three situations. By preparing a blueprint of these three situations, the management may decide what must be done in each of these situations.
- It helps in avoiding business shocks and surprises and helps the company in preparing for the future.
- It helps in coordinating various business functions like production, sales, etc. by providing policies and procedures.

Case Study 10

Though Ran Apparels is making huge profits every year on a regular basis, it is not able to provide sufficient dividend to its shareholders. As a result, EPS remains low. Identify and explain the concept that can help to resolve the problem.

Ans. The concept that can help to resolve the problem is trading on equity. Trading on equity means the use of fixed cost sources of finance such as preference shares, debentures and long-term loans in the capital structure, so as to increase the return on equity shares. This is also known as financial leverage. It is advisable to use trading on equity when the rate of return on investment is more than the rate of interest payable on debentures and loans.

Case Study 11

The Return on Investment (RoI) of a company ranges between 10-12% for the past three years. To finance its future fixed capital needs, it has the following options for borrowing debt. Option 'A' : Rate of interest 9% Option 'B' : Rate of interest 13%. Which source of debt, 'Option A' or 'Option B', is better? Give reason in support of your answer. Also, state the concept being used in taking the decision.

Ans. The company should use 'Option A' as in this case, the Return on Investment (10-12%) will be more than the cost of Debt (9%). The concept being used in the above case is trading on equity.

The use of debt alongwith equity increases Earnings Per Share (EPS). This use of fixed financial charge, i.e. interest, increases the profit earned by shareholders. This concept is known as trading on equity.

If the company opts for Option A, it will lead to favourable trading on equity as in this case, RoI > CoD, where RoI-Return on Investment (10-12%) CoD-Cost of Debt (9%).

Case Study 12

Company 'A' has the debt-equity ratio of 3 :1. Another Company 'B' has the debt-equity ratio of 2.5 : 1. Both the companies are part of an industry where the operating costs are high. Many of the companies in this industry are vulnerable to high business risk.

Which one of the two companies is going to have higher chances of financial risk?

Why do you think the financial risk in the above mentioned industry is going to be dangerous for the companies?

Ans. The Company A is going to have higher chances of financial risk as the debt component is higher. Due to the higher debt component there will be an increase in the fixed financial costs. In case a company is unable to bear fixed financial costs the financial risk increases.

If a company is unable to bear operating costs then business risk gets generated. In an industry where there is already a chance of higher business risk an additional financial risk will increase the total risk to a dangerous level.

Case Study 13

Kanav, after passing out of college with specialisation in renewable energy, was determined to start a solar power plant. The venture required heavy investment in plant and machinery and less on manual labour. Kanav invested in the latest solar panel technology and infrastructure and purchased the latest solar panels, inverters and battery storage systems. Despite the high risk and substantial investment, Kanav's business had good expansion possibilities.

The world was increasingly moving towards clean energy solutions and there was a growing demand for sustainable power sources. So, Kanav decided to create a higher capacity to meet the anticipated demand quickly. This entailed further investment in fixed assets which Kanav was able to arrange. As the years passed, the solar power plant did very well and played a pivotal role in the city's transition towards a greener and more sustainable future.

Identify and explain the two factors affecting the fixed capital requirements discussed in the above case. **CBSE 2024**

Ans. The factors affecting the fixed capital requirements discussed is the case are

(i) **Technology Upgradation**
Industries in which assets becomes obsolete sooner due to technology upgradation, need higher investment in fixed assets to replace older assets. While companies whose assets are not or least affected by technology upgradation, needs lesser investment.

(ii) **Growth Prospects**
Higher growth of an organisation requires higher investment in fixed assets. A company expecting such growth may expand its production capacity in order to meet the anticipated higher demand quickly. This entails larger investment in fixed assets and consequently, larger fixed capital.

Case Study 14

Pinnacle Ltd. deals in the sale of stationery and office furniture. They source the finished products from reputed brands who give them four to six months credit. Seeing the demand for electronic items, they are also planning to market these items by opening outlets throughout India. For this, they decided to join hands with a Japanese electronic goods manufacturer.

Identify and state any two factors that would affect fixed capital requirement of Pinnacle Ltd. as discussed above.

Ans. Two factors that would affect the fixed capital requirement are

(i) **Diversification**
When a company wants to diversify its operations or enter into a new business other than that of its current product, it requires more fixed capital.

(ii) **Level of Collaboration**
The collaborations between the organisations to use one another's facilities and assets reduce the need for fixed capital.

Case Study 15

KJ Ltd. is manufacturing trucks at its manufacturing unit in Kolkata. The demand of its trucks is high as the economic growth is about 7% to 8%.

The company has estimated a 20% increase in the demand of its trucks. It is planning to set-up a new truck manufacturing unit.

For this the company will require approximately ₹ 2,000 crore as fixed capital and ₹ 500 crore as working capital. The company has already arranged for its fixed capital.

State any three factors that the finance manager of the company should keep in mind while arranging its working capital.

Ans. Following are the factors that the finance manager of the company should keep in mind while arranging its working capital

(i) **Scale of Operations**
Organisations which operate on a large scale, generally need to maintain high level of inventory and debtors. Such organisations, therefore, require large amount of working capital as compared to the organisations which operate on a lower scale.

(ii) **Production Cycle**
It is the time span between receipt of raw material and their conversion into finished goods. Companies with longer processing cycle require more working capital and *vice-versa*.

(iii) **Inflation**
Price level changes also affect the working capital requirement. With rising prices, large amount is required even to maintain a constant volume of production and sales.
Thus, working capital requirement becomes higher with higher rate of inflation.

Case Study 16

Verma Ltd. has various warehousing arrangements. The services provided by the company help the businesses to decrease their overheads, increase efficiency and reduce the distribution time.

(i) State whether the working capital requirements of Verma Ltd. will be high or low. Give reason.

(ii) Explain any two factors affecting working capital requirement.

Ans.

(i) The working capital requirement of Verma Ltd. will be low as it is a service industry which usually does not have to maintain inventory.

(ii) Factors affecting working capital requirement are as follows

- **Credit Allowed**
  Different firms allow different credit terms to their customers. These terms depend upon the level of competition that a firm faces, as well as the credit worthiness of their clientele. Liberal credit policy means more working capital requirement while strict credit policy means less working capital requirement.
- **Credit Availed**
  Just as a firm allows credit to its customers, it also may get credit from its suppliers. To the extent, it avails the credit on purchases, the working capital requirement is reduced and *vice-versa*.

Case Study 17

KJ Ltd. is manufacturing trucks at its manufacturing unit in Kolkata. The demand of its trucks is high as the economic growth is about 7% to 8%. The company has estimated a 20% increase in the demand of its trucks. It is planning to set-up a new truck manufacturing unit. For this the company will require approximately 2,000 crores as fixed capital and 500 crores as working capital.

The company has already arranged for its fixed capital. State any three factors that the finance manager of the company should keep in mind while arranging its working capital.

Ans. Following are the factors that affect the working capital requirement

(i) **Business Cycle**
Different phases of business cycles affect the requirement of working capital by a firm. In case of a boom, the sales as well as production are likely to be larger thus, larger amount of working capital is required.
In case of depression, the requirement for working capital will be lower, since the sales as well as production will be less.

(ii) **Nature of Business**
The basic nature of a business influences the amount of working capital required. A trading organisation and a service industry firm usually needs a smaller amount of working capital as compared to a manufacturing organisation. This is because operating cycle of trading company is small in comparison to manufacturing company which have to convert raw material into finished goods before any sale become possible.

(iii) **Operating Efficiency**
Companies manage their operations with varied degrees of efficiency. A firm that manages its raw materials efficiently may require less working capital. This is reflected in a higher inventory turnover ratio. Similarly, a better debtor turnover ratio can be achieved reducing the amount tied up in receivables.

Long Case Studies

Case Study 18

S Ltd. is manufacturing steel at its plant in India. It is enjoying a buoyant demand for its products as economic growth is about 7-8% and the demand for steel is growing. It is planning to set-up a new steel plant to cash on the increased demand.

It is estimated that it will require about ₹ 5,000 crore to set-up and about ₹ 500 crore of working capital to start the new plant. **NCERT Modified**

(i) Describe the role and objectives of financial management for this company.

(ii) Explain the importance of having a financial plan for this company. Give an imaginary plan to support your answer.

Ans.

(i) **Role of Financial Management**
Financial management decisions has a bearing on the financial health of business by affecting the following

- **Size and Composition of Fixed Assets**
  'S' Ltd. requires ₹ 5,000 crore, which is a huge sum. Financial management will have to ensure that composition is carefully decided. Since, it is into infrastructure industry, it has a long gestation period between investments and returns. Thus, the goal should be to minimise the risk with investing into most productive assets and latest technology, which in no case should remain idle.
- **Quantum of Current Assets and their Break-up**
  ₹ 500 crore are required for current assets to finance working capital.

  Thus, the company should ensure correct break-up and optimum utilisation.

- **Amount of Long-term and Short-term Financing to be Used**
  Long-term assets require long-term financing, whereas, short-term assets require short-term financing. The choice is between liquidity and profitability. An optimum mix of two is required.
- **Break-up of Long-term Financing into Debt and Equity**
  Since, setting-up of new steel plant is a long-term task, therefore, large amount of debt is required. Accordingly, debt and equity ratio might be more.
- **Items of Profit and Loss Account**
  Higher debt is likely to increase interest expense of the company. This and other likely expenses must be kept in mind before taking financing decision.

  Objective of Financial Management
  The objective of financial management is maximisation of shareholders' wealth. The investment decision, financial decision and dividend decision helps an organisation to achieve this objective. In the given situation, S Ltd. envisages growth prospects of steel industry due to the growing demand. To expand the production capacity, the company needs to invest. However, investment decision will depend on the availability of funds, the financing decision and the dividend decision.

  Thus, the company will take those financial, decisions which will result in value addition, i.e. the benefits are more than the cost. This will lead to an increase in the market value of the shares of the company.

(ii) Importance of financial plan for the company is as follows
- It helps in forecasting what may happen in future under different business situations. By this, it helps the firms to face the eventual situation in a better way.
- It helps in avoiding business shocks and surprises and helps the company in preparing for the future.
- It helps in coordinating various business' functions.
- It tries to link the present with the future.
- It provides a link between investment and financing decisions on a continuous basis.
- It helps in reducing waste, duplication of efforts and gaps in planning through detailed plans of action.
- It makes the evaluation of actual performance easier by spelling out the objectives of various business segments.

Financial Plan of S Ltd. An imaginary financial plan for steel plant (in form of anticipated balance sheet)

Balance Sheet (Anticipated)

Particulars	₹ (in crores)
I. EQUITY AND LIABILITIES	
1. Shareholders' Funds	
(i) Share Capital	600
(ii) Reserves and Surplus	400
2. Non-current Liabilities	
(i) Secured Loans	2,000
(ii) Unsecured Loans	2,000
3. Current Liabilities	
(i) Trade Payables	400
(ii) Provisions	100
Total	5,500
II. ASSETS	
1. Non-current Assets	
(i) Fixed Assets	3,000
(ii) Non-current Investments	1,000
2. Current Assets	
(i) Short-term Loans and Advances	1,000
(ii) Misc. Expenditure	300
(iii) Profit and Loss A/c (Debit balance)	200
Total	5,500

Note
- It is an imaginary financial plan.
- The total capital is ₹ 5,500 crores.
- Fixed capital is ₹ 5,000 crore and working capital is ₹ 500 crores.
- Debt equity ratio of 4 : 1 has been assumed.
- Since, steel plant is an infrastructure project, having a long gestation period, therefore, company has to borrow. Thus, ₹ 4,000 crore has been borrowed in form of secured and unsecured loans.
- It is an old company, thus is having reserves and surplus of ₹ 400 crore.
- Long gestation period can call for miscellaneous expenditure of ₹ 300 debit balance of profit and loss account in normal situations.
- Current ratio of 2 : 1 is quite good.

Case Study 19

'Neeraj Exports Ltd.' is engaged in the export of electronic goods. The company has been expanding its operations for the last few years and is now planning to set-up a new manufacturing unit. It is faced with the decision of how to finance this new project.

The company has a solid cash flow position and has been consistently generating profits. However, it already has significant fixed operating costs in the form of rent, salaries and other expenses. The current shareholders are not in favour of issuing additional equity shares as they fear losing control of the company. Meanwhile, the stock market is experiencing a downturn, which makes raising funds through equity challenging. In light of these factors, the company is considering its financing options.

Quoting lines from the above discussion, identify and explain any four factors affecting the financing decision.

Ans. Factors affecting the financing decision are as follows

(i) **"The company has a solid cash flow position and has been consistently generating profits."**

This reflects the **cash flow position** of the business. A company with strong cash flows can opt for debt financing since it will be able to meet the obligations of interest and principal repayments. If the company had poor cash flow, it would prefer equity financing, which does not require regular payments.

(ii) **"The company already has significant fixed operating costs in the form of rent, salaries and other expenses."**

This highlights the **fixed operating costs** of the business. Companies with higher fixed operating costs may prefer to keep their financing costs low by reducing debt. This is because adding more debt would increase the burden of fixed financing costs, making the business more vulnerable to fluctuations in earnings.

(iii) **"The current shareholders are not in favour of issuing additional equity shares as they fear losing control of the company."**

This reflects the **control considerations** of the company. When shareholders want to retain control over the company, they may prefer debt financing, as it does not dilute ownership. Issuing more equity would mean sharing control with new shareholders, which is undesirable for current owners.

(iv) **"The stock market is experiencing a downturn, which makes raising funds through equity challenging."**

This relates to the **state of the capital market**. When the stock market is down, it becomes difficult for companies to raise funds through the issue of shares, as investors are hesitant to invest in equity. In such situations, companies may prefer debt financing, as it can be a more reliable source of funding.

Case Study 20

Abhishek Ltd. is manufacturing cotton clothes. It has been consistently earning good profits for many years. This year too, it has been able to generate profits. There is availability of enough cash in the company and good prospects for growth in future.

It is a well managed organisation and believes in quality, equal employment opportunities and good remuneration practices. It has many shareholders who prefer to receive a regular income form their investments.

It has taken a loan of ₹ 50 lakhs from ICICI Bank and is bound by certain restrictions on the payment of dividend according to the terms of the loan agreement.

The above discussion about the company leads to various factors which decide how much of the profits should be retained and how much has to be distributed by the company.

Quoting the lines from the above discussion, identify and explain any four such factors.

Ans. Factors affecting divided decision are as follows

(i) **"Consistently earning good profits."**

It relates to the stability of earnings of the company as a company having stable income is always in a better position to pay higher dividend. A company having regular and stable earnings can declare higher dividends, while a company with unstable earnings is likely to pay smaller dividends.

(ii) **"There is availability of enough cash in the company."**

The above line reflects the cash flow position of the business which is another major factor influencing the dividend decision. Payment of dividend involves an outflow of cash.

A company may be earning profit but may be short on cash. Thus, company having surplus cash may declare higher dividend while during shortage of cash, company may declare low dividend.

(iii) **"It has many shareholders who prefer to receive a regular income."**

Shareholders' preference is highlighted in the above statement.

While declaring dividends, management must keep in mind the preferences of the shareholders. If the shareholders in general, desire that atleast a certain amount is paid as dividend, the companies are likely to declare the same.

There are always some shareholders' who depends upon a regular income from their investments like retired people, middle class shareholders, etc.

(iv) **"It has taken a loan of ₹ 50 lakhs from ICICI Bank and is bound by certain restrictions on the payment of dividend."**

The above statement highlights contractual constraints due to which the company is bound by certain restrictions on the payment of dividend. While granting loans to a company, sometimes, the lender may impose certain restrictions on the payment of dividends in future.

The companies are required to ensure that the dividend payout does not violate the terms of the loan agreement in this regard.

Case Study 21

'Sarah Ltd.' is a company manufacturing cotton yarn. It has been consistently earning good profits for many years. This year too, it has been able to generate enough profits. There is availability of enough cash in the company and good prospects for growth in future. It is a well managed organisation and believes in quality, equal employment opportunities and good remuneration practices. It has many shareholders who prefer to receive a regular income from their investments.

It has taken loan of ₹ 40 lakh from IDBI and is bound by certain restrictions on the payment of dividend according to the terms of loan agreement. The above discussion about the company leads to various factors which decide how much of the profits should be retained and how much has to be distributed by the company. Quoting the lines from the above discussion identify and explain any four such factors.

Ans. The factors identified in the above lines are given below

(i) The line "It has been consistently earning goods profits for many years' indicated stability of earnings."

Stability of earnings of a business unit also affects the dividend decision. A company having stable earnings can declare higher dividend whereas a company having unstable earnings is likely to pay smaller dividend.

(ii) The line "This year too, it has been able to generate enough profits" indicates 'earnings' as a factor affecting dividend decision. Companies generally have a policy of stabilising dividends, i.e. increase in dividend is only done when the earning potential of the company has gone up and not just the current year's earnings. Thus, dividend per share is not altered when the change is small or temporary in nature.

(iii) The line "There is availability of enough cash in the company and good prospects for growth in future" indicates 'growth opportunities'. Companies which are intended to grow, generally pay less dividend and retain more money out of profits to invest in profitable projects. On the contrary, companies which are not intended to grow and have enough earnings and cash, can pay higher dividends.

(iv) The line "It has many shareholders who prefer to receive a regular income from their, investments' indicates 'shareholders' preference'.

While declaring dividends, management must keep in mind the preferences of the shareholders in this regard. If the shareholders in general desire that at least a certain amount is paid as dividend, the companies are likely to declare the same. There are always some shareholders who depend upon a regular income from their investments.

Case Study 22

Mr. Shah is the owner of Shah Marble Ltd. Within a short span of time, the company could generate cash flow which not only covered fixed cash payment obligations but also create sufficient buffer.

The company is on the growth path and a new breed of consumers is eager to buy the Italian marble sold by Shah Marble Ltd. To meet the increasing demand, Mr. Shah decided to expand his business by acquiring a mine. This required an investment of ₹ 120 crore. To seek advice in this matter, he called his financial advisor Mr. Seth who advised him about the judicious mix of equity (40%) and debt (60%).

Mr. Seth also suggested him to take loan from a financial institution as the cost of raising funds nor from financial institutions is low. Though this will increase the financial risk but will also raise the return to equity shareholders. He also apprised him that issue of debt will not dilute the control of equity shareholders.

At the same time, the interest on loan is a tax deductible expense for computation of tax liability. After due deliberations with Mr. Seth, Mr. Shah decided to raise funds from a financial institution.

(i) Identify and explain the concept of financial management as advised by Mr. Seth in the above situation.

(ii) State any four factors affecting the concept as identified in part (i) above which have been discussed between Mr. Shah and Mr. Seth.

Ans.

(i) The concept of financial management as advised by Mr. Seth is capital structure. It refers to the relative proportion between owners and borrowed fund.

(ii) Following are the factors that affect the capital structure

- **Control**

  Issue of more equity leads to dilution of shareholders' control over the business. Debt financing has no such implication.

  Thus, if existing shareholders do not want to lose control, then they can prefer more of debt in capital structure and *vice-versa*.

- **Regulatory Framework**

  The Companies Act and SEBI guidelines must be observed while raising funds from the public. e.g. Public issue of shares and debentures have to be made as per the SEBI guidelines. Borrowings from banks and other financial institutions require fulfilment of certain norms, which has an impact on the choice of the source of finance.

  The company prefers that source of finance which have less and flexible legal requirements.

- **Stock Market Condition**
  If the stock market is rising, i.e. bullish period, then it is easy to raise funds through issue of shares as more people invest in equity. However, depressed capital market, i.e. bearish period, may make issue of equity shares difficult for any company and the company has to opt for debt financing.
- **Cash Flow Position**
  Cash flows must not only cover fixed cash payment obligations but there should be sufficient buffer also.

  Company must have enough cash for normal business operations, investment in fixed assets, meeting the debt service commitments, like interest payment and repayment of principal. Thus, company which is confident of generating required cash flows can opt for more of debt in its capital structure and *vice-versa*.

Case Study 23

Mania Industries Ltd manufactures steel. Its plants are located in Gujarat. It produces around two million tonnes of saleable steel. With the increase in demand for steel, it is planning to expand the capacity of the existing steel plants. It will require ₹ 1,500 crore of fixed capital and ₹ 100 crore of working capital. The company is considering whether it should issue equity shares or 7% debentures of ₹ 1,600 crore.

The capital structure at present comprises of equity only. The finance manager of the company suggested that since the stock markets are undergoing a bearish phase, it should issue debentures.

(i) Is it justified to raise funds by issuing debentures? Give reason.

(ii) Explain the impact of issue of debentures on the risk faced by the company.

(iii) Explain the impact of cost of debt and cost of equity on the capital structure of the company.

Ans.

(i) It is justified to raise funds by issuing debentures. It is because during the bearish phase in the capital market, a company may find raising of equity capital more difficult and it may opt for debt.

(ii) The issue of debentures will increase the financial risk faced by the company as the payment of interest and the return of principle is obligatory for the business. Any default in meeting these commitments may force the business to go into liquidation.

(iii) **Impact of Cost of Debt on the Capital Structure of the Company**

- A company having ability to borrow at a lower rate is in a better position to employ higher debt.
- Thus, more debt can be used if debt can be raised at a lower rate and *vice-versa*.

Impact of Cost of Equity on the Capital Structure of the Company

When a company increases debt, the financial risk faced by the equity holders increases and thus, the cost of equity also increases which discourages the use of debt beyond a certain limit.

Case Study 24

ABC Tech Solutions is a growing software company that specialises in developing innovative technology solutions for various industries. The company has recently decided to expand its operations by opening a new development center in a different city. To set-up this center, ABC Tech needs to invest in advanced computer systems, office infrastructure, and various other fixed assets.

While planning this expansion, the management faces the challenge of efficiently managing its fixed capital, which includes these long-term assets. The CEO, Mr. Rajesh, emphasises the importance of this decision, as it will directly impact the company's future profitability and growth. Additionally, the company needs to evaluate how much capital will be required to ensure the smooth functioning of the new center.

The finance team begins analysing factors while setting-up in a new location. They also consider the cost of acquiring fixed assets and the company's future expansion plans to ensure they allocate sufficient capital. Mr. Rajesh stresses the importance of managing fixed capital to ensure that assets are used efficiently, financial stability is maintained and the company can remain competitive in the market.

(i) Give any four reasons why management of fixed capital is important.

(ii) State any two factors that affect the requirement of fixed capital.

Ans.

(i) Management of fixed capital is important because of the following reasons

- **Long-term Growth**
  These decisions have bearing on the long-term growth of business. The funds invested in long-term assets are likely to yield returns in the future which affect the future prospects of the business.
- **Large Amount of Funds Involved**
  These decisions result in a substantial portion of capital funds being blocked in long-term projects. Therefore, these investments are planned after undertaking a detailed analysis which may involve decisions like where to procure funds from and at what rate of interest.
- **Risk Involved**
  Fixed capital involves investment of huge amount. It affects the returns of the firm as a whole in the long-term. Therefore, investment decisions involving fixed capital influence the overall business risk of the firm.

- **Irreversible Decisions**
  These decisions once taken, are not reversible without incurring heavy losses. These decisions should be taken only after careful evaluation of each detail, as abandoning a project after heavy investment, is quite costly in terms of wastage of funds.

(ii) Factors that affect the requirement of fixed capital are as follows

- **Technology Upgradation**
  Industries in which assets becomes obsolete sooner due to technology upgradation, need higher investment in fixed assets to replace older assets. While companies whose assets are not or least affected by technology upgradation, needs lesser investment. e.g. Computers become obsolete faster and are replaced much sooner than say, furniture.
- **Growth Prospects**
  Higher growth of an organisation requires higher investment in fixed assets. A company expecting such growth may expand its production capacity in order to meet the anticipated higher demand quickly. This entails larger investment in fixed assets and consequently, larger fixed capital.

Case Study 25

Vikram Automobiles Pvt. Ltd. a leading manufacturer of electric two-wheelers in India, has witnessed an extraordinary surge in demand over the past 12 months. "It's been an exciting period for us, with sales hitting record levels," says the CFO of Vikram Automobiles.

The company caters to the growing urban population eager to shift to eco-friendly modes of transport.

Interestingly, working capital management has been smooth, with a turnover of trade receivables averaging between 10 and 20 days.

One of the key reasons working capital remained in control was the pre-orders for their new range of electric scooters. Customers had placed advanced orders months in advance, with deposits paid, which helped boost the company's cash flow.

The quick turnover of finished products and the company's efficient inventory management kept storage costs low.

"As soon as the scooters are manufactured, they are immediately shipped to dealers, keeping inventory at minimal levels," said the CFO.

Moreover, favourable banking relationships further supported the company's strong cash flow position, aiding in efficient working capital management.

(i) Explain the concept of working capital.

(ii) Identify and explain any four factors that affect the requirement of working capital.

Ans.

(i) Working capital refers to the capital required for carrying out day-to-day activities of the business. It is required to bear the operating costs of business.
WC = CA – CL
Working Capital = Current Assets – Current Liabilities

(ii) Following are the factors that affect the requirement of working capital

- **Credit Allowed**
  Different firms allow different credit terms to their customers. These terms depend upon the level of competition that a firm faces, as well as the credit worthiness of their clientele.
  Liberal credit policy means more working capital requirement while strict credit policy means less working capital requirement.
- **Availability of Raw Materials**
  If the raw materials are easily and readily available, lower stock levels can be maintained, thus require less working capital.
  Whereas, when the raw materials are scarce or not readily available, higher stock levels will have to be maintained, thus increasing the need for working capital requirement. In addition, the time lag between the placement of order and actual receipt of material (also called lead time) is also relevant.
- **Growth Prospects**
  The companies which have a possibility of growth potential or are planning to expand, will require larger amount of working capital to meet higher production and sales target whenever required.
- **Level of Competition**
  Higher level of competitiveness may necessitate companies to maintain larger stock of finished goods to meet urgent demand from customers. This increases the working capital requirement. Whereas, company having less competition will require lesser amount of working capital.

SELF ASSESSMENT TEST

Objective Type Questions

1. Which of the following is not a factor affecting financing decision of a company?
   (a) Cost
   (b) Risk
   (c) Cash flow position of a company
   (d) Growth opportunities
2. Avni Textiles earned a net profit of ₹ 5 crore and wants to appropriate these profits. Which of the following decisions will help in deciding it?
   (a) Investment decision (b) Financing decision
   (c) Dividend decision (d) None of these
3. Dividend policy that should be followed by a company having growth opportunities is
   (a) conservative dividend policy
   (b) regular dividend policy
   (c) stable dividend policy
   (d) None of the above
4. A decision to acquire a new and modern plant to upgrade an old one is known as ……… decision.
   (a) financing decision
   (b) working capital decision
   (c) investment decision
   (d) dividend decision
5. Investment in fixed assets is essential in which type of organisation?
   (a) Trading (b) Manufacturing
   (c) Both (a) and (b) (d) None of these
6. Net working capital will be ……… if current assets are of ₹ 4,00,000 and current liabilities are of ₹ 50,000.
   (a) ₹ 6,00,000 (b) ₹ 3,00,000
   (c) ₹ 2,50,000 (d) ₹ 3,50,000

Answers 1. (d) 2. (c) 3. (a) 4. (c) 5. (b) 6. (d)

Short Answer Type Questions

7. Explain the main objectives of financial management.
8. "Financial management is based on three major decisions." Explain.
9. "Investment criteria is one of the factors, which affect capital budgeting decision." Comment.
10. Rohan wants to decide how much of the profit earned by his company should be distributed to shareholders and how much should be retained in the business. Explain any three factors that he should consider that can affect dividend decision.
11. How is debt different from equity on the basis of cost and risk?
12. "The amount of dividend that is paid by a company does not involve any restrictions." Comment.
13. Fixed capital refers to investment in long-term assets. Explain any two factors affecting the fixed capital requirements of an enterprise.

Long Answer Type Questions

14. "Sound financial planning is essential for the success of any enterprise." Explain this statement by giving any six reasons.
15. When the return on investment of the company is higher than interest rate on debt, it can use more debt in the capital structure of the company in order to increase its earning per share. Explain the given situation with the help of a suitable example.
16. Amri Ltd. wants to meet the urgent demand of customers and need stock of finished goods. Explain any five factors that Amri Ltd. should take into consideration that can affect the requirements of working capital.

10

CHAPTER

Financial Markets

A business is a part of an economy which comprises of two major sectors, households which save funds, called as *savers* and business firms which invest the funds, called as *investors.*

▼ YOUR STUDY GOALS

10.1 Concept of Financial Market
10.2 Stock Exchange
10.3 Securities and Exchange Board of India (SEBI)

▼ YOUR PRACTICE GOAL

- Objective Type Questions (57 Qs ; MCQs, A-R, Statements, Matching)
- Subjective Questions (14 SAs, 6 LAs)
- Case Study Based Questions (Short Case Studies-10, Long Case Studies-5)
- Self Assessment Test (6 MCQs, 7 SAs, 3 LAs)

10.1 Concept of Financial Market

Financial market acts as an intermediary or a link between the savers (households) and the investors (business firms) by mobilising funds between them. It helps savers to allocate their surplus funds for investment and simultaneously helps investors to borrow funds to meet their requirements.

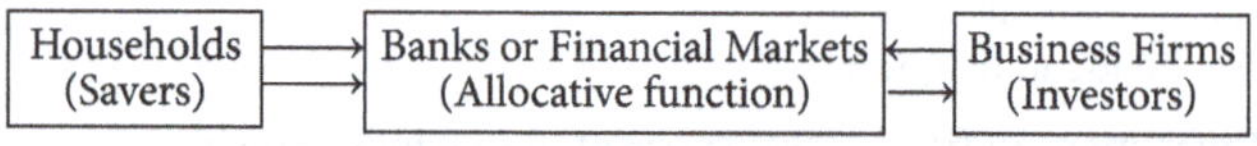

There are mainly two mechanisms which can be used for allocation of funds, *viz.* banks or financial markets.

- Households or savers can deposit their surplus funds with **banks**, who in turn lend these funds to business firms.
- Households can also buy the securities offered by a business using **financial markets**.

The process through which allocation of funds is done, is known as **financial intermediation**.

Classification of Financial Market

Financial market can be broadly classified under two heads, which are as follows

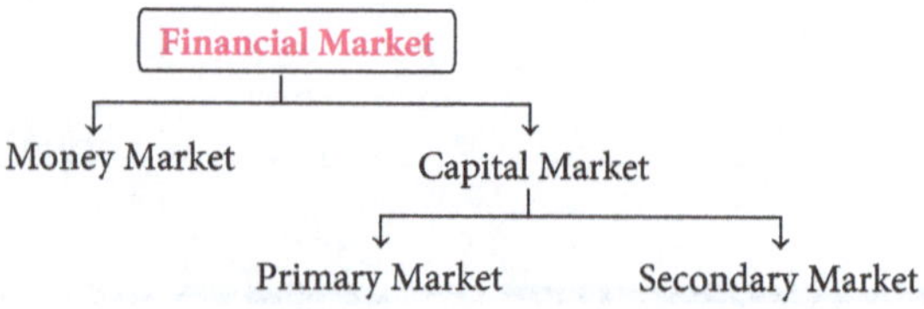

Money Market

It is a market for short-term funds, which deals in monetary assets whose period of maturity is upto one year.

Various instruments in this market include treasury bills, certificate of deposit, commercial paper, call money, etc. Instruments are highly liquid and less risky. There is no fixed geographical location and it is a market for short-term funds.

The **major participants** in this market are Reserve Bank of India, commercial banks, non-banking finance companies, state governments, large corporate houses and mutual funds.

Capital Market

It is a market for medium and long-term funds. This market facilitates the institutional arrangements through which long-term funds, both debt and equity are raised and invested. It includes a network of all the organisations, institutions and instruments which provide medium and long-term funds.

The **instruments** in this market include shares, debentures, bonds, public deposits, etc.

Ideal Capital Market

An ideal capital market is where

- Finance is available at reasonable cost.
- Financial institutions are sufficiently developed.
- Market operations are free, fair, competitive and transparent.
- Provide sufficient information to investors.
- Allocate capital most productively.
- Minimise transaction costs.

Types of Capital Market

1. **Primary Market**

It is also known as the new issues market, as this market deals with the new securities being issued for the first time. The **investors** in primary market include banks, insurance companies, mutual funds and individuals.

2. **Secondary Market**

It is a market where purchase and sale of existing securities takes place. It is also known as stock market or stock exchange.

It also contributes to economic growth by channelising funds into the most productive investments, through the process of **disinvestment** by existing investors and **reinvestment** by new investors.

Primary Market

Company X wants to raise funds to expand its operations. To do this, it issues new shares for the first time to the public in the primary market. Banks, mutual funds and individual investors can buy these shares directly from the ompany, which helps the company to raise the necessary capital for growth.

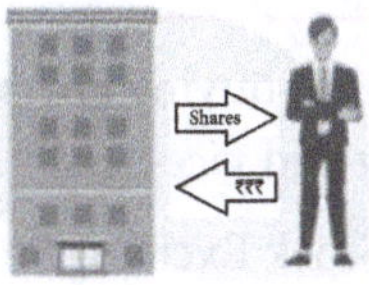

Secondary Market

Once the shares of the company are issued and sold in the primary market, investors who own these shares can trade them in the secondary market, like the stock exchange. Here, people buy and sell already existing shares. Arun, an investor bought shares of the company earlier, he can now sell them to others on the stock exchange.

Money Market Vs Capital Market

Basis	Money Market	Capital Market
Meaning	It is a market dealing in securities of short-term funds, whose maturity period is upto one year.	It is a market dealing in securities for long-term funds, whose maturity period is more than one year.
Participants	Major participants are RBI, commercial banks, financial institutions and finance companies.	Participants of capital market are financial institutions, banks, corporate entities, foreign investors and ordinary retail investors from the members of public.
Instruments	Instruments traded are T-bills, commercial bills, certificate of deposits, etc.	Main instruments traded are shares, debentures, bonds, preference shares, etc.
Investment Outlay	In money market, instruments require huge sum of money, because these are quite expensive.	It does not require huge capital outlay, as the value of units of securities is generally low, i.e. ₹ 10 or ₹ 100. Even the trading lot is kept low at ₹ 5, ₹ 50, ₹ 100 or so.
Duration	They have a tenure of maximum one year and may even be traded for a single day.	Deals with medium-term and long-term securities with a maturity period of more than one year.
Liquidity	They are highly liquid and have an arrangement for providing liquidity, which is provided by Discount and Finance House of India (DFHI).	They are less liquid, e.g. A person wanting to sell shares may not get a buyer.
Risk/Safety of Funds	Money market instruments are generally safe due to shorter duration and credibility of issuers.	Capital market instruments are riskier both in terms of returns and repayment of principal.
Expected Returns	The expected rate of return is less due to short duration.	The expected returns are high and there is even a possibility of capital gain.

Primary Market Vs Secondary Market

Basis	Primary Market	Secondary Market
Nature of Securities	It deals in new issue of securities, issued by new companies or further issue by existing companies.	Existing securities, i.e. securities already sold are traded in stock exchange.
Type of contact with Investor	Securities are issued directly to the investors or through intermediaries.	Ownership of existing securities is exchanged between the investors, where the company is not involved.
Capital Formation	It promotes capital formation directly.	It indirectly promotes capital formation by providing liquidity.
Buying and Selling	Only buying of securities takes place.	Both buying and selling of existing securities take place.
Pricing	Prices of securities are decided by the company	Prices are decided by the demand and supply of securities.
Location	There is no fixed geographical location.	It is located at specified places.

10.2 Stock Exchange

A stock exchange is an institution which provides a platform for buying and selling of existing securities. It provides liquidity by facilitating the exchange of securities into money and *vice-versa*.

According to **Securities Contracts Regulation Act, 1956,** "Stock Exchange means any body of individuals, whether incorporated or not, constituted for the purpose of assisting, regulating or controlling the business of buying and selling or dealing in securities."

Functions of Stock Exchange

1. **Provides Liquidity and Marketability to Existing Securities** Stock exchange provides ready and continuous market where securities can be bought and sold. It gives investors the chance to disinvest and reinvest.
2. **Pricing of Securities** Share prices are determined by the forces of demand and supply, providing constant value information to both buyers and sellers.

3. **Safety of Transactions** Regulated dealings within the legal framework ensure safe and fair deal in the market for the investors.
4. **Contributes to Economic Growth** Disinvestment and reinvestment in stock exchanges channelise savings into most productive investment avenues which promotes capital formation and economic growth.
5. **Spreading of Equity Cult** Stock exchanges educate the public and regulate new issues, promoting broader share ownership. It helps in promoting better and safe trading practices.
6. **Provides Scope for Speculation** Stock exchange provides sufficient scope within the provisions of law for speculative activity in a restricted and controlled manner.

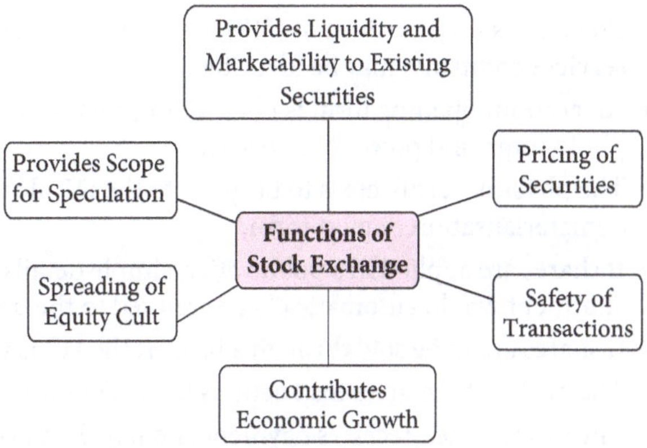

Trading and Settlement Procedure on Stock Exchange

Trading in securities is executed through an online, **screen based electronic trading system**. All the securities are now bought and sold electronically in the broker's office through a computer terminal, which is connected to the computer system of the main stock exchange. In this type of trading, any member can log on to the site and feed the information about the shares he wants to buy or sell and the price into the computer.

The computer in the brokers' office constantly matches the orders at the best bid and offer price. Those that are not matched, remain on the screen and are open for future matching during the day.

Advantages of Screen Based Trading System

1. **Transparency** Screen-based trading ensures that participants can see real time prices during transactions.
2. **Efficient Pricing** Information on prices and market developments is quickly shared using computer screens, helping fix prices effectively.
3. **Operational Efficiency** Reduction time, cost and risk of error, enhances overall efficiency of trade.
4. **Wide Participation** It allows large number of participants, even globally, to buy or sell securities through brokers or members, improving market liquidity.
5. **Unified Trading Platform** All trading centers across the country are connected to a single computer-based stock exchange platform.

Dematerialisation

Dematerialisation is a process where securities held by the investor in the physical form are cancelled and the investor is given an electronic entry or number so that he/she can hold it as an electronic balance in his account.

For this, investor has to open a demant account with an organisation, called a **depository**.

Following are its benefits

- Convenient, similar to a bank account.
- Physical shares can be converted to electronic form and *vice-versa*.
- Demat securities can be pledged for loans.
- Eliminates risk of loss, theft or forgery of shares certificates
- Brokers ensure accurate share credits to the investor's account.

Depository

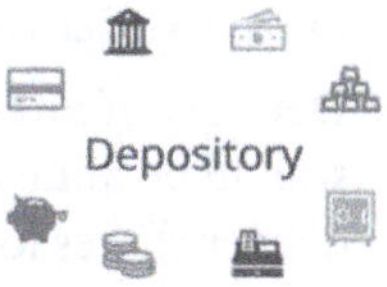

Depository is an institution or organisation which holds securities (e.g. Shares, debentures, bonds, mutual funds, etc.) of investors in electronic form.

A securities account can be opened in a depository, where all securities can be deposited, withdrawn or sold at any time as well as instruction to deliver or receive securities on behalf of the investor can also be given.

There are two depositories in India

- National Securities Depository Limited
- Central Depository Services (India) Limited

Working of the Demat System

- The Depository Participant (DP), either a bank, broker or financial services company, may be identified.
- An account opening form is filled giving details of PAN card, photograph and power of attorney.
- The physical certificate is to be given to the DP alongwith a dematerialisation request form.
- If shares are applied in a public offer, simple details of DP and demat account are to be given and the shares on allotment would automatically be credited to the demat account.
- If shares are to be sold through a broker, the DP is to be instructed to debit the account with the number of shares.
- The broker, then gives instructions to his DP for delivery of shares to the stock exchange.
- The broker, then receives payment and pay the person for the shares sold.
- All these transactions are to be completed within 2 days, i.e. delivery of shares and payment received from the buyer is on a T+2 basis, settlement period.

Depository Participant (DP)

- DP serves as an intermediary between the investor and the depository, who is authorised to maintain the accounts of dematerialised shares.
- All the buying and selling of securities under depository are done through DP only.
- Financial institutions, banks, clearing corporations, stock brokers and non-banking finance corporations can become depository participants.

Steps in Trading and Settlement Procedure

1. **Approaching a Broker** Investor signs a broker-client agreement and provides required details (like PAN (mandatory), address, bank account, depository account, etc). The broker then opens a trading account in the name of investor.
2. **Opening a Demat Account** After signing agreement; investor opens a demat or Beneficial Owner (BO) accout for holding and transferring securities. A bank account is also opened for cash transactions.
3. **Placing an Order** Investor specifies the number and price of shares to the broker, who in return provides an order confirmation slip.
4. **Finding a Deal** Broker then matches the order on the stock exchange online for the best available price of shares.
5. **Execution of Order** Once matched, the order is executed electronically and broker will issue a trade confirmation slip to investor.
6. **Issuing Contract Note** Within 24 hours, the broker issues a contract note with transaction details, including a **unique order code.**
7. **Delivery of Shares by Investor** Investor has to deliver the shares sold or pay cash for the shares bought. This should be done immediately after receiving contract note or before the day when broker shall make payment or deliver shares to exchange. This is called **pay-in day**.
8. **Settlement Cycle** Cash is paid or securities are delivered on pay-in day, which is before the T + 1 day as the deal has to be settled and finalised on the T + 1 day.
9. **Payment to Broker** On T+1 day, the exchange will deliver the shares or make payment to the broker. This is called the **pay-out day**. The broker, then has to make the payment to the investor within 24 hours of the pay-out day.
10. **Delivery of Shares by Broker** The broker transfers shares directly to the investor's demat account. The investor has to give details about his demat account and instruct his depository participant to take delivery of securities directly into his beneficial owner account.

10.3 Securities and Exchange Board of India (SEBI)

It was established by the Government of India on 12th April, 1988. It got statutory status on 30th January, 1992. For issuers, it provides a market place in which they can raise finance fairly and easily. For investors, it provides protection and supply of accurate and correct information. For intermediaries, it provides a competitive professional market.

Establishment of SEBI

The tremendous growth in capital market due to increasing participation of the public led to a variety of malpractices by companies, brokers, investment consultants, etc. such as

- Unofficial private placements.
- Unofficial premium on new issues.
- Non-adherence of provisions of the Companies Act.
- Delay in delivery of shares.
- **Price Rigging** Manipulating the market price of shares by increasing or decreasing their prices.
- **Insider Trading** The insiders of the company like directors, promoters, etc. use inside information to make personal profits.

These malpractices eroded the investors' confidence as government and stock exchanges were helpless in redressing their problems due to the lack of proper penal provisions in the legislation. Thus, to overcome this issue, government decided to set-up a separate regulatory body known as SEBI.

Objectives of SEBI

- To regulate stock exchanges and the securities industry to promote their orderly functioning.
- To protect the rights and interests of investors, and to guide and educate them.
- To prevent fraudulent activities and malpractices.
- To regulate and develop a code of conduct for intermediaries like brokers, merchant bankers, etc. with a view to make them competitive and professional.

Functions of SEBI

Regulatory Functions	Development Functions	Protective Functions
• Registration of brokers, sub-brokers and other players in the market. • Registration of collective investment schemes and mutual funds. • Regulation of stock brokers, portfolio exchanges, underwriters and merchant bankers and the business in stock exchanges. • Regulation of takeover bids by companies. • Levy fee or other charges for carrying out the purposes of the Act. • SEBI conducts inspections, enquiries and audits of stock exchanges and intermediaries. • Perform and exercise such power under Securities Contracts (Regulation) Act, 1956, as may be delegated by the Government of India.	• Training of intermediaries of the securities market. • Conducting research and publishing information useful to all market participants. • Undertaking measures to develop the capital markets by adopting a flexible approach.	• Prohibition of fraudulent and unfair trade practices. • Controlling insider trading and imposing penalties for such practices. • Undertaking steps for investor protection. • Promotion of fair practices and code of conduct in securities market.

Mind Map

FINANCIAL MARKETS

1 Concept of Financial Market

Financial market acts as an intermediary or a link between the savers (households) and the investors (business firms) by mobilising funds between them.

2 Money Market

It is a market for short-term funds, which deals in monetary assets whose period of maturity is up to one year.
Various instruments include treasury bills, certificate of deposit, commercial paper, call money, etc.

3 Capital Market

It is a market for medium and long-term funds. Instruments include shares, debentures, bonds, public deposits, etc.

Types

- **Primary** It is also known as the new issues market, as this market deals with the new securities being issued for the first time
- **Secondary** It is a market where purchase and sale of existing securities takes place. It is also known as stock market or stock exchange

4 Stock Exchange

A stock exchange is an institution which provides a platform for buying and selling of existing securities.

Functions

- **Providing Liquidity and Marketability to Existing Securities** Gives investors the chance to disinvest and reinvest
- **Pricing of Securities** Share prices are determined by forces of demand and supply
- **Safety of Transactions** Stock exchange is well regulated and dealings are well defined
- **Contributes to Economic Growth** Leads to capital formation
- **Spreading of Equity Cult** Guide and educate public about investments
- **Providing Scope for Speculation** Necessary to ensure liquidity and price continuity

5 Trading Procedure on a Stock Exchange

- Approaching a broker
- Opening a demat account
- Placing an order
- Finding a deal
- Execution of order
- Issuing contract note
- Delivery of shares by investor
- Settlement cycle
- Payment to broker
- Delivery of shares by broker

6 Objectives of SEBI

Securities and Exchange Board of India (SEBI) was established by government on 12th April, 1988.
It's objectives are

- To regulate stock exchanges and the securities industry to promote their orderly functioning
- To protect the rights and interests of investors and to guide and educate them
- To prevent fraudulent activities and malpractices
- To regulate and develop a code of conduct for intermediaries like brokers, merchant bankers, etc. with a view to make them competitive and professional

7 Functions of SEBI

- **Regulatory Functions**
  Includes registration of brokers, sub-brokers, collective investment schemes, regulation of stock brokers, portfolio exchanges, takeover bids, levying fees, etc.
- **Development Functions**
  Includes training of intermediaries of securities market, conducting research and undertaking measures to develop capital markets
- **Protective Functions**
  Includes prohibition of fraudulent and unfair trade practices, controlling insider trading, undertaking steps for investor protection and promotion of fair practices

EXAM PATTERN QUESTIONS

Objective Type Questions

Multiple Choice Questions (MCQs)

1. Financial market .... financial assets.

(a) creates (b) exchanges
(c) creates and exchanges (d) None of these

2. Supply side of finance includes

(a) financial institutions
(b) insurance companies
(c) financial institutions and insurance companies
(d) industry

3. Which of the following performs the functions of giving inputs to saving and transfer them to more productive uses?

(a) Wholesale market (b) Retail market
(c) Financial market (d) Financial institutions

4. Mr. Sharma, a retired government employee, has recently received a lump sum amount from his pension fund. He wants to ensure that his savings are invested in a way that not only keeps his money safe but also provides him with regular returns. Mr. Sharma has two options: he can deposit his savings in a bank, which will lend it to businesses, or he can directly invest in securities through the financial market.

By choosing to invest in securities, he becomes part of the financial intermediation process, which channels funds from savers like him to investors needing capital. What role does the financial market play for Mr. Sharma in the case above? Competency Based Que

(a) Acts as a lender of last resort to Mr. Sharma
(b) Serves as an intermediary, linking his savings with investment opportunities
(c) Ensures government protection for all his investments
(d) Offers guaranteed returns on his investments

5. Analyse the below picture and fill in the blank.

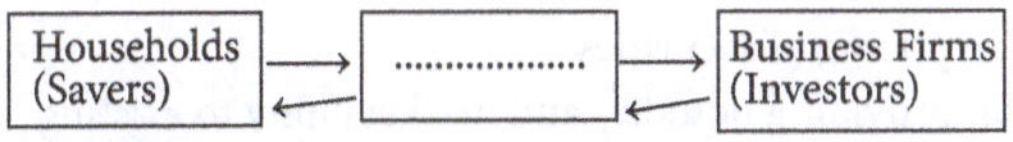

(a) Business (b) Customers
(c) Government (d) Financial Markets

6. Identify the market in the below picture where trading of securities occur including stock market, bond market, etc.

(a) Secondary market (b) Money market
(c) Financial market (d) None of these

7. .... has been established with the specific objective of providing a ready market for money market instruments. CBSE 2023

(a) Discount Finance House of India
(b) Securities and Exchange Board of India
(c) Reserve Bank of India
(d) State Bank of India

8. A government decides to issue short-term treasury bills with a maturity period of 3 months to raise funds for immediate expenses. Investors, including commercial banks and financial institutions, are buying and selling these securities for a quick return.

The market operates with high liquidity and short-term investment focus. Identify the type of market. Competency Based Que

(a) Money market (b) Capital market
(c) Primary market (c) None of these

9. Identify the concept of financial management depicted in the below picture.

(a) Money market (b) Capital market
(c) Primary market (d) Secondary market

10. Adapting to a change in consumer preference towards online shopping, Zeta started a grocery delivery app. It is a platform that ensures 5 minute delivery of groceries. Because of this service, Zeta earned huge profit within a year.

It planned to expand its operations and decided to raise funds by directly issuing its securities to investors. The market through which Zeta has decided to raise funds for its expansion is **Competency Based Que**

(a) money market (b) primary market
(c) secondary market (d) Both (b) and (c)

11. Amit is a new investor exploring ways to invest in the stock market. He learns that there are two main markets where securities are traded i.e. the primary and secondary markets. In the primary market, companies issue new securities directly to investors to raise funds, with prices set by the company.

Meanwhile, in the secondary market, investors buy and sell existing securities among themselves, with prices fluctuating based on demand and supply. Amit is also informed that while the primary market has no fixed location, the secondary market is located at specific stock exchanges.

In which market are prices of securities determined by demand and supply? **Competency Based Que**

(a) Primary market
(b) Secondary market
(c) Both primary and secondary markets
(d) Neither primary nor secondary markets

12. Identify the type of market highlighted in the below picture.

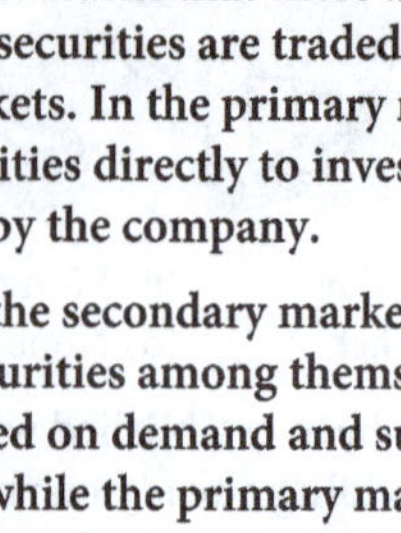

(a) Money market (b) Primary market
(c) Secondary market (d) None of these

13. Mohan wants to buy shares of Limunt Ltd. which are being traded at the National Stock Exchange. He feels that the share prices will go up in the future. Which market should he approach for this purpose? **CBSE 2023; Competency Based Que**

(a) Money market
(b) Primary market
(c) Secondary market
(d) Both (b) and (c)

14. Which of the following statements is incorrect?

(a) The money market deals with short-term funds and includes instruments such as treasury bills and commercial paper
(b) The capital market is responsible for medium and long-term funds and includes shares, debentures and bonds
(c) The primary market deals with the trading of existing securities and is also known as the stock market
(d) The secondary market, also known as the stock exchange, involves the purchase and sale of existing securities

15. The stock exchange protects the interest of

(a) investor
(b) company
(c) government
(d) None of the above

16. Priya recently attended a seminar on investing, where she learned about the role of stock exchanges in the economy. She was fascinated to find out that stock exchanges provide a platform for buying and selling existing securities, making it easier for investors to reinvest their money.

The prices of securities in the exchange are determined by demand and supply, which helps investors stay updated on the value of their investments.

Priya was also reassured to know that all transactions are regulated to ensure safety and that stock exchanges contribute to economic growth by channeling savings into productive investments. Additionally, she learned that stock exchanges promote an equity culture by educating the public on safe trading practices.

Which of the following is a function of a stock exchange? **Competency Based Que**

(a) Setting the prices of newly issued securities
(b) Providing liquidity and marketability to existing securities
(c) Issuing new securities on behalf of companies
(d) Offering only long-term investment options

17. The function of stock exchange which helps in creating a continuous market where securities are bought and sold is **CBSE 2023**

(a) safety of transactions
(b) pricing of securities
(c) providing liquidity and marketability to existing securities
(d) contribution to economic growth

18. For stock exchanges, the services of SEBI are ....

(a) optional (b) necessary
(c) unnecessary (d) essential

19. **Meenu's father has gifted his daughter the shares of a large cement company, with which he had been working. The securities were in the physical form. She already has a bank account and does not possess any other forms of securities. She wished to sell the shares and approached a registered broker for the purpose.**

Mention one mandatory detail which she will have to provide with the broker. **Competency Based Que**

(a) Date of birth and address (b) PAN number
(c) Bank account details (d) Residential status

20. **Meera decided to invest in stocks and bonds for the first time. Her financial advisor suggested she open a demat account to make the process of holding her investments more secure and convenient. Meera learned that with a demat account, she could hold all her securities in electronic form rather than as physical certificates. This way, she could avoid risks associated with physical securities, like loss or forgery.**

Additionally, if she ever needed a loan, her demat securities could be pledged as collateral. She also appreciated that her account functions similarly to a bank account, allowing her to easily track and manage her investments without needing to handle physical documents.

Which of the following is not a benefit of dematerialisation? **Competency Based Que**

(a) Eliminates the risk of loss or forgery
(b) Provides physical share certificates for easier access
(c) Allows securities to be pledged for loans
(d) Enables convenient tracking similar to a bank account

21. **Aruna's grandmother gave her shares worth ₹ 35 crore in her name and told her that these were gifted to her by Aruna's late grandfather. When Aruna opened the bank locker to get the share certificates, she found many crumpled share certificates inside.**

To overcome this problem, financial market has adopted a new concept called **Competency Based Que**

(a) demutualisation (b) dematerialisation
(c) Both (a) and (b) (d) None of these

22. **Identify the malpractice done in securities market from the picture given below.**

(a) Price rigging
(b) Misleading statement in prospectus
(c) Insider trading (d) Forgery

23. **Mohani is a Company Secretary in Feelings Ltd. During the course of meeting with directors, she came to know that as against the previous years, this year company will declare higher dividend. She observed that once the news will be out among the public, share prices will rise. Thus, she purchased large number of compnay's shares before this news reached the public.**

Identify the type of malpractice used by Mohani.

Competency Based Que

(a) Price rigging
(b) Insider trading
(c) Unofficial private placement
(d) Both (a) and (b)

24. **SEBI recently called for information and issued a show cause notice to NSE and its 14 officials seeking explanation on the preferential access allegations at the exchange's co-location facility. State the function that SEBI performed by doing so.**

(a) Protective function (b) Regulatory function
(c) Developmental function (d) None of these

25. **Which of the following statements is incorrect?**

(a) Providing liquidity to securities is one the functions of stock exchange
(b) Process of holding shares in electronic form is known as dematerialisation
(c) SEBI performs the regulatory function of controlling insider trading and imposing penalties for such practices
(d) Capital market consists of commercial banks, development banks and stock exchanges

26. **Vikram recently started investing in the stock market and wanted to better understand the role of SEBI, the regulatory authority of India's securities market. He learned that SEBI performs various functions to maintain the smooth operation and integrity of the market.**

SEBI is responsible for registering and regulating brokers, sub-brokers and mutual funds, ensuring they follow the necessary guidelines.

Additionally, SEBI protects investors by prohibiting fraudulent activities, like insider trading and takes steps to maintain fair practices. Vikram also found that SEBI actively works on market development through initiatives like training intermediaries and publishing research for market participants. Through these efforts, SEBI aims to safeguard investors while supporting market growth.

Which of the following protective functions of SEBI is highlighted in the above case? Competency Based Que

(a) Conducting training for intermediaries
(b) Regulating stock exchanges and brokers
(c) Prohibiting fraudulent and unfair trade practices
(d) Registration of collective investment schemes

27. Which of the following statements is incorrect? CBSE 2023

(a) The protective functions of the Securities and Exchange Board of India include levying fee or other charges for carrying out the purposes of the Act
(b) The development functions of the Securities and Exchange Board of India include training of intermediaries of the securities market
(c) The regulatory functions of the Securities and Exchange Board of India include registration of collective investment schemes and mutual funds
(d) The objectives of the Securities and Exchange Board of India include protecting the rights and interests of investors, particularly individual investors and to guide and educate them

28. XYZ Ltd. issued prospectus for the subscription of its shares for ₹ 500 crore in 2008. The issue was oversubscribed by 20 times. The company issued shares to all the applicants on pro-rata basis.

Later SEBI inspected the prospectus and found some misleading statement about the management of the company in it. SEBI imposed a penalty of ₹ 5 crore and banned its three executive directors for dealing in securities market for three years.

Identify the function performed by SEBI in the above case. Competency Based Que

(a) Protective function (b) Developmental function
(c) Regulatory function (d) None of these

29. Rajeev was unwilling to buy shares in the stock market as he was told by someone that stock market is a place where various malpractices take place. He decides to discuss the matter with his friend who explains to him how SEBI takes care of the interests of the investors. Identify the type of function of SEBI. Competency Based Que

(a) Protective function (b) Regulatory function
(c) Developmental function (d) None of these

Direction *Read the following case study and answer the questions 30 to 33 on the basis of the same*

Reena's grandfather was unwell. He called Reena and gave her a box containing cash and certain papers which were crumbled. She saw them carefully and found that these were share certificates. Reena now wants to know the process through which she can trade in these shares. She also learnt about the trading procedures and got to know about SEBI as well.

She told her friend Rekha, "SEBI regularly inspects the various elements of trading and also conducts the brokers' enquiries. SEBI also promotes fair trade practices for investor protection. It also controls insider trading and imposes penalties in case of such malpractices."

She also told her friend about many instruments such as commercial papers or bills which are not traded on stock exchange.

30. Which process would have been done by Reena to facilitate trading?

(a) Demutualisation (b) Remutualisation
(c) Dematerialisation (d) Rematerialisation

31. Which function is highlighted in the lines, "SEBI regularly inspects the various elements of trading and also conducts the brokers' enquiries"?

(a) Protective (b) Developmental
(c) Regulatory (d) None of these

32. Which function is highlighted in the lines, "SEBI also promotes fair trade practices for investor protection. It also considers trading and imposes penalties in case of such malpractices"?

(a) Protective (b) Developmental
(c) Regulatory (d) None of these

33. Reena told her friend about many instruments such as commercial papers or bills which are not traded on stock exchange. Which instruments of market Reena is referring to?

(a) Stock market
(b) Capital market
(c) Money market (d) Both (b) and (c)

Assertion-Reason

Direction (Q.No. 34 to 43) *Read the following Assertion (A) and Reason (R) and choose the correct alternative from the following* **Alternatives**

(a) Both Assertion (A) and Reason (R) are true and Reason (R) is the correct explanation of Assertion (A)
(b) Both Assertion (A) and Reason (R) are true, but Reason (R) is not the correct explanation of Assertion (A)
(c) Assertion (A) is true, but Reason (R) is false
(d) Assertion (A) is false, but Reason (R) is true

34. Assertion (A) Financial market reduces the cost of transactions.

Reason (R) Financial market helps in saving time, effort and money of buyers by providing them valuable information.

35. Assertion (A) Money market instruments are less risky.

Reason (R) Instruments of money market have shorter duration and issuers are financially sound.

36. **Assertion** (A) Capital market instruments are risky from the perspective of return and principal repayment.

Reason (R) Capital market deals in medium and long-term securities.

37. **Assertion** (A) Primary market is also known as the new issues market.

Reason (R) Primary market deals with the securities already traded in market.

38. **Assertion** (A) Secondary market provides the platform to existing investors to disinvest and fresh investors to enter the market.

Reason (R) It is a market for the purchase and sale of existing securities.

39. **Assertion** (A) Forces of demand and supply influence the share prices on a stock exchange.

Reason (R) A stock exchange is a mechanism of constant valuation through which the prices of securities are determined.

40. **Assertion** (A) Secondary markets help in providing liquidity to securities.

Reason (R) Secondary markets facilitate the sale and purchase of new securities issued by companies.

41. **Assertion** (A) Depository participant acts as an intermediary between the investor and the depository.

Reason (R) Only banks are permitted to become depository participants.

42. **Assertion** (A) SEBI was established to protect the rights and interests of investors and to guide and educate them.

Reason (R) SEBI ensures that only the stock exchanges are regulated while other intermediaries remain unregulated.

43. **Assertion** (A) SEBI undertakes steps for investor protection as part of its developmental functions.

Reason (R) SEBI also imposes penalties on fraudulent trade practices to protect investors.

Two Statement Based MCQs

Direction (Q.No. 44 to 53) *Read the following statements carefully and choose the correct alternative*

Alternatives

(a) Statement I is correct and Statement II is incorrect
(b) Statement II is correct and Statement I is incorrect
(c) Both the statements are correct
(d) Both the statements are incorrect

44. **Statement I** Financial market creates and exchanges financial assets.

Statement II Money market deals in short-term securities.

45. **Statement I** Primary market is a part of capital market.

Statement II Primary market is associated with old issues.

46. **Statement I** Capital market instruments are considered riskier both with respect to returns and principal repayment.

Statement II Capital market investment generally yields a higher return for investors. **CBSE 2023**

47. **Statement I** Capital market deals in medium and long-term securities.

Statement II Equity shares, preference shares, debentures, bonds are the instruments of money market.

48. **Statement I** Secondary market directly promotes capital formation.

Statement II Capital market deals in medium and long-term securities such as equity shares and debentures. **CBSE SQP 2025**

49. **Statement I** Secondary market involves the sale and purchase of existing securities only.

Statement II Stock exchange provides sufficient scope for speculation.

50. **Statement I** Stock exchange promotes capital formation by directly issuing new securities.

Statement II Stock exchange enhances liquidity and marketability of securities through trading of existing shares.

51. **Statement I** Trading on stock exchanges today is screen-based and electronic, enhancing transparency.

Statement II The stock exchange ensures operational efficiency by reducing errors and the time taken for transactions.

52. **Statement I** SEBI's protective functions include the prohibition of fraudulent and unfair trade practices, as well as controlling insider trading.

Statement II SEBI's development functions involve training intermediaries, conducting research and adopting a flexible approach to develop capital markets.

53. **Statement I** SEBI was set-up with the main purpose of keeping a check on malpractices and to protect the interest of investors.

Statement II As per the development function, SEBI can levy fee or other charges for carrying out the purposes of the Act.

Matching

54. Match the following

Column I	Column II
A. Money market	(i) It deals in short-term securities.
B. Capital market	(ii) It is also known as the stock market.
C. Primary market	(iii) It deals in long-term securities.
D. Secondary market	(iv) It is also known as the new issues market.

Codes

	A	B	C	D		A	B	C	D
(a)	(ii)	(i)	(iii)	(iv)	(b)	(iii)	(iv)	(i)	(ii)
(c)	(i)	(iii)	(iv)	(ii)	(d)	(i)	(ii)	(iii)	(iv)

55. Match the following

Column I	Column II
A. Spreading equity cult	(i) A stock exchange is a mechanism of constant valuation.
B. Safety of transactions	(ii) It gives investors the chance to disinvest and reinvest.
C. Pricing of securities	(iii) The membership of a stock exchange is well regulated.
D. Providing liquidity and market ability to existing securities	(iv) A stock exchange ensures wider share ownership.

Codes

	A	B	C	D		A	B	C	D
(a)	(ii)	(i)	(iii)	(iv)	(b)	(iii)	(iv)	(i)	(ii)
(c)	(iv)	(iii)	(i)	(ii)	(d)	(i)	(ii)	(iii)	(iv)

56. Match the steps of trading of securities with their correct option

Column I	Column II
A. Step 1	(i) Broker will go online and connect to the stock exchange.
B. Step 2	(ii) Approach a registered broker.
	(iii) Open a demat account.

Codes

	A	B		A	B
(a)	(i)	(ii)	(b)	(ii)	(iii)
(c)	(i)	(iii)	(d)	(ii)	(i)

57. Match the following

Column I	Column II
A. Regulatory function	(i) To register the brokers, sub-brokers and other players of the stock market.
B. Developmental function	(ii) To control the insiders trading in securities.
C. Protective function	(iii) To impart training to the intermediaries.

Codes

	A	B	C		A	B	C
(a)	(i)	(iii)	(ii)	(b)	(iii)	(ii)	(i)
(c)	(ii)	(iii)	(i)	(d)	(iii)	(i)	(ii)

Answers

1. (c) creates and exchanges
2. (c) financial institutions and insurance companies
3. (c) Financial market
4. (b) Serves as an intermediary, linking his savings with investment opportunities
5. (d) Financial Markets
6. (c) Financial market
7. (a) Discount Finance House of India
8. (a) Money market
9. (c) Primary market
10. (c) secondary market
11. (b) Secondary market
12. (c) Secondary market
13. (c) Secondary market
14. (c) The secondary market deals with the trading of existing securities and is also known as the stock market
15. (a) investor
16. (b) Providing liquidity and marketability to existing securities
17. (c) providing liquidity and marketability to existing securities
18. (d) essential
19. (b) PAN number
20. (b) Provides physical share certificates for easier access

21. (b) dematerialisation
22. (c) Insider trading
23. (b) Insider trading
24. (b) Regulatory function
25. (c) SEBI performs the protective function of controlling insider trading and imposing penalties for such practices
26. (c) Prohibiting fraudulent and unfair trade practices
27. (a) The regulatory functions of the Securities and Exchange Board of India include levying fee or other charges for carrying out the purposes of the Act
28. (a) Protective function
29. (a) Protective function
30. (c) Dematerialisation
31. (c) Regulatory
32. (a) Protective
33. (c) Money market
34. (a) Both Assertion (A) and Reason (R) are true and Reason (R) is the correct explanation of Assertion (A)
35. (a) Both Assertion (A) and Reason (R) are true and Reason (R) is the correct explanation of Assertion (A)
36. (b) Both Assertion (A) and Reason (R) are true, but Reason (R) is not the correct explanation of Assertion (A)
37. (c) Secondary market deals with the securities already traded in market.
38. (a) Both Assertion (A) and Reason (R) are true and Reason (R) is the correct explanation of Assertion (A)
39. (a) Both Assertion (A) and Reason (R) are true and Reason (R) is the correct explanation of Assertion (A)
40. (c) Secondary markets provide liquidity to securities, but they do not deal with new securities. New securities are dealt with in the primary market.
41. (c) Depository participants act as intermediaries between the investor and the depository, but it is not true that only banks are allowed to become depository participants.
    Other entities like financial institutions, stockbrokers and custodians can also become depository participants.
42. (c) SEBI regulates not just stock exchanges, but also other intermediaries like brokers, underwriters and merchant bankers.
43. (c) Investor protection is a part of SEBI's protective functions, not developmental functions.
44. (c) Both the statements are correct
45. (a) The primary market deals with new issues of securities, not old ones.
46. (c) Both the statements are correct
47. (a) Equity shares, preference shares, debentures, bonds are the instruments of capital market.
48. (b) Statement II is correct and Statement I is incorrect
49. (c) Both the statements are correct
50. (b) Stock exchange does not issue new securities directly. This process is handled by the primary market.
51. (c) Both the statements are correct
52. (c) Both the statements are correct
53. (a) As per the regulatory function, SEBI can levy fee or other charges for carrying out the purposes of the Act.
54. (c) (i) (iii) (iv) (ii)
55. (c) (iv) (iii) (i) (ii)
56. (b) (ii) (iii)
57. (a) (i) (iii) (ii)

Subjective Questions

Short Answer Type Questions

1. "Money market plays an important role as it is a market for short-term funds."
In the light of this statement, state any four features of money market. Competency Based Que

Ans. Following are the features of money market

(i) It is a market for short-term funds.

(ii) Instruments of money market are highly liquid and less risky.

(iii) Money market instruments are quite expensive and their maturity period is upto one year.

(iv) It has no fixed geographical location.

2. Define capital market. State the two types of capital market.

Ans. Capital market is a market for medium and long-term funds.

This market facilitates the institutional arrangements through which long-term funds, both debt and equity are raised and invested.

Instruments include shares, debentures, bonds, etc.

Following are the types of capital market

(i) **Primary Market**
It is also known as the new issues market, as this market deals with the new securities being issued for the first time.
Investors in primary market include banks, insurance companies, mutual funds, etc.

(ii) **Secondary Market**
It is a market where purchase and sale of existing securities takes place. It is also known as stock market or stock exchange.
It also contributes to economic growth by channelising funds into the most productive investments.

3. Nature of 'capital market' can be explained well with the help of its features. State any three such features of capital market.

Ans. Capital market is a market for medium and long-term funds. It includes all the institutions and organisations that provide long-term and medium-term funds. The common instruments used in capital market are shares, debentures, bonds, mutual funds, etc.

Features of capital market are

(i) The capital market consists of series of channels through which savings of the public are made available for industrial and commercial enterprises.

(ii) The capital market directs the savings of the public (investor) into their most productive investment plan, leading to growth and development of the economy.

(iii) Participants in the capital market include corporate entities, stock exchanges, development banks, commercial banks, financial institutions, foreign investors and ordinary retail investors from members of the public.

4. Give the meaning of capital market. Distinguish between capital market and money market on the basis of the following

(i) Participants (ii) Duration

(iii) Investment outlay **CBSE 2024 C**

Or **Give the meaning of 'capital market'. Differentiate between 'capital market' and 'money market' on the basis of** **CBSE 2025**

(i) Participants (ii) Instruments

Or **Give the meaning of 'money market'. Differentiate between capital market and money market on the basis of the following** **CBSE 2025**

(i) Investment outlay (ii) Duration

Ans. Capital Market

It is a market dealing in securities for long-term funds, whose maturity period is more than one year.

Money Market

It is a market for short-term funds, which deals in monetary assets whose period of maturity is upto one year.

Following are the differences between capital market and money market

Basis	Capital Market	Money Market
Participants	Participants of capital market are financial institutions, banks, corporate entities, foreign investors and ordinary retail investors from the members of public.	Major participants are RBI, commercial banks, financial institutions and finance companies.
Duration	Deals with medium-term and long-term securities with a maturity period of more than one year.	They have a tenure of maximum one year and may even be traded for a single day.
Investment Outlay	It does not require huge capital outlay, as the value of units of securities is generally low, i.e. ₹ 10 or ₹ 100. Even the trading lot is kept low at ₹ 5, ₹ 50, ₹ 100 or so.	In money market, instruments require huge sums of money, because these are quite expensive.
Instruments	Main instruments traded are shares, debentures, bonds, preference shares, etc.	Instruments traded are T-bills, commercial bills, certificate of deposits, etc.

5. Explain the recent capital reform in the trading and settlement procedure.

Ans. Earlier, trading on a stock exchange used to take place on the floor of stock exchange, where prices were shouted out and shares were sold to the highest bidder. However, now-a-days, trading is done electronically in the broker's office through a computer terminal, which is connected to the main computer system of the stock exchange.

Any member can log on to the site, feed the information about the shares he wants to buy or sell and the price into the computer. Accordingly, the transaction is executed by matching the orders at the best bid and offer price.

6. Discuss the merits of screen based trading system.

Ans. Following are the merits of screen based trading system

(i) It ensures transparency as it allows participants to see the prices of securities in the market while business is being transacted.

(ii) It increases efficiency of information being passed on, thus helps in fixing prices efficiently. The computer screens display information on prices and also capital market developments that influence share prices. It increases the efficiency of operations because of reduction in time, cost and risk of error.

(iii) It enables a large number of participants to trade with each other. People from all over the country and even abroad can buy or sell securities through brokers or members without knowing each other, leading to improvement of liquidity of the market.

(iv) It has provided a single trading platform. All the trading centres spread across the country have been brought onto one trading platform, i.e. the stock exchange, on the computer.

7. Name the document prepared in the process of online trading of securities that is legally enforceable and helps to settle disputes/claims between the investor and the broker.

Ans. The document that is prepared in the process of online trading of securities is contract note. It is issued by the broker within 24 hours of execution of order. This note contains details of the number of shares, their price, date and time of deal and the brokerage charged. A unique order code number is assigned to each transaction by the stock exchange and is mentioned on the note.

8. State the meaning of dematerialisation. Discuss any two benefits of dematerialisation.

Ans. Dematerialisation is a process where securities held by the investor in the physical form are cancelled and the investor is given an electronic entry or number so that he/she can hold it as an electronic balance in his account.

Following are the benefits of dematerialisation

(i) It is very convenient as it is just like a bank account.

(ii) Physical shares can be converted into electronic form or electronic holdings can be reconverted into physical certificates (i.e. rematerialisation).

9. State the role of depository participant. List two depositories that are operational in India.

Ans. Following is the role of depository participant

(i) DP serves as an intermediary between the investor and the depository, who is authorised to maintain the accounts of dematerialised shares.

(ii) All the buying and selling of securities under depository are done through DP only.

(iii) Financial institutions, banks, clearing corporations, stock brokers and non-banking finance corporations can become depository participants.

The two depositories that are operational in India include National Securities Depositories Limited and Central Depositories Service (India) Limited.

10. What is a depository and what services they offer to the investors?

Ans. Depository is an institution or organisation, which holds securities (e.g. Shares, debentures, bonds, etc.) in electronic form, in which trading is done. Depositories provide following services

(i) Maintain records of shareholding in electronic form.

(ii) Enable deposit and withdrawal of securities to and from the depository through the process of dematerialisation and rematerialisation.

(iii) Effect the transfer of securities traded in the depository mode on a stock exchange.

11. State some of the benefits, which are offered by depository system.

Ans. Benefits of a depository system are as follows

(i) The risk of loss/tearing up of share certificate is eliminated.

(ii) Risk of bad deliveries is totally eliminated.

(iii) Investment in shares become more liquid.

(iv) There is immediate transfer of ownership of securities.

12. List some examples of the malpractices in capital market, which forced government to set-up a separate regulatory body SEBI. Competency Based Que

Ans. Malpractices such as existence of self-styled merchant bankers, unofficial private placements, rigging of prices, unofficial premium on new issues, non-adherence of provisions of the Companies Act, violation of rules and regulations of stock exchanges and listing requirements, delay in delivery of shares, etc. had eroded investors' confidence and multiplied investor grievances. In order to fight with such problems, government established SEBI as a separate regulatory body.

13. State any three objectives of Securities and Exchange Board of India. CBSE 2023

Ans. Following are the three objectives of Securities and Exchange Board of India

(i) To protect the rights and interests of investors and to guide and educate them.

(ii) To prevent fraudulent activities and malpractices.

(iii) To regulate and develop a code of conduct for intermediaries like brokers, merchant bankers, etc. with a view to make them competitive and professional.

14. State any three protective functions of Securities and Exchange Board of India (SEBI). CBSE 2025; 2024 C; 23

Ans. Following are the protective functions of Securities and Exchange Board of India (SEBI) (any three)

(i) Prohibition of fraudulent and unfair trade practices.

(ii) Controlling insider trading and imposing penalties for such practices.

(iii) Undertaking steps for investor protection.

(iv) Promotion of fair practices and code of conduct in securities market.

Long Answer Type Questions

15. What are the various differences between primary and secondary market? Explain.

Or **Differentiate between 'primary market' and 'secondary market' on the basis of any three points.** CBSE 2025

Ans. Following are the various differences between primary and secondary market

Basis	Primary Market	Secondary Market
Nature of Securities	It deals in new issue of securities, issued by new companies or further issue by existing companies.	Existing securities, i.e. securities already sold are traded in stock exchange.
Type of Contact with Investor	Securities are issued directly to the investors or through intermediaries.	Ownership of existing securities is exchanged between the investors, where the company is not involved.

Basis	Primary Market	Secondary Market
Capital Formation	It promotes capital formation directly.	It indirectly promotes capital formation by providing liquidity.
Buying and Selling	Only buying of securities takes place.	Both buying and selling of existing securities take place.
Pricing	Prices of securities are decided by the company	Prices are decided by the demand and supply of securities.
Location	There is no fixed geographical location.	It is located at specified places.

16. "The stock exchange serves as the beating heart of the financial market, where shares, bonds and securities pulsate through the economy, ensuring liquidity, price discovery and investment opportunities.

In light of this, elucidate the key functions performed by a stock exchange. Competency Based Que

Or **Explain the following functions of stock exchange** CBSE 2025

(i) Providing liquidity and marketability to existing securities

(ii) Pricing of securities (iii) Safety of transaction

Ans. Following are the key functions performed by a stock exchange

(i) **Provides Liquidity and Marketability to Existing Securities**
A basic function of stock exchange is to provide a ready and continuous market where securities can be bought and sold. It gives investors the chance to disinvest and reinvest. Thus, regular dealing provides both liquidity and easy marketability to existing securities in the market.

(ii) **Pricing of Securities**
Share prices on a stock exchange are determined by the forces of demand and supply. It makes a constant valuation of securities and provides important information to both buyers and sellers in the market.

(iii) **Safety of Transactions**
Stock exchange is well-regulated and its dealings are well-defined according to the existing legal framework. This ensures that the investing public gets a safe and fair deal in the market.

(iv) **Contributes to Economic Growth**
In stock exchange, the process of disinvestment and reinvestment channelise the savings into their most productive investment avenues. This leads to capital formation and economic growth.

(v) **Spreading of Equity Cult**
Stock exchange takes various steps to guide and educate public about investments, ensures wider share ownership by regulating new issues and promotes better and safe trading practices.

(vi) **Provides Scope for Speculation**
It is generally accepted that a certain degree of speculation is necessary to ensure liquidity and price continuity in the stock market. Thus, it provides sufficient scope within the provisions of law for speculative activity in a restricted and controlled manner.

17. What are the various steps in the trading and settlement procedure? Discuss.

Ans. Following are the steps involved in the trading and settlement procedure

(i) **Approaching a Broker**
The first step undertaken by an investor is to approach a registered broker or sub-broker and enter into an agreement with him.
He has to sign a broker-client agreement and a client registration form along with certain other details and information, which are as follows

- PAN number (mandatory) • Date of birth and address
- Bank account details
- Educational qualification and occupation
- Residential status (Indian/NRI)
- Depository account details
- Name of any other broker with whom registered
- Client code number in client registration form

The broker then opens a trading account in the name of the investor.

(ii) **Opening a Demat Account**
The investor, then has to open a demat account or Beneficial Owner (BO) account with a DP for holding and transferring securities in demat form. He also has to open a bank account for cash transactions in the securities market.

(iii) **Placing an Order**
The investor places an order with the broker to buy or sell securities. For this, he has to specify the number of shares and the price at which the shares should be bought or sold. The broker will then issue an order confirmation slip to the investor.

(iv) **Finding a Deal**
The broker then goes to the online stock exchange and match the shares with the best prices available.

(v) **Execution of Order**
The broker's terminal will be informed when shares can be bought/sold at the mentioned price and the order will be executed electronically.

After this, he will issue a trade confirmation slip to the investor.

(vi) **Issuing Contract Note**
Within 24 hours of execution of order, the broker issues a contract note, containing details of the number of shares, their price, date and time of deal and the brokerage charged.

A Unique Order Code number is assigned to each transaction by the stock exchange and is printed on the note. Contract note is an important document as it is legally enforceable and helps to settle disputes between the investor and the broker.

(vii) **Delivery of Shares by Investor**
Investor has to deliver the shares sold or pay cash for the shares bought. This should be done immediately after receiving the contract note or before the day when the broker shall make payment or delivery of shares to the exchange. This is called pay-in day.

(viii) **Settlement Cycle**
Cash is paid or securities are delivered on pay-in day, which is before the T +2 days as the deal has to be settled and finalised on the T + 2 days. The settlement cycle is on T + 2 days on a rolling settlement basis, w.e.f. 1st April, 2003.

(ix) **Payment to Broker**
On T+2 days, the exchange will deliver the share or make payment to the broker. This is called the pay-out day. The broker, then has to make the payment to the investor within 24 hours of the pay-out day.

(x) **Delivery of Shares by Broker**
Finally, the broker can make delivery of shares in demat form directly to the investor's demat account.

18. Explain the working of the demat system.

Ans. Following is the working of the demat system

(i) The Depository Participant (DP), either a bank, broker or financial services company, may be identified.
(ii) An account opening form is filled giving details of PAN card, photograph and power of attorney.
(iii) The physical certificate is to be given to the DP along with a dematerialisation request form.
(iv) If shares are applied in a public offer, simple details of DP and demat account are to be given and the shares on allotment would automatically be credited to the demat account.
(v) If shares are to be sold through a broker, the DP is to be instructed to debit the account with the number of shares.
(vi) The broker, then, gives instructions to his DP for delivery of shares to the stock exchange.
(vii) The broker then receives payment and pay the person for the shares sold.
(viii) All these transactions are to be completed within 2 days, i.e. delivery of shares and payment received from the buyer is on a T+2 basis, settlement period.

19. SEBI plays a crucial role in regulating the securities market to ensure fairness and transparency. Discuss the key regulatory functions of SEBI that help maintain the integrity and smooth functioning of the financial market. Competency Based Que

Or **State any three 'regulatory functions' of Securities and Exchange Board of India.** CBSE 2025

Ans. Following are the key regulatory functions of SEBI

(i) Registration of brokers, sub-brokers and other players in the market.
(ii) Registration of collective investment schemes and mutual funds.
(iii) Regulation of stock brokers, portfolio exchanges, underwriters and merchant bankers and the business in stock exchanges.
(iv) Regulation of takeover bids by companies.
(v) Levy fee or other charges for carrying out the purposes of the Act.
(vi) SEBI conducts inspections, enquiries and audits of stock exchanges and intermediaries.
(vii) Perform and exercise such power under Securities Contracts (Regulation) Act, 1956, as may be delegated by the Government of India.

20. It was established by the Government of India on 12th April, 1988 as an interim administrative body to promote orderly and healthy growth of the securities market and for investor protection.

It was given statutory status in 1992 through an Act of Parliament.

(i) Identify the regulatory body which has been highlighted above.
(ii) State the three objectives of the regulatory body identified in part (i).
(iii) State any two functions that are performed for the development of the securities market by the regulatory body identified in part (i). CBSE SQP 2025

Ans.

(i) Securities Exchange Board of India (SEBI)
(ii) **Objectives of SEBI**
Refer to Q.No. 13 of short answer type questions.
(iii) Development functions of SEBI includes
- Training of intermediaries of the securities market.
- Conducting research and publishing information useful to all market participants.

Case Study Based Questions

Short Case Studies

Case Study 1

Identify the type of financial market in the following cases

(i) In this financial market there is a higher degree of liquidity of the financial instruments available to the investors as there is an institute which takes guarantee of this action.

The name of this institute is DFHI (Discount Finance House of India).

(ii) The securities return in this market is riskier in relation to both the returns as well as principal amount. The reason is the performance of the issuing companies. When these companies perform well there are chances of high return but when the other way round happens the returns may go down and result in loss of money to the investors.

Ans.

(i) The type of financial market mentioned in the case is money market. It is a market dealing in securities of short-term funds, whose maturity period is upto one year.

(ii) The type of financial market mentioned in the case is capital market. It is a market dealing in securities for long-term funds, whose maturity period is more than one year.

Case Study 2

'Hitesh Ltd.' is a well-known company in the cement industry since 1999. The company has an authorised capital of ₹ 100 crore and is listed with a reputed stock exchange. The value of its shares is increasing day-by-day due to increase in the demand for cement.

Now the company wants to enter into car manufacturing business. For this it requires ₹ 200 crore. The finance manager of the company decides to raise this capital by a public issue.

(i) Identify the market in which the company's existing securities are being traded.

(ii) Name the market through which the company wants to raise its capital of ₹ 200 crore for its new business.

(iii) Distinguish between the markets identified in (i) and (ii) above on the basis of any two points. **CBSE 2023**

Ans.

(i) The market in which the company's existing securities are being traded is secondary market.

(ii) The market through which the company wants to raise its capital of ₹ 200 crore for its new business is primary market.

(iii) Following are the differences between primary and secondary market

Basis	Primary Market	Secondary Market
Nature of Securities	It deals in new issue of securities, issued by new companies or further issue by existing companies.	Existing securities, i.e. securities already sold are traded in stock exchange.
Type of Contact with Investor	Securities are issued directly to the investors or through intermediaries.	Ownership of existing securities is exchanged between the investors, where the company is not involved.

Case Study 3

These days, the development of a country is also judged by its system of transferring finance from the sector where it is in surplus to the sector where it is needed the most. To give strength to the economy, SEBI is undertaking measures to develop the capital market.

In addition to this, there is another market in which unsecured and short-term debt instruments are actively traded every day. These markets together help the savers and investors in directing the available fund into their most productive investment opportunity.

(i) Name the function being performed by the market in the above case.

(ii) Name the market segment other than the capital market segment in which unsecured and short-term debt instruments are traded. Also, give any three points of difference between the two.

Ans.

(i) The function performed by the market in the above case is mobilisation of savings and channelising them into the most productive use or allocative function.

(ii) Money market is the market segment where unsecured, short-term debt instruments are traded.

Following are the points of difference between money and capital market

Basis	Money Market	Capital Market
Meaning	It is a market dealing in securities of short-term funds, whose maturity period is upto one year.	It is a market dealing in securities for long-term funds, whose maturity period is more than one year.

Basis	Money Market	Capital Market
Liquidity	They are highly liquid and have an arrangement for providing liquidity, which is provided by Discount and Finance House of India (DFHI).	They are less liquid, e.g. A person wanting to sell shares may not get a buyer.
Risk/Safety of Funds	Money market instruments are generally safe due to shorter duration and credibility of issuers.	Capital market instruments are riskier both in terms of returns and repayment of principal.

Case Study 4

In 2nd five year plan, 'industrialisation' was the 'main focus'. But the major problem was saving and investment-household used to invest in gold and property only. Government had to take initiative for establishing Infrastructure and other basic industries.

With pace of economic development, small savings were promoted by establishing an organised market. This market is regulated by SEBI and has attributed a lot in economic development.

(i) Identify the market referred in the case.

(ii) State two functions of this market.

Ans.

(i) The market referred in the case is secondary market.

(ii) Two functions of the secondary market are as follows

- **Contributes to Economic Growth**
  In stock exchange, the process of disinvestment and reinvestment channelise the savings into their most productive investment avenues. This leads to capital formation and economic growth.
- **Spreading of Equity Cult**
  Stock exchange takes various steps to guide and educate public about investments, ensures wider share ownership by regulating new issues and promotes better and safe trading practices.

Case Study 5

Raman who is a broker in a stock exchange has to face challenging questions from society. His own family sometimes asks him to think about his decision to become a broker. He however, has full faith in the stock exchange.

He knows that the membership of a stock exchange is properly regulated abiding the legal system and the public doing investment is safe in making deals. His children one day asked him the reason behind the ups and downs in the stock market.

He clarified their doubt by telling them that forces of supply and demand decide the prices of securities in the secondary market.

Off late he has decided to write a book on the functioning of stock exchange and its significance in the Indian economy. He is trying to highlight in his book, how through the process of investment and disinvestment, existing securities are sold and resold and savings are channelised into the most productive opportunities.

Definitely Raman is justifying his presence in his job.

(i) What is the meaning of stock exchange?

(ii) Identify and briefly explain the functions of stock exchange discussed in the above case.

Ans.

(i) Stock exchange is a collection of individuals, formed as a body or not, constituted for the objective of helping, controlling and regulating the dealings related to buying and selling of securities.

(ii) The different functions of stock exchange highlighted in the above case are

- **Ensures Safety of Transaction**
  Stock exchange is well regulated and its dealings are well-defined according to the existing legal framework. This ensures that the investing public gets a safe and fair deal in the market.
- **Helps in Deciding Pricing of Securities**
  Share prices on a stock exchange are determined by the forces of demand and supply.

  It makes a constant valuation of securities and provides important information to both buyers and sellers in the market.
- **Helps in Contributing to the Economic Growth**
  In stock exchange, the process of disinvestment and reinvestment channelise the savings into their most productive investment avenues. This leads to capital formation and economic growth.

Case Study 6

Rajiv, a small investor from a remote town, is looking to invest in stocks for the first time. He accesses the stock market through an online platform that allows him to view real-time prices, make quick trades and track his portfolio from his home.

The platform he uses is highly efficient, with minimal errors and quick order executions. Rajiv is amazed by how he can trade alongside investors from different parts of the world, all on the same platform, without physically visiting any stock exchange office.

Based on the case above, list any three advantages of the screen-based trading system.

Ans. Following are the advantages of the screen-based trading system

(i) It ensures transparency as it allows participants to see the prices of securities in the market while business is being transacted.

(ii) It increases efficiency of information being passed on, thus helps in fixing prices efficiently. The computer screens display information on prices and also capital market developments that influence share prices.

(iii) It increases the efficiency of operations because of reduction in time, cost and risk of error.

Case Study 7

Supriya's grandmother, who was unwell, called her and gave her a gift packet. Supriya opened the packet and saw many crumpled share certificates inside. Her grandmother told her that they had been left behind by her grandfather. As no trading is now done in physical form, Supriya wants to know the process by adopting which she is in a position to deal with these certificates.

(i) Identify and state the process.

(ii) Also give two reasons to Supriya why dealing with shares in physical form had been stopped.

Ans.

(i) The process is dematerialisation. It is a process where securities held by the investor in the physical form are cancelled and the investor is given an electronic entry or number so that he/she can hold it as an electronic balance in his account.

(ii) Dealing with shares in physical form had been stopped due to the following reasons

- **Theft**
  When shares were in physical form, they were vulnerable to theft as they were tangible documents. If someone stole the physical share certificates, they could be used fraudulently, potentially sold or transferred without the owner's consent.
- **Forgery**
  Physical shares were also prone to forgery, where individuals could create counterfeit share certificates to cheat investors or companies.

Case Study 8

Mr. Patel, a director of ABC Ltd. was privy to confidential information that the company was planning to issue bonus shares in its upcoming board meeting. Anticipating that this announcement would lead to a rise in the company's stock price, Mr. Patel took advantage of this insider information. He decided to buy 12,000 shares of ABC Ltd. from the stock market before the announcement was made public.

Once the announcement was made, as expected, the stock price surged by ₹ 10 due to increased demand from investors excited by the bonus share issue. After a few months, when the stock price had risen considerably, Mr. Patel sold all 12,000 shares and made a substantial profit, leveraging his access to confidential company information that was not available to general investors.

(i) Name the act of Mr. Patel.

(ii) Is it permitted?

Ans.

(i) Mr. Patel is indulged in insider trading. Insider trading means buying and selling of securities by those persons (directors, promoters, etc.) who have some secret information about the company and who wish to take advantage of such secret information. This hurts the interests of the general investors. It was very essential to check this tendency. Many steps have been taken to check insider trading through the medium of the SEBI.

(ii) Insider trading is illegal and is not permitted. Regulatory bodies like the Securities and Exchange Board of India (SEBI) have stringent measures in place to detect and penalise insider trading activities to protect the interests of the general public and maintain fair practices in the stock market.

Case Study 9

Due to various malpractices and exploitation of investors in the securities market, the Indian Government established a separate regulatory body to protect the investors and to develop and regulate the securities market.

(i) Identify the regulatory body set-up by the government.

(ii) Discuss its various objectives.

Ans.

(i) The regulatory body set-up by the government is Securities and Exchange Board of India (SEBI).

(ii) Following are the three objectives of Securities and Exchange Board of India

- To protect the rights and interests of investors and to guide and educate them.
- To prevent fraudulent activities and malpractices.
- To regulate and develop a code of conduct for intermediaries like brokers, merchant bankers, etc. with a view to make them competitive and professional.

Case Study 10

Identify and explain the type of function of SEBI in the following cases

(i) Rajeev was unwilling to buy shares in the stock market as he was told by someone that stock market is a place where various malpractices take place. He decides to discuss the matter with his friend who explains to him how SEBI takes care of the interests of the investors.

(ii) Pankaj wants to become a stock broker. When he approaches people and asks them to get started as investor through him they ask for a certificate which the SEBI must have given him. He becomes aware of the fact that in order to function as a stock broker he will have to get registered with SEBI.

Ans.

(i) The type of function discussed in the case is protective function. It includes

- Prohibition of fraudulent and unfair trade practices.
- Controlling insider trading and imposing penalties for such practices.
- Undertaking steps for investor protection.
- Promotion of fair practices and code of conduct in securities market.

(ii) The type of function discussed in the case is regulatory function. It includes

- Registration of brokers, sub-brokers and other players in the market, registration of collective investment schemes and mutual funds.
- Regulation of stock brokers, portfolio exchanges, under-writers and merchant bankers and the business in stock exchanges, regulation of takeover bids by companies.
- Levy fee or other charges for carrying out the purposes of the Act.
- SEBI conducts inspections, enquiries and audits of stock exchanges and intermediaries.
- Perform and exercise such power under Securities Contracts (Regulation) Act, 1956, as may be delegated by the Government of India.

Long Case Studies

Case Study 11

Shreya is a student of 10+2 (Commerce). Her two friends Sugandha and Sakshi are 10+2 (Non-medical) students. Shreya has full knowledge of capital market. Both her friends are interested in it, but they do not have even an iota of knowledge about it. Shreya gives them the knowledge about capital market in the following manner

"In order to meet its financial requirements, company issues shares. Shares are issued in capital market. The company issue a prospectus and invites the general public to invest in shares. It is called Initial Public Offer (IPO). It is not the case that by investing once the investors are entrapped.

If they so desire, they can sell their shares, at the current market price, to other investors and thus can withdraw their own capital.

Another important feature is that the market in which the company issues shares has no particular place. However, the market wherein the shareholders sell shares does have a particular place, called stock exchange."

(i) In the above paragraph, two types of capital market have been mentioned. Identify them.

(ii) Of the identified type of capital market, give two characteristics of each by way of quotation.

Ans.

(i) The two types of capital market that have been mentioned in the case are primary market and secondary market.

(ii) Following are the characteristics of primary market

- "Company issues .... called Initial Public Offer." It is related to new issues.
- "Market in which .... no particular place." It has no particular geographical location.

Following are the characteristics of secondary market

- "If they so desire........... withdraw their capital." It creates liquidity.
- "However.........called stock exchange." It has a particular geographical location.

Case Study 12

Reena got ₹ 10,00,000 after selling her parental property, which she had got as a gift from her grandmother. Her friend advised her to invest in securities in the stock market.

Reena was unaware of the procedure for the same. Her friend introduced her to a stock broker, who was registered with the National Stock Exchange. Reena approached the broker.

The broker guided her to open a DEMAT account with a depository, as well as a bank account. Reena opened a bank account and DEMAT account with Exim Bank.

(i) Identify and state the steps in the trading procedure for buying and selling of securities which have been discussed above.

(ii) State the next four steps of the trading procedure.

Ans.

(i) Following are the steps in the trading procedure for buying and selling of securities which have been discussed above.

- **Approaching a Broker**
  The first step undertaken by an investor is to approach a registered broker or sub-broker and enter into an agreement with him. He has to sign a broker-client agreement and a client registration form along with certain other details and information, which are as follows
  - PAN number (mandatory)
  - Date of birth and address

- Bank account details
- Educational qualification and occupation
- Residential status (Indian/NRI)
- Depository account details
- Name of any other broker with whom registered
- Client code number in client registration form the broker then opens a trading account in the name of the investor.

- **Opening a Demat Account**
  The investor, then has to open a demat account or Beneficial Owner (BO) account with a DP for holding and transferring securities in demat form. He also has to open a bank account for cash transactions in the securities market.

(ii) The next four steps of the trading procedure are as follows

- **Placing an Order**
  The investor places an order with the broker to buy or sell securities. For this, he has to specify the number of shares and the price at which the shares should be bought or sold. The broker will then issue an order confirmation slip to the investor.
- **Finding a Deal**
  The broker then goes to the online stock exchange and match the shares with the best prices available.
- **Execution of Order**
  The broker's terminal will be informed when shares can be bought/sold at the mentioned price and the order will be executed electronically. After this, he will issue a trade confirmation slip to the investor.
- **Issuing Contract Note**
  Within 24 hours of execution of order, the broker issues a contract note, containing details of the number of shares, their price, date and time of deal and the brokerage charged.

  A Unique Order Code number is assigned to each transaction by the stock exchange and is printed on the note. Contract note is an important document as it is legally enforceable and helps to settle disputes between the investor and the broker.

Case Study 13

Rahul, an avid investor, was following the stock market closely. One day, he read about a company that suddenly halted trading of its shares due to an order from SEBI (Securities and Exchange Board of India). The company was found guilty of manipulating stock prices, which created artificial demand for its shares.

SEBI's intervention not only suspended trading but also imposed penalties on the company's officials involved in these malpractices.

Rahul was curious about how SEBI ensures such activities don't go unchecked and how it helps in maintaining transparency in the securities market.

This incident made him wonder about the actual role of SEBI and how it contributes to the overall development of the securities market.

He began researching SEBI's functions and its impact on both investors and companies.

(i) Explain the purpose and role of SEBI to Rahul in the Indian securities market.

(ii) State the developmental and protective functions of SEBI and how they contribute to the growth of the securities market.

(iii) State any one objective of SEBI.

Ans.

(i) Following is the purpose and role of SEBI in the Indian securities market

The basic purpose of SEBI is to create an environment to facilitate efficient mobilisation and allocation of resources through the securities markets. It also aims to stimulate competition and encourage innovation.
SEBI aims to meet the needs of following mentioned groups

- **Issuers**
  For issuers, provides a market place in which they can raise finance fairly and easily.
- **Investors**
  For investors, provides protection and supply of accurate and correct information.
- **Intermediaries**
  For intermediaries, provides a competitive professional market.

(ii) Following are the developmental functions of SEBI

- Training of intermediaries of the securities market.
- Conducting research and publishing information useful to all market participants.
- Undertaking measures to develop the capital markets by adopting a flexible approach.

Following are the protective functions of SEBI

- Prohibition of fraudulent and unfair trade practices.
- Controlling insider trading and imposing penalties for such practices.
- Undertaking steps for investor protection.
- Promotion of fair practices and code of conduct in securities market.

(iii) The objective of SEBI is to regulate stock exchanges and the securities industry to promote their orderly functioning.

Case Study 14

Rajiv Malhotra was the managing director of 'Finvest Securities,' a leading financial services firm. The firm primarily dealt with portfolio management, mutual funds and stock market investments. Rajiv ensured that all regulatory guidelines were followed diligently.

His firm was known for registering brokers and intermediaries according to the rules set by SEBI. Rajiv also paid close attention to the company's responsibilities, ensuring that Finvest Securities was fully compliant with all the necessary regulations and levies.

However, during a stock market boom, there was an increase in fraudulent practices, insider trading and speculative activities in the industry. Despite these developments, Finvest Securities continued to follow their strict regulatory framework and refused to participate in unfair trade practices. Their conservative approach limited their short-term profits but earned them a solid reputation for ethical behaviour.

In contrast, 'Market Flow Investments,' a competitor, saw rapid growth by exploiting loopholes and engaging in aggressive trading strategies. This allowed them to generate high profits in the short-term. However, when SEBI launched an inquiry and audited the intermediaries involved, market flow was penalised for insider trading, while Finvest Securities was praised for upholding ethical standards.

Quoting lines from the above paragraph, identify and explain two regulatory functions and two protective functions of SEBI as discussed in the case above.

Ans. Following are the regulatory functions discussed in the case

(i) **Registration of Market Intermediaries**

Quoting from the case "Rajiv ensured that all regulatory guidelines were followed diligently. His firm was known for registering brokers and intermediaries according to the rules set by SEBI."

SEBI regulates the securities market by ensuring that brokers, sub-brokers and other intermediaries in the market are registered and operate according to established guidelines.

This helps in maintaining transparency and professionalism in the market.

(ii) **Levying Fees and Charges**

Quoting from the case "Rajiv also paid close attention to the company's responsibilities, ensuring that Finvest Securities was fully compliant with all the necessary regulations and levies."

SEBI has the authority to levy fees and charges for various market-related activities to ensure compliance and maintain orderly functioning in the stock exchanges.

Following are the protective functions discussed in the case

(i) **Prohibition of Fraudulent and Unfair Trade Practices**

Quoting from the case "Despite these developments, Finvest Securities continued to follow their strict regulatory framework and refused to participate in unfair trade practices."

SEBI protects investors by prohibiting fraudulent and unfair trade practices, ensuring that market activities are ethical and in line with the law.

(ii) **Controlling Insider Trading and Imposing Penalties**

Quoting from the case "However, when SEBI launched an inquiry and audited the intermediaries involved, Market flow was penalised for insider trading, while Finvest Securities was praised for upholding ethical standards."

SEBI actively monitors and controls insider trading by imposing penalties on those who engage in such practices, safeguarding investor interests and promoting fair market practices.

Case Study 15

R Ltd. is a real estate company which was formed in 1950. In about 56 years of its existence, the company has managed to carve out a niche for itself in this sector. Lately, this sector is witnessing a boom due to the fact that the Indian economy is on the rise. The incomes of middle class are rising. More people can afford to buy homes for themselves due to easy availability of loans and accompanying tax concessions.

To expand its business in India and abroad, the company weighs various options to raise money through equity offerings in India. Whether to tap equity or debt market, whether to raise money from domestic market or international market or combination of both? When to raise the necessary finance from money market or capital market? It is also planning to list itself in New York Stock Exchange to raise money through ADRs.

To make its offerings attractive, it is planning to offer host of financial plans and products to its stakeholders and investors and also expand its listing at stock exchange after complying with the regulations of SEBI.

(i) What benefits will the company derive from listing at stock exchange?

(ii) What are the regulations of SEBI that the company must comply with?

(iii) How does the SEBI exercise control over R Ltd. in the interest of investors?

Ans.

(i) Following are the benefits the company can derive from listing at stock exchange

- It provides nationwide trading facility for all types of securities.
- The liquidity and best available prices for the securities are ensured by the processing speed of the exchange.

(ii) Following are the regulations of the SEBI for new issue that the company must comply with

- Prospectus has to be attached with every application.
- Objective of the issue and cost of project should be mentioned in the prospectus.
- Company's management, past history and present business of the firm should be highlighted in the prospectus.
- Subscription list for public issue should be kept open for a minimum of 3 days and maximum of 10 days.
- Collections agents are not allowed to collect application money in cash. Issue should make adequate disclosure regarding the terms and conditions of redemption, security conversion and other relevant features of the new instrument, so that an investor can make reasonable determination of risks, returns, safety and liquidity of the instrument. The disclosure shall be vetted by SEBI in this regard.

(iii) SEBI will exercise control over R Ltd. by

- Prohibiting fraudulent and unfair trade practices in the securities market. Unfair trade practices include price rigging, making misleading statements, etc.
- Prohibiting insider trading, i.e. restricts the persons having access to price sensitive information about the company to take undue advantage of it.
- Examining that adequate disclosure about the terms and conditions of redemption, security conversion and other relevant features of the new instrument at the time of issue is made, so that an investor can make reasonable determination of risks, returns, safety and liquidity of the instrument.

SELF ASSESSMENT TEST

Objective Type Questions

1. .... is a link between savers and borrowers which helps to establish a link between savers and investors.
   (a) Marketing (b) Financial market
   (c) Money market (d) None of these

2. Manan wants to buy shares of Tata Steel which are being traded at National Stock Exchange. He thinks that prices will increase. Which market should he approach for this purpose?
   (a) Money market (b) Primary market
   (c) Secondary market (d) Both (b) and (c)

3. The settlement cycle for trading of equity is
   (a) T+3 (b) T+2
   (c) T+5 (d) T+1

4. After the trade has been executed, the broker issues a contract note to the investor within
   (a) 52 hours (b) 24 hours
   (c) 48 hours (d) 12 hours

5. It acts like a bank and keeps securities in electronic form on behalf of the investor.
   (a) Depository participant
   (b) Depository
   (c) Stock exchange
   (d) None of the above

6. SEBI is a regulator of
   (a) capital market (b) money market
   (c) commodity market (d) oversees market

Answers 1. (b) 2. (c) 3. (d) 4. (b) 5. (b) 6. (a)

Short Answer Type Questions

7. Differentiate between capital market and money market on any three basis.
8. State any three features of money market.
9. State any three functions of stock exchange.
10. Explain the working of a demat account.
11. " Screen based trading has become popular in today's era." Enumerate the various benefits offered by screen-based trading.
12. Mr. Mahesh is one of the directors of ABC Ltd. He purchases bonus shares in anticipation of price rise and sold them to earn profit. Identify the act committed by Mahesh. Is it permitted?
13. The Indian Government established a separate regulatory body to protect the investors and to develop and regulate the securities market. Identify the regulatory body and state any three objectives of the regulatory body.

Long Answer Type Questions

14. Mohan wants to engage in trading of securities and is confused between primary and secondary market. As a consultant, how would you explain the differences between primary and secondary market.
15. Rohan wants to buy shares of one of the companies, through a broker. Discuss the steps involved in screen-based trading for buying and selling of securities in this case.
16. State any four regulatory and two developmental functions of SEBI.

11

CHAPTER

> Business is not financial science, it's about trading, buying and selling. It's about creating a product or service so good that people will pay for it.
>
> — *Anta Roddick*

▼ **YOUR STUDY GOALS**

11.1 Concept of Marketing
11.2 Concept of Marketing Mix
11.3 Product
11.4 Pricing
11.5 Place/Physical Distribution
11.6 Promotion

▼ **YOUR PRACTICE GOAL**

- Objective Type Questions (72 Qs ; MCQs, A-R, Statements, Matching)
- Subjective Questions (20 SAs, 8 LAs)
- Case Study Based Questions (Short Case Studies-13, Long Case Studies-9)
- Self Aassessment Test (6 MCQs, 7 SAs, 3 LAs)

Marketing

11.1 Concept of Marketing

Traditionally, marketing has been referred to as performance of business activities that direct the flow of goods and services from producers to consumers. 'Merchandising', 'selling' and distribution are all parts of a large number of activities undertaken by a firm, collectively called marketing.

In modern times, marketing is described as a social process, where by people exchange goods and services for money or for something of value to them.

According to **Philip Kotler**, marketing can be defined as, "a social process by which individual groups obtain what they need and want through creating offerings and freely exchanging products and services of value with other."

Features of Marketing

1. **Needs and Wants** The process of marketing helps individuals and groups in obtaining what they need and want. A need is a state of felt deprivation or feeling of being deprived of something. Needs are basic to human beings and do not pertain to a particular product. Wants, on the other hand, are culturally defined objects that are potential satisfiers of needs.
2. **Creating a Market Offering** Market offering refers to a complete offer for a product or service, having given features like size, quality, taste, etc. at a certain price, available at a given outlet or location and so on. A good 'market offer' is the one which is developed after analysing the needs and preferences of the potential buyers.

3. **Customer Value** A product will be purchased only if it is perceived to be giving greatest benefit or value for the money. Thus, the job of a marketer is to add to the value of the product, so that the customers prefer it in relation to the competing products and decide to purchase it.
4. **Exchange Mechanism** The process of marketing works through the exchange mechanism. Exchange refers to the process through which two or more parties come together to obtain the desired product or service from someone, by giving something in return. In the present world, goods are produced at different places and distributed over a wide geographical area involving exchanges at different levels of distribution. Therefore, exchange is referred to as **essence of marketing.**

Conditions to be Satisfied for an Exchange to take Place

- Presence of atleast two parties, *viz.* the buyer and the seller.
- Each party should be capable of offering something of value to each other.
- Each party should have the ability to communicate and deliver the goods or services.
- Each party should have the freedom to accept or reject the offer.
- Each party should be willing to enter into a transaction with each other, i.e. the acceptance or rejection of the offer takes place on voluntary basis rather than on the basis of any compulsion.

Related Concepts of Marketing

1. **Market** In the traditional sense, the term 'market' refers to the place where buyers and sellers gather to enter into transactions involving the exchange of goods and services.

   In modern marketing sense, the term market refers to a set of actual and potential buyers of a product or service. The other ways in which this term is being used is in the context of a product market (cotton market, gold or share market), geographic market (national and international market), type of buyers (consumer market and industrial market) and the quantity of goods transacted (retail market and wholesale market).
2. **Marketer** It refers to a person who takes more active part in the process of exchange.
3. **Marketing Management** It involves selecting the right customer groups and building lasting relationships with them. This is done by creating, delivering and effectively sharing value that meets customers' needs and encourages loyalty and growth.

Marketing Management Philosophies

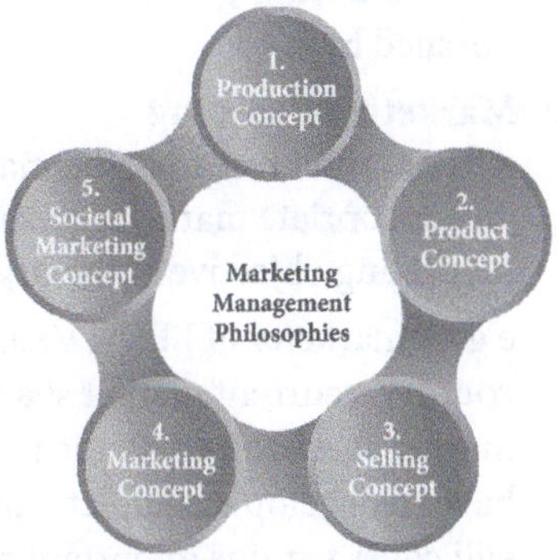

1. **Production Concept** Under this concept, the assumption was that profits could be maximised by producing at a large scale, thereby, minimising the cost of production per unit. The focus was to improve the firm's efficiency of production and distribution. In this concept, availability and affordability of the product were considered to be the key to success of a firm.
2. **Product Concept** Under this concept, the focus shifted from quantity of production to quality of products. Product improvement in terms of its quality and features became the key to profit maximisation of a firm, under the product concept.
3. **Selling Concept** Under this concept, firms began to undertake aggressive selling and promotional efforts to attract and persuade customers to buy the product. The focus of firms shifted to pushing up sales through aggressive selling techniques like advertising, personal selling and sales promotion.

4. **Marketing Concept** This concept emphasises that in the long-run, profits can be maximised by identifying the needs of present and potential customers and satisfying them in an effective way. In this concept, the basic roleof a firm is to 'identify the need and fill it'.
5. **Societal Marketing Concept** This concept pays attention to social, ecological and ethical aspects of marketing for dealing with problems like environmental pollution, deforestation, shortage of resources, population explosion, etc. It is an extension of marketing concept as customer satisfaction is supplemented by welfare of the society.

Functions of Marketing

Marketing performs number of functions, which can be categorised as

Functions of Marketing

- Gathering and analysing market information
- Product designing and development
- Packaging and labelling
- Customer support services
- Promotion
- Transportation
- Marketing planning
- Standardisation and grading
- Branding
- Pricing of product
- Physical distribution
- Storage or warehousing

1. **Gathering and Analysing Market Information**
   It is necessary to identify the needs of the customers and take various decisions for the successful marketing of products and services.
   It is also important to make an analysis of the available opportunities and threats as well as strengths and weaknesses of the organisation as it helps in deciding what opportunities can best be pursued by it.
2. **Marketing Planning**
   After market research, the marketer has to develop an appropriate marketing plan to achieve the marketing objective of the organisation.
   e.g. A marketer of LED TV, having 15% of the country's current market share, aims to enhance his market share to 30% in the next two years. So, he will have to develop a complete marketing plan which will cover various important aspects like plan for increasing the level of production, products promotion, etc. and specify the action programmes to achieve these objectives.
3. **Product Designing and Development**
   A good design of a product not only helps to make it attractive, but also helps in improving its performance and also give it a competitive advantage over the similar products present in the market.
   e.g. When we plan to buy refrigerator, we not only see its features like cost, storage capacity, but also the design aspects like its shape, style, etc.
4. **Standardisation and Grading**
   Standardisation refers to producing goods of pre-determined specifications or standards regarding quality, price, packaging, technology, equipment, etc. This ensures uniformity and consistency in output.
   Grading is the process of classifying the products into different groups, on the basis of some of its important characteristics such as quality, size, etc. It ensures quality of goods and helps in realising higher value for high quality output.
5. **Packaging and Labelling**
   Packaging refers to designing and developing the package for a product. Labelling refers to designing and developing the label to be put on the package.
   In modern day marketing, packaging and labelling have become so important that these are considered as the pillars of marketing.
6. **Branding**
   It refers to the process of giving a name, sign, symbol or a combination of all to a product for creating its identification. It helps to differentiate the product from other products available in the market.
7. **Customer Support Services**
   One of the important functions of marketing management is to develop the customer support services like after sales services, handling of complaints, credit services, maintenance services, technical services and consumer information, etc. which aims to provide maximum satisfaction to the customer.
8. **Pricing of Product**
   Pricing refers to the process of determining the price of a product. Price of a product refers to the amount of money that the customer has to pay to obtain a product. The marketers have to analyse a number of factors such as pricing objectives, pricing strategies, demand, cost, competition, etc. to decide the price of a product.

9. **Promotion**
   It refers to the process of informing the customers about the product and then persuading them to buy it. The popular methods of promotion are advertising, sales promotion, personal selling and public relations.
10. **Physical Distribution**
    It covers all the activities required to physically move the goods from manufacturers to the customers. It involves major decisions areas and activities like channels of distribution, physical movement of goods, storage, warehousing, inventory control, transportation, etc.
11. **Transportation**
    It involves physical movement of goods from one place to another. It is necessary to make available the goods to places where they are needed.

    e.g. Tea produced in Assam has to be transported not only within the State but to other far-off places also, where it is consumed. Thus, transportation helps to create *'place utility'*.
12. **Storage or Warehousing**
    Usually, there is a time gap between production or procurement of goods and their sales. It may be because of irregular demand for the products such as woollen garments or there may be irregular supply because of seasonal production such as rice, wheat or cotton, etc. Thus, arrangement for storage of goods is necessary.

    It also helps to avoid delays in delivery, meeting contingencies in demand and stabilising the prices of products in the market. Thus, it helps to create *'time utility'*.

11.2 Concept of Marketing Mix

Marketing management decisions are based on a number of controllable and non-controllable factors. Controllable factors can be influenced at the level of firm such as price of the product, packaging decision, etc. Non-controllable factors are beyond the control of the firm such as rate of inflation, credit policy, etc. The combination of different variables chosen by a firm to prepare its market offering, is called **marketing mix**.

According to "**Philip Kotler**, "Marketing mix is the set of marketing tools that the firm uses to pursue its marketing objectives in the target market."

Elements of Marketing Mix

- **Product** Product means goods or services or 'anything of value', which is offered to the market for sale. e.g. Hindustan lever offers number of consumer products like toiletries (Close-Up toothpaste, Lifebuoy soap, etc.), detergent powder (Surf, Wheel), food products (Refined Vegetable Oil), etc.

  It also includes extended product or what is offered to the customer as after-sales services, handling complaints, credit services, etc.

4Ps of Marketing Mix

- **Price** Price is the amount of money that the customers have to pay to obtain the product. Decisions are also required to be taken in respect of discounts to customers, traders and credit terms, etc. so that customers perceive the price to be in line with the value of the product.
- **Place** Place or physical distribution include all the activities required to physically move firm's products to target customers. Important decision areas in this respect include selection of dealers or intermediaries to reach the customers, providing support to the intermediaries, etc.
- **Promotion** Promotion refers to the process of informing the customers about the availability, features, merits, etc. of the product and then persuading them to buy it.

11.3 Product

From the customer's point of view, a product is a bundle of utilities, which is purchased because of its capability to provide satisfaction of certain need.

A customer may seek to satisfy the following benefits from a product

- Functional benefits
- Psychological benefits
- Social benefits

e.g. Purchase of a motorcycle provides functional utility of transportation, but at the same time satisfies the need for prestige and esteem and provides social benefit by the way of acceptance from a group.

Products may be broadly classified as

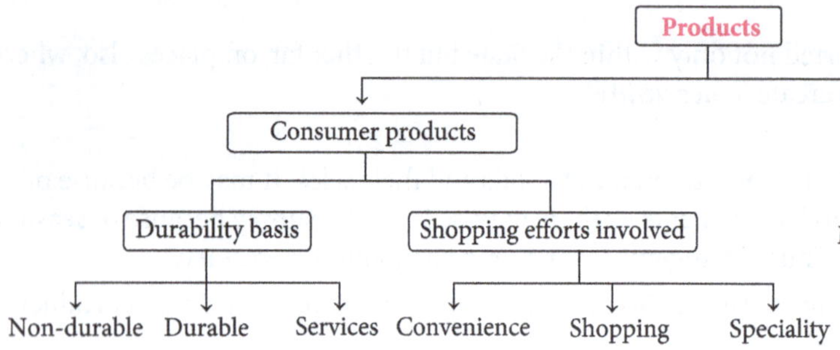

Product Mix

A product is a 'bundle of utilities associated with the utilisation of the product. Apart from the physical product/ service, product mix also consists of branding, packaging and labelling.

Branding

The process of giving a name or a sign or a symbol, etc. to a product is called branding.

Firm has to decide whether to sell its products under a brand name or generic name. Generic name is the name of the whole class of the product, such as camera.

Terms related to Branding

- **Brand** A brand is a name, term, sign, symbol, design or some combination of them, used to identify the products (goods or services) of one seller or group of sellers and to differentiate them from those of the competitors. e.g. Bata, Parker, etc. Brand consists of two components
  (a) **Brand Name** The part of a brand, which can be spoken, is called a brand name. In other words, brand name is the verbal component of a brand. e.g. Maggi, Lux, etc.
  (b) **Brand Mark** The part of a brand which can be recognised but which is not utterable, is called brand mark. It appears in the form of a symbol, design, distinct colour scheme or lettering. e.g. Red and blue ball of Pepsi, etc.
- **Trademark** A brand or part of a brand that is given legal protection is called trademark. The protection is given against its use by other firms. e.g. Maruti Suzuki sign sign on Maruti Cars.

Advantages of Branding to Marketers

1. **Enables Product Differentiation** Branding helps a firm to distinguish its product from the other competing products available in the market.
2. **Helps in Advertising and Display Programmes** Without a brand, the advertiser cannot promote and create awareness and sell his product.
3. **Differential Pricing** By building brand acceptance and brand loyalty, a firm can charge a different price for its product from that of its competitors.
4. **Ease in Introduction of New Product** If a new product is introduced under an established brand name, it is likely to be accepted easily and get a quick start.

Advantages of Branding to Customers

1. **Helps in Product Identification** Branding helps the customer to easily identify the product and reduces the requirement of inspection.
2. **Ensures Quality** Branding ensures a particular level of quality of the product and helps in building the confidence of the customers.
3. **Status Symbol** Certain brands become status symbols and customers feel proud and satisfied in purchasing them.

Characteristics of a Good Brand Name

Characteristics	Explanation
Short and Easy	A brand name should be short, easy to pronounce, spell, recognise and remember. e.g. Vim, Ponds, Lux, etc.
Suggestive	A brand should suggest the product's quality and benefits. It should be appropriate to the product's function. e.g. Ujala, Fair and Lovely, etc.
Distinct	A brand name should be distinct from the other brands present in the market. e.g. Liril, Sprite, Raymonds, etc.
Adaptable to Packaging	A brand name should be adaptable to packaging and labelling requirements to different advertising media and to different languages.
Versatile	A brand name should be versatile enough to accommodate new products, which are added to the product line.
Capable of Registration	A brand name should be capable of being registered and legally protected.
Staying Power	A brand name should have long-lasting staying power and should not get out of date.

Packaging

Packaging refers to the act of designing and producing the container or wrapper of a product. Various kinds of goods are placed or packed into appropriate containers for protection and convenient handling.

Levels of Packaging

- **Primary Package** It means the immediate container of a product. It may be kept till the customer is ready to use the product. e.g. Toothpaste tube or bottle of perfume. It provides protection and facilitates the use of the product.
- **Secondary Packaging** It means additional layer of protection that is kept till the product is ready for use. e.g. A toothpaste tube is packed in a cardboard box. When the consumer begins to use the product, the box is disposed-off.
- **Transportation Packaging** It means packaging done to protect the product and help in the process of transportation and storage. e.g. Toothpaste boxes are sent to retailers in corrugated boxes each containing 20, 50 or 100 units.

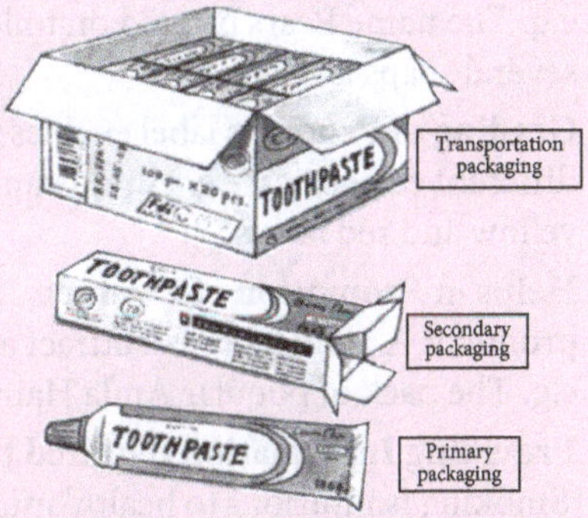

Importance of Packaging

1. **Rising Standards of Health and Sanitation** Because of increasing consciousness about health and sanitation, people now prefer to buy packaged goods as the chances of adulteration in such goods are minimised.
2. **Self-service Outlets** The self-service outlets are becoming very popular, particularly in major cities and towns. Because of this, some of the traditional role assigned to personal selling in respect of promotion has gone to packaging.
3. **Innovational Opportunity** The recent innovation and developments in packaging have completely changed the marketing scene in the country. e.g. Milk can now be stored for 4-5 days without refrigeration.
4. **Product Differentiation** Packaging helps to create differentiation amongst products on the basis of different colour, size, material, etc. of the package. e.g. By looking at the package of food products, hair oil, etc. one can make some guess about quality of the product contained in it.

Functions of Packaging

1. **Product Identification** The package of a product helps the customer to easily identify the product in the market. e.g. Red Label tea in a red colour packing, Taj Mahal tea in blue box pack, etc.
2. **Product Protection** The package of a product protects it from spoilage, breakage, pilferage, leakage, damage, etc. This kind of protection is required during storing, distribution and transportation of the product. e.g. Oil in plastic bottles.
3. **Facilitating Use of the Product** The size and shape of the package should be convenient to open, handle and use for the consumers. e.g. Toothpaste tubes, handwash soap dispenser, etc.
4. **Product Promotion** Packaging is also used for promotion purposes. An eye-catching colour scheme, photograph or typeface may be used to attract attention of the people at the point of purchase. Packaging also plays an important role in self-service stores.

Functions of Packaging
- → Product identification
- → Product protection
- → Facilitating use of the product
- → Product promotion

Labelling

The term 'labelling' means designing a label to be put on the package. A label describes the product, its usage and specifies its contents. Label can be a simple tag or a descriptive label.

Functions of Labelling

1. **Describe the Product and Specify its Contents** A label helps to describe the product, its usage, cautions in use, contents, manufacturing and expiry dates, etc.
2. **Identification of the Product or Brand** Label gives a definite identity to the product or brand and therefore, the identification of a product becomes easy. e.g. The name Pears printed on toilet soaps helps us to know which soap out of several soaps is Pears.
3. **Grading of Products** label enables the manufacturer to grade the products into different categories. e.g. Hindustan lever sells different grades of tea under green, yellow and red labels.
4. **Helps in Promotion of Products** Label helps to aid in promotion of the products. A good label can attract attention, describe the product and stimulate the buyer to buy the product. e.g. The pack of popular Amla Hair Oil states, 'Baalon mein Dum, Life mein Fun'.
5. **Providing Information required by Law** Label provides information required under law. e.g. Statutory warning 'Smoking is injurious to health' must be stated on the package of cigarettes. Such information is considered necessary on processed foods, drugs and tobacco products. In case of hazardous or poisonous material, appropriate safety warning need to be put on the label.

11.4 Pricing

Pricing refers to the process of determining the price of a product.

Price of a product refers to the amount of money that the customer has to pay to obtain a product from the market. Pricing is considered as a regulator of demand of a product, because, when the price of the product is increased, demand falls and *vice-versa.*

Factors affecting Price Determination

Important factors that affect the price of product are

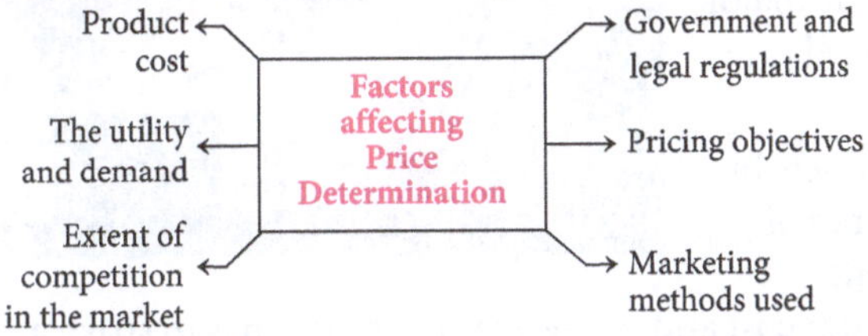

1. **Product Cost**

   The total cost of product includes production, selling and distribution costs. The cost sets the minimum level or floor price for a product.

   Costs can be broadly divided into three categories

   - **Fixed costs**, which do not vary with change in production, like rent of a building, etc.
   - **Variable costs**, which vary at all levels of production, like cost of raw material, etc.
   - **Semi-variable costs**, which vary with production, but not in direct proportion with it, like salary plus commission, etc.

   Total cost is sum total of fixed, variable and semi-variable cost. Price is determined by adding a profit to the average cost of a product.

2. **The Utility and Demand**

   While the product costs set the lower limits of the price, the utility provided by the product and the intensity of demand of the buyer sets the upper limit of price, which a buyer would be prepared to pay. According to the law of demand, consumers usually purchase more units at a low price than at a high price.

3. **Extent of Competition in the Market**

   The price of a product is affected by the nature and the degree of competition.

   The price can be set upto the higher limit, if the extent of competition is low in the market and *vice-versa.*

   Competitors' price, their reactions, their product, quality and features must be considered before fixing the price.

4. **Goverment and Legal Regulations**

   To protect the interest of public against unfair practices in the field of price fixing, the government has all the rights to control the prices of various products and services by including the products in the category of essential commodities such as drugs, some food items, LPG, etc.

5. **Pricing Objectives**

   Pricing objectives of firm also affect the fixation of the price of a product. Generally, firm's objective is to maximise the profits.

   But, there is a difference in maximising profit in short-run and in the long-run, which is stated below

   - If the firm decides to maximise profits in the short-run, it would tend to charge maximum price for its products.
   - If the firm decides to maximise profits in long-run, it would opt for a lower per unit price so that it can capture larger share of the market and earn greater profits through increased sales.

   Apart from this, the firm's other pricing objectives may be obtaining market share leadership, surviving in a competitive market and attaining product quality leadership.

6. **Marketing Methods Used**

   Price fixation process is also affected by various elements of marketing such as distribution system, quality of salesmen employed, quality and amount of advertising, sales promotion efforts, the type of packaging, product differentiation, credit facility and customer services provided.

11.5 Place/Physical Distribution

Physical distribution covers all the activities required to make the goods and services available at the right place, so that people can purchase the same. Two important decisions related to physical distribution include channels of distribution and physical movement of goods.

Components of Physical Distribution

1. **Order Processing** It involves time and steps required to deliver the goods as per the order received from customers. A good physical distribution system should provide for an accurate and speedy processing of orders.
2. **Transportation** It is the means of carrying goods and raw materials from the point of production to the point of sale. It is one of the major elements in the physical distribution of goods as unless the goods are physically made available, the sale cannot be completed.
3. **Warehousing** It refers to the act of storing and assorting products in order to create *'time utility'* in them. Firms having large number of warehouses will take less time in serving customers at different locations. However, large number of warehouses involve greater cost and *vice-versa*. Thus, firm has to strike a balance between the cost of warehousing and the level of customer service.
4. **Inventory Control** It is related to an important decision of about deciding the level of inventory. Higher the level of inventory, higher will be level of service to customers but the cost of carrying the inventory will also be high as lot of capital would be tied up in the stock. Thus, a balance is to be maintained in respect of the cost and customer satisfaction.

Channels of Distribution

These are a set of individuals and firms that take title or assist in transferring title of particular goods and services as they move from producers to consumers. They help to cover wide geographical area, provide convenience to customers and provide economy of efforts by reducing distribution efforts of producer and shopping efforts of customers.

Types of Channels of Distribution

Major types of distribution channels involve the following

1. Direct Channel (Zero Level Channel)

The most simple mode of distribution is direct distribution, where the goods are directly made available to consumers from the manufacturers, without use of any intermediary. e.g. Bata selling through its own retail outlets, similarly, mail order selling, internet selling and selling through its own sales force (Amway) are examples of direct selling.

Manufacturer → Consumer

2. Indirect Channels

When one or more intermediary is involved in the distribution network, then it is referred to as indirect channels. The various indirect channels are

(i) **Manufacturer-Retailer-Consumer** (One Level Channel) In this method, an intermediary is used. Here, manufacturer sells the goods to the retailer who sells them to the final consumers.

This method is used for expensive products and also useful for selling Fast Moving Consumer Goods (FMCG). e.g. Maruti sells its cars through company approved retailers.

Manufacturer → Retailer → Consumer

(ii) **Manufacturer-Wholesaler-Retailer-Consumer** (Two Level Channel) In this method, manufacturer sells the goods to the wholesaler, wholesaler sells them in small quantity to retailer and then retailer sells them to the consumer. This medium is mainly used to sell consumer non-durable goods like soap, tea, salt, sugar, ghee, etc. Through this channel, manufacturer covers the large market area.

Manufacturer → Wholesaler → Retailer → Customer

(iii) **Manufacturer-Agent-Wholesaler-Retailer-Consumer** (Three level channel) In this case, manufacturers use their own agents or brokers who connect them to wholesalers and then to the retailer. This is done when the line of product is limited and wide coverage is required.

Manufacturer → Agent → Wholesaler → Retaitler → Consumer

11.6 Promotion

Promotion refers to the use of communication with the twin objective of informing potential customers about a product and persuading them to buy it. Promotion is an important element of marketing mix by which marketers makes use of various tools of communication to encourage exchange of goods and services in the market.

Elements of Promotion Mix

Promotion mix refers to combination of promotional tools used by an organisation to achieve its communication objectives.

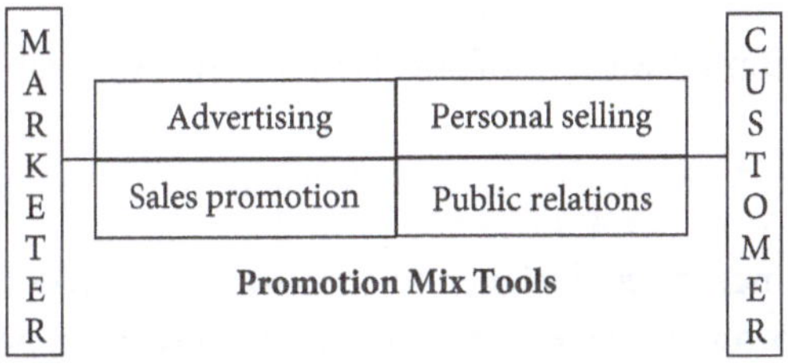

Promotion Mix Tools

These tools are also called elements of promotion mix and can be used in different combinations to achieve the goals of promotion.

Advertising

It is an impersonal form of communication, which is paid for by the marketers to promote some goods or services.

Features of Advertising

1. **Paid Form** Advertising is a paid form of communication, i.e. the sponsor has to bear the cost of communicating with the prospects.
2. **Impersonality** There is no direct face-to-face contact between the prospect and the advertiser. It is therefore, referred to as non-personal form of promotion. Advertising creates a monologue and not a dialogue.
3. **Identified Sponsor** Advertising is undertaken by some identified individual or company, who makes the advertising efforts and also bears the cost of it.

Merits of Advertising

1. **Mass Reach** Advertising is a medium through which a large number of people can be reached over a vast geographical area.
2. **Enhancing Customer Satisfaction and Confidence** Advertising creates confidence amongst prospective buyers as they feel more comfortable and assured about the product quality and hence feel more satisfied.
3. **Expressiveness** With the developments in art, computer designs graphics, etc. advertising has developed into one of the most forceful medium of communication.
4. **Economy** Because of its wide reach, the overall cost of advertising gets spread over numerous communication links established, causing the per-unit cost to decline significantly.

Personal Selling

Personal selling involves oral presentation of message in the form of conversation with one or more prospective customers for the purpose of making sales. It is a personal form of communication.

Features of Personal Selling

1. **Personal Form** Personal selling involves a direct face-to-face communication between the seller and the buyer.
2. **Development of Relationship** Personal selling helps to develop a personal and friendly relationship between the salesperson and the customer, which may become important in making sale.

Merits of Personal Selling

1. **Flexibility** The salesman can adjust/change his message according to the needs of the customers.
2. **Direct Feedback** Since, there is a direct face-to-face contact between the buyer and seller, it provides immediate feedback from the customer.
3. **Minimum Wastage** There is minimum wastage of efforts as the company can decide the target customers before making any contact with them.

Sales Promotion

Sales promotion refers to short-term incentives, designed to encourage the buyers to make immediate purchase of a product or service. These include all promotional efforts other than advertising, personal selling and public relations.

Sales promotion activities include offering cash discounts, sales contests, free gift offers and free sample distribution.

Companies use sales promotion tools designed specifically to promote sales among different groups as

1. **Customers** Through free samples, discounts and contests.
2. **Traders or Middlemen** Through cooperative advertising, dealer discounts, incentives and contests.
3. **Salespersons** Through bonus, special offers and contests.

Sales promotion includes only those activities that are used to provide short-term incentives to boost the sales of a firm.

Public Relations

Public relations involve a variety of programmes designed to promote or protect a company's image and its individual products in the eyes of the public.

Many organisations have separate public relations department or they take services of outside public relations agency. Such department or outside agency helps the firms in the following ways

- They help to disseminate information and build goodwill about the business.
- They monitor the attitude of the general public and generate positive publicity.
- They are especially useful when there is negative publicity about the company or its products. At that time, they tackle the situation like an emergency to protect and improve the company's image.
- They also advise top management to adopt certain programmes which will add to their public image and ensure that negative publicity does not take place at all.

Ways/Methods/ Tools of Public Relations

- **Newsletters Print or Emailed Newsletters** These are the important and most attractive way to promote the business and build public relations.
- **Social Media** Using social networking sites such as Facebook, Twitter, can help to easily build up the relations with public.
- **Press Release** It is the most common medium to interact with general public.
- **Special Events** By sponsoring the social events, one can easily build up the relations with public and use such events in future for publicity and propaganda.

Mind Map

MARKETING

1 Concept of Marketing

Marketing is a social process where people exchange goods and services for money or for something of value to them.

2 Feature of Marketing

- **Needs and Wants** Focus of marketing is on the satisfaction of the needs and wants of individuals and organisations
- **Creating a Market Offering** It refers to a complete offer for a product or service
- **Customer Value** Job of the marketer is to add value to the product
- **Exchange Mechanism** Exchange refers to the process through which two or more parties come together to obtain the desired product or service

3 Market Management Philosophies

- Production concept (Producing at a large-scale)
- Product concept (Focus on quality of products)
- Selling concept (Involves aggressive selling and promotional efforts)
- Marketing concept (Identifying the needs of present and potential customers)
- Societal marketing concept (Pays attention to social, ecological and ethical aspects of marketing)

4 Function of Marketing

- Gathering and analysing market information to identify the needs of the customers
- Marketing planning to achieve the marketing objectives
- Product designing and development to achieve a competitive advantage
- Standardisation and grading to ensure uniformity, consistency and to meet specifications
- Packaging and labelling to attract customers and convey information
- Branding to differentiate the products
- Customer support services to provide maximum satisfaction
- Pricing of products to determine the price
- Promotion
- Physical distribution includes storage, warehouse, etc.
- Transportation to make the goods available
- Storage or warehousing to make arrangement for storage of goods

5 Elements of Marketing Mix

Marketing mix consists of various elements which are classified into four categories, also known as '4Ps of marketing'.

Place Mix

Physical distribution covers all the activities required to make the goods and service available at the right place.

Channels of Distribution

- Direct channel
- Indirect channels
  - One level channel
  - Two level channel
  - Three level channel

Components of Physical Distribution

- **Order Processing** Involves time and steps required to deliver the goods
- **Transportation** Carrying goods and raw materials from the point of production to point of sale
- **Warehousing** Storing and assorting products
- **Inventory Control** Deciding the level of inventory

Product Mix

A product is a bundle of utilities associated with the utilisation of product. Product mix consists of

- **Branding** Process of giving a name or a sign or a symbol to a product
- **Packaging** Act of designing and producing the container or wrapper of a product. Three levels include primary, secondary and transportation
- **Labeling** Designing a label to be put on the package

Price Mix

Pricing refers to the process of determining the price of a product.

Factors Affecting Price Determination

- **Product Cost** Total cost includes production, selling and distribution costs
- **Utility and Demand of Product** Product cost sets lower limit, utility and demand sets upper limit
- **Extent of Competition in the Market** Price is affected by nature and degree of competition
- **Government and Legal Regulations** Control the price of products
- **Pricing Objectives** To maintain profits in short-run or long-run
- **Marketing Methods Used** Distribution system, quality of salesmen employed, etc.

Promotion Mix

Promotion refers to the use of communication with twin objective of informing potential customers about a product and persuading them to buy it. It includes

- **Advertising** Impersonal form of communication which is paid for by the marketers to promote some goods or services
- **Personal Selling** Involves oral presentation of message in the form of conversion with one or more prospective customers for the purpose of making sales
- **Sales Promotion** Refers to short-term incentives designed to encourage the buyers to make immediate purchase of a product or service
- **Public Relations** Variety of programmes designed to promote or protect a company's image and its individual products in the eyes of the public. Tools include newsletters print, social media, press release and special events

EXAM PATTERN QUESTIONS

Objective Type Questions

Multiple Choice Questions (MCQs)

1. Which of the following is the feature of the marketing?

(a) Needs and wants
(b) Creating a market offering
(c) Customer value
(d) All of the above

2. .... is called marketer.

(a) Satisfaction seeker
(b) Satisfaction provider
(c) Seller
(d) Service provider

3. "A company creates a product with specific features such as size, quality and taste, which is made available at a certain price and location to meet the needs and preferences of potential buyers." The important feature of marketing illustrated above is **Competency Based Que**

(a) market offering
(b) customer value
(c) exchange mechanism (d) needs and wants

4. A person feeling hungry may get food by offering to give money or some other product or service in return to someone who is willing to accept the same for food. The important feature of marketing illustrated above is **Competency Based Que**

(a) exchange mechanism
(b) customer value
(c) creating a market offering
(d) needs and wants

5. 'Buy one get one free' is printed on the label of the package of a mosquito repellant. Identify the labelling function being performed by this statement.

(a) Grading of products
(b) Helps in promotion of products
(c) Identification of product or brand
(d) None of the above

6. A marketer of colour TV having 20% of the current market share of the country aims at enhancing the market share to 50% in next 3 years. For achieving this objective he specified an action programme. Name the function of marketing being discussed above. **NCERT Modified; Competency Based Que**

(a) Marketing planning (b) Standardisation
(c) Packaging (d) Grading

7. A leading smartphone manufacturer has observed a declining market share despite a significant increase in production and marketing efforts. The company realises that it has not effectively gathered sufficient market information regarding customer preferences, trends and competitor activities. The company decides to conduct in-depth market research to identify customer needs and opportunities, as well as its own strengths and weaknesses.

Based on this research, the company aims to develop a comprehensive marketing plan that focuses on improving product design, promotional strategies and pricing policies. The goal is to regain lost market share and create a more competitive presence in the market within the next year.

What is the first step the company should take to improve its market position? **Competency Based Que**

(a) Developing a marketing plan
(b) Designing and developing the product
(c) Conducting market research
(d) Setting pricing strategies

8. Kumar wanted to purchase a fuel efficient car having the latest standards regarding minimisation of pollution. He saw an advertisement offering such a car and visited the showroom of the company wherein the car was displayed.

In his discussion, the marketing manager told him that the company is providing credit facilities, maintenance services and many other effective services which are helping in bringing repeat sales and developing brand loyalty.

Identify the marketing function which the marketing manager was discussing with Kumar. **Competency Based Que**

(a) Branding (b) Physical distribution
(c) Promotion (d) Customer support services

9. Kamlesh Singh opened a jewellery store 'Fashion Jewels' offering workwear, light jewellery with modern designs for young working women. Good jewellery designs not only made the jewellery attractive for young working women, but also gave him a competitive edge in the market. The jewellery was a hit with working women and 'Fashion Jewels' was able to report a profit of ₹ 3 crore in the first year itself.

The function of marketing performed by Kamlesh Singh in the above case was **Competency Based Que**

(a) packaging and labelling
(b) promotion
(c) customer support service
(d) product designing and development

10. **Identify the function of marketing illustrated in the below picture.**

(a) Branding (b) Packaging and labelling
(c) Promotion
(d) Product designing and development

11. **Atul was a pen manufacturer. He used to make ball point pens in a small factory in the basement of his house. Daily, he would go to the market place and distribute pens to the retailers. Some of the pens were sold by him of his own by meeting persons on road. He had not kept any name for his pens.**

They were just blue, black and red pens. One of his friends suggested him to keep a good name of his pens. He kept his own name and started selling pens with the name of Atul Pens. Then there were three categories of pens – Atul Red, Atul Blue and Atul Black. Gradually his business started to pick up even more and he made good revenue.

Identify the function of marketing highlighted in the above case. **Competency Based Que**

(a) Branding (b) Packaging
(c) Grading (d) Customer support service

12. **The process of classification of products into different groups, on the basis of some of the important characteristics such as quality, size, etc. is known as** **CBSE SQP 2025**

(a) branding (b) standardisation
(c) grading (d) marketing planning

13. **"A company carefully selects a specific group of customers to focus on and tailors its products and marketing efforts to meet their specific needs." Identify the concept of marketing management highlighted by this statement.** **Competency Based Que**

(a) Production concept (b) Product concept
(c) Societal marketing concept
(d) Marketing concept

14. **The focus of .... concept is 'attracting consumers' while the focus of .... concept is 'consumer's satisfaction'.**

(a) product, selling (b) selling, production
(c) marketing, selling (d) selling, marketing

15. **Large-scale production done to reduce the average cost of production is the essence of .... concept of marketing management.**

(a) product (b) selling
(c) production (d) marketing

16. **Jasdeep, a dealer in school uniforms, decided to maximise his profit by using different aggressive promotional efforts. Identify the marketing management philosophy adopted in the above case.** **Competency Based Que**

(a) Selling concept (b) Production concept
(c) Product concept (d) Marketing concept

17. **Aman microwaves produce microwaves but they do not try to understand the needs of the customers. Their main focus is always on the quality of the product but never on customer requirement. They try to include as many features as possible in their product. This year they have added a special type of alarm in their product which is a unique feature.**

The alarm is available in ten varieties. However, the customers say that the product is not of much use to them as it consumes a lot of electricity. Identify the marketing management philosophy involved in the given situation. **Competency Based Que**

(a) Production concept (b) Product concept
(c) Selling concept (d) Marketing concept

18. **One of the following is considered to be an extension of the marketing concept, which apart from customer satisfaction pays attention to ethical and ecological aspects of marketing. Identify the concept.**

(a) Selling concept (b) Product concept
(c) Production concept (d) Societal marketing concept

19. **A popular beverage company has been focusing on large-scale production to reduce the cost per unit and make the product more affordable. While the company has successfully minimised production costs, it has started facing competition from a newer brand that emphasises high quality ingredients and unique flavours.**

The newer brand's customers seem more loyal, even though its products are priced higher. The company is now considering shifting its approach to focus more on product quality and customer preferences rather than just mass production.

Which marketing concept is the company most likely to adopt in order to compete with the newer brand? **Competency Based Que**

(a) Production concept (b) Product concept
(c) Selling concept (d) Marketing concept

20. **A buyer buys a product for service for what it does for him/her or the benefit it provides to him/her. There can be three type of benefits, a consumer may seek to satisfy from the purchase of a product : (i) Functional benefits (ii) Social benefits end (iii)…..** **CBSE 2025**

(a) Technological benefits
(b) Economic benefits
(c) Psychological benefits
(d) Environmental benefits

21. **Maria Vena Ltd. entered into the market with coloured television and has now introduced products like audio system, air conditioners, washing machines, etc. The company is not only offering the products but also handling complaints and offering after-sales services. Identify the element of marketing mix discussed here.** **Competency Based Que**

(a) Place (b) Product
(c) Promotion (d) Price

22. **The symbol which appears on all 'Audi' cars as shown in figure below and which is not utterable is known as its**

(a) brand (b) brand name
(c) brand mark (d) trademark

23. **Identify the important term related to branding illustrated in picture below.**

(a) Brand name (b) Brand mark
(c) Both brand mark and trademark
(d) Trademark

24. **Arjun has decided to start a business of creating customised stationery items, such as planners and notebooks. To establish a strong market presence and ensure easy recognition, he has chosen the brand name 'NoteCraft.' This name will help him create a distinct identity for his products and set them apart from those of competitors.**

Identify the relative advantage of branding to the marketers being described in the above case. **Competency Based Que**

(a) Facilitates differential pricing
(b) Ease in the launching of new products
(c) Facilitates product differentiation
(d) Assists in advertising and display programmes

25. **A well-established shoe company has recently launched a new line of sports shoes. The company has created a distinctive logo featuring a stylised swoosh, which is unique to their brand. The logo is now prominently displayed on all marketing materials, advertisements and product packaging. Additionally, the company has applied for trademark protection to prevent other brands from using similar symbols. This new logo helps differentiate their shoes from other competitors in the market.**

What part of the brand is represented by the stylised swoosh logo in the case? **Competency Based Que**

(a) Brand name (b) Brand mark
(c) Trade mark (d) Brand

26. **A renowned cosmetics company launches a new line of skincare products under its well-established brand name. Due to the brand's strong reputation for quality and customer loyalty, the new products quickly gain popularity. Customers easily identify the brand and trust its promise of high quality ingredients. The company also uses its established brand image to charge premium prices for the new line, knowing that loyal customers are willing to pay for the trusted quality. Additionally, the new products enjoy quick acceptance in the market due to the brand's influence.**

Which advantage of branding is most evident in the case of the new skincare line? **Competency Based Que**

(a) Ease in introduction of new product
(b) Differential pricing
(c) Helps in advertising and display programmes
(d) Ensures quality

27. **Nishita Verma has set-up a factory to manufacture herbal hand sanitizers in Gwalior. The size and shape of the bottles in which the products are packed are specially designed so that it should be convenient to handle and use by the consumers.**

The bottles in which the sanitizer are packed in part of **Competency Based Que**

(a) primary packaging (b) secondary packaging
(c) tertiary packaging
(d) Both secondary and tertiary packaging

28. Identify the level of packaging in the below picture.

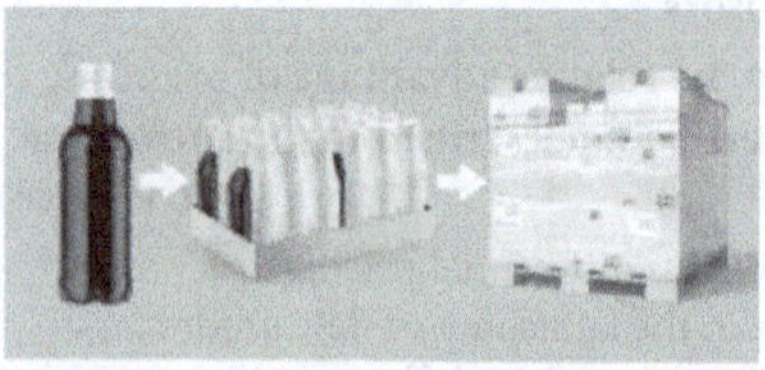

(a) Primary package (b) Secondary package
(c) Transportation package (d) Both (a) and (b)

29. Which of the following is not the function of packaging?

(a) Product protection (b) Pricing objectives
(c) Promotion (d) Product identification

30. A new juice brand introduces its product in a unique, eco-friendly bottle that not only protects the juice but also stands out on store shelves. The packaging design is eye-catching, helping to differentiate it from competitors. Additionally, the brand emphasises that the packaging ensures the juice remains fresh for several days without refrigeration.

Which importance of packaging is highlighted by the juice brand's use of eco-friendly packaging? Competency Based Que

(a) Rising standards of health and sanitation
(b) Product differentiation
(c) Innovational opportunity
(d) Self-service outlets

31. The level(s) of packaging shown in the picture given below is/are CBSE 2024 C

(a) primary level only
(b) primary and secondary levels
(c) primary, secondary and transportation packaging levels
(d) primary and transportation packaging levels

32. Which of the following statements is incorrect?

(a) Branding helps to differentiate a product from others in the market.
(b) Customer support services include handling complaints and providing technical assistance.
(c) Pricing of a product does not consider competition as a factor.
(d) Promotion involves informing customers about the product to persuade them to buy it.

33. As soon as CocaCola reduced its selling price on 2 litre to ₹ 75, soon Pepsi followed with a price reduction in its selling price and priced its 2 litre per bottle at ₹ 74.50. Which factor of pricing is being discussed here?

(a) The utility and demand Competency Based Que
(b) Extent of competition in the market
(c) Marketing methods used
(d) Pricing objectives

34. 'Product cost' as a factor affecting price determination of a product includes

(a) cost of producing, distributing and selling the product
(b) utility provided by the product
(c) nature and degree of competition
(d) maximising profit in the short-run

35. Prakhar Ltd. is the manufacturer of life-saving drugs. There was an outbreak of flu two years back that spread quickly and affected many people. Prakhar Ltd. made huge investment on research and development and was able to develop a medicine for the same. The medicine was very effective in controlling the flu and now it has become a necessity for the patients. As a result, the demand for the medicine increased manifold. Considering the demand, the company increased the price of the medicine. The government observed the situation. Since it was the only available medicine to combat flu, the government declared it as an essential medicine and regulated its price to make it affordable for the public.

From the following, identify the factor(s) affecting the determination of price discussed in the above case.

I. Product cost II. Marketing methods used
III. Utility and demand
IV. Government and legal regulations

CBSE 2024 C; Competency Based Que

Codes

(a) Only IV (b) I, III and IV
(c) III and IV (d) I, II and III

36. Which of the following is not a component of 'physical distribution'? CBSE 2024

(a) Inventory control (b) Order processing
(c) Standardisation and grading
(d) Transportation

37. .... refers to time and steps involved between receipt of order from customer and delivery of goods.

(a) Inventory control (b) Order processing
(c) Transportation (d) Warehousing

38. When the products are sold by a manufacturer to the end consumer without involving any intermediary, the type of channel of distribution used is CBSE 2024 C

(a) zero level channel (b) one level channel
(c) two level channel (d) three level channel

39. **Which of the following statements is incorrect?**
(a) Advertising is a personal form of communication
(b) Advertising is a paid form of communication
(c) Advertising is a mass selling technique
(d) Advertising is inflexible as the message cannot be adjusted to the needs of the buyer

40. **Reena Limited has hired 200 salesmen who will be assigned the task of contacting prospective buyers and creating awareness about the new range of organic incenses introduced by the company.**

Identify the element of promotion described in the given lines. Competency Based Que
(a) Advertising
(b) Sales promotion
(c) Personal selling
(d) Public relation

41. **Which of the following statements is incorrect about sales promotion?** CBSE 2023
(a) It includes short-term incentives which are designed to encourage the buyers to make immediate purchase of a product or services
(b) It includes all promotional efforts other than advertising, personal selling and public relations
(c) It includes only those activities that are used to provide long-term incentives to boost the sales of a firm
(d) It includes the activities which are undertaken to supplement other promotional efforts such as advertising and personal selling

42. **Beenu had a bookstore in Sabad called 'Bookmark'. For years, the bookstore was doing reasonably well but with the rise of digital books and online retailers, her sales had declined. Beenu's daughter, who had just completed her MBA with a specialisation in marketing decided to launch a marketing campaign to revive the bookstore.**

The campaign's focus was on the joy of reading books in physical form, the joy of turning pages and the warm atmosphere of the bookstore. She organised story writing and other competitions every weekend. The information of these was given to the parents and children through television, radio, children's magazines, etc. Attractive prizes were offered to the winners.

This increased the footfall of the children and their parents and the bookstore soon became popular. The tool of communication used by Beenu's daughter to revive the bookstore was CBSE 2024; Competency Based Que
(a) advertising
(b) sales promotion
(c) personal selling
(d) public relations

43. **Identify the promotion tool illustrated by the picture.**

(a) Sales promotion (b) Personal selling
(c) Advertising (d) Public relations

Direction *Read the following case study and answer the questions 44 to 47 on the basis on the same*

Sagar Snacks, a well-known snack manufacturer in Jaipur, Rajasthan, initially specialised in Aloo Tikki. This crispy potato snack quickly became popular among the locals and tourists visiting the city. As the business grew, Sagar Snacks expanded its product line by introducing various regional snacks, sweets and beverages. Despite the diversification, Aloo Tikki remained the flagship product, generating the highest revenue for the brand.

To maintain its market position, Sagar Snacks offered competitive pricing and exceptional customer services, such as custom orders for events and loyalty discounts for regular customers. Over time, the brand became synonymous with quality snacks, with customers often asking for Sagar's Aloo Tikki specifically rather than just any Aloo Tikki.

In recent years, Sagar Snacks has developed a robust distribution network, establishing both physical stores and an online platform to reach a broader audience.

Due to increasing competition in the market, the company decided to enhance its promotional strategies by collaborating with a reputed advertising agency, AdBoost Pvt. Ltd. Following their advice, Sagar Snacks has focused on managing its public image by sponsoring local festivals, organising food fairs and supporting community initiatives like waste management programmes.

44. **"As the business grew, Sagar Snacks expanded its product line by introducing various regional snacks, sweets and beverages." Legal protection was also given. The brand name Sagar Snacks serves as a**
(a) brand value (b) trademark
(c) trade name (d) brand mark

45. **"Sagar Snacks offered competitive pricing and exceptional customer services, such as custom orders for events and loyalty discounts for regular customers." Identify the factor affecting the element of the marketing mix being discussed above.**
(a) Marketing methods used (b) Objectives
(c) Extent of competition in the market
(d) Product cost

46. **"Sagar Snacks has developed a robust distribution network, establishing both physical stores and an online platform to reach a broader audience."**

Identify the decision related to the element of the marketing mix being discussed above.

(a) Sorting and assorting products to create time utility
(b) Regarding the channels or using intermediaries
(c) Both (a) and (b)
(d) One regarding branding, packaging and labelling

47. **"Sagar Snacks has focused on managing its public image by sponsoring local festivals, organising food fairs and supporting community initiatives."**

Name the department in the organisation generally responsible for performing the above important task of managing public opinion.

(a) Marketing department
(b) A separate department created in the firm for the purpose
(c) An outside agency
(d) All of the above

Assertion-Reason

Direction (Q.No. 48 to 57) *Read the following Assertion (A) and Reason (R) and choose the correct alternative from the following*

Alternatives

(a) Both Assertion (A) and Reason (R) are true and Reason (R) is the correct explanation of Assertion (A)
(b) Both Assertion (A) and Reason (R) are true, but Reason (R) is not the correct explanation of Assertion (A)
(c) Assertion (A) is true, but Reason (R) is false
(d) Assertion (A) is false, but Reason (R) is true

48. **Assertion** (A) The marketing process helps individuals and groups obtain what they need and want through exchange mechanisms.

Reason (R) Exchange is the process where two or more parties come together to obtain a desired product or service by giving something in return.

49. **Assertion** (A) A well-developed marketing plan is essential to achieve the marketing objectives of an organisation.

Reason (R) Marketing planning helps in specifying the action programmes related to production, promotion and other aspects to achieve set targets.

50. **Assertion** (A) Standardisation reduces the need for inspection, testing and evaluation of the products.

Reason (R) Standardisation ensures the buyers that goods conform to the pre-determined standards of quality, price, packaging, etc.

51. **Assertion** (A) Warehousing creates time utility.

Reason (R) Warehousing bridges the time gap between production and consumption of goods.

52. **Assertion** (A) According to the product concept of marketing, the focus of the firms shifted from quantity of production to quality of products.

Reason (R) With the decrease in supply of products, customers started looking for products which were superior in quality.

53. **Assertion** (A) The societal marketing concept extends the marketing concept by emphasising not only customer satisfaction but also the welfare of society.

Reason (R) The societal marketing concept addresses issues like environmental pollution, resource shortages and ethical considerations in marketing.

54. **Assertion** (A) A good brand name should be short, easy to pronounce and distinct from other brands in the market.

Reason (R) A good brand name must also be capable of being registered and legally protected to prevent unauthorised use by other firms.

55. **Assertion** (A) A trademark provides legal protection to a brand or part of a brand, preventing its unauthorised use by other firms.

Reason (R) A trademark is a part of a brand that can be spoken and identified verbally.

56. **Assertion** (A) Packaging and labelling are considered as pillars of modern day marketing.

Reason (R) Packaging refers to designing the package for a product, while labelling involves developing the label to be put on the package.

57. **Assertion** (A) Sales promotion is mostly executed to support only personal selling.

Reason (R) Sales promotion only consists of those activities that provide short-term incentives to boost sales.

Two Statements Based MCQs

Direction (Q.No. 58 to 67) *Read the following statements carefully and choose the correct alternative*

Alternatives

(a) Statement I is correct and Statement II is incorrect
(b) Statement II is correct and Statement I is incorrect
(c) Both the statements are correct
(d) Both the statements are incorrect

58. **Statement I** Warehousing helps in creating 'time utility' by storing goods until they are needed.

Statement II Firms with fewer warehouses can serve customers more quickly but incur lower costs.

59. **Statement I** The concept of product relates to not only the physical product but also the benefits offered by it from customer's point of view.

Statement II The concept of product does not include the extended product by way of after-sale services, availability of spare parts, handling complaints, etc.

CBSE 2023

60. **Statement I** Packaging helps in product differentiation by using different colours, sizes and materials.

Statement II Packaging plays no role in protecting the product during transportation and distribution.

61. **Statement I** Labelling helps in grading products by categorising them into different levels of quality.

Statement II Labelling does not play a role in providing information required by law.

62. **Statement I** Packaging serves as a silent salesperson by attracting customers and influencing their purchase decisions.

Statement II Warehousing is primarily concerned with the transfer of ownership from producer to consumer.

63. **Statement I** The price of a product can be set higher if the competition in the market is low.

Statement II Government intervention can influence price determination for products classified as essential commodities.

64. **Statement I** Variable costs are costs that do not change with the level of production.

Statement II Fixed costs are those costs that remain the same regardless of the level of production.

65. **Statement I** Direct distribution channels involve intermediaries like wholesalers and retailers.

Statement II Indirect channels of distribution can involve multiple levels such as wholesaler, retailer and agent.

66. **Statement I** Promotion aims to persuade potential customers to buy products through communication.

Statement II Promotion is not a part of the marketing mix.

67. **Statement I** Advertising helps in building customer confidence and satisfaction.

Statement II Personal selling reaches a large audience over a vast geographical area.

Matching

68. Match the following CBSE 2023

Column I	Column II
A. The product concept	(i) It emphasises on increasing the profit through increased sales volumes by adopting aggressive selling techniques.
B. The production concept	(ii) It emphasises on quality performance and features of product and thus profit maximisation through product improvement.
C. The selling concept	(iii) It emphasises on profit maximisation through volume of production, thereby reducing the cost of production.
D. The marketing concept	(iv) It emphasises on profit maximisation through customer satisfaction, i.e. identifying the needs of its present and prospective buyers and satisfying them in an effective manner.

Codes

	A	B	C	D
(a)	(ii)	(i)	(iii)	(iv)
(b)	(iii)	(iv)	(i)	(ii)
(c)	(iv)	(iii)	(i)	(ii)
(d)	(ii)	(iii)	(i)	(iv)

69. Match the following

Column I	Column II
A. Primary packaging	(i) A big cardboard box containing say 50 units of toothpaste tubes.
B. Secondary packaging	(ii) A toothpaste tube
C. Transportation packaging	(iii) A cardboard box of toothpaste

Codes

	A	B	C
(a)	(i)	(ii)	(iii)
(b)	(ii)	(iii)	(i)
(c)	(i)	(iii)	(ii)
(d)	(ii)	(i)	(iii)

70. Match the following

Column I	Column II
A. Branding	(i) Act of designing and producing the container or wrapper of a product.
B. Packaging	(ii) Putting identification marks on the package.
C. Labelling	(iii) Process of giving a name or a sign or a symbol to the product.

Codes

	A	B	C
(a)	(ii)	(i)	(iii)
(b)	(iii)	(i)	(ii)
(c)	(i)	(iii)	(ii)
(d)	(ii)	(iii)	(i)

71. Match the following

Column I		Column II	
A.	Social process	(i)	Market
B.	Set of potential customers	(ii)	Marketing
C.	Controllable variables	(iii)	Trademark
D.	A registered brand name	(iv)	Marketing mix

Codes

	A	B	C	D
(a)	(ii)	(i)	(iv)	(iii)
(b)	(iii)	(ii)	(i)	(iv)
(c)	(i)	(iii)	(iv)	(ii)
(d)	(ii)	(i)	(iii)	(iv)

72. Match the following

Column I		Column II	
A.	Public relations	(i)	It refers to short-term incentive to make immediate purchase.
B.	Advertising	(ii)	It is a one-way method of promotion.
C.	Sales promotion	(iii)	It is used to manage the public opinion.
D.	Personal selling	(iv)	In it, a direct face-to-face dialogue takes place.

Codes

	A	B	C	D
(a)	(ii)	(i)	(iii)	(iv)
(b)	(iii)	(ii)	(i)	(iv)
(c)	(i)	(iii)	(iv)	(ii)
(d)	(i)	(ii)	(iii)	(iv)

Answers

1. (d) All of the above
2. (b) Satisfaction provider
3. (a) market offering
4. (a) exchange mechanism
5. (b) Helps in promotion of products
6. (a) Marketing planning
7. (c) Conducting market research
8. (d) Customer support services
9. (d) product designing and development
10. (d) Product designing and development
11. (a) Branding
12. (c) grading
13. (d) Marketing concept
14. (d) selling, marketing
15. (c) production
16. (a) Selling concept
17. (b) Product concept
18. (d) Societal marketing concept
19. (b) Product concept
20. (c) Psychological benefits
21. (b) Product
22. (c) brand mark
23. (c) Both brand mark and trademark
24. (c) Facilitates product differentiation
25. (b) Brand mark
26. (a) Ease in introduction of new product
27. (a) primary packaging
28. (a) Primary package
29. (b) Pricing objectives
30. (b) Product differentiation
31. (d) primary and transportation packaging levels
32. (c) Pricing of a product does not consider competition as a factor
33. (b) Extent of competition in the market
34. (a) cost of producing, distributing and selling the product
35. (b) I, III and IV
36. (c) Standardisation and grading
37. (b) Order processing
38. (a) zero level channel
39. (a) Advertising is an impersonal form of communication
40. (c) Personal selling
41. (c) It includes only those activities that are used to provide long-term incentives to boost the sales of a firm
42. (d) public relations
43. (a) Sales promotion
44. (b) trademark
45. (a) Marketing methods used
46. (b) Regarding the channels or using intermediaries
47. (d) All of the above
48. (a) Both Assertion (A) and Reason (R) are true and Reason (R) is the correct explanation of Assertion (A)
49. (a) Both Assertion (A) and Reason (R) are true and Reason (R) is the correct explanation of Assertion (A)
50. (a) Both Assertion (A) and Reason (R) are true and Reason (R) is the correct explanation of Assertion (A)
51. (a) Both Assertion (A) and Reason (R) are true and Reason (R) is the correct explanation of Assertion (A)
52. (c) With the increase in supply of products, customers started looking for products which were superior in quality.
53. (a) Both Assertion (A) and Reason (R) are true and Reason (R) is the correct explanation of Assertion (A)
54. (b) Both Assertion (A) and Reason (R) are true, but Reason (R) is not the correct explanation of Assertion (A)
55. (c) Trademarks provide legal protection, but a trademark is not limited to the verbal component of a brand. Instead, it can include symbols or logos.
56. (b) Both packaging and labelling are crucial, Reason (R) merely defines the terms rather than explaining why they are pillars of marketing.

57. (d) Sales promotion also supplement advertising alongwith personal selling.
58. (a) Warehousing creates time utility, but firms with fewer warehouses will take more time to serve customers, not less.
59. (a) The concept of a product indeed includes the physical product as well as the benefits perceived by the customer and it also encompasses the extended product, which includes after-sale services and other aspects that enhance customer satisfaction.
60. (a) Packaging helps in product differentiation and protects the product from spoilage, breakage and damage.
61. (a) Labelling helps in grading products and providing information required by law.
62. (a) Warehousing is primarily concerned with the storage of goods rather than the transfer of ownership.
63. (c) Both the statements are correct
64. (b) Fixed costs remain the same regardless of production, while variable costs change with production levels.
65. (b) Indirect channels involve intermediaries, while direct channels bypass them.
66. (a) Promotion is part of the marketing mix and aims to persuade customers.
67. (a) Advertising enhances customer satisfaction, while personal selling is limited to one-on-one communication.
68. (d) (ii) (iii) (i) (iv)
69. (b) (ii) (iii) (i)
70. (b) (iii) (i) (ii)
71. (a) (ii) (i) (iv) (iii)
72. (b) (iii) (ii) (i) (iv)

Subjective Questions

Short Answer Type Questions

1. Which functions of marketing help to create 'time utility' and 'place utility'? Explain.

Ans. The following functions of marketing help to create 'time utility' and 'place utility'

(i) **Storage and Warehousing**
Usually, there is a time gap between production or procurement of goods and their sales.
Therefore, it is necessary to make arrangements for storage of goods, so that a regular supply of goods is maintained in the market. It also helps to avoid delays in delivery and meeting contingencies in demand. This also helps in stabilising the prices of products in the market. Thus, it helps to create 'time utility'.

(ii) **Transportation**
It involves physical movement of goods from one place to another. While production of a good takes place at a place, its consumers are spread over a vast area. Therefore, it is necessary to make available these goods at places where they are needed. Thus, transportation helps to create 'place utility'.

2. Explain the following functions of marketing
(i) Product designing and development
(ii) Standardisation and grading

Ans.

(i) **Product Designing and Development**
A good design of a product not only helps to make it attractive, but also helps in improving its performance and also give it a competitive advantage over the similar products present in the market.
e.g. When we plan to buy refrigerator, we not only see its features like cost, storage capacity, but also the design aspects like its shape, style, etc.

(ii) **Standardisation and Grading**
Standardisation refers to producing goods of pre-determined specifications or standards regarding quality, price, packaging, technology, equipment, etc. This ensures uniformity and consistency in output and reduces the need for inspection, testing and evaluation of the products. Grading is the process of classifying the products into different groups, on the basis of some of its important characteristics such as quality, size, etc. Grading is necessary for such goods which are not produced according to pre-determined specifications, such as agricultural goods. Grading ensures that the goods belong to a particular quality and helps in realising higher prices for high quality output.

3. Differentiate between 'product' and 'production' concepts of marketing philosophies on the following basis
(i) Starting point **(ii) Main focus**
(iii) Means **(iv) Ends**

Ans. Following are the differences between product and production concept

Basis	Product Concept	Production Concept
Starting Point	The marketing efforts start after the product is produced in the factory.	The marketing efforts start after the product is produced in the factory.
Main Focus	Its focus in on quality, features, performance of the product.	Its focus in on quantity of product.

Basis	Product Concept	Production Concept
Means	It uses product improvement as a means to achieve the objective.	It uses availability and affordability of the product as as means to achieve the objective.
Ends	Its objective is to earn profit through product quality.	Its objective is to earn profit through production volume.

4. Explain the essence of the selling concept in marketing.

Ans. Selling concept assumes that the customers would not buy enough, unless they are adequately convinced and motivated to do so. It is believed that aggressive selling and promotional efforts are important to make customers buy their products.

The focus of business firms shifted to pushing the sale of products through aggressive selling techniques with a view to persuade, lure or coax the buyers to buy the products. Making sale through any means became important. It was assumed that buyers can be manipulated but what was forgotten was that in the long-run what matters most is the customer satisfaction, rather than anything else.

5. Distinguish between marketing and selling concepts on any four basis.

Ans. Following are the differences between marketing and selling concepts

Basis	Marketing Concept	Selling Concept
Concept	Find wants and fill them.	Create products and sell them.
Focus	It focuses on maximum satisfaction of customer needs and wants.	It focuses on transferring the title and ownership of goods from seller to the buyer.
Aim	It aims at increasing profit by satisfying the consumers.	It aims at maximising profits by increasing sales.
Scope	It has wider scope. It is concerned with identifying customer needs, developing the product, pricing, selling and providing after-sales services to satisfy the customers.	It has a limited scope. It is concerned with transfer of ownership of goods from the sellers to the buyers through promotion and salesmanship. Thus, it is just a part of marketing.

6. State the pillars, on which marketing concept is based.

Ans. Marketing concept is based on the following pillars

(i) Identification of market or customer who are chosen as the target of marketing effort.

(ii) Understanding needs and wants of customers in the target market.

(iii) Development of products or services with the aim to satisfy the need of customers.

(iv) Providing information and making the goods available to the final users.

7. Elaborate on the key components of the marketing mix, often referred to as the 4Ps.

Or **Explain the four elements of marketing mix.**

CBSE SQP 2025

Ans. Marketing mix refers to the combination of four basic elements, which constitute the core of a company's marketing system. 4Ps/Elements of marketing mix are as follows

(i) **Product**
It refers to goods or services or anything of value, which is offered in the market for exchange.

(ii) **Price**
It refers to the amount of money, which the customer pays for the products or services.

(iii) **Place**
It is concerned with the availability of products and services at right time and at right place, so that the customers find it convenient to purchase.

(iv) **Promotion**
It refers to the use of communication tools to provide information to the customer about a product and persuade them to buy it.

8. Product is a bundle of utilities. Explain.

NCERT; Competency Based Que

Ans. Yes, product is a bundle of utilities. It can be explained with the help of an example. On wearing a shirt, we get the following satisfactions

(i) **Functional Satisfaction**
To wear the shirt and cover the body with it.

(ii) **Psychological Satisfaction**
To feel more confident and active after wearing the shirt provides psychological satisfaction.

(iii) **Social Satisfaction**
Getting recognition after wearing shirt from a group of known people is social satisfaction.

9. Define brand, brand name, brand mark and trademark.

Ans. Brand

A brand is a name, term, sign, symbol, design or some combination of them, used to identify the products (goods or services) of one seller or group of sellers and to differentiate them from those of the competitors. e.g. Bata, Parker.

Brand Name

The part of a brand, which can be spoken, is called a brand name. In other words, brand name is the verbal component of a brand. e.g. Maggi, Lux.

Brand Mark

The part of a brand which can be recognised but which is not utterable is called brand mark. It appears in the form of a symbol, design, distinct colour scheme or lettering. e.g. Red and blue ball of Pepsi.

Trademark

A brand or part of a brand that is given legal protection is called trademark. The protection is given against its use by other firms. e.g. Maruti Suzuki sign on Maruti Cars.

10. Explain how branding benefits customers and improves their shopping experience.

Ans. The three advantages of branding to the customers are as follows

(i) **Product Identification**
Branding helps customers in identifying the product. e.g. A customer, who is satisfied with 'Lux' soap need not buy any other product. Thus, branding facilitates repeated purchases and reduces the time and effort involved therein.

(ii) **Ensures Quality**
Branding ensures a specific level of quality to customers. This builds up confidence of customers and increases their level of satisfaction. Branded products are well packed to prevent adulteration.

(iii) **Status Symbol**
Some brands become status symbols due to their quality. The consumers of these brands feel proud and enjoy status in using them.

11. State any four characteristics of good brand name.

Ans. Following are the characteristics of good brand name (any four)

(i) **Distinct**
A brand name should be distinct from the other brands present in the market. e.g. Liril, Sprite, Raymonds, etc.

(ii) **Adaptable to Packaging**
A brand name should be adaptable to packing and labelling requirements to different advertising media and to different languages.

(iii) **Versatile**
A brand name should be versatile enough to accommodate new products, which are added to the product line.

(iv) **Capable of Registration**
A brand name should be capable of being registered and legally protected.

(v) **Staying Power**
A brand name should have long lasting staying power and should not get out of date.

12. "The main goal of label is to draw consumer attention and spreading company's name with logo." In the light of this statement, state the advantages of labelling. Competency Based Que

Or **Describe the functions of labelling in the marketing of products.** NCERT

Ans. Functions of labelling are

(i) **Describe the Product and Specify its Contents**
It specifies the contents and other features of the product. It enables the manufacturer to give clear instructions to the consumer about the proper use of his product. It helps to describe the product, its usage, cautions in use, contents, manufacturing and expiry dates, price, quantity, etc.

(ii) **Identification of the Product or Brand**
It gives a definite identity to the product or brand and therefore, the identification of a product becomes easy. e.g. The name Pears printed on toilet soaps helps us to know which soap out of several' soaps is Pears.

(iii) **Grading of Products**
It enables the manufacturer to grade the product into different categories. e.g. Hindustan Lever sells different grades of tea under green, yellow and red labels.

13. "Packaging refers to wrapping and crating the goods to protect them." Discuss in brief. Competency Based Que

Ans. Packaging refers to wrapping, crating, filling or compressing of goods to protect them from spoilage, pilferage, breakage, leakage, etc. Various kinds of goods are placed or packed into appropriate containers for protection and convenient handling. Bulky materials like cotton and jute are compressed into bales. Liquid materials like oil and wine are put into bottles, barrels and heavy goods are crated and fragile products are placed in boxes, tins or special containers.

On the other hand, packaging involves designing and producing appropriate packages for products. It is concerned with the determination of convenient size lots in which the product is to be put in the market and the creation of proper packages for different lot sizes. The importance of packaging includes

(i) It provides innovational opportunity.
(ii) It provides protection to the product.

14. In the competitive landscape of modern business, packaging plays a crucial role in delivering both utility and visual appeal to consumers. Discuss the three levels of packaging.

Ans. Following are the three levels of packaging

(i) **Primary Packaging**
It means the immediate container of a product. It may be kept till the customer is ready to use the product, e.g. Plastic package for socks or throughout the life of a product, toothpaste tube or bottle of perfume. It provides protection and facilitates the use of the product.

(ii) **Secondary Packaging**
It means additional layer of protection that is kept till the product is ready for use. e.g. A toothpaste tube is packed in a cardboard box. When the consumer begins to use the product, the box is disposed-off.

(iii) **Transportation Packaging**
It means packaging done to protect the product and help in the process of transportation and storage.
e.g. Toothpaste boxes are sent to retailers in corrugated boxes each containing 20, 50 or 100 units.

15. State any four functions of packaging.

Ans. Following are the functions of packaging

(i) **Product Identification**
The package of a product helps the customer to easily identify the product in the market.
e.g. Red Label tea in a red colour packing, Taj Mahal tea in blue box pack, etc.

(ii) **Product Protection**
The package of a product protects it from spoilage, breakage, pilferage, leakage, damage, etc.
This kind of protection is required during storing, distribution and transportation of the product.
e.g. Oil in plastic bottles.

(iii) **Facilitating Use of the Product**
The size and shape of the package should be convenient to open, handle and use for the consumers.
e.g. Toothpaste tubes, handwash soap dispenser, etc.

(iv) **Product Promotion**
Packaging is also used for promotion purposes. An eye-catching colour scheme, photograph or typeface may be used to attract attention of the people at the point of purchase.
Packaging also plays an important role in self-service stores.

16. What is meant by 'indirect channels of distribution'? Explain any two methods of indirect channels of distribution.

Ans. Indirect Channels
When a manufacturer takes help of one or more middlemen to move goods from production place to the consumption place, the distribution channel is called indirect channel.
Following are the types of indirect channel

(i) **One Level Channel**
In this method, an intermediary is used. Here, manufacturer sells the goods directly to the retailer instead of selling it to agents or wholesalers. This method is used for expensive products.

(ii) **Two Level Channel**
In this method, manufacturer sells the material to the wholesaler, wholesaler to the retailer and the retailer to the consumer.
Here, wholesaler after purchasing material in large quantity from the manufacturer sells in small quantity to the retailer.
Then retailers make the products available to consumers. This medium is mainly used to sell consumer non-durable goods like soap, tea, salt, sugar, ghee, etc.

17. Define advertising. What are its main features? Explain. NCERT

Ans. Advertising is an impersonal form of communication, which is paid for by the marketers to promote some goods or services.
Following are the features of advertising

(i) **Paid Form**
Advertising is a paid form of communication. That is, the sponsor has to bear the cost of communicating with the prospects.

(ii) **Impersonality**
There is no direct face-to-face contact between the prospect and the advertiser. It is therefore, referred to as impersonal method of promotion. Advertising creates a monologue and not a dialogue.

(iii) **Identified Sponsor**
Advertising is undertaken by some identified individual or company, who makes the advertising efforts and also bears the cost of it.

18. Discuss the key features of personal selling.

Ans. Following are the features of personal selling

(i) **Personal Form**
Personal selling involves a direct face-to-face communication between the seller and the buyer.

(ii) **Development of Relationship**
Personal selling helps to develop a personal and friendly relationship between the salesperson and the customer, which may become important in making sale.

(iii) **Customised Presentation**
Personal selling allows the salesperson to tailor the sales pitch according to the specific needs, preferences and buying behaviour of each customer, making it a more personalised and effective approach.

19. Discuss the role of sales promotion as an element of promotion mix. NCERT

Ans. Sales promotion refers to short-term incentives, which are designed to encourage the buyers to make immediate purchase of a product or service. These include all promotional efforts other than advertising, personal selling and public relations, used by a company to boost its sales. Sales promotion activities include offering cash discounts, sales contests, free gift offers and free sample distribution.

Sales promotion is usually undertaken to supplement other promotional efforts such as advertising and personal selling. e.g. 20% off on branded clothes, free samples with new products, gold coin inside the bag of tea leaves, etc.

20. **What are the various methods of public relation? Explain.**

Ans. Following are the various methods of public relation

(i) **Newsletters Print or Emailed Newsletters**
These are the important and most attractive way to promote the business and build public relations.

(ii) **Social Media**
Using social networking sites such as Facebook, Twitter, can help to easily build up the relations with public.

(iii) **Press Release**
It is the most common medium to interact with general public.

(iv) **Special Events**
By sponsoring the social events, one can easily build up the relations with public and use such events in future for publicity and propaganda.

Long Answer Type Questions

21. **Explain the following functions of marketing**
(i) **Gathering and analysing market information**
(ii) **Marketing planning**
(iii) **Customer support services**

Ans.

(i) **Gathering and Analysing Market Information**
It is one of the important functions of a marketer. It is necessary to identify the needs of the customers and take various decisions for the successful marketing of products and services. It is also important to make an analysis of the available opportunities and threats as well as strengths and weaknesses of the organisa- tion as it helps in deciding what opportunities can best be pursued by it.

A new trend has emerged in the collection of market information due to the growth of computers. Many companies are using interactive sites on the internet, to gather views and opinions of customers, before taking important business decisions.

(ii) **Marketing Planning**
After market research, the marketer has to develop an appropriate marketing plan to achieve the marketing objective of the organisation. e.g. A marketer of LED TV, having 15% of the country's current market share, aims to enhance his market share to 30% in the next two years.

So, he will have to develop a complete marketing plan which will cover various important aspects like plan for increasing the level of production, products promotion, etc. and specify the action programmes to achieve these objectives.

(iii) **Customer Support Services**
One of the important functions of marketing management is to develop the customer support services like after-sales services, handling of complaints, credit services, maintenance services, technical services and consumer information.

All these services aim at providing maximum customer satisfaction.

22. **What is marketing concept? How does it help in the effective marketing of goods and services?** NCERT

Ans. **Marketing Concept**
This concept emphasises that in the long-run, profits can be maximised by identifying and satisfying the needs of present and potential customers. Therefore, customer satisfaction became the focal point of all business decisions.

It helps in the effective marketing of goods and services in the following ways

(i) **Role in a Firm**
Marketing emphasises customer satisfaction as the key to survival and growth of an organisation. It helps to focus the activities of the organisation on fulfilling the needs and wants of consumers, by designing the product according to them. This helps to develop brand loyalty and bring prosperity for the firm.

(ii) **Role in the Economy**
Marketing acts as a catalyst in economic development of a country and helps in raising living standard of the people. Marketing inspires people to undertake various activities and to set-up enterprises for producing goods that are demanded in the market and ensure smooth flow of goods through efficient distribution system. It helps to establish linkages between the business, accelera- ting economic activity, leading to higher incomes, more consumption, increased savings and investment.

23. **Mention/State the five philosophies, by which the marketing efforts be guided. Also differentiate between them on any four basis.**

Ans. Marketing philosophies are
(i) Production concept
(ii) Product concept
(iii) Selling concept
(iv) Marketing concept
(v) Societal marketing concept

Difference between different marketing philosophies

Basis	Production Concept	Product Concept	Selling Concept	Marketing Concept	Societal Marketing Concept
Starting Point	Factory	Factory	Factory	Market	Market, society
Main Focus	Quantity of product	Quality performance and features of product	Existing product	Customer needs	Customer needs and society's well-being
Means	Availability and affordability of products	Product improvements	Selling and promoting	Integrated marketing	Integrated marketing
Ends	Profit through volume of production	Profit through product quality	Profit through sales volume	Profit through customer satisfaction	Profit through customer satisfaction and social welfare

24. What are the factors affecting determination of the price of a product or service? Explain. NCERT

Or **Explain any four factors affecting determination of the price of a product or service.** CBSE SQP 2025

Ans. The important factors that affect the price of a product are

(i) **Product Cost**
The total cost of product includes production, selling and distribution costs. In the long-run the firm strives to coven all their costs. The cost sets the minimum level or floor price for a product.
In addition to that firm aims to earn profit margin over and above the costs. Costs can be broadly divided into three categories
- Fixed costs, which do not vary with change in production.
- Variable costs, which vary at all levels of production.
- Semi-variable costs, which vary with production, but not in direct proportion with it. Total cost is the sum total of fixed, variable and semi-variable cost, at a specific level of activity. Price is determined by adding a profit to the average cost of a product.

(ii) **The Utility and Demand**
It is necessary to anticipate the utility and demand of a product, while fixing the price, as if a product is offering higher utility, one can easily charge high price from the customer. Whereas, if utility is low, one cannot charge high price for such products.
On the other hand, if the demand is elastic, price should be set at a lower level and if the demand is less elastic or inelastic, price can be set at a higher level.

(iii) **Extent of Competition in the Market**
The price can be set upto the higher limit, if the extent of competition is low in the market and *vice-versa*. Competitors' price, their reactions, their product, quality and features must be considered before fixing the price.

(iv) **Government and Legal Regulations**
To protect the interest of public, the government has all the rights to control the prices of various products and services by including the products in the category of essential commodities such as drugs, some food items, LPG, etc.
With government intervention, there can be a check on the activity of monopolist as they cannot charge unfairly high price for essential commodities.

(v) **Pricing Objectives**
If the objective of the firm is to maximise sales, price will be set at a lower level, whereas, if the firm's objective is profit maximisation, price will be set at a higher level. Apart from this, the firm's other pricing objectives may be
- Obtaining market share leadership by setting the price at lower levels.
- Surviving in a competitive market by setting price at lower levels, in order to face intense competition efficiently.
- For attaining product quality leadership higher prices are set to cover high quality and cost of research and development.

(vi) **Marketing Methods Used**
The price of the product also gets affected by various techniques and methods of marketing used to promote the products. If the company is using intensive advertising to promote the sale of product, then it will charge high price. Other marketing methods, which affect price of a product are type of packaging, distribution system, salesmen employed, customer support services, etc.

25. The physical handling and movement of goods from the place of production to the place of distribution is an important element of marketing mix.
(i) Name and state the element.
(ii) Explain any three main components of this element. CBSE 2023; Competency Based Que

Ans.

(i) The element is physical distribution. Physical distribution covers all the activities required to make the goods and services available at the right place, so that people can purchase the same. Two important decisions include channels of distribution and physical movement of goods.

(ii) Following are the three components of physical distribution

- **Transportation**
  Transportation is the means of carrying goods and raw materials from the point of production to the point of sale. It is one of the major elements in the physical distribution of goods as unless the goods are physically made available, the sale cannot be completed.
- **Warehousing**
  It refers to the act of storing and assorting products in order to create 'time utility' in them. Important points related to warehousing are as follows. Firms having large number of warehouses will take less time in serving customers at different locations. However, large number of warehouses involve greater cost and *vice-versa*. Thus, firm has to strike a balance between the cost of warehousing and the level of customer service.
- **Inventory Control**
  It is related to an important decision of about deciding the level of inventory. Higher the level of inventory, higher will be level of service to customers but the cost of carrying the inventory will also be high as lot of capital would be tied up in the stock. Thus, a balance is to be maintained in respect of the cost and customer satisfaction.

26. Explain the major activities involved in the physical distribution of products. NCERT

Ans. The physical handling and movement of goods from place of production to the place of distribution, is called physical distribution. It covers all the activities required to physically move the goods from the manufacturers to the customers.

Components of Physical Distribution

The main components of the process of physical distribution are

(i) **Order Processing**
A good physical distribution system should provide for an accurate and speedy processing of orders.

In the absence of this, goods would reach the customers in wrong quality or quantity, resulting in dissatisfaction of customers.

(ii) **Transportation**
It means carrying raw materials and finished goods from one place to another.

It helps in creating 'place utility', by making available the goods where they are required.

(iii) **Warehousing**
It refers to the act of storing and assorting products in order to create 'time utility'. It helps in proper placement of goods and providing facilities to store them, so that they can be made available as and when demanded by the market.

(iv) **Inventory Control**
An important decision in physical distribution is deciding about the level of inventory. Higher the level oil inventory, higher will be level of service and cost of carrying the inventory and *vice-versa*.

Various factors which are considered for determining inventory levels are

- Firm's policy regarding level of customer' service.
- Degree of accuracy of sales forecast.
- Responsiveness of distribution system.
- Cost of holding inventory.
  A good inventory decision aims at timely fulfillment of demand at minimum cost.

27. Identify and explain the promotional tool of marketing mix, which involves oral presentation of message with one or more prospective customers for the purpose of making sales. Also, explain any three benefits of this tool. Competency Based Que

Ans. Personal selling involves oral presentation of message in the form of conversation with one or more prospective customers for the purpose of making sales. It is a personal form of communication.

Under this technique, companies appoint salespersons to contact prospective buyers for the purpose of creating awareness about the product and developing product preferences with the aim of making sale.

Following are the three benefits of this tool

(i) **Flexibility**
The salesman can adjust/change his message according to the needs of the customers. This makes the communication more relevant and effective, as the approach can be customised to match the customer's interests and concerns.

Flexibility also allows the salesperson to handle objections and offer solutions tailored to the customer's specific situation.

(ii) **Direct Feedback**
Since there is a direct face-to-face contact between the buyer and seller, it provides immediate feedback from the customer.
This real time interaction allows the salesperson to evaluate the customer's level of interest and address any concerns or hesitations promptly, ensuring a more dynamic and responsive sales process.

(iii) **Minimum Wastage**
There is minimum wastage of efforts as the company can decide the target customers before making any contact with them. This selective targeting ensures that resources are invested in high potential prospects, thereby improving the efficiency of the sales process and reducing unnecessary effort. Additionally, it allows sales teams to focus on individuals most likely to make a purchase.

28. **Advertising and personal selling both are communication tools that help in promotion of the products. However, the kind of approach followed by the tools differ. Differentiate between these two tools by giving any six points.** Competency Based Que

Or Distinguish between advertising and personal selling. **NCERT**

Or Give any four points of difference between advertising and personal selling. **CBSE SQP 2025**

Ans. Following are the differences between advertising and personal selling

Basis	Advertising	Personal Selling
Form	Advertising is an impersonal form of communication.	Personal selling is a personal form of communication
Meaning	Advertising involves transmission of standardised messages, i.e. same message is sent to all the customers in a market segment.	In personal selling, the sales talk is adjusted keeping view customer's background and needs.
Flexibility	Advertising is inflexible as the message can' t be adjusted to the needs of the buyer.	Personal selling is highly flexible as the message can be adjusted.
Reach	It reaches masses, i.e. a large number of people can be approached.	Only a limited number of people can be contacted because of time and cost considerations.
Cost	In advertising the cost per person reached is very low.	The cost per person is quite high in the case of personal selling.
Time	Advertising can cover the market in a short time.	Personal selling efforts take a lot of time to cover the entire market.

Case Study Based Questions

Short Case Studies

Case Study 1

Sonaza watch manufacturing company is a renowned company in marketing watches. It performs various activities like market analysis, product designing or merchandising, packaging, warehousing, branding, pricing, promotion and selling. The company maintains good customer relations through various follow-up activities. This helps the company in procuring repeat sales orders.

(i) Name and define the concept related to the activities mentioned in the above paragraph.

(ii) Explain any three features of this concept identified in part (i).

Ans.

(i) The concept related to the activities mentioned in the above paragraph is marketing. It can be defined as, "a social process by which individual groups obtain what they need and want through creating offerings and freely exchanging products and services of value with others."

(ii) Following are the features of marketing (any three)

- **Needs and Wants**
The process of marketing helps individuals and groups in obtaining what they need and want. A need is a state of felt deprivation or feeling of being deprived of something. Needs are basic to human beings and do not pertain to a particular product. Wants, on the other hand, are culturally defined objects that are potential satisfiers of needs.
- **Creating a Market Offering**
Market offering refers to a complete offer for a product or service, having given features like size, quality, taste, etc. at a certain price; available at a given outlet or location and so on. A good 'market offer' is the one which is developed after analysing the needs and preferences of the potential buyers.

- **Customer Value**
  A product will be purchased only if it is perceived to be giving greatest benefit or value for the money. The job of a marketer is to add to the value of the product so that the customers prefer it in relation to the competing products and decide to purchase it.
- **Exchange Mechanism**
  The process of marketing works through the exchange mechanism. Exchange refers to the process through which two or more parties come together to obtain the desired product or service from someone offering the same by giving something in return.

Case Study 2

Arnav is a distributer of tea to far-off places. He has opened a company which deals in tea selling. He has categorised his tea to be sold into three categories–green, yellow and red. His brother Ramesh on the other hand is running a mobile manufacturing company.

His company strictly produces mobile according to the pre-determined specifications. The mobiles of each variety are of same size, looks and performance.

(i) In the above case which function of marketing has been highlighted?

(ii) Name the four advantages of the above highlighted function.

Ans.

(i) In the above case the function of marketing which has been highlighted is 'standardisation' and 'grading'.

(ii) The advantages of standardisation and grading are

- The buyers get standard quality products which are according to the given standards.
- The time of buyer is saved as there is no need to inspect the product.
- Grading helps in categorising products which are not produced as per standards e.g. Natural products like wheat, rice, etc.
- Grading helps in getting good price for premium quality products and saves time of seller as well as buyer.

Case Study 3

Ginika, Tanish and Rohit were friends from college days and now they are doing different kinds of business. They regularly meet and discuss their business ideas and exchange notes on customer satisfaction, marketing efforts, product designing, selling techniques, social concerns, etc.

In one of such meetings, Ginika drew the attention of Tanish and Rohit towards the exploitation of consumers.

She told that most of the sellers were exploiting the consumers in various ways and were not paying attention towards the social, ethical and ecological aspects of marketing, whereas she was not doing so.

Tanish told that they were under pressure to satisfy the consumers, but stated that the consumers would not buy or not buy enough unless they were adequately convinced and motivated for the same.

Rohit stressed that a company cannot achieve its objectives without understanding the needs of the customers.

It was the duty of the businessmen to keep consumer satisfaction in mind because business is run by the resources made available to them by the society.

He further stated that he himself was taking into consideration the needs of the customers.

Identify the various types of thinking that guided Ginika, Tanish and Rohit in the marketing efforts of their business. Also, state one more feature of the various types of thinking identified that is not given in the above para.

Ans. Various types of thinking that guided the marketing efforts were

Ginika Societal marketing concept/thinking/ philosophy. Societal marketing concept or philosophy aims at identifying the needs and wants of the target market and delivering the desired customer satisfaction in an effective and efficient manner so that a business is able to take care of the long-term well-being of the consumers and the society.

Tanish Selling concept/thinking/philosophy.
Firms following this philosophy undertake aggressive selling and promotional efforts to make customers buy their products.

Rohit Marketing concept/thinking/philosophy.

Firms following this concept or thinking take all the decisions from the point of view of satisfaction of customers. It involves development of products for satisfying needs of the target market better than the competitors.

Case Study 4

Rohan is a dedicated shoe manufacturer specialising in affordable school shoes for students. Observing an opportunity to maximise his profit, Rohan decides to scale-up his production. His goal is to produce a high quantity of shoes, aiming to distribute them across a broad market at affordable prices.

By increasing production volume, he believes he can lower the average cost of manufacturing each pair, which would allow him to sell his shoes at competitive prices, making them widely available to school students across different regions.

Rohan's approach is focused on maximising output and reaching as many customers as possible by keeping prices low, thus ensuring easy availability.

(i) Identify the marketing management philosophy adopted by Rohan.

(ii) Explain the philosophy on the basis of main focus and means and ends.

Ans.

(i) The marketing management philosophy adopted by Rohan is production philosophy.

(ii) The main focus of the production philosophy is quantity of production. In Rohan's case, his priority is to produce a high number of shoes, aiming to supply them at a large-scale, reaching a broad market of school students. To achieve his goal, Rohan uses balanced pricing and easy accessibility as his means. By reducing production costs through high volume manufacturing, he can afford to price the shoes competitively, making them affordable and accessible to a wide range of customers. The ultimate goal (or end) of the production philosophy is to gain profit through maximum production.

Case Study 5

GreenTech Solutions, a company focused on sustainable products, has launched a new line of eco-friendly gadgets designed to reduce environmental impact. They aim to balance consumer needs with environmental welfare, ensuring minimal harm to nature while offering high quality products.

The company emphasises the importance of using recyclable materials, minimising carbon footprints and supporting environmental causes with every purchase. To create a strong market presence, GreenTech has branded its products with a unique logo and distinct packaging that highlights its green initiatives.

As a result, the brand stands out from competitors, allowing the company to charge premium prices due to the growing demand for eco-conscious products.

(i) Identify the marketing management philosophy adopted by GreenTech Solutions.

(ii) Explain the advantages of branding to marketers as identified in the case.

Ans.

(i) The marketing management philosophy adopted by GreenTech Solutions is societal marketing concept.

(ii) Following are the advantages of branding to marketers as identified in the case

- **Enables Product Differentiation**
  Branding helps a firm to distinguish its product from the other competing products available in the market.
- **Helps in Advertising and Display Programmes**
  Without a brand, the advertiser cannot promote and create awareness for and sale his product.
- **Differential Pricing**
  By building brand acceptance and brand loyalty, a firm can charge a different price for its product from that of its competitors.

Case Study 6

Ramesh has purchased a car. He is from lower middle class and teaches in a college. He has purchased a luxury car and has definitely prevented himself from buying a house for another 5 years. There were many reasons which stimulated him to take this expensive decision of life. His friends are from rich backgrounds and have access to all luxuries in their lives.

In order to gain importance in his friend circle he knew he will have to purchase a car which improves his stature in their eyes.

His mother thinks that his son's decision was not good. She considers it as wastage of money. She thinks that the purpose of a car is only as a transportation vehicle.

However, the views of his wife differ to that of her mother's. She thinks that since he has purchased this car his confidence level has gone high and he is mentally more equipped as he can rely on his car for several benefits like transportation, prestige, etc.

Definitely people have their different perceptions to a situation. Similar is the case with his family members.

(i) In the above case, which concept of marketing has been highlighted throughout the paragraph?

(ii) Which benefits have been highlighted in the above case related to the concept in the previous part of this question?

Ans.

(i) The concept of marketing which is highlighted in the above case is 'product is a bundle of utilities'.

(ii) The benefits highlighted in the above case are

- **Social Benefit**
  In order to gain importance in his friend circle, Ramesh knew he will have to purchase a car which improves his stature in their eyes.
- **Functional Benefit**
  Ramesh's mother thinks that the purpose of a car is only as a transportation vehicle.
- **Psychological Benefit**
  Ramesh's mother thinks that since he has purchased this car his confidence level has gone high and he is mentally more equipped as he can rely on his car for several benefits like transportation, prestige, etc.

Case Study 7

Rahul recently bought a premium branded shirt for an important office meeting. He carefully chose a colour and style that suited his personality and paid attention to the quality of the fabric.

On the day of the meeting, he wore the shirt, feeling comfortable and well-dressed. As he arrived at the office, Rahul felt an added sense of confidence and readiness to face the day.

During the meeting, he noticed several colleagues complimenting him on his attire, which made him feel recognised and appreciated within his team.

Identify the three types of satisfaction Rahul experienced after wearing the shirt and briefly explain each.

Competency Based Que

Ans. On wearing a shirt, Rahul experienced the following satisfactions

(i) **Functional Satisfaction**
To wear the shirt and cover the body with it.

(ii) **Psychological Satisfaction**
To feel more confident and active after wearing the shirt provides psychological satisfaction.

(iii) **Social Satisfaction**
Getting recognition after wearing shirt from a group of known people is social satisfaction.

Case Study 8

Raunak soap is an established soap in the market. The soap has shown great growth in terms of repeated purchase and addition of new customers. Now that the company has grown the top management of the company has decided to launch new products. The names to be kept for the new products are giving them new challenges.

The company has decided to launch a cream named 'soother' as it is very good for skin and makes it very soft and removes dryness. There are other products also which are on its list. One is hair oil. Since the oil will be sold in different packagings, on different media and in different regions the name of the oil should suit this requirement.

The third new product to be launched is shampoo. The company wants a name for the shampoo which stands out different from other players in the market as if it doesn't happen then it will be just another shampoo in the market. The company is also considering the release of a detergent powder.

For this the company has decided that the name should be easily remembered as the people of all sections of society will need it for washing clothes and might find a long or tough name easily forgettable. The last new product on the list they have decided to launch is a prickly heat powder.

They have invested a lot in the manufacturing of this powder and want to sell this product like they have been selling Raunak soap for years that is for a long period of time.

In the above case, identify the various characteristics of good brand name highlighted.

Ans. Following are the various characteristics of good brand name

(i) **Short and Easy**
A brand name should be short, easy to pronounce, spell, recognise and remember. e.g. Vim, Ponds, Lux, etc.

(ii) **Suggestive**
A brand should suggest the product's quality and benefits. It should be appropriate to the product's function. e.g. Ujala, Fair and Lovely, etc.

(iii) **Distinct**
A brand name should be distinct from the other brands present in the market. e.g. Liril, Sprite, Raymonds, etc.

(iv) **Adaptable to Packaging**
A brand name should be adaptable to packing and labelling requirements to different advertising media and to different languages.

(v) **Staying Power**
A brand name should have long lasting staying power and should not get out of date.

Case Study 9

Lighting Ltd. a fire cracker manufacturing company launched some new products on eve of Diwali which attracted many buyers.

To meet the increased demand, the company employed children from nearby villages. Although the product was in great demand, appropriate safety warnings for use were not mentioned on the packets that led to many accidents.

(i) Identify and explain the important product related decision that was not taken into consideration by the company.

(ii) State any three functions of the product related decision identified in (i).

Ans.

(i) The important product related decision that was not taken into consideration by the company is labelling. The term 'labelling' means designing a label to be put on the package. A label describes the product, its usage and specifies its contents.

(ii) Following are the functions of labelling (any three)

- **Describe the Product and specify its Contents**
  A label helps to describe the product, its usage, cautions in use, contents, manufacturing and expiry dates. etc.
- **Identification of the Product or Brand**
  Label gives a definite identity to the product or brand and therefore, the identification of a product becomes easy. e.g. The name Pears printed on toilet soaps helps us to know which soap out of several soaps is Pears.
- **Grading of Products**
  Label enables the manufacturer to grade the products into different categories. e.g. Hindustan lever sells different grades of tea under green, yellow and red labels.
- **Providing Information Required by Law**
  Label provides information required under law. e.g. Statutory warning 'Smoking is injurious to health' must be stated on the package of cigarettes. Such information is considered necessary on processed foods, drugs and tobacco products. In case of hazardous or poisonous material, appropriate safety warning need to be put on the label.

Case Study 10

Sharmila is the founder of a new FMCG company. She wants her products to speak to the potential customers. For this she is working a lot on the packaging of her products. She has decided to cut down the personal selling efforts of her company by reducing the number of sales men as she wants that the packaging should speak for itself thus gaining the attention of the potential customers. She has made other efforts also.

She has brought an R&D department in her organisation and has asked them to invent new types of packaging in order to increase the scope of marketing as new packaging would ensure safety, environment friendliness and attractiveness.

She knows she will face a lot of competition in the market as already there are many players in the market who are ready to give challenge to her products.

She wants her packaging to be such that her product should stand apart, be recognised easily and not be lost in the pool of different products in the market. Their packaging should convey their quality. The nature of the potential customers has changed over the years. They have become more demanding and informed.

They have more choices now. One thing that the customers always look for in an FMCG product is the hygiene and purity; these two traits can only be conveyed to the potential customers by proper packaging. Sharmila's perception about packaging is really noteworthy.

(i) Which concept of marketing has been highlighted in the above case?

(ii) State any three benefits of concept identified in (i).

Ans.

(i) The concept of marketing highlighted in the above case is 'importance of packaging'.

(ii) The different benefits of packaging are

- **Rising Standards of Health and Sanitation**
  Because of increasing consciousness about health and sanitation, people now prefer to buy packaged goods as the chances of adulteration in such goods are minimised.
- **Self-service Outlets**
  The self-service outlets are becoming very popular, particularly in major cities and towns. Because of this, some of the traditional role assigned to personal selling in respect of promotion has gone to packaging.
- **Innovational Opportunity**
  The recent innovation and developments in packaging have completely changed the marketing scene in the country.

  e.g. Milk can now be stored for 4-5 days without refrigeration. Similarly, lots of new innovations have come in the area of pharma- ceuticals, soft drinks, etc. As a result, the scope for marketing of such products has increased.

Case Study 11

"Every time I travelled, my friends asked me to bring chocolates and coffee from all over the world," says Raveena.

Finally, she and her colleague, Rahul, decided to start a business out of it. They posted on social media platforms, asked people for their opinions and formulate a list of 100 places. They tied up with the different vendors. They started servicing people from Mumbai who wanted coffee from Chennai, people from Kolkata who wanted chocolates from Delhi. They wanted to bridge the gap between buyers and sellers through the business.

Explain any two important activities that Raveena and Rahul will have to be involved in for making the goods available to the customers at the right place, in the right quantity and at the right time.

Ans. Following are the important activities/components of physical distribution

(i) **Order Processing**
A good physical distribution system should provide for an accurate and speedy processing of orders. In the absence of this, goods would reach the customers in wrong quality or quantity, resulting in dissatisfaction of customers.

(ii) **Transportation**
It means carrying raw materials and finished goods from one place to another. It helps in creating 'place utility', by making available the goods where they are required.

Case Study 12

EcoPure products is a company specialising in environmentally friendly cleaning supplies. Founded by a group of sustainability enthusiasts, the company prides itself on producing high quality, eco-friendly products that are safe for both people and the planet.

To maintain a close connection with its customers and ensure that they understand the benefits of its products, EcoPure sells its cleaning supplies directly to consumers through its own website. The company provides detailed information about each product, including ingredients, usage instructions and environmental impact.

The company has also set-up a subscription service, allowing customers to receive their favourite products delivered to their homes on a regular basis.

Identify the type of channel of distribution used by EcoPure Products.

Ans. The type of channel of distribution used by EcoPure Products is direct channel (zero level channel).

The most simple mode of distribution is direct distribution, where the goods are directly made available to consumers from the manufacturers, without the use of any intermediary.

e.g. EcoPure Products sells directly through its website and engages with customers through workshops and demonstrations.

Other examples of direct selling include mail order selling, internet selling, and selling through a company's own sales force (e.g. Amway).

Case Study 13

Going to gym and following a protein diet has become a popular trend those days. However, with the busy work culture, many people, especially the youth struggle to find time for weight loss programmes. Allikkas working in a multi-national company, wanted to join a gym for weight loss but could not find time. There is no good gym near her house. One day, Aika was walking out of the office during lunch time and saw an attractive poster of a gym which was near her house. Anika was curious to enquire about their weight loss programme.

Next day, when he went to the gym, she was surprised to know about various schemes offered by the gym. They were not only offering 50% discount on the fee of weight loss programme: but also providing free coach facility and free protein diet for the customer. But these offers were valid only for 10 days. Attracted by these schemes Anika immediately submitted the fee end joined the gym.

CBSE 2025

(i) Identify and give the meaning of the element of marketing mix discussed above.

(ii) The element of marketing-mix identified in (i) above includes various tools of communication. Identify and explain the tools highlighted in the above para.

Ans.

(i) The element of marketing mix discussed in the case is 'promotion'. Promotion refers to the use of communication with the twin objective of informing potential customers about a product and persuading them to buy it. Promotion is an important element of marketing mix by which marketers makes use of various tools of communication to encourage exchange of goods and services in the market.

(ii) The element of promotion includes various tools of communication. The tools highlighted in the above paragraph are

- **Advertising**
The gym used an attractive poster to catch Anika's attention and inform her about its services. It is an impersonal form of communication, which is paid for by the marketers to promote some goods or services.
- **Sales Promotion**
The gym offered a 50% discount on the weight loss programme fee, free coaching and a free protein diet for a limited period (10 days).
Sales promotion refers to short-term incentives, designed to encourage the buyers to make immediate purchase of a product or service.

Long Case Studies

Case Study 14

Ananya, a student of Class XII Business Studies, belonged to a family of farmers who specialised in cultivating wheat. Her family grew different types of wheat and were known for their high quality produce. Her father, who was experienced in wheat farming, suggested that she explore the possibility of selling their produce directly to consumers as a part of her project. She noticed that wheat production occurred seasonally, but its demand remained steady throughout the year.

Ananya recognised that this gap between production and sales needed proper planning. To maintain the quality of the wheat, she rented a warehouse for proper storage until it could be sold in the market. She used eco-friendly packaging with clear labels that provided information about the type of wheat, nutritional value, and the product's authenticity. Additionally, she gave her product a unique brand name, 'Golden Grain', to distinguish it from other wheat brands in the market.

Explain the three functions of marketing as identified in the above case study.

Ans. Following are the three functions of marketing as identified in the above case study

(i) **Packaging and Labelling**

Packaging refers to designing and developing the package for a product.

Package refers to the wrapper or container, which not only provides protection to the product, but also acts as a promotional tool for it. Labelling refers to designing and developing the label to be put on the package. A label is a carrier of information. It may be a simple tag or a complex graphic providing details about the product. In modern day marketing, packaging and labelling have become so important that these are considered as the pillars of marketing.

(ii) **Branding**

It refers to the process of giving a name, sign, symbol or a combination of all to a product for creating its identification. It helps to differentiate the product from other products available in the market. It also helps to build the customer's loyalty and promote sales.

(iii) **Storage or Warehousing**

Usually, there is a time gap between production or procurement of goods and their sales. It may be because of irregular demand for the products such as woollen garments or there may be irregular supply because of seasonal production such as rice, wheat or cotton, etc. It also helps to avoid delays in delivery, meeting contingencies in demand and stabilising the prices of products in the market. Thus, it helps to create time utility. It is performed by intermediaries such as wholesalers, retailers, manufacturers, etc.

Case Study 15

BJ Pvt. Ltd. is a company manufacturing organic shampoos with the brand name 'Pure Shine'. This name will help the company in creating product differentiation. To satisfy the needs of the customers in the target market the company used natural ingredients like curry leaves, neem, rice, etc. The focus of the company is on satisfaction of customers needs.

To have higher demand of shampoo it decided to fix a lower price in comparison to the other shampoos available in the market. To inform the customers about the shampoo and its features, etc. the company used various promotional tools.

For maximum satisfaction of customers, the company provides the contact details of the customer care centre to handle customer complaints.

Identify and explain any three functions of marketing discussed in the above paragraph. **CBSE 2024 C**

Ans. Functions of marketing are

(i) **Branding**

For explanation, refer to case study 14.

(ii) **Pricing**

Pricing refers to determining the price of a product i.e. the amount of money customers have to pay to obtain a product from the market pricing is considered as a regulator of demand of a product, because when the price of the product is increased, demand falls and *vice-versa*.

(iii) **Promotion**

Promotion of products and services involves informing the customers about the firm's product, its features, etc. and persuading them to purchase these products. Promotion is an important element of marketing mix by which marketers make use of various tools of communication to encourage exchange of goods and services in the market.

Case Study 16

Ayush and Rhea were passionate about sustainable agriculture and healthy living. They wanted to start a business selling organic produce. They had a small farm in a rural area where they began growing fresh organic produce and herbs.

In the beginning, they faced challenges in marketing their organic products. They realised that their high quality produce needed better presentation and a strong identity to stand out in a competitive market.

They named the business Earthy Store' which indicated the products' benefits and qualities and reflected the values of the business sustainablility and health. They chose a logo' that incorporated elements of nature and used, earthy colours to convey their organic commitment.

They designed' and developed eco-friendly biodegradable bags and reusable containers to courier their products to the customers.

They also added personal touch by including handwritten notes in each bag. They also designed and developed product stickers with detailed information about organic certification, nutritional benefits, date of manufacture, date of expiry, etc. The stickers so developed were put on the bags and reusable containers for customers convenience.

Earthy Store' created a user friendly website and established strong media presence to inform potential customers about their products and persuading them to buy the same. Within a couple of months, they had built a loyal customer base which made them earn profits even in a competitive environment. In a year, they were able to secure contracts with local grocery stores and restaurants. Quoting lines from the above paragraph, identify and explain the three functions of marketing discussed in the above case.

Ans. By quoting the lines from the paragraph, the functions of marketing discussed here are as follows

(i) They realised that .... competitive market.

Marketing Planning

After market research, the marketer has to develop an appropriate marketing plan to achieve the marketing objective of the organisation.

e.g. A marketer of LED TV, having 15% of the country's current market share, aims to enhance his market share to 30% in the next two years. So, he will have to develop a complete marketing plan which will cover various important aspects like plan for increasing the level of production, products promotion, etc. and specify the action programmes to achieve these objectives.

(ii) They named .... the organic commitment.

Branding

It refers to the process of giving a name, sign, symbol or a combination of all to a product for creating its identification.

It helps to differentiate the product from other products available in the market. It also helps to build customer's loyalty and promoting its sales.

The important decision areas in respect of branding include deciding the brand strategy i.e. whether each product will be given a separate brand name such as Kitkat, Milkybar, etc. or the same brand name will be extended to all products, like Whirlpool fridge, Whirlpool LED TV, etc.

(iii) They designed .... customer convenience.

Packaging and Labelling

Packaging refers to designing and developing the package for a product. Package refers to the wrapper or container, which not only provides protection to the product, but also acts as a promotional tool for it. Labelling refers to designing and developing the label to be put on the package.

A label is a carrier of information. It may be a simple tag or a complex graphic providing details about the product. In modern day marketing, packaging and labelling have become so important that these are considered as the pillars of marketing.

Case Study 17

Choco Ltd. offers a wide variety of chocolate products. It has an action programme of not selling its products by their generic name but under different names like Choco-silk bar, Choco-munchy and Choco-crunchy, etc. for different customer segments.

All these names have great popularity and acceptability in the markets. As the company policy, the products were offered at reasonable and affordable prices for targeting a mass customer base. During the festive season, the company launched a massive promotional campaign to increase its revenue and achieve its communication objectives.

The company introduced free gifts for the customers. Their on-ground sales team delivers the product not only to the departmental stores but also to small shops, so that all segments of customers can easily get the products.

They also provide information and support services to customers to ensure repeat sales.

From the view point of the management function, briefly explain any four activities of marketing which the firm will be involved in, apart from the above mentioned ones it's already performing.

Ans. Functions of marketing, apart from the ones Choco Ltd. is already performing are (any four)

(i) **Gathering and Analysing Market Information**
This is necessary to identify the needs of the customers and make various decisions for the successful marketing of the products and services.
This is important for making an analysis of the available opportunities and threats as well as strengths and weaknesses of the organisation and help in deciding what opportunities can best be pursued by it.

(ii) **Product Designing and Development**
The design of the product contributes to making the product attractive to the target customers. A good design can improve performance of a product and give it a competitive advantage in the market.

(iii) **Packaging and Labeling**
Packaging refers to designing and developing the package for the products. Labelling refers to designing and developing the label to be put on the product.

(iv) **Transportation**
It involves physical movement of goods from one place to another. While production of a good takes place at a place, its consumers are spread over a vast area. Therefore, it is necessary to make available these goods to places where they are needed. Thus, transportation helps to create 'place utility'.

(v) **Standardisation**
It refers to producing goods of pre-determined specifications which help in achieving uniformity and consistency in the output.

Case Study 18

Aryan and Rohan were passionate about sustainable agriculture and healthy living. They wanted to start a business selling organic produce. They had a small farm in a rural area where they began growing fresh organic produce and herbs.

In the beginning, they faced challenges in marketing their organic products. They realised that their high quality produce needed better presentation and a strong identity to stand out in a competitive market. They named the business 'Earthy Store,' which indicated the products' benefits and qualities and reflected the values of the business sustainability and health.

They chose a logo that incorporated elements of nature and used earthy colours to convey their organic commitment. They designed and developed eco-friendly biodegradable bags and reusable containers to courier their products to the customers.

They also added a personal touch by including handwritten notes in each bag. They designed and developed product stickers with detailed information about organic certification, nutritional benefits, date of manufacture, date of expiry, etc.

The stickers were put on the bags and reusable containers for customers' convenience. 'Earthy Store' created a user friendly website and established a strong media presence to inform potential customers about their products and persuade them to buy them.

Within a couple of months, they had built a loyal customer base, allowing them to earn profits even in a competitive environment. In a year, they secured contracts with local grocery stores and restaurants. Quoting lines from the above paragraph, identify and explain the three marketing philosophies discussed in the above case.

Ans.

(i) **Product Concept**
Aryan and Rohan focused on the quality of their organic produce, as indicated by the line, "they realised that their high quality produce needed better presentation and a strong identity to stand out in a competitive market."
This reflects their belief in delivering superior products to attract customers. Under this concept, the focus shifted from quantity of production to quality of products. Product improvement became the key to profit maximisation of a firm, under the product concept.

(ii) **Marketing Concept**
They recognised the importance of understanding and meeting customer needs, demonstrated by their efforts to create a user-friendly website and a strong media presence to "inform potential customers about their products and persuade them to buy."
This indicates their commitment to aligning their marketing strategies with customer preferences. This concept emphasises that in the long-run profits can be maximised by identifying the needs of present and potential customers and satisfying them in an effective way. The basic role of a firm is to identify the need and fill it.

(iii) **Societal Marketing Concept**
Their commitment to sustainability and health is highlighted in the line, "which indicated the products' benefits and qualities and reflected the values of the business: sustainability and health."

This shows that they aimed to provide not just value to customers but also benefit to society and the environment through their business practices. This concept pays attention to social, ecological and ethical aspects of marketing for dealing with problems like environmental pollution, deforestation, shortage of resources, population explosion, etc. It is an extension of marketing concept as customer satisfaction is supplemented by welfare of the society.

Case Study 19

Ravi and Megha started 'Energy lights' a company mnnufacturing energy efficient LED lighting after realising an increasing demand for the same. Manufacturing high quality LED lights with some unique features required substantial investment in technology and high grade material.

This pushed up their cost of manufacturing. To determine the price of their LED lights they not only wanted to cover all costs but also wanted to earn a margin of profit over and above the costs.

This will set for them the minimum level or the floor price at which the LED lights would be sold. The high demand and the utility provided by these lights will set the upper limit of the price. Though there was enough competition in LED lights business, even then they kept the price of their lights higher than the competitors because of good quality and its features.

They justified the higher price because of the product differentiation and unique methods of advertising and sales promotion, etc.

Quoting lines from the above para, identify and explain any three factors which were taken into consideration by Ravi and Megha to determine the price of their LED lights.

CBSE 2025

Ans. Following are the three factors which were taken into consideration by Ravi and Megha 'to determine the price of their LED lights

(i) **Product Cost**
"To determine the price of their LED lights they not only wanted to cover all costs but also wanted to earn a margin of profit over and above the costs. This will set for them the minimum level or the floor price at which the LED lights would be sold." The total cost of product includes production, selling and distribution costs. The cost sets the minimum level or floor price for a product. Total cost is sum total of fixed, variable and semi-variable cost. Price is determined by adding a profit to the average cost of a product.

(ii) **Utility and Demand**
"The high demand and the utility provided by these lights will set the upper limit of the price." While the product costs set the lower limits of the price, the utility provided by the product and the intensity of demand of the buyer sets the upper limit of price, which a buyer would be prepared to pay.

(iii) **Marketing Methods Used**
"They justified the higher price because of the product differentiation and unique methods of advertising and sales promotion etc."

Price fixation process is also affected by various elements of marketing such as distribution system, quality of salesmen employed, quality and amount of advertising, sales promotion efforts, the type of packaging, product differentiation, credit facility and customer services provided.

Case Study 20

Maruti Udyog sells its cars and vans through company approved retailers and covers a wide area of market. Identify the channel adopted by Maruti and discuss in brief the other two channels also.

Ans. Maruti Udyog has adopted one level or manufacturer-retailer-consumer channel. Under this channel, the manufacturer sells to one or more retailers who in turn sell to the ultimate consumers.

Various marketing functions are performed by the producer and the retailers.

This channel is popular when the retailers are big and buy in large quantities.

e.g. Departmental stores, chain stores and supermarkets. This channel is often used for the distribution of consumer durables and products of high value.

Automobiles, home appliances, readymade garments, shoes and perishable products are often sold through this channel.

Other two channels are

(i) **Manufacturer-Wholesaler-Retailer-Consumer**
(Two level channel)
This is the 'traditional' or normal channel for the distribution of consumer goods.

This channel is suitable where the producer has limited finance and a narrow product line or where the wholesalers are specialised and provide strong promotional support.

Small producers and small retailers find this channel most convenient especially in case of products with widely scattered markets.

(ii) **Manufacturer-Agent-Wholesaler-Retailer-Consumer** (Three level channel)

When the retailers are few or geographically concentrated, distribution through agents may be more economical than through wholesalers.

For instance, a manufacturer may employ selling agents or brokers to sell his products to retailers. Sometimes, even the retailer is bypassed and the agent sells directly to institutional buyers like consumer cooperatives, business firms, educational institutions and government agencies or departments. This channel is commonly used to sell textiles, agricultural products, machinery and equipments, etc.

Case Study 21

AutoX Pvt. Ltd. is a company that specialises in the production of electric motorcycles. After conducting a market survey, they discovered that consumers are seeking an environmentally friendly alternative to conventional fuel powered motorcycles.

Taking into account consumer needs as well as social, ethical and ecological aspects of marketing, the company introduced a new electric motorcycle model powered by renewable energy sources.

The launch event received significant media coverage from top news channels and newspapers to spread awareness about the product and enhance the company's reputation. AutoX Pvt. Ltd. recognises the importance of managing public perception and maintaining strong relations with the public consistently.

(i) Identify and explain the marketing philosophy involved in the above case.

(ii) Identify and explain the communication tool that was used by the company.

(iii) Explain any two other promotional tools that can be used by X Ltd. to achieve its objectives.

Or

Kumar and Sons Ltd. is engaged in the manufacturing of cars. The company surveyed the market and found that customers need a car which runs on eco-friendly fuel instead of petrol or diesel. Keeping the needs of customers as well as social, ethical and ecological aspects of marketing in mind, the company launched a new model of car that runs on bio-diesel.

The launch event was covered by the top news channels and newspapers.

This was done to disseminate information about the car and build goodwill of the business. Kumar and Sons Ltd. understands that it is imperative to manage public opinion and company's relations with the public on a regular basis.

(i) Identify and explain the marketing philosophy involved in above case.

(ii) Identify and explain the communication tool involved in the above case.

(ii) Explain any two other promotional tools that can be used by Kumar and Sons Ltd. to achieve its objectives.

Ans.

(i) The marketing philosophy involved in the above case is societal marketing concept. This concept pays attention to social, ecological and ethical aspects of marketing for dealing with problems like environmental pollution, deforestation, shortage of resources, population explosion, etc.

It is an extension of marketing concept as customer satisfaction is supplemented by welfare of the society.

(ii) The communication tool used by the company is public relations. It refers to that non-sales communication which a business has with its various audiences with a view to manage public opinion.

(iii) Two other promotional tools that can be used by AutoX Pvt Ltd. to achieve its objectives are

- **Advertising**
  It is an impersonal form of communication, which is paid for by the marketers to promote some goods or services. There is no direct face-to-face contact between the prospect and the advertiser.
- **Sales Promotion**
  It refers to short-term incentives, designed to encourage the buyers to make immediate purchase of a product or service. These include all promotional efforts other than advertising, personal selling and public relations. Sales promotion activities include offering cash discounts, sales contests, free gift offers and free sample distribution.

Case Study 22

A company was marketing 'juicers' which were very popular due to their quality and after-sale services provided to the customers.

The company was a leading company in the market and earning huge profits. Because of huge profits, the company ignored the after-sales services. As a result its relations with the customers got spoiled and the image of the company in the public was damaged.

Top management became concerned when the profits for the current quarter fell steeply. On analysis, it was revealed that ignoring the after-sales services was its reason.

Therefore, the company took all possible measures to protect and promote its favourable image.

As a result the goodwill of the company improved in the society.

(i) Name and state the communication tool used by the marketer in the above case to improve its image.

(ii) Also explain role of the tool as identified in part (i).

Ans.

(i) The communication tool used by the marketer in the above case is 'public relations'. It is an important element of marketing. It means maintaining relations with public.

By maintaining such relations, companies create goodwill.

Public relations evaluate public attitudes, identify the policies and procedures of an organisation with the public interest to earn public understanding and acceptance.

Public does not mean only customers, but it includes shareholders, suppliers, intermediaries, customers, etc.

Thus, it helps in maintaining and establishing mutual understanding between an organisation and public.

(ii) The role of public relations can be discussed with respect to functions performed by public relations department.

These functions are

- **Smooth Functioning of Business**
  It helps in analysing trends, predicting their consequences, counselling organisational leaders and implementing planned programme of action and thus helps in smooth functioning of business and achievement of objectives.
- **Building Corporate Image and Brand Equity**
  Public relations covers a wide range of tactics, tools and programmes to promote and protect company's image and products. It uses the tools to build corporate image which ultimately affects favourably on its products.
- **Launching New Products**
  The good image promotion itself lends credibility to new launches of the organisations.
- **Press Relations**
  The public relations department is in contact with the media to present true facts and a correct picture about the company, otherwise, news can get distorted if it is taken from some other source.

SELF ASSESSMENT TEST

Objective Type Questions

1. Identify the process of classification of products into different groups, on the basis of some of its important characteristics.
   (a) Standardisation (b) Grading
   (c) Product mix (d) Grouping
2. Which product-related decision is concerned with providing detailed information about the product on its package?
   (a) Branding (b) Packaging
   (c) Labelling
   (d) Both branding and packaging
3. Which of the following act as a silent salesman?
   (a) Product (b) Price
   (c) Packaging (d) Promotion
4. Cardbox of shaving Cream is an example of
   (a) primary packaging (b) secondary packaging
   (c) transport packaging (d) None of these
5. Which of the following is not a component of the marketing communication mix?
   (a) Advertising (b) Personal selling
   (c) Pricing (d) Sales promotion
6. It involves use of short-term incentives to encourage the buyers to make immediate purchase. Identify the tool of promotion.
   (a) Advertising (b) Personal selling
   (c) Sales promotion (d) Public relations

Answers 1. (b) 2. (c) 3. (c) 4. (b) 5. (c) 6. (c)

Short Answer Type Questions

7. State any three differences between marketing and selling concept.
8. "Marketing mix is a combination of 4Ps." Identify and explain the 4Ps in detail.
9. "Product is a bundle of utilities." Do you agree? Comment.
10. State any four characteristics of a good brand name.
11. Packaging plays an important role in attracting the attention of the customers. In the light of the given statement, explain the various levels of packaging.
12. What information is generally placed on the package of a food product? Explain.
13. Mohan uses one of the promotional techniques where he gets direct feedback. Identify and explain the technique in detail.

Long Answer Type Questions

14. ABC organics has recently launched a new herbal shampoo and included a detailed description of ingredients, usage instructions and benefits on the product's packaging. In the context of the case, explain what is labelling? State the advantages of labelling.
15. "Pricing is a single most important element affecting the revenue and profits of a firm." In the light of the given statement, explain any six factors that affect the determination of price.
16. Explain the various activities involved in the physical distribution of goods.

12

CHAPTER

Consumer Protection

Consumer protection is necessary as a consumer might be exposed to risk due to unsafe products, might be cheated because of misleading advertisements or might have to pay a higher price, etc.

▼ **YOUR STUDY GOALS**

12.1 Concept of Consumer Protection

12.2 Consumer Protection Act, 2019

- Consumer Rights and Responsibilities
- Redressal Agencies
- Reliefs/Remedies Available to Consumers

12.3 Consumer Awareness

▼ **YOUR PRACTICE GOAL**

- Objective Type Questions (63 Qs ; MCQs, A-R, Statements, Matching)
- Subjective Questions (13 SAs, 5 LAs)
- Case Study Based Questions (Short Case Studies-10, Long Case Studies-5)
- Self Assessment Test (6 MCQs, 7 SAs, 3 LAs)

12.1 Concept of Consumer Protection

The concept of consumer protection is to safeguard the interests of the consumers. It is a very wide term which aims at

- Educating consumers about their rights and responsibilities.
- Providing them protection against unscrupulous, unfair trade practices of traders, etc.
- Speedy redressal of their grievances.

Importance of Consumer Protection

Consumer protection has assumed great importance for consumers as well as businesses in the following ways

From Consumers' Point of View

1. **Consumer Ignorance** In the light of widespread ignorance of consumers about their rights and reliefs available to them, it becomes necessary to educate them about the same so as to achieve consumer awareness.
2. **Unorganised Consumers** Consumers need to be organised in the form of consumer organisations which would take care of their interests.

Though, in India there are few consumer organisations, still adequate protection is required to be given to consumers till these organisations become powerful to protect and promote the interests of consumers.

3. **Widespread Exploitation of Consumers** Consumers might be exploited by unscrupulous, exploitative and unfair trade practices like defective and unsafe products, adulteration, false and misleading advertising, hoarding, black marketing, etc. Consumer protection provides safety to consumers against such exploitations.

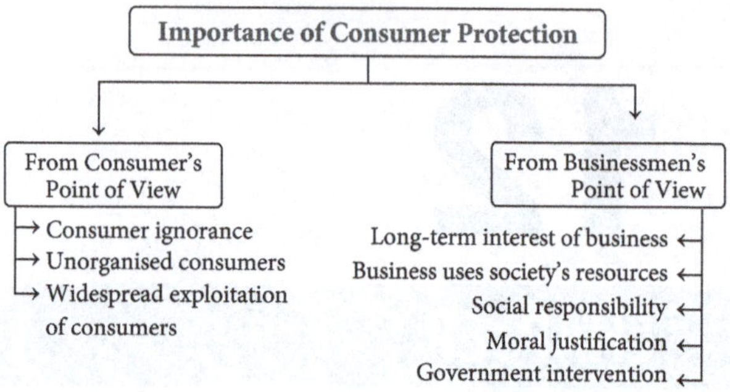

From the Businessmen's Point of View

1. **Long-term Interest of Business** Satisfied customers not only lead to repeat sales but also provide good feedback to prospective customers. Thus, help in increasing the customer-base of business which contributes to the long-term interest of the business.
2. **Business uses Society's Resources** Business firms use resources that belong to the society. Therefore, it is the responsibility of businesses to convert these resources into useful goods and services which are in public interest.
3. **Social Responsibility** Business organisation makes money by selling their products to consumers. It is the social responsibility of businessman to provide satisfaction to their customers and take care of their interests.
4. **Moral Justification** It is the moral duty of a businessman to serve their customers well and keep them away from exploitative and unfair trade practices. Therefore, business must avoid unfair trade practices such as adulteration, misleading advertising, hoarding, black marketing, etc.
5. **Government Intervention** If a business organisation engages in any form of exploitative trade practices, it would invite government intervention, which can tarnish the image of the company. Therefore, it is in the interest of business itself, to voluntarily take care of consumer needs and interests.

12.2 Consumer Protection Act, 2019

The Consumer Protection Act, 2019 seeks to protect and promote the consumers' interest through speedy and inexpensive redressal of their grievances.

It's **scope** is very wide. It extends to the whole of India. It is applicable to all types of businesses whether a manufacturer or a trader and supplying goods or providing services including e-commerce firms.

The main **features** of this act are as follows

- The act has provided various rights and responsibilities of consumers to protect their interest.
- The act provides safeguards to the consumers against defective goods, substandard services, unfair trade practices and other forms of their exploitation.
- The act stresses on setting-up of a three-tier machinery, consisting of District Commission, State Commission and National Commission.
- It also provides a framework for the formation of consumer protection councils in every District and State and also at the apex level.

Concept of Consumer

A 'consumer' is generally understood as a person who uses or consumes goods or avails of any service.

Under the Consumer Protection Act, 2019, a consumer is a person, who buys any good or avails any service for a consideration which has been paid or promised, or partly paid and partly promised, or under any scheme of deferred payment.

The term includes any other user of such goods or services when such use is made with the approval of the buyer. It applies to both offline and online transactions through electronic means or by teleshopping or direct selling or multilevel marketing. The term 'consumer', however, does not include a person, who obtains goods for resale or for any commercial purpose, or a person, who avails such services for any commercial purpose.

Consumer Rights

The Consumer Protection Act provides following six rights to consumers to safeguard their interests

1. **Right to Safety** According to this right, a consumer has a right to be protected against the marketing of such goods and services that are hazardous to life and health. Thus, consumers are educated to use standardised goods, such as electrical goods with ISI mark, food products with FPO mark, etc. as such goods would be an assurance of meeting quality specifications.
2. **Right to be Informed** According to this right, a consumer has the right to get true and complete information about the ingredients, quality, quantity, price, expiry date of the goods and services, etc. which he intends to buy.
3. **Right to be Assured** According to this right, consumers have the freedom to access variety of products at competitive prices. This implies that the marketers should offer a wide variety of products in terms of quality, brand, size, etc. so that the consumer can make a wise choice.

4. **Right to be Heard** According to this right, a consumer has a right to file a complaint and to be heard in case of dissatisfaction with a good or a service. It is because of this reason, many enlightened business firms have set-up their own consumer service and grievance cells.
5. **Right to Seek Redressal** According to this right, consumer has the right to get relief in case the product falls short of his expectations. The act provides various reliefs to the consumers like compensation for any loss or injury suffered by the consumers, replacement of goods or removal of defects in the goods, etc.
6. **Right to Consumer Education** According to their right, consumer has the right to acquire knowledge and to be a well-informed consumer throughout his life. He should be aware about his rights and reliefs available to him in case of a product or service falling short of his expectations.

Responsibilities of Consumers

A consumer should fulfil the following responsibilities, while purchasing, using and consuming goods and services

- A consumer should be aware about the various goods and services available in the market, so that he can make a wise choice by comparing their features and prices.
- A consumer must always buy standardised goods as they provide quality assurance. Thus, a consumer should always look for ISI mark on electrical goods, FPO mark on food products, hallmark on jewellery, etc.
- A consumer must learn about the various risks associated with the use and maintenance of goods. He must follow the manufacturer's instructions carefully.

- A consumer must read the labels carefully, so as to have complete information about the price, quantity, ingredients, usage, contents, expiry date, etc.
- A consumer must ensure that he gets a fair deal.
- A consumer should be honest in his dealings. He should choose legal goods and discourage unscrupulous (unethical) practices like black marketing, hoarding, etc.
- A consumer should always ask for a cash memo, as it serves as a proof of purchase required at the time of taking any action against a fraudulent seller or manufacturer.
- A consumer must file a complaint in case of any shortcoming in goods or services availed.
- A consumer should take initiative to form consumer societies that can take active part in educating consumers and safeguarding their interests.
- A consumer should respect the environment and avoid creating pollution.

Marks Indicating Products Quality

Electrical appliances which are manufactured with substandard products or do not conform to the safety norms might cause serious injury. Thus, consumers are educated to use standardised goods, such as electrical goods with ISI mark, food products with FPO mark, etc.

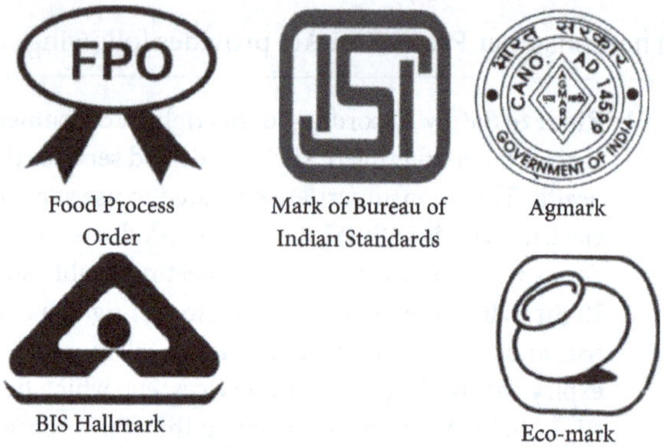

Marks indicating quality in different products

Who can File a Complaint?

The following can file a complaint under the Act

- A consumer.
- Any voluntary registered consumer association.
- The Central Government or any State Government.
- One or more consumers, where there are numerous consumers having the same interest.
- A legal heir or representative of a deceased consumer.

Against Whom a Complaint can be Filed?

- A complaint can be filed against seller, manufacturer or dealer of goods, whose goods are defective.

Defect means any fault, imperfection or shortcoming in the quality, quantity or purity of goods.

- It can be filed against the provider of services, if they are deficient in any manner.

Deficiency means any imperfection, shortcoming or inadequacy in the quality, nature and manner of services.

Redressal Agencies

For the redressal of consumer grievances, the Consumer Protection Act, 2019 provides for setting up of a three-tier machinery at the District, State and the National levels.

Three-Tier Redressal Agencies

- District Commission (Entertain claims upto ₹ 1 crore)
- State Commission (Entertain claims exceeding ₹ 1 crore but less than ₹ 10 crore)
- National Commission (Entertain claims exceeding ₹ 10 crore)

District Commission	State Commission	National Commission
The State Governments are required to establish District Consumer Disputes Redressal Commission or District Commission in each district.	State Consumer Disputes Redressal Commission or State Commission is set up by the State Government and its jurisdiction is restricted to the boundaries of the State concerned.	National Consumer Disputes Redressal Commission or National Commission has territorial jurisdiction over the whole country. It is set up by the Central Government.
Each District Commission consists of a President and two members appointed by the State Government.	It shall consist of a President, who is or has been a judge of a High Court and four other members.	It shall consist of a President, who is or has been a judge of the Supreme Court and four other members.
A District Commission can receive consumer complaints, where the value of goods or services and the compensation claimed is not more than ₹ 1 crore.	Only those complaints can be filed, where the value of goods or services and compensation claimed is more than ₹ 1 crore but does not exceed ₹ 10 crore.	All complaints pertaining to those goods or services and compensation whose value is more than ₹ 10 crore can be filed.
On receiving the complaint, the District Commission shall refer the complaint to the party against whom complaint is filed. If required, sample of goods can also be sent for testing in a laboratory.	On receiving complaint, the State Commission refers the complaint to the party against whom complaint is filed and if required, goods or their sample is sent to laboratory for testing.	On receiving complaint, the National Commission refers the complaint to the party against whom complaint is filed and if required, goods or their sample is sent to laboratory for testing.
District Commission shall pass an order after considering the test report from laboratory and hearing to the party against whom the complaint is filed.	State Commission shall pass an order after considering the test report from laboratory and hearing to the party against whom the complaint is filed.	After considering the laboratory test report and hearing to the party against whom the complaint is filed, the National Commission shall pass an order.
If the aggrieved party is not satisfied with the order of District Commission, then it can file an appeal before the State Commission within 45 days of the passing of the order.	If the aggrieved party is not satisfied with the order of the State Commission, it can file an appeal before the National Commission within 30 days of the passing of the order.	An order passed by the National Commission in a matter of its original jurisdiction is appealable before the Supreme Court within 30 days of the passing of the order.

Setting-up of Consumer Mediation Cell

The Chapter V of the Consumer Protection Act of 2019 provides for a mediation process for settlement of disputes at three levels–National, State and District with all three being attached to the respective commissions. It is a new provision in the Act 2019 as an alternate mechanism to ensure faster and speedy dispute settlements by respective commissions.

Reliefs/Remedies Available to Consumers

If the consumer court is satisfied about the genuineness of the complaint, it can issue one or more of the following directions to the opposite party

- To remove the defect in goods or deficiency in services.
- To replace the defective product with a new one, free from any defect.
- To refund the price paid for the product or the charges paid for the service.
- To pay a reasonable amount of compensation for any loss of injury suffered by the consumer due to the negligence of the opposite party.
- To pay punitive damages in appropriate circumstances.
- To discontinue the unfair/restrictive trade practice and not to repeat it in the future.
- Not to offer hazardous goods for sale.
- To withdraw the hazardous goods from the market.
- To cease manufacture of hazardous goods and to refrain from offering hazardous services.

- To pay any amount (not less than 5% of the value of the defective goods or deficient services provided), to be credited to the Consumer Welfare Fund or any other organisation/person, to be utilised in the prescribed manner.
- To issue corrective advertisement to neutralise the effect of a misleading advertisement.
- To pay adequate costs to the appropriate party.

12.3 Consumer Awareness

A consumer's awareness about the rights and responsibilities can help to achieve the objective of consumer protection. In India, several consumer organisations and Non-government Organisations (NGOs) have been set up for the protection and promotion of consumers' interest.

They aim at promoting the welfare of the people. They have their own Constitution and are free from government interference.

Some Important Consumer Organisations and NGOs

- Voluntary Organisation in Interest of Consumer Education (VOICE), Delhi
- Common Cause, New Delhi
- Consumer Guidance Society of India, Mumbai
- Consumer Education and Research Centre (CERC), Ahmedabad
- Consumer Utility and Trust Society (CUTS), Jaipur

Role of Consumer Organisations and NGOs

- Educating the general public about consumer rights by organising training programmes, seminars and workshops.
- Imparting knowledge about consumer problems, legal reporting, reliefs available and other matters of interest by publishing periodicals and publications.
- Carrying out comparative testing of consumer products in accredited laboratories to test relative qualities of competing brands and publishing the test results for the benefit of consumers.
- Encouraging consumers to strongly protest and take action against any unscrupulous, exploitative and unfair trade practice of the seller.
- Providing legal assistance to consumers by providing aid, advice, etc. to seek legal remedy.
- Filing complaints in appropriate consumer courts on behalf of the consumers.
- Taking an initiative in filing cases in consumer courts in the interest of general public, not for any individual.

Mind Map

CONSUMER PROTECTION

1 Concept of Consumer Protection

Consumer protection aims at
- Educating consumers about their rights and responsibilities
- Providing them protection against unscrupulous, unfair trade practices of traders
- Speedy redressal of their grievances

2 Importance of Consumer Protection

From Consumer's Point of View
- **Consumer Ignorance** It is necessary to educate the consumers about their rights and redressal agencies which are available
- **Unorganised Consumers** Consumers need to be organised in the form of consumer organisations
- **Widespread Exploitation of Consumers** Consumer protection provides safety to consumers from exploitation

From the Point of View of Business
- **Long-term Interest of Business** Should aim at long-term profit maximisation
- **Business uses Society's Resources** Responsibility to convert into useful goods
- **Social Responsibility** To provide satisfaction to consumers
- **Moral Justification** Moral duty of businesses to serve consumers well
- **Government Intervention** It can hamper the image of business

3 Consumer Protection Act, 2019

It seeks to protect and promote the consumers' interest through speedy and inexpensive redressal of their grievances.
It is applicable to all types of businesses including e-commerce firms.

4 Concept of Consumer

A consumer is a person, who buys any good or avails any service for a consideration which has been paid or promised, or partly paid and partly promised, or under any scheme of deferred payment. The term includes any other user of such goods or services when such use is made with the approval of the buyer.

5 Consumer Rights

- **Right to Safety** To protect from goods that are hazardous
- **Right to be Informed** To get true and complete information about price, quality, etc.
- **Right to be Assured** Consumers have the freedom to access variety of products at competitive prices
- **Right to be Heard** To file a complaint and to be heard in case of dissatisfaction
- **Right to seek Redressal** To get relief in case product falls short of expectations
- **Right to Consumer Education** To acquire knowledge about various rights and reliefs

6 Responsibilities of Consumers

- Consumer should have knowledge about market
- Consumer must be quality conscious
- Use the products safely
- Consumer must refer labels carefully
- Insist on cash memo
- Consumer must be honest
- Consumer must file a complaint
- Form consumer organisations
- Consumer must respect the environment
- Assert yourself to ensure that you get a fair deal

7 Redressal Agencies

- District Commission (Entertain claims upto ₹ 1 crore)
- State Commission (Entertain claims more than ₹ 1 crore but less than ₹ 10 crore)
- National Commission (Entertain claims more than ₹ 10 crore)

8 Reliefs Available to Consumers

- To remove the defects in good or deficiency in services
- To replace the defective product with a new one
- To refund the price paid of the product
- To pay punitive damages in appropriate circumstances
- Not to offer hazardous goods for sale
- To withdraw the hazardous goods from the market
- To pay adequate costs to the appropriate party
- To issue corrective advertisement to neutralise the effect of misleading advertisement

9 Role of Consumer Organisations and NGOs

- Educating the general public about consumer rights
- Imparting knowledge about consumer problems
- Carrying out comparative testing of consumer products
- Encouraging consumers to protest
- Providing legal assistance to consumers
- Filing complaints in appropriate consumer courts
- Taking an initiative in filing cases

EXAM PATTERN QUESTIONS

Objective Type Questions

Multiple Choice Questions (MCQs)

1. When a single consumer fails to get his rights protected, he seeks the help of

(a) trade union (b) consumer association
(c) labour union (d) None of these

2. Providing protection to the consumers against the improper behaviour of the producers and sellers is called ....

(a) Consumer Protection Act
(b) consumer protection
(c) consumer welfare
(d) consumer education

3. "The Consumer Protection Act aims to inform consumers about their rights and available remedies, helping them to approach redressal agencies when necessary." Which importance of consumer protection is being highlighted in this statement?

Competency Based Que

(a) Widespread exploitation of consumers
(b) Consumer ignorance (c) Unorganised consumers
(d) Long-term interest of business

4. A group of residents in a town came together to form a consumer organisation after facing repeated issues with local businesses selling sub-standard goods. They noticed that many products were overpriced and often defective. The organisation aimed to advocate for consumer rights, educate the public and take legal action against dishonest businesses.

What is the primary benefit of forming a consumer organisation as seen in this case? **Competency Based Que**

(a) Increase in product prices
(b) Protection of consumer interests
(c) Decrease in product variety
(d) Higher advertising costs

5. Anita Sharma, a 27 year old graphic designer, recently purchased a new smartphone after seeing advertisements that highlighted its amazing features. However, upon receiving the phone, she found that many advertised features were either non-functional or misleading. Frustrated, Anita tried to contact customer service but faced long wait times and unhelpful responses. Realising she had little knowledge about her consumer rights, Anita felt helpless.

Which consumer issue is highlighted by Anita's experience with misleading advertisements?

Competency Based Que

(a) Consumer ignorance
(b) Unorganised consumers
(c) Widespread exploitation
(d) Ineffective customer service

6. Which of the following statements is incorrect regarding the importance of consumer protection?

(a) Consumer protection is necessary to educate consumers due to widespread ignorance about their rights and available reliefs
(b) Consumers are highly organised and therefore, no further protection is required to safeguard their interests
(c) Satisfied customers help in the long-term interest of businesses by leading to repeat sales and positive feedback
(d) Business firms are responsible for using society's resources to produce goods and services that benefit the public

7. Which of the following statements is incorrect regarding the Consumer Protection Act, 2019?

(a) A consumer is defined as a person who buys goods or avails services for consideration that has been paid, promised or is part of a deferred payment scheme
(b) The Act applies only to offline transactions and does not cover online transactions
(c) A person using goods or services with the approval of the buyer is also considered a consumer
(d) Individuals obtaining goods for resale or availing services for commercial purposes are not included in the definition of a consumer

8. Identify the incorrect statement with respect to consumer protection in India. **CBSE SQP 2025**

(a) It not only includes educating consumers about their rights and responsibilities but also helps in getting their grievances redressed
(b) It not only requires a judicial machinery for protecting the interest of consumers but also requires the consumers to get together and form themselves into consumer associations for protection and promotion of their interests

(c) It is the moral duty of any business to take care of consumers' interest and avoid any form of exploitation
(d) The provisions of Consumer Protection Act came into force from 1981

9. **TechSol Inc., a well-known electronics manufacturer, has consistently focused on enhancing customer satisfaction. The company believes that happy customers not only return for more purchases but also recommend their products to others, expanding the company's reach. TechSol is also committed to responsible use of resources; it sources raw materials sustainably and works to reduce waste, acknowledging that these resources belong to society. Furthermore, the company understands its social responsibility to meet customers' expectations by offering high quality products and excellent service.**

What is TechSol Inc. focusing on by prioritising customer satisfaction, sustainable resource usage and meeting social responsibilities? **Competency Based Que**

(a) Legal responsibility
(b) Financial profit
(c) Long-term interest of business
(d) Marketing

10. **Which of the following will not be considered as consumers as per Consumer Protection Act, 2019?** **CBSE 2023**

(a) A person, who avails any service for a consideration which has been partly paid
(b) Any user of goods if such use is made with the approval of the buyer
(c) A person who purchases goods through online means
(d) A person who obtains goods for resale purposes

11. **Ravi ordered a smartphone from an online shopping website, paying in instalments as per the platform's deferred payment scheme. After a few days, the phone developed issues with its camera and battery. Ravi contacted the customer service team, but they did not resolve the issue despite multiple follow-ups.**

He decided to file a complaint under the Consumer Protection Act, 2019, claiming his rights as a consumer. He argued that, as per the Act, he is entitled to quality goods and appropriate service.

Under the Consumer Protection Act, 2019, which of the following correctly describes a 'consumer'? **Competency Based Que**

(a) A person who buys goods solely for resale
(b) A person who buys goods or services for consideration, not for commercial use
(c) A person who buys goods on a commercial basis
(d) A person who avails of services for business promotion

12. **Reena bought a heater of a reputed brand for ₹ 2,000 but it caused an electric shock while it was being used. Reena wants to exercise her 'right'. Identify the right under which she can be protected.** **Competency Based Que**

(a) Right to safety
(b) Right to be assured
(c) Right to be heard
(d) Right to seek redressal

13. **Neha Patel, a 30 year old software engineer, was excited about purchasing a new washing machine from Brand Z after seeing their catchy advertisements online. However, when she visited the store, she found that the model was unavailable. Upon asking the salesperson, she learned that it was out of stock and would take weeks to restock.**

Neha was frustrated as she had planned to use it immediately. Moreover, the product's packaging did not provide any information about energy efficiency.

Which consumer right is violated by the absence of energy efficiency information on the packaging? **Competency Based Que**

(a) Right to be heard
(b) Right to be informed
(c) Right to safety
(d) Right to seek redressal

14. **"As per Consumer Protection Act, 2019, the consumer has a right to get relief in case the product or service falls short of his expectations."**

Which consumer right is discussed in the above statement? **CBSE 2023**

(a) Right to be heard
(b) Right to be assured
(c) Right to seek redressal
(d) Right to safety

15. **Which consumer right is depicted in the below picture?**

(a) Right to be heard
(b) Right to consumer education
(c) Right to safety
(d) Right to seek redressal

16. **"In case of dissatisfaction with goods or services, consumers have the right to file a complaint and have their concerns addressed." What does this statement illustrate about consumer rights?**

(a) Right to be assured
(b) Right to consumer education
(c) Right to be heard
(d) Right to seek redressal

17. Coka Crackers Ltd., a fire cracker manufacturing company, launched some new products on the eve of Diwali which attracted many customers. To meet the increased demand, the company employed children from nearby villages and in the urgency of work, they ignored to specify safety warnings on packets of crackers.

Identify which consumer right is being ignored? **Competency Based Que**

(a) Right to be assured
(b) Right to be heard
(c) Right to be informed
(d) Right to seek redressal

18. Consumers can ask anything regarding the date of manufacturing, MRP, etc. about the product that he intend to buy.

Identify the consumer right highlighted in the above lines. **CBSE SQP 2025**

(a) Right to be informed
(b) Right to be assured
(c) Right to be heard
(d) Right to safety

19. As per the Consumer Protection Act, 2019, the consumer has a right to file a complaint and to be heard in case of dissatisfaction with a good or a service. The consumer right being referred to here is .... **CBSE 2024 C**

(a) right to safety
(b) right to be heard
(c) right to be informed
(d) right to seek redressal

20. 'Assert yourself', this is an important .... of the consumer.

(a) responsibility (b) right
(c) act (d) All of these

21. Sapna wants to buy a gold bangle. As an aware consumer, how can she be sure about the quality of gold bangle she is going to buy. **Competency Based Que**

(a) She should check hallmark on the jewellery
(b) She should check agro mark on the jewellery
(c) She should check FPO mark on the jewellery
(d) She can ask from another jewellery shop

22. Ms. Meera wants to buy a Strawberry drink. As a responsible consumer, she should check which mark on the label of the strawberry drink? **Competency Based Que**

(a) BSI mark (b) ISI mark
(c) FPO mark (d) None of these

23. Identify the responsibility of consumer being highlighted in the picture given below

(a) Be honest in dealing (b) Be aware
(c) Buy only standardised goods
(d) Ask for cash memo

24. Which of the following statements is incorrect regarding the responsibilities of a consumer?

(a) A consumer should be aware of the various goods and services available in the market to make informed choices
(b) It is unnecessary for a consumer to check for quality assurance marks like ISI, FPO or hallmark on products
(c) A consumer must learn about the risks associated with the use and maintenance of goods and follow manufacturer's instructions
(d) A consumer should read labels carefully to gather complete information about price, quantity and expiry date

25. Identify the responsibility of consumer from the picture below in which the doctor is suggesting the surgery to his patient.

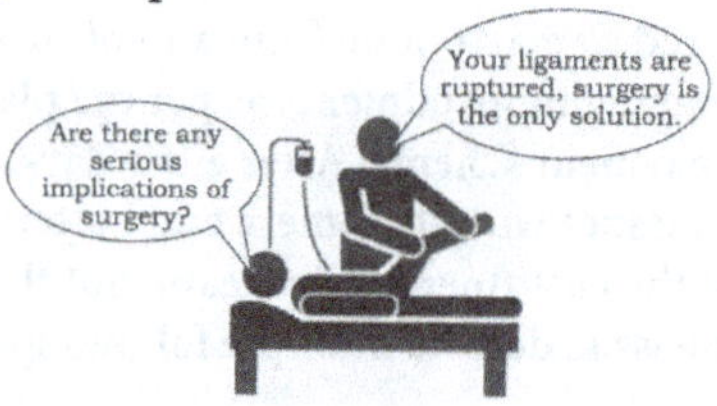

(a) Assert yourself to ensure that you get a fair deal
(b) Be honest in your dealings
(c) Learn about the risk associated with products and services
(d) Respect the environment

26. Identify the type of product to which the symbol illustrated by the picture given below is related.

(a) Fruit and vegetable products
(b) Metal products
(c) Agricultural commodities
(d) Electrical goods

27.

Identify the responsibility that a consumer fulfills when he looks for the quality marks given above. **CBSE SQP 2025**

(a) Assert yourself to ensure that you get a fair deal
(b) Getting a proper receipt
(c) Buy only standardised products
(d) Be honest in your dealings

28. Radhika recently bought a packaged food product from a local store. While at the store, she carefully checked the label on the package to make sure it had the price, quantity, ingredients, usage instructions and expiry date. She also made sure to ask for a cash memo to keep a record of her purchase.

As an aware consumer, Radhika believes in buying products only from reputable sources and discourages unethical practices like black marketing or hoarding.

Which of the following consumer responsibilities did Radhika fulfill by her actions? **Competency Based Que**

(a) Avoiding misleading advertisements
(b) Reading the label carefully for complete information
(c) Supporting only local products
(d) Buying only from online stores

29. "A complaint can be filed by various entities, including a consumer, a registered voluntary consumer association or the government." Who among the following is not allowed to file a complaint under the Consumer Protection Act?

(a) A consumer
(b) A legal heir of a deceased consumer
(c) A voluntary consumer association
(d) A friend of the consumer

30. As per the Consumer Protection Act, 2019 which of the following statement is correct? **CBSE 2025**

(a) In case the aggrieved party is not satisfied with the order of the District Commission, he can directly appeal before the National Commission.
(b) In case the aggrieved party is not satisfied with the order of the District Commission, he can directly appeal before the Supreme Court.
(c) In case the aggrieved party is not satisfied with the order' of the State Commission, he can directly appeal before the Supreme Court.
(d) In case the aggrieved party is not satisfied with the order of the National Commission, he can appeal before the Supreme Court.

31. Sarita bought a flat from Sugan Developers for ₹ 5 crore and was shocked to discover that the quality of construction was bad, roof leaked during the rainy season and plaster was coming off at various places. Which consumer forum should she approach for redressal of her grievance? **CBSE 2023; Competency Based Que**

(a) District Commission (b) State Commission
(c) National Commission (d) Supreme Court

32. Mr. Bhushan has purchased a product and found it defective. The seller denied taking it back. Mr. Bhushan can file complaint under the Consumer Protection Act, 2019. Within how much time, complaint can be filed from the date on which the cause of action has arisen? **Competency Based Que**

(a) Within three months
(b) Within six months
(c) Within a year
(d) Within two years

33. State Commission has the jurisdiction to entertain complaints where value of goods and services paid as consideration is .... **CBSE SQP 2025**

(a) more than ₹ 1 crore and not more than ₹ 5 crore
(b) more than ₹ 10 crore
(c) less than ₹ 1 crore
(d) more than ₹ 1 crore and not more than ₹ 10 crore

34. Look at the picture below and find, where the consumer would have complained at first?

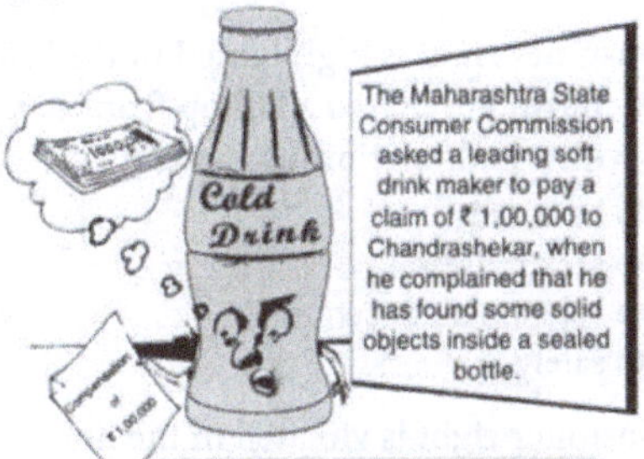

Compensation for impurities in cold drinks.

(a) State Commission
(b) District Commission
(c) National Commission
(d) Supreme Court

Direction *Read the following case study and answer the questions 35 to 38 on the basis of the same*

Riya Sharma, a 27-year-old online shopper, was discussing her recent experiences about electronic gadgets with her friend, Meera Verma. Riya mentioned, "I saw a lot of advertisements for Brand Y's new smartphone on social media, highlighting its amazing features and offers. However, when I tried to buy it online, the product was listed as 'out of stock' for weeks.

It's frustrating that the company promotes its product so heavily when they can't fulfill demand. Additionally, the smartphone packaging didn't include any warranty details, which makes me question how long it will last."

Meera chimed in, "I had a similar experience. I wanted to buy a wireless speaker from Brand Y, but the salesperson insisted that I should buy a different brand instead, even though I was interested in Brand Y's product. It felt like my choice was taken away from me. Furthermore, when my cousin purchased a laptop from Brand Y, it arrived with a malfunctioning battery. After she contacted customer service, they quickly arranged for a technician to fix it, but it was a hassle for her."

35. Which consumer right is highlighted in the lines, "the smartphone packaging didn't include any warranty details, which makes me question how long it will last"?

(a) Right to be heard
(b) Right to be informed
(c) Right to safety
(d) Right to be assured

36. Which consumer right is violated in the lines, "when I tried to buy it online, the product was listed as 'out of stock' for weeks"?

(a) Right to be heard
(b) Right to be informed
(c) Right to safety
(d) Right to be assured

37. Which consumer right is highlighted in the lines, "when my cousin purchased a laptop from Brand Y, it arrived with a malfunctioning battery"?

(a) Right to be heard
(b) Right to seek redressal
(c) Right to consumer education
(d) Right to safety

38. Which consumer right is violated in the line, "the salesperson insisted that I should buy a different brand instead, even though I was interested in Brand Y's product"?

(a) Right to information
(b) Right to be assured
(c) Right to be heard
(d) Right to consumer education

Assertion-Reason

Direction (Q.No. 39 to 48) *Read the following Assertion (A) and Reason (R) and choose the correct alternative from the following*

Alternatives

(a) Both Assertion (A) and Reason (R) are true and Reason (R) is the correct explanation of Assertion (A)
(b) Both Assertion (A) and Reason (R) are true, but Reason (R) is not the correct explanation of Assertion (A)
(c) Assertion (A) is true, but Reason (R) is false
(d) Assertion (A) is false, but Reason (R) is true

39. **Assertion** (A) Consumer ignorance about their rights makes it necessary to educate them to achieve consumer awareness.

Reason (R) Educating consumers will protect them against unscrupulous trade practices.

40. **Assertion** (A) Consumers in India are well-organised to safeguard their interests.

Reason (R) Consumer organisations are powerful enough to protect and promote the interests of consumers.

41. **Assertion** (A) Satisfied customers lead to repeat sales and increased customer base for the business.

Reason (R) Providing customer satisfaction helps businesses in the long-term.

42. **Assertion** (A) The government will intervene only if businesses adopt fair trade practices.

Reason (R) Businesses must voluntarily protect consumers to avoid government intervention.

43. **Assertion** (A) Businesses should ignore consumer protection as long as they are making profits.

Reason (R) Satisfied consumers help build a positive business reputation.

44. **Assertion** (A) Under the Consumer Protection Act, 2019, a consumer includes a person who buys goods for commercial purposes.

Reason (R) The Consumer Protection Act excludes consumers who obtain goods for resale.

45. **Assertion** (A) Consumers have the freedom to choose products of their choice.

Reason (R) Right to be assured allows consumers to choose from different products available at competitive prices.

46. **Assertion** (A) Buy only standardised goods.

Reason (R) They provide quality assurance.

47. **Assertion** (A) The marketers should offer a wide variety of products to the consumers.

Reason (R) The consumer has the freedom to choose from a variety of products at competitive prices.

48. **Assertion** (A) NGOs play a role in educating the public about consumer rights.

Reason (R) NGOs organise training programmes and publish periodicals to impart knowledge to consumers.

Two Statements Based MCQs

Direction (Q.No. 49 to 59) *Read the following statements carefully and choose the correct alternative*

Alternatives

(a) Statement I is correct and Statement II is incorrect
(b) Statement II is correct and Statement I is incorrect
(c) Both the statements are correct
(d) Both the statements are incorrect

49. **Statement I** Consumers are often unaware of their rights and the reliefs available to them, making it important to educate them about consumer protection.

Statement II Widespread consumer ignorance makes consumer protection unnecessary, as consumers do not face significant exploitation.

50. **Statement I** Businesses should focus only on profit making without regard to consumer protection, as it does not affect their long-term interests.

Statement II Consumer protection contributes to the long-term interest of businesses by ensuring customer satisfaction and repeat sales.

51. **Statement I** Consumer Protection Act, 2019 is applicable to all the areas whether private, public or cooperative.

Statement II An individual consumer cannot file a complaint under the Consumer Protection Act, 2019.

52. **Statement I** The right to safety ensures that consumers are protected from hazardous goods and services that could harm life or health.

Statement II The right to safety encourages consumers to purchase goods marked with ISI and FPO for assurance of quality.

53. **Statement I** The right to be heard ensures that consumers can file complaints and be heard if they are dissatisfied with a product or service.

Statement II Enlightened business firms have set-up grievance cells to address consumer complaints as a part of the right to be heard.

54. **Statement I** The right to seek redressal allows consumers to claim compensation, replacement of goods or removal of defects when the product does not meet expectations.

Statement II The right to seek redressal only applies to defective goods, not deficient services.

55. **Statement I** Consumers have the responsibility to be well-informed about the product they intend to purchase.

Statement II Consumers do not need to check for certification marks like ISI or Agmark before purchasing products.

56. **Statement I** Consumers should file a complaint if they are dissatisfied with a product or service.

Statement II Consumers are not required to ask for a receipt or invoice as proof of purchase.

57. **Statement I** The consumer courts can order the withdrawal of hazardous goods from the market.

Statement II If a product is found to be defective, punitive damages can be awarded in all circumstances.

58. **Statement I** A consumer can ask for a replacement of a defective product with a new one free from any defects.

Statement II If a service is deficient, the consumer can only receive compensation for damages and cannot ask for a refund.

59. **Statement I** As per the Consumer Protection Act, 2019, the District Commission has a jurisdiction to entertain complaints where value of goods or services paid as consideration does not exceed ₹ 10 crores.

Statement II If any of the parties is not satisfied by the order of the District Commission, they can appeal against such order to the State Commission on the grounds of facts or law within a period of forty-five days from the date of order. **CBSE 2024 C**

Matching

60. Match the following

Column I		Column II	
A.	Consumer ignorance	(i)	Safety from unfair trade practices
B.	Unorganised consumers	(ii)	Long-term profit maximisation
C.	Widespread exploitation of consumers	(iii)	Awareness of rights and redressal agencies
D.	Long-term interest of business	(iv)	Need for consumer organisations

Codes

	A	B	C	D		A	B	C	D
(a)	(iii)	(iv)	(i)	(ii)	(b)	(iii)	(ii)	(i)	(iv)
(c)	(ii)	(iii)	(i)	(iv)	(d)	(iv)	(iii)	(ii)	(i)

61. Match the following

Column I		Column II	
A.	Right to safety	(i)	Right to acquire knowledge and skills to be an informed consumer
B.	Right to be heard	(ii)	Right to know the MRP, expiry date, etc

Column I	Column II
C. Right to be informed	(iii) Many enlightened firms have set-up their own consumer service and grievance cells
D. Right to consumer education	(iv) A consumer has the right to be protected from goods and services which are hazardous to life and health

Codes

	A	B	C	D
(a)	(ii)	(i)	(iii)	(iv)
(b)	(iii)	(iv)	(i)	(ii)
(c)	(iv)	(iii)	(i)	(ii)
(d)	(iv)	(iii)	(ii)	(i)

62. Match the following

Column I	Column II
A. Agmark	(i) Food products
B. ISI Mark	(ii) Jewellery
C. FPO Mark	(iii) Electrical goods
D. Hallmark	(iv) Agricultural commodities

Codes

	A	B	C	D
(a)	(ii)	(i)	(iii)	(iv)
(b)	(iii)	(iv)	(i)	(ii)
(c)	(iv)	(iii)	(i)	(ii)
(d)	(ii)	(iii)	(i)	(iv)

63. Match the following

Column I	Column II
A. To acquire knowledge and skills to be an informed consumer	(i) Consumer responsibility
B. To refund the price paid for the product or the charges paid for the service	(ii) Consumer right
C. Buy only standardised products	(iii) Relief available to consumers

Codes

	A	B	C
(a)	(ii)	(i)	(iii)
(b)	(iii)	(i)	(ii)
(c)	(iii)	(ii)	(i)
(d)	(ii)	(iii)	(i)

Answers

1. (b) consumer association **2.** (b) consumer protection
3. (b) Consumer ignorance
4. (b) Protection of consumer interests
5. (c) Widespread exploitation
6. (b) It is important to protect the consumers as they are not fully organised
7. (b) The Act also applies to online transactions
8. (d) The provisions of Consumer Protection Act came into force from 1986
9. (c) Long-term interest of business
10. (d) A person who obtains goods for resale purposes
11. (b) A person who buys goods or services for consideration, not for commercial use.
12. (a) Right to safety **13.** (b) Right to be informed
14. (c) Right to seek redressal
15. (a) Right to be heard **16.** (c) Right to be heard
17. (c) Right to be informed
18. (a) Right to be informed
19. (b) right to be heard **20.** (a) responsibility
21. (a) She should check hallmark on the jewellery
22. (c) FPO mark
23. (c) Buy only standardised goods
24. (b) It is important for consumer to check for quality assurance marks
25. (c) Learn about the risk associated with products and services
26. (a) Fruit and vegetable products
27. (c) Buy only standardised products
28. (b) Reading the label carefully for complete information
29. (d) A friend of the consumer
30. (d) In case the aggrieved party is not satisfied with the order of the National Commission, he can appeal before the Supreme Court.
31. (b) State Commission **32.** (d) Within two years
33. (d) more than ₹ 1 crore and not more than ₹ 10 crore
34. (b) District Commission **35.** (b) Right to be informed
36. (d) Right to be assured **37.** (d) Right to safety
38. (b) Right to be assured
39. (a) Both Assertion (A) and Reason (R) are true and Reason (R) is the correct explanation of Assertion (A)
40. (d) Consumers are not yet well-organised to safeguard their interests.
41. (a) Both Assertion (A) and Reason (R) are true, and Reason (R) is the correct explanation of Assertion (A)

42. (d) Government intervention occurs when businesses engage in unfair practices, not when they adopt fair ones.
43. (d) Businesses should not ignore consumer protection.
44. (d) Consumer Protection Act does not consider individuals buying goods for commercial purposes as consumers.
45. (a) Both Assertion (A) and Reason (R) are true and Reason (R) is the correct explanation of Assertion (A)
46. (a) Both Assertion (A) and Reason (R) are true and Reason (R) is the correct explanation of Assertion (A)
47. (a) Both Assertion (A) and Reason (R) are true and Reason (R) is the correct explanation of Assertion (A)
48. (a) Both Assertion (A) and Reason (R) are true and Reason (R) is the correct explanation of Assertion (A)
49. (a) Consumers are often unaware of their rights, so education is crucial. Due to widespread consumer ignorance, consumer protection becomes necessary.
50. (b) Consumer protection helps businesses in the long-term through customer satisfaction and repeat sales, so profit should not be the only focus.
51. (a) An individual consumer can file a complaint under the Consumer Protection Act, 2019 if they feel their rights have been violated.
52. (c) Both the statements are correct
53. (c) Both the statements are correct
54. (a) The right to seek redressal applies to both defective goods and deficient services, allowing consumers to claim various reliefs.
55. (a) Consumers should be well informed about products and check for certification marks to ensure quality.
56. (a) Consumers must file a complaint if dissatisfied and always request a receipt or invoice as proof of purchase.
57. (a) Hazardous goods can be withdrawn, but punitive damages are awarded only in appropriate circumstances.
58. (a) Consumers can request a replacement of defective goods and they are also entitled to refunds for deficient services.
59. (b) Statement II is correct and Statement I is incorrect
60. (a) (iii) (iv) (i) (ii)
61. (d) (iv) (iii) (ii) (i)
62. (c) (iv) (iii) (i) (ii)
63. (d) (ii) (iii) (i)

Subjective Questions

Short Answer Type Questions

1. State any four features of Consumer Protection Act, 2019.

Ans. Following are the features of Consumer Protection Act, 2019

(i) The act has provided various rights and responsibilities of consumers to protect their interest.

(ii) The act provides safeguards to the consumers against defective goods, deficient services, unfair trade practices and other forms of their exploitation.

(iii) The act stresses on setting up of a three tier machinery, consisting of District Commission, State Commission and National Commission.

(iv) It also provides a framework for the formation of consumer protection councils in every District and State and also at the apex level.

2. What is the objective of the Consumer Protection Act, 2019?

Ans. The main objective of the Consumer Protection Act, 2019 is to protect the interests of consumers in India. It aims to provide a speedy and simple redressal to consumers' grievances. It provides effective safeguards to consumers against various types of exploitations and unfair trade practices.

The Act has created special consumer courts for enforcement of the rights of consumers. It provides a convenient and inexpensive procedure for redressal of grievances of consumers.

3. Explain any three points of importance of consumer protection from the point of view of consumer.

Ans. Importance of consumer protection from the point of view of consumer can be explained with the help of the following points

(i) **Consumer Ignorance**
In the light of widespread ignorance of consumers about their rights and reliefs available to them, it becomes necessary to educate them about the same so as to achieve consumer awareness.

(ii) **Unorganised Consumers**
Consumers need to be organised in the form of consumer organisations which would take care of their interests. Adequate protection is required to be given to consumers till these organisations become powerful enough to protect and promote the interests of consumers.

(iii) **Widespread Exploitation of Consumers**
Consumers might be exploited by unscrupulous, exploitative and unfair trade practices like defective and unsafe products, adulteration, false and misleading advertising, hoarding, black-marketing, etc. Consumers need protection against such malpractices of the sellers.

4. "Consumer protection is important for businesses as it helps build trust, ensures customer satisfaction and boosts brand reputation." In the light of the statement, explain any two points of importance of consumer protection from business point of view. Competency Based Que

Ans. Consumer protection is important from business point of view because of the following reasons

(i) **Moral Justification**
Business exists to serve human beings. It is the moral duty of a businessman to serve their customers well and keep them away from exploitative and unfair trade practices. Therefore, business must avoid unfair trade practices such as adulteration, misleading advertising, hoarding, black marketing, etc.

(ii) **Government Intervention**
If a business organisation engages in any form of exploitative trade practices, it would invite government intervention, which can tarnish the image of the company. Therefore, it is in the interest of business itself, to voluntarily take care of consumer needs and interests.

5. "The Consumer Protection Act provides a comprehensive framework to safeguard consumers against unfair trade practices and defective goods or services."
In the light of the statement, elaborate on the scope of the Act. Competency Based Que

Ans. The Consumer Protection Act, 2019 seeks to protect and promote the consumers' interest through speedy and inexpensive redressal of their grievances. It extends to the whole of India. It is applicable to all types of businesses whether a manufacturer or a trader and whether supplying goods or providing services including e-commerce firms.

The Act confers certain rights to consumers with a view to empowering them and to protect their interests.

6. Define a 'consumer' according to the provisions of the Consumer Protection Act, 2019.

Or Who is a consumer as per CPA? NCERT

Ans. Consumer is a person, who buys any good or avails any service for a consideration which has been paid or promised, or partly paid and partly promised, or under any scheme of deferred payment.

The term includes any other user of such goods or services when such use is made with the approval of the buyer.

The term 'consumer', however does not include a person, who obtains such goods for resale or for any commerical purpose or a person, who avails such services for any commercial purpose.

7. Explain the following rights of a consumer CBSE 2023

(i) Right to be heard
(ii) Right to seek redressal

Ans.

(i) **Right to be Heard**
According to this right, a consumer has a right to file a complaint and to be heard in case of dissatisfaction with a good or a service. It is because of this reason, many enlightened business firms have set-up their own consumer service and grievance cells.

(ii) **Right to Seek Redressal**
According to this right, consumer has the right to get relief in case the product falls short of his expectations. The Act provides various reliefs to the consumers like compensation for any loss or injury suffered by the consumers, replacement of goods or removal of defects in the goods, etc.

8. Explain the following rights of consumers as provided under Consumer Protection Act, 2019

(i) Right to be informed (ii) Right to safety

Ans.

(i) **Right to be Informed**
According to this right, a consumer has the right to get true and complete information about the ingredients, quality, quantity, price, expiry date of the goods and services etc. which he intends to buy.

(ii) **Right to Safety**
According to this right, a consumer has a right to be protected against the marketing of such goods and services that are hazardous to life and health. Thus, consumers are educated to use standardised goods, such as electrical goods with ISI mark, food products with FPO mark, etc as such goods would be an assurance of meeting quality specifications.

9. State any four responsibilities that a consumer should discharge while purchasing, using and consuming goods and services.

Or What are the responsibilities of a consumer? NCERT

Ans. Following are the responsibilities that a consumer should discharge while purchasing, using and consuming goods and services

(i) A consumer should always ask for a cash memo, as it serves as a proof of purchase required at the time of taking any action against a fraudulent seller or manufacturer.

(ii) A consumer must file a complaint in case of any shortcoming in goods or services availed.

(iii) A consumer should take initiative to form consumer societies that can take active part in educating consumers and safeguarding their interests.

(iv) A consumer should respect the environment and avoid creating pollution.

10. How does consumer awareness protect consumers from exploitation? Competency Based Que

Ans. Self-help is the ideal way to overcome problems. If every consumer become aware of his/her rights and the remedies available against exploitation and unscrupulous activities, then businessmen will not be able to exploit consumers.

Therefore, consumers should be made aware and educated about their rights. They should know how to protect themselves against malpractices in the market.

11. Who can file a complaint in a consumer court? NCERT

Ans. The following can file a complaint under the Consumer Protection Act

(i) A consumer.
(ii) Any voluntary registered consumer association.
(iii) The Central Government or any State Government.
(iv) One or more consumers, where there are numerous consumers having the same interest.
(v) A legal heir or representative of a deceased consumer.

12. Explain in brief the procedure for filing a complaint under the Consumer Protection Act, 2019.

Ans. A complaint may be filed by the complainant or his authorised agent in person or by post.

There is no fee for filing a complaint. A complaint should be in writing and it should contain the following information

(i) The name, description and address of the complainant.
(ii) The name, description and address of the opposite party or parties, as far as they can be ascertained.
(iii) The facts relating to complaint and when and where it arose.
(iv) Documents if any, in support of the allegations contained in the complaint.
(v) Details of the relief which a complainant is seeking.

13. State any four reliefs available to consumers if the consumer court is satisfied about the genuineness of the complaint. CBSE 2023

Ans. Following are the reliefs available to consumers of the consumer court is satisfied about the genuineness of the complaint

(i) To remove the defect in goods or deficiency in services.
(ii) To replace the defective product with a new one, free from any defect.
(iii) To refund the price paid for the product or the charges paid for the service.
(iv) To pay a reasonable amount of compensation for any loss of injury suffered by the consumer due to the negligence of the opposite party.

Long Answer Type Questions

14. What is meant by consumer protection? State any three points of importance of consumer protection from the business point of view.

Or **Explain the importance of consumer protection from the point of view of a business.** NCERT

Ans. The concept of consumer protection is to safeguard the interests of the consumers. It is a very wide term which aims at educating consumers about their rights and responsibilities, providing them protection against unscrupulous, unfair trade practices of traders, etc. and speedy redressal of their grievances.

Consumer protection is important from the business point of view because of the following reasons

(i) **Long-term Interest of Business**
Satisfied customers not only lead to repeat sales but also provide good feedback to prospective customers and thus, help in increasing the customer base of business which contributes to the long-term interest of the business.

(ii) **Business uses Society's Resources**
Business firms use resources that belong to the society. Therefore, it is the responsibility of businesses to convert these resources into useful goods and services which are in public interest.

(iii) **Social Responsibility**
Business organisation makes money by selling their products to consumers. It is the social responsibility of businessman to provide satisfaction to their customers and take care of their interests.

15. State any six responsibilities that a consumer should keep in mind while purchasing goods and services.

Ans. Following are the responsibilities that a consumer should keep in mind while purchasing goods and services

(i) A consumer should be aware about the various goods and services available in the market, so that he can make a wise choice by comparing their features and prices.
(ii) A consumer must always buy standardised goods as they provide quality assurance. Thus, a consumer should always look for ISI mark on electrical goods, FPO mark on food products, hallmark on jewellery, etc.
(iii) A consumer must learn about the various risks associated with the use and maintainance of goods. He must follow the manufacturer's instructions carefully.
(iv) A consumer must read the labels carefully, so as to have complete information about the price, quantity, ingredients, usage, contents, expiry date, etc.
(v) A consumer must ensure that he gets a fair deal.

(vi) A consumer should be honest in his dealings. He should choose legal goods and discourage unscrupulous practices like black-marketing, hoarding, etc.

16. Explain the redressal mechanism available to consumers under the Consumer Protection Act, 2019. NCERT

Ans. Following is the redressal mechanism available to consumers under the Consumer Protection Act, 2019.

(i) **District Commission**

- The State Governments are required to establish District Consumer Disputes Redressal Commission or District Commission in each district.
- Each District Commission consists of a President and two members appointed by the State Government.
- A District Commission can receive consumer complaints, where the value of goods or services and the compensation claimed is not more than ₹ 1 crore.
- On receiving the complaint, the District Commission shall refer the complaint to the party against whom complaint is filed. If required, sample of goods can also be sent for testing in a laboratory.
- District Commission shall pass an order after considering the test report from laboratory and hearing to the party against whom the complaint is filed.
- If the aggrieved party is not satisfied with the order of District Commission, then it can file an appeal before the State Commission within 45 days of the passing of the order.

(ii) **State Commission**

- State Consumer Disputes Redressal Commission or State Commission is set-up by the State Government and its jurisdiction is restricted to the boundaries of the State concerned.
- The State Commission shall consist of a President, who is or has been a judge of a High Court and four other members. All the three shall be appointed by the State Government.
- Only those complaints can be filed, where the value of goods or services and compensation claimed is more than ₹ 1 crore but does not exceed ₹ 10 crore. The appeals against the orders of any District Commission can also be filed before the State Commission.
- On receiving complaint, the State Commission refers the complaint to the party against whom complaint is filed and if required, goods or their sample is sent to laboratory for testing.
- State Commission shall pass an order after considering the test report from laboratory and hearing to the party against whom the complaint is filed.
- If the aggrieved party is not satisfied with the order of the State Commission, it can file an appeal before the National Commission within 30 days of the passing of the order.

(iii) **National Commission**

- National Consumer Disputes Redressal Commission or National Commission has territorial jurisdiction over the whole country. It is set-up by the Central Government.
- It shall consist of a President, who is or has been a judge of the Supreme Court and four other members.
- All complaints pertaining to those goods or services and compensation whose value is more than ₹ 10 crore can be filed. Appeals against the order of any State Commission can also be filed before the National Commission.
- On receiving complaint, the National Commission refers the complaint to the party against whom complaint is filed and if required, goods or their sample is sent to laboratory for testing.
- After considering the laboratory test report and hearing to the party against whom the complaint is filed, the National Commission shall pass an order.
- An order passed by the National Commission in a matter of its original jurisdiction is appealable before the Supreme Court within 30 days of the passing of the order.

17. Various remedies are available to a consumer under the Consumer Protection Act, 2019. Explain these remedies which are available to a consumer for redressing their grievances.

Ans. Following remedies are available to a consumer for redressing their grievances

(i) To remove the defect in goods or deficiency in services.
(ii) To replace the defective product with a new one, free from any defect.
(iii) To refund the price paid for the product or the charges paid for the service.
(iv) To pay a reasonable amount of compensation for any loss of injury suffered by the consumer due to the negligence of the opposite party.
(v) To pay punitive damages in appropriate circumstances.
(vi) To discontinue the unfair/restrictive trade practice and not to repeat it in the future.
(vii) Not to offer hazardous goods for sale.
(viii) To withdraw the hazardous goods from the market.
(ix) To cease manufacture of hazardous goods and to desist from offering hazardous services.
(x) To pay any amount (not less than 5% of the value of the defective goods or deficient services provided), to be credited to the Consumer Welfare Fund or any other organisation/person, to be utilised in the prescribed manner.

(xi) To issue corrective advertisement to neutralise the effect of a misleading advertisement.

(xii) To pay adequate costs to the appropriate party.

18. Explain the role of consumer organisations and NGOs in protecting and promoting consumers interest. NCERT

Ans. Consumer organisations and NGOs are established or formed to protect and promote the consumer interest. They perform following functions

(i) Educating the general public about consumer rights by organising training programmes, seminars and workshops.

(ii) Imparting knowledge about consumer problems, legal reporting, reliefs available and other matters of interest by publishing periodicals and publications.

(iii) Carrying out comparative testing of consumer products in accredited laboratories to test relative qualities of competing brands and publishing the test results for the benefit of consumers.

(iv) Encouraging consumers to strongly protest and take action against any unscrupulous, exploitative and unfair trade practices of the seller.

(v) Providing legal assistance to consumers by providing aid, advice, etc. to seek legal remedy.

(vi) Filing complaints in appropriate consumer courts on behalf of the consumers.

(vii) Taking an initiative in filing cases in consumer courts in the interest of general public.

Case Study Based Questions

Short Case Study

Case Study 1

FSSAI (Food Safety and Standards Authority of India) has made a proposal for hotels and other food outlets to declare the kind of oil/fat used in cooking each of the food items on their menus. Name and explain the consumer right being reinforced by this proposal. NCERT

Ans. The consumer right being reinforced in the case is 'right to be informed'. According to this right, a consumer has the right to get true and complete information about the ingredients, quality, quantity, price, expiry date of the goods and services, etc. which he intends to buy. Therefore, the legal framework in India has made it compulsory for manufacturers to provide all such information on the package and label of the product. Right to be informed is fundamental to consumer protection, empowering individuals with the knowledge they need to make safe and well informed choices about the goods and services they consume.

Case Study 2

Mohan purchase a scooter from Sarang Automobiles with a written guarantee to repair or replace, if necessary, within six months or 5,000 kms of distance travelled whichever is earlier.

After covering the distance of 400 kms in two months, the gears of the bike started giving problems. Mohan took the scooter to the dealer who refused to listen to his complaint. He was confused about what he should do.

(i) Suggest the rights that Mohan may exercise in the above case.

(ii) Discuss briefly, the rights suggested in point (i).

Ans.

(i) The rights that Mohan may exercise in the above case are right to safety and right to seek redressal.

(ii) Following are the rights suggested in point (i)

- **Right to Safety**
  According to this right, a consumer has a right to be protected against the marketing of such goods and services that are hazardous to life and health. Thus, consumers are educated to use standardised goods, such as electrical goods with ISI mark, food products with FPO mark, etc as such goods would be an assurance of meeting quality specifications.
- **Right to Seek Redressal**
  According to this right, consumer has the right to get relief in case the product falls short of his expectations. The Act provides various reliefs to the consumers like compensation for any loss or injury suffered by the consumers, replacement of goods or removal of defects in the goods, etc.

Case Study 3

Ramesh, after completing his graduation, started working with a multinational company in Delhi. But due to ill health of his parents, he had to go back to his village. There he noticed that the villagers were literate but ignorant about their rights. Many vegetable vendors were using stones as weights to sell their vegetables. Some shopkeepers were selling food items without having the 'FPO Mark'. The villagers did not find anything wrong with these practices. So, to create awareness among the villagers, Ramesh decided to publish a weekly journal 'Jan Jagriti.' State the right which Ramesh has exercised by doing so.

Ans. Ramesh has exercised 'right to consumer education'. Consumer should have knowledge about the various rights and reliefs provided by the legislations to protect their interest. Every consumer has the right to be well informed about his rights, and to spread awareness and education by forming consumer organisations and associations.

Case Study 4

Nikita buys a packet of cake from a cake shop without asking for the bill. The pack does not bear any information other than the name of the shop. After reaching home she finds the cake to be stale.

(i) Identify the consumer right that has been violated.
(ii) State any three responsibilities that a consumer must keep in mind while purchasing any good.

Ans.

(i) The consumer right that has been violated is 'right to be informed'.

According to this right, a consumer has the right to get true and complete information about the ingredients, quality, quantity, price, expiry date of the goods and services etc. which he intends to buy.

(ii) Following are the responsibilities that a consumer must keep in mind while purchasing any good (any three)

- A consumer should always ask for a cash memo, as it serves as a proof of purchase required at the time of taking any action against a fraudulent seller or manufacturer.
- A consumer must file a complaint in case of any shortcoming in goods or services availed.
- A consumer should take initiative to form consumer societies that can take active part in educating consumers and safeguarding their interests.
- A consumer should respect the environment and avoid creating pollution.

Case Study 5

Shobhit wants to purchase a sandwich maker. He goes to a nearby mall and enters the shop where electric gadgets are kept. He asks the salesman about the area where sandwich makers are kept.

The sales man takes him to that place where different types of sandwich makers are kept. He very patiently observes all the electronic gadgets, sees their functions, reads their instructions, compares their prices and sees their warranty periods.

After some time when he pays the concerned person, tells him to note his home address and telephone number for future contact. He also asks him to inform him about any new products in the market.

(i) In the above case, name one consumer responsibility Shobhit should follow and the consumer right that is maintained.
(ii) Which mark should be checked by Shobhit on the electronic appliance as he purchases it?

Ans.

(i) The consumer responsibility that Shobhit should follow is collecting cash memo as it serves as a proof of purchase required at the time of taking any action against a fraudulent seller or manufacturer. When Shobhit reads instructions, his 'right to be informed' is maintained.

(ii) The mark which should be checked in the case of any electrical appliance is an 'ISI' mark.

Case Study 6

Aman, a young graduate was living away from home in another city. He had problems in cooking and heating food. He decided to purchase a microwave oven for the same. He went to the market, visited many shops and compared various microwave oven brands available in the market.

He compared features, price, after-sale service and customer reviews, etc. to make an informed choice as per his needs.

After selecting the oven, he checked that it should have an ISI mark. This gave him confidence about the safety, standards and quality of the oven. After reaching home he followed the manufacturer's instructions for safe installation and use of microwave oven. This helped him in avoiding any risk associated with the usage of microwave oven.

By doing all this Aman kept in mind various responsibilities while purchasing and using the microwave oven. Still he left some of the responsibilities that were not fulfilled by him. State any three such responsibilities. **CBSE 2025**

Ans. Aman fulfilled several consumer responsibilities while purchasing and using the microwave oven, such as comparing products, checking for the ISI mark and following manufacturer instructions. However, he did not fulfill the following responsibilities

(i) A consumer must read the labels carefully, so as to have complete information about the price, quantity, ingredients, usage, contents, expiry date, etc.

(ii) A consumer should be honest in his dealings. He should choose legal goods and discourage unscrupulous (unethical) practices like black marketing, hoarding, etc.

(iii) A consumer should always ask for a cash memo, as it serves as a proof of purchase required at the time of taking any action against a fraudulent seller or manufacturer.

Case Study 7

Sameeksha is a Class XII student having Business Studies as one of her subjects. After studying 'consumer protection' as one of the chapters in Business Studies, she tried to apply the acquired knowledge while purchasing and using the goods.

She is very fond of cooking and always tries new recipies. This time she wants to purchase a 'bread maker' to prepare homemade bread. She checked online about the various brands of 'bread maker' available in the market and compared their price, so that an intelligent and wise choice can be made. Then she went to a near by market to buy it. Being an informed consumer, she looked for the standardisation mark, negotiated the price printed on the label, checked the date of manufacturing and asked for guarantee or warranty of the product. After satisfying with all the concerned information, she purchased the 'bread maker' and as a responsible consumer asked for the cash memo.

After coming back home, she opened the packaging of the 'bread maker' and found an instruction booklet inside.

She carefully read all the instructions and operated the bread maker step-by-step and succeeded in making nice 'atta bread' for her family. Sameeksha has fulfilled many responsibilities of a consumer while purchasing and using the 'bread maker'. State any four responsibilities fulfilled by Sameeksha besides asking for a cash memo. **CBSE 2023**

Or

Ishaan wanted to buy five litres of mustard oil. Before he went to the market, he surfed the internet to find out about the various brands of mustard oil available in the market. On visiting the retail shop, he could find five different brands of mustard oil but to his surprise, only one of them had 'FSSAI' certification mark, which he decided to buy. He read the label on the oil container to find out the price and weight of the oil. While paying for the oil he ensured that the cashier gave him the cash memo.

Ishaan was a responsible consumer. State any four responsibilities that Ishaan kept in mind while purchasing the mustard oil. **CBSE 2024 C**

Ans. Following are the four responsibilities fulfilled by Sameeksha besides asking for a cash memo/Ishaan kept in mind

(i) A consumer should be aware about the various goods and services available in the market, so that he can make a wise choice by comparing their features and prices.

(ii) A consumer must always buy standardised goods as they provide quality assurance. Thus, a consumer should always look for ISI mark on electrical goods, FPO mark on food products, hallmark on jewellery, etc.

(iii) A consumer must read the labels carefully, so as to have complete information about the price, quantity, ingredients, usage, contents, expiry date, etc.

(iv) A consumer must learn about the various risks associated with the use and maintenance of goods. He must follow the manufacturer's instructions carefully.

Case Study 8

Raghu purchased a truck worth ₹1.5 crore. The truck had some inbuilt problems and after some days stopped starting. Since it was in the guarantee period, it was shown to the company. The people in the company refused to attend to his complaints.

It was heart breaking for him so he decided to file a complaint in the State Commission. The State Commission on hearing the pleas from both the parties gave decision in favour of the truck company. It was shockingly bad news for Raghu.

(i) At what level of authority should Raghu file a complaint now?

(ii) In how many days should he file his complaint at the next level?

(iii) Which right of the consumer is being exercised by Raghu in this case?

Ans.

(i) Raghu should now file a complaint at the level of 'National Commission' as it is an appeal against the order of the State Commission.

(ii) Raghu should file his complaint at the National Commission level within 30 days of the passing of the order.

(iii) The right being exercised by Raghu is the 'right to seek redressal', which allows consumers to file complaints and seek compensation for unfair practices or unsatisfactory services.

Case Study 9

Anuj, after a lot of research, paid SS Developers' an advance of ₹ 2 crore to build a lavish house for him. They promised to deliver the property within 18 months. At the end of 18 months, Anuj asked for the delivery of the property many times but the developer did not respond. Anuj realised that SS Developers' was not in a position to hand over the property to him.

Anuj asked for a refund of the money with interest, which SS Developers' refused. Anuj approached the consumer court with his complaint. **CBSE 2024**

(i) Which grievance redressal agency had Anuj approached?

(ii) State any three reliefs Anuj is likely to get, if the consumer court is satisfied with the complaint.

Ans.

(i) Anuj had approached to 'State Commission'.

(ii) If the consumer court is satisfied about the genuineness of the complaint, it can issue one or more of the following directions to the opposite party (any three)

- To refund the price paid for the product or the charges paid for the service.
- To pay a reasonable amount of compensation for any loss suffered by the consumer due to the negligence of the opposite party.
- To pay punitive damages in appropriate circumstances.
- To discontinue the unfair/restrictive trade practice and not to repeat it in the future.

Case Study 10

Rajneesh purchased a 500 ml bottle of fruit juice for ₹ 60 in Ahmedabad from a local store. While consuming it, he found an insect floating in it.

He sent a legal notice to the company immediately and decided to approach a Consumer Dispute Redressal Agency for a relief of ₹ 2 lakh. **CBSE 2023**

(i) Which Consumer Dispute Redressal Agency did Rajneesh approach, out of the three-tier machinery set-up under Consumer Protection Act, 2019 for redressal?

(ii) If Rajneesh is not satisfied by the order of the above Agency, where can he appeal against such order and within how many days?

(iii) State any two reliefs that can be granted to Rajneesh in the above case.

Ans.

(i) Rajneesh approached the District Consumer Disputes Redressal Commission (District Commission).

(ii) If Rajneesh is not satisfied by the order of District Consumer Disputes Redressal Commission (District Commission), he can appeal against such order to the State Consumer Disputes Redressal Commission (State Commission) within 45 days from such order.

(iii) Reliefs that can be granted to Rajneesh in the above case are

- To replace the defective product with a new one.
- To refund the price paid for the product.

Long Case Studies

Case Study 11

Ravi was a regular customer at 'FreshMart,' a grocery store chain known for offering a wide range of products at competitive prices. However, during one of his visits, he realised that the store was selling some defective products, and their advertisements about certain discounts were misleading. Many customers like Ravi were unaware of their rights and continued to purchase the defective items without raising complaints. Moreover, the customers lacked any unified platform to voice their concerns effectively.

Ravi felt that consumers like him were being taken advantage of due to their lack of knowledge and unorganised status. Meanwhile, certain consumer organisations were working hard to protect consumers' interests but were still not powerful enough to address these widespread issues.

This situation highlighted the need for stricter protection and consumer awareness to safeguard their rights and interests. Quoting lines from the above paragraph, identify and explain three importance of consumer protection discussed in the above case.

Ans. Consumer protection is important because of the following reasons as indicated in the case

(i) **Consumer Ignorance**

"Many customers like Ravi were unaware of their rights and continued to purchase the defective items without raising complaints."

This highlights the importance of educating consumers about their rights and the reliefs available to them.

Consumer protection is necessary to raise awareness and ensure consumers are informed about the products they purchase and the actions they can take in case of unfair treatment.

(ii) **Unorganised Consumers**

"Moreover, the customers lacked any unified platform to voice their concerns effectively." Consumers often lack the organisation needed to protect their interests. Consumer protection emphasises the importance of organising consumers into powerful consumer organisations that can advocate for their rights and safeguard their interests against unfair practices.

(iii) **Widespread Exploitation of Consumers**

"Ravi felt that consumers like him were being taken advantage of due to their lack of knowledge and unorganised status." This points out how consumers are vulnerable to exploitative practices like defective products and misleading advertisements. Consumer protection is vital to prevent such exploitation by ensuring strict regulations against unfair trade practices and offering consumers proper channels for redressal.

Case Study 12

Vivek is engaged in trading of Refrigerator. He purchases these refrigerators from Mohan Electronics, the manufacturer. All the refrigerators are certified by 'Bureau of Indian Standards'. During Diwali season, Mohan Electronics supplied some defective refrigerators to Vivek.

Vivek is getting complaints about the refrigerators from almost all customers.

(i) Who amongst the following can exercise his/her 'Right' and against whom?
  (a) Vivek (b) Mohan Electronics
  (c) Consumers

(ii) Define 'Consumer' as per the provisions of the Consumer Protection Act, 2019 and state the right that can be exercised to get relief.

Ans.

(i) Consumers can exercise their rights against Mohan Electronics.

(ii) Under the Consumer Protection Act, 2019, a consumer is a person, who buys any good or avails any service for a consideration which has been paid or promised, or partly paid and partly promised, or under any scheme of deferred payment.

The term includes any other user of such goods or services when such use is made with the approval of the buyer. It applies to both offline and online transactions through electronic means or by teleshopping or direct selling or multilevel marketing.

The term 'consumer', however, does not include a person, who obtains goods for resale or for any commercial purpose, or a person, who avails such services for any commercial purpose.

The right which can be exercised to get relief is Right to Seek Redressal. According to this right, consumer has the right to get relief in case the product falls short of his expectations. The Act provides various reliefs to the consumers like compensation for any loss or injury suffered by the consumers, replacement of goods or removal of defects in the goods, etc.

Case Study 13

Meera was excited to buy a new food processor for her kitchen. She visited a local store, which was offering a huge discount on electrical appliances. While browsing, she noticed that many of the appliances, including the food processor she was interested in, did not have the ISI mark. Despite the store's claims of quality, she was concerned about the safety of these products. Additionally, when she inquired about the specifications and ingredients of the products, the salesperson gave vague and incomplete information.

Meera wanted to ensure that she was buying a safe and reliable product, but she felt misinformed. She also noticed that the store offered limited brands and varieties of food processors, giving her fewer options to choose from. Meera felt that her rights as a consumer were not being respected and considered reporting this issue to a consumer protection organisation.

Quoting lines from the above paragraph, identify and explain three rights of consumers discussed in the case.

Ans. Following are the three rights of consumers discussed in the case

(i) **Right to Safety**

"She noticed that many of the appliances, including the food processor she was interested in, did not have the ISI mark." This highlights the Right to Safety, which ensures consumers are protected from goods that are hazardous to life and health. In this case, Meera was concerned about the absence of standard safety marks (ISI), which serve as an assurance of quality and safety for electrical products.

(ii) **Right to be Informed**

"When she inquired about the specifications and ingredients of the products, the salesperson gave vague and incomplete information."

This reflects the right to be informed, which entitles consumers to complete and accurate information about the product, such as its quality, ingredients, price and expiry date.

Meera's dissatisfaction with the lack of clear details shows that her right to receive proper product information was violated.

(iii) **Right to be Assured**

"She also noticed that the store offered limited brands and varieties of food processors, giving her fewer options to choose from."

This relates to the right to be assured, which ensures consumers have access to a variety of products at competitive prices.

Meera's concern about the limited variety of food processors indicates that she was not provided with enough options to make an informed and wise purchase decision.

Case Study 14

Mrs. Mathur sent a jacket to a laundry shop in January, 2018. The jacket was purchased at a price of ₹ 4,500. She had previously sent the jacket for dry cleaning with Shine Dry Cleaners and the jacket was cleaned well. However, she noticed that her jacket had white discolouration marks when she collected the jacket this time.

On informing the dry cleaner, Mrs. Mathur received a letter confirming that discolouration indeed appeared after the jacket was dry cleaned.

She contacted the dry cleaner multiple times and requested for compensation for discoloured jacket but to no avail. Upon consumer court's intervention, Shine Dry Cleaners agreed to compensate ₹ 2,500 to Mrs. Mathur for the discoloured jacket. NCERT

(i) Which right was exercised by Mrs. Mathur at the first instance?
(ii) Name and explain the right which helped Mrs. Mathur to avail the compensation.
(iii) State which consumer responsibility has been fulfilled by Mrs. Mathur in the above case.
(iv) State any other two responsibilities to be assumed by the consumers.

Ans.

(i) Right that was exercised by Mrs. Mathur at the first instance was right to be heard.
(ii) Right to seek redressal helped Mrs Mathur to avail the compensation. According to this right, consumer has the right to get relief in case the product falls short of his expectations.

The Act provides various reliefs to the consumers like compensation for any loss or injury suffered by the consumers, replacement of goods or removal of defects in the goods, etc.

(iii) Mrs. Mathur filed a complaint in an appropriate consumer court due to the defect of discolouration marks on her jacket.
(iv) Two other responsibilities of consumers are
- A consumer must ensure that he/she gets a fair deal.
- A consumer should always ask for a cash memo, as it serves as a proof of purchase required at the time of taking any action against a fraudulent seller/ manufacturer.

Case Study 15

Suresh has opened an NGO for the welfare of the consumers. He has got a degree in law. In order to utilise his education he quite often helps people in their legal affairs. Now that he has started an NGO he assures that whenever a consumer in his knowledge is deprived of his consumer rights he should file a complaint on his behalf in the consumer court and fight for his cause. His organisation has some of the people with journalist background.

The three of them along with Suresh from the side of their NGO have launched a monthly magazine which creates awareness about the rights, reliefs and responsibilities of the consumers.

All the members of this NGO work with a lot of enthusiasm. Recently in the central part of the city they organised a training program in which all the information related to the exploitation of consumers, consumer ignorance, consumer rights and reliefs available to the consumers were the key highlights. The government has also provided support to their organisation. The government laboratories are easily in touch with them and are ready for any type of confirmation of results related to the purity of products.

More and more members are getting attached with the organisation. The membership is increasing.

The organisation recently helped few ladies stage a demonstration outside the showroom of a company responsible for selling a fake electrical appliance responsible for the death of one man.

In totality the NGO is doing a great job. State the various functions performed by NGOs for the protection of the interest of consumers.

Ans. Following are the functions performed by NGOs for the protection of the interest of consumers.

(i) Educating the general public about consumer rights by organising training programmes, seminars and workshops.
(ii) Imparting knowledge about consumer problems, legal reporting, reliefs available and other matters of interest by publishing periodicals and publications.
(iii) Carrying out comparative testing of consumer products in accredited laboratories to test relative qualities of competing brands and publishing the test results for the benefit of consumers.
(iv) Encouraging consumers to strongly protest and take action against any unscrupulous, exploitative and unfair trade practice of the seller.
(v) Providing legal assistance to consumers by providing aid, advice, etc. to seek legal remedy.
(vi) Filing complaints in appropriate consumer courts on behalf of the consumers.
(vii) Taking an initiative in filing cases in consumer courts in the interest of general public, not for any individual.

SELF ASSESSMENT TEST

Objective Type Questions

1. Golu bought an iron from 'Sidhu Electricals'. She got an electric shock while using the iron. Which consumer right has been violated here?
   (a) Right to be heard (b) Right to seek redressal
   (c) Right to safety (d) Right to choose
2. National Commission government is actively advertising for 'Jago Grahak Jago'. Which consumer right is highlighted in the given statement?
   (a) Right to be heard
   (b) Right to consumer education
   (c) Right to seek redressal
   (d) Right to be informed
3. Informing consumer about the contents of the product, its usage, etc. is part of
   (a) right to safety
   (b) right to information
   (c) right to consumer education
   (d) right to be heard
4. Mention the quality mark which a consumer should look for while purchasing jewellery.
   (a) ISI Mark (b) FSSAI Mark
   (c) Eco Mark (d) Hall Mark
5. A complaint can be filed against a seller, manufacturer or a dealer of goods whose goods are .... in any manner.
   (a) perfect (b) flawless
   (c) defective (d) None of these
6. A consumer is not certain satisfied with State Commission. In how many days, he/she can challenge the same and approach the National Commission?
   (a) 20 days (b) 30 days
   (c) 40 days (d) 50 days

Answers 1. (c) 2. (b) 3. (b) 4. (d) 5. (c) 6. (b)

Short Answer Type Questions

7. What is the objective of the Consumer Protection Act, 2019?
8. Explain any three points of importance of consumer protection from the point of view of consumer.
9. Discuss any three rights of the consumer under the Consumer Protection Act.
10. Explain in brief the procedure for filing a complaint under the Consumer Protection Act, 2019.
11. Raj purchases a machine for ₹ 3 crore and it was not as per specifications. The defect was not rectified even after many complaints. Suggest appropriate authority to file complaint. Can he appeal to Supreme Court if not satisfied with the order of appropriate authority?
12. "Consumer is entitled to certain reliefs if the consumer court is satisfied about the genuineness of the complaint". State any four such reliefs.
13. Explain the role of consumer organisations and Non-Governmental Organisations (NGOs) in safeguarding and promoting consumer interests, highlighting any four key points.

Long Answer Type Questions

14. Explain the importance of consumer protection from the point of view of a business.
15. Mohan saw an advertisement on television regarding purchase and sale of electronic items. In this context, as an informed consumer, what responsibilities can Mohan exercise?
16. "Consumer Protection Act, 2019 provides a proper redressal mechanism to the consumer for their protection."

    In the light of the given statement, discuss in detail the redressal mechanism and its functioning.

PROJECT WORK

PROJECT 1
Principles of Management

PROJECT 2
Marketing

PROJECT Report

A project report is a written statement of what the analyser analyses in his/her evaluation. The project report needs to be prepared with great care and consideration.

A project report should

- be handwritten
- be concise
- be clear
- have diagrammatic presentation
- have a length of 25 to 30 pages
- have topics with suitable headings
- end up with conclusion

Elements

Try to ensure that your report contains the following elements

Title Page

This should include the project title, name of the company on which you are conducting your research and name of the student. You can also list the name of your school, class and subject teacher.

Acknowledgement

It is usual to thank those individuals, who have provided particularly useful assistance, technical or otherwise, during your project. In this, you pleased your supervisor as he/she will have invested quite a lot of time in overseeing your progress. You can also give a note of thank to the department of the company, which provides you a relevant data.

Content Page

This should list the main sections and sub-sections of your report. Choose self-explanatory titles with their respective pages and use double spacing for clarity. Content should be impressive and explanatory so that the reader would clearly understand the motto of the project.

Try to avoid too many levels of sub-heading.

Introduction

This is one of the most important component of the project report. It should begin with a clear statement of what the project is about, so that the nature and scope of the project can be understood by a reader. It should summarise everything which you set out to achieve and provide a clear summary of the project's background, relevance and main contributions. The introduction should set the context for the project and should provide the reader with a summary of the key things to look out for in, the remainder of the report. It is useful in stating the main objectives of the project as part of the introduction.

Background

The background section of the report should set the project into action, it specifies the problem of the company, what remedial actions were taken by the company, what are its effects. It proposes the layout of whole project.

Body of Report

The central part of the report usually consists of three or four sections detailing the technical work undertaken during the project. The structure of these sections is highly project dependent. They can reflect the chronological development of the project. It includes the detailed description regarding the matter of the project.

Evaluation

This might involve quantitative and qualitative evaluation such as expressibility, functionality, ease-of-use, etc of a product. At some point, you should also evaluate the strengths and weaknesses of what you have done. It includes certain questionnaires, sampling test which help in evaluating the result on the basis of truths and facts.

Conclusion

The conclusion should list the things, which have been learnt as a result of the work you have done. It shows the ultimate response of the project undertaken by a student. It should be expressive and impressive so that a reader would clearly evaluate the result and rated you on the basis of your presentation.

PROJECT WORK

Title of the project	Project Report on Application of Principles of Management
Company Chosen for the Project	Domino's
Name	....
School	....
Year	....
Class	XII A
Submitted to	....

Yeh Hai
Rishton Ka Time

Project Work

Contents

Acknowledgement

I would like to express my profound gratitude towards many individuals, as without their kind support, it would not be possible for me to complete this project report. I would like to extend my sincere thanks to my teacher, who gave me the golden opportunity in enhancing my hidden capabilities.

Unfortunately, I addressed several difficulties in coordinating the activities of the project but I am highly indebted to Mrs .... for her guidance and constant supervision, as well as for providing necessary information regarding the project and also for her support in completing the project.

I would also like to express my gratitude towards my parents and subject teacher for their kind co-operation and encouragement as they helped me a lot in completion of this project.

I would love if you appreciate the quality and performance of this work.

At last, I end up by thanking all who helped me in finalising the project within the limited time frame.

Introduction of Henri Fayol
(1841-1925)

Henri Fayol was a French management theorist, whose theories concerning scientific organisation of labour were widely influencial in the beginning of twentieth century. He graduated from the Mining Academy of St Etienne in 1860 in mining engineering. The 19 year old engineer started at the mining company, 'Compagnie de Commentary-Fourchambean-Decazeville, ultimately acting as its managing director during 1888-1918.

Fayol was the first to introduce four functions of management - Planning, Organising, Directing and Controlling, although his version was a bit different - Plan, Organise, Command, Coordinate and Control. According to Fayol, all activities of an industrial undertaking could be divided into – Technical, Commercial, Financial, Security, Accounting and Managerial. He also suggested that a manager must possess qualities like physical, moral, education, knowledge and experience.

Based on his experience, he developed his own concept of administration. The principles propounded by Fayol were published in 1917 in his book 'Administration Industrielle at Generale'. For his contribution, he is also known as 'Father of General Management'. Henri Fayol developed 14 principles of general management, which provide guidelines for decision-making and action.

Principles of General Management

1. **Division of Work**

   Fayol has advocated the division of work. According to him, if work is divided into small tasks and assigned to trained specialists, then it will help in taking the advantage of specialisation.

   The intent of division of work is to produce more and better work with the same effort. It is the most efficient way to use human effort. Because of this principle, an organisation is divided into separate departments, viz production, sales, finance, marketing, etc.

2. **Authority and Responsibility**

   Authority means the right to give orders and obtain obedience. On the other hand, responsibility means obligation to complete the assigned task on time.

   According to Fayol, there must be a balance between authority and responsibility. Excess of authority without matching responsibility may result in misuse of authority, whereas excess responsibility without adequate authority may lead to failure of organisational goals.

3. **Discipline**

   It is the sincerity and obedience towards organisational rules and regulations, as these are necessary for the smooth functioning of an organisation. According to Fayol, good superiors at all levels, fair agreements and judicious application of penalties are helpful in maintaining discipline.

   It means obedience on part of workers as well as managers.

4. **Unity of Command**

   The principle of unity of command states that each participant in a formal organisation should receive orders and is responsible to only one superior.

   If in any case, employee gets orders from two superiors at the same time, the principle of unity of command is violated and it will result in confusion and chaos.

5. **Unity of Direction**

It implies that there should be one head and one plan for a group of activities having the same objective. In other words, the related activities should be put under one group, there should be one plan of action for them and they should be in the control of one manager.

6. **Subordination of Individual Interest to General Interest**

The interest of an organisation is to achieve its goals. These goals are achieved after integrating the efforts of different individuals who are working in the organisation to satisfy their own personal needs.

Thus, the interests of various stakeholders, i.e. owners, shareholders, creditors, financers and the society cannot be sacrificed for one individual.

7. **Remuneration of Employees**

According to Fayol, the quantum and methods of remuneration payable to employees should be fair and reasonable. It should be satisfactory to both employers and employees, which gives them a reasonable standard of living and should be within the paying capacity of the company.

8. **Centralisation and Decentralisation**

The concentration of decision-making authority is called centralisation whereas its dispersal among more than one person is known as decentralisation.

According to Fayol, an organisation should strive to achieve a proper balance between centralisation and decentralisation according to size of organisation, ability of superiors, ability of subordinates, etc.

9. **Scalar Chain**

According to Fayol, scalar chain refers to the chain of authority and communication that runs from top to bottom and should be followed by managers and their subordinates.

Gang plank refers to an arrangement in which two managers working at the same level can communicate with each other directly for quick communication.

10. **Order**

As per this principle, there should be an orderly arrangement of men and material which implies that there is a fixed place for everything and everyone in the organisation.

A place for everything, called material order, and a place for everyone, called social order, ensures that there is no hindrance in the activity going on in the organisation.

11. **Equity**

This principle emphasises kindliness and justice in the behaviour of managers towards workers. It will bring loyalty and devotion in the behaviour of employees and they will put their best to achieve the targets.

There should be no discrimination against anyone on account of sex, religion, language, caste or belief and equal opportunities should be available for all.

12. **Stability of Personnel**

According to Fayol, employee turnover should be minimised to maintain organisational efficiency. Therefore, suppose an individual gets selected for a post, then he should be given appropriate time to prove his abilities.

We can say, he should be kept at the post for a minimum fixed tenure. This ensures stability and thus, he can get proper time to explore his skills.

13. **Initiative**

Fayol suggested that employees at all levels should take initiatives or actions without any force or boundations. They should be encouraged to develop and carry out plans for improvements. Initiative means taking the first step with self-motivation. This will help to motivate them and they will work hard for the betterment of the organisation.

14. **Esprit De Corps**

It means union is strength. Fayol emphasised on team work. He suggested that every employee must consider himself as part of team. This spirit brings harmony in the groups and they strive to work hard to achieve the targets of an organisation. For this, managers should replace 'I' with 'We' in all his conversations.

About Domino's

Domino's Pizza is an American restaurant chain and international franchise pizza delivery corporation, headquartered at the Domino Farms Office Park (the campus being owned by Domino's Pizza co-founder Tom Monaghan) in Ann Arbor Charter Township, Michigan, United States, near Ann Arbor, Michigan.

Founded in 1960, Domino's is the second largest pizza chain in the United States (after Pizza Hut) and the largest worldwide, with more than 10,000 corporate and franchised stores in 70 countries. Domino's Pizza was sold to Bain Capital in 1998 and went public in 2004.

Domino's Pizza

The current Domino's logo introduced in 2012

DOMINO'S

Type	Public
Traded as	NYSE : DPZ
Founded	Ypsilanti, Michigan on June 10, 1960
Headquarters	Domino Farms Office Park, Ann Arbor Charter Township, Michigan, United States
Area Served	Worldwide
Key People	Tom Monaghan, Founder; J Patrick Doyle, CEO
Products	Italian-American cuisine, pizza, pasta, chicken wings, submarine sandwihces, wraps, desserts
Revenue	$ 2.47 billion USD (2017)
Employees	2,90,000 (January 2017)
Website	www.dominos.com (http://www.dominos.com)

Early Years

In 1960, Tom Monaghan and his brother, James, purchased Domi'Nick's, a small pizza store in Ypsilanti, Michigan, near Eastern Michigan University. The deal was secured by a $500 down payment and the brothers borrowed $900 to pay for the store. The brothers planned to split the work hours evenly, but James didn't want to quit his job as a full-time mailman to keep up with the demands of the new business. Within eight months, James traded his half of the business to Tom for the Volkswagen Beetle, they used for pizza deliveries.

By 1965, Tom Monaghan had purchased two additional pizzerias; he now had a total of three locations in the same country. Monaghan wanted the stores to share the same branding but the original owner forbade him from using the DomiNick's name. One day, an employee returned from a pizza delivery and suggested the name Domino's. Monaghan immediately loved the idea and officially renamed the business Domino's Pizza, Inc in 1965.

The company logo originally had three dots, representing the three stores in 1965. Monaghan planned to add a new dot with the addition of every new store, but this idea quickly faded, as Domino's experienced rapid growth.

Domino's Pizza opened its first franchise location in 1967 and by 1978, the company expanded to 200 stores. In 1975, Domino's faced a lawsuit by Amstar Corporation, the maker of Domino Sugar, alleging trademark infringement and unfair competition. On 2nd May 1980, the Fifth Circuit Court of Appeals in New Orleans found in favour of Domino's Pizza.

International Expansion

On 12th May, 1983, Domino's opened its first international store in Winnipeg, Manitoba, Canada. That same year, Domino's opened its 1000th store overall. In 1997, Domino's opened its 1500th international location, opening seven stores in one day across five continents. From 2007 to 2012, Domino's gradually established a presence in India with atleast 1000 locations by 2012. By 2014, the company had grown to 6000 international locations.

Potential for over 2,800 additional restaurants in Domino's top 10 international markets

Top 10 Markets	YE 2011 Store Count	Delivery Market Position	Potential Store Count
United Kingdom	670	1	1100
Mexico	577	1	700
Australia	450	1	650
India	439	1	1000
South Korea	358	2	400
Canada	354	3	400
Turkey	220	1	500
Japan	205	3	700
France	195	1	850
Taiwan	141	2	150
TOTAL	**3,609**		**6450**

International Operations

Domino's Pizza currently has locations in 73 countries. It has its stores in 5700 cities worldwide (2900 international and 2,800 in the US). Domino's has 10988 stores as of the first quarter of 2014, with 774 in the UK, 4986 in the US and 715 in India. In most cases, Domino's has master franchise agreements with one company per country, but three companies have acquired multiple master franchise agreements, covering a number of countries:

- The master franchises for India, Nepal, Sri Lanka and Bangladesh are currently owned by the Indian company Jubilant Food Works.
- India has become the largest international market for Domino's outside its home market. Indian pizza flavours like paneer pizza, chicken tikka masala pizza and kheema do pyaza pizza are selling internationally.
- In 2013, Domino's UK and Ireland published a video showing a proof-of-concept 'DomiCopter', a drone capable of delivering a pizza.

Sale of the Company

In 1998, after 38 years of ownership, Domino's Pizza founder Tom Monaghan announced his retirement, sold 93% of the company to Bain Capital Inc, for about $ 1 billion, and ceased being involved in day-to-day operations of the company. A year later, the company named David A Brandon, as the CEO.

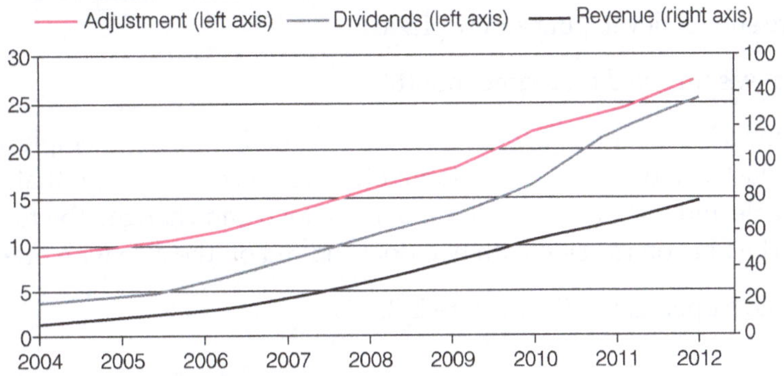

Current Era

In 2004, after 44 years as a privately held company, Domino's began trading common stock on the New York Stock Exchange under the ticker symbol 'DPZ'. Industry trade publication Pizza Today magazine named Domino's Pizza 'Chain of the Year' in 2003, 2010, and 2011. In a simultaneous celebration in January 2006, Domino's opened its 5000th US store in Huntley, Illinois and its 3000th international store in Panama City, Panama making 8000 total stores for the system. In August 2006, the Domino's location in Tallaght, Dublin, Ireland, became the first store in Domino's history to hit a turnover of $3 million (2.35 million) per year. As of September 2006, Domino's has 8238 stores worldwide, which totalled $1.4 billion in gross income.

Innovations

- In 2007, Domino's introduced its 'Veterans delivering the dream' franchising programme and also rolled out its online and mobile ordering sites.
- In 2008, Domino's introduced the 'Pizza Tracker', an online application, that allows customers to view the status of their order in a simulated 'real time' progress bar.
- The first Domino's with a dining room opened in Stephenville, Texas, giving the customers the option to either eat in or take their pizza home.
- Domino's announced plans to entirely reinvent its pizza. It began a self-criticising ad campaign in which consumers were filmed criticising the then-current pizza's quality and chefs were shown developing a new pizza.
- The new pizza was unveiled that same month.
- In 2012, Domino's Pizza removed the word 'Pizza' from their logo, to emphasise their non-pizza products. At the same time, Domino's introduced a new logo that removed the blue rectangle and text under the domino in the logo and changed the formerly all-red domino to be blue on the side with two dots and red on the side with one dot.
- In 2016, Domino's opened its 1000th store in India.

Menu

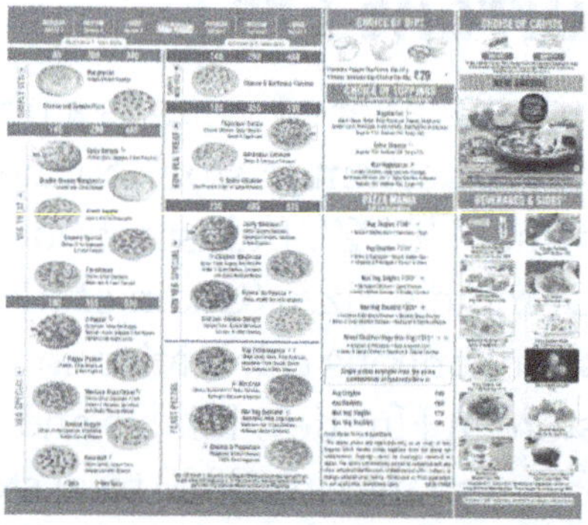

The Domino's menu varies by region. The current Domino's menu in the United States features a variety of Italian-American entrees and side dishes. Pizza is the primary focus, with traditional, speciality and custom pizzas available in a variety of crust styles and toppings. In 2011, Domino's launched artisan-style pizzas. Additional entrees include pasta, bread bowls, and oven-baked sandwiches. The menu offers chicken side dishes, breadsticks, as well as beverages and desserts.

Domino's constantly strives to develop products that suit the tastes of the consumers and hence delighting them. Domino's believes strongly in the strategy of 'Think global and act local'. Thus, time and again they have been innovating with delicious new products such as crusts, toppings and flavours suitable to the taste buds of Indian consumers. Further providing value for money and affordable products to their consumers has been an important part of their efforts. The initiatives such as Fun Meal and Pizza Mania have been extremely popular with consumers looking for an affordable and value for money meal option.

Corporate Governance Philosophy

The corporate governance philosophy of the company is driven by the interest of stakeholders and business needs of the organisation. Aligning itself to this philosophy and in order to sustain the shareholders' trust, the company has placed corporate governance on a high priority.

The highlights of the company's corporate governance regime are:

- At the core of the company's corporate governance practice is Board of Directors, which oversees how the management serves and protects the long-term interests of all the stakeholders. The company believes that an active, well-informed and independent board is necessary to ensure high standards of corporate governance. To ensure the independence of the board, the majority of the Board members, four out of seven, are independent directors.
- Constitution of several committees, such as Audit Committee, Nomination, Remuneration and Compensation Committee, Stakeholders Relationship Committee, Sustainability and Corporate Social Responsibility Committee, etc for focused attention, enables the company to ensure expedient resolution of diversified matters.
- The Code of Conduct for directors and senior management, along with the code for prevention of insider trading formulated in terms of the SEBI Guidelines, constitute strong parameters of company's corporate governance philosophy.
- Establishment of whistle blower policy to ensure utmost transparency in business. This policy acts as a neutral and unbiased forum for the directors, employees and business partners of the company and its subsidiaries (both Indian and foreign) to voice concerns in a responsible and effective manner without fear of reprisal.
- Strong focus on hiring, retaining and nurturing best talent and on promoting a culture of excellence across the organisation. Exhaustive HRD policies cover succession planning, training and development, employee grievance handling. Employee stock option plans - to attract, reward and retain key senior executives.
- Regular communication with shareholders, including e-mailing of financial performance, to enhance the trust and confidence of the shareholders.

Charitable Activities

- In 2001, Domino's launched a two-year national partnership with the Make-A-Wish Foundation of America. That same year, company stores in New York city and Washington DC provided more than 12000 pizzas to relief workers following the 11th September attacks on the World Trade Center and The Pentagon.
- Through a matching funds programme, the corporation donated $350000 to the American Red Cross' disaster relief effort.
- In 2004, Domino's began a partnership with St Jude Children's Research Hospital, participating in the hospital's 'Thanks and Giving' campaign, since the campaign began in 2004 and raising more than $ 1.3 million in 2006.

Advertising

In the 1980s, Domino's Pizza was well known for its advertisements featuring the Noid. That concept was created by Group 243 Inc who then hired Will Vinton Studios, to produce the television commercials that they created. The catchphrase associated with the commercials was 'Avoid the Noid'.

Sponsorship

Domino's sponsored CART's Doug Shierson Racing, which was driven by Arie Luyendyk and won the 1990 Indianapolis 500. In 2003, Domino's teamed up with NASCAR for a multi-year partnership to become the 'Official Pizza of NASCAR'.

Domino's also sponsored Michael Waltrip Racing and driver David Reutimann during the 2007 season in the NASCAR Sprint Cup Series.

International Store Growth Since YE 2008

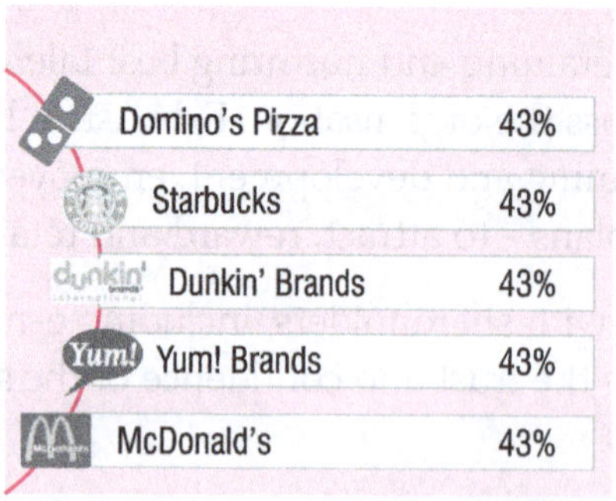

Applications of Fayol's Principles in Domino's

1. **Division of Work**

   This principle is certainly implemented in Domino's as all employees are divided into departments according to their capabilities and expertise to indulge in an activity. People with special talent are placed in the appropriate department so that they may practice such activities repetitively and achieve specialisation. On this basis, its functioning has been divided into a number of departments, viz:

   - Human resource department
   - Payroll department
   - Complaint department
   - Marketing department
   - Property department

   As per my survey, the employees of Domino's work for two or more jobs, i.e. job rotation, as it acts as an incentive to them and at the same time, they get an opportunity to learn newer activities. Thus, division of work in Domino's is quite evident from the working of the organisation.

2. **Authority and Responsibility**

   In Domino's, it was observed that each employee is given adequate authority to perform his tasks along with the responsibility to complete it in time. e.g. the chef in the outlet is given full authority to use the materials and products, but is responsible to prepare the order within the requisite time. Thus, there is a balance between authority and responsibility of each employee. The employees give efficient performance with the presence of required authority, but do not have scope for misuse of authority.

3. **Discipline**

   Good discipline is an essential in all successful organisations. On the basis of my survey, I came to a realisation that Domino's has clear and fair agreements regarding working conditions and regulations in the organisation with respect to working hours, timings, leave rules, code of conduct, etc. Discipline ensures obedience to the employment terms and conditions, in order to maintain coordination in activities and ensures systematic working.

4. Unity of Command

An analysis of the organisation structure of Domino's clearly exhibits unity of command, being followed at all levels of the organisation. There is a clear superior at each level of individual subordinates. e.g. the branch manager of each branch has full control over the employees working in the particular branch, while, he himself is accountable to the higher level authorities. Thus, it clearly shows that each subordinate work under the command of a superior, so that there is no confusion in the works to be done and no conflict among superiors, which lead to smooth functioning of the organisation.

5. Unity of Direction

This principle is evident in the working of Domino's. The major objective of Domino's is to maintain its position in the market and achieve specialisation, for which production and sales departments keep struggling, so that the organisational goals are achieved. This helps the employees to realise the goals that they have to work for and work for its success. They believe in unity is strength, whereas, teamwork and collaboration help to achieve even the unexpected. e.g. when the company undertook an advertising campaign of '30 minutes or free' offer, to broaden its customer base, the top level made the plan while the middle and lower levels facilitated the implementation of such plan successfully.

6. Remuneration of Employees

On the basis of the information supplied by employees in the questionnaire, it is discovered that the remuneration paid to employees are just and equitable. Equal wages are provided to people working at the same levels. Employees are satisfied with the compensation and incentive plan of the company. This ensure employees a reasonable standard of living. In case of work overtime, they are paid wages at a higher rate. Employees are encouraged to work for extra time to achieve targets because of such schemes. At the same time, it is within the paying capacity of Domino's.

7. Centralisation and Decentralisation

Domino's concentrates on centralised structure, so that control is maintained over all their outlets with uniformity. It is necessary to ensure consistency of customer need satisfaction, service and quality at each outlet. Centralisation helps the management to implement common policies and practices with uniformity all over its branches. This facilitates control and coordination among various outlets. It facilitates in achieving economies of scale, but leads to delayed decision-making. Employees lack initiative due to lack of authority to take decisions. The subordinates and employees lack recognition, authority and sense of belongingness in the organisation.

8. Scalar Chain

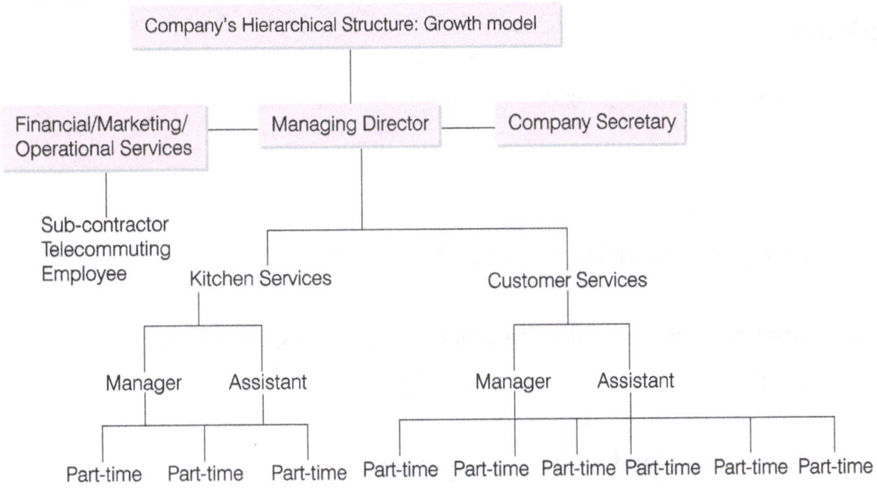

Within each branch of Domino's, there is a formal organisation structure, defining clear relationships among superiors and subordinates. At the top is the managing director, wholly responsible and accountable for their branch, working along with a company secretary and other managers in financial, marketing and operational areas. Further, the structure is divided into kitchen and customer services, looked after by managers as well as assistants.

9. Order

There is strict obedience of principle of order in Domino's, as there is a predetermined fixed place for all materials, food items, equipments, etc in each outlet. This helps the staff to do the work effectively and efficiently without any obstruction.

10. Esprit de Corps

This principle is undoubtedly followed in Domino's, as the staff in each outlet works with unity and harmony within the organisation. The reason behind the company's success is enthusiastic participation of each member like a family in the attainment of company's objectives. Since, there are clear lines of authority and opportunities provided to employees to take initiative, success of the company is an obvious occurence.

Questionnaire

A questionnaire was developed by the investigator to be filled by the employees:

1. Name of the employee ....

2. Job profile ....

3. Number of working years (in Domino's) ....

4. Are you satisfied with the working of the organisation?
   (a) Yes (b) No

5. Are you satisfied with your superiors?
   (a) Yes (b) No

6. Are you satisfied with your compensation?
   (a) Yes (b) No

7. Are you satisfied with the incentive plan of the company?
   (a) Yes (b) No

8. Do you find that rules and regulations equally applicable on all employees?
   (a) Yes (b) No

9. Any suggestion for improvement in working ....

Observation

According to the survey and the information gathered from the employees through the questionnaire, I observed the following:

Level of Satisfaction with regard to compensation	Number of Employees
Highly Satisfied	....
Satisfied	....
Dissatisfied	....

Level of satisfaction with regard to working conditions	Number of Employees
Highly Satisfied	....
Satisfied	....
Dissatisfied	....

Level of satisfaction with regard to discipline	Number of Employees
Highly Satisfied	....
Satisfied	....
Dissatisfied	....

Level of satisfaction with regard to working hours	Number of Employees
Highly Satisfied	....
Satisfied	....
Dissatisfied	....

Conclusion

According to the survey, that I conducted for the customers and employees of Domino's, I conclude that the 14 principles of management propounded by Henri Fayol are applicable and followed in Domino's. It follows the principles of division of work, authority and responsibility, discipline, unity of command, unity of direction, remuneration of employees, centralisation and decentralisation, scalar chain, order and esprit de corps.

As a result, they have gained benefits of specialisation, better working, systematic operations, loyal employees, coordinated work and order and discipline in the organisation. This is the base of the success of Domino's, as the market leader in the industry.

Viva Questions

1. Who was Henri Fayol?
2. State two major contributions of Fayol to management.
3. What is 'division of work'? State its positive effects.
4. What are the adverse effects of violating principle of 'discipline'?
5. What does 'unity of command' ensure?
6. What is 'scalar chain' meant for? Where is it used?
7. What are the positive effects of following principle of 'order' and 'equity'?
8. Who was the founder of Domino's and how it came into existence?
9. State two innovations in Domino's over the years.
10. List few countries where Domino's has spread its operations.
11. List few reasons that you consider as the reason for its success.
12. State one example of a principle of management followed in Domino's.

PROJECT WORK

Title of the Project	Project Report on Marketing
Product Chosen for the Project	**Toothpaste**
Name	....
School	....
Year	....
Class	XII A
Submitted to	....

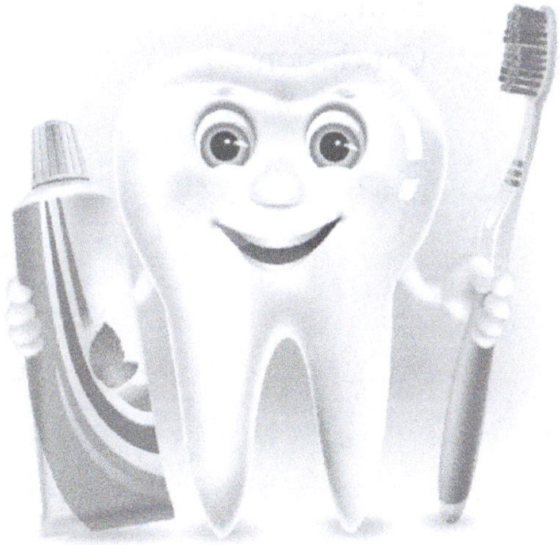

Contents

Acknowledgement

I would like to express my profound gratitude towards many individuals, as without their kind support, it would not be possible for me to complete this project report. I would like to extend my sincere thanks to my teacher, who gave me the golden opportunity in enhancing my hidden capabilities.

Unfortunately, I addressed several difficulties in coordinating the activities of the project but I am highly indebted to Mrs .... for her guidance and constant supervision, as well as for providing necessary information regarding the project and also for her support in completing the project.

I would also like to express my gratitude towards my parents and subject teacher for their kind cooperation and encouragement, as they helped me a lot in completion of this project.

I would love if you appreciate the quality and performance of this work.

At last, I end up by thanking all who helped me in finalising the project within the limited time frame.

Introduction

Marketing

Marketing, as we all are aware of, is the process of identification and understanding the needs and wants of customers, developing goods or services to satisfy them, offering them something better than the competitors, at a profit. It facilitates exchange of goods and services that satisfies people's needs and wants.

Marketing has profoundly affected our day-to-day lives. It is a part of everything we do viz, the things we use, the food we eat, the services we use and the environment we live in.

For a firm, marketing is a very important process, as it helps not only to create a place for the product in the market, but also make it survive for a long time, generating recurring sales, brand loyalty and profits for the firm.

Beginning with the decision of what to produce, its quality, features, standards, manufacturing process, branding, packaging, labelling, transportation, promotion and after sales services, all constitute the process of successful marketing.

Product Chosen for Marketing

Product	:	Toothpaste
Brand Name	:	Freshine
Tag Line	:	More Fresh, More Shine
Nature	:	Consumer : Non-durable
Range of the Product	:	Oral Care, Whitening and Herbal Toothpastes
Competing Brands	:	Close-up, Colgate, Pepsodent, Dabur-Red Sensodyne
Types of Oralcare	:	Toothpaste and Tooth Powder
Social Message	:	'Healthy People, Healthy India'

Toothpaste

Toothpaste is a paste or gel dentifrice used with a toothbrush as an accessory to clean and maintain the aesthetics and health of teeth. Toothpaste is used to promote oral hygiene: it serves as an abrasive that aids in removing the dental plaque and food from the teeth, assists in suppressing halitosis and delivers active ingredients (most commonly fluoride) to help prevent tooth and gum disease (gingivitis). Most of the cleaning is achieved by the mechanical action of the toothbrush, and not by the toothpaste. Salt and sodium bicarbonate (baking soda) are among materials that can be substituted for commercial toothpaste. Toothpaste is not intended to be swallowed due to the fluoride content, but is generally not very harmful if accidentally swallowed in small amounts. However, one should seek medical attention after swallowing abnormally large amounts.

A Consumer Product

Toothpaste is considered as a non-durable consumer product because it has the following features:

(i) It is consumed in single/few act of consumption.

(ii) It has a regular demand.

(iii) The price level and profit margin is usually low.

(iv) These are usually available at convenient locations. Therefore, they are called 'convenience goods'.

(v) The marketers have to advertise heavily for such a product.

(vi) Sales promotion techniques play an important role in the promotion of the product.

Benefits of a Toothpaste

(i) A toothpaste prevents tooth decay.

(ii) It prevents tartar build-up.

(iii) It freshens your breath.

(iv) It prevents gum disease.

(v) It makes your teeth feel clean.

(vi) It leaves a nice taste in your mouth.

(vii) It can be used to dry up spots.

(viii) It prevents gingivitis.

(ix) If you have sensitive teeth, you can use a senstivity toothpaste.

(x) It tastes nice.

(xi) It promotes good oral hygiene.

(xii) It helps your teeth stay white.

(xiii) It prevents foul smell.

(xiv) It prevents tooth decay.

Types of Toothpaste

There are many different types of toothpaste available in the market. Their various functions depend on the active ingredients they contain. The following are the common types of toothpaste:

(i) Anti-decay Toothpaste

They contain fluoride compounds such as sodium fluoride (NaF), stannous fluoride (SnF2), or Monofluorophosphate (MFP2), etc. If the fluoride content is 1000 ppm (parts per million) or above, they are all effective in preventing tooth decay. Children's toothpaste contains 500 ppm fluoride and is usually flavoured, e.g. fruit flavour, candy flavour, which is more appealing to children.

(ii) Desensitizing Toothpaste

The active ingredients provide relief from dentine hypersensitivity symptoms in two ways. First, they interrupt the neurone response to pain stimuli; second, they occlude the dentinal tubules of dentine. Active ingredients such as Potassium Nitrate or Arginine, etc are used by different product manufacturers. There are many different types of desensitizing toothpastes marketed by different brand names.

(iii) Anti-calculus Toothpaste

The manufacturer claims that the calcification of dental plaque could be retarded by this kind of toothpaste, thus it reduces the rate of calculus formation. The active ingredient is Pyrophosphate or Zinc Citrate, etc.

(iv) Anti-plaque Toothpaste

This kind of toothpaste inhibits plaque accumulation, reduces the toxic effects of the bacterial toxin on the tooth surrounding tissues, thereby reducing the chances of getting gum disease. In the market, there are different anti-plaque toothpastes which contain different active ingredients, e.g. Triclosan or Zinc Citrate, etc.

(v) Whitening Toothpaste

This kind of toothpaste contains relatively coarse abrasives which function by abrading the stains on the tooth surface, giving a whitening effect. The effects of the long-term use of this kind of toothpaste are still unknown.

(vi) Herbal and Natural Toothpastes

Companies such as Tom's of Maine, among others, manufacture natural and herbal toothpastes and market them to consumers who wish to avoid the artificial ingredients commonly found in regular toothpastes. Many herbal toothpastes do not contain fluoride or sodium lauryl sulphate. The ingredients found in natural toothpastes vary widely but often include baking soda, aloe, eucalyptus oil, myrrh, plant extract (strawberry extract), and essential oils.

Ingredients

In addition to 20-42% water, toothpastes are derived from a variety of components, the three main ones are:

(i) **Abrasives** Abrasives constitute atleast 50% of a typical toothpaste. These insoluble particles help to remove plaque from the teeth. The removal of plaque and calculus helps in minimising cavities and periodontal disease.

Abrasives, like the dental polishing agents' used in dentists offices, also cause a small amount of enamel erosion which is termed 'polishing' action. Some brands contain powdered white mica, which acts as a mild abrasive and also adds a cosmetically pleasing glittery shimmer to the paste.

(ii) **Fluorides** Fluoride in various forms is the most popular active ingredient in toothpaste to prevent cavities. Fluoride occurs in small amounts in plants, animals and some natural water sources. The additional fluoride in toothpaste has beneficial effects on the formation of dental enamel and bones.

(iii) **Surfactants** Many, although not all, toothpastes contain Sodium Lauryl Sulfate (SLS) or related surfactants (detergents). SLS is found in many other personal care products, as well, such as shampoo, and is mainly a foaming agent, which enables uniform distribution of toothpaste, improving its cleansing power.

Other Components

(i) **Antibacterial Agents** Triclosan, an antibacterial agent, is a common toothpaste ingredient in the United Kingdom. Triclosan or zinc chloride prevents gingivitis and according to the American Dental Association, helps to reduce tartar and bad breath.

(ii) **Flavourants** Toothpaste comes in a variety of colours and flavours intended to encourage use of the product. Three most common flavourants are peppermint, spearmint and wintergreen. More exotic flavours include anethole anise, apricot, bubblegum, cinnamon, fennel, lavender, neem, ginger, vanilla, lemon, orange and pine.

(iii) **Remineralizers** Hydroxyapatite nanocrystals and calcium phosphate are included in some formulations for remineralisation, i.e. the reformation of enamel.

(iv) **Miscellaneous Components** Agents are added to suppress the tendency of toothpaste to dry into a powder. Included are various sugar alcohols, such as glycerol, sorbitol or xylitol or related derivatives, such as 1, 2-propylene glycol and polyethyleneglycol.

Safety

Fluoride

Although water fluoridation has been praised as one of the top medical achievements of the 20th century, fluoride-containing toothpaste can be acutely toxic, if swallowed in large amounts. The risk of using fluoride is low enough that the use of 'full-strength' toothpaste (1350-1500 ppm fluoride) is advised for all ages (although smaller volumes are used for young children; a 'smear' of toothpaste until three years old). A major concern of dental fluorosis is for children under 12 months ingesting excessive fluoride through toothpaste. Several non-fluoride toothpastes are also available.

Diethylene Glycol

The inclusion of sweet-tasting but toxic diethylene glycol in Chinese-made toothpaste led to a several nation, multiple brand toothpaste recall in 2007. The world outcry made Chinese officials ban the practice of using diethylene glycol in toothpaste.

Triclosan

Reports have suggested triclosan, an active ingredient in many toothpastes, can combine with chlorine in tap water to form chloroform, which the United States Environmental Protection Agency classifies as a probable human carcinogen. An animal study revealed the chemical might modify hormone regulation and many other lab researches proved bacteria might be able to develop resistance to triclosan in a way which can help them to resist antibiotics, also.

Production Process

The production process of 'freshine' can be defined as follows:

(i) The liquid base is prepared first with water, sorbitol or glycerine and other liquid ingredients used.

(ii) Rheology modifiers may be pre-mixed with a non-aqueous liquid ingredient such as glycerin or the flavouring oil or dry blended with other powdered ingredients to aid dispersion.

(iii) The active ingredient, sweetener and preservative are added and dispersed.

(iv) The abrasive/filler is then added.

(v) Flavouring and colouring are added.

(vi) The detergent is added last under slow speed agitation to minimise foaming. It is typically in solid form to avoid adding water to the formulation at this stage.

Market Research

Need to Carry Out Market Research

Market research is necessary to be conducted as many organisations are described as product oriented or market oriented. Here, the marketer is market oriented which means that the whole organisation focuses on the needs of its consumers. It is, therefore, essential that it identifies and anticipates changing consumer needs before the development of new products.

Market research adds value to businesses by identifying consumers' needs. It helps them to plan ahead. e.g. looking at what products or extensions it should develop and for whom. It focuses the business on the needs of its consumers. An organisation that does this can improve its competitive advantage.

In addition to the resources required during development, suppliers must produce an advertising campaign to raise awareness of the product among consumers and encourage retailers to stock the product. Launching a new product can be a risky business. In order to reduce risks, market research is essential. A good research will help in new product extensions, gives more choice to consumers and helps them to feel more favourably about the existing brands.

Role of Market Research

Market research is the collection and analysis of data in the following order

(i) To identify and satisfy consumer needs.

(ii) The main purpose is to reduce risk and facilitate decision-making.

(iii) It is particularly useful while launching a new product and ensures that the right goods are produced.

(iv) Market research provides information on consumer needs and wants, competitors, the marketing mix and potential sales.

(v) By knowing all such crucial issues, firms are able to estimate the correct amount to produce/supply. This will reduce the financial risk involved and ensures the maximum return on investment.

Stage of Market Research

In order to develop the new toothpaste 'Freshine', the marketer undertook three distinct stages of research :

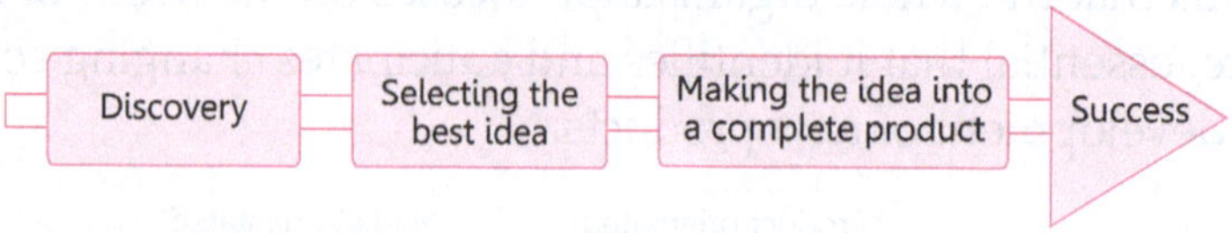

Stage 1 Discovery

Initial research aimed to identify a set of new ideas that would be suitable for developing a new product. Secondary research was used to find out about innovation trends in the toothpaste market. It was also used to find out about new products, types and brands available around the world.

Stage 2 Selecting the Best Idea

This stage aimed to select the best idea arising from the stage 1 research. The marketer puts the ideas among the Board members. The Board had pictures showing product ideas and a description of what the new product would be like. These were then shown to a large group of representative consumers in a quantitative survey. They were asked to rate those ideas against a number of scales, so that they could identify which product ideas, consumers liked the best or disliked.

Stage 3 Making the Idea into a Complete Product

When the best idea is selected from stage 2, the marketer uses this idea to make a real product. The research helped the marketer to explore the taste and features of the new product in more detail. The marketer needed to understand the 'experience' of the consumer before a decision could be made about how to develop the product in more detail.

Questionnaire

In order to conduct market research, the marketer has prepared the following questionnaire:

Dear Respondent,

We are conducting a survey on the types and brands of toothpastes available in the market, for the purpose of knowing the customers' needs and wants with regard to our new product.

(i) Your name : __________

(ii) Gender : __________

(iii) Number of members in the family : __________

(iv) Address : __________

(v) Brand of toothpaste presently used : __________

(vi) Reason for using that brand : __________

(vii) Which other brands are conveniently available at your location : __________

(viii) If provided a new product, what quality would you look for? __________

(ix) Price that you are paying for the product : __________

(x) Are you satisfied with the product : [Yes] [No]

(xi) Are you satisfied with the price : [Yes] [No]

Above mentioned interview questions will help in assessing the market situation and the existing information about the competitors.

Industry experts conducted such surveys to analyse the potential strength of the consumers and market.

Competiting Brands in Market

1. Plus White 

2. Sensodyne 

3. Colgate 

4. Oral-B 

5. Pepsodent 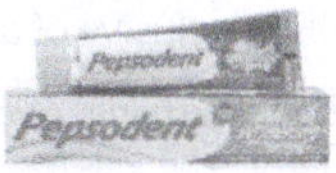

Branding

Branding refers to the process of giving a name, sign, symbol or a combination of all, to give an identity to the product. It helps the customers to identify the product in the market and distinguish it from the other products available in the market. It helps the marketer in advertising/display programmes and introduce new products easily in the market. A brand ensures quality and acts a status symbol for its customers.

As a marketer, I have chosen Freshine as the brand name of the toothpaste, because of the following reasons:

(i) **Simple and easy** 'Freshine' is short, simple, easy to remember, prounounce and use word, which can be used as a brandname.

(ii) **Suggestive** 'Freshine' is suggestive, as it indicates that the product provides freshness and shine, when used.

(iii) **Distinctive** It is different from the other brands of toothpaste in the market.

(iv) **Adaptable** It is a word, which is very much adaptable to the packaging and labelling of the product.

(v) **Versatile** It is a versatile name, as it can include a large range of products in it such as soap, detergents, toothbrush, cleaners, shoe-polish, etc.

(vi) **Staying power** 'Freshine' is a word that has a staying power, which would not get out of date in a short time period.

Labelling

Labelling is the process of designing and creating a 'label' for a product. A label can be a simple tag or a complex graphic, containing detailed information about the product, its contents, use, ingredients, weight, price, taxes, brand name, brand mark, tag line, social message and promotional message.

Following is the label of the toothpaste as designed by the marketer.

Ingredients	Directions	Other Information
....	Do not swallow	Batch No : ....
....	For adults and children above 2years	Date of Mfg : ....
....	Brush after 2 main meals.	Expiry Date : ....
Warning Keep Out of Reach of Children Under 6 Years of Age	Rinse well to avoid swallowing	MRP (inclusive of all taxes : ....

WARNING : Keep out of the reach of children under 6 years of age.
If you accidentally more than used for brushing, get medical help or contact a poison control center right away.

Packaging

Packaging refers to the process of designing and creating a wrapper or container for a product. There are three levels of packaging assigned to 'Freshine' by the marketer.

These are:

(i) **Primary package** It is the immediate container, in which a product is stored. For 'Freshine', the marketer has decided to use a 'tube' as the primary package which would:

(a) protect the paste from spoilage, leakage, damage and adulteration.

(b) help/facilitate in usage of product by the users.

(ii) **Secondary package** The marketer has decided to give a secondary package also to its product as it would:

(a) provide the product with an additional layer of protection.

(b) provide detailed information about the product by acting as a label.

(iii) **Transportation package** The marketer has also provided a third layer of packaging for the purpose of storage and transportation of product in bulk. It is in the form of large cardboard boxes, known as transportation package.

Pricing

Pricing refers to the process of setting the price for a product. It is a very crucial decision as it affects the sale and revenue of the firm. Various strategies of pricing used by marketers are :

(i) Absorption pricing
(ii) Contribution margin-based pricing
(iii) Skimming pricing
(iv) Decoy pricing
(v) High-low pricing
(vi) Limit pricing
(vii) Marginal cost pricing
(viii) Penetration pricing
(ix) Predatory pricing
(x) Premium pricing

The marketer has used penetration policy for pricing its product. It includes setting the price low with the goals of attracting customers and gaining market share. This price will be raised later, once the product captures the market. The following pricing decision has been taken by the marketer :

Quantity Selling Price	50 gms	100 gms	200 gms
To wholesaler	–	–	–
To retailer	–	–	–
To customer	–	–	–

Channels of Distribution

Various channels of distributions are used by marketers for the physical distribution of goods. These are:

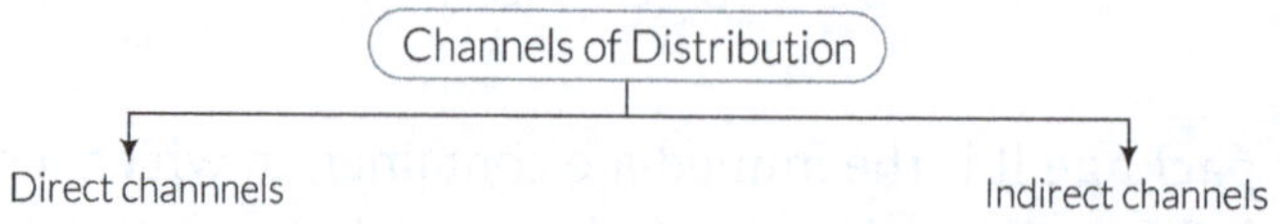

The marketer, in case of toothpaste, will choose indirect channel because of the following reasons :

(i) **Size of the market** Since the size of the market for a consumer non-durable product is large, it must use indirect channels of distribution.

(ii) **Nature of the product** When products are standardised, less bulky and non-technical, indirect channels must be used.

(iii) **Value of the product** Since the value of product is not high, indirect channels should be used.

(iv) **Regular demand Products** like toothpaste are non durable, frequently consumed and have a regular demand . Thus, indirect channels must be used.

(v) **Non-perishable** Since toothpaste is not perishable, it can be distributed through indirect channels.

On the basis of the above factors, it is advised that the marketer should make use of three-level channel of distribution.

Transportation and Warehousing

Transportation is the means of carrying goods and raw materials from the point of production to the point of sale. It is important because unless the goods are physically made available, the sale cannot be completed. It helps to create place utility by making the goods available, where they are required.

The marketer has decided to use the following modes of transportation:

(i) **Water transport** For transporting the goods abroad.

(ii) **Rail and road transport** For domestic transportation of goods to the markets.

The marketer would also make proper arrangements for warehousing in order to create time utility, i.e. making the goods available at the right time to the markets, as and when demanded by the consumers. Warehousing would depend on the following aspects:

(a) Time lag between production and consumption.

(b) Nearness to the markets and production sites.

(c) Nature of product.

(d) Arrangement for protection of goods.

Ways of Promotion

Promotion refers to the use of communication with the twin objectives of informing potential customers about a product and persuading them to buy it.

Promotion Techniques Opted by Company

(i) **Advertising on television** The company has used a 30 second TV commercial to promote the product over a wide area at economical cost per person.

(ii) **Advertising in newspapers** The company has used a weekly advertising plan to spread product information to those who do not pay attention to advertising on television.

(iii) **Personal selling** The company has planned to provide commissions to salesmen for promoting the product and achieve specific sales targets. Fringe benefits and free gifts are also offered on achieving targets.

(iv) **Sales promotion** The company uses sales promotion measures such as product combination, quantity gifts, sampling and contests from time to time to boost the sales in a short period.

(v) **Publicity** The company publicises its product by organising events, sponsoring programmes and working for social cause.

Unique Selling Proposition 'USP'

In order to face the stringent competition, the marketer has adopted two promotional measures as its USP. They are:

(i) **Direct selling through catalogues and internet** The marketer is promoting the sale of its product by offering it to customers at special prices through catalogues and internet.

(ii) **Attractive incentives to wholesalers and retailers** The marketer is promoting the sale of its product by offering gifts/attractive packages of tours and incentives to wholesalers and retailers. Since personal selling is an effective tool of promotion, it would help the product to generate a long lasting demand for it.

Social Message

The social message spread by the marketer for the promotion of the product is:

'Clean people will make India cleaner'.

Conclusion

By undertaking this project, I learnt about the process of manufacturing and marketing of a toothpaste, as a complete market offer for the customer. It helped me to know the pricing and promotion policy of the company. Social responsibility of the business has been fulfilled in various ways by proper labelling, packaging and spreading of social message amongst consumers. Competition for the product is too much in the industry, but it has great scope also.

Viva Questions

(i) Why have you chosen 'toothpaste' as the subject matter of your project?

(ii) What is marketing?

(iii) Why have you chosen 'freshine' as the brand name of your product?

(iv) Why is the competition so tough in this industry?

(v) What all information have you included in the label of your product ?

(vi) What packaging levels have you used for it and why?

(vii) Why have you selected three–level channel of distribution?

(viii) What factors are considered while taking decision regarding warehousing?

(ix) What is the firm's USP?

(x) Which sales promotion measures are being used for promoting the product?

3 Sample Question Papers

SAMPLE QUESTION PAPER 1

A Highly Simulated Sample Question Paper for CBSE Class XII Examination

BUSINESS STUDIES

Time : 3 Hours **Max. Marks : 80**

General Instructions

1. This question paper contains 34 questions. All questions are compulsory.
2. Marks are indicated against each question.
3. Answers should be brief and to the point.
4. Answers to the questions carrying 3 marks may be from 50 to 75 words.
5. Answers to the questions carrying 4 marks may be about 150 words.
6. Answers to the questions carrying 6 marks may be about 200 words.

1. The earlier approach of caveat emptor which means 'Let the buyer beware', has now been changed to .... (1)

(a) caveat venditor (b) caveat marketer
(c) caveat buyer (d) None of these

2. Rahul Mehta purchased a car for ₹ 17 lakh from an automobile company. Later on, he found defects in its engine. Suggest him the appropriate authority, where he could file a complaint under Consumer Protection Act. (1)

(a) District Commission (b) State Commission
(c) National Commission (d) Supreme Court of India

3. Span of management refers to .... (1)

(a) the number of superiors that a manager can effectively supervise
(b) the number of customers that a manager can effectively supervise
(c) the number of subordinates that a manager can effectively supervise
(d) the number of creditors that a manager can effectively supervise

4. Harish bought a pain relieving ointment after seeing it being displayed in the chemist's shop. The ointment tube has packet in a cardboard box.

The tubes were received by the chemist from the wholeseller in corrugated boxes containing 30 units. Identify the level of packaging involved in the above mentioned case. (1)

(a) Primary packaging
(b) Secondary packaging
(c) Transportation packaging
(d) All of the above

5. "If a manager wants to introduce new accounting system, then there may be initial resistance from accounting staff. But, if manager explains the purpose, provides training and motivates them with incentive, the staff may cooperate with manager."

Which importance of directing is highlighted here? (1)

(a) Initiate action (b) Means of motivation
(c) Facilitates change (d) Provides stability

6. Choose the statement that correctly highlights the feature of the business environment. (1)

(a) It consists of a single, straightforward factor influencing business decisions.
(b) It is a static concept, unaffected by changes in technology or government policies.
(c) It is aggregative in nature and includes social, political, economic, legal and technological influences.
(d) It is easy to predict future events, such as changes in consumer preferences or government policies.

7. In which of the following aspects, money market is different from capital market? (1)

(a) Participants
(b) Tenure of securities traded
(c) Liquidity of securities traded
(d) All of the above

8. Which of the following statements is incorrect about the Securities Exchange Board of India (SEBI)? **(1)**
(a) It is a non-statutory body
(b) It is established in 1992
(c) It is established to protect the right of investors
(d) None of the above

9.

Identify the quality mark illustrated in the above picture. **(1)**
(a) Mark of Bureau of Indian Standards
(b) BIS Hallmark
(c) Food Process Order
(d) Agmark

10. "Government of India set-up a regulatory body to check on various unfair trade practices like price rigging, unofficial premium in new issues, unofficial private placements, etc." Identify it. **(1)**
(a) SEBI (b) NSDL
(c) RBI (d) ASSOCHAM

11. Which of the following statements is not true? **(1)**
(a) Formal organisation originates as a result of company's rules and policies
(b) Informal organisation arises out of personal qualities of individuals
(c) Under formal organisation, flow of communication takes place in any direction
(d) Formal organisation is rigid in nature

12. Madhuban Oils Ltd. has the largest share of 60% in the market. The company's policy is to sell only for cash. In 2021, for the first time company's number one position in the industry has been threatened because other companies started selling oil on credit also.

But, the manager of Madhuban Oils Ltd. continued to rely on its previously tried and tested successful plans, which didn't work because the environment is not static. This led to decline in sales of Madhuban Oils Ltd.

The above said case highlights the limitation(s) of planning which led to decline in its sales. Identify such limitation(s). **(1)**
(a) Planning does not guarantee success
(b) Planning may not work in dynamic environment
(c) Planning leads to rigidity
(d) Both (a) and (b)

13. Match the following **(1)**

Column I	Column II
A. Overseeing the activities of subordinates	(i) Motivation
B. Influencing the behaviour of subordinates	(ii) Leadership
C. Making subordinates to act in a desired manner	(iii) Supervision

Codes

	A	B	C		A	B	C
(a)	(i)	(ii)	(iii)	(b)	(ii)	(iii)	(i)
(c)	(iii)	(ii)	(i)	(d)	(i)	(iii)	(ii)

14. Statement I Not only employee-turnover, but frequent termination of rotation must also be avoided.

Statement II Employee must be provided the feeling of job security. With feeling of insecurity of job, the employees cannot contribute their maximum. **(1)**

Alternatives
(a) Statement I is correct and Statement II is incorrect
(b) Statement II is correct and Statement I is incorrect
(c) Both statements are correct
(d) Both statements are incorrect

15. Assertion (A) Finance is the life blood of business.

Reason (R) Finance is very essential for the smooth running of the business. **(1)**

Alternatives
(a) Both Assertion (A) and Reason (R) are true and Reason (R) is the correct explanation of Assertion (A)
(b) Both Assertion (A) and Reason (R) are true, but Reason (R) is not the correct explanation of Assertion (A)
(c) Assertion (A) is true, but Reason (R) is false
(d) Assertion (A) is false, but Reason (R) is true

16. What are the factors that affect the dividend decision? **(1)**
(i) Amount of earnings
(ii) Stability in earnings
(iii) Contractual constraints
(iv) Cost of debt
(v) Floatation cost

Codes
(a) (i), (ii) and (iii) (b) (i), (iii) and (iv)
(c) (ii), (iii) and (v) (d) (i), (iv) and (v)

17. Statement I Planning seeks to bridge the gap between where we are and where we want to go.

Statement II Planning is basically an intellectual activity of thinking. **(1)**

Alternatives

(a) Statement I is correct and Statement II is incorrect

(b) Statement II is correct and Statement I is incorrect

(c) Both statements are correct

(d) Both statements are incorrect

18. **Assertion** (A) Depository holds securities in electronic form.

Reason (R) Depository is formed for the purpose of free transferability of securities with speed, accuracy and security. (1)

Alternatives

(a) Both Assertion (A) and Reason (R) are true and Reason (R) is the correct explanation of Assertion (A)

(b) Both Assertion (A) and Reason (R) are true, but Reason (R) is not the correct explanation of Assertion (A)

(c) Assertion (A) is true, but Reason (R) is false

(d) Assertion (A) is false, but Reason (R) is true

19. "Organising is a crucial function of management that ensures efficient workflow and clarity in roles. After tasks are identified and divided, they are grouped into departments. Specific duties are then assigned and clear authority and reporting relationships are established."

Place the steps of organising in the correct order. (1)

(a) Departmentalisation, establishing authority and reporting relationships, assignment of duties, identification and division of work

(b) Identification and division of work, departmentalisation, assignment of duties, establishing authority and reporting relationships

(c) Identification and division of work, assignment of duties, departmentalisation, establishing authority and reporting relationships

(d) Departmentalisation, identification and division of work, assignment of duties, establishing authority and reporting relationships

20. For the purpose of selecting employees for the post of 'sales executives' for its retail outlets, Reliance Fresh conducted a recruitment programme at Rajasthan University.

Considering the vast number of job seekers, group discussions were conducted and the candidates who were selected had to face interviews and then they were offered job if they passed such interviews.

Such programmes are often known as (1)

(a) advertisement

(b) campus recruitment

(c) campus selection

(d) direct recruitment

21. "To manage is to forecast and plan, to organise, to command, to coordinate and to control," enunciated by Fayol. Comment. (3)

Or What do you understand by the technique 'standardisation of work'? Also, mention its objectives.

22. Priya purchased a new electric kettle from a local store. Within a week of using it, the kettle started emitting smoke due to a wiring defect. Despite reporting the issue to the store, they refused to replace the kettle or provide a refund, claiming it was not their responsibility. When Priya escalated the issue to the manufacturer, they also denied any liability, leaving her with no resolution. Furthermore, Priya faced multiple follow-ups with both parties, causing significant inconvenience. Identify and explain the consumer rights that have been violated in the above case. (3)

23. What do you understand by dematerialisation of securities and demat account? (3)

Or To avoid the problem of shortage and surplus of funds, what is required in financial management? Name the concept and explain any two points of its importance.

24. Ashutosh runs a locks manufacturing factory. He wants to expand his business. For expansion, he contemplates to enter into the manufacturing of locks for bikes as an ancillary company. By doing this, his company will be able to provide many products to bike manufacturers.

(i) Which type of organisational structure will he choose for his factory?

(ii) State any two advantages of this organisational structure. (3)

25. Rajat had opened an internet cafe in the 90's to cash in on the boom of the internet. In the initial years, he got good profits. This made him carefree and he started taking his success for granted. But lately for the last few years, he is finding it difficult to even bear the expenses of his cafe, leave alone earning profits.

(i) Which aspect or feature of business environment has Rajat ignored?

(ii) What changes in the macro environment has affected his business? (4)

26. State any four functions performed by the Securities and Exchange Board of India (SEBI) to regulate and protect the interests of investors. (4)

Or "The stock exchange serves as the beating heart of the financial market, where shares, bonds and securities pulsate through the economy, ensuring liquidity, price discovery and investment opportunities."

Elucidate the key functions performed by a stock exchange.

27. Mohit, the owner of a shoe manufacturing factory, plans to diversify into leather bags and western formal wear while continuing his existing business of shoes. To manage this expansion effectively, he needs an organisation structure that can accommodate the new ventures while maintaining the existing operations seamlessly.

(i) Which organisation structure will you suggest him and why?

(ii) Mention the suitability of the organisation structure suggested. (4)

28. "Management is the systematised body of knowledge that explains certain general truths." Explain the statement by giving any two reasons to support your answer. (4)

29. Differentiate between recruitment and selection on any four basis. (4)

Or

Enlist any four needs as per Maslow's theory alongwith individual and organisational examples.

30. Arnav is the production manager of Technomart Corporation. Due to heavy demand of the company's product and excessive load on production department, Arnav delegated part of his authority and work to his subordinate supervisor. Since, the supervisor was not proficient in handling the work, work quality degraded resulting in poor quality output.

Thereafter, the manager is of the view that he is not responsible for the quality of work, as he has delegated responsibility to his subordinate. Do you agree with his view point? Justify your answer by giving proper arguments. (4)

31. Bharti Enterprises, a small manufacturing firm in India, was initially struggling to compete in the highly competitive market. However, with the rapid changes in technology and increased demand for eco-friendly products, the company identified a unique opportunity to develop sustainable packaging solutions. By closely monitoring market trends and environmental factors, the firm was able to introduce biodegradable packaging, giving them a significant first-mover advantage.

Additionally, the firm recognised early warning signals when competitors started adopting similar sustainable practices, prompting them to innovate further in order to maintain their competitive edge. Over time, this helped Bharti Enterprises not only improve its performance but also expand its market share.

Quoting the lines from the above paragraph, identify and explain any three points highlighting the importance of the business environment for Bharti Enterprises. (6)

32. XYZ Ltd., a manufacturing company, has experienced a sudden increase in production output. To ensure smooth workflow and maintain employee motivation, the manager has been providing clear instructions, supervising tasks and guiding the team to achieve organisational goals effectively. Additionally, regular team meetings are conducted to address challenges and provide feedback, fostering a collaborative work environment. The manager ensures that employees are well-supported through regular communication and encouragement, promoting a sense of trust and engagement.

(i) Identify the function of management indicated in the case. (1)

(ii) State any two elements of the function identified in (i). (2)

(iii) State any three points of importance of function identified in (i). (3)

33. "Every action in the organisation is initiated through directing." In the light of this statement, explain the term directing and mention any five points of it's importance. (6)

Or Discuss the following limitations of controlling.

(i) Costly affair

(ii) Resistance from employees

(iii) Little control on external factors

34. What are the factors affecting determination of the price of a product or service? Explain. (6)

Or Marketing is a social process wherein people interact with each other, in order to persuade them to act in a particular way. However, there are certain distinguishing features of marketing. Explain them.

Answers

1. (a)	**2.** (a)	**3.** (c)	**4.** (d)	**5.** (c)	**6.** (c)	**7.** (d)	**8.** (a)	**9.** (b)	**10.** (a)
11. (c)	**12.** (d)	**13.** (c)	**14.** (c)	**15.** (a)	**16.** (a)	**17.** (c)	**18.** (a)	**19.** (b)	**20.** (b)

SAMPLE QUESTION PAPER 2

A Highly Simulated Sample Question Paper for CBSE Class XII Examination

BUSINESS STUDIES

Time : 3 Hours **Max. Marks : 80**

General Instructions

1. This question paper contains 34 questions. All questions are compulsory.
2. Marks are indicated against each question.
3. Answers should be brief and to the point.
4. Answers to the questions carrying 3 marks may be from 50 to 75 words.
5. Answers to the questions carrying 4 marks may be about 150 words.
6. Answers to the questions carrying 6 marks may be about 200 words.

1. In Mumbai, Salman found impurities in a bottle of soft drink which he had bought. He approached the redressal forum. Which right is exercised by him? (1)

(a) Right to be heard (b) Right to be informed
(c) Right to seek redressal
(d) Right to consumer education

2. In Tysfo Ltd., the purchase department purchased 20 tonnes of raw material for the production department. However, the production department required only 15 tonnes.

Due to this reason, goods were produced beyond required level and were not accepted by sales department. As a result, many goods remained unsold. Identify the aspect of management lacking in the given case. (1)

(a) Planning (b) Coordination
(c) Directing (d) None of these

3. How many principles were given by Henry Fayol? (1)

(a) 12 (b) 13
(c) 14 (d) 15

4. "Motivation at the workplace begins when an employee experiences an unsatisfied need, which creates tension leading to the formation of drives. This results in search behaviour to fulfill the unmet need." Arrange the following stages of motivation in the correct order. (1)

(a) Drives, search behaviour, tension, unsatisfied need
(b) Tension, drives, search behaviour, unsatisfied need
(c) Unsatisfied need, tension, drives, search behaviour
(d) Drives, unsatisfied need, tension, search behaviour

5. Budgets are known as .... financial plans made for a period of one year or less. (1)

(a) long-term
(b) short-term
(c) medium-term
(d) Both (b) and (c)

6. Which of the following statements is/are incorrect? (1)

(a) Business finance refers to the money required for carrying out business activities.
(b) Dividend decision relates to the relative proportion of various sources of finance.
(c) From the company point of view, the use of equity share capital results in more cost but less of risk.
(d) Capital structure represents the proportion of debt capital and equity capital to make up the total capital of the firm.

7. "The manager of 180 Ltd. calculated total sales and revenue earned by each sales executive to conduct appraisals at the end of the year." Which step of controlling is highlighted here? (1)

(a) Setting performance standards
(b) Measurement of actual performance
(c) Comparing actual performance with standards
(d) Analysing deviations

8. **Statement I** Advertising is the impersonal communication in case of promotion.

Statement II Production cost is the only important component while fixing up the price. (1)

Alternatives

(a) Statement I is correct and Statement II is incorrect
(b) Statement II is correct and Statement I is incorrect
(c) Both statements are correct
(d) Both statements are incorrect

9. Choose the statement that correctly highlights the benefit of financial planning. (1)

(a) It increases the risk of business shocks and surprises and helps the company in preparing for the future
(b) It helps in coordinating various business functions like production, sales, etc. by providing policies and procedures
(c) It does not link the present with the future
(d) It leads to waste and duplication of efforts

10. The top management of Raheja Ltd. focuses on maintaining an effective two-way communication with their employees. The aim is to keep everyone well informed and involve employees in company's activities and provide opportunities for them to give their feedback. What will the company achieve by following such a network of communication? (1)

(a) Smooth functioning of the enterprise
(b) Managerial efficiency
(c) Both (a) and (b)
(d) None of the above

11. Assertion (A) Planning provides the base for controlling.

Reason (R) Planning establishes the standards against which the actual performance is evaluated. (1)

Alternatives

(a) Both Assertion (A) and Reason (R) are true and Reason (R) is the correct explanation of Assertion (A)
(b) Both Assertion (A) and Reason (R) are true, but Reason (R) is not the correct explanation of Assertion (A)
(c) Assertion (A) is true, but Reason (R) is false
(d) Assertion (A) is false, but Reason (R) is true

12. What explains informal organisation the best? (1)

(a) All departments in an organisation reports to a coordinating head
(b) Network of personal and social relationships that arise as people associate with other people in a work environment
(c) This structure is created intentionally by the managers for achievement of organisational goal
(d) None of the above

13. Assertion (A) Finance is the life blood of business.

Reason (R) Finance is very essential for the smooth running of the business. (1)

Alternatives

(a) Both Assertion (A) and Reason (R) are true and Reason (R) is the correct explanation of Assertion (A)
(b) Both Assertion (A) and Reason (R) are true, but Reason (R) is not the correct explanation of Assertion (A)
(c) Assertion (A) is true, but Reason (R) is false
(d) Assertion (A) is false, but Reason (R) is true

14. Identify the incorrect statement about marketing among the following. (1)

(a) Marketing mix is a wider term than product mix
(b) Marketing is a social process
(c) The focus of marketing activities is on customer needs
(d) Marketing is merely a post production activity

15. Thirthankar Pvt. Ltd is a school bag manufacturing company. For the purpose of profit maximisation, Nisha added a laptop pocket to the existing bag design. Which marketing management philosophy is adopted by Nisha? (1)

(a) Production concept
(b) Product concept
(c) Selling concept
(d) Marketing concept

16. What are the important characteristics of an effective brand name? (1)

(i) Distinctive
(ii) Adaptable to packaging
(iii) Versatile for new products
(iv) Not capable of legal registration
(v) Having short-term popularity
(vi) Easily outdated

Codes

(a) (i), (ii) and (iii)
(b) (ii), (iii) and (v)
(c) (i), (iii) and (vi)
(d) (i), (iii) and (iv)

17. Match the following on the basis of functions of marketing. (1)

Column I	Column II
A. Gathering market information	(i) Conduct SWOT analysis
B. Promotion	(ii) To persuade customers
C. Product designing	(iii) Competitive advantage

Codes

	A	B	C		A	B	C
(a)	(i)	(ii)	(iii)	(b)	(ii)	(iii)	(i)
(c)	(iii)	(ii)	(i)	(d)	(i)	(iii)	(ii)

18. 

Analyse the picture in which Mrs. Rekha is asking about the functions and warranty period of the Mixer from the shopkeeper.

Choose the correct option reflected in picture. (1)

(a) Consumer organisations

(b) Consumer awareness

(c) Both (a) and (b)

(d) None of the above

19. **Statement I** Labelling is also an important feature of the product.

Statement II It not only protects the product but also serves as a promotional tool. (1)

Alternatives

(a) Statement I is correct and Statement II is incorrect

(b) Statement II is correct and Statement I is incorrect

(c) Both statements are correct

(d) Both statements are incorrect

20. Ganga's grandfather was unwell. He called Ganga and gave her a box containing cash and certain papers which were crumbled. He saw them carefully and found that these were share certificates. Ganga now wants to know the process through which he can trade in these shares. He also learnt about the trading procedures and got to know about SEBI as well.

Which process would have been done by Ganga to facilitate trading? (1)

(a) Demutualisation (b) Remutualisation

(c) Dematerialisation (d) Rematerialisation

21. Distinguish between marketing and selling concepts on any three basis. (3)

Or As per the concept of marketing, mention any three items that can be marketed.

22. Sakshi purchased a bottle of soy-souce from the local grocery shop. The information provided on the bottle was not clear. She fell sick on consuming it. She filed a case in the District Commission under Consumer Protection Act and got the relief.

(i) Identify the important aspect neglected by the marketer in the above case.

(ii) Explain briefly any two functions of the aspect identified in (i) above. (3)

23. Vatikes Jewellers, a leading brand in the jewelry industry, is planning to open a new manufacturing unit equipped with advanced machinery to produce intricate designs. The management is carefully evaluating the type of machinery, the cost of setting-up the unit and the technology required for consistent production.

Based on the above scenario, state any three factors affecting the requirements of fixed capital. (3)

24. Explain 'direct recruitment' and 'advertisement' as external sources of recruitment. (3)

Or How does recruitment takes place through recommendations and employment exchange?

25. Nature of money market can be well explained with the help of its features. State any four such features of money market. (4)

Or Define capital market. State the two types of capital market.

26. Riya recently purchased a smartphone online. Upon receiving it, she noticed that the device was defective and did not match the product description. She contacted the company for a replacement but faced delays and unresponsive customer service.

Frustrated, she decided to read about consumer protection laws to understand her rights and responsibilities as a buyer.

(i) What is consumer protection?

(ii) State any three responsibilities of a consumer. (4)

27. Rahul, a young entrepreneur, recently launched a tech start-up providing AI-based solutions for businesses. However, within a few months, he noticed that new government regulations on data privacy had been introduced, requiring compliance with stricter standards.

Additionally, growing awareness among customers about ethical AI practices started influencing their choices.

Rahul decided to adapt his operations by incorporating transparent data policies and ethical AI principles to align with these changes and sustain his business in the competitive market.

(i) Identify the dimension of business environment is highlighted in the case.

(ii) State any three points of components of the concept identified in (i). (4)

28. Moko Yoko Ltd. is a manufacturing company who manufactures two wheelers for domestic Indian market as well as for export. It had enjoyed a substantial market share and also had a loyal customer base. But, now it is experiencing issue as it is unable to meet its targets with regard to sales and customers satisfaction. Also, automobile industry in India has grown tremendously and many new players have come with better technology and pricing, which has increased the problems for the company.

It is now planning to revamp its controlling system and take other steps necessary to rectify the problems it is facing. You are required to identify and explain the benefits that the organisation will drive from a good control system. (4)

29. SEBI, as a watch dog performs various functions which protects the investors. Name and explain any two functions. (4)

Or Distinguish between money market and capital market.

30. 'Staffing is an inherent part of human resource management'. Discuss. (4)

31. Differentiate between delegation and decentralisation on the basis of any six points. (6)

Or "Planning provides direction to managers and employees, facilitating a smooth workflow in achieving organisational objectives. It involves developing various types of plans that guide action at different levels of the organisation."

In light of the above statement, explain three types of plans in the planning function of management.

32. Shubh, a manager, maintains open communication with people across all levels, including his own and other departments. However, he expects his subordinates to work solely for personal satisfaction and contentment, disregarding the importance of monetary rewards.

Additionally, he demands immediate results from his subordinates without allowing them adequate time to adapt to a new environment.

Furthermore, Shubh is lenient with his employees regarding adherence to work timings and the completion of assigned targets.

Identify the principles of management violated in the above case and explain them. (6)

33. "Management act as a crucial factor in steering an organisation towards its strategic goals, productivity and ensuring its competitive advantage."

Explain how management is important in the functioning of an organisation. (6)

Or

Explain any five characteristics of coordination which helps in integrating the efforts of various departments.

34. A company X Ltd. manufacturing cosmetics, which enjoyed a pre-eminent position in business, has grown in size. Its business was very good till 1991. But after that, new liberalised environment has seen entry of many MNC's in the sector. With the result, the market share of X Ltd. has declined.

The company followed a very centralised business model with directors and divisional heads making even minor decisions.

Before 1991, this business model had served the company very well as consumers has no choice. But now, the company is under pressure to reform and decentralise.

(i) What do you understand by decentralisation? (1)

(ii) Can an organisation in general, be fully centralised or fully decentralised? (2)

(iii) Explain any three advantages of decentralisation. (3)

Answers

1. (a)	**2.** (b)	**3.** (c)	**4.** (c)	**5.** (b)	**6.** (b)	**7.** (b)	**8.** (b)	**9.** (b)	**10.** (c)
11. (a)	**12.** (b)	**13.** (a)	**14.** (d)	**15.** (b)	**16.** (a)	**17.** (a)	**18.** (b)	**19.** (a)	**20.** (c)

SAMPLE QUESTION PAPER 3

A Highly Simulated Sample Question Paper for CBSE Class XII Examination

BUSINESS STUDIES

Time : 3 Hours **Max. Marks : 80**

General Instructions

1. This question paper contains 34 questions. All questions are compulsory.
2. Marks are indicated against each question.
3. Answers should be brief and to the point.
4. Answers to the questions carrying 3 marks may be from 50 to 75 words.
5. Answers to the questions carrying 4 marks may be about 150 words.
6. Answers to the questions carrying 6 marks may be about 200 words.

1. "Planning is an essential process in an organisation to achieve its objectives effectively. It involves a sequence of steps that ensure a clear path towards the desired goals. The process begins with setting objectives, followed by several logical steps."

Place the subsequent steps of the planning process in the correct order. (1)

(a) Developing premises, identifying alternative courses of action, evaluating alternative courses, setting objectives

(b) Setting objectives, developing premises, evaluating alternative courses, identifying alternative courses of action

(c) Setting objectives, developing premises, identifying alternative courses of action, evaluating alternative courses

(d) Identifying alternative courses of action, setting objectives, developing premises, evaluating alternative courses

2. Which function of channels of distribution refers to the process of creating desired combinations of products to fulfil varied needs of customers such as cricket kit? (1)

(a) Sorting (b) Accumulation

(c) Allocation (d) Assorting

3. Which principle of scientific management discards the old approach of rule of thumb? (1)

(a) Harmony, not discord

(b) Cooperation, not individualism

(c) Science, not rule of thumb

(d) Either (a) or (c)

4. Alokik Ltd. is engaged in manufacturing plastic containers. The objective of the company is to manufacture 150 containers a day. To achieve this, the efforts of all departments are coordinated and interlinked and authority-responsibility relationship is established among various job positions. There is a clarity on who is to report to whom. Identify the function of management highlighted in the given case.

(a) Planning (b) Directing (1)

(c) Organising (d) Controlling

5. 'Shirt Up' is a company engaged in the production of men's shirt. The company follows Taylor's differential wage rate payment method and has the following piece rate wages.

(i) ₹ 15 per shirt to every worker who is able to produce the standard output of 8 shirts or more, per day.

(ii) ₹ 12 per shirt to every worker who is not able to produce the standard output.

Calculate the wages payable to Satish, who produced 11 shirts. (1)

(a) ₹ 132 (b) ₹ 165

(c) ₹ 33 (d) None of these

6. Which of the following is/are true about functional structure? (1)

(a) It is economical as there is minimal duplication of resources

(b) It is costlier due to duplication of resources

(c) It is easier to fix responsibility on each division

(d) Both (b) and (c)

7. Ravi is a supervisor at 'Dhyan Medicos Ltd'. The company manufactures cancer related medicines. Ravi's job is to make sure that the work goes on smoothly and there is no interruption in production. He is a good leader who give orders only after consulting his subordinates and work out the policies with the acceptance of the group. Identify the leadership style adopted by Ravi. (1)

(a) Autocratic leadership (b) Democratic leadership
(c) Free-rein leadership (d) None of these

8. Computer education is an example of .... being marketed. (1)

(a) ideas (b) information
(c) experience (d) services

9. **Statement I** Management principles are derived after observation and experimentation when certain conditions are present.

Statement II Principles of management are behavioural in nature and these can be applied to human beings only. (1)

Alternatives

(a) Statement I is correct and Statement II is incorrect
(b) Statement II is correct and Statement I is incorrect
(c) Both statements are correct
(d) Both statements are incorrect

10 Match the impact of decisions in Column I with their correct option in Column II (1)

	Column I		Column II
A.	Financing decision	(i)	Affects retained earnings
B.	Dividend decision	(ii)	Increase in size of assets
C.	Working capital decision	(iii)	Increase the financial risk of company
D.	Capital budgeting decision	(iv)	Affects liquidity and profitability

Codes

	A	B	C	D		A	B	C	D
(a)	(iii)	(i)	(iv)	(ii)	(b)	(iv)	(iii)	(ii)	(i)
(c)	(ii)	(i)	(iv)	(iii)	(d)	(i)	(ii)	(iii)	(iv)

11. Kalash Dairy Products Ltd. is a successful business of making milk. They decided to put a hologram seal on the packet to ensure that product is not tampered with. Which decision is taken here? (1)

(a) Labelling (b) Branding
(c) Standardising (d) Packaging

12. **Assertion** (A) Capital budgeting decisions are important and must be taken carefully.

Reason (R) Investment decisions affect the earning capacity of firm over the long-run and are not reversible except at huge cost. (1)

Alternatives

(a) Both Assertion (A) and Reason (R) are true and Reason (R) is the correct explanation of Assertion (A)
(b) Both Assertion (A) and Reason (R) are true, but Reason (R) is not the correct explanation of Assertion (A)
(c) Assertion (A) is true, but Reason (R) is false
(d) Assertion (A) is false, but Reason (R) is true

13. **Assertion** (A) Demand for sarees may be fairly high in India whereas it may be almost non-existent in France.

Reason (R) Business environment consists of numerous inter-related and dynamic conditions of forces which arise from different sources. (1)

Alternatives

(a) Both Assertion (A) and Reason (R) are true and Reason (R) is the correct explanation of Assertion (A)
(b) Both Assertion (A) and Reason (R) are true, but Reason (R) is not the correct explanation of Assertion (A)
(c) Assertion (A) is true, but Reason (R) is false
(d) Assertion (A) is false, but Reason (R) is true

14. "Gupta Ltd. offers employment to widows and weaker sections of the society."

Identify the objective of the organisation in the given case. (1)

(a) Personal objective (b) Social objective
(c) Organisational objective (d) Both (a) and (b)

15.

Identify the quality mark highlighted in the above picture. (1)

(a) BIS Hallmark (b) Food Process Order
(c) Ecomark (d) Agmark

16. Identify the incorrect statement with respect to the redressal mechanism under the Consumer Protection Act, 2019. (1)

(a) District Commissions are established by State Governments in every district and consist of a President and two members appointed by the Central Government.
(b) A District Commission can entertain consumer complaints where the value of goods or services and the compensation claimed is not more than ₹ 1 crore.
(c) If the aggrieved party is not satisfied with the order of the District Commission, an appeal can be filed before the State Commission within 45 days.

(d) District Commissions can send samples of goods for testing in a laboratory if required while investigating complaints.

17. Management plays a crucial role in the success of any organisation by ensuring effectiveness and efficiency. Which of the following correctly highlights the importance of management? (1)

(i) It aligns individual efforts towards achieving group goals.

(ii) It contributes to decline in productivity by reducing costs through planning and control.

(iii) It creates adaptability within the organisation to deal with a dynamic environment.

(iv) It focuses on individual growth rather than on organisational objectives.

(v) It contributes to societal development by fulfilling social responsibilities.

Codes

(a) (i), (iii) and (v) (b) (ii), (iv) and (v)

(c) (i), (ii) and (iv) (d) (i), (iv) and (v)

18. Which of the following is incorrect with regard to the National Commission? (1)

(a) The members are appointed by central government.

(b) Where the aggrieved party was not satisfied with the order of the National Commission, the case can be taken to the Supreme Court of India.

(c) A complaint can be made to the National Commission when compensation exceeds ₹ 1 crore.

(d) None of the above

19. **Statement I** Method study means finding the one best way of doing a task.

Statement II Fatigue study means eliminating the unnecessary movements. (1)

Alternatives

(a) Statement I is correct and Statement II is incorrect

(b) Statement II is correct and Statement I is incorrect

(c) Both statements are correct

(d) Both statements are incorrect

20. Ananya's grandfather while telling her about the past of Indian economy told her that even after opening up of our economy in 1991, foreign companies found it very difficult to cut through the bureaucratic red tape to get permits for doing business in India. Sometimes it took months to process even their application in process.

As a result, these companies were discouraged from inves- ting in India but the situation has improved overtime.

Identify the element of business environment which was the cause for discouragement to foreign companies based on above case. (1)

(a) Economical (b) Social

(c) Political (d) Legal

21. "Coordination is the essence of management." Explain. (3)

Or Name and explain that principle of Fayol which suggest that communication from top to bottom should follow the official lines of command.

22. Bhagyashri Enterprises is a company engaged in the marketing of air purifiers of a famous brand. The company has a functional structure with four main functions; purchases, sales, finance and staffing. To ensure the proper and optimum functioning of employees, company appointed a new personnel manager.

However, the newly appointed personnel manager is of the view that there is no need for training the workers.

Do you agree with the views of the personnel manager? Give reasons in support of your answer. (3)

23. Mr. Sharma purchased a book from a bookseller and took the cash memo of ₹ 1,000 which he paid for the book. Later, he found that the actual price of the book is ₹ 800, but the bookseller had put a sticker of ₹ 1,000 on the original price.

(i) Can Mr. Sharma recover the extra money that he paid?

(ii) What other options are available to him against bookseller? (3)

24. Explain giving reasons why firms with high debtors turnover ratio and high inventory turnover ratio require lesser amount of working capital. (3)

Or

Explain the meaning of capital structure.

25. MRTU Group of Hotels, an abroad based company, decided to establish a chain of new hotels in India, only after a careful study of the business industry. They felt that tourism industry was the biggest industry in the world.

Its future is particularly bright in India and gives certain social advantages too.

This will help in giving employment and generating revenue in the country.

(i) Identify the components of business environment reflected in this case.

(ii) Explain the components of business environment identified in (i). (4)

26. A company comprised of competing divisions, allows its top management to frame policies or sound strategic thinking on various aspects like allocation of resources, funds, etc. In the light of the above statement, state the disadvantages of divisional structure. (4)

Or Organisation is the harmonious adjustment of specialised parts for the accomplishment of some common purpose or desired goals. In the light of this statement, explain any four points of importance of organising.

27. Explain the following types of plan using suitable examples
(i) Objective (ii) Policy (4)

28. 'Tulsi Herbal Ltd.' is engaged in the manufacturing and distribution of medicines. The company has set-up an objective of increasing its sales turnover by 15%. To achieve this objective, the company has decided to diversify into ayurvedic medicines. Since, the company has already set its objectives, developed the premises based on the same as well as identified alternative couses of action, it wants your help for the remaining steps to be taken in this process. Explain briefly these steps. (4)

29. 'SEBI is the watch dog of security market'. Do you agree? Give three reasons to support your answer. (4)

Or Briefly mention the advantages of screen-based trading system.

30. You are an HR in TRIMX Ltd. You have recruited 20 candidates for the post of senior executive without conducting the written test due to which the working of a company suffers as unprofessionals are hired for senior positions.
(i) In context to this, explain the importance of conducting test during selection process.
(ii) Also, state the various types of tests conduction in this process. (4)

31. Explain the various steps involved in the process of controlling. (6)

Or Planning and controlling are considered to be inseparable twins of management. Explain.

32. Ramesh has recently joined a manufacturing company as a human resources manager. He notices that several employees have been leaving the organisation due to dissatisfaction with their work environment. To address this, Ramesh starts analysing the needs of employees at different levels in the organisation.

He observes that a group of workers often complain about their inability to afford basic necessities like food and shelter due to low wages.

Another group frequently discusses their concerns about job stability and fear of sudden layoffs.

In a separate instance, he sees that the office staff often prefer working in teams and value friendships and group activities. Some senior employees express their desire for recognition and status through promotions and appreciation, while a few high performing employees talk about achieving personal goals and striving to reach their full potential in their careers.

Ramesh decides to design motivational policies based on these observations to ensure employee satisfaction and retention. Quoting the lines from the above case, identify and explain the needs highlighted by Ramesh based on Maslow's hierarchy of needs. (6)

33. Explain how the following factors affect the requirement of fixed capital.
(i) Level of collaboration
(ii) Financing alternatives
(iii) Diversification (6)

Or "Effective financial planning serves as a blueprint for the success of any business enterprise, ensuring optimal resource utilisation and minimising risks."

In light of the above statement, explain how effective financial planning contributes to the achievement of business objectives by providing any six reasons.

34. A company was marketing 'Mixer Grinders' which were very popular due to their quality and after-sale services provided to the customers. The company was a leading company in the market and earning huge profits. Because of huge profits, the company ignored the after-sales services. As a result, its relations with the customers got spoiled and the goodwill of the company in market was damaged. Top management became concerned when the profits fell steeply. On analysis, it was revealed that ignoring after-sales services was its reason. Therefore, the company took all possible measures to protect and promote its favourable image. As a result, goodwill of the company improved in the society.
(i) Name the communication tool used by the marketer in the abovesaid case. (1)
(ii) State the meaning of the communication tool identified in (i). (2)
(iii) Discuss the role of the tool identified in part (i) above. (3)

Answers

1. (c)	**2.** (d)	**3.** (c)	**4.** (c)	**5.** (b)	**6.** (a)	**7.** (b)	**8.** (d)	**9.** (c)	**10.** (a)
11. (d)	**12.** (a)	**13.** (b)	**14.** (b)	**15.** (c)	**16.** (a)	**17.** (a)	**18.** (c)	**19.** (a)	**20.** (c)

CBSE

Code **66/2/1**

Examination Paper 2025

BUSINESS STUDIES

Time : 3 Hours **Max. Marks : 80**

General Instructions

1. This question paper contains 34 questions. All questions are compulsory.
2. Marks are indicated against each question.
3. Answers should be brief and to the point.
4. Answers to the questions carrying 3 marks may be from 50 to 75 words.
5. Answers to the questions carrying 4 marks may be about 150 words.
6. Answers to the questions carrying 6 marks may be about 200 words.

Set I

1. "It is the process of designing and maintaining an environment in which individuals, working together in groups, efficiently accomplish selected aims." Identify the process. (1)

(a) Management (b) Organising
(c) Staffing (d) Directing

2. Kavi works as a marketing manager in stationery mart. It deals in various types of stationery items for many schools across the country. When new session starts in schools, Kavi forecasts the sales of different stationery products for each school for every month.

All items are represented in numbers so that it becomes easier for him to compare the actual sales with expected sales. The type of plan discussed above is (1)

(a) strategy (b) policy (c) programme (d) budget

3. Assertion (A) Directing facilitates introduction of needed changes in the organisation.

Reason (R) Directing increases resistance to changes in the organisation. (1)

Alternatives

(a) Both Assertion (A) and Reason (R) are true and Reason (R) is the correct explanation of Assertion (A)
(b) Assertion (A) is true, but Reason (R) is false
(c) Assertion (A) is false, but Reason (R) is true
(d) Both Assertion (A) and Reason (R) are true, but Reason (R) is not the correct explanation of Assertion (A)

4. CVX Ltd. was a leading company, manufacturing home appliances like food processors, juicers and mixer grinders. The company was earning good profits and was paying high dividends to its shareholders consistently. The company now decided to manufacture soup-making machines, pop-up toasters and electric irons. The company wanted to enter into emerging markets out of India also. Entering these markets will require additional capital investment which will facilitate in production and distribution infrastructure, etc. For this, the management decided to retain money out of their earnings to finance the required investment and distribute smaller dividend to the shareholders.

The factor affecting dividend decision which was kept in mind by the management of CVX Ltd. for entering into emerging markets and launching new products was (1)

(a) amount of earnings
(b) stability of earnings
(c) stability of dividends (d) growth opportunities

5. Statement I Staffing is that part of the process of management which is concerned with obtaining, utilising and maintaining a satisfied and satisfactory workforce.

Statement II Staffing is a continuous process. (1)

Alternatives

(a) Both the statements are true
(b) Both the statements are false
(c) Statement I is true, but Statement II is false
(d) Statement II is true, but Statement I is false

6. Choose the statement that correctly highlights the benefit of using internal sources of recruitment. (1)

(a) It helps in simplifying the process of selection
(b) It provides wider choice while selecting the employees
(c) It brings new blood in the organisation
(d) It is an expensive and time consuming source

7. Atul was working as an employee in a readymade garments factory. He was very sincere and dedicated and always completed his work in time. It pained him to see that his colleagues were reluctant to do the work even though they had the ability to do it.

Due to his good behaviour and willingness to work, he was promoted to the post of the supervisor of the same team in which he was a worker earlier. He understood very well that it was not always possible to get the best of work from employees merely by exercising formal authority. He had insights into the causes of behaviour of of people. He knew how to get the work done by the workers in a desired manner to achieve the organisational objectives. Under his supervision even the workers who were reluctant to work started working efficiently and effectively.

From the following, identify the concept used by Atul, as a supervisor to get the work completed (1)

(a) Leadership (b) Financial incentives
(c) Motivation (d) Non-financial incentives

8. 'Isha Sweets' was set by Isha Sharma to prepare and sell organic, vegan and healthy sweets alternatives like hazelnuts date ladoos, dry fruit date burfi, stuffed mejdool date, etc. For the last many years, the demand for her products was very high as people these days prefer to buy healthier alternatives for consumption as well as gifting purposes. But this year suddenly, the cost of dates, dry fruits and other ingredients used for preparing these healthy sweets had increased. With rising prices of raw materials, larger amounts of funds were required to maintain a constant volume of production and sales.

As a result, the working capital requirement of 'Isha Sweets' became higher.

The factor which led to an increase in the working capital requirements of 'Isha Sweets' was (1)

(a) availability of raw material
(b) inflation
(c) scale of business (d) production cycle

9. "The process of organising allows a business enterprise to accommodate changes in the business environment. It allows the organisation structure to be suitably modified to pave the way for a smooth transition."

The point of importance of organizing function of management highlighted in the above lines is (1)

(a) benefits of specialisation
(b) clarity in working relationships
(c) optimum utilisation of resources
(d) adaptation to change

10. A buyer buys a product or service for what it does for him/her or the benefit it provides to him/her. There can be three type of benefits, a consumer may seek to satisfy from the purchase of a product: (i) Functional benefits (ii) Social benefits and (iii) .... (1)

(a) technological benefits (b) economic benefits
(c) psychological benefits (d) environmental benefits

11. Nimesh was working as a production manager in HL Ltd., an electrical wire manufacturing company. One of the vendors who was. supplying copper to HL Ltd. wanted to close down his business within 15 days as he had to go abroad to live with his son. The vendor was selling all his stocks at 60% discount. Nimesh wrote a letter to the general manager to seek approval for procurement of this material. But due to rigid rules and cumbersome procedures there was delay in getting sanction and order could not be placed.

The type of communication barrier that led to procedural delay was (1)

(a) semantic barrier (b) psychological barrier
(c) organizational barrier (d) personal barrier

12. "The right of an individual to command his subordinates and to take action within the scope of his position' is called (1)

(a) decentralisation (b) authority
(c) responsibility (d) accountability

13. As per the Consumer Protection Act, 2019 which of the following statement is correct? (1)

(a) In case the aggrieved party is not satisfied with the order of the District Commission, he can directly appeal before the National Commission.
(b) In case the aggrieved party is not satisfied with the order of the District Commission, he can directly appeal before the Supreme Court.
(c) In case the aggrieved party is not satisfied with the order of the State Commission, he can directly appeal before the Supreme Court.
(d) In case the aggrieved party is not satisfied with the order of the National Commission, he can appeal before the Supreme Court.

14. Identify the dimension of business environment illustrated by the given picture. (1)

(a) Social (b) Political
(c) Technological (d) Economic

15. Assertion (A) Planning involves looking ahead and preparing for the future.

Reason (R) The purpose of planning is to meet future events effectively to the best advantage of an organisation. (1)

Alternatives

(a) Both Assertion (A) and Reason (R) are true and Reason (R) is the correct explanation of Assertion (A)
(b) Both Assertion (A) and Reason (R) are true, but Reason (R) is not the correct explanation of Assertion (A)
(c) Assertion (A) is true, but Reason (R) is false
(d) Assertion (A) is false, but Reason (R) is true

16. Match the techniques of scientific management given in Column I with their meaning given in Column II (1)

Column I	Column II
A. Method study	(i) It refers to the study of movements like lifting, putting objects, sitting and changing positions, etc. which are undertaken while doing a typical job.
B. Motion study	(ii) It determines the amount and frequency of rest intervals in completing a task.
C. Time study	(iii) It determines the standard time taken to perform a well defined job.
D. Fatigue study	(iv) It determines one best way of doing a job.

Codes

	A	B	C	D		A	B	C	D
(a)	(ii)	(iii)	(i)	(iv)	(b)	(i)	(iv)	(ii)	(iii)
(c)	(iv)	(i)	(iii)	(ii)	(d)	(iii)	(ii)	(iv)	(i)

17. Akshara runs a business the name of 'AK Solutions' in a well reputed area of her city where people provide spaces to students as library, as study centres and as training and event centres to businesses. Akshara provides only conference halls to big and small enterprises for their meetings and events.

Suddenly, in July 2024, floods affected some libraries and study centres in her neighbouring area. The exams were fast approaching and studenta were facing a lot of problems as these study centres and libraries had to be closed.

Taking advantage of this opportunity and to help the students 'AK Solutions' adapted itself to the needs of the environment, they decided to convert some of their conference halls into libraries and study centres. They also decided to provide food and other facilities required by the students at subsidised rates. This initiative increased their business manifold and earned them significant goodwill.

The feature of management highlighted in the above case is (1)

(a) management is a continuous process
(b) management is an intangible force
(c) management is a dynamic function
(d) management is a group activity

18. 'Increase in the profit earned by the equity shareholders due to the presence of fixed financial charges like interest' is called (1)

(a) financial planning (b) dividend decision
(c) financing decision (d) trading on equity

19. Statement I The cost of debt is more than the cost of equity.

Statement II Lenders risk is lower than the equity shareholders risk. (1)

Alternatives

(a) Both the statements are true
(b) Both the statements are false
(c) Statement I is true, but statement II is false
(d) Statement I is false, but statement II is true

20. "To ensure that enough funds are available at right time to honour the commitments and to carry out the plans" is discussed in which of the following concepts? (1)

(a) Capital structure (b) Financial leverage
(c) Financial planning (d) Investment decision

21. Explain the following functions of stock exchange
(i) Providing liquidity and marketability to existing securities
(ii) Pricing of securities
(iii) Safety of transaction (3)

Or Differentiate between 'primary market' and 'secondary market' on the basis of any three points.

22. Radhika started a business of supplying high class facial kits to beauty parlours in various cities of the country. Initially, the business was doing well and her products were popular.

Despite the high quality of the products, Radhika faced difficulties in certain parlours, especially in Kagpur city, where her products failed to gain a strong market presence.

To understand the cause, she appointed a qualified marketing manager. The marketing manager discovered that there was no proper exchange of facts, ideas and views, etc. between the incharge of Kagpur city and the employees at different parlours at Kagpur. Vicky, who was the incharge and responsible for overseeing all parlours in Kagpur, was unable to effectively foster a common understanding of the product among the employees.

As a result, the employees did not grasp the key benefits and features of the high class facial kits. In turn, the employees were not able to convince potential clients about the product's value.

(i) Identify the concept discussed in the above case.

(ii) The concept identified in (i) above can be defined as a process having various elements. State first five elements of this process. (3)

23. Give the meaning of 'capital market'. Differentiate between 'capital market' and 'money market' on the basis of

(i) Participants (ii) Instruments

Or State any three 'Regulatory functions' of Securities and Exchange Board of India.

24. Aman, a young graduate was living away from home in another city. He had problems in cooking and heating food. Ho decided to purchase a microwave oven for the same. He went to the market, visited many shops and compared various microwave oven brands available in the market. He compared features, price, after- sale service and customer reviews, etc. to make an informed choice as per his needs.

After selecting the oven, he checked that it should have an ISI mark. This gave him confidence about the safety, standards and quality of the oven.

After reaching home he followed the manufacturer's instructions for safe installation and use of microwave oven. This helped him in avoiding any risk associated with the usage of microwave oven.

By doing all this Aman kept in mind various responsibilities while purchasing and using the microwave oven. Still he left some of the responsibilities that were not fulfilled by him. State any three such responsibilities. (3)

25. Explain the following principles of management given by Fayol

(i) Division of work

(ii) Authority and responsibility (4)

Or Explain the following points of significance of principles of management

(i) Providing managers with useful insights into reality.

(ii) Optimum utilisation of resources and effective administration

26. Explain the following features of coordination (4)

(i) Coordination integrates group efforts

(ii) Coordination is the responsibility of all managers

Or Explain the following features of management

(i) Management is a goal-oriented process

(ii) Management is a continuous process

27. Nisha had given some old dresses of her own to her house-helper Beenu. After a few days, Nisha was happily surprised when she saw Beenu wearing one of the dresses beautifully refurbished. On enquiry, Beenu told Nisha that this was done by her daughter who had just completed her class 12th studies. Beenu also told Nisha that she was a little concerned as her daughter did not want to study further.

Nisha was very much impressed by the creativity of Beenu's daughter, so she decided to setup a small business for her. Nisha bought 15 sewing machines and appointed 15 girls to refurbish the old dresses. Nisha also arranged old dresses from various sources and employed a person who will sell these dresses at a very low cost for the one's who could not purchase new dresses due to their low income.

Nisha divided the girls in three equal groups, each having five sewing machines. Each group was given a target of refurbishing 150 old dresses in a fortnight with a cost of ₹ 30 per dress.

After a fortnight, Nisha who was supervising this business with Beenu was informed that group I was able to meet the target by refurbishing 150 old dresses at a cost of ₹ 30 per dress. Group II was able to refurbish 150 old dresses at a cost of ₹ 35 per dress, whereas group III could refurbish only 140 old dresses but at a cost of ₹ 27 per dress.

(i) Identify the concepts of management discussed above for each of the three groups giving reason in support of your answer.

(ii) Give meaning of the concepts identified in (i) above and state which one is important for the management and why? (4)

28. Prachi is working as an academic counsellor for specially abled students at one of the top school to provide special support and guidance to these students. She clearly states in advance the methods of teaching and tackling the students. She ensures that the goals are clearly stated for each and every teacher so that they act as a guide for deciding what action should be taken and in which direction.

Her well laid plans will serve as a basis for coordinating the activities and efforts of teachers teaching different subjects to these students. It helps the teachers in bringing clarity of thought and action to their work.

Identify and explain the two points of importance of 'Planning' function of management highlighted in the above para. (4)

29. Going to gym and following a protein diet has become a popular trend these days. However, with the busy work culture, many people, especially the youth struggle to find time for weight loss programmes.

Anika was working in a multi-national company, wanted to join a gym for weight loss but could not find time. There is no good gym near her house. One day, Anika was walking out of the office during lunch time and saw an attractive poster of a gym which was near her house.

Anika was curious to enquire about their weight loss programme. Next day, when she went to the gym, she was surprised to know about various schemes offered by the gym. They were not only offering 50% discount on the fee of weight loss programme, but were also providing free coach facility and fres protein diet for the customer. But these offers were valid only for 10 days. Attracted by these schemes Anika immediately submitted the fee and joined the gym.

(i) Identify and give the meaning of the element of marketing mix discussed above.

(ii) The element of marketing mix identified in (i) above includes various tools of communication. Identify and explain the tools highlighted in the above para. (4)

30. The demand for take away food business is increasing day-by-day. People working in multi-national companies have to work till night very often and they are reluctant to cook food. Taking advantage of this opportunity, Amit and Bijoy started 'Langar', a take away food business. The food became famous because of its good quality and standards of hygiene followed by them.

Over the years, the business became very profitable. They decided to expand the business by opening more branches in different cities. To ensure consistent food quality at all branches and to maintain the hygiene and quality they planned to import machines with advanced technology.

The cost of each machine was ₹ 12 crores. They knew that this decision has to be taken very carefully, as it involves a huge cost and that the decision, once taken is irreversible.

(i) Identify and state the financial decision discussed in the above para.

(ii) Explain any two factors affecting the decision identified in (i) above. (4)

31. Explain the following steps in the process of selection (6)

(i) Preliminary screening

(ii) Selection tests

(iii) Employment interview

(iv) Reference and background checks

Or Explain the following non-financial incentives

(i) Status

(ii) Organisational climate

(iii) Job enrichment

(iv) Employee participation

32. Asha was running a business of producing and selling pickles, murabbas and papad etc. She was earning a good profit for the last many years. Now, she wanted to add some new products in her product line. Seeing the growing demand of millets, she decided to add some millet products. After doing a lot of market research, she found out that the demand for millet noodles, pasta and ready to eat millet cereals was increasing day-by-day. To give a different taste and to have uniqueness in her products, she prepared a new tasty herb based sauce for cooking these products and decided to launch this along with millet products in the market.

For this Asha hired 10 additional women workers specially trained for the same. However, despite adding more workers, to her surprise, production was not upto the mark.

Concerned about this and to ensure that the activities were performed as per the plans and that the resources were being used effectively and efficiently for the achievement of predetermined goals, Asha appointed a supervisor Nabita. Nabita monitored the activities and discovered that two of the newly hired workers were spending their whole day gossiping and distracting the other workers. As a result the production was low.

(i) Identify and state the function of management discussed above.

(ii) State any five points of importance of the function identified in (i) above. (6)

33. State any three advantages and any three limitations of formal organisation. (6)

Or State any six advantages of functional structure of organisation.

34. Ravi and Megha started 'Energylights' a company manufacturing energy efficient LED lighting after realising an increasing demand for the same.

Manufacturing high quality LED lights with some unique features required substantial investment in technology and high grade materials. This pushed up their cost of manufacturing. To determine the price of their LED lights they not only wanted to cover all costs but also wanted to earn a margin of profit over and above the costs. This will set for them the minimum level or the floor price at which the LED lights would be sold. The high demand and the utility provided by these lights will set the upper limit of the price.

Though there was enough competition in LED lights business, even then they kept the price of their lights higher than the competitors because of good quality and its features. They justified the higher price because of the product differentiation and unique methods of advertising and sales promotion etc.

Quoting lines from the above para, identify and explain any three factors which were taken into consideration by Ravi and Megha to determine the price of their LED lights. (6)

Set II Uncommon Questions from Set I

12. "The obligation of a subordinate to properly perform the assigned duty" is called (1)

(a) delegation (b) authority
(c) responsibility (d) accountability

23. Give the meaning of 'money market'. Differentiate between 'capital market' and 'money market' on the basis of

(i) Investment outlay (ii) Duration (3)

Or State any three 'Development functions' of securities and Exchange Board of India.

25. Explain the following principles of management given by Fayol

(i) Unity of command (ii) Order (4)

Or Explain the following points of significance of principle of management

(i) Scientific decision (ii) Fulfilling social responsibility

26. Explain the following features of coordination

(i) Coordination ensures unity of action
(ii) Coordination is a continuous process (4)

Or Explain the following features of management

(i) Management is a group activity
(ii) Management is an intangible force

33. State any three advantage and any three limitations of informal organisation. (6)

Or State any three advantages and any three disadvantage of divisional structure of organisation.

Set III Uncommon Questions from Set I & II

12. 'Answerability for outcome of the assigned task' is called (1)

(a) decentralisation (b) authority
(c) responsibility (d) accountability

23. Differentiate between 'capital market' and 'money market' on the basis of

(i) Liquidity (ii) Safety
(iii) Expected return (3)

Or State any three 'protective functions' of Securities and Exchange Board of India.

25. Explain the following principles of management given by Fayol

(i) Equity (ii) Initiative (4)

Or Explain the following points of significance of principles of management

(i) Meeting changing environment requirements
(ii) Management training, education and research

26. Explain the following features of co-ordination

(i) Coordination is an all pervasive function
(ii) Coordination is a deliberate function (4)

Or 'Management is multidimensional' is one of the features of management. Explain its following dimensions

(i) Management of work (ii) Management of people

31. Explain the following steps in the process of staffing

(i) Placement and orientation
(ii) Training and development
(iii) Performance appraisal
(iv) Promotion and career planning (6)

Or Explain the following non-financial incentives

(i) Career advancement opportunity
(ii) Employee recognition programmes
(iii) Job security (iv) Employee empowerment

33. Give meaning of 'formal organisation'. State any five features of formal organisation. (6)

Or Differentiate between 'functional structure' and 'divisional structure' of organisation on any six basis.

Answers

Set I

1. (a) Management
2. (d) budget
3. (b) Directing does not increase resistance to change; instead, it helps in overcoming resistance by providing proper communication, motivation and leadership.
4. (d) growth opportunities
5. (a) Both the statements are true
6. (a) It helps in simplifying the process of selection
7. (a) Leadership
8. (b) inflation
9. (d) adaptation to change
10. (c) psychological benefits
11. (c) organisational barrier
12. (b) authority
13. (d) In case the aggrieved party is not satisfied with the order of the National Commission, he can appeal before the Supreme Court.
14. (c) Technological
15. (a) Both Assertion (A) and Reason (R) are true and Reason (R) is the correct explanation of Assertion (A)
16. (c) (iv) (i) (iii) (ii)
17. (c) management is a dynamic function
18. (d) trading on equity
19. (d) The cost of debt is generally **lower** than the cost of equity. This is because interest payments on debt are tax deductible and debt holders have a fixed claim on assets, making it a lower risk investment compared to equity.
20. (c) Financial planning
21. Refer to Q.No. 16 of long answer type questions in chapter 10.

Or Refer to Q.No. 15 of long answer type questions in chapter 10.

22. (i) The concept discussed in the given case is Communication.

    (ii) Refer to Q.No. 18 case study based questions in chapter 7.
23. Refer to Q.No. 4 of short answer type questions in chapter 10.

Or Refer to Q.No. 19 of long answer type questions in chapter 10.

24. Refer to Q.No. 6 of case study based questions in chapter 12.
25. Refer to Q.No. 21 of long answer type questions in chapter 2.

Or Refer to Q.No. 18 of long answer type questions in chapter 2.

26. Refer to Q.No. 19 of long answer type questions in chapter 1.

Or Refer to Q.No. 1 of short answer type questions in chapter 1.

27. Refer to Q.No. 3 of case study based questions in chapter 1.
28. Refer to Q.No. 2 of case study based questions in chapter 4.
29. Refer to Q.No. 13 of case study based questions in chapter 11.
30. Refer to Q.No. 2 of case study based questions in chapter 9.
31. Refer to Q.No. 25 of long answer type questions in chapter 6.

Or Refer to Q.No. 27 of long answer type questions in chapter 7.

32. Refer to Q.No. 11 of case study based questions in chapter 8.
33. Following are the advantages of formal organisation

    (i) Unity of command is maintained through an established chain of command.

    (ii) Role and duties of each member are clearly specified which avoids confusion and duplication of effort.

    (iii) It helps in effective accomplishment of goals by providing a framework for the operations to be performed.

    Following are the limitations of formal organisation

    (i) It may lead to procedural delays and delayed decision-making as the established chain of command has to be followed.

    (ii) Creativity gets reduced, as it does not allow any deviations from the rigidly laid down policies.

    (iii) It places more emphasis on structure and work and ignores human relationships as well as social needs of the employees.

Or Refer to Q.No. 4 of short answer type questions in chapter 5.

34. Refer to Q.No. 19 of case study based questions in chapter 11.

Set II

12. (c) Responsibility
23. Refer to Q.No. 4 of short answer type questions in chapter 10.

Or Following are the three developmental functions of Securities and Exchange Board of India

(i) Training of intermediaries of the securities market.

(ii) Conducting research and publishing information useful to all market participants.

(iii) Undertaking measures to develop the capital markets by adopting a flexible approach.

25. (i) **Unity of Command** According to the principle of unity of command, an employee should receive orders from one superior at a time and that employee should be answerable only to that superior.

If this principle is violated, then authority is undermined, discipline is in jeopardy, order disturbed and stability threatened. If unity of command is maintained in organisation, it would help to avoid confusion among workers, conflict among superiors and create better relations between workers and managers.

(ii) **Order** This principle states that there should be an orderly 'arrangement and specific place, for everything (material order) and everyone (social order) in the organisation. Essentially, it means orderliness.

Or

(i) **Scientific Decision** Management principles help in thoughtful decision-making which should be based on facts and justifiable in terms of intended purposes. They emphasise logic and are based on objective assessment of the situation.

(ii) **Fulfilling Social Responsibility** The increased awareness of public has forced business organisations to fulfill their social responsibilities. Management principles are also evolved to serve these demands of society. These principles not only guide managers to achieve organisational goals but also guide them to perform social responsibilities.

26. Refer to topic 'Characteristics of Coordination' on Page 8 in chapter 1.

Or Refer to Q.No. 1 of short answer type questions in chapter 1.

33. Refer to Q.No. 23 of long answer type questions in chapter 5.

Or Refer to Q.No. 20 of long answer type questions in chapter 5.

Set III

12. (d) Accountability

23. Refer to difference 'Money Market vs Capital Market' on page 286 in chapter 10.

Or

Following are the protective functions of Securities and Exchange Board of India (SEBI)

(i) Prohibition of fraudulent and unfair trade practices.

(ii) Controlling insider trading and imposing penalties for such practices.

(iii) Undertaking steps for investor protection.

25. (i) **Equity** Refer to Q.No. 8 of short answer type questions in chapter 2.

(ii) **Initiative** Refer to Q.No. 20 of long answer type questions in chapter 2.

Or Refer to Q.No. 19 of long answer type questions in chapter 2.

26. Refer to Q.No. 19 of long answer type questions in chapter 1.

Or Refer to Q.No. 2 of long answer type questions in chapter 1.

31. Refer to Q.No. 21 of long answer type questions in chapter 6.

Or

(i) **Career Advancement Opportunity** Every individual wants to grow to the higher level in the organisation. When employees are provided opportunities to grow in status and responsibility. they are satisfied and are committed to organisational goals. Appropriate skill development programmes and sound promotion policy help employees to exhibit improved performance.

(ii) **Employee Recognition Programmes** Recognition means acknowledgement of work with a show of appreciation.

When such appreciation is given to the work performed by employees, they feel motivated.

(iii) **Job Security** Employees want their job to I be secure. They want certain stability of income and work, which will motivate them to work with greater zeal.

However. it has one negative aspect i.e. when individuals feel that they are not likely to lose their jobs they may become complacent and careless.

(iv) **Employee Empowerment** It means giving more autonomy and power to subordinates., It makes people feel that their jobs are important as a result of which they contribute positively to the use of skills and talents in the job performance.

33. Refer to Q.No. 22 of long answer type questions in chapter 5.

Or Refer to Q.No. 21 of long answer type questions in chapter 5.

CBSE

Code
66/5/1

Examination Paper 2025

BUSINESS STUDIES

Time : 3 Hours **Max. Marks : 80**

General Instructions

1. This question paper contains 34 questions. All questions are compulsory.
2. Marks are indicated against each question.
3. Answers should be brief and to the point.
4. Answers to the questions carrying 3 marks may be from 50 to 75 words.
5. Answers to the questions carrying 4 marks may be about 150 words.
6. Answers to the questions carrying 6 marks may be about 200 words.

Set I

1. "The task of management is to make people work towards achieving the organisational goals, by making their strengths effective and their weaknesses irrelevant."

The dimension of management discussed above is (1)

(a) management of work (b) management of people
(c) management of operations
(d) Both (a) and (c)

2. "Management helps in providing good quality products and services, creates employment opportunities, adopts new technology for the greater good of the people and leads to the path towards growth and development."

The point of importance of management highlighted above is (1)

(a) management helps in achieving group goals
(b) management increases efficiency
(c) management helps in achieving personal objectives
(d) management helps in development of society

3. "Business environment includes both specific and general forces."

Which of the following force is not included in specific forces? (1)

(a) Legal conditions (b) Investors
(c) Competitors (d) Suppliers

4. **Statement I** Organising is the process of defining and grouping the activities of the enterprise and establishing authority relationships among them.

Statement II Process of organising involves a series of steps that need to be taken in order to achieve the desired goals. (1)

Alternatives

(a) Both the statement are true
(b) Both the statement are false
(c) Statement I is true and Statement II is false
(d) Statement I is false and Statement II is true

5. 'Monitoring plans is important to ensure that objectives are achieved' is one of the steps in the process of planning.

Identify the step from the following (1)

(a) Setting objectives (b) Developing premises
(c) Implementing the plan
(d) Follow-up action

6. Match the type of plan given in Column I with its meaning given in Column II (1)

Column I		Column II
A. Policy	(i)	A comprehensive plan for accomplishing an organisation's objectives.

Column I		Column II
B. Procedure	(ii)	A detailed statement about a project which outlines the objectives, policies, procedures, rules, tasks, human and physical resources required and the budget to implement any course of action.
C. Programme	(iii)	A general statement that guides thinking or channelises energies towards direction.
D. Strategy	(iv)	Routine steps on how to carry out activities.

Codes

	A	B	C	D
(a)	(iii)	(iv)	(ii)	(i)
(b)	(i)	(iii)	(iv)	(ii)
(c)	(ii)	(i)	(iii)	(iv)
(d)	(iv)	(ii)	(i)	(iii)

7. **Assertion** (A) Marketing is only a post production activity.

Reason (R) Marketing includes activities like identification of customer needs, collection of information for developing the product, designing suitable product package and giving it a brand name. (1)

Alternatives

(a) Both Assertion (A) and Reason (R) are true and Reason (R) is the correct explanation of Assertion (A)
(b) Both Assertion (A) and Reason (R) are false
(c) Assertion (A) is true, but Reason (R) is false
(d) Assertion (A) is false, but Reason (R) is true

8. Ramesh and Harish are best friends, both working at 'Anuja Garments Ltd.', a company manufacturing designer clothing for women. Ramesh works in the marketing department and aims to increase the sales by 15% by offering discounts. However, Harish, the finance manager is not giving approval for this discount as it would mean loss of revenue for the company. This kind of conflict arises in organisations where each department performs activities in isolation from the other. To resolve such issues, there is a need for linking the activities of various departments. The concept of management which integrates the efforts of different departments and at different levels, is (1)

(a) efficiency
(b) effectiveness
(c) controlling
(d) coordination

9. **Assertion** (A) Training enhances employee productivity, both in terms of quality and quantity, leading to high profits for the organisation.

Reason (R) Training is a systematic learning which is always better, as hit and trial methods without systematic learning lead to wastage of efforts and money. (1)

Alternatives

(a) Both Assertion (A) and Reason (R) are false
(b) Assertion (A) is true, but Reason (R) is false
(c) Both Assertion (A) and Reason (R) are true and Reason (R) is the correct explanation of Assertion (A)
(d) Both Assertion (A) and Reason (R) are true, but Reason (R) is not the correct explanation of Assertion (A)

10. **Statement I** Workload analysis would enable an assessment of the number and types of human resources available for the performance of various jobs.

Statement II Workforce analysis would reveal the number and types of human resources necessary for the performance of various jobs. (1)

Alternatives

(a) Both the statements are true
(b) Both the statements are false
(c) Statement I is true, but Statement II is false
(d) Statement I is false, but Statement II is true

11. .... is the instrument, which is traded in money market. (1)

(a) Equity share (b) Debenture
(c) Commercial paper (d) Bond

12. The process of holding securities in an electronic form is known as (1)

(a) rolling settlement
(b) registration
(c) dematerialisation (d) depository

13. "If the shareholders in general desire that at least a certain amount is paid as dividend, the companies are likely to declare the same."

The above statement hihghlights which of the following factors affecting dividend decision? (1)

(a) Amount of earning
(b) Shareholders' preference
(c) Stability of earnings
(d) Stability of dividends

14. Which of the following statement is incorrect in respect of responsibility of a consumer while purchasing, using and consuming goods and services? (1)

(a) Check ISI mark on food products before buying
(b) Ask for a cash-memo on purchase of goods and services
(c) Read labels carefully so as to have information about prices, net weight, manufacturing and expiry dates, etc.
(d) Assert yourself to ensure that you get a fair deal

15. Identify the external source of recruitment displayed in the picture given below. (1)

(a) Advertisement (b) Direct recruitment
(c) Web publishing (d) Labour contractors

16. 'ABC Ltd., a large multinational company had approximately 1,000 employees in each of its departments. The company had five departments. In this organisation, leave applications of the employees had to be approved by the departmental heads. This approval is delayed due to large number of leave applications in each department. This led to a lot of dissatisfaction amongst the employees. To resolve this problem, the chief executive officer of the organisation called a meeting of all departmental heads.

It was decided to assign the approval of leave applications up to 10 days to the managers at all levels. It was also decided that it will be assigned till the lowest level throughout the organisation. Since the decision-making authority was shared with lower levels and placed nearest to the point of action, they could approve or deny leave applications without requiring higher level approval. After the policy change, employees at all levels noticed an improvement in the sanctioning of leave applications.

The concept of management which led to an improvement in the speed and flexibility of leave approval is (1)

(a) organising (b) delegation
(c) decentralisation (d) authority

17. 'XYZ Ltd.' is using registers to record attendance of the employees even in this new tech era. The human resource manager is facing problems due to the dishonest behaviour of employees as they are writing wrong working hours. Not only this, the production manager is also reporting about the theft of raw materials every day.

To resolve these types of problems, the company started using biometric attendance system and installed cameras at important areas to keep an eye on the activities of the employees. This helped in reducing dishonest behaviour of the employees to a large extent.

The point of importance of controlling highlighted in the above case is (1)

(a) improving employee motivation
(b) ensuring order and discipline
(c) making efficient use of resources
(d) accomplishing organisational goals

18. Veena received ₹ 40 lakhs as a gift from her father. She was discussing various avenues of investing her money with her brother. He advised Veena to invest her money in shares of Moreso Ltd., a reputed company. He further added that it would not only generate good returns over the long-term, but could easily be sold whenever required.

Identify the function of stock exchange being highlighted by Veena's brother in the above case. (1)

(a) Pricing of securities
(b) Providing liquidity and marketability to existing securities
(c) Safety of transactions
(d) Providing scope for speculation

19. 'Payal Ltd.' plans to start manufacturing solar panels which will require a significant amount of investment in machinery. The machinery which they intend to purchase is newly launched in the market. It will not only reduce the cost per unit, but also double the production as compared to the machines used by other solar panel manufacturers already existing in this business.

The chief executive officer of 'Payal Ltd.' asked the finance manager to forecast the fund requirements for purchasing the above machinery to ensure that enough funds are available at the right time.

From the following, identify the concept about which the chief executive officer is discussing with the finance manager (1)

(a) Capital budgeting (b) Trading on equity
(c) Financial planning (d) Wealth maximisation

20. 'Maira Electronics' is a manufacturer of smartphones and famous for its quality. It is a large organisation, so each and every piece produced cannot be checked. So the company made a policy that out of 500 smartphones produced a day, 20 smartphones would be randomly selected for a quality lity check. Identify the step of controlling process discussed above (1)

(a) Setting performance standards
(b) Measurement of actual performance
(c) Comparing actual performance with standards
(d) Taking corrective action

21. Differentiate between 'primary market' and 'secondary market' on any three basis. (3)

Or Differentiate between 'capital market' and 'money market' on the following basis

(i) Duration (ii) Liquidity

(iii) Safety

22. Vani, after completing her course in 'nutrition and fitness', wanted to launch millet-based healthy snacks. She researched a lot and started manufacturing a range of healthy, crunchy millet namkeens and named them 'pure millets'. The name reflected natural ingredients, appealing to health conscious consumers. The millet snacks were packaged in eco-friendly, biodegradable packets with a reasonable feature, ensuring freshness and convenience. The stickers on the packets displayed the name with the tagline 'Power Your Health' and nutritional information and certifications like 'Organic Certified' to establish the product's health benefits. Pure Millets' got off to a good start.

In addition to features and quality, various other product related important decisions are discussed in the above case. Identify and give the meaning of any three such decisions. (3)

23. Explain the following factors affecting the fixed capital requirements of a company (3)

(i) Nature of business

(ii) Choice of technique

(iii) Growth prospects

Or Explain the following factors affecting financing decision of a company.

(i) Fixed operating costs

(ii) Control considerations

(iii) State of capital market

24. 'Essential Ltd.' is a company that has been manufacturing cooking oil for the past 20 years and 700 employees are working in it. Recognising the growing demand for hair care products, they developed a unique formula for hair growth useful even for people who are bald. They want to keep the formula confidential to maintain a competitive edge. As they plan to immediately launch the hair oil in the market, they needed reliable people who could be evaluated more accurately and be placed in this specialised department quickly.

For this, the chief executive officer consulted the Human Resource Manager, Karn. Karn suggested that there are five reliable and hard working employees who will be a good fit for this specialised department. Also, there are two employees in the production department to whom they can give the responsibility of heading this department with higher pay.

The company is committed to improve motivation, loyalty and satisfaction level of employees.

Explain any two sources of recruitment discussed above which will help 'Essential Ltd.' to recruit reliable people in this specialised department. (3)

25. 'AK Ltd.' is a large company with 4,000 workers engaged in production of wide varieties of spices used in the Indian Kitchen. The company has been struggling with a persistent issue of workers making unreasonable demands and going on strike frequently. To address the issue, the chief executive officer appointed a management expert who will analyse the situation and suggest solutions to overcome the problem. The management expert analysed the situation and suggested that the company could resolve the issue by following Taylor's principle of scientific management which suggested complete mental revolution on the part of both management and workers. It means that management and workers should transform their thinking, where even trade unions will not think of going on strike. It emphasises that prosperity of the employer cannot exist for a long time unless it is accompanied by the prosperity for the employees and *vice-versa.*

(i) Identify and explain the principle of scientific management discussed in the above case by the management expert.

(ii) Also, explain another principle suggested by Taylor, which is an extension of the principle identified in (i) above. (4)

26. 'Omara Ltd. is a garments company that produces jackets from organic, recycled and sustainable materials. The sourcing of eco-friendly fabrics, slower production process and focus on ethical labour practices result in big time gap between receipt of fabrics and their conversion into jackets. Since 'Omara Ltd.' faces intense competition in the garment industry, it has to hold large stocks of jackets to meet urgent orders from customers. To further attract and retain customers, 'Omara Ltd.' offers liberal credit terms to them. Thus 'Omara Ltd.' is able to perform much better than its competitors.

(i) State whether the total working capital requirement of 'Omara Ltd. will be high or low.

(ii) Justify your answer given in (i) above by identifying and stating any three factors affecting working capital requirements discussed in the above case. (4)

27. 'Smart Aids' was a reputed company manufacturing e-walking sticks. It is now providing e-walking sticks with sensors or voice feedback for helping people with vision or mobility issues to move around more safely and easily.

The company has been earning good profits. After its great success, it wants to diversify and enter into the manufacturing of high class smart watches. These smart watches will help older people to live independently and safely while staying connected to their loved ones. These smart watches would also monitor their health by sending emergency alerts, reminding them to take medicines, etc. and help in managing their health issues. It will encourage physical activity and offer voice assistance for easy use and keep them connected with family through calls and messages.

Though there are very homogeneous functions in both the products, they set-up a separate business unit for these watches. Both units will have separate managers responsible for the performance of their units and have authority over the unit. Each manager would be accountable for profits, revenues and costs of their unit. This type of organisational structure would help the organisation to add new units without interrupting the existing operations.

(i) State the type of organisational structure suitable for 'Smart Aids, giving reason in support of your answer.

(ii) Give two advantages of the organisational structure, which are highlighted in the above case. **(4)**

28. Explain the following features of 'management'. **(4)**

(i) Management is a dynamic function

(ii) Management is an intangible force

Or Explain the following features of 'Principles of Management'.

(i) General guidelines

(ii) Cause and effect relationship

29. Explain the following principles of 'general management'. **(4)**

(i) Division of work

(ii) Unity of command

Or Explain the following points of importance of principles of management

(i) Providing managers with useful insights into reality

(ii) Optimum utilisation of resources and effective administration

30. Sara decided to purchase vegetables online from 'Desi Store' which is a popular online store. She ordered 1 kg carrots, 1 kg potatoes and 2 kg tomatoes. After receiving the order, Sara realised that the weight of the vegetables was much less than what she had ordered. On checking the website again, she found that on the website, only price of each item is stated, but the weight or quantity of the vegetables against the price is not specified.

She contacted the customer care center for her grievance. The customer care center representative simply told that weight of the vegetables varies, so it is not indicated against the price.

Sara asked the representative many times to speak to a supervisor, but every time the representative stated that no one is available. Sara was disappointed and left a review on the website and filed a case in the district forum.

Identify and explain the two rights of the consumer discussed above. **(4)**

31. Explain any four points of importance of 'Planning function of management'. **(6)**

Or Explain any four points that highlight the importance of 'delegation'.

32. Identify and explain the communication barrier discussed in each of the following cases and name the broad category of each communication barrier to which they relate

(i) 'MNB Ltd.' launches a new software programme using artificial intelligence. Ajit, the project manager, explains the new software system to employees in the organisation, using terms like 'cloud computing', 'machine learning', etc. Since the employees are not specialists in this field, they cannot understand the actual meaning of many words used by the project manager.

(ii) Rajesh, working as production manager in 'KLM Ltd.', approaches the general manager, Kumar to discuss the problems he is having at work. Rajesh tells him about the increasing workload and the need for additional support. However, Kumar who is working on an important file, keeps glancing at it while nodding occasionally. He does not make eye contact with Rajesh or stop reading the file. He responds saying 'Okay Rajesh, just try to manage'. Rajesh leaves the office feeling disappointed.

(iii) Suresh is a senior technician at a company manufacturing spare parts of a car. He suggests a new method for reducing the idle time on machines to increase efficiency. He presents his idea during a team meeting and is appreciated by everyone. But the manager Pankaj, does not offer any appreciation award for his brilliant idea. **(6)**

33. Explain any four features of 'directing' function of management. **(6)**

Or Explain any four features of 'motivation', an element of directing.

34. 'Sound-it' is a start-up planning to launch a line of wireless earbuds.

Before launching, the company decides to gather feedback from customers through online surveys and interactive websites. From this research, they identify their target market as young, tech-savvy people, who value good sound quality, durability and comfort. The research also shows that customers want earbuds with long battery life, water resistance and the ability to easily connect with other devices.

Using this information, 'Sound-it' designs earbuds that meet these needs of the customer. The earbuds are comfortable with soft eartips, include advanced noise-cancelling technology, a lightweight design and good water resistance, making them perfect for sports and outdoor activities.

The design not only improves sound and comfort, but also gives it a competitive edge in the market.

It decides to charge an amount lower than their competitors to attract customers who want good quality at an affordable price after evaluating various factors like production costs, competitor prices, the product's utility and demand, etc.

To inform the customers about its earbuds, 'Sound-it', runs digital advertisement on social media and offers special discounts and free gift offers on its earbuds.

Identify and explain the four marketing functions discussed in the above case. (6)

Set II Uncommon Questions from Set I

23. Explain the following factors affecting the fixed capital requirements of a company (3)

(i) Scale of operations

(ii) Technology upgradation

(iii) Diversification

Or Explain the following factors affecting the capital budgeting decision of a company

(i) Cash flows of the project

(ii) The rate of return

(iii) The investment criteria involved

28. Explain the following features of management (4)

(i) Management is a goal-oriented process

(ii) Management is a group activity

Or Explain the following features of 'principles of management'

(i) Universal applicability

(ii) Flexible

29. (a) Explain the following principles of 'general management' (4)

(i) Authority and responsibility

(ii) Unity of direction

Or Explain the following points of importance of principles of management

(i) Scientific decisions

(ii) Meeting changing environment requirements

31. Explain any four limitations of 'planning' function of management. (6)

Or Explain any four points of importance of 'organising' function of management.

33. Explain any four points of importance of 'directing function of management. (6)

Or Explain the following styles of 'Leadership'.

(i) Autocratic leadership (ii) Democratic leadership

(iii) Laissez-faire leadership

Set III Uncommon Questions from Set I & II

1. 'In order to survive, every management has some basic product or service to provide. This requires a production process which entails the flow of input material and the technology for transforming this input into the desired output for consumption.'

The dimension of management discussed above is (1)

(a) management of work

(b) management of people

(c) management of operations

(d) None of the above

21. Give the meaning of 'financial market', 'capital market' and 'money market'. (3)

Or Differentiate between 'capital market' and 'money market' on the basis of the following

(i) Investment outlay

(ii) Expected return

(iii) Participants

28. Explain the following features of 'management' (4)

(i) Management is a continuous process.

(ii) Management is all pervasive.

Or Explain the following features of 'Principles of management'
(i) Mainly behavioural
(ii) Contingent

29. Explain the following principles of 'general management'
(i) Discipline (ii) Equity (4)

Or Explain the following points of importance of principles of management.
(i) Fulfilling social responsibilities
(ii) Management training, education and research

31. Explain any four features of 'planning'. (6)

Or Explain any four points of importance of 'decentralisation'.

33. Explain any four suitable measures to overcome communication barriers and improve communication effectiveness. (6)

Or

Explain the following non-financial incentives
(i) Job security
(ii) Career advancement opportunity
(ii) Job enrichment

Answers

Set I

1. (b) management of people
2. (d) management helps in development of society
3. (a) Legal conditions
4. (a) Both the statements are true
5. (d) Follow-up action
6. (a) (iii) (iv) (ii) (i)
7. (d) Marketing is not only a post-production activity. It begins even before production, with activities such as market research, identifying customer needs and product development. It continues after production with promotion, distribution and customer feedback.
8. (d) Coordination
9. (c) Both Assertion (A) and Reason (R) are true and Reason (R) is the correct explanation of Assertion (A)
10. (b) Workload analysis helps a manager to assess the number and type of human resources necessary to perform various jobs in the organisation. Workforce analysis helps to know the number and type of human resource already available in the organisation.
11. (c) Commercial paper
12. (c) dematerialisation
13. (b) Shareholders' preference
14. (a) Check ISI mark on food products before buying
15. (c) Web publishing
16. (c) decentralisation
17. (b) ensuring order and discipline
18. (b) Providing liquidity and marketability to existing securities
19. (c) Financial planning
20. (b) Measurement of actual performance
21. Refer to Q.No. 15 of long answer type questions in chapter 10.

Or Refer to difference 'Money Market vs Capital Market' on page 286 in chapter 10.

22. The case highlights various product related decisions that are crucial for marketing.

Three such decisions are

(i) **Branding** The process of giving a name or a sign or a symbol, etc. to a product is called branding. Firm has to decide whether to sell its products under a brand name or generic name. Generic name is the name of the whole class of the product, such as camera.

(ii) **Packaging** Packaging refers to the act of designing and producing the container or wrapper of a product. Various kinds of goods are placed or packed into appropriate containers for protection and convenient handling.

(iii) **Labelling** The term 'labelling' means designing a label to be put on the package. A label describes the product, its usage and specifies its contents. Label can be a simple tag or a descriptive label.

23. (i) **Nature of Business** The nature of business has a great influence upon the fixed capital requirements. e.g. A trading company requires lower investment in fixed assets as compared to a manufacturing organisation, since it does not require to purchase plant and machinery, etc.

(ii) **Choice of Technique** Some organisations are capital intensive, whereas, others are labour intensive.

A capital intensive organisation requires more investment in plant and machinery as it rely less on manual labour. On the other hand, labour intensive organisations require less investment in fixed assets.

(iii) **Growth Prospects** Higher growth of an organisation requires higher investment in fixed assets. A company expecting such growth may expand its production capacity in order to meet the anticipated higher demand quickly. This entails larger investment in fixed assets and consequently, larger fixed capital.

Or (i) **Fixed Operating Cost** If a firm is having a higher fixed operating cost like payment of interests, premiums, salaries, rent, etc. then, it should redue fixed financing costs like , payment of interest on debt. Hence, lower debt financing is better.

(ii) **Control Considerations** When existing shareholders do not want to lose control over the business, they may prefer debt to equity as debt financing has no such implication.

(iii) **State of Capital Market** If the stock market is rising, then it is easy to raise funds through issue of shares as more people invest in equity. However, depressed capital market may make issue of equity shares difficult for any company and the company has to opt for debt financing.

24. Two sources of recruitment which will help Essential Ltd. to recruit reliable people in the specialised department are as follows

(i) **Transfer** It refers to shifting of an employee from one job or department to another without a significant change in salary, responsibilities or status. It is a horizontal movement that can address staffing imbalances and help to avoid terminations and removing individual problems and grievances.

(ii) **Promotions** It means shifting an employee to a higher position with increased responsibilities, status and pay. This vertical shift boosts motivation and loyalty among employees.

25. (i) 'Harmony, not Discord' has been discussed in the case. It states that there should be complete harmony between management and workers. For this, Taylor called for complete mental revolution which means a change in the mindset of both management and workers. It implies that management should share the gains with workers and workers should work hard for the betterment of the business.

(ii) 'Cooperation, not Individualism' is an extension of Harmony, not Discord. It states that there should be complete cooperation between the labour and the management instead of individualism. This principle is an extension of principle of 'harmony, not discord'.

According to this principle, competition should be replaced by cooperation. Management and workers both should realise that they need each other.

According to Taylor, there should be an almost equal division of work and responsibility between workers and management.

26. (i) The total working capital of Omara Ltd. will be high.

(ii) Factors affecting the working capital requirement in the case which leads to higher working capital requirement are as follows

(a) **Production Cycle** Production cycle is the time span between the receipt of raw material and their conversion into finished goods. Some businesses have a longer production cycle while some have a shorter one. Duration and the length of production cycle affects the amount of funds required for raw materials and expenses.

(b) **Credit Allowed** Different firms allow different credit terms to their customers. These terms depend upon the level of competition that a firm faces, as well as the credit worthiness of their clientele. Liberal credit policy means more working capital requirement while strict credit policy means less working capital requirement.

(c) **Level of Competition** Higher level of competitiveness may necessitate companies to maintain larger stock of finished goods to meet urgent demand from customers. This increases the working capital requirement. Whereas, company having less competition will require lesser amount of working capital.

27. (i) The type of organisational structure suitable for 'Smart Aids' is 'divisional organisational structure'. It is because the company is diversifying into a new product line (smartwatches) while continuing its existing operations (walking sticks). Each product line is being treated as a separate business unit with its own manager responsible for its performance, including profits, revenue and costs. This structure allows the company to add new business units without disrupting existing operations, making it an ideal choice for diversification.

(ii) Divisional organisational structure has the following advantages

(a) Divisional heads are accountable for profits, as revenue and costs are easily identifiable. Thus, fixation of responsibility and accountability is easy.

(b) It facilitates growth by allowing new divisions to be added without disrupting existing operations.

28. Refer to Q.No. 1 of short answer type questions in chapter 1.

Or (i) **General Guidelines** Management principles are guidelines to action and cannot be used as tailor made tools, i.e. they do not provide readymade, straitjacket solutions. This is so because real business situations are very complex and dynamic.

So, principles of management are general guidelines and cannot be applied strictly as the principles of physical sciences.

(ii) **Cause and Effect Relationship** The principles of management are intended to establish relationship between cause and effect so that they can be used in similar situations in a large number of cases. It means, principles help in predicting the outcome of managerial actions.

29. (i) **Division of Work** As per this principle, if work is divided into small tasks and assigned to trained specialists, then it will help in taking the advantage of 'specialisation'. According to Fayol, "The intent of division of Work is to produce more and better work for the same effort. Specialisation is the most efficient way to use human effort." Because of this principle, an organisation is divided into separate departments *viz.* Production, sales, finance, marketing, etc. This principle is applicable to all kinds of technical as well as managerial work.

(ii) **Unity of Command** According to the principle of unity of command, an employee should receive orders from one superior at a time and that employee should be answerable only to that superior. If this principle is violated, then authority is undermined, discipline is in jeopardy, order disturbed and stability threatened. If unity of command is maintained in organisation, it would help to avoid confusion among workers, conflict among superiors and create better relations between workers and managers.

Or Refer to Q.No. 18 of long answer type questions in chapter 2.

30. The two rights discussed in the case are as follows

(i) **Right to be Informed** According to this right, a consumer has the right to get true and complete information about the ingredients, quality, quantity, price, expiry date of the goods and services, etc. which he intends to buy.

(ii) **Right to Seek Redressal** According to this right, consumer has the right to get relief in case the product falls short of his expectations. The act provides various reliefs to the consumers like compensation for any loss or injury suffered by the consumers, replacement of goods or removal of defects in the goods, etc.

31. Refer to Q.No. 18 of long answer type questions in chapter 4.

Or Refer to Q.No. 16 of short answer type questions in chapter 5.

32. Here are the communication barriers in each case along with their broad categories

(i) **Case 1** (MNB Ltd.) Employees fail to understand technical terms like 'cloud computing' and 'machine learning' used by the project manager. The barrier is technical jargon. Specialists often use technical terms which can confuse non-experts to understand the actual meaning of such terms, causing miscommunication. It is a type of semantic barrier.

(ii) **Case 2** (KLM Ltd.) The General Manager, Kumar, is distracted while listening to Rajesh and does not give full attention to his concerns. The barrier is lack of attention. Distractions or preoccupation of receiver's mind can prevent proper listening and understanding of the message. It is a type of psychological barrier.

(iii) **Case 3** (Manufacturing company) The manager, Pankaj, does not acknowledge or reward Suresh's innovative idea, leading to a lack of motivation. The barrier is lack of proper incentives.

Without motivation or rewards, subordinates may lack initiative to communicate or offer suggestions. It is a type of personal barrier.

33. Refer to Q.No. 1 of short answer type questions in chapter 7.

Or Refer to Q.No. 3 of short answer type questions in chapter 7.

34. The four marketing functions discussed in the case are as follows

(i) **Gathering and Analysing Market Information** The company conducts online surveys and uses an interactive website to gather feedback from customers. It is necessary to identify the needs of the customers and take various decisions for the successful marketing of products and services. It is also important to make an analysis of the available opportunities and threats as well as strengths and weaknesses of the organisation as it helps in deciding what opportunities can best be pursued by it.

(ii) **Product Designing and Development** Based on the research findings, 'Sound-it' designs earbuds with features like noise cancellation, lightweight design and comfort enhancing eartips. A good design of a product not only helps to make it attractive, but also helps in improving its performance and also give it a competitive advantage over the similar products present in the market.

e.g. When we plan to buy refrigerator, we not only see its features like cost, storage capacity, but also the design aspects like its shape, style, etc.

(iii) **Pricing of Product** The company sets a competitive price lower than its rivals. Pricing refers to the process of determining the price of a product.

Price of a product refers to the amount of money that the customer has to pay to obtain a product. The marketers have to analyse a number of factors such as pricing objectives, pricing strategies, demand, cost, competition, etc. to decide the price of a product.

(iv) **Promotion** It refers to the process of informing the customers about the product and then persuading them to buy it. The popular methods of promotion are advertising, sales promotion, personal selling and public relations. 'Sound-it' runs digital advertisements on social media and offers special discounts and free gifts to create awareness and attract customers to their earbuds.

Set II

23. (i) **Scale of Operations** A larger organisation operating at a larger scale needs higher investment in fixed assets as compared to a small organisation.

(ii) **Technology Upgradation** Industries in which assets becomes obsolete sooner due to technology upgradation, need higher investment in fixed assets to replace older assets.

While companies whose assets are not or least affected by technology upgradation, needs lesser investment. e.g. Computers become obsolete faster and are replaced much sooner than say, furniture.

(iii) **Diversification** When a company wants to diversify its operations or enter into a new business other than that of its current product, it requires more fixed capital. e.g. An apparel company diversifying into cosmetic business, will certainly require more fixed capital for investing into plant and machinery, building, etc.

Or (i) **Cash Flows of the Project** When a business invests huge amount of money in a certain project, then it expects to generate some cash flows in the form of cash receipts and payments over the life of an investment.

These cash flows should be carefully analysed before selecting the desired project.

(ii) **The Rate of Return** Each project is selected keeping in mind the expected returns or income for the company and the degree of risk involved. So, before investing in a project, the firm should critically compare the expected returns from different projects and then invest accordingly.

e.g. If there are two projects A and B (with the same risk involved), with a rate of return of 15% and 20% respectively, then project B is more preferable.

(iii) **The Investment Criteria Involved** The basic criteria to invest in a particular project involves amount of investment, interest rate, cash flows and rate of return. The other criteria like availability of labour, machinery, technology, etc. also helps in selecting an investment proposal. There are number of capital budgeting techniques which are applied to evaluate investment proposals before selecting a particular project.

28. (i) **Management is a Goal-oriented Process** The basic aim of management is to achieve the organisational goals.

These should be simple and clearly stated. Different organisations have different set of goals.

Management achieve these goals through uniting the efforts of the individuals in the organisation.

(ii) **Management is a Group Activity** An organisation is a collection of diverse individuals with different needs. Through coordination and teamwork, management unites the efforts of individuals to achieve organisational goals, alongwith the growth and development of individuals as needs and opportunities change.

Or (i) **Universal Applicability** The principles of management can be applied to all kinds of organisations, irrespective of size (small or large) and nature (business, government or social organisation). However, extent of application varies depending on nature and size of organisation.

(ii) **Flexible** Management principles are not as rigid as in case of pure science principles. They are flexible and can be modified by the manager as per changes in the business environment. These principles cannot be applied blindly, even in an identical situation.

29. (i) **Authority and Responsibility** According to this principle, there should be a proper balance between authority and responsibility. Authority is the right to give orders to subordinates and responsibility is the duty, which a subordinate is expected to perform by virtue of his position in organisation. Authority and responsibility go hand in hand. An organisation should build safeguards against abuse of managerial power. At the same time, a manager should have necessary authority to carry out his responsibility.

(ii) **Unity of Direction** It implies that there should be one head and one plan for a group of activities having the same objective. All the related activities should be put under one group and they should be in the control of one manager.

Or Refer to Q.No. 18 of long answer type questions in chapter 2.

31. Refer to Q.No. 20 of long answer type questions in chapter 4.

Or Following are the four points of importance of organising function of management

(i) **Optimum Utilisation of Resources** It leads to proper usage of all materials, financial and human resources. Proper assignment of jobs to workers reduces duplication of work which helps to prevent confusion, minimises wastages and allows the best possible use of resources.

(ii) **Effective Administration** It gives a clear description of jobs and duties as well as responsibilities of each individual. This helps to avoid confusion and duplication of activities. Clarity in working relationships enables proper execution of work and brings effectiveness in administration.

(iii) **Benefits of Specialisation** Organising leads to a systematic allocation of job amongst the workforce. This reduces the work load as well as enhances productivity. Repetitive performance of a particular task by a worker helps him to gain experience and attain specialisation.

(iv) **Adaptation to Change** It facilitates modification in organisational structure and revision of inter-relationships among people in order to adapt to environmental changes. It also helps to provide stability to the enterprise, so that it can continue to survive and grow inspite of changes.

33. Refer to Q.No. 25 of long answer type questions in chapter 7.

Or Refer to Q.No. 28 of long answer type questions in chapter 7.

Set III

1. (c) Management of operations

21. **Financial market** It acts as an intermediary or a link between the savers (households) and the investors (business firms) by mobilising funds between them. It helps savers to allocate their surplus funds for investment and simultaneously helps investors to borrow funds to meet their requirements.

Capital Market It is a market for medium and long-term funds. This market facilitates the institutional arrangements through which long-term funds, both debt and equity are raised and invested.

It includes a network of all the organisations, institutions and instruments which provide medium and long-term funds.

Money Market It is a market for short-term funds, which deals in monetary assets whose period of maturity is upto one year.

Various instruments in this market include treasury bills, certificate of deposit, commercial paper, call money, etc. Instruments are highly liquid and less risky. There is no fixed geographical location and it is a market for short-term funds.

Or Following are the differences between money market and capital market

Basis	Money Market	Capital Market
Investment Outlay	In money market, instruments require huge sum of money, because these are quite expensive.	It does not require huge capital outlay, as the value of units of securities is generally low, i.e. ₹ 10 or ₹ 100. Even the trading lot is kept low at ₹ 5, ₹ 100 or so.
Expected Returns	The expected rate of return is less due to short duration.	The expected returns are high and there is even a possibility of capital gain.
Participants	Major participants are RBI, commercial banks, financial institutions and finance companies.	Particpants of capital market are financial institutions, banks corporate entities, foreign investors and ordinary retail investors from the members of public.

28. (i) **Management is a Continuous Process** Management is an ongoing process of continuous, composite, but separate functions (planning, organising, staffing, directing and controlling). These functions are simultaneously performed by all managers on a continuous basis.

(ii) **Management is All Pervasive** Management is necessary to conduct all types of activities whether it is a business or non-business activity. It is universally applicable in all types of organisation whether political, economic or social.

Or (i) **Mainly Behavioural** Principles of management aim at influencing human behaviour because all work is done by human beings. Human behaviour is very complex and dynamic in nature. Management principles aim to influence such unpredictable behaviour in order to achieve organisational goals. Therefore, principles of management are mainly behavioural in nature. Principles also enable a better understanding of relationship between human and material resources in accomplishing organisational purposes.

(ii) **Contingent** The application of management principles is dependent or contingent upon the prevailing conditions at a particular point of time. They have to be suitably applied as per the situation.

29. (i) **Discipline** It is the sincerity and obedience towards organisational rules and employment agreement, necessary, for the smooth functioning of an organisation. According to Fayol, good superiors at all levels, clear and fair agreements and judicious application of penalties are required in maintaining discipline.

(ii) **Equity** According to this principle, there should be no discrimination against anyone on account of sex, religion, language, caste, belief or nationality and 'equal opportunities should be available for all. This principle emphasises kindliness and justice pin the behaviour of managers towards workers. This will ensure loyalty and devotion.

Or Refer to Q.No. 18 of long answer type questions in chapter 2.

31. Refer to Q.No. 1 of short answer type questions in chapter 4.

Or Refer to Q.No. 26 of long answer type questions in chapter 5.

33. Following are the measures to overcome barriers to effective communication

(i) **Be Aware of Languages, Tone and Content of Message** The language, tone and content used for conveying the message must be understandable to the receiver and should not offend the sentiments of the listener.

(ii) **Convey Things of Help and Value to Listeners** While conveying the message, it is better to know the interests and needs of the receiver. If the message relates directly or indirectly to such interests and needs, it certainly evokes response from communicatee.

(iii) **Ensure Proper Feedback** The communicator may ensure the success of communication by asking questions regarding the message conveyed. The receiver of communication should also be encouraged to respond to communication.
The communication process may be improved by the feedback received to make it more responsive.

(iv) **Communicate for Present as well as Future** Besides meeting the present commitments, communication should also aim at future goals of the enterprise.

Or (i) **Job Security** Employees want their job to be secure. They want certain stability of income and work, which will motivate them to work with greater zeal.
However. it has one negative aspect i.e. when individuals feel that they are not likely to lose their jobs they may become complacent and careless.

(ii) **Career Advancement Opportunity** Every individual wants to grow to the higher level in the organisation. When employees are provided opportunities to grow in status and responsibility. they are satisfied and are committed to organisational goals. Appropriate skill development programmes and sound promotion policy help employees to exhibit improved performance.

(iii) **Job Enrichment** It is concerned with designing of jobs that include greater variety of work content, requiring higher level of knowledge and skill.
This provides opportunity for growth and development of an employee on one hand and more autonomy and responsibility on the other, which becomes a source of motivation to the individual.